7.1 Financial Planning Online: **Personal Credit Counseling**
http://www.phil.frb.org/consumers/establish.html

7.2 Financial Planning Online: **Obtaining a Free Credit Report**
http://www.ftc.gov/bcp/conline/pubs/credit/freereports.htm

7.3 Financial Planning Online: **Identity Theft**
http://www.consumer.gov/idtheft

8.1 Financial Planning Online: **Your Credit Card Report**
http://finance.yahoo.com/creditreports

8.2 Financial Planning Online: **Eliminating Credit Card Debt**
http://cgi.money.cnn.com/tools/debtplanner/debtplanner.jsp

8.3 Financial Planning Online: **Your Rights When Using Credit**
http/www.chicagofed.com/consumer_information/personal_finance_information.cfm

8.4 Financial Planning Online: **The Best Credit Card for You**
http://www.bankrate.com/brm/rate/cc_home.asp

8.5 Financial Planning Online: **Establishing and Protecting Credit**
http://www.chicagofed.com/consumer_information/budgeting_and_saving.cfm

8.6 Financial Planning Online: **Estimating the Time Necessary to Pay Off Your Balance**
http://www.free-financial-advice.net/time-to-pay-debt.html

9.1 Financial Planning Online: **Loan Request Online**
http://www.lendingtree.com

9.2 Financial Planning Online: **Applying for a Home Equity Loan**
http://www.ditech.com

9.3 Financial Planning Online: **Prices of New Cars**
http://autos.yahoo.com/

9.4 Financial Planning Online: **Trade-in and Retail Values of Used Cars**
http://www.kbb.com/

9.5 Financial Planning Online: **Car Loan Interest Rate Quotation**
http://www.bankrate.com/brm/rate/auto_home.asp?link=8

9.6 Financial Planning Online: **Prevailing Car Loan Interest Rates**
http://biz.yahoo.com/b/r/a.html

9.7 Financial Planning Online: **What Is the Optimal Loan Maturity?**
http://www.bankrate.com/brm/auto-loan-calculator.asp

9.8 Financial Planning Online: **Should You Lease or Buy?**
http://www.bloomberg.com/analysis/calculators/leasebuy.html

10.1 Financial Planning Online: **How Much Money Can You Borrow?**
http://www.calcbuilder.com/cgi-bin/calcs/HOM1.cgi/ excite

10.2 Financial Planning Online: **Recent Sales Prices of Nearby Homes**
http://realestate.yahoo.com/re/homevalues/

10.3 Financial Planning Online: **Listing of Homes Nearby for Sale**
http://www.realtor.com

(continued inside the back cover)

PERSONAL FINANCE

THIRD EDITION

THE ADDISON-WESLEY SERIES IN FINANCE

PERSONAL
FINANCE

THIRD EDITION

JEFF MADURA
Florida Atlantic University

Boston San Francisco New York
London Toronto Sydney Tokyo Singapore Madrid
Mexico City Munich Paris Cape Town Hong Kong Montreal

Detailed Contents

Chapter 8   Managing Your Credit 197

The Most Interactive Book on the Market

The Third Edition of Personal Finance *integrates the Building Your Own Financial Plan and case study worksheets into each chapter, helping students to create their own personalized plan for financial success.*

BUILDING YOUR OWN FINANCIAL PLAN

Personal Finance's structure mirrors a comprehensive financial plan, teaching students the skills they need to build their own financial plan. The Building Your Own Financial Plan chapter-ending case studies are presented as an integrated series of exercises and worksheets that represent a portion of a financial plan. At the end of the course, students will have completed a financial plan that they can continue implementing beyond the school term. All of the worksheets are also available on the Financial Planning CD-ROM, which is packaged with each new book.

BUILDING YOUR OWN FINANCIAL PLAN

Loans to finance purchases such as automobiles and homes may be obtained from a variety of sources, each of which has advantages and disadvantages. For example, automob... financed through the dea... union, or a Revi... rently have or anticipate having up...

tify as many sources of these loans as possible. Evaluate the advantages and disadvantages of each source to assist you in determining where to best meet your various borrowing needs.

...this chapter, and to the ...to continue building

NAME _____ DATE _____

Liabilities and Net Worth

Current Liabilities

Loans
Credit card balance
Other current liabilities
Total current liabilities

Long-Term Liabilities

Mortgage
Car loan
Other long-term liabilities
Total long-term liabilities

Total Liabilities

Net Worth

3. Reevaluate the goals you set in Chapter 1. Based on your person... much you can save each year to reach your goals.

Personal Financial Goals

Financial Goal	Dollar Amount	Savin...
Short-Term Goals		
1.		
2.		
3.		
Intermediate-Term Goals		
1.		
2.		
3.		
Long-Term Goals		
1.		
2.		
3.		

NAME _____ DATE _____

2. Prepare your personal balance sheet.

Personal Balance Sheet

Assets

Liquid Assets

Cash
Checking account
Savings account
Other liquid assets
Total liquid assets

Household Assets

Home
Car
Furniture
Other household assets
Total household assets

Investment Assets

Stocks
Bonds
Mutual Funds
Other investments
Total investment assets

Real Estate

Residence
Vacation home
Other
Total real estate

Total Assets

NAME _____

Chapter 2: Building Your Own Financial ...

GOALS

1. Determine how to increase net cash flows in the near future.
2. Determine how to increase net cash flows in the distant fut...

ANALYSIS

1. Prepare your personal cash flow statement.

Personal Cash Flow Statement

Cash Inflows

Disposable (after-tax) income
Interest on deposits
Dividend payments
Other
Total Cash Inflows

Cash Outflows

Rent/Mortgage
Cable TV
Electricity and water
Telephone
Groceries
Health care insurance and expenses
Clothing
Car expenses (insurance, maintenance, and gas)
Recreation
Other
Total Cash Outflows
Net Cash Flows

If you enter your cash flow information in the Excel worksheet, the software will create a pie chart of your cash outflows.

An Interactive Approach

Personal Finance's interactive approach incorporates Internet-based resources along with many examples, problems, and ongoing case studies, all of which focus on providing students with hands-on practice applying financial concepts.

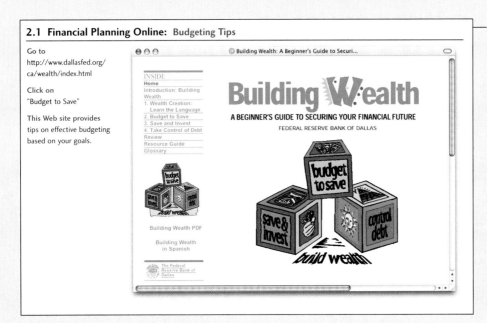

2.1 Financial Planning Online: Budgeting Tips

Go to
http://www.dallasfed.org/
ca/wealth/index.html

Click on
"Budget to Save"

This Web site provides
tips on effective budgeting
based on your goals.

Financial Planning Online features in every chapter highlight Internet resources. Each includes a full-color picture of a Web site, its Internet address, and a description of what the Web site provides.

Financial Planning Online Exercises show students how to obtain, critically evaluate, and use Internet-based resources in making personal finance decisions.

FINANCIAL PLANNING ONLINE EXERCISES

1. Go to http://www.calcbuilder.com/cgi-bin/calcs/
SAV13.cgi/FinanCenter and go to "What's it worth to reduce my spending?"

   You can input various expenses that can be reduced and determine the savings that will accrue over time. Input your age, your age at retirement, 2 percent for the rate you can earn on savings, and 25 percent and 6 percent for the federal and state tax rates, respectively.

   a. If you waited to buy a car, you could, perhaps, save $220 monthly. Enter this information and go to the Results page to find out what this savings would amount to at retirement.

   b. If you ate out less, you could save, say, $150 monthly. Enter this information and go to the Results page to find out what this adds up to by retirement.

FINANCIAL PLANNING PROBLEMS

1. Angela earns $2,170 per month before taxes in her full-time job and $900 before taxes in her part-time job. About $650 per month is needed to pay taxes. What is Angela's disposable income?

2. Angela (from problem 1) inspects her checkbook and her credit card bills and determines that she has the following monthly expenses:

Rent	$500
Cable TV	30
Electricity	100
Water	25
Telephone	40
Groceries	400
Car expenses	350
Health insurance	200
Clothing and personal items	175
Recreation	300

   What is Angela's net cash flow?

Financial Planning Problems require students to demonstrate knowledge of mathematically-based concepts to perform computations in order to make well-informed personal finance decisions.

Real-Life Scenarios

EXAMPLE

Stephanie Spratt graduated from college last year with a degree in marketing. After job searching for several months, she was just hired by the sales department of an advertising firm at an annual salary of $38,000. She is eager to have money from her salary to spend and to give up her interim part-time job waiting tables.

Stephanie plans to save a portion of every paycheck so that she can invest money to build her wealth over time. She realizes that by establishing a financial plan to limit her spending today, she can increase her wealth and therefore her potential spending in the future. At this point, Stephanie decides to develop an overview of her current financial position, establish her goals, and map out a plan for how she might achieve those goals, as shown in Exhibit 1.10.

A running example of Stephanie Spratt, a recent college graduate and new entrant into the workforce, helps students apply concepts to real-life situations. Students are commonly faced with dilemmas similar to those Stephanie faces, such as how to control recreational spending or whether to buy or lease a car.

THE SAMPSONS—A CONTINUING CASE

After about 10 months of saving $500 a month, the Sampsons have achieved their goal of saving $5,000 that they will use as a down payment on a new car. (They have also been saving an additional $300 per month over the last year for their children's college education.) Sharon's new car is priced at $25,000 plus 5 percent sales tax. She will receive a $1,000 trade-in credit on her existing car and will make a $5,000 down payment on the new car. The Sampsons would like to allocate a maximum of $500 per month to the loan payments on Sharon's new car. The annual interest rate on a car loan is currently 7 percent. They would prefer to have a relatively short loan maturity, but cannot afford a monthly payment higher than $500.

Go to the worksheets at the end of this chapter, and to the CD-ROM accompanying this text, to continue this case.

Build a financial plan for the Sampson family! The parents of two children, Dave and Sharon Sampson have made few plans regarding their financial future and are eager to start saving towards a new car, their children's college education, and their retirement. Students apply chapter concepts to counsel the Sampsons on the accompanying worksheets.

PART 4: BRAD BROOKS—A CONTINUING CASE

Brad tells you about his plans to upgrade his auto insurance. Specifically, he would like to add several types of coverage to his policy, such as uninsured motorist coverage and rental car coverage. Recall that Brad is 30 years old. Brad also has a driving record that contains several speeding tickets and two accidents (one of which he caused). He realizes that adding coverage will increase the cost of his insurance. Therefore, he is thinking about switching insurance companies to a more inexpensive carrier.

Brad mentions that he is generally happy with the HMO he is insured with through the technology company he works for. However, Brad also mentions that he does not particularly like to see his primary care physician each time he requires a consultation with a specialist. Brad tells you that his company also offers a PPO, but that he did not choose that plan because he knows little about it.

Brad is trying to decide between term life insurance and whole life insurance. Brad likes whole life insurance, as he believes that the loan feature on that policy will give him an option for meeting his liquidity needs.

At the end of each part, students are prompted to **build a financial plan for Brad Brooks** using the accompanying worksheets. Brad has expensive tastes—as evidenced by his soaring credit card balance—and he needs assistance in gaining control over his finances.

Learning Tools

Chapter 2

Planning with Personal Financial Statements

W here does it all go? It seems like the last paycheck is gone before the next one comes in. Money seems to burn a hole in your pocket, yet you don't believe that you are living extravagantly. Last month you made a pledge to yourself to spend less than the month before. Somehow, though, you are in the same position as you were last month. Your money is gone. Is there any way to plug the hole in your pocket?

What are your expenses? For many people, the first obstacle is to correctly assess their true expenses. Each expense seems harmless and worthwhile. But combined they can be a pack of piranhas that quickly gobble up your modest income. What can you do to gain control of your personal finances?

Just read on in this chapter and you will see how to take control of your finances. However, your task is not easy because it takes self-discipline and there may be no immediate reward. The result is often like a diet: easy to get started, but hard to carry through.

Your tools are the personal balance statement, the personal cash flow statement, and a budget. These three personal financial statements show you where you are, predict where you will be after three months or a year, and help you control expenses. The potential benefits are reduced spending, increased savings and investments, and peace of mind from knowing that you are in control.

24

The objectives of this chapter are to:

- Explain how to create your personal cash flow statement
- Identify the factors that affect your cash flows
- Show how to create a budget based on your forecasted cash flows
- Describe how to create your personal balance sheet
- Explain how your net cash flows are related to your personal balance sheet (and therefore affect your wealth)

Chapter Introductions
The opening of each chapter provides an interest-grabbing scenario that previews the chapter's content.

Learning Objectives
Corresponding to the main headings in each chapter, the list of learning objectives guides students through the material.

EXAMPLE   Suppose your ancestors settled in the American colonies in 1693. At that time, one of them invested $20 in a savings account at a local bank earning 5 percent interest annually. Also assume that this ancestor never informed his family members of this transaction and that the money remained in the account accumulating interest of 5 percent annually until the year 2006, when the bank locates you and informs you of the account. Over this time period, the $20 would have accumulated to $86 million.

As a more realistic example, consider that an investment today of just $2,000 in an account ....rns 6 percent a year will be worth about $11,487 in 30 years.

mutual funds
Investment companies that sell shares to individuals and invest the proceeds in investment instruments such as bonds or stocks.

real estate
Rental property and land.

rental property
Housing or commercial property that is rented out to others.

Marginal Glossary
Throughout the text, key terms and their definitions appear in the text margin where they are first introduced.

Explanation by Example
Practical examples applying concepts in realistic scenarios throughout chapters help cement student understanding.

Ethical Dilemmas

Real-life ethical situations are presented along with questions to encourage students' critical thinking about ethics.

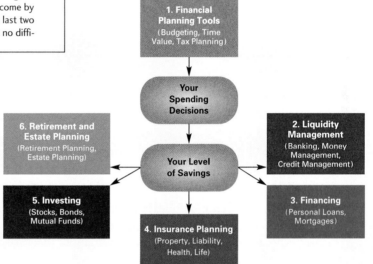

Summary

In paragraph form, the chapter summary presents the key points of the chapter to aid in student study.

Integrating the Key Concepts

This section emphasizes the relationship between chapter topics and the six components of a financial plan.

Review Questions

Test knowledge of material by comparing and contrasting concepts, interpreting financial quotations, and understanding how financial data can be used to make personal finance decisions.

INSTRUCTOR AND STUDENT SUPPORT PACKAGE

The following array of supplementary materials is available to help busy instructors teach more effectively and to allow busy students to learn more efficiently.

Instructor's Manual

Prepared by Dianne R. Morrison, University of Wisconsin, La Crosse, this comprehensive manual pulls together a wide variety of teaching tools. Each chapter contains an overview of key topics, teaching tips, and detailed answers and step-by-step solutions to the Review Questions, Financial Planning Problems, and Sampson family case questions. Each part concludes with answers to the Brad Brooks case questions.

The manual's teaching resources also includes an essay on key considerations when restructuring a course from lecture to online, instructions for setting up a fantasy stock market game, and a guide to the *Right on the Money*™ videos.

Test Bank

Prepared by Stephen L. Christian of Jackson Community College and Terry L. Christian, the Test Bank contains over 2000 questions in true-false, multiple-choice, and short-essay format that can be used for quick test preparation. Qualifiers with each multiple-choice question indicate the level of difficulty. Every question has been scrutinized for accuracy and clarity.

Instructor's Resource Disk

Fully compatible with the Windows and Macintosh operating systems, this CD-ROM provides a number of resources.

- *PowerPoint Lecture Presentation.* Authored by Barbara Rice, Florida College, this useful tool provides slides illustrating key points and exhibits as well as Web site information from the text in lecture note format. The slides can be easily converted to transparencies or viewed electronically in the classroom. Many slides have Excel spreadsheets embedded in them so that instructors can manipulate spreadsheets in the classroom with ease.

- *Computerized Test Bank.* The easy-to-use testing software (Test-Gen EQ with QuizMaster-EQ for Windows and Macintosh) is a valuable test preparation tool that allows instructors to view, edit, and add questions.

- *Instructor's Manual and Test Bank.* For added convenience, the Instructor's Resource Disk also includes Microsoft Word files for the entire contents of the Instructor's Manual and Test Bank.

Video Series

A series of twelve videos from the PBS series *Right on the Money*™ hosted by award-winning journalist and financial expert Chris Farrell is available to qualified adopters of the text. An insightful journey through the world of personal finance, the half-hour segments take viewers on the road and around the country to learn valuable lessons through the personal experiences of people working through financial issues. The program is produced by TPT, Twin Cities Public Television, St. Paul/Minneapolis, with the exclusive national sponsorship of ING/ReliaStar, Inc. In its first five seasons, *Right on the Money*™ has been carried on more than 130 public television stations and seen by millions of viewers. The following episodes are available from

Addison-Wesley: Your Bank Account; Credit Cards; Debt 101; Buying or Leasing a Car; Managing Your Student Loans; Credit Report Repairs; Buying or Renting a Home; Insuring Your Home; Investment Basics; Mutual Fund Basics; Picking Single Stocks; and Preparing for Retirement.

Please contact your local Addison-Wesley sales representative for details. For information on the *Right on the Money*™ series, point your browser to **http://www.rightonthemoney.org**. This comprehensive, interactive Web site complements the series and includes many useful financial resources, tips, suggested readings, and links.

Financial Planning Workbook and CD-ROM

The workbook has been fully integrated into the text for the Third Edition. At the end of each chapter the student is prompted to complete the Building Your Own Financial Plan exercises and the Sampson family continuing case. At the end of each part, the student is prompted to complete the Brad Brooks continuing case. Students can easily rip out the perforated worksheets to build their financial plan. Each new copy of the text is also packaged with a Financial Planning CD-ROM, which is designed to run on Excel 97, Excel 2000, and Excel XP.

The software templates prompt students through the key steps in the financial decision-making process as they complete the Building Your Own Financial Plan exercises. The software's true power lies in the linking of all the worksheets; students are prompted to revise their goals, cash flow statement, and personal balance sheet to demonstrate their understanding of the interrelationships among their financial decisions. Creating a complete and integrated plan has never been this easy!

Additional software features include the following:

- New calculation-based templates on topics such as determining your federal income tax liability, reconciling a checking account, estimating the time it will take to pay off credit card debt, and determining disability insurance needs.

- For decisions that require time value of money analysis, the software directs students for input and then performs the calculations.

- Enhanced graphics such as pie charts and bar graphs that are generated based on user input aid students in visualizing their cash outflows and asset allocation.

Write Down the Money! Diary

Take control of your spending and budgeting with the *Write Down the Money! Diary* from the makers of the *Right on the Money*™ video series. Each new copy of the textbook is packaged with a pocket-size diary that you can use to track your cash outflows over a thirty-day period. With this detailed record of your spending, you will be prepared to budget more precisely for the next month and beyond. Check out the companion downloadable calculator at **http://www.rightonthemoney.org**.

Companion Website

Available at **http://www.aw-bc.com/madura**, the Web site provides online access to innovative teaching and learning tools, including:

- Online Study Guide featuring true/false, multiple choice, and essay questions, as well as two mini-case problems per chapter.

- Sample midterm and final exams.

- Complete e-book version of the text, which allows for easy navigation to the Financial Planning Online resources, viewing of video clips, and quick searches for key terms.

- Up-to-date links to the Financial Planning Online features and Financial Planning Online Exercises.
- *Right on the Money*™ video clip index and a link to the Write Down the Money! budget calculator.

Superior Support for Online Course Management

With *Personal Finance*, you can incorporate technology into the classroom—be it virtual or physical—with ease. In addition to the Companion Website, the Web content is available pre-loaded in CourseCompass, WebCT, and Blackboard.

CourseCompass allows you to easily build and manage online course materials. All it requires is an Internet connection and a Web browser; CourseCompass is nationally hosted, so there is no need for anyone at your academic institution to have to set up and maintain CourseCompass. Powered by the Blackboard online learning system, CourseCompass includes all the powerful Blackboard features for teaching and learning: Instructors can set up a course calendar to post assignments and assess student performance with the gradebook; assign students quizzes with time limits; use communication tools such as e-mail and a course discussion board; and direct students to submit documents electronically in the digital drop box.

Course materials tailored to the Madura text that are included with the CourseCompass, WebCT, and Blackboard course management systems include:

- All of the supplementary items available with the text.
- Ten-question homework sets and two mini-case problems per chapter that you can assign to students.
- True/false and multiple-choice quizzes for each chapter, as well as sample midterm and final exams.

Please contact your local sales representative for more information on obtaining Web content in these various formats.

Wall Street Journal Edition

Order *The Wall Street Journal* Edition of this text and your students will receive a 10-week subscription to *The Wall Street Journal* and access to *The Wall Street Journal* Online Edition. And for adopting The *Wall Street Journal* Edition, professors will receive a complimentary full-year subscription to *The Wall Street Journal* and access to *The Wall Street Journal* Online Edition at **http://online.wsj.com**. Please contact your Addison-Wesley sales representative for details.

Online Trading and Investment Simulator (OTIS)

A truly exciting addition to our teaching/learning assets is the use of OTIS, a powerful trading and investment simulator developed at the Alfred P. West, Jr., Learning Lab at the Wharton School of the University of Pennsylvania. This Web-based simulator makes the student a virtual fund manager. Students learn how to construct and manage portfolios; understand the mechanics, risks, and requirements of margin trading; appreciate the benefits of short selling; and grasp the concept of liquidity as it applies to meeting a portfolio's short- and long-term needs, among other skills.

The simulator enables the student fund manager to make trades, view holdings, assess performance, and evaluate performance against that of fellow classmates. A true innovation to the art and science of trading and investment, OTIS will quickly propel students into a hands-on, interactive learning environment.

For more information about OTIS visit **http://www.aw-bc.com/wharton**. To order OTIS please contact your Addison-Wesley sales representative for details at **http://www.aw-bc.com/replocator/**.

LIST OF REVIEWERS

Addison-Wesley sought the advice of many excellent reviewers, all of whom strongly influenced the organization, substance, and approach of this book. The following individuals provided extremely useful evaluations:

Eddie Ary,
Ouachita Baptist University

Charles Blaylock,
Lamar University

Kathleen Bromley,
Monroe Community College

Charles E. Downing,
Massasoit Community College

Brenda Eichelberger,
Portland State University

Michael Finke,
University of Missouri

Daniel Klein,
Bowling Green State University

John R. Ledgerwood,
Bethune-Cookman College

Diann Moorman,
Iowa State University

Dianne Morrison,
University of Wisconsin – La Crosse

Susan L. Pallas,
Southeast Community College

Aimee D. Prawitz,
Northern Illinois University

Gerald Silver,
Purdue University

Carolyn Strauch,
Crowder College

Timothy Strudell,
University of Texas at San Antonio

Wayne Williams,
University of North Florida

Addison-Wesley would also like to thank the following individuals who provided feedback in previous editions:

Tim Alzheimer,
Montana State University, Bozeman

Pat Andrus,
University of Louisiana, Lafayette

Albert L. Auxier,
University of Tennessee, Knoxville

H. David Barr,
Blinn College

John Blaylock,
Northeast Community College

Lyle Bowlin,
University of Northern Iowa

Ted Caldwell,
California State University, Fullerton

Margaret A. Camp,
University of Nebraska, Kearney

Joyce Cantrell,
Kansas State University

Steven L. Christian,
Jackson Community College

Conrad Ciccotello,
Georgia State University

Bruce A. Costa,
University of Montana

ACKNOWLEDGMENTS

I benefited from the insight of John Bernardin, Dave Brooks, Ed Everhart, Marianne Hudson, and Victor Kalafa regarding various personal finance issues. I also benefited from many individuals who I surveyed to identify the personal finance concepts that were most important to them, and to determine how I could most effectively communicate common personal finance dilemmas and solutions.

Special acknowledgment is due to several individuals whose contributions to this Third Edition and expertise are great assets: to Steven L. Christian of Jackson Community College and Terry L. Christian for developing content for the Building Your Own Financial Plan exercises and workbook templates, writing the Ethical Dilemmas, and revising the Test Bank; to Michael P. Griffin, University of Massachusetts, Dartmouth, for developing the Excel-based Financial Planning Software; to Barbara Rice of Florida College for preparing the PowerPoint Lecture Note Presentation; and to Dianne R. Morrison of the University of Wisconsin, La Crosse for authoring the Instructor's Manual. I am especially indebted to Michael J. Woodworth for his role on the Third Edition, his skilled work as an accuracy checker, and for his contributions to the tax chapter.

I wish to acknowledge the help and support of many people associated with Addison-Wesley who made this textbook possible. First and foremost, the contributions of Peg Monahan, development editor, were invaluable. I also wish to thank Donna Battista, finance editor, for her continual support. The efforts of Bridget Page, media producer, Heather McNally, supplements editor, and Allison Stendardi, editorial assistant, are also noteworthy.

I greatly appreciated the copyediting by Kathy Cantwell. Other contributors in the production process whose commitment to quality benefited the project are Meredith Gertz, production supervisor, Chuck Spaulding, designer, and Gillian Hall, project manager at The Aardvark Group.

Finally, I wish to thank my wife, Mary, and my parents for their moral support.

Overview of a Financial Plan

*I*magine that you are taking a vacation next year. This is a major event for you and you wish to plan thoroughly so that nothing goes wrong. You have many choices to make. Where should you go? How big is your vacation budget and how do you want to allocate it? Vacations require detailed planning. You choose your itinerary, carefully save your money and vacation time, and have the time of your life.

Now, imagine that you are planning your financial future. You have major events ahead of you and you wish to plan thoroughly so that nothing goes wrong. You have many choices to make. Should you invest in a retirement account? What type of house should you buy? How much of your budget should be allocated to food and utilities? How much can you afford to spend on clothes? Should you spend all of your money as you earn it, or should you use some money for investment opportunities? When do you want to retire? Do you want to leave an estate for your heirs? All of these decisions require detailed planning.

In a world where there are few guarantees, thorough financial planning, prudent financial management, and careful spending can help you achieve your financial goals.

The personal financial planning process enables you to understand a financial plan and to develop a personal financial plan. The simple objective of financial planning is to make the best use of your resources to achieve your financial goals. The sooner you develop your goals and a financial plan to achieve those goals, the easier it will be to achieve your objectives.

The objectives of this chapter are to:

- Explain how you benefit from personal financial planning
- Identify the key components of a financial plan
- Outline the steps involved in developing your financial plan

HOW YOU BENEFIT FROM AN UNDERSTANDING OF PERSONAL FINANCE

personal finance
The process of planning your spending, financing, and investing to optimize your financial situation.

personal financial plan
A plan that specifies your financial goals and describes the spending, financing, and investing plans that are intended to achieve those goals.

Personal finance (also referred to as **personal financial planning**) is the process of planning your spending, financing, and investing to optimize your financial situation. A **personal financial plan** specifies your financial goals and describes the spending, financing, and investing plans that are intended to achieve those goals. Although the U.S. is one of the wealthiest countries, many Americans do not manage their financial situations well. Consequently, they tend to rely too much on credit and have excessive debt. Consider these statistics:

- More than 1.6 million people filed for personal bankruptcy in 2004.
- The level of savings in the U.S. is only about 2 percent of income earned.
- About half of all surveyed people in the U.S. who are working full-time state that they live from one paycheck to the next, without a plan for saving money.
- About 40 percent of people who work full time do not save for retirement. Those who do typically save a relatively small amount of money.

The lack of savings is especially problematic given the increasing cost of health care and other necessities. You will have numerous options regarding the choice of bank deposits, credit cards, loans, insurance policies, investments, and retirement plans. With an understanding of personal finance, you will be able to make decisions that can enhance your financial situation. An understanding of personal finance is beneficial to you in many ways, including the following:

Make Your Own Financial Decisions

opportunity cost
What you give up as a result of a decision.

An understanding of personal finance enables you to make informed decisions about your financial situation. Each of your spending decisions has an **opportunity cost,** which represents what you give up as a result of that decision. By spending money for a specific purpose, you forgo alternative ways that you could have spent the money and also forgo saving the money for a future purpose. For example, if your decision to use your cell phone costs $100 per month, you have forgone the possibility of using that money to buy concert tickets or to save for a new car. Informed financial decisions increase the amount of money that you accumulate over time and give you more flexibility to purchase the products and services you want in the future.

Judge the Advice of Financial Advisers

The personal financial planning process will enable you to make informed decisions about your spending, saving, financing, and investing. Nevertheless, you may prefer to rely on advice from various types of financial advisers. An understanding of personal finance allows you to judge the guidance of financial advisers and to determine whether their advice is in your best interest (or in their best interest).

EXAMPLE   You want to invest $10,000 of your savings. A financial adviser guarantees that your investment will increase in value by 20 percent (or by $2,000) this year, but he will charge you 4 percent of the investment ($400) for his advice. If you have a background in personal finance, you would know that no investment can be guaranteed to increase in value by 20 percent in one year. Therefore, you would realize that you should not trust this financial adviser. You could either hire a more reputable financial adviser or review investment recommendations made by financial advisers on the Internet (often for free).

Become a Financial Adviser

An understanding of personal finance may interest you in pursuing a career as a financial adviser. Financial advisers are in demand because many people lack an understanding of personal finance or are not interested in making their own financial decisions. A single course in personal finance is insufficient to start a career as a financial adviser, but it may interest you in taking additional courses to obtain the necessary qualifications.

COMPONENTS OF A FINANCIAL PLAN

A complete financial plan contains your personal finance decisions related to six key components:

1. Budgeting and tax planning

2. Managing your liquidity

3. Financing your large purchases

4. Protecting your assets and income (insurance)

5. Investing your money

6. Planning your retirement and estate

These six components are very different; decisions concerning each are captured in separate plans that, taken together, form your overall financial plan. To begin your introduction to the financial planning process, let's briefly explore each component.

A Plan for Your Budgeting and Tax Planning

budget planning (budgeting)
The process of forecasting future expenses and savings.

Budget planning (also referred to as **budgeting**) is the process of forecasting future expenses and savings. That is, it requires you to decide whether to spend or save money. If you receive $750 in income during one month, your amount saved is the amount of money (say, $100) that you do not spend. The relationship between income received, spending, and saving is illustrated in Exhibit 1.1. Some individuals are "big spenders": they focus their budget decision on how to spend most or all of their income and there-

Exhibit 1.1 How a Budget Plan Affects Savings

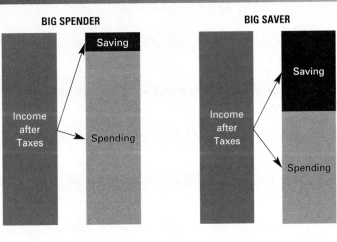

fore have little or no money left for saving. Others are "big savers": they set a savings goal and consider spending their income received only after allocating a portion of it toward saving. Budgeting can help you estimate how much of your income will be required to cover monthly expenses so that you can set a goal for saving each month.

The first step in budget planning is to evaluate your current financial position by assessing your income, your expenses, your **assets** (what you own), and your **liabilities** (debt, or what you owe). Your **net worth** is the value of what you own minus the value of what you owe. You can measure your wealth by your net worth. As you save money, you increase your assets and therefore increase your net worth. Budget planning enables you to build your net worth by setting aside part of your income to either invest in additional assets or reduce your liabilities.

Your budget is influenced by your income, which in turn is influenced by your education and career decisions. Individuals who pursue higher levels of education tend to have smaller budgets during the education years. After obtaining their degrees, however, they typically are able to obtain jobs that pay higher salaries and therefore have larger budgets.

A key part of budgeting is estimating the typical expenses that you will incur each month. If you underestimate expenses, you will not achieve your savings goals. Achieving a higher level of future wealth requires you to sacrifice by keeping spending at a lower level today.

Many financial decisions are affected by tax laws, as some forms of income are taxed at a higher rate than others. By understanding how your alternative financial choices would be affected by taxes, you can make financial decisions that have the most favorable effect on your cash flows. Budgeting and tax planning are discussed in Part 1 because they underpin decisions about all other parts of your financial plan.

A Plan to Manage Your Liquidity

You should have a plan for how you will cover your daily purchases. Your expenses can range from your morning cup of coffee to major car repairs. You need to have **liquidity**, or access to funds to cover any short-term cash needs. You can enhance your liquidity by using money management and credit management.

Money management involves decisions regarding how much money to retain in a liquid form and how to allocate the funds among short-term investments. If you do not have access to money to cover cash needs, you may have insufficient liquidity. That is, you have the assets to cover your expenses, but the money is not easily accessible. Finding an effective liquidity level involves deciding how to invest your money so that you can earn a return, but also have easy access to cash if needed. At times, you may be unable to avoid cash shortages because of unanticipated expenses.

Credit management involves decisions about how much credit you need to support your spending and which sources of credit to use. Credit is commonly used to cover both large and small expenses when you are short on cash, so it enhances your liquidity. Credit should be used only when necessary, however, as you will need to pay back borrowed funds with interest (and the interest expenses may be very high). The use of

assets
What you own.

liabilities
What you owe; your debt.

net worth
The value of what you own minus the value of what you owe.

liquidity
Access to funds to cover any short-term cash deficiencies.

money management
Decisions regarding how much money to retain in a liquid form and how to allocate the funds among short-term investment instruments.

credit management
Decisions regarding how much credit to obtain to support your spending and which sources of credit to use.

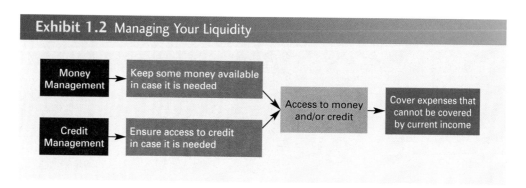

Exhibit 1.2 Managing Your Liquidity

money management and credit management to manage your liquidity is illustrated in Exhibit 1.2.

A Plan for Your Financing

Loans are typically needed to finance large expenditures, such as the payment of college tuition or the purchase of a car or a home. The amount of financing needed is the difference between the amount of the purchase and the amount of money you have available, as illustrated in Exhibit 1.3. Managing loans includes determining how much you can afford to borrow, deciding on the maturity (length of time) of the loan, and selecting a loan that charges a competitive interest rate.

A Plan for Protecting Your Assets and Income

insurance planning
Determining the types and amount of insurance needed to protect your assets.

To protect your assets, you can conduct **insurance planning**, which determines the types and amount of insurance that you need. In particular, automobile insurance and homeowner's insurance protect your assets, while health insurance limits your potential medical expenses. Disability insurance and life insurance protect your income.

A Plan for Your Investing

Any funds that you have beyond what you need to maintain liquidity should be invested. Because these funds normally are not used to satisfy your liquidity needs, they can be invested with the primary objective of earning a high return. Potential investments include stocks, bonds, mutual funds, and real estate. You must determine how much of your funds you wish to allocate toward investments and what types of investments you wish to consider. Most investments are subject to **risk** (uncertainty surrounding their potential return), however, so you need to manage them so that your risk is limited to a tolerable level.

risk
Uncertainty surrounding the potential return on an investment.

A Plan for Your Retirement and Estate

retirement planning
Determining how much money you should set aside each year for retirement and how you should invest those funds.

Retirement planning involves determining how much money you should set aside each year for retirement and how you should invest those funds. Retirement planning must begin well before you retire so that you can accumulate sufficient money to invest and support yourself after you retire. Money contributed to various kinds of retirement plans is protected from taxes until it is withdrawn from the retirement account.

estate planning
Determining how your wealth will be distributed before or upon your death.

Estate planning is the act of planning how your wealth will be distributed before or upon your death. Effective estate planning protects your wealth against unnecessary taxes, and ensures that your wealth is distributed in the manner that you desire.

How the Text Organization Relates to the Financial Plan's Components

Each of the six parts of this text covers one specific component of the financial plan. The relationship among the components of the financial plan is illustrated in Exhibit 1.4.

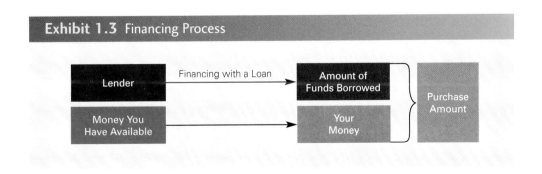

Exhibit 1.3 Financing Process

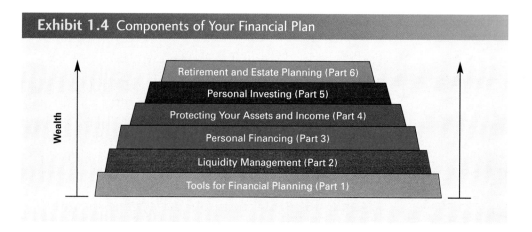

Part 1 (Tools for Financial Planning) describes budgeting, which focuses on how cash received (from income or other sources) is allocated to saving, spending, and taxes. Budget planning serves as the foundation of the financial plan, as it is your base for making personal financial decisions.

The next component is liquidity management (Part 2) because you must have adequate liquidity before financing or investing. Once your budget plan and your liquidity are in order, you are in a position to plan your financing (Part 3) for major purchases such as a new car or a home. Part 4 explains how to use insurance to protect your assets and your income. Next, you can consider investment alternatives such as stocks, bonds, and mutual funds (Part 5). Finally, planning for retirement (Part 6) focuses on the wealth that you will accumulate by the time you retire.

An effective financial plan enhances your net worth and therefore builds your wealth. In each part of the text, you will have the opportunity to develop a component of your financial plan. At the end of each chapter, the Building Your Own Financial Plan exercise offers you guidance on the key decisions that you can make after reading that chapter. Evaluate your options and make decisions using the Excel-based software on the CD-ROM available with your text. By completing the Building Your Own Financial Plan exercises, you will build a financial plan for yourself by the end of the school term. Exhibit 1.5 lists examples of the decisions you will make for each component.

How the Components Relate to Your Cash Flows. Exhibit 1.6 illustrates the typical types of cash inflows (cash that you receive) and cash outflows (cash that you spend). This exhibit also shows how each component of the financial plan reflects decisions on how to obtain or use cash. You receive cash inflows in the form of income from your employer and use some of that cash to spend on products and services. Income (Part 1) focuses on the relationship between your income and your spending. Your budgeting decisions determine how much of your income you spend on products and services. The residual funds can be allocated for your personal finance needs. Liquidity management (Part 2) focuses on depositing excess cash or obtaining credit if you are short on cash. Financing (Part 3) focuses on obtaining cash to support your large purchases. Protecting your assets and income (Part 4) focuses on determining your insurance needs and spending money on insurance premiums. Investing (Part 5) focuses on using some of your cash to build your wealth. Planning for your retirement (Part 6) focuses on periodically investing cash in your retirement account.

If you need more cash inflows beyond your income, you may decide to rely on savings that you have already accumulated or obtain loans from creditors. If your income exceeds the amount that you wish to spend, you can use the excess funds to make more investments or to repay some or all of the principal on existing loans. Thus, your investment decisions can serve as a source of funds (selling your investments) or a way of using additional funds (making additional investments). Your financing decisions can serve as a source of funds (obtaining additional loans) or a use of funds (repaying existing loans).

Exhibit 1.5 Examples of Decisions Made in Each Component of a Financial Plan

A Plan for:	Types of Decisions
1. Managing your income	What expenses should you anticipate?
	How much money should you attempt to save each month?
	How much money must you save each month toward a specific purchase?
	What debt payments must you make each month?
2. Managing your liquidity	How much money should you maintain in your checking account?
	How much money should you maintain in your savings account?
	Should you use credit cards as a means of borrowing money?
3. Financing	How much money can you borrow to purchase a car?
	Should you borrow money to purchase a car or should you lease a car?
	How much money can you borrow to purchase a home?
	What type of mortgage loan should you obtain to finance the purchase of a house?
4. Protecting your assets and income	What type of insurance do you need?
	How much insurance do you need?
5. Investing	How much money should you allocate toward investments?
	What types of investments should you consider?
	How much risk can you tolerate when investing your money?
6. Your retirement and estate	How much money will you need for retirement?
	How much money must you save each year so that you can retire in a specific year?
	How will you allocate your estate among your heirs?

Exhibit 1.6 How Financial Planning Affects Your Cash Flows

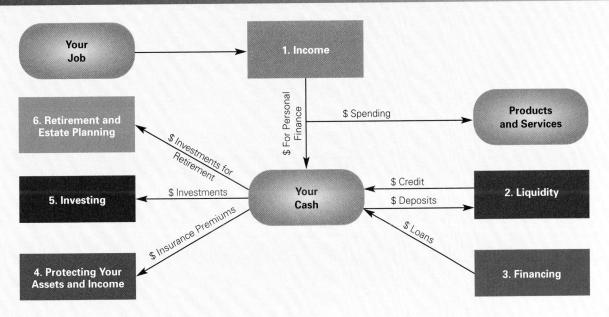

DEVELOPING THE FINANCIAL PLAN

Six steps are involved in developing each component of your financial plan.

Step 1. Establish Your Financial Goals

You must determine your financial goals.

Types of Goals. You can specify your goals in the form of purchases that you wish to make someday, or your goals may simply be to get out of debt or improve your credit history. For example, you may want to pay off your student loans or make regular payments on your credit card debt. These goals in turn influence the amount of money that you will need. Your goals may also be specified in the form of an amount of wealth that you hope to have someday, such as a goal to have $200,000 in wealth by age 40. You may simply want to accumulate a specific amount of savings over time so that you can afford to do whatever you want in the future, help other family members, or contribute to a worthy cause.

Set Realistic Goals. You need to be realistic about your goals so that you can have a strong likelihood of achieving them. A financial plan that requires you to save almost all of your income is useless if you are unable or unwilling to follow that plan. When this overly ambitious plan fails, you may become discouraged and lose interest in planning. By reducing the level of wealth you wish to attain to a realistic level, you will be able to develop a more viable plan.

Timing of Goals. Financial goals can be characterized as short term (within the next year), intermediate term (typically between one and five years), or long term (beyond five years). For instance, a short-term financial goal may be to accumulate enough money to purchase a car within six months. An intermediate-term goal would be to pay off a school loan in the next three years. A long-term goal would be to save enough money so that you can maintain your lifestyle and retire in 20 years. The more aggressive your goals, the more ambitious your financial plan will need to be.

Step 2. Consider Your Current Financial Position

Your decisions about how much money to spend next month, how much money to place in your savings account, how often to use your credit card, and how to invest your money depend on your financial position. A person with little debt and many assets will clearly make different decisions than a person with mounting debt and few assets. And a single individual without dependents will have different financial means than a couple with children, even if the individual and the couple have the same income. The appropriate plan also varies with your age and wealth. If you are 20 years old with zero funds in your bank account, your financial plan will be different than if you are 65 years old and have saved much of your income over the last 40 years.

Since your financial planning decisions are dependent on your financial position, they are dependent on your education and career choice, as explained next.

How Your Future Financial Position Is Tied to Your Education. Your financial position is highly influenced by the amount of education you pursue. The more education you have, the higher your earnings will likely be. As Exhibit 1.7 shows, the difference in earnings between a high school graduate and bachelor's degree holder in 2000 was $17,500. Before you choose a major, consider your skills, interests, and the career paths that different majors will prepare you for. A major in biology or chemistry may allow you to pursue careers in the biotechnology industry, while a major in English may allow you to pursue a career in journalism.

How Your Future Financial Position Is Tied to Your Career Choice. Your career choices also affect your income and potential for spending and saving money. If you become a social worker, you will be in a different financial position than if you choose to work as

Exhibit 1.7 Comparison of Income among Education Levels

Education	Median Level of Annual Income
Master's degree	$55,300
Bachelor's degree	46,300
Associate degree	35,400
Some college, no degree	32,400
High-school graduate	28,800
Some high school, no degree	21,400

Source: Bureau of Labor Statistics, U.S. Department of Labor.

an electrical engineer. As a social worker, you will need to save a much higher proportion of your income to achieve the same level of savings that you could amass as an electrical engineer. If you choose a career that pays a low income, you will need to set attainable financial goals. Or you may reconsider your choice of a career in pursuit of a higher level of income. However, be realistic. You should not decide to be a doctor just because doctors' salaries are high if you dislike health-related work. You should choose a career that will be enjoyable and that your skills are suited to. If you like your job, you are more likely to perform well. Since you may be working for 40 years or longer, you should seriously think about the career that will satisfy your financial and personal needs.

The fastest-growing occupations in 2000–2010 are identified in the first column of Exhibit 1.8. The expected change in the employment level for each of these positions is shown in the second column, while the percentage change in employment is shown in the third column. Earnings are ranked in the fourth column, and the main source of education is shown in the fifth column. Notice that many of the fastest-growing occupations are in computer- and health-related fields, and that education requirements range from on-the-job training to a doctoral degree.

Many people change their career over time. As the demand for occupations changes, some jobs are eliminated and others are created. In addition, some people grow tired of their occupation and seek a new career. Thus, career choices are not restricted to students who are just completing their education. As with your initial career decision, a shift to a new career should be influenced by your views of what will satisfy you.

Various Web sites can help you estimate the income level for a specific career. Additional information about careers and Web site links on salary levels for various types of careers are provided at http://www.aw-bc.com/madura. Even if the income level in a particular career you desire is less than what you expected, you may be able to maintain the same financial goals by extending the period in which you hope to achieve those goals.

Step 3. Identify and Evaluate Alternative Plans That Could Achieve Your Goals

You must identify and evaluate the alternative financial plans that could achieve your financial goals (specified in Step 1), given your financial position (determined in Step 2). For example, to accumulate a substantial amount of money in 10 years, you could decide either to save a large portion of your income over those years or to invest your initial savings in an investment that may grow in value over time. The first plan is a more conservative approach, but requires you to save money consistently over time. The second plan does not require as much discipline, because it relies on the initial investment to grow substantially over time. However, the second plan is more likely to fail because there is risk related to whether the value of the initial investment will increase as expected.

Exhibit 1.8 Fastest-Growing Occupations, 2000–2010

Occupation	Number (in 1000s)	Change Percent	Quartile Rank by 2000 Median Annual Earnings[1]	Most Significant Source of Education or Training
Computer software engineers, applications	380	100	1	Bachelor's degree
Computer support specialists	490	97	2	Associate degree
Computer software engineers, systems software	284	90	1	Bachelor's degree
Network and computer systems administrators	187	82	1	Bachelor's degree
Network systems and data communications analysts	92	77	1	Bachelor's degree
Desktop publishers	25	67	2	Postsecondary vocational award
Database administrators	70	66	1	Bachelor's degree
Personal and home care aides	258	62	4	Short-term on-the-job training
Computer systems analysts	258	60	1	Bachelor's degree
Medical assistants	187	57	3	Moderate-term on-the-job training
Social and human service assistants	147	54	3	Moderate-term on-the-job training
Physician assistants	31	53	1	Bachelor's degree
Medical records and health information technicians	66	49	3	Associate degree
Computer and information systems managers	150	48	1	Bachelor's or higher degree, plus work experience
Home health aides	291	47	4	Short-term on-the-job training
Physical therapist aides	17	46	3	Short-term on-the-job training
Occupational therapist aides	4	45	3	Short-term on-the-job training
Physical therapist assistants	20	45	2	Associate degree
Audiologists	6	45	1	Master's degree
Fitness trainers and aerobics instructors	64	40	3	Postsecondary vocational award
Computer and information scientists, research	11	40	1	Doctoral degree
Veterinary assistants and laboratory animal caretakers	22	40	4	Short-term on-the-job training
Occupational therapist assistants	7	40	2	Associate degree
Veterinary technologists and technicians	19	39	3	Associate degree
Speech-language pathologists	34	39	1	Master's degree
Mental health and substance abuse social workers	33	39	2	Master's degree
Dental assistants	92	37	2	Moderate-term on-the-job training
Dental hygienists	54	37	1	Associate degree
Special education teachers, preschool, kindergarten, and elementary school	86	37	1	Bachelor's degree
Pharmacy technicians	69	36	3	Moderate-term on-the-job training

[1]The quartile rankings of Occupational Employment Statistics annual earnings data are presented in the following categories: 1=very high ($39,700 and over), 2=high ($25,760 to $39,660), 3=low ($18,500 to $25,760), and 4=very low (up to $18,490).

Source: Bureau of Labor Statistics, U.S. Department of Labor.

Step 4. Select and Implement the Best Plan for Achieving Your Goals

You need to analyze and select the plan that will be most effective in achieving your goals. Individuals in the same financial position with the same financial goals may decide on different financial plans. For example, you may be willing to save a specific amount of money every month to achieve a particular level of wealth in 10 years. Another individual may prefer to make some risky investments today (rather than save money every month) in order to achieve the same level of wealth in 10 years. The type of plan you select to achieve your financial goals is influenced by your willingness to take risk and your self-discipline.

Using the Internet. The Internet provides you with valuable information for making financial decisions. Your decision to spend money on a new stereo or to save the money may be dependent on how much you can earn from depositing the money. Your decision of whether to purchase a new car depends on the prices of new cars and financing rates on car loans. Your decision of whether to purchase a home depends on the prices of homes and financing rates on home loans. Your decision of whether to invest in stocks is influenced by the prices of stocks. Your decision of where to purchase insurance may be influenced by the insurance premiums quoted by different insurance agencies. All of these financial decisions require knowledge of prevailing prices or interest rates, which are literally at your fingertips on the Internet.

The Internet also provides updated information on all parts of the financial plan, such as:

- Current tax rates and rules that can be used for tax planning

- Recent performances of various types of investments

- New retirement plan rules that can be used for retirement planning

Many Web sites offer online calculators that you can use for a variety of financial planning decisions, such as:

- Estimating your taxes

- Determining how your savings will grow over time

- Determining whether buying or leasing a car is more appropriate

Special features in each chapter called Financial Planning Online illustrate how the Internet facilitates the creation of the various parts of the financial plan. Financial Planning Online exercises are also provided at the end of each chapter so that you can practice using the Internet for financial planning purposes. URLs in this text are available and updated on the text's Web site for easy navigation.

When you use online information for personal finance decisions, keep in mind that some information may not be accurate. Use reliable sources, such as Web sites of government agencies or financial media companies that have a proven track record for reporting financial information. Also, recognize that free personal finance advice provided online does not necessarily apply to every person's situation. Get a second opinion before you follow online advice, especially when the advice recommends that you spend or invest money.

Focus on Ethics: Personal Financial Advice

Many individuals have a limited background in financial planning and rely on professionals in the financial services industry for advice when developing their financial plan. While most advisers take their responsibilities seriously and are very ethical, there are some unethical and incompetent advisers.

One of the facets of financial services products that creates a potential conflict of interest for your adviser is the many fee and commission structures available on even a

single product such as a life insurance policy. Your objective is to get the best advice appropriate for your needs. The adviser's objective should be the same, but the method (or product) selected could possibly be chosen because of the commission structure the product offers. Let's face it: there is always a conflict of interest any time a salesperson charges a fee or commission. Normally this conflict is not a problem, since fees and commissions are regulated and are subject to competitive pressure. You certainly should inquire as to the amount of commission or fees involved in any transaction. If they are unreasonable, take your business elsewhere.

There are two things to be wary of: unethical behavior and incompetent advice. Unethical behavior can range from touting a stock as a "Buy" when it clearly is not, to outright theft or fraud. Incompetent advice is hard to discern. If you clearly state that you have a low risk tolerance and you are persuaded to buy a risky stock, you probably are receiving incompetent advice, or perhaps even unethical advice.

How do you avoid unethical and incompetent advisers? The solution is to do your homework. By being alert, asking questions, and carefully considering the advice, you may be able to avoid advisers who do not have your interests first on their priority lists. Ask questions of them and ask questions of their current clients. In many cases you will hear of an adviser through a friend or acquaintance. Ask about their experience with the adviser. After you meet the adviser, you can make your own judgments. Check the credentials of the adviser. Financial services professionals are licensed for the products they sell and they must meet continuing education requirements to maintain those licenses.

1.1 Financial Planning Online: Financial Planning Tools for You

Go to
http://finance.yahoo.com/

This Web site provides much information and many tools that can be used for all aspects of financial planning, including tax rates, bank deposit rates, loan rates, credit card information, mortgage rates, and quotations and analysis of stocks, bonds, mutual funds, and insurance policies. It also provides information for creating retirement plans and wills.

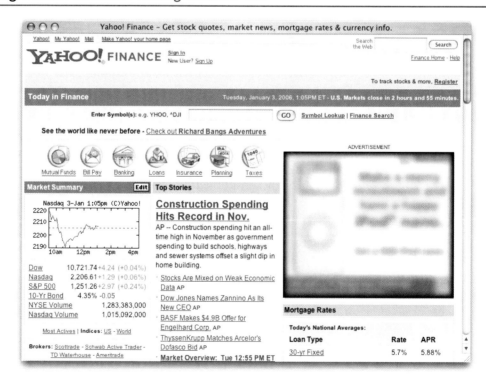

There are special certifications such as the CFP®, the Certified Financial Planner designation, and the CLU, Chartered Life Underwriter, that indicate a level of competence in some aspects of financial planning.

While most financial services professionals are indeed professionals and knowledgeable in their field, it is still your responsibility to monitor your investments. In the final analysis, it should be your decision which product to buy, how much insurance coverage you should have, and when you should change investments. Educating yourself on these financial products is key to making sound decisions.

Step 5. Evaluate Your Financial Plan

After you develop and implement each component of your financial plan, you must monitor your progress to ensure that the plan is working as you intended. Keep your financial plan easily accessible so that you can evaluate it over time.

Step 6. Revise Your Financial Plan

If you find that you are unable or unwilling to follow the financial plan that you developed, you need to revise the plan to make it more realistic. Of course, your financial goals may have to be reduced as well if you are unable to maintain the plan for achieving a particular level of wealth.

As time passes, your financial position will change, especially upon specific events such as graduating from college, marriage, a career change, or the birth of a child. As your financial position changes, your financial goals may change as well. You need to revise your financial plan to reflect such changes in your means and priorities.

The steps in developing a financial plan are summarized in Exhibit 1.9. To see how the steps can be applied, consider the example on the next page.

Exhibit 1.9 Summary of Steps Used to Develop a Financial Plan

1. Establish your financial goals.

   - What are your short-term financial goals?
   - What are your intermediate-term financial goals?
   - What are your long-term financial goals?

2. Consider your current financial position.

   - How much money do you have in savings?
   - What is the value of your investments?
   - What is your net worth?

3. Identify and evaluate alternative plans that could achieve your goals.

   - Given your goals and existing financial position described in the previous steps, how can you obtain the necessary funds to achieve your financial goals?
   - Will you need to reduce your spending to save more money each month?
   - Will you need to make investments that generate a higher rate of return?

4. Select and implement the best plan for achieving your goals.

   - What are the advantages and disadvantages of each alternative plan that could be used to achieve your goals?

5. Evaluate your financial plan.

   - Is your financial plan working properly? That is, will it enable you to achieve your financial goals?

6. Revise your financial plan.

   - Have your financial goals changed?
   - Should parts of the financial plan be revised in order to increase the chance of achieving your financial goals? (If so, identify the parts that should be changed, and determine how they should be revised.)

EXAMPLE

Stephanie Spratt graduated from college last year with a degree in marketing. After job searching for several months, she was just hired by the sales department of an advertising firm at an annual salary of $38,000. She is eager to have money from her salary to spend and to give up her interim part-time job waiting tables.

Stephanie plans to save a portion of every paycheck so that she can invest money to build her wealth over time. She realizes that by establishing a financial plan to limit her spending today, she can increase her wealth and therefore her potential spending in the future. At this point, Stephanie decides to develop an overview of her current financial position, establish her goals, and map out a plan for how she might achieve those goals, as shown in Exhibit 1.10.

Key financial planning decisions that relate to Stephanie's financial plan will be summarized at the end of each chapter. Your financial planning decisions will differ from Stephanie's or anyone else's. Nevertheless, the process of building the financial plan is the same. You need to establish your goals, assess alternative methods for achieving your goals, and decide on a financial plan that can achieve your goals.

Exhibit 1.10 Overview of Stephanie Spratt's Financial Plan

Step 1. Current Financial Position:

I have very little savings at this time and own an old car. My income, which is about $30,000 a year after taxes, should increase over time.

Step 2. Financial Goals:

I would like to:

- *buy a new car within a year,*
- *buy a home within two years,*
- *make investments that will allow my wealth to grow over time, and*
- *build a large amount of savings for retirement in 20 to 40 years.*

Step 3. Plans to Achieve the Goals:

Since my current financial position does not provide me with sufficient funds to achieve these financial goals, I need to develop a financial plan for achieving these goals. One possible plan would be to save enough money until I could purchase the car and home with cash. With this plan, however, I would not have sufficient savings to purchase a home for many years. An alternative is to save enough money to make a down payment on the car and home and to obtain financing to cover the rest of the cost. This alternative plan allows me to allocate some of my income toward investments.

My financing decisions will determine the type of car and home that I will purchase and the amount of funds I will have left to make other investments so that I can build my wealth over time.

Step 4. Selecting and Implementing the Best Plan:

Financing the purchase of a car and a home is a more appropriate plan for me. I will prepare a budget so that over time I can accumulate savings that will be used to make a down payment on a new car. Then, I will attempt to accumulate savings to make a down payment on a new home. I need to make sure that I can afford financing payments on any money that I borrow.

Step 5. Evaluating the Plan:

Once I establish a budget, I will monitor it over time to determine whether I am achieving the desired amount of savings each month.

Step 6. Revising the Plan:

If I cannot save as much money as I desire, I may have to delay my plans for purchasing a car and a home until I can accumulate enough funds to make the down payments. If I am able to exceed my savings goal, I may be able to purchase the car and the home sooner than I had originally expected.

SUMMARY

Personal financial planning is the process of planning your spending, financing, and investing to optimize your financial situation. Your financial planning decisions allow you to develop a financial plan, which involves a set of decisions on how you plan to manage your spending, financing, and investments.

A financial plan has six components: (1) budgeting, (2) managing your liquidity, (3) financing large purchases, (4) protecting your assets and income, (5) investing, and (6) planning beyond your career.

The financial planning process involves six steps: (1) establishing your financial goals, (2) considering your current financial position, (3) identifying and evaluating alternative plans that could achieve your goals, (4) selecting and implementing the best plan for achieving your financial goals, (5) evaluating the financial plan over time to ensure that you are meeting your goals, and (6) revising the financial plan when necessary.

INTEGRATING THE KEY CONCEPTS

All of the components of the financial plan are related. In general, the financial planning tools (such as budgeting and tax planning) are used for the financial planning decisions discussed in the following parts. For example, your budget (discussed in Part 1) determines how much money you can set aside to maintain liquidity (Part 2) or to invest in long-term investments (Part 5). The other components of the financial plan are also related. The way you obtain funds to finance large purchases such as a car or a home (discussed in Part 3) is dependent on whether you sell any of your existing investments (discussed in Part 5) to obtain all or a portion of the funds needed. Your need for insurance (discussed in Part 4) is dependent on the types of assets you own (e.g., a car or a home). Your ability to save for retirement each month (discussed in Part 6) is dependent on the amount of funds you need to pay off any existing credit balance (discussed in Part 2) or loans (discussed in Part 3).

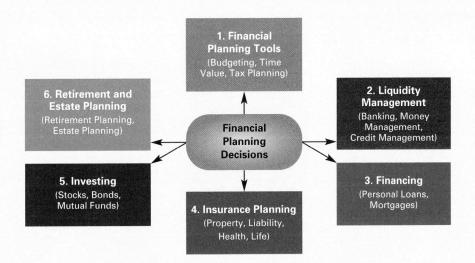

REVIEW QUESTIONS

1. Define personal financial planning. What types of decisions are involved in a personal financial plan?

2. What is an opportunity cost? What might be some of the opportunity costs of spending $10 per week on the lottery?

3. How can an understanding of personal finance benefit you?

4. What are the six key components of a financial plan?

5. Define budget planning. What elements must be assessed in budget planning?

6. How is your net worth calculated? Why is it important?

7. What factors influence income? Why is an accurate estimate of expenses important in budget planning? How do tax laws affect the budgeting process?

8. What is liquidity? What two factors are considered in managing liquidity? How are they used?

9. What factors are considered in managing financing?

10. What is the primary objective of investing? What else must be considered? What potential investment vehicles are available?

11. What are the three elements of planning to protect your assets? Define each element.

12. How does each element of financial planning affect your cash flows?

13. What are the six steps in developing a financial plan?

14. How do your financial goals fit into your financial plan? Why should goals be realistic? What are three time frames for goals? Give an example of a goal for each time frame.

15. Name some factors that might affect your current financial position.

16. How do your current financial position and goals relate to your creation of alternative financial plans?

17. Once your financial plan has been implemented, what is the next step? Why is it important?

18. Why might you need to revise your financial plan?

19. List some information available on the Internet that might be useful for financial planning. Describe one way you might use some of this information for financial planning purposes.

20. What are some of the different types of unethical behavior financial advisers might engage in? How can an understanding of personal financial planning help you deal with this potential behavior?

FINANCIAL PLANNING PROBLEMS

1. Julia brings home $1,600 per month after taxes. Julia's rent is $350 per month, her utilities are $100 per month, and her car payment is $250 per month. Julia is currently paying $200 per month to her orthodontist for her braces. If Julia's groceries cost $50 per week and she estimates her other expenses to be $150 per month, how much will she have left each month to put toward savings to reach her financial goals?

2. Julia (from problem 1) is considering trading in her car for a new one. Her new car payment will be $325 per month, and her insurance cost will increase by $60 per month. Julia determines that her other car-related expenses (gas, oil) will stay about the same. What is the opportunity cost if Julia purchases the new car?

3. Mia has $3,000 in assets, a finance company loan for $500, and an outstanding credit card balance of $135. Mia's monthly cash inflows are $2,000, and she has monthly expenses of $1,650. What is Mia's net worth?

4. At the beginning of the year, Arianne had a net worth of $5,000. During the year she set aside $100 per month from her paycheck for savings and borrowed $500 from her cousin that she must pay back in January next year. What was her net worth at the end of the year?

5. Anna has just received a gift of $500 for her graduation, which increased her net worth by $500. If she uses the money to purchase a stereo, how will her net worth be affected? If she invests the $500 at 10 percent interest per year, what will it be worth in one year?

6. Jason's car was just stolen, and the police informed him that they will probably be unable to recover it. His insurance will not cover the theft. Jason has a net worth of $3,000, all of which is easily convertible to cash. Jason requires a car for his job and his daily life. Based on Jason's cash flow, he can currently not afford more than $200 in car payments. What options does he have? How will these options affect his net worth and cash flow?

Ethical Dilemma

7. Sandy and Phil have recently married and are both in their early 20s. In establishing their financial goals, they determine that their three long-term goals are to purchase a home, to provide their children with college education, and to plan for their retirement.

   They decide to seek professional assistance in reaching their goals. After considering several financial advisers who charge an annual fee based on the size of their portfolio, they decide to go to Sandy's cousin Larry, who is a stockbroker. Larry tells them that he is happy to help them, and the only fee he will charge is for transactions. In their initial meeting, Larry recommends stocks of several well-known companies that pay high dividends, which they purchase. Three months later, Larry tells them that due to changing market conditions, they need to sell the stocks and buy several others. Three months later, the same thing happens. At the end of the year Phil and Sandy, who had sold each of the stocks for more than they had paid for them, were surprised to see that the total dollar value of their portfolio had declined. After careful analysis, they found the transaction fees exceeded their capital gains.

   a. Do you think Larry behaved ethically? Explain.

   b. Would Larry have a personal reason for handling Sandy and Phil's portfolio as he did? Explain.

FINANCIAL PLANNING ONLINE EXERCISES

1. Go to http://www.careers-in-finance.com/fpskill.htm.

   a. What are the most important skills needed to perform the job of a financial planner? Which skills are your strengths and which are your weaknesses?

   b. How can you obtain the skills you lack?

   c. Review the job listings in your area and the information on salaries. Is a career as a financial planner appealing to you? Why or why not?

2. The purpose of this exercise is to familiarize you with the wide variety of personal finance resources on Yahoo!. Go to http://finance.yahoo.com/?u.

   a. Determine how inflation and taxes will affect your investments. Go to the tax center to answer this question. How well are your investments doing after inflation and taxes if your current investments are valued at $50,000, you expect an average annual return of 8 percent on your investments, you expect to hold your investments for 25 years, your combined federal and state income tax rate is 30 percent, and the estimated annual inflation rate is 3 percent?

   b. Return to http://finance.yahoo.com/?u. Go to "Calculators" under "Banking." How large a line of credit can you obtain assuming the appraised value of your home is $125,000 and your mortgage is $75,000? Change the value of the home and the mortgage to $100,000 and $70,000, respectively, and check the line of credit you can obtain.

   c. Use the Back option in your browser to return to http://finance.yahoo.com/?u. Under "Loans," find the current rates for your region. Compare your rates with the national auto loan rates. Why are the rates different?

   d. Under "Loans," what is the monthly payment for a 48-month auto loan of $10,000 at both the lowest rate and the highest rate in your region? Use the sales tax rate in your state or assume 6 percent. Assume zero down payment and no trade-in or rebates.

BUILDING YOUR OWN FINANCIAL PLAN

These end-of-chapter exercises are designed to enable you to create a working lifelong financial plan. Like all plans, your personal plan will require periodic review and revision. In this first exercise, you should review your current financial situation; if you are a full-time student, base your review on what you anticipate your financial situation will be upon your graduation. After carefully reviewing your current or anticipated financial situation, create three short-term goals and three intermediate-term and long-term goals.

Your short-term goals should be goals that you can realistically accomplish in one year. They may include, but are not limited to, paying off credit card balances, beginning a 401(k) or other retirement-type savings program, or getting your cash inflows and outflows in balance.

Your intermediate-term goals are goals that you should realistically be able to accomplish in one to five years. They may include, but are not limited to, purchasing a new vehicle or paying off school loans.

Long-term goals will take longer than five years to accomplish realistically. They may include, but are not limited to, purchasing a home, taking a major trip (such as a summer in Europe), or saving sufficient funds to retire at a predetermined age.

The goals that you develop are a first draft and may be added to or modified as you proceed through this course. This course is designed to provide you with information and insight that will help you make informed decisions about your financial future. As you gain experience in financial planning, new goals may emerge, and existing goals may change. Once you have completed your financial plan, you should review your goals annually or whenever a significant change occurs in your life (e.g., marriage, divorce, birth of a child, or a significant change in employment circumstances).

Go to the worksheets at the end of this chapter and to the CD-ROM accompanying this text to begin building your financial plan.

THE SAMPSONS—A CONTINUING CASE

Dave and Sharon Sampson are 30 years old and have two children, who are 5 and 6 years old. Since marrying seven years ago, the Sampsons have relied on Dave's salary, which is currently $48,000 per year. They have not been able to save any money, as Dave's income is just enough to cover their mortgage loan payment and their other expenses.

Dave and Sharon feel they need to take control of their finances. Now that both children are in school, they have decided that Sharon will look into getting a part-time job. She was just hired for a part-time position at a local department store at a salary of $12,000 per year. Dave and Sharon are excited by the prospect of having additional cash inflows—they now feel they have the leeway to start working toward their financial goals.

The Sampsons own a home valued at about $100,000, and their mortgage is $90,000. They have a credit card balance of $2,000. Although they own two cars and do not have any car loans, Sharon's car is old and will need to be replaced soon. Sharon would really like to purchase a new car within the next year; she hopes to save $500 each month until she has accumulated savings of $5,000 to use for a down payment.

The Sampsons are also concerned about how they will pay for their children's college education. Sharon plans to save an additional $300 each month that will be set aside for this purpose.

The Sampsons also know they need to save for their retirement over time. Yet they do not have a plan right now to achieve that goal because they are focused on saving for a new car and their children's education. If the Sampsons were to start saving for retirement, they would probably consult a financial adviser.

The Sampsons have decided to develop a financial plan. They realize that by formally identifying their main goals, they will be able to implement and monitor their plan over time. At the end of every chapter, you will help the Sampsons develop their financial plan using the key concepts presented in the chapter.

Go to the worksheets at the end of this chapter, and to the CD-ROM accompanying this text to begin this case.

Chapter 1: Building Your Own Financial Plan

GOALS

1. Evaluate your current financial situation.
2. Set short-term, intermediate-term, and long-term goals.

ANALYSIS

1. Complete the Personal Financial Goals worksheet below.

Personal Financial Goals

Financial Goal	Dollar Amount to Accomplish	Priority (Low, Medium, High)
Short-Term Goals		
1.		
2.		
3.		
Intermediate-Term Goals		
1.		
2.		
3.		
Long-Term Goals		
1.		
2.		
3.		

2. A key part of the process of establishing your goals is evaluating your financial situation and career choices. Go to the "Occupational Outlook Handbook, 2004–05 Edition" (http://www.bls.gov/oco/home.htm) and research two careers that interest you. Complete the worksheet on the next page with the information you find on this Web site.

Personal Career Goals

	Career One	Career Two
Job Title		
Educational Requirements		
Advancement Potential		
Job Outlook		
Salary Range		
Continuing Education Requirements		
Related Occupations		
Brief Description of Working Conditions		
Brief Job Description		

DECISIONS

Describe your strategies for reaching your goals.

_____

_____

_____

_____

_____

_____

_____

_____

_____

_____

_____

_____

_____

_____

_____

_____

Chapter 1: The Sampsons—A Continuing Case

CASE QUESTION

Help the Sampsons summarize their current financial position, their goals, and their plans for achieving their goals by filling out the following worksheets.

Current Financial Position

Major Assets	Amount
Savings (High, Medium, or Low)	
Money Owed	
Salary	

Financial Goals

Goal 1. Purchase a new car for Sharon this year

How to Achieve the Goal	
How to Implement the Plan	
How to Evaluate the Plan	

Goal 2. Pay for the children's college education in 12–17 years from now

How to Achieve the Goal	
How to Implement the Plan	
How to Evaluate the Plan	

Goal 3. Set aside money for retirement

How to Achieve the Goal	
How to Implement the Plan	
How to Evaluate the Plan	

Tools for Financial Planning

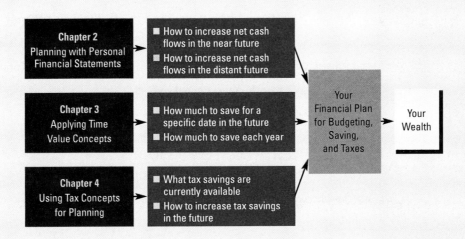

THE CHAPTERS IN THIS PART INTRODUCE THE KEY TOOLS USED TO make financial planning decisions. Chapter 2 describes the personal financial statements that help you to monitor your spending and guide your budgeting decisions. Chapter 3 illustrates how you can use time value of money concepts to make decisions about saving. Chapter 4 explains how to use tax concepts to assess and minimize your tax liability. Your budget, saving, and tax plans all influence your cash flows and wealth.

Planning with Personal Financial Statements

Where does it all go? It seems like the last paycheck is gone before the next one comes in. Money seems to burn a hole in your pocket, yet you don't believe that you are living extravagantly. Last month you made a pledge to yourself to spend less than the month before. Somehow, though, you are in the same position as you were last month. Your money is gone. Is there any way to plug the hole in your pocket?

What are your expenses? For many people, the first obstacle is to correctly assess their true expenses. Each expense seems harmless and worthwhile. But combined they can be a pack of piranhas that quickly gobble up your modest income. What can you do to gain control of your personal finances?

Just read on in this chapter and you will see how to take control of your finances. However, your task is not easy because it takes self-discipline and there may be no immediate reward. The result is often like a diet: easy to get started, but hard to carry through.

Your tools are the personal balance statement, the personal cash flow statement, and a budget. These three personal financial statements show you where you are, predict where you will be after three months or a year, and help you control expenses. The potential benefits are reduced spending, increased savings and investments, and peace of mind from knowing that you are in control.

The objectives of this chapter are to:

- Explain how to create your personal cash flow statement
- Identify the factors that affect your cash flows
- Show how to create a budget based on your forecasted cash flows
- Describe how to create your personal balance sheet
- Explain how your net cash flows are related to your personal balance sheet (and therefore affect your wealth)

PERSONAL CASH FLOW STATEMENT

personal cash flow statement
A financial statement that measures a person's cash inflows and cash outflows.

As mentioned in Chapter 1, budgeting is the process of forecasting future expenses and savings. When budgeting, the first step is to create a **personal cash flow statement,** which measures your cash inflows and cash outflows. Comparing your cash inflows and outflows allows you to monitor your spending and determine the amount of cash that you can allocate toward savings or other purposes.

Cash Inflows
The main source of cash inflows for working people is their salary, but there can be other important sources of income. Deposits in various types of savings accounts can generate cash inflows in the form of interest income. Some stocks also generate quarterly dividend income.

Cash Outflows
Cash outflows represent all of your expenses. Expenses are both large (for example, monthly rent) and small (for example, dry cleaning costs). It is not necessary to document every expenditure, but you should track how most of your money is spent. Recording transactions in your checkbook when you write checks helps you to identify how you spent your money. Using a credit card for your purchases also provides a written record of your transactions. Many people use software programs such as Quicken and Microsoft Money to record and monitor cash outflows.

Creating a Personal Cash Flow Statement
You can create a personal cash flow statement by recording how you received cash over a given period and how you used cash for expenses.

EXAMPLE

Stephanie Spratt tried to limit her spending in college but never established a personal cash flow statement. Now that she has begun her career and is earning a salary, she wants to monitor her spending on a monthly basis. She decides to create a personal cash flow statement for the last month.

Stephanie's Monthly Cash Inflows. Stephanie's present salary is about $3,170 per month ($38,000 annually) before taxes. For budgeting purposes, she is interested in the cash inflow she receives from her employer after taxes.

About $670 per month of her salary goes to taxes, so her disposable (after-tax) income is:

Monthly Salary	$3,170
−Monthly Taxes	−$670
Monthly Cash Inflow	$2,500.

Then Stephanie considers other potential sources of cash inflows. She does not receive any dividend income from stock and she does not have any money deposited in an account that pays interest. Thus, her entire monthly cash inflows come from her paycheck. She inserts the monthly cash inflow of $2,500 at the top of her personal cash flow statement.

Stephanie's Monthly Cash Outflows.   Stephanie looks in her checkbook register to see how she spent her money last month. Her household payments for the month were as follows:

- $600 for rent

- $50 for cable TV

- $60 for electricity and water

- $60 for telephone expenses

- $300 for groceries

- $130 for a health care plan provided by her employer (this expense is deducted directly from her pay)

Next Stephanie reviews several credit card bills to estimate her other typical expenses on a monthly basis:

- About $100 for clothing

- About $200 for car expenses (insurance, maintenance, and gas)

- About $600 for recreation (including restaurants and a health club membership)

Stephanie uses this cash outflow information to complete her personal cash flow statement, as shown in Exhibit 2.1. Her total cash outflows were $2,100 last month.

Stephanie's Net Cash Flows. Monthly cash inflows and outflows can be compared by estimating **net cash flows**, which are equal to the cash inflows minus the cash outflows. Stephanie estimates her net cash flows to determine how easily she covers her expenses and how much

net cash flows
Cash inflows minus cash outflows.

Exhibit 2.1 Personal Cash Flow Statement for Stephanie Spratt

Cash Inflows	Last Month
Disposable (after-tax) income	$2,500
Interest on deposits	0
Dividend payments	0
Total Cash Inflows	**$2,500**

Cash Outflows	Last Month
Rent	$600
Cable TV	50
Electricity and water	60
Telephone	60
Groceries	300
Health care insurance and expenses	130
Clothing	100
Car expenses (insurance, maintenance, and gas)	200
Recreation	600
Total Cash Outflows	**$2,100**
Net Cash Flows	**+$400**

excess cash she has to allocate to savings or other purposes. Her net cash flows during the last month were:

Net Cash Flows	=	Cash Inflows	–	Cash Outflows
	=	$2,500	–	$2,100
	=	$400.		

Stephanie enters this information at the bottom of her personal cash flow statement.

FACTORS THAT AFFECT CASH FLOWS

To enhance your wealth, you want to maximize your (or your household's) cash inflows and minimize cash outflows. Your cash inflows and outflows depend on various factors, as will be described next.

Factors Affecting Cash Inflows

Cash inflows are highly influenced by factors that affect your income level. The key factors to consider are the stage in your career path and your job skills.

Stage in Your Career Path. The stage you have reached in your career path influences cash inflows because it affects your income level. Cash inflows are relatively low for people who are in college or just starting a career (like Stephanie Spratt). They tend to increase as you gain job experience and progress within your chosen career.

Your career stage is closely related to your place in the life cycle. Younger people tend to be at early stages in their respective careers, whereas older people tend to have more work experience and are thus further along the career path. It follows that cash inflows tend to be lower for younger individuals and much higher for individuals in their 50s.

There are many exceptions to this tendency, however. Some older people switch careers and therefore may be set back on their career path. Other individuals who switch careers from a low-demand industry to a high-demand industry may actually earn higher incomes. Many women put their careers on hold for several years to raise children and then resume their professional lives.

The final stage in the life cycle that we will consider is retirement. The cash flows that come from a salary are discontinued at the time of retirement. After retirement, individuals rely on Social Security payments and interest or dividends earned on investments as sources of income. Consequently, retired individuals' cash inflows tend to be smaller than when they were working. Your retirement cash inflows will come from income from your investments and from your retirement plan. The manner in which age commonly affects cash inflows is summarized in Exhibit 2.2. Notice that there are three distinct phases.

Type of Job. Income also varies by job type. Jobs that require specialized skills tend to pay much higher salaries than those that require skills that can be obtained very quickly and easily. The income level associated with specific skills is also affected by the demand for those skills. The demand for people with a nursing license has been very high in recent years, so hospitals have been forced to pay high salaries to outbid other hospitals for nurses. Conversely, the demand for people with a history or an English literature degree is low because more students major in these areas than there are jobs.

Number of Income Earners in Your Household. If you are the sole income earner, your household's cash inflows will typically be less than if there is a second income earner. Many households now have two income earners, a trend that has substantially increased the cash flows to these households.

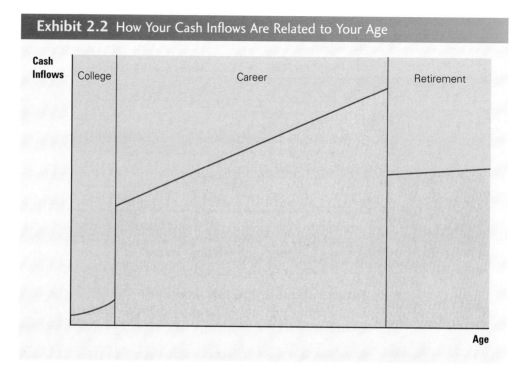

Exhibit 2.2 How Your Cash Inflows Are Related to Your Age

Factors Affecting Cash Outflows

The key factors that affect cash outflows are a person's family status, age, and personal consumption behavior.

Size of Family. A person who is supporting a family will normally incur more expenses than a single person without dependents. The more family members, the greater the amount of spending, and the greater the amount of cash outflows. Expenses for food, clothing, day care, and school tuition are higher for families with many dependents.

Age. As people get older, they tend to spend more money on expensive houses, cars, and vacations. This adjustment in spending may result from the increase in their income (cash inflows) over time as they progress along their career path.

Personal Consumption Behavior. People's consumption behavior varies substantially. At one extreme are people who spend their entire paycheck within a few days of receiving it, regardless of the size of the paycheck. Although this behavior is understandable for people who have low incomes, it is also a common practice for some people who have very large incomes, perhaps because they do not understand the importance of saving for the future. At the other extreme are "big savers" who minimize their spending and focus on saving for the future. Most people's consumption behavior is affected by their income. For example, a two-income household tends to spend more money when both income earners are working full-time.

budget
A cash flow statement that is based on forecasted cash flows for a future time period.

CREATING A BUDGET

The next step in the budgeting process is an extension of the personal cash flow statement. You can forecast net cash flows by forecasting the cash inflows and outflows for each item on the personal cash flow statement. We refer to a cash flow statement that is based on forecasted cash flows for a future time period as a **budget.** For example, you may develop a budget to determine whether your cash inflows will be sufficient to cover your cash outflows. If you expect your cash inflows to exceed your cash outflows, you can also use the budget to determine the amount of excess cash that you will have available to invest in additional assets or to make extra payments to reduce your personal debt.

EXAMPLE

Stephanie Spratt wants to determine whether she will have sufficient cash inflows this month. She uses the personal cash flow statement she developed last month to forecast this month's cash flows. However, she adjusts that statement for the following additional anticipated expenses:

1. Total health care expenses will be $430 this month, due to a minor health care procedure she received recently that is not covered by her insurance.

2. Car maintenance expenses will be $500 this month, primarily due to the need to purchase new tires for her car.

Stephanie revises her personal cash flow statement from last month to reflect the expected changes this month, as shown in Exhibit 2.3. The numbers in boldface type show the revised cash flows as a result of the unusual circumstances for this month.

The main effects of the unusual circumstances on Stephanie's expected cash flows for this month are summarized in Exhibit 2.4. Notice that the expected cash outflows for this month are $2,700, or $600 higher than the cash outflows in a typical month. In this month, the expected net cash flows are:

Expected Net Cash Flows   =   Expected Cash Inflows   –   Expected Cash Outflows

$$= \$2,500 \quad\quad - \quad \$2,700$$

$$= -\$200.$$

The budgeting process has alerted Stephanie to this $200 cash shortage.

Exhibit 2.3 Stephanie Spratt's Revised Personal Cash Flow Statement

Cash Inflows	Actual Amounts Last Month	Expected Amounts This Month
Disposable (after-tax) income	$2,500	$2,500
Interest on deposits	0	0
Dividend payments	0	0
Total Cash Inflows	**$2,500**	**$2,500**

Cash Outflows	Actual Amounts Last Month	Expected Amounts This Month
Rent	$600	$600
Cable TV	50	50
Electricity and water	60	60
Telephone	60	60
Groceries	300	300
Health care insurance and expenses	130	**430**
Clothing	100	100
Car expenses (insurance, maintenance, and gas)	200	**500**
Recreation	600	600
Total Cash Outflows	**$2,100**	**$2,700**
Net Cash Flows	**+$400**	**–$200**

Exhibit 2.4 Summary of Stephanie Spratt's Revised Cash Flows

	Last Month's Cash Flow Situation	Unusual Cash Flows Expected This Month	This Month's Cash Flow Situation
Cash inflows	$2,500	$ 0	$2,500
Cash outflows	$2,100	$600	$2,700
Net cash flows	$ 400	–$600	–$200

Anticipating Cash Shortages

In a month with a large amount of unexpected expenses, you may not have sufficient cash inflows to cover your expected cash outflows. If the cash shortage is small, you would likely withdraw funds from your checking account to make up the difference. If you expect a major deficiency for a future month, however, you might not have sufficient funds available to cover it. The budget can warn you of such a problem well in advance so that you can determine how to cover the deficiency. You should set aside funds in a savings account that can serve as an emergency fund in the event that you experience a cash shortage.

Assessing the Accuracy of the Budget

Periodically compare your actual cash flows over a recent period (such as last month) to the forecasted cash flows in your budget to determine whether your forecasts are on target. Many individuals tend to be overly optimistic about their cash flow forecasts. They overestimate their cash inflows and underestimate their cash outflows; as a result, their net cash flows are less than expected. By detecting such forecasting errors, you can take steps to improve your budgeting. You may decide to limit your spending to stay within your budgeted cash outflows. Or you may choose not to adjust your spending habits, but increase your forecast of cash outflows to reflect reality. By budgeting accurately, you are more likely to detect any future cash flow shortages and therefore can prepare in advance for any deficiencies.

EXAMPLE

Recall that Stephanie Spratt forecasted cash flows to create a budget for this coming month. Now it is the end of the month, so she can assess whether her forecasts were accurate. Her forecasted cash flows are shown in the second column of Exhibit 2.5. She compares the actual cash flows (third column) to her forecast and calculates the difference between them (shown in the fourth column). This difference between columns two and three is referred to as the forecasting error; a positive difference means that the actual cash flow level was less than forecasted, while a negative difference means that the actual cash flow level exceeded the forecast.

Reviewing the fourth column of Exhibit 2.5, Stephanie notices that total cash outflows were $100 more than expected. Her net cash flows were –$300 (a deficiency of $300), which is worse than the expected level of –$200. Stephanie assesses the individual cash outflows to determine where she underestimated. Although grocery expenses were slightly lower than expected, her clothing and recreation expenses were higher than she anticipated. She decides that the expenses were abnormally high in this month only, so she believes that her budgeted cash flows should be reasonably accurate in most months.

Forecasting Net Cash Flows over Several Months

To forecast your cash flows for several months ahead, you can follow the same process as for forecasting one month ahead. Whenever particular types of cash flows are expected to be normal, they can be forecasted from previous months when the levels were normal. You can make adjustments to account for any cash flows that you expect to be unusual in a specific month in the future. (For example, around the winter holidays you can expect to spend more on gifts and recreation.)

Exhibit 2.5 Comparison of Stephanie Spratt's Budgeted and Actual Cash Flows for This Month

Cash Inflows	Expected Amounts (forecasted at the beginning of the month)	Actual Amounts (determined at the end of the month)	Forecasting Error
Disposable (after-tax) income	$2,500	$2,500	$0
Interest on deposits	0	0	0
Dividend payments	0	0	0
Total Cash Inflows	**$2,500**	**$2,500**	**$0**
Cash Outflows	**Expected Amounts**	**Actual Amounts**	**Forecasting Error**
Rent	$600	$600	$0
Cable TV	50	50	0
Electricity and water	60	60	0
Telephone	60	60	0
Groceries	300	280	+20
Health care insurance and expenses	430	430	0
Clothing	100	170	−70
Car expenses (insurance, maintenance, and gas)	500	500	0
Recreation	600	650	−50
Total Cash Outflows	**$2,700**	**$2,800**	**−$100**
Net Cash Flows	**−$200**	**−$300**	**−$100**

Expenses such as health care, car repairs, and household repairs often occur unexpectedly. Although such expenses are not always predictable, you should budget for them periodically. You should assume that you will likely incur some unexpected expenses for health care as well as for repairs on a car or on household items over the course of several months. Thus, your budget may not be perfectly accurate in any specific month, but it will be reasonably accurate over time. If you do not account for such possible expenses over time, you will likely experience lower net cash flows than expected over time.

Creating an Annual Budget

If you are curious about how much money you may be able to save in the next year, you can extend your budget out for longer periods. You should first create an annual budget and then adjust it to reflect anticipated large changes in your cash flows.

EXAMPLE

Stephanie Spratt believes her budget for last month (except for the unusual health care and car expenses) is typical for her. She wants to extend it to forecast the amount of money that she might be able to save over the next year. Her cash inflows are predictable because she already knows her salary for the year. Some of the monthly cash outflows (such as rent and the cable bill) in her monthly budget are also constant from one month to another. To forecast these types of cash outflows, she simply multiplies the monthly amount by 12 (for each month of the year) to derive an estimate of the annual expenses, as shown in the third column of Exhibit 2.6.

Exhibit 2.6 Annual Budget for Stephanie Spratt

Cash Inflows	Typical Month	This Year's Cash Flows (equal to the typical monthly cash flows × 12)
Disposable (after-tax) income	$2,500	$30,000
Interest on deposits	0	0
Dividend payments	0	0
Total Cash Inflows	**$2,500**	**$30,000**
Cash Outflows	**Typical Month**	**This Year's Cash Flows**
Rent	$600	$7,200
Cable TV	50	600
Electricity and water	60	720
Telephone	60	720
Groceries	300	3,600
Health care insurance and expenses	130	1,560
Clothing	100	1,200
Car expenses (insurance, maintenance, and gas)	200	2,400
Recreation	600	7,200
Total Cash Outflows	**$2,100**	**$25,200**
Net Cash Flows	**+$400**	**$4,800** (difference between cash inflows and outflows)

Some other items vary from month to month, but last month's budgeted amount seems a reasonable estimate for the next 12 months. Over the next 12 months Stephanie expects net cash flows of $4,800. Therefore, she sets a goal of saving $4,800, which she can place in a bank account or invest in stocks.

Improving the Budget

As time passes, you should review your budget to determine whether you are progressing toward the financial goals that you established. To increase your savings or pay down more debt so that you can more easily achieve your financial goals, you should identify the components within the budget that you can change to improve your budget over time.

EXAMPLE

Recall that Stephanie Spratt expects to spend about $2,100 and invest the remaining $400 in assets (such as bank accounts or stocks) each month. She would like to save a substantial amount of money so that she can purchase a new car and a home someday, so she considers how she might increase her net cash flows.

Stephanie assesses her personal income statement to determine whether she can increase her cash inflows or reduce her cash outflows. She would like to generate more cash inflows than $2,500, but she is already paid well, given her skills and experience. She considers pursuing a part-time job on weekends, but does not want to use her limited free time to work. Therefore, she realizes that given her present situation and preferences, she will not be able to increase her monthly cash inflows. She decides to reduce her monthly cash outflows so that she can save more than $400 per month.

2.1 Financial Planning Online: Budgeting Tips

Go to
http://www.dallasfed.org/
ca/wealth/index.html

Click on
"Budget to Save"

This Web site provides
tips on effective budgeting
based on your goals.

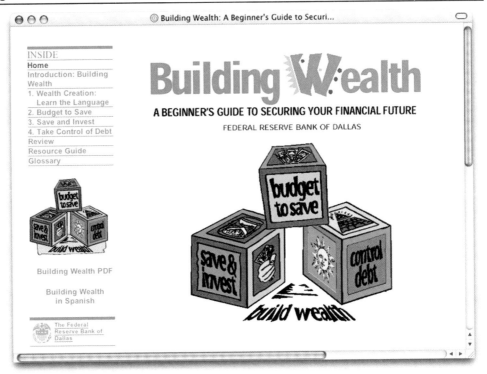

Stephanie reviews the summary of cash outflows on her budget to determine how she can reduce spending. Of the $2,100 that she spends per month, about $1,500 is spent on what she considers necessities (such as her rent and utilities). The remainder of the cash outflows (about $600) is spent on recreation; Stephanie realizes that any major reduction in spending will have to be in this category of cash outflows.

Most of her recreation spending is on her health club membership and on eating at restaurants. She recognizes that she can scale back her spending while still enjoying these activities. Specifically, she observes that her health club is upscale and overpriced. She can save about $60 per month by going to a different health club that offers essentially the same services. She also decides to reduce her spending at restaurants by about $40 per month. By revising her spending behavior in these ways, she can reduce her cash outflows by $100 per month, as summarized here:

	Previnus Cash Flow Situation	Planned Cash Flow Situation
Monthly cash inflows	$2,500	$2,500
Monthly cash outflows	$2,100	$2,000
Monthly net cash flows	$400	$500
Yearly net cash flows	$4,800	$6,000

This reduction in spending will increase net cash flows from the present level of about $400 per month to a new level of $500 per month. Over the course of a year, her net cash flows will now be $6,000. Although Stephanie had hoped to find a solution that would improve her personal cash flow statement more substantially, she believes this is a good start. Most importantly, her budget is realistic.

Focus on Ethics: Excessive Financial Dependence

Have you ever been faced with a large unexpected expense that forced you to ask for financial assistance from your family or your friends? Such a situation could result from a failure to maintain a budget or to even set a budget. Other causes are unexpected expenses. Perhaps your car breaks down and needs some expensive repairs. Or perhaps you see something that you would really like to buy, but you know you cannot afford it. If you have not planned for such a large expenditure, you may not have money to pay for it. Faced with a looming debt, it may seem easy to fall back on your family for support. Beware of relying too much on such support. When you fail to control your own budget, your reliance on others over long periods of time can create tension with your relatives and can ultimately destroy family relationships.

You must become self-reliant. While there are times when an emergency may force you to rely on family or friends for financial assistance, you should not take such help for granted on a regular and long-term basis. Create a budget and stay within it. Build and maintain an emergency fund so that you need not rely on others in times of financial crisis. Remember, they are making a sacrifice to help you. Their opportunity cost is either forgone consumption or perhaps an investment opportunity delayed. So, before you seek help from family members or friends, ask yourself if you have done all you can on your own. Are you a careful spender or are you buying luxury items that you really cannot afford? Is your financial crisis an unforeseen emergency or did you spend the money earlier instead of saving it for this expense? Careful budgeting and controlled spending lead to self-reliance and a feeling of financial freedom.

PERSONAL BALANCE SHEET

The next step in the budgeting process is to create a personal balance sheet. A budget tracks your cash flows over a given period of time, whereas a personal balance sheet

---

2.2 Financial Planning Online: The Impact of Reduced Spending

Go to
http://www.calcbuilder.com/
cgi-bin/calcs/SAV13.cgi/
intrustbank

This Web site provides
an estimate of the savings
that you can accumulate over
time if you can reduce your
spending on one or more of
your monthly expenses.

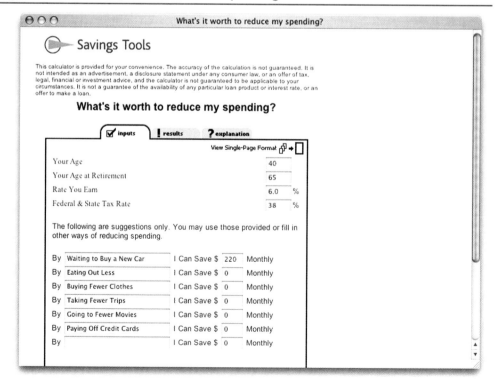

personal balance sheet
A summary of your assets (what you own), your liabilities (what you owe), and your net worth (assets minus liabilities).

provides an overall snapshot of your wealth at a specific point in time. The **personal balance sheet** summarizes your **assets** (what you own), your **liabilities** (what you owe), and your net worth (assets minus liabilities).

Assets

The assets on a balance sheet can be classified as liquid assets, household assets, and investments.

liquid assets
Financial assets that can be easily sold without a loss in value.

Liquid Assets. **Liquid assets** are financial assets that can be easily sold without a loss in value. They are especially useful for covering upcoming expenses. Some of the more common liquid assets are cash, checking accounts, and savings accounts. Cash is handy to cover small purchases, while a checking account is convenient for larger purchases. Savings accounts are desirable because they pay interest on the money that is deposited. For example, if your savings account offers an interest rate of 4 percent, you earn annual interest of $4 for every $100 deposited in your account. The management of liquid assets for covering day-to-day transactions is discussed in Part 2.

household assets
Items normally owned by a household, such as a home, car, and furniture.

Household Assets. **Household assets** include items normally owned by a household, such as a home, car, and furniture. The financial planning involved in purchasing large household assets is discussed in Part 3. These items tend to make up a larger proportion of your total assets than the liquid assets.

When creating a personal balance sheet, you need to assess the value of your household assets. The market value of an asset is the amount you would receive if you sold the asset today. For example, if you purchased a car last year for $20,000, the car may have a market value of $14,000 today, meaning that you could sell it to someone else for $14,000. The market values of cars can easily be obtained from various sources on the Internet, such as http://kbb.com/. Although establishing the precise market value of some assets such as a house may be difficult, you can use recent selling prices of other similar houses nearby to obtain a reasonable estimate.

2.3 Financial Planning Online: Budgeting Advice

Go to
http://www.calcbuilder.com/
cgi-bin/calcs/BUD3.cgi/
FinanCenter

This Web site provides a means for comparing your actual budget versus your desired budget (based on your income and spending habits) and shows how you could improve your budget.

How Much Am I Spending?	Current Spending	Desired Spending
Home Payment	$ 900	$ 900
Home Maintenance	$ 50	$ 50
Utilities	$ 160	$ 130
Auto Payments	$ 300	$ 300
Auto Expenses	$ 120	$ 90
Insurance Payments	$ 250	$ 250
Child Care	$ 300	$ 300
Alimony	$ 0	$ 0
Education	$ 150	$ 150
Food	$ 260	$ 180
Clothing	$ 140	$ 100
Gifts and Charity	$ 60	$ 80
Entertainment	$ 200	$ 120
Travel	$ 60	$ 60
Credit Card Interest	$ 40	$ 0
Miscellaneous	$ 0	$ 0
Your Monthly Income After Taxes		$ 3000

Investments.   Some of the more common investments are in bonds, stocks, and rental property.

bonds
Certificates issued by borrowers to raise funds.

Bonds are certificates issued by borrowers (typically, firms and government agencies) to raise funds. When you purchase a $1,000 bond that was just issued, you provide a $1,000 loan to the issuer of the bond. You earn interest while you hold the bond for a specified period. (Bonds are the subject of Chapter 17.)

stocks
Certificates representing partial ownership of a firm.

Stocks are certificates representing partial ownership of a firm. Firms issue stock to obtain funding for various purposes, such as purchasing new machinery or building new facilities. Many firms have millions of shareholders who own shares of the firm's stock.

The investors who purchase stock are referred to as shareholders or stockholders. You may consider purchasing stocks if you have excess funds. You can sell some of your stock holdings when you need funds.

The market value of stocks changes daily. You can find the current market value of a stock at many Web sites, including http://finance.yahoo.com/?u. Stock investors can earn a return on their investment if the stock's value increases over time. They can also earn a return if the firm pays dividends to its shareholders.

Investments such as stocks normally are not considered liquid assets because they can result in a loss in value if they have to be sold suddenly. Stocks are commonly viewed as a long-term investment and therefore are not used to cover day-to-day expenses. (Stocks will be discussed in detail in Chapters 15 and 16.)

mutual funds
Investment companies that sell shares to individuals and invest the proceeds in investment instruments such as bonds or stocks.

Mutual funds sell shares to individuals and invest the proceeds in an overall portfolio of investment instruments such as bonds or stocks. They are managed by portfolio managers who decide what securities to purchase so that the individual investors do not have to make the investment decisions themselves. The minimum investment varies depending on the particular fund, but it is usually between $500 and $3,000. The value of the shares of any mutual fund can be found in periodicals such as *The Wall Street Journal* or on various Web sites. We'll examine mutual funds in detail in Chapter 18.

real estate
Rental property and land.

Real estate includes holdings in rental property and land. **Rental property** is housing or commercial property that is rented out to others. Some individuals purchase a second home and rent it out to generate additional income every year. Others purchase apartment complexes for the same reason. Some individuals purchase land as an investment.

rental property
Housing or commercial property that is rented out to others.

Liabilities
Liabilities represent debt (what you owe) and can be segmented into current liabilities and long-term liabilities.

current liabilities
Debt that will be paid within a year.

Current Liabilities. **Current liabilities** are debt that you will pay off in the near future (within a year). The most common example of a current liability is a credit card balance that will be paid off in the near future. Credit card companies send the cardholder a monthly bill that itemizes all the purchases made in the previous month. If you pay your balance in full upon receipt of the bill, no interest is charged on the balance. The liability is then eliminated until you receive the next monthly bill.

long-term liabilities
Debt that will be paid over a period longer than one year.

Long-Term Liabilities. **Long-term liabilities** are debt that will be paid over a period beyond one year. A common long-term liability is a student loan, which reflects debt that a student must pay back to a lender over time after graduation. This liability requires you to pay an interest expense periodically. Once you pay off this loan, you eliminate this liability and do not have to pay any more interest expenses. In general, you should limit your liabilities so that you can limit the amount of interest owed.

Other common examples of long-term liabilities are a car loan and a mortgage (housing) loan. Car loans typically have a maturity of between 3 and 5 years, while mortgages typically have a maturity of 15 or 30 years. Both types of loans can be paid off before their maturity.

Net Worth
Your net worth is the difference between what you own and what you owe.

Net Worth = Value of Total Assets − Value of Total Liabilities

In other words, if you sold enough of your assets to pay off all of your liabilities, your net worth would be the amount of assets you would have remaining. Your net worth is a measure of your wealth because it represents what you own after deducting any money that you owe. If your liabilities exceed your assets, your net worth is negative. Excessive liabilities and spending beyond your means can lead to bankruptcy.

Creating a Personal Balance Sheet

You should create a personal balance sheet to determine your net worth. Update it periodically to monitor how your wealth changes over time.

EXAMPLE

Stephanie Spratt wants to determine her net worth by creating a personal balance sheet that identifies her assets and her liabilities.

Stephanie's Assets. Stephanie owns:

- $500 in cash
- $3,500 in her checking account
- Furniture in her apartment that is worth about $1,000
- A car that is worth about $1,000
- 100 shares of stock that she just purchased for $3,000 ($30 per share), which does not pay dividends

Stephanie uses this information to complete the top of her personal balance sheet, shown in Exhibit 2.7. She classifies each item that she owns as a liquid asset, a household asset, or an investment asset.

Stephanie's Liabilities. Stephanie owes $2,000 on her credit card. She does not have any other liabilities at this time, so she lists the one liability on her personal balance sheet under "Current Liabilities" because she will pay off the debt soon. Since she has no long-term liabilities at this time, her total liabilities are $2,000.

Stephanie's Net Worth. Stephanie determines her net worth as the difference between her total assets and total liabilities. Notice from her personal balance sheet that her total assets are valued at $9,000, while her total liabilities are valued at $2,000. Thus, her net worth is:

Net Worth	= Total Assets	− Total Liabilities
	= $9,000	− $2,000
	= $7,000.	

Changes in the Personal Balance Sheet

If you earn new income this month but spend all of it on products or services such as rent, food, and concert tickets that are not personal assets, you will not increase your net worth. As you invest in assets, your personal balance sheet will change. In some cases, such as when you purchase a home, your assets increase while at the same time your liabilities increase by taking on a mortgage. In any case, your net worth will not grow unless the increase in the value of your assets exceeds the increase in your liabilities.

EXAMPLE

Stephanie Spratt is considering purchasing a new car for $20,000. To make the purchase, she would:

- Trade in her existing car, which has a market value of about $1,000.
- Write a check for $3,000 as a down payment on the car.
- Obtain a five-year loan for $16,000 to cover the remaining amount owed to the car dealer.

Her personal balance sheet would be affected as shown in Exhibit 2.8 and explained next.

Exhibit 2.7 Stephanie Spratt's Personal Balance Sheet

Assets

Liquid Assets

Cash	$500
Checking account	3,500
Savings account	0
Total liquid assets	$4,000

Household Assets

Home	$0
Car	1,000
Furniture	1,000
Total household assets	$2,000

Investment Assets

Stocks	$3,000
Total investment assets	$3,000
Total Assets	**$9,000**

Liabilities and Net Worth

Current Liabilities

Credit card balance	$2,000
Total current liabilities	$2,000

Long-Term Liabilities

Mortgage	$0
Car loan	0
Total long-term liabilities	$0
Total Liabilities	**$2,000**
Net Worth	**$7,000**

Change in Stephanie's Assets. Stephanie's assets would change as follows:

- Her car would now have a market value of $20,000 instead of $1,000.
- Her checking account balance would be reduced from $3,500 to $500.

Thus, her total assets would increase by $16,000 (her new car would be valued at $19,000 more than her old one, but her checking account would be reduced by $3,000).

Change in Stephanie's Liabilities. Stephanie's liabilities would also change:

- She would now have a long-term liability of $16,000 as a result of the car loan.

Therefore, her total liabilities would increase by $16,000 if she purchases the car.

Change in Stephanie's Net Worth. If Stephanie purchases the car, her net worth would be:

Net Worth = Total Assets − Total liabilities

= $25,000   − $18,000

= $7,000.

Exhibit 2.8 Stephanie's Personal Balance Sheet if She Purchases a New Car

Assets

	Present Situation	If She Purchases a New Car
Liquid Assets		
Cash	$500	$500
Checking account	3,500	500
Savings account	0	0
Total liquid assets	$4,000	$1,000
Household Assets		
Home	$0	$0
Car	1,000	20,000
Furniture	1,000	1,000
Total household assets	$2,000	$21,000
Investment Assets		
Stocks	$3,000	$3,000
Total investment assets	$3,000	$3,000
Total Assets	**$9,000**	**$25,000**

Liabilities and Net Worth

	Present Situation	If She Purchases a New Car
Current Liabilities		
Credit card balance	$2,000	$2,000
Total current liabilities	$2,000	$2,000
Long-Term Liabilities		
Mortgage	$0	$0
Car loan	0	16,000
Total long-term liabilities	$0	$16,000
Total Liabilities	**$2,000**	**$18,000**
Net Worth	**$7,000**	**$7,000**

Stephanie's net worth would remain unchanged as a result of buying the car because her total assets and total liabilities would increase by the same amount.

Stephanie's Decision. Because the purchase of a new car will not increase her net worth, she decides not to purchase the car at this time. Still, she is concerned that her old car will require high maintenance in the future, so she will likely buy a car in a few months once she improves her financial position.

Analysis of the Personal Balance Sheet

The budgeting process helps you monitor your cash flows and evaluate your net worth. In addition, by analyzing some financial characteristics within your personal balance sheet or cash flow statement, you can monitor your level of liquidity, your amount of debt, and your ability to save.

Liquidity. Recall that liquidity represents your access to funds to cover any short-term cash deficiencies. You need to monitor your liquidity over time to ensure that you have sufficient funds when they are needed. Your liquidity can be measured by the liquidity ratio, which is calculated as:

$$\text{Liquidity Ratio} = \text{Liquid Assets/Current Liabilities}$$

A high liquidity ratio indicates a higher degree of liquidity. For example, a liquidity ratio of 3.0 implies that for every dollar of liabilities that you will need to pay off in the near future, you have $3 in liquid assets. Thus, you could easily cover your short-term liabilities.

A liquidity ratio of less than 1.0 means that you do not have sufficient liquid assets to cover your upcoming payments. In this case, you might need to borrow funds.

E X A M P L E

Based on the information in her personal balance sheet shown in Exhibit 2.7, Stephanie measures her liquidity:

Liquidity Ratio	=	Liquid Assets/Current Liabilities
	=	$4,000/$2,000
	=	2.0.

Stephanie's liquidity ratio of 2.0 means that for every dollar of current liabilities, she has $2 of liquid assets. This means that she has more than enough funds available to cover her current liabilities, so she is maintaining sufficient liquidity to cover her current liabilities.

Debt Level. You also need to monitor your debt level to ensure that it does not become so high that you are unable to cover your debt payments. A debt level of $20,000 would not be a serious problem for a person with assets of $100,000, but it could be quite serious for someone with hardly any assets. Thus, your debt level should be measured relative to your assets, as shown here:

$$\text{Debt-to-Asset Ratio} = \text{Total Liabilities/Total Assets}$$

A high debt ratio indicates an excessive amount of debt and should be reduced over time to avoid any debt repayment problems. Individuals in this position should review their cash flows to maximize inflows and minimize outflows.

E X A M P L E

Based on her personal balance sheet, Stephanie calculates her debt-to-asset ratio as:

Debt-to-Asset Ratio	=	Total Liabilities/Total Assets
	=	$2,000/$9,000
	=	22.22%.

This 22.22 percent debt level is not overwhelming. Even if Stephanie lost her job, she could still pay off her debt.

Savings Rate. To determine the proportion of disposable income that you save, you can measure your savings over a particular period in comparison to your disposable income (income after taxes are taken out) using the following formula:

$$\text{Savings Rate} = \text{Savings during the Period/Disposable Income during the Period}$$

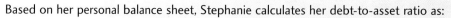

EXAMPLE

Based on her cash flow statement, Stephanie earns $2,500 in a particular month and expects to have net cash flows of $400 for savings or investments. She calculates her typical saving rate per month as:

Savings Rate = Savings during the Period/Disposable Income during the Period

= $400/$2,500

= 16%.

Thus, Stephanie saves 16 percent of her disposable income.

RELATIONSHIP BETWEEN CASH FLOWS AND WEALTH

The relationship between the personal cash flow statement and the personal balance sheet is shown in Exhibit 2.9. This relationship explains how you build wealth (net worth) over time. If you use net cash flows to invest in more assets, you increase the value of your assets without increasing your liabilities. Therefore, you increase your net worth. You can also increase your net worth by using net cash flows to reduce your liabilities. So, the more of your income that you allocate to investing in assets or to reducing your debt, the more wealth you will build.

Your net worth can change even if your net cash flows are zero. For example, if the market value of your car declines over time, the value of this asset is reduced and your net worth will decline. Conversely, if the value of a stock that you own increases, the value of your assets will rise, and your net worth will increase.

HOW BUDGETING FITS WITHIN YOUR FINANCIAL PLAN

The key budgeting decisions for building your financial plan are:

- How can I improve my net cash flows in the near future?

- How can I improve my net cash flows in the distant future?

These decisions require initial estimates of your cash inflows and outflows and an assessment of how you might change your spending behavior to improve your budget over time. By limiting your spending, you may be able to increase your net cash flows and your net worth. Exhibit 2.10 provides an example of how the budgeting decisions apply to Stephanie Spratt's financial plan.

Exhibit 2.9 How Net Cash Flows Can Be Used to Increase Net Worth

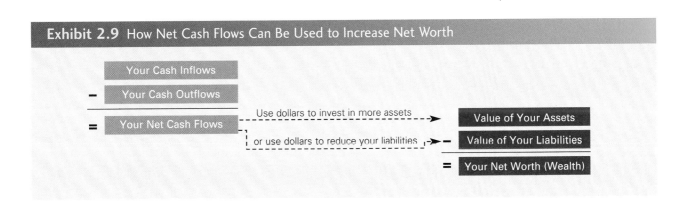

Exhibit 2.10 Application of Budgeting Concepts to Stephanie Spratt's Financial Plan

GOALS FOR A BUDGETING PLAN

1. *Determine how I can increase my net cash flows in the near future.*
2. *Determine how I can increase my net cash flows in the distant future.*

ANALYSIS

Present Situation:

Cash Inflows = *$2,500 per month*	
Cash Outflows = *$2,100 per month*	
Net Cash Flows = *$400 per month*	
Estimated Savings per Year = *$4,800 ($400 per month × 12 months)*	

Increase Net Cash Flows by:

Increasing my salary? (New job?)	*No. I like my job and have no plans to search for another job right now, even if it would pay a higher salary.*
Increasing my income provided by my investments?	*No. My investments are small at this point. I cannot rely on them to provide much income.*
Other? (If yes, explain.)	*No.*

Reduce Cash Outflows by:

Reducing my household expenses?	*No.*
Reducing my recreation expenses?	*Yes (by $100 per month).*
Reducing my other expenses?	*No.*

Overall, I identified only one adjustment to my budget, which will increase monthly net cash flows by $100.

DECISIONS

Decision to Increase Net Cash Flows in the Near Future:

I initially established a budget to save $4,800 per year. During the next year, I can attempt to save an additional $100 per month by reducing the amount I spend on recreation. I can increase my savings if I reduce cash outflows. By reducing cash outflows by $100 per month, my savings will increase from $400 to $500 per month. The only way that I can reduce cash outflows at this point is to reduce the amount I spend for recreation purposes.

Decision to Increase Net Cash Flows in the Distant Future:

My cash inflows will rise over time if my salary increases. If I can keep my cash outflows stable, my net cash flows (and therefore my savings) will increase. When I buy a new car or a home, my monthly cash outflows will increase as a result of the monthly loan payments. If I buy a new car or a home, I need to make sure that I limit my spending (and therefore limit the loan amount) so that I have sufficient cash inflows to cover the monthly loan payments along with my other typical monthly expenses.

If I get married someday, my husband would contribute to the cash inflows, which would increase net cash flows. We would be able to save more money and may consider buying a home. If I marry, my goal will be to save even more money per month than I save now, to prepare for the possibility of raising a family in the future.

DISCUSSION QUESTIONS

1. How would Stephanie's budgeting decisions be different if she were a single mother of two children?

2. How would Stephanie's budgeting decisions be affected if she were 35 years old? If she were 50 years old?

SUMMARY

The personal cash flow statement measures your cash inflows, your cash outflows, and their difference (net cash flows) over a specific period. Cash inflows result from your salary or from income generated by your investments. Cash outflows result from your spending.

Your cash inflows are primarily affected by your stage in your career path and your type of job. Your cash outflows are influenced by your family status, age, and personal consumption behavior. If you develop specialized skills, you may be able to obtain a job position that increases your cash inflows. If you limit your consumption, you can limit your spending and therefore reduce your cash outflows. Either of these actions will increase net cash flows and thus allow you to increase your wealth.

You can forecast net cash flows (and therefore anticipate cash deficiencies) by creating a budget, which is based on forecasted cash inflows and outflows for an upcoming period.

The budgeting process allows you to control spending. Comparing your forecasted and actual income and expenses will show whether or not you were able to stay within the budget. By examining the difference between your forecast and the actual cash flow, you can determine areas of your budget that may need further control or areas of your budget that required less in expenditures than you predicted. This analysis will help you modify your spending in the future or perhaps adjust your future budgets.

The personal balance sheet measures the value of your assets, your liabilities, and your net worth. The assets can be categorized into liquid assets, household assets, and investments. Liabilities can be categorized as current or long-term liabilities. The difference between total assets and total liabilities is net worth, which is a measure of your wealth.

The net cash flows on the personal cash flow statement are related to the net worth on the personal balance sheet. When you have positive net cash flows over a period, you can invest that amount in additional assets, which results in an increase in your net worth (or your wealth). Alternatively, you may use the net cash flows to pay off liabilities, which also increases your wealth.

INTEGRATING THE KEY CONCEPTS

Budgeting is a starting point for developing your financial plan. Before you can look for ways to improve your cash flows, you need to recognize how you spend or save your money. Your budget decisions dictate your level of spending and saving and therefore affect the other parts of the financial plan. The amount you save affects your liquidity (Part 2), the amount of financing necessary (Part 3), the amount of insurance that you can afford and need (Part 4), the amount of funds that you can invest (Part 5), and the level of wealth that you will need for retirement (Part 6).

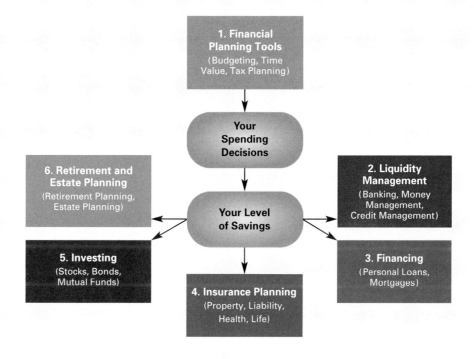

REVIEW QUESTIONS

1. What two personal financial statements are most important to personal financial planning?

2. Define cash inflows and cash outflows and identify some sources of each. How are net cash flows determined?

3. In general, how can you modify your cash flows to enhance your wealth?

4. Identify some factors that affect cash inflows.

5. Identify some factors that affect cash outflows.

6. What is a budget? What is the purpose of a budget? How can a budget help when you are anticipating cash shortages or a cash surplus?

7. How do you assess the accuracy of your budget? How can finding forecasting errors improve your budget?

8. How should unexpected expenses be handled in your budget? How might these expenses affect your budget for a specific month? Over time?

9. Describe the process of creating an annual budget.

10. Suppose you want to change your budget to increase your savings. What could you do?

11. How do you think people who do not create a budget deal with cash deficiencies? How can this affect their personal relationships?

12. What is a personal balance sheet?

13. Name three classifications of assets. Briefly define and give examples of each.

14. What are bonds? What are stocks? What are mutual funds? Describe how each of these provides a return on your investment.

15. Describe two ways real estate might provide a return on an investment.

16. What are liabilities? Define current liabilities and long-term liabilities.

17. How is net worth a measure of wealth?

18. When does your net worth increase? Will the purchase of additional assets always increase your net worth? Why or why not?

19. What three financial characteristics can be monitored by analyzing your personal balance sheet?

20. What is the liquidity ratio? What does it indicate? How is the debt-to-asset ratio calculated? What does a high debt ratio indicate? How is your savings rate determined? What does it indicate?

21. Describe how wealth is built over time. How do your personal cash flow statement and your personal balance sheet assist in this process?

FINANCIAL PLANNING PROBLEMS

1. Angela earns $2,170 per month before taxes in her full-time job and $900 before taxes in her part-time job. About $650 per month is needed to pay taxes. What is Angela's disposable income?

2. Angela (from problem 1) inspects her checkbook and her credit card bills and determines that she has the following monthly expenses:

Rent	$500
Cable TV	30
Electricity	100
Water	25
Telephone	40
Groceries	400
Car expenses	350
Health insurance	200
Clothing and personal items	175
Recreation	300

   What is Angela's net cash flow?

3. Angela makes a budget based on her personal cash flow statement. In two months, she must pay $375 for tags and taxes on her car. How will this payment affect her net cash flow for that month? Suggest ways that Angela might handle this situation.

4. From the information in problems 1 through 3, how much can Angela expect to save in the next 12 months?

5. Angela analyzes her personal budget and decides that she can reduce her recreational spending by $50 per month. How much will that increase her annual savings? What will her annual savings be now?

6. If Angela is saving $350 per month, what is her savings rate (i.e., savings as a percentage of disposable income)?

7. Peter is a college student. All of Peter's disposable income is used to pay his college-related expenses. While he has no liabilities (Peter is on a scholarship), he does have a credit card that he typically uses for emergencies. He and his friend went on a shopping spree in New York City costing $2,000, which Peter charged to his credit card. Peter has $20 in his wallet, but his bank accounts are empty. What is Peter's liquidity ratio? What does this ratio indicate about Peter's financial position?

8. Peter (from problem 7) has an old TV worth about $100. Peter's other assets total about $150. What is

Peter's debt-to-asset ratio? What does this indicate about Peter's financial position?

9. Bill and Ann have the following assets:

Fair Market Value

Home	$85,000
Cars	22,000
Furniture	14,000
Stocks	10,000
Savings account	5,000
Checking account	1,200
Bonds	15,000
Cash	150
Mutual funds	7,000
Land	19,000

What is the value of their liquid assets? What is the value of their household assets? What is the value of their investments?

10. Bill and Ann have the following liabilities:

Mortgage	$43,500
Car loan	2,750
Credit card balance	165
Student loans	15,000
Furniture note (6 months)	1,200

What are their current liabilities? What are their long-term liabilities? What is their net worth?

11. Bill and Ann would like to trade in one of their cars with a fair market value of $7,000 for a new one with a fair market value of $21,500. The dealer will take their car and provide a $15,000 loan for the new car. If they make this deal, what will be the effect on their net worth?

12. What is Bill and Ann's liquidity ratio? What is their debt-to-asset ratio? Comment on each ratio.

Ethical Dilemma

13. Dennis and Nancy are in their early 20s and have been married for three years. They are eager to purchase their first house, but they do not have sufficient money for a down payment. Nancy's Uncle Charley has agreed to loan them the money to purchase a small house. Uncle Charley requests a personal balance sheet and cash flow statement as well as tax returns for the last two years to verify their income and their ability to make monthly payments.

For the past two years, Dennis has been working substantial overtime, which has increased his income by over 25%. The cash flow statements for the last two years show that Nancy and Dennis will have no diffi-

culty making the payments Uncle Charley requires. However, Dennis' company has informed their employees that the overtime will not continue in the coming year. Nancy and Dennis are concerned that if they prepare their personal cash flow statement based on Dennis' base salary that Uncle Charley will not loan them the money because it will show the loan payments can only be made with very strict cost cutting and financial discipline. Therefore they elect to present just what Uncle Charley requested, which were the last two years' personal cash flow statements and tax returns. They decide not to provide any additional information unless he asks.

a. Comment on Nancy and Dennis' decision not to provide the information underlying their cash flow statement. What potential problems could result from their decision?

b. Discuss in general the disadvantages of borrowing money from relatives.

FINANCIAL PLANNING ONLINE EXERCISES

1. Go to http://www.calcbuilder.com/cgi-bin/calcs/SAV13.cgi/FinanCenter and go to "What's it worth to reduce my spending?"

You can input various expenses that can be reduced and determine the savings that will accrue over time. Input your age, your age at retirement, 2 percent for the rate you can earn on savings, and 25 percent and 6 percent for the federal and state tax rates, respectively.

a. If you waited to buy a car, you could, perhaps, save $220 monthly. Enter this information and go to the Results page to find out what this savings would amount to at retirement.

b. If you ate out less, you could save, say, $150 monthly. Enter this information and go to the Results page to find out what this adds up to by retirement.

c. If you went to fewer movies and reduced expenses by $50 monthly, how much extra could you save by retirement? Enter this information and go to the Results page to find out the impact.

d. If you paid off credit card balances and reduced interest costs by $100 monthly, how much could you accumulate by retirement? Enter this information and go to the Results page to find out.

e. If you took all these measures to reduce your spending, what is the total savings you could accrue at retirement? To find out, look at the bottom section on the Results page.

2. Go to http://www.calcbuilder.com/cgi-bin/calcs/ BUD3.cgi/themotleyfool and go to "How much am I spending?"

Do you want to know how your spending habits affect your future wealth? Using this information, you can fine-tune your budget.

a. Enter an actual home payment or rent of $600 per month and a desired amount of $550. Determine the impact of only this difference on future wealth. You can also view the impact graphically by clicking on the Graph tab.

b. Enter an actual expense for utilities of $350 per month and your desired amount of $250. Calculate the effect of only this change on future wealth. You can also view the impact graphically by clicking on the Graph tab.

c. Enter an actual expense for food of $600 monthly and a desired amount of $500. Determine the financial consequences of only this change in figures. You can also view the results graphically by clicking on the Graph tab.

d. Enter actual entertainment expenses of $250 monthly and a desired amount of $175. Determine the financial impact of only this change on future wealth. You can also view the results graphically by clicking on the Graph tab.

BUILDING YOUR OWN FINANCIAL PLAN

Two major components of any good personal financial plan are a personal cash flow statement and a balance sheet. If you are a full-time student, prepare your cash flow statement based upon your anticipated cash flow at graduation.

To prepare your personal balance sheet and cash flow statement, turn to the worksheets at the end of this chapter and to the CD-ROM accompanying this text. In most cases, you will not have all of the cash inflows and outflows or assets and liabilities listed on the worksheet.

When listing your liabilities, be sure to include any educational loans even if they are not payable until after graduation.

When preparing your personal cash flow statement, break down all expenses into the frequency in which you are/will be paid. For example, if your car insurance is $700 per year and you are paid monthly, divide the $700 by 12. If you

are paid biweekly, divide the $700 by 26. Personal cash flow statements should be set up based upon the frequency of your pay. This way, each time you are paid, you can distribute your paycheck to the appropriate cash outflow categories.

If, after preparing your personal cash flow statement, you have an excess of cash outflows over cash inflows, you should review in detail each cash outflow to determine its necessity and whether it can realistically be reduced in order to balance your cash inflows and outflows. Using Web sites like http://www.firsttechcu.com/Calculators/budget/ calculators_budget.html (click on "What's it worth to reduce my spending?"), you can also estimate the savings that you can accumulate over time by reducing your cash outflows.

Personal financial statements should be reviewed annually or whenever you experience a change that affects your cash inflows such as getting a raise, obtaining a new job, marrying, or getting divorced.

THE SAMPSONS—A CONTINUING CASE

The Sampsons realize that the first step toward achieving their financial goals is to create a budget capturing their monthly cash inflows and outflows. Dave and Sharon's combined income is

now about $4,000 per month after taxes. With the new cash inflows from Sharon's paycheck, the Sampsons have started spending more on various after-school programs for their children such as soccer leagues and tennis lessons. In Chapter 1, they resolved to save a total of $800 per month for a new car and for their children's education.

Reviewing their checking account statement from last month, Dave and Sharon identify the following monthly household payments:

- $900 for the mortgage payment ($700 loan payment plus home insurance and property taxes).
- $60 for cable TV.
- $80 for electricity and water.
- $70 for telephone expenses.
- $500 for groceries.
- $160 for a health care plan provided by Dave's employer (this expense is deducted directly from Dave's salary).

The Sampsons also review several credit card bills to estimate their other typical monthly expenses.

- About $180 for clothing.
- About $300 for car expenses (insurance, maintenance, and gas).
- About $100 for school expenses.
- About $1,000 for recreation and programs for the children.
- About $20 as a minimum payment on their existing credit card balance.

To determine their net worth, the Sampsons also assess their assets and liabilities, which include the following:

- $300 in cash.
- $1,700 in their checking account.
- Home valued at $100,000.
- Furniture worth about $3,000.
- Sharon's car, which needs to be replaced soon, is worth about $1,000. Dave's car is worth approximately $8,000.
- They owe $90,000 on their home mortgage and about $2,000 on their credit cards.

Go to the worksheets at the end of this chapter, and to the CD-ROM accompanying this text, to continue this case.

Chapter 2: Building Your Own Financial Plan

GOALS

1. Determine how to increase net cash flows in the near future.
2. Determine how to increase net cash flows in the distant future.

ANALYSIS

1. Prepare your personal cash flow statement.

Personal Cash Flow Statement

Cash Inflows	This Month
Disposable (after-tax) income	
Interest on deposits	
Dividend payments	
Other	
Total Cash Inflows	

Cash Outflows	
Rent/Mortgage	
Cable TV	
Electricity and water	
Telephone	
Groceries	
Health care insurance and expenses	
Clothing	
Car expenses (insurance, maintenance, and gas)	
Recreation	
Other	
Total Cash Outflows	
Net Cash Flows	

If you enter your cash flow information in the Excel worksheet, the software will create a pie chart of your cash outflows.

2. Prepare your personal balance sheet.

Personal Balance Sheet

Assets

Liquid Assets

Cash	
Checking account	
Savings account	
Other liquid assets	
Total liquid assets	

Household Assets

Home	
Car	
Furniture	
Other household assets	
Total household assets	

Investment Assets

Stocks	
Bonds	
Mutual Funds	
Other investments	
Total investment assets	

Real Estate

Residence	
Vacation home	
Other	
Total real estate	
Total Assets	

Liabilities and Net Worth

Current Liabilities

Loans	
Credit card balance	
Other current liabilities	
Total current liabilities	

Long-Term Liabilities

Mortgage	
Car loan	
Other long-term liabilities	
Total long-term liabilities	
Total Liabilities	
Net Worth	

3. Reevaluate the goals you set in Chapter 1. Based on your personal cash flow statement, indicate how much you can save each year to reach your goals.

Personal Financial Goals

Financial Goal	Dollar Amount	Savings per Year	Number of Years
Short-Term Goals			
1.			
2.			
3.			
Intermediate-Term Goals			
1.			
2.			
3.			
Long-Term Goals			
1.			
2.			
3.			

DECISIONS

1. Describe the actions you will take to increase your net cash flows in the near future.

_____

_____

_____

_____

_____

_____

_____

_____

2. Detail your plans to increase your net cash flows in the distant future.

_____

_____

_____

_____

_____

_____

_____

_____

Chapter 2: The Sampsons—A Continuing Case

CASE QUESTIONS

1. Using the information in the case, prepare a personal cash flow statement for the Sampsons.

Personal Cash Flow Statement

Cash Inflows	This Month
Total Cash Inflows	

Cash Outflows

Include categories for cash outflows as follows:

Rent/Mortgage	
Cable TV	
Electricity and water	
Telephone	
Groceries	
Health care insurance and expenses	
Clothing	
Car expenses (insurance, maintenance, and gas)	
School expenses	
Recreation	
Credit card minimum payments	
Other	
Total Cash Outflows	
Net Cash Flows	

2. Based on their personal cash flow statement, will the Sampsons be able to meet their savings goals? If not, how do you recommend that they revise their personal cash flow statement in order to achieve their savings goals?

_____

_____

_____

_____

_____

_____

3. Prepare a personal balance sheet for the Sampsons.

Personal Balance Sheet

Assets

Liquid Assets

Cash	
Checking account	
Savings account	
Total liquid assets	

Household Assets

Home	
Car	
Furniture	
Total household assets	

Investment Assets

Stocks	
Bonds	
Mutual Funds	
Total investment assets	
Total Assets	

Liabilities and Net Worth

Current Liabilities

Loans	
Credit card balance	
Total current liabilities	

Long-Term Liabilities

Mortgage	
Car loan	
Total long-term liabilities	
Total Liabilities	
Net Worth	

4. What is the Sampsons' net worth? Based on the personal cash flow statement that you prepared in question 2, do you expect that their net worth will increase or decrease in the future? Why?

Applying Time Value Concepts

Armin Santori is a million-dollar kid. He has pledged not to smoke from his present age of 18 until retirement at age 67. Armin has no idea of the economic value of his decision, nor does he yet have a grasp of the time value of money. Just how much money could he accumulate based on the value of two packs of cigarettes per day and a modest rate of return?

Let's assume that Armin will save an amount equivalent to the cost of two packs per day at $3.00 per pack. Each year for 49 years Armin would have available $2,190 to invest (2 packs × $3.00/pack × 365 days). Assuming a rate of return of 8 percent per year, Armin would accumulate $1,161,450 by age 67! Armin Santori has stumbled upon a fundamental financial planning tool that will benefit him: The time value of money.

A dollar received today is worth more than a dollar received tomorrow because it can be saved and invested. Personal financial planning decisions are commonly based on time value of money calculations. Should you accept a lump sum at retirement or take a monthly payment for life? How much should you invest each month to accumulate your down payment for a house five years from now? If you accumulate a nest egg by retirement, how much can you withdraw from your retirement funds each month during retirement? The concept of the time value of money can help you solve problems such as these and allow you to develop a financial plan based on realistic calculations.

The objectives of this chapter are to:

- Calculate the future value of a dollar amount that you save today
- Calculate the present value of a dollar amount that will be received in the future
- Calculate the future value of an annuity
- Calculate the present value of an annuity

THE IMPORTANCE OF THE TIME VALUE OF MONEY

The time value of money is a powerful principle. In fact, it is so powerful that Albert Einstein stated that it was one of the strongest forces on earth. The time value is especially important for estimating how your money may grow over time.

EXAMPLE   Suppose your ancestors settled in the American colonies in 1693. At that time, one of them invested $20 in a savings account at a local bank earning 5 percent interest annually. Also assume that this ancestor never informed his family members of this transaction and that the money remained in the account accumulating interest of 5 percent annually until the year 2006, when the bank locates you and informs you of the account. Over this time period, the $20 would have accumulated to $86 million.

As a more realistic example, consider that an investment today of just $2,000 in an account that earns 6 percent a year will be worth about $11,487 in 30 years.

These examples show how money grows over time when you receive a return on your investment. When you spend money, you incur an opportunity cost of what you could have done with that money had you not spent it. In the previous example, if you had spent the $2,000 on a vacation rather than saving the money, you would have incurred an opportunity cost of the alternative ways that you could have used the money. That is, you can either have a vacation today or have that money accumulate to be worth $11,487 in 30 years (among other possible choices). Whatever decision you make, you will forgo some alternative uses of those funds.

The time value of money is most commonly applied to two types of cash flows: a single dollar amount (also referred to as a lump sum) and an annuity. An **annuity** is a stream of equal payments that are received or paid at equal intervals in time. For example, a monthly deposit of $50 as new savings in a bank account at the end of every month is an annuity. Your telephone bill is not an annuity, as the payments are not the same each month. This chapter will discuss the time value of money computations related to the future and present value of both lump-sum and annuity cash flows. Calculations are illustrated using both time value tables and a financial calculator.

**annuity
(or ordinary annuity)**
A series of equal cash flow payments that are received or paid at equal intervals in time.

FUTURE VALUE OF A SINGLE DOLLAR AMOUNT

When you deposit money in a bank savings account, your money grows because the bank pays interest on your deposit. The interest is a reward to you for depositing your money in the account, and is normally expressed as a percentage of the deposit amount and is paid annually.

You may want to know how your money will grow to determine whether you can afford specific purchases in the future. For example, you may want to estimate how your existing bank balance will accumulate in six months when you will need to make a tuition payment. Alternatively, you may want to estimate how that money will accumulate in one year when you hope to make a down payment on a new car. To do this, you can apply the interest rate that you expect to earn on your deposit to the deposit amount.

To determine the future value of an amount of money you deposit today, you need to know:

- The amount of your deposit (or other investment) today
- The interest rate to be earned on your deposit
- The number of years the money will be invested

EXAMPLE

If you created a bank deposit of $1,000 that earned 4 percent annually, the deposit will earn an annual interest of:

Interest rate times deposit

4 percent $\times$ $1,000 = $40.

Thus, your deposit will accumulate to be worth $1,040 by the end of one year.

compounding
The process of earning interest on interest.

In the next year, the interest rate of 4 percent will be applied not only on your original $1,000 deposit, but also on the interest, that you earned in the previous year. The process of earning interest on interest is called **compounding**.

EXAMPLE

Assuming that the interest rate is 4 percent in the second year, it will be applied to your deposit balance of $1,040, which results in interest of $41.60 (computed as 4 percent $\times$ $1,040). Thus, your balance by the end of the second year would be $1,081.60.

Notice that the interest of $41.60 paid in the second year is more than the interest paid in the first year, even though the interest rate is the same. This is because the interest rate was applied to a larger deposit balance.

In the third year, a 4 percent interest rate would result in interest of $43.26 (computed as 4 percent of $1,081.60). Your deposit balance would be $1,124.86 by the end of the third year.

future value interest factor (FVIF)
A factor multiplied by today's savings to determine how the savings will accumulate over time.

In some cases, you may want to know how your deposit will accumulate over a long period of time, such as 20 or 30 years. You can quickly determine the future value for any period of time by using the **future value interest factor (FVIF)**, which is a factor multiplied by today's savings to determine how the savings will accumulate over time. It is dependent on the interest rate and the number of years the money is invested. Your deposit today is multiplied by the FVIF to determine the future value of the deposit.

Using the Future Value Table

Exhibit 3.1 shows the *FVIF* for various interest rates (*i*) and time periods (*n*). Each column in Exhibit 3.1 lists an interest rate and each row lists a possible time period. By reviewing any column of Exhibit 3.1, you will notice that as the number of years increases, the *FVIF* becomes higher. This means that the longer the time period in which your money is invested at a set rate of return, the more your money will grow.

By reviewing any row of Exhibit 3.1, you will notice that as the interest rate increases, the *FVIF* becomes higher. This means that the higher the rate of return, the more your money will grow over a given time period.

Exhibit 3.1 Future Value of $1 (*FVIF*)

Year	1%	2%	3%	4%	5%	6%	7%	8%	9%
1	1.010	1.020	1.030	1.040	1.050	1.060	1.070	1.080	1.090
2	1.020	1.040	1.061	1.082	1.102	1.124	1.145	1.166	1.188
3	1.030	1.061	1.093	1.125	1.158	1.191	1.225	1.260	1.295
4	1.041	1.082	1.126	1.170	1.216	1.262	1.311	1.360	1.412
5	1.051	1.104	1.159	1.217	1.276	1.338	1.403	1.469	1.539
6	1.062	1.126	1.194	1.265	1.340	1.419	1.501	1.587	1.677
7	1.072	1.149	1.230	1.316	1.407	1.504	1.606	1.714	1.828
8	1.083	1.172	1.267	1.369	1.477	1.594	1.718	1.851	1.993
9	1.094	1.195	1.305	1.423	1.551	1.689	1.838	1.999	2.172
10	1.105	1.219	1.344	1.480	1.629	1.791	1.967	2.159	2.367
11	1.116	1.243	1.384	1.539	1.710	1.898	2.105	2.332	2.580
12	1.127	1.268	1.426	1.601	1.796	2.012	2.252	2.518	2.813
13	1.138	1.294	1.469	1.665	1.886	2.113	2.410	2.720	3.066
14	1.149	1.319	1.513	1.732	1.980	2.261	2.579	2.937	3.342
15	1.161	1.346	1.558	1.801	2.079	2.397	2.759	3.172	3.642
16	1.173	1.373	1.605	1.873	2.183	2.540	2.952	3.426	3.970
17	1.184	1.400	1.653	1.948	2.292	2.693	3.159	3.700	4.328
18	1.196	1.428	1.702	2.026	2.407	2.854	3.380	3.996	4.717
19	1.208	1.457	1.754	2.107	2.527	3.026	3.617	4.316	5.142
20	1.220	1.486	1.806	2.191	2.653	3.207	3.870	4.661	5.604
25	1.282	1.641	2.094	2.666	3.386	4.292	5.427	6.848	8.623
30	1.348	1.811	2.427	3.243	4.322	5.743	7.612	10.063	13.268

EXAMPLE   Suppose you want to know how much money you will have in five years if you invest $5,000 now and earn an annual return of 9 percent. The present value of money (*PV*) is the amount invested, or $5,000. The *FVIF* for an interest rate of 9 percent and a time period of five years is 1.539 (look down the column 9%, and across the row for 5 years). Thus, the future value (*FV*) of the $5,000 in five years will be:

$$FV = PV \times FVIF_{i,n}$$

$$FV = PV \times FVIF_{9\%,5}$$

$$= \$5,000 \times 1.539$$

$$= \$7,695.$$

Using a Financial Calculator

There are a variety of financial calculators available for purchase that greatly simplify time value calculations as the following example shows.

10%	12%	14%	15%	16%	18%	20%	25%	30%
1.100	1.120	1.140	1.150	1.160	1.180	1.200	1.250	1.300
1.210	1.254	1.300	1.322	1.346	1.392	1.440	1.563	1.690
1.331	1.405	1.482	1.521	1.561	1.643	1.728	1.953	2.197
1.464	1.574	1.689	1.749	1.811	1.939	2.074	2.441	2.856
1.611	1.762	1.925	2.011	2.100	2.288	2.488	3.052	3.713
1.772	1.974	2.195	2.313	2.436	2.700	2.986	3.815	4.827
1.949	2.211	2.502	2.660	2.826	3.185	3.583	4.768	6.276
2.144	2.476	2.853	3.059	3.278	3.759	4.300	5.960	8.157
2.358	2.773	3.252	3.518	3.803	4.435	5.160	7.451	10.604
2.594	3.106	3.707	4.046	4.411	5.234	6.192	9.313	13.786
2.853	3.479	4.226	4.652	5.117	6.176	7.430	11.642	17.922
3.138	3.896	4.818	5.350	5.936	7.288	8.916	14.552	23.298
3.452	4.363	5.492	6.153	6.886	8.599	10.699	18.190	30.288
3.797	4.887	6.261	7.076	7.988	10.147	12.839	22.737	39.374
4.177	5.474	7.138	8.137	9.266	11.974	15.407	28.422	51.186
4.595	6.130	8.137	9.358	10.748	14.129	18.488	35.527	66.542
5.054	6.866	9.276	10.761	12.468	16.672	22.186	44.409	86.504
5.560	7.690	10.575	12.375	14.463	19.673	26.623	55.511	112.46
6.116	8.613	12.056	14.232	16.777	23.214	31.948	69.389	146.19
6.728	9.646	13.743	16.367	19.461	27.393	38.338	86.736	190.05
10.835	17.000	26.462	32.919	40.874	62.669	95.396	264.70	705.64
17.449	29.960	50.950	66.212	85.850	143.371	237.376	807.79	2620.00

EXAMPLE

Suppose you have $5,687 to invest in the stock market today. You like to invest for the long term and plan to choose your stocks carefully. You will invest your money for 12 years in certain stocks on which you expect a return of 10 percent annually. Although financial calculators can vary slightly in their setup, most would require inputs as shown at left.

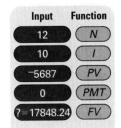

Where:

N	=	number of periods
I	=	interest rate
PV	=	present value, which is the initial amount deposited
PMT	=	payment, which is not applicable in this problem
FV	=	future value of the deposit you make today, which is computed by the calculator

The PV is a negative number here, reflecting the outflow of cash to make the investment. The calculator computes the future value to be $17,848.24, which indicates that you will have $17,848.24 in your brokerage account in 12 years if you achieve a return of 10 percent annually on your $5,687 investment.

Use a financial calculator to determine the future value of $5,000 invested at 9 percent for five years. (This is the previous example used for the *FVIF* table.) Your answer should be $7,695. Any difference in answers using the *FVIF* table versus using a financial calculator is due to rounding.

Focus on Ethics: Delaying Payments

Based on the time value of money, it seems rational to delay payment obligations. If you invest your money while delaying the payment, you could earn interest on your funds. You might be tempted to invest money before making your rent payment at the beginning of each month, or before making a car payment each month. However, delaying your payments too long can lead to late fees and penalties that can damage your credit rating. You could also be evicted from your apartment or your car could be repossessed.

What alternative will still allow you to take advantage of the time value of money? You should invest your money in an interest-bearing account before you need to make payments. By paying bills electronically you can delay payments and still ensure on-time payment. You can even use settings on many bill-paying Web sites that allow you to set a future date for a payment once you receive a bill. Make use of your money while you have it, but always make payments by the obligation dates.

PRESENT VALUE OF A DOLLAR AMOUNT

discounting
The process of obtaining present values.

In many situations, you will want to know how much money you must deposit or invest today to accumulate a specified amount of money at a future point in time. The process of obtaining present values is referred to as **discounting**. Suppose that you want to have $20,000 for a down payment on a house in three years. You want to know how much money you need to invest today to achieve $20,000 in three years. That is, you want to know the present value of $20,000 that will be received in three years, based on some interest rate that you could earn over that period.

3.1 Financial Planning Online: Paying Your Bills Online

Go to
http://finance.yahoo.com/
bp

This Web site provides an online bill paying service.

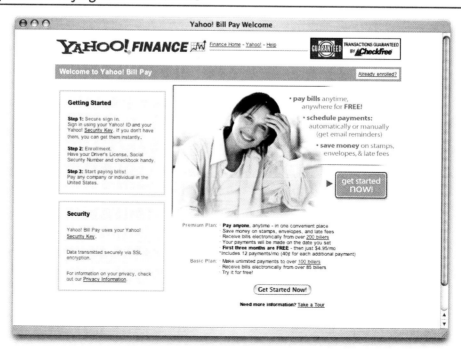

To determine the present value of an amount of money received in the future, you need to know:

- The amount of money to be received in the future
- The interest rate to be earned on your deposit
- The number of years the money will be invested

present value interest factor (PVIF)
A factor multiplied by a future value to determine the present value of that amount.

The present value can be calculated by using a **present value interest factor (PVIF)**, which is a factor multiplied by the future value to determine the present value of that amount. It is dependent on the interest rate and the number of years the money is invested.

Using the Present Value Table

Exhibit 3.2 shows the *PVIF* for various interest rates (i) and time periods (n). Each column in Exhibit 3.2 lists an interest rate, while each row lists a time period.

You will notice that in any column of Exhibit 3.2 the *PVIF* is lower as the number of years increases. This means that less money is needed to achieve a specific future value when the money is invested for a greater number of years.

Similarly, an inspection of any row in Exhibit 3.2 will reveal that less money is needed to achieve a specific future value when the money is invested at a higher rate of return.

EXAMPLE   You would like to accumulate $50,000 in five years by making a single investment today. You believe you can achieve a return from your investment of 8 percent annually. What is the dollar amount that you need to invest today to achieve your goal?

The *PVIF* in this example is .681 (look down the column 8% and across the row for 5 years). Using the present value table, the present value (*PV*) is:

$$PV = FV \times PVIF_{i,n}$$
$$PV = FV \times PVIF_{8\%,5}$$
$$= \$50,000 \times 0.681$$
$$= \$34,050.$$

Thus, you need to invest $34,050 today to have $50,000 in five years if you expect an annual return of 8 percent.

Using a Financial Calculator

Using a financial calculator, present values can be obtained quickly by inputting all known variables and solving for the one unknown variable.

EXAMPLE   Loretta Callahan would like to accumulate $500,000 by the time she retires in 20 years. If she can earn an 8.61 percent return annually, how much must she invest today to have $500,000 in 20 years? Since the unknown variable is the present value (*PV*), the calculator input will be as shown at left.

Input	Function
20	N
8.61	I
?	PV
0	PMT
500000	FV
Solution	
$95,845.94	

Where:

N	=	20 years
I	=	8.61%
PV	=	present value, or the amount that would have to be deposited today
PMT	=	payment, which is not applicable in this problem
FV	=	amount of money desired at a future point in time

Thus, Loretta would have to invest $95,845.94 today to accumulate $500,000 in 20 years if she really earns 8.61 percent annually.

Exhibit 3.2 Present Value of $1 (*PVIF*)

Year	1%	2%	3%	4%	5%	6%	7%	8%	9%
1	.990	.980	.971	.962	.952	.943	.935	.926	.917
2	.980	.961	.943	.925	.907	.890	.873	.857	.842
3	.971	.942	.915	.889	.864	.840	.816	.794	.772
4	.961	.924	.888	.855	.823	.792	.763	.735	.708
5	.951	.906	.863	.822	.784	.747	.713	.681	.650
6	.942	.888	.837	.790	.746	.705	.666	.630	.596
7	.933	.871	.813	.760	.711	.665	.623	.583	.547
8	.923	.853	.789	.731	.677	.627	.582	.540	.502
9	.914	.837	.766	.703	.645	.592	.544	.500	.460
10	.905	.820	.744	.676	.614	.558	.508	.463	.422
11	.896	.804	.722	.650	.585	.527	.475	.429	.388
12	.887	.788	.701	.625	.557	.497	.444	.397	.356
13	.879	.773	.681	.601	.530	.469	.415	.368	.326
14	.870	.758	.661	.577	.505	.442	.388	.340	.299
15	.861	.743	.642	.555	.481	.417	.362	.315	.275
16	.853	.728	.623	.534	.458	.394	.339	.292	.252
17	.844	.714	.605	.513	.436	.391	.317	.270	.231
18	.836	.700	.587	.494	.416	.350	.296	.250	.212
19	.828	.686	.570	.475	.396	.331	.276	.232	.194
20	.820	.673	.554	.456	.377	.312	.258	.215	.178
25	.780	.610	.478	.375	.295	.233	.184	.146	.116
30	.742	.552	.412	.308	.231	.174	.131	.099	.075

Use a financial calculator to determine the present value of a single sum by calculating the present value of $50,000 in five years if the money is invested at an interest rate of 8 percent. This is the example used earlier to illustrate the present value tables. Your answer should be $34,050. Your answer may vary slightly due to rounding.

FUTURE VALUE OF AN ANNUITY

Earlier in the chapter, you saw how your money can grow from a single deposit. An alternative way to accumulate funds over time is through an ordinary annuity, which represents a stream of equal payments (or investments) that occur at the end of each period. For example, if you make a $30 deposit at the end of each month for 100 months, this is an ordinary annuity. As another example, you may invest $1,000 at the end of each year for 10 years. There is a simple and quick method to determine the future value of an annuity. If the payment changes over time, the payment stream does not reflect an annuity. You can still determine the future value of a payment stream that does not reflect an annuity, but the computation process is more complicated.

annuity due
A series of equal cash flow payments that occur at the beginning of each period.

An alternative to an ordinary annuity is an **annuity due**, which is a series of equal cash flow payments that occur at the beginning of each period. Thus, an annuity due

10%	12%	14%	15%	16%	18%	20%	25%	30%
.909	.893	.877	.870	.862	.847	.833	.800	.769
.826	.797	.769	.756	.743	.718	.694	.640	.592
.751	.712	.675	.658	.641	.609	.579	.512	.455
.683	.636	.592	.572	.552	.516	.482	.410	.350
.621	.567	.519	.497	.476	.437	.402	.328	.269
.564	.507	.456	.432	.410	.370	.335	.262	.207
.513	.452	.400	.376	.354	.314	.279	.210	.159
.467	.404	.351	.327	.305	.266	.233	.168	.123
.424	.361	.308	.284	.263	.225	.194	.134	.094
.386	.322	.270	.247	.227	.191	.162	.107	.073
.350	.287	.237	.215	.195	.162	.135	.086	.056
.319	.257	.208	.187	.168	.137	.112	.069	.043
.290	.229	.182	.163	.145	.116	.093	.055	.033
.263	.205	.160	.141	.125	.099	.078	.044	.025
.239	.183	.140	.123	.108	.084	.065	.035	.020
.218	.163	.123	.107	.093	.071	.054	.028	.015
.198	.146	.108	.093	.080	.060	.045	.023	.012
.180	.130	.095	.081	.069	.051	.038	.018	.009
.164	.116	.083	.070	.060	.043	.031	.014	.007
.149	.104	.073	.061	.051	.037	.026	.012	.005
.092	.059	.038	.030	.024	.016	.010	.004	.001
.057	.033	.020	.015	.012	.007	.004	.001	.000

timelines
Diagrams that show payments received or paid over time.

differs from an ordinary annuity in that the payments occur at the beginning instead of the end of the period.

The best way to illustrate the future value of an ordinary annuity is through the use of **timelines**, which show the payments received or paid over time.

EXAMPLE   You plan to invest $100 at the end of every year for the next three years. You expect to earn an annual interest rate of 10 percent on the funds that you invest. Using a timeline, the cash flows from this annuity can be represented as follows:

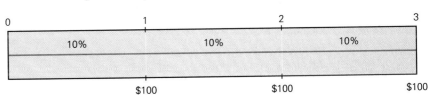

You would like to know how much money will be in your investment account at the end of the third year. This amount is the future value of the annuity. The first step in calculating the future value of the annuity is to treat each payment as a single sum and determine the future value of each payment individually. Next, add up the individual future values to obtain the future value of the annuity.

Since the first payment will be invested from the end of year 1 to the end of year 3, it will be invested for two years. Since the second payment will be invested from the end of year 2 to the end of year 3, it will be invested for one year. The third payment is made at the end of year 3, the point in time at which we want to determine the future value of the annuity. Hence, the third-year payment will not accumulate any interest. Using the future value in Exhibit 3.1 to obtain the future value interest factor for two years and 10 percent ($FVIF_{10\%,2} = 1.21$) and the future value interest factor for one year and 10 percent ($FVIF_{10\%,1} = 1.10$), the future value of your annuity can be determined as follows:

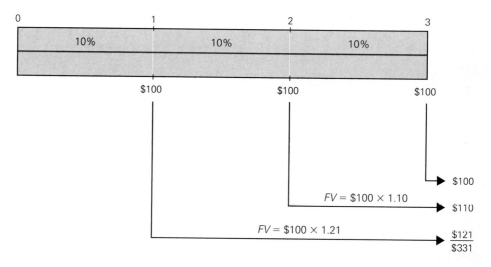

Adding up the individual future values shows that the future value of this annuity is $331 (i.e., you will have $331 in your account at the end of the third year). Notice that $300 of the $331 represents the three $100 payments. Thus, the remaining $31 of the $331 is the combined interest you earned on the three payments.

Using the Future Value Annuity Table

future value interest factor for an annuity (FVIFA)
A factor multiplied by the periodic savings level (annuity) to determine how the savings will accumulate over time.

Computing the future value of an annuity by looking up each individual single-sum future value interest factor (*FVIF*) is rather tedious. Consequently, Exhibit 3.3 lists the factors for various interest rates and periods (years). These factors are referred to as **future value interest factors for an annuity ($FVIFA_{i,n}$)**, where *i* is the periodic interest rate and *n* is the number of payments in the annuity. The annuity payment (*PMT*) can be multiplied by the *FVIFA* to determine the future value of the annuity (*FVA = PMT × FVIFA*). Each column in Exhibit 3.3 lists an interest rate, while each row lists the period of concern.

EXAMPLE

Suppose that you have won the lottery and will receive $150,000 at the end of every year for the next 20 years. As soon as you receive the payments, you will invest them at your bank at an interest rate of 7 percent annually. How much will be in your account at the end of 20 years (assuming you do not make any withdrawals)?

To find the answer, you must determine the future value of an annuity. (The stream of cash flows is in the form of an annuity since the payments are equal and equally spaced in time.) Using Exhibit 3.3 to determine the factor, look in the *i* = 7% column and the *n* = 20 periods row. Exhibit 3.3 shows that this factor is 40.995.

The next step is to determine the future value of your lottery annuity:

$$FVA = PMT \times FVIFA_{i,n}$$

$$= PMT \times FVIFA_{7,20}$$

$$= \$150,000 \times 40.995$$

$$= \$6,149,250.$$

Thus, after 20 years, you will have $6,149,250 if you invest all your lottery payments in an account earning an interest rate of 7 percent.

As an exercise, use the future value annuity table to determine the future value of five $172 payments, received at the end of every year, and earning an interest rate of 14 percent. Your answer should be $1,137.

Using a Financial Calculator to Determine the Future Value of an Annuity

Using a financial calculator to determine the future value of an annuity is similar to using the calculator to determine the future value of a single dollar amount. As before, the known variables must be input in order to solve for the unknown variable.

The following example illustrates the use of a financial calculator to determine the future value of an annuity.

EXAMPLE   You have instructed your employer to deduct $80 from your paycheck every month and automatically invest the money at an annual interest rate of 5 percent. You intend to use this money for your retirement in 30 years. How much will be in the account at that time?

3.2 Financial Planning Online: Estimating the Future Value of Your Savings

Go to
http://moneycentral.msn.com/
investor/calcs/n_savapp/
main.asp

This Web site provides
an estimate of the future
value of your savings,
based on your initial balance, the amount saved
per period, the interest
rate, and the number of
periods.

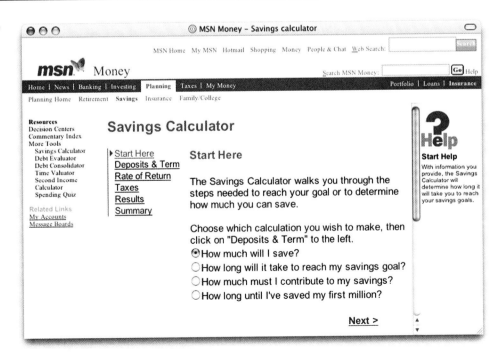

Exhibit 3.3 Future Value of a $1 Ordinary Annuity (FVIFA)

Year	1%	2%	3%	4%	5%	6%	7%	8%	9%
1	1.000	1.000	1.000	1.000	1.000	1.000	1.000	1.000	1.000
2	2.010	2.020	2.030	2.040	2.050	2.060	2.070	2.080	2.090
3	3.030	3.060	3.091	3.122	3.152	3.184	3.215	3.246	3.278
4	4.060	4.122	4.184	4.246	4.310	4.375	4.440	4.506	4.573
5	5.101	5.204	5.309	5.416	5.526	5.637	5.751	5.867	5.985
6	6.152	6.308	6.468	6.633	6.802	6.975	7.153	7.336	7.523
7	7.214	7.434	7.662	7.898	8.142	8.394	8.654	8.923	9.200
8	8.286	8.583	8.892	9.214	9.549	9.897	10.260	10.637	11.028
9	9.369	9.755	10.159	10.583	11.027	11.491	11.978	12.488	13.021
10	10.462	10.950	11.464	12.006	12.578	13.181	13.816	14.487	15.193
11	11.567	12.169	12.808	13.486	14.207	14.972	15.784	16.645	17.560
12	12.683	13.412	14.192	15.026	15.917	16.870	17.888	18.977	20.141
13	13.809	14.680	15.618	16.627	17.713	18.882	20.141	21.495	22.953
14	14.947	15.974	17.086	18.292	19.599	21.015	22.550	24.215	26.019
15	16.097	17.293	18.599	20.024	21.579	23.276	25.129	27.152	29.361
16	17.258	18.639	20.157	21.825	23.657	25.673	27.888	30.324	33.003
17	18.430	20.012	21.762	23.698	25.840	28.213	30.840	33.750	36.974
18	19.615	21.412	23.414	25.645	28.132	30.906	33.999	37.450	41.301
19	20.811	22.841	25.117	27.671	30.539	33.760	37.379	41.466	46.018
20	22.019	24.297	26.870	29.778	33.066	36.786	40.995	45.762	51.160
25	28.243	32.030	36.459	41.646	47.727	54.865	63.249	73.106	84.701
30	34.785	40.568	47.575	56.805	66.439	79.058	94.461	113.283	136.308

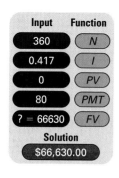

Input	Function
360	N
0.417	I
0	PV
80	PMT
? = 66630	FV

Solution

$66,630.00

This problem differs from the problems we have seen so far, in that the payments are received on a monthly (not annual) basis. You would like to obtain the future value of the annuity and consequently need the number of periods, the periodic interest rate, the present value, and the payment. Because there are 12 months in a year, there are $30 \times 12 = 360$ periods. Furthermore, since the annual interest rate is 5 percent, the monthly interest rate is $5/12 = 0.417$ percent. Also, note that to determine the future value of an annuity, most financial calculators require an input of 0 for the present value. The payment in this problem is 80.

The input for the financial calculator would be as shown at the left.

Thus, you will have $66,630 when you retire in 30 years as a result of your monthly investment.

PRESENT VALUE OF AN ANNUITY

Just as the future value of an annuity can be obtained by compounding the individual cash flows of the annuity and then adding them up, the present value of an annuity can be obtained by discounting the individual cash flows of the annuity and adding them up.

Referring to our earlier example of an ordinary annuity with three $100 payments and an interest rate of 10 percent, we can graphically illustrate the process as follows:

10%	12%	14%	16%	18%	20%	25%	30%
1.000	1.000	1.000	1.000	1.000	1.000	1.000	1.000
2.100	2.120	2.140	2.160	2.180	2.200	2.250	2.300
3.310	3.374	3.440	3.506	3.572	3.640	3.813	3.990
4.641	4.779	4.921	5.066	5.215	5.368	5.766	6.187
6.105	6.353	6.610	6.877	7.154	7.442	8.207	9.043
7.716	8.115	8.536	8.977	9.442	9.930	11.259	12.756
9.487	10.089	10.730	11.414	12.142	12.916	15.073	17.583
11.436	12.300	13.233	14.240	15.327	16.499	19.842	23.858
13.579	14.776	16.085	17.518	19.086	20.799	25.802	32.015
15.937	17.549	19.337	21.321	23.521	25.959	33.253	42.619
18.531	20.655	23.044	25.733	28.755	32.150	42.566	56.405
21.384	24.133	27.271	30.850	34.931	39.580	54.208	74.327
24.523	28.029	32.089	36.786	42.219	48.497	68.760	97.625
27.975	32.393	37.581	43.672	50.818	59.196	86.949	127.91
31.772	37.280	43.842	51.660	60.965	72.035	109.69	167.29
35.950	42.753	50.980	60.925	72.939	87.442	138.11	218.47
40.545	48.884	59.118	71.673	87.068	105.931	173.64	285.01
45.599	55.750	68.394	84.141	103.740	128.117	218.05	371.52
51.159	63.440	78.969	98.603	123.414	154.740	273.56	483.97
57.275	72.052	91.025	115.380	146.628	186.688	342.95	630.17
98.347	133.334	181.871	249.214	342.603	471.981	1,054.80	2,348.80
164.494	241.333	356.787	530.312	790.948	1,181.882	3,227.20	8,730.00

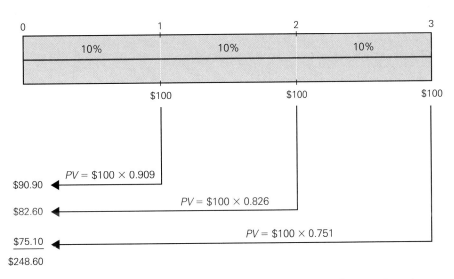

Adding up the individual present values leads to the conclusion that the present value of this annuity is $248.60. Therefore, three $100 payments received at the end of each of the next three years are worth $248.60 to you today if you can invest your money at an interest rate of 10 percent.

present value interest factor for an annuity (PVIFA)
A factor multiplied by a periodic savings level (annuity) to determine the present value of the annuity.

Using the Present Value Annuity Table

Exhibit 3.4 shows the **present value interest factors for an annuity (PVIFA$_{i,n}$)** for various interest rates (*i*) and time periods (*n*) in the annuity. Each column in Exhibit 3.4 lists an interest rate, while each row lists a time period.

EXAMPLE You have just won the lottery. As a result of your luck, you will receive $82,000 at the end of every year for the next 25 years. Now, a financial firm offers you a lump sum of $700,000 in return for these payments. If you can invest your money at an annual interest rate of 9 percent, should you accept the offer?

This problem requires you to determine the present value of the lottery annuity. If the present value of the annuity is higher than the amount offered by the financial firm, you should reject the offer. Using Exhibit 3.4 to determine the factor, we look in the *i* = 9% row and the *n* = 25 periods column. Exhibit 3.4 shows that this factor is 9.823.

The next step is to determine the present value of the annuity:

$$PVA = PMT \times PVIFA_{i,n}$$
$$= PMT \times PVIFA_{9,25}$$
$$= \$82,000 \times 9.823$$
$$= \$805,486.$$

Exhibit 3.4 Present Value of $1 Ordinary Annuity (PVIFA)

Year	1%	2%	3%	4%	5%	6%	7%	8%	9%
1	0.990	0.980	0.971	0.962	0.952	0.943	0.935	0.926	0.917
2	1.970	1.942	1.913	1.886	1.859	1.833	1.808	1.783	1.759
3	2.941	2.884	2.829	2.775	2.723	2.673	2.624	2.577	2.531
4	3.902	3.808	3.717	3.630	3.546	3.465	3.387	3.312	3.240
5	4.853	4.713	4.580	4.452	4.329	4.212	4.100	3.993	3.890
6	5.795	5.601	5.417	5.242	5.076	4.917	4.767	4.623	4.486
7	6.728	6.472	6.230	6.002	5.786	5.582	5.389	5.206	5.033
8	7.652	7.325	7.020	6.733	6.463	6.210	5.971	5.747	5.535
9	8.566	8.162	7.786	7.435	7.108	6.802	6.515	6.247	5.995
10	9.471	8.983	8.530	8.111	7.722	7.360	7.024	6.710	6.418
11	10.368	9.787	9.253	8.760	8.306	7.887	7.499	7.139	6.805
12	11.255	10.575	9.954	9.385	8.863	8.384	7.943	7.536	7.161
13	12.134	11.348	10.635	9.986	9.394	8.853	8.358	7.904	7.487
14	13.004	12.106	11.296	10.563	9.899	9.295	8.745	8.244	7.786
15	13.865	12.849	11.938	11.118	10.380	9.712	9.108	8.559	8.061
16	14.718	13.578	12.561	11.652	10.838	10.106	9.447	8.851	8.313
17	15.562	14.292	13.166	12.166	11.274	10.477	9.763	9.122	8.544
18	16.398	14.992	13.754	12.659	11.690	10.828	10.059	9.372	8.756
19	17.226	15.678	14.324	13.134	12.085	11.158	10.336	9.604	8.950
20	18.046	16.351	14.877	13.590	12.462	11.470	10.594	9.818	9.129
25	22.023	19.523	17.413	15.622	14.094	12.783	11.654	10.675	9.823
30	25.808	22.397	19.600	17.292	15.372	13.765	12.409	11.258	10.274

Thus, the 25 payments of $82,000 each are worth $805,486 to you today if you can invest your money at an interest rate of 9 percent. Consequently, you should reject the financial firm's offer to purchase your future lottery payments for $700,000.

As an exercise, use the present value annuity table to determine the present value of eight $54 payments, received at the end of every year and earning an interest rate of 14 percent. Your answer should be $250.50, which means that the eight payments have a present value of $250.50.

Using a Financial Calculator to Determine the Present Value of an Annuity

Determining the present value of an annuity with a financial calculator is similar to using the calculator to determine the present value of a single-sum payment. Again, the values of known variables are inserted in order to solve for the unknown variable.

EXAMPLE   A recent retiree, Dave Buzz receives his $600 pension monthly. He will receive this pension for 20 years. If Dave can invest his funds at an interest rate of 10 percent, he should be just as satisfied receiving this pension as receiving a lump-sum payment today of what amount?

10%	12%	14%	16%	18%	20%	25%	30%
0.909	0.893	0.877	0.862	0.847	0.833	0.800	0.769
1.736	1.690	1.647	1.605	1.566	1.528	1.440	1.361
2.487	2.402	2.322	2.246	2.174	2.106	1.952	1.816
3.170	3.037	2.914	2.798	2.690	2.589	2.362	2.166
3.791	3.605	3.433	3.274	3.127	2.991	2.689	2.436
4.355	4.111	3.889	3.685	3.498	3.326	2.951	2.643
4.868	4.564	4.288	4.039	3.812	3.605	3.161	2.802
5.335	4.968	4.639	4.344	4.078	3.837	3.329	2.925
5.759	5.328	4.946	4.607	4.303	4.031	3.463	3.019
6.145	5.650	5.216	4.833	4.494	4.193	3.571	3.092
6.495	5.938	5.453	5.029	4.656	4.327	3.656	3.147
6.814	6.194	5.660	5.197	4.793	4.439	3.725	3.190
7.103	6.424	5.842	5.342	4.910	4.533	3.780	3.223
7.367	6.628	6.002	5.468	5.008	4.611	3.824	3.249
7.606	6.811	6.142	5.575	5.092	4.675	3.859	3.268
7.824	6.974	6.265	5.668	5.162	4.730	3.887	3.283
8.022	7.120	6.373	5.749	5.222	4.775	3.910	3.295
8.201	7.250	6.467	5.818	5.273	4.812	3.928	3.304
8.365	7.366	6.550	5.877	5.316	4.843	3.942	3.311
8.514	7.469	6.623	5.929	5.353	4.870	3.954	3.316
9.077	7.843	6.873	6.097	5.467	4.948	3.985	3.329
9.427	8.055	7.003	6.177	5.517	4.979	3.995	3.332

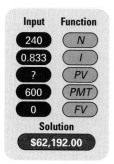

Input	Function
240	N
0.833	I
?	PV
600	PMT
0	FV
Solution	
$62,192.00	

This problem requires us to determine the present value of the pension annuity. Because there are 20 × 12 = 240 months in 20 years, *n* = 240. The monthly (periodic) interest rate is 10/12 = 0.833 percent. Thus, *i* = 0.833. Using these inputs with a financial calculator, we obtain the inputs shown to the left.

The present value is $62,192. If Dave is offered a lump sum of $62,192 today, he should accept it if he can invest his funds at an interest rate of 10 percent.

USING TIME VALUE TO ESTIMATE SAVINGS

Now that you understand the various time value calculations, you can apply them to financial planning. The key time value tools for building your financial plan are estimating the future value of annual savings and determining the amount of annual savings necessary to achieve a specific amount of savings in the future. Recognizing how much savings you can accumulate over time can motivate you to save money every month.

Estimating the Future Value from Savings

The future value of an annuity is especially useful when determining how much money you will have saved by a future point in time if you periodically save a specific amount of money every year. You can apply this process when you are saving for a large purchase (such as a down payment on a home) in the near future or even for your retirement in the distant future.

EXAMPLE

Stephanie Spratt believes that she may be able to save about $5,000 per year. She wants to know how much she will have in 30 years if she earns 6 percent annual interest on her investment. The annuity in this example is $5,000. The future value annuity factor based on a 30-year period and a 6 percent interest rate is 79.058. Thus, the future value is:

$5,000 × 79.058 = $395,290.

If she could earn 7 percent instead of 6 percent on her savings, the future value annuity factor would be 94.461, and the future value would be:

$5,000 × 94.461 = $472,305.

Estimating the Annual Savings That Will Achieve a Future Amount

The future value of annuity tables are also useful for determining how much money you need to save each year to achieve a specific amount of savings at a designated future point in time. Thus, you can estimate the size of the annuity that is necessary to achieve a specific future value of savings that you desire. Because *FVA = PMT × FVIFA*, the terms can be rearranged to solve for the annuity:

$$FVA/FVIFA = PMT$$

Exhibit 3.5 shows how Stephanie Spratt uses the time value tools to develop a financial plan. Stephanie developed a tentative plan to save $5,000 per year. After applying the time value tools, however, she recognizes that she could accumulate $600,000 in 30 years by saving $6,352 per year. She decides to strive for this higher level of annual savings. Because she realizes that this goal is ambitious, she sets a minimum goal of saving $5,000 per year.

EXAMPLE

Stephanie Spratt now wants to know how much money she must save every year to achieve $600,000 in 30 years, based on a 7 percent interest rate. In this example, the future value is $600,000, and the future value interest factor is 94.461. The unknown variable is the annuity.

$$PMT = FVA/FVIFA$$
$$= \$600,000/94.461$$
$$= \$6,352.$$

Thus, Stephanie would need to invest $6,352 each year to accumulate $600,000 in 30 years.

HOW A SAVINGS PLAN FITS WITHIN YOUR FINANCIAL PLAN

The key savings decisions for building your financial plan are:

- How much should I attempt to accumulate in savings for a future point in time?
- How much should I attempt to save every month or every year?

These decisions require an understanding of the time value of money. Exhibit 3.5 shows how these savings decisions apply to Stephanie Spratt's financial plan.

Exhibit 3.5 How Time Value of Money Decisions Fit within Stephanie Spratt's Financial Plan

GOALS FOR A SAVINGS PLAN

1. *Calculate how much savings I will accumulate by various future points in time.*
2. *Determine how much I need to save each year to ensure a comfortable living upon retirement.*

ANALYSIS

Present Situation:

Expected Savings per Year = *$5,000*

Expected Annual Rate of Return = *6% or 7%*

Estimated Amount of Savings to Be Accumulated:

Savings Accumulated over:	Assume Annual Return = 6%	Assume Annual Return = 7%
5 years	$28,185	$28,753
10 years	65,905	69,080
15 years	116,380	125,645
20 years	183,930	204,975
25 years	274,325	316,245
30 years	395,290	472,305

Annual Savings Needed to Achieve a Specific Savings Goal:

Savings Goal = *$80,000 in 10 years, $200,000 in 20 years, $500,000 in 30 years*

Expected Annual Rate of Return = *6% or 7%*

Savings Goal	Assume Annual Return = 6%	Assume Annual Return = 7%
$80,000 in 10 years	$6,069	$5,790
$200,000 in 20 years	5,437	4,879
$500,000 in 30 years	6,324	5,293

To achieve a savings goal of $80,000 in 10 years, I would need to save $6,069 per year (assuming an annual return of 6 percent on my money). To achieve a goal of $200,000 in 20 years, I would need to save $5,437 per year (assuming a 6 percent annual return).

DECISIONS

Decision on My Savings Goal in the Future:

If I can save $5,000 a year, I should accumulate $28,185 in 5 years and $65,905 in 10 years. These estimates are based on an assumed annual return of 6 percent. If my annual return is higher, I should accumulate even more than that. The estimated savings for longer time periods are much higher.

A comparison of the third column with the second column in the table shows how much more savings I could accumulate if I can earn an annual return of 7 percent instead of 6 percent.

Decision on My Savings Goal per Year:

Although my initial plan was to develop a budget for saving about $5,000 a year, I will try to save more so that I can achieve my savings goals. I will use a minimum savings goal of $5,000, but will try to save about $6,000 per year.

DISCUSSION QUESTIONS

1. How would Stephanie's savings decisions be different if she were a single mother of two children?

2. How would Stephanie's savings decisions be affected if she were 35 years old? If she were 50 years old?

SUMMARY

You can estimate the future value of a single dollar amount to determine the future value of a bank deposit or a fund established for retirement. It is determined by estimating the compounded interest that is generated by the initial amount. The future value can be determined by using a future value table or a financial calculator.

You can estimate the present value of a single dollar amount so that you know what a future payment would be worth if you had it today. The present value of a single dollar amount to be received in the future is determined by discounting the future value. The present value of a future amount to be received can be determined by using a present value table or a financial calculator.

You can estimate the future value of an annuity so that you can determine how much a stream of payments will be worth at a specific time in the future. This involves determining the future value of every single dollar amount contained within the annuity, which is easily estimated by using a future value annuity table or a financial calculator.

You can estimate the present value of an annuity so that you can determine how much a stream of future payments is worth today. This involves determining the present value of every single dollar amount contained within the annuity, which is easily estimated by using a present value annuity table or a financial calculator.

INTEGRATING THE KEY CONCEPTS

Time value tools can be applied to all parts of your financial plan. When you borrow money for liquidity reasons or to finance your use of credit cards, the amount of debt grows over time if it is not paid off. When you save money for liquidity reasons or for investment purposes, your money will grow over time if you earn a positive return. The time value tools are especially useful for retirement planning because they allow you to estimate the future value of

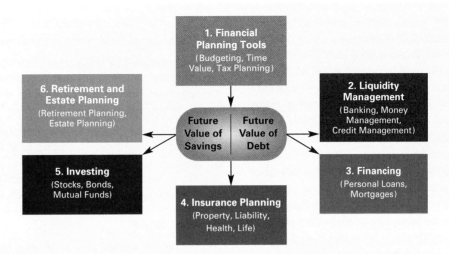

retirement funds if you follow a particular savings pattern over time.

REVIEW QUESTIONS

1. What is the time value of money? How is it related to opportunity costs?

2. To what types of cash flows is the time value of money concept most commonly applied?

3. What is an annuity?

4. Define compounding. How is it used in financial planning?

5. What two methods can be used to calculate future values?

6. What is the formula for determining the future value of a single sum when using the future value interest factor table? What information must be known in order to find the correct future value interest factor?

7. What is discounting?

8. Describe some instances when determining the present value of an amount is useful.

In questions 9 through 12, indicate whether you would use the table for determining the future value of a single sum (FVIF), the present value of a single sum (PVIF), the future value of an annuity (FVIFA), or the present value of an annuity (PVIFA).

9. You want to know how much you must deposit today to have $5,000 in five years.

10. You plan to contribute $300 per month to your company's retirement plan and want to know how much you will have at retirement.

11. You received $500 as a gift for graduation, and you want to know how much it will be worth in three years if you deposit it in a savings account.

12. You must decide between accepting a lump-sum settlement and annual payments.

13. What formula is used to determine the present value of an annuity? What does the present value of an annuity indicate?

14. How would you modify the *FVA* equation to determine how much you would need to save each month to have a specific amount at a specific time in the future?

15. In determining the future value of an annuity to be invested monthly over a five-year period, what number of periods should you use?

FINANCIAL PLANNING PROBLEMS

Questions 2, 5, 6, 7, 13, 14, and 15 require a financial calculator.

1. Rodney has $1,000 in cash received as graduation gifts from various relatives. He wants to invest it in a certificate of deposit (CD) so that he will have a down payment on a car when he graduates from college in five years. His bank will pay 6 percent for the five-year CD. How much will Rodney have in five years to put down on his car?

2. Michelle is attending college and has a part-time job. Once she finishes college, Michelle would like to relocate to a metropolitan area. She wants to build her savings so that she will have a "nest egg" to start her off. Michelle works out her budget and decides she can afford to set aside $50 per month for savings. Her bank will pay her 3 percent on her savings account. What will Michelle's balance be in five years?

3. Twins Jessica and Joshua, both 25, graduated from college and began working in the family restaurant business. The first year, Jessica began putting $2,000 per year in an individual retirement account and contributed to it for a total of 10 years. After 10 years she made no further contributions until she

Chapter 3: Building Your Own Financial Plan

GOALS

1. Determine how much savings you will accumulate by various future points in time.
2. Estimate how much you will need to save each year in order to achieve your goals.

ANALYSIS

1. For each goal you set in Chapter 1, make the calculations using an interest rate that you believe you can earn on your invested savings. Then recalculate the amount you will need for each goal based on a rate that is one point higher and a rate that is one point lower than your original rate. (The Excel worksheet will perform the calculations based on your input.)

Time Value of Money

Future Value of a Present Amount

Present Value	
Number of Periods	
Interest Rate per Period	
Future Value	

Future Value of an Annuity

Payment per Period	
Number of Periods	
Interest Rate per Period	
Future Value	

Present Value of a Future Amount

Future Amount	
Number of Periods	
Interest Rate per Period	
Present Value	

Present Value of an Annuity

Payment per Period	
Number of Periods	
Interest Rate per Period	
Present Value	

Chapter 3: The Sampsons—A Continuing Case

CASE QUESTIONS

1. Help the Sampsons determine how much they will have for their children's education by calculating how much $3,600 in annual savings will accumulate to if they earn interest of (a) 5 percent and (b) 7 percent. Next, determine how much $4,800 in annual savings will accumulate to if they earn interest of (a) 5 percent and (b) 7 percent.

Savings Accumulated over the Next 12 Years
(Based on Plan to Save $3,600 per Year)

Amount Saved per Year	$3,600	$3,600
Interest Rate	5%	7%
Years	12	12
Future Value of Savings		

Savings Accumulated over the Next 12 Years
(Based on Plan to Save $4,800 per Year)

Amount Saved per Year	$4,800	$4,800
Interest Rate	5%	7%
Years	12	12
Future Value of Savings		

2. What is the impact of the higher interest rate of 7 percent on the Sampsons' accumulated savings?

_____

_____

_____

_____

3. What is the impact of the higher savings of $4,800 on their accumulated savings?

_____

_____

_____

_____

4. If the Sampsons set a goal to save $70,000 for their children's college education in 12 years, how would you determine the yearly savings necessary to achieve this goal? How much would they have to save by the end of each year to achieve this goal, assuming a 5 percent annual interest rate?

Calculator: Savings Needed Each Year

Future Value	$70,000
Interest Rate	5%
Years	12
Savings Needed Each Year	

Using Tax Concepts for Planning

F aced with $22,000 of unreimbursed medical expenses, the Ricardos pledged to pay off the debt as soon as possible. With a combined income of $150,000 per year they managed to pay $2,000 per month over eleven months. An example of financial responsibility? Yes. A success story? No. What did they do wrong?

Unfortunately for the Ricardos, they paid off the debt over a period of time that fell into two calendar years. They paid $10,000 in the first calendar year and $12,000 in the second calendar year, unaware that medical expenses representing the first 7.5 percent of adjusted gross income in a tax year is not included in itemized deductions. Since 7.5% of $150,000 is $11,250, they were unable to claim a dime of the medical expenses paid the first year. In the second year they were able to claim a mere $750. Had they paid the entire $22,000 in one tax year they would have been able to claim an itemized deduction of $10,750. Since their marginal tax rate is 30 percent, they could have reduced their taxes by 30 percent of $10,750 or a total tax savings of $3,225.

Now you might ask, "Yes, but could they afford to pay off the entire medical bill in the first year?" The Ricardos did possess sufficient assets to pay off their medical expenses in one calendar year. But by the time their accountant became aware of the situation, it was too late. The moral of this story is that you as a taxpayer may be able to take advantage of significant tax breaks. However, while an accountant can help you complete your taxes correctly, it is your responsibility to take actions during the tax year that take full advantage of available tax-reduction strategies.

This chapter explains the basics of individual taxation. Knowledge of the tax laws can help you conserve your income, enhance your investments, and protect the transfer of wealth when you die. Understanding the taxation of income and wealth is crucial to sound financial planning.

The objectives of this chapter are to:

- Explain how to determine your tax filing status
- Demonstrate how to calculate your gross income
- Show how deductions and exemptions can be used
- Explain how to determine your taxable income, tax liability, and refund or additional taxes owed
- Illustrate how to fill out a tax form and determine your tax liability

BACKGROUND ON TAXES

Taxes are an integral part of our economy. They are paid on earned income, consumer purchases, wealth transfers, and capital assets. Special taxes are levied on certain consumer products such as cigarettes, alcohol, and gasoline. Corporations pay corporate income taxes on corporate profits. Homeowners pay property taxes on the value of their homes and land. Hundreds of billions of dollars are paid in taxes each year in the United States. These taxes are a significant source of funding for governments and governmental agencies. Taxes are used to pay for a wide variety of governmental services and programs including national defense, Social Security, fire and police protection, government employees, road construction and maintenance, and our education systems.

Individuals pay taxes at the federal, state, and local levels. The federal tax system is administered by a branch of the U.S. Treasury Department called the Internal Revenue System (IRS). While Congress passes federal tax laws, it is the IRS that enforces those laws and prepares the forms and publications that taxpayers use to calculate their income taxes.

Many taxes, such as sales taxes, are paid at the time of a transaction. Income taxes are generally paid as income is earned in a process called withholding. Taxes are withheld as income is earned throughout the year. Self-employed individuals have to estimate the amount of taxes to withhold and therefore pay estimated tax withholdings. Employees file a form with their employer, which helps the employer calculate the amount of taxes to withhold. Individuals are allowed to withhold more than the minimum from each pay cycle, but are not allowed to reduce the amount of withholding below the amount specified by the IRS.

The tax year for federal income taxes ends on December 31 of each calendar year. Individual income taxes must be filed and paid by April 15 of the following year. The IRS allows taxpayers to file for an extension beyond April 15, but all taxes due for the tax year must be paid by April 15.

Tax Relief Acts

Economic Growth and Tax Relief Reconciliation Act of 2001
Tax cut package designed to provide short-term economic stimulus through tax relief for taxpayers.

In the summer of 2001, Congress passed the **Economic Growth and Tax Relief Reconciliation Act of 2001** (more commonly referred to as the Tax Relief Act of 2001). Provisions of the $1.35 trillion tax cut package began taking effect in 2001 and were scheduled to be phased in gradually until the law expires in 2011. Designed to provide a short-term stimulus to the economy and long-term tax relief for individual taxpayers, the Act reduced inequalities in the tax code, simplified several sections of the tax code, and provided educational incentives to a broad range of taxpayers. Tax relief for parents included an increase in the child tax credit and an expansion of the dependent care credit. The 2001 tax reform measures also expanded contributions to retirement plans. All of the measures of the 2001 law are scheduled to end in 2011. Unless these provisions of the tax law are made permanent, the tax rates will revert to pre-2001 levels.

Jobs and Growth Tax Relief Act of 2003
An act that accelerated much of the tax relief resulting from the 2001 Tax Relief Act.

On May 6, 2003, Congress passed the **Jobs and Growth Tax Relief Reconciliation Act of 2003**. The Act accelerated much of the tax relief scheduled to occur as a result of the 2001 Tax Relief Act. Specifically, individual tax rates were lowered by 2–3 percent, the

4.1 Financial Planning Online: Internal Revenue Service

Go to
http://www.irs.gov

This Web site provides
information about tax
rates, guidelines, and
deadlines.

child tax credit was increased to $1,000 per child for 2003 and 2004, the standard deduction for married taxpayers was increased to twice the standard deduction for single taxpayers, the 15 percent tax bracket for married taxpayers was increased to twice that of single taxpayers, and investors were rewarded with lower long-term capital gains and dividend tax rates.

These laws do not change the process for computing taxes; instead, they have an impact on various adjustments made to determine your personal income taxes. As the process to determine your personal taxes is described in this chapter, pertinent new tax provisions are identified. (Changes that affect retirement and estate planning are discussed in Chapters 20 and 21.)

Social Security and Medicare Taxes

FICA (Federal Insurance Contributions Act)
Taxes paid to fund the Social Security System and Medicare.

Medicare
A government health insurance program that covers people over age 65 and provides payments to health care providers in the case of illness.

Your **earned income** (wages or salary) is subject to **FICA (Federal Insurance Contributions Act)** taxes that fund Social Security and Medicare. Your employer withholds FICA taxes from each of your paychecks. The Social Security system uses the funds to make payments to you upon your retirement (subject to age and other requirements). The Social Security tax is equal to 6.20 percent of your salary up to a maximum level (the level was $90,000 in 2005 and changes over time). There is no Social Security tax on income beyond this maximum level. **Medicare** is a government health insurance program that covers people 65 years of age and older and some people with disabilities under age 65. Medicare provides payments to health care providers in the case of illness. Medicare taxes are 1.45 percent of your earned income, regardless of the amount. Your employer pays the same amount of FICA and Medicare taxes on your behalf.

The taxes described above also apply if you are self-employed. However, self-employed persons serve not only as the employee but also as the employer. Their FICA taxes are equal to 15.3 percent, which represents the 7.65 percent FICA tax paid by the employee plus the 7.65 percent FICA tax paid by the employer. The Social Security tax rate is again capped at the maximum limit, while the Medicare tax rate applies to the entire earnings. One-half of the FICA taxes paid by the self-employed is tax-deductible (i.e., half can be deducted from income when determining the federal income tax).

EXAMPLE

Stephanie Spratt earned a salary of $38,000 this year. She is subject to total FICA taxes of 7.65 percent, which is based on 6.20 percent for Social Security and 1.45 percent for Medicate. Thus, her Social Security taxes and Medicare taxes are

	Social Security Tax	Medicare Tax
Tax rate	6.2% (up to a maximum of 90,000)	1.45%
Tax amount	.062 × $38,000 = $2,356	0145 × $38,000 = $551

Her total FICA taxes are $2,907 (computed as $2,356 + $551).

personal income taxes
Taxes imposed on income earned.

Personal Income Taxes

Your income is also subject to **personal income taxes**, which are taxes imposed on income you earn. For any year that you earn income, you must file a tax return that consists of a completed Form 1040 or 1040EZ, plus supporting documents. Your tax return will show whether a sufficient amount of taxes was already withheld from your paycheck, whether you still owe some taxes, or whether the government owes you a refund. If you still owe taxes, you should include a check for the taxes owed along with your completed tax return.

Form 1040EZ, the simplest tax form to use, is an appropriate alternative to Form 1040 in some cases. Generally, this form is used by individuals whose filing status is either single or married filing jointly, who have no dependents, and whose taxable income is less than $100,000. Tax forms can be downloaded from several Web sites, including http://www.yahoo.com. Several software programs, including TurboTax, MacInTax, and Quicken, are also available to help you prepare your return. An example of Form 1040 is shown in Exhibit 4.1. Refer to this form as you read through the chapter.

Notice from Exhibit 4.1 that determining taxes requires you to address filing status, gross income, adjusted gross income, exemptions, itemized deductions, standard deduction, taxable income (adjusted gross income), tax credits, and capital gains and losses. Each of these topics is covered in this chapter so that you will be equipped to fill out Form 1040 to determine your taxes.

FILING STATUS

Each year, taxpayers must specify a filing status when submitting their income tax return. The alternatives are:

- Single
- Married filing joint return
- Married filing separate return
- Head of household
- Qualifying widow(er) with dependent child

Married people usually combine their incomes and file a joint return. However, each may file a separate tax return in some circumstances. The "head of household" status can be selected by single people who have at least one dependent in their household. The tax rates applied when using this status may be more favorable than when filing under the "single" status. If you are a qualifying widow(er) with a dependent child, you are entitled to use the joint tax rates for two years following the death of your spouse, assuming that you do not remarry, have a child for whom you can claim an exemption, and pay more than half the cost of maintaining your residence.

Exhibit 4.1 Form 1040

Form **1040**

Department of the Treasury—Internal Revenue Service

U.S. Individual Income Tax Return 2005 (99) IRS Use Only—Do not write or staple in this space.

For the year Jan. 1–Dec. 31, 2005, or other tax year beginning ____, 2005, ending ____, 20 ____

OMB No. 1545-0074

Label (See instructions on page 16.) **Use the IRS label.** Otherwise, please print or type.

LABEL HERE

Your first name and initial	Last name
If a joint return, spouse's first name and initial	Last name
Home address (number and street). If you have a P.O. box, see page 16.	Apt. no.
City, town or post office, state, and ZIP code. If you have a foreign address, see page 16.	

Your social security number

Spouse's social security number

▲ You **must** enter your SSN(s) above. ▲

Checking a box below will not change your tax or refund.

Presidential Election Campaign ▶ Check here if you, or your spouse if filing jointly, want $3 to go to this fund (see page 16) ▶ ☐ **You** ☐ **Spouse**

Filing Status

Check only one box.

1 ☐ Single
2 ☐ Married filing jointly (even if only one had income)
3 ☐ Married filing separately. Enter spouse's SSN above and full name here. ▶
4 ☐ Head of household (with qualifying person). (See page 17.) If the qualifying person is a child but not your dependent, enter this child's name here. ▶
5 ☐ Qualifying widow(er) with dependent child (see page 17)

Exemptions

6a ☐ **Yourself.** If someone can claim you as a dependent, **do not** check box 6a
b ☐ **Spouse**
c **Dependents:**

(1) First name Last name	(2) Dependent's social security number	(3) Dependent's relationship to you	(4) ✔ if qualifying child for child tax credit (see page 19)
	:		☐
	:		☐
	:		☐
	:		☐

If more than four dependents, see page 19.

Boxes checked on 6a and 6b ____
No. of children on 6c who:
• lived with you ____
• did not live with you due to divorce or separation (see page 20) ____
Dependents on 6c not entered above ____
Add numbers on lines above ▶ ____

d Total number of exemptions claimed

Income

Attach Form(s) W-2 here. Also attach Forms W-2G and 1099-R if tax was withheld.

If you did not get a W-2, see page 22.

Enclose, but do not attach, any payment. Also, please use **Form 1040-V.**

7	Wages, salaries, tips, etc. Attach Form(s) W-2	7
8a	**Taxable** interest. Attach Schedule B if required	8a
b	**Tax-exempt** interest. **Do not** include on line 8a 8b	
9a	Ordinary dividends. Attach Schedule B if required	9a
b	Qualified dividends (see page 23) 9b	
10	Taxable refunds, credits, or offsets of state and local income taxes (see page 23)	10
11	Alimony received	11
12	Business income or (loss). Attach Schedule C or C-EZ	12
13	Capital gain or (loss). Attach Schedule D if required. If not required, check here ▶ ☐	13
14	Other gains or (losses). Attach Form 4797	14
15a	IRA distributions 15a b Taxable amount (see page 25)	15b
16a	Pensions and annuities 16a b Taxable amount (see page 25)	16b
17	Rental real estate, royalties, partnerships, S corporations, trusts, etc. Attach Schedule E	17
18	Farm income or (loss). Attach Schedule F	18
19	Unemployment compensation	19
20a	Social security benefits 20a b Taxable amount (see page 27)	20b
21	Other income. List type and amount (see page 29) ____	21
22	Add the amounts in the far right column for lines 7 through 21. This is your **total income** ▶	22

Adjusted Gross Income

23	Educator expenses (see page 29)	23
24	Certain business expenses of reservists, performing artists, and fee-basis government officials. Attach Form 2106 or 2106-EZ	24
25	Health savings account deduction. Attach Form 8889	25
26	Moving expenses. Attach Form 3903	26
27	One-half of self-employment tax. Attach Schedule SE	27
28	Self-employed SEP, SIMPLE, and qualified plans	28
29	Self-employed health insurance deduction (see page 30)	29
30	Penalty on early withdrawal of savings	30
31a	Alimony paid b Recipient's SSN ▶ ____	31a
32	IRA deduction (see page 31)	32
33	Student loan interest deduction (see page 33)	33
34	Tuition and fees deduction (see page 34)	34
35	Domestic production activities deduction. Attach Form 8903	35
36	Add lines 23 through 31a and 32 through 35	36
37	Subtract line 36 from line 22. This is your **adjusted gross income** ▶	37

For Disclosure, Privacy Act, and Paperwork Reduction Act Notice, see page 78.   Cat. No. 11320B   Form **1040** (2005)

Exhibit 4.1 Form 1040 (*continued*)

Form 1040 (2005)   Page **2**

			38	
Tax and Credits	38	Amount from line 37 (adjusted gross income)	38	

39a	Check if:	☐ **You** were born before January 2, 1941, ☐ Blind.	Total boxes
		☐ **Spouse** was born before January 2, 1941, ☐ Blind.	checked ▶ 39a

Standard Deduction for—

b If your spouse itemizes on a separate return or you were a dual-status alien, see page 35 and check here ▶39b ☐

- People who checked any box on line 39a or 39b **or** who can be claimed as a dependent, see page 36.

- All others:

Single or Married filing separately, $5,000

Married filing jointly or Qualifying widow(er), $10,000

Head of household, $7,300

40	**Itemized deductions** (from Schedule A) **or** your **standard deduction** (see left margin) .	40	
41	Subtract line 40 from line 38	41	
42	If line 38 is over $109,475, or you provided housing to a person displaced by Hurricane Katrina, see page 37. Otherwise, multiply $3,200 by the total number of exemptions claimed on line 6d	42	
43	**Taxable income.** Subtract line 42 from line 41. If line 42 is more than line 41, enter -0-	43	
44	**Tax** (see page 37). Check if any tax is from: **a** ☐ Form(s) 8814 **b** ☐ Form 4972 . . .	44	
45	**Alternative minimum tax** (see page 39). Attach Form 6251	45	
46	Add lines 44 and 45 . . . . ▶	46	

47	Foreign tax credit. Attach Form 1116 if required . . .	47	
48	Credit for child and dependent care expenses. Attach Form 2441	48	
49	Credit for the elderly or the disabled. Attach Schedule R .	49	
50	Education credits. Attach Form 8863	50	
51	Retirement savings contributions credit. Attach Form 8880 . .	51	
52	Child tax credit (see page 41). Attach Form 8901 if required	52	
53	Adoption credit. Attach Form 8839	53	
54	Credits from: **a** ☐ Form 8396 **b** ☐ Form 8859 . .	54	
55	Other credits. Check applicable box(es): **a** ☐ Form 3800 **b** ☐ Form 8801 **c** ☐ Form _____	55	

56	Add lines 47 through 55. These are your **total credits** . . .	56	
57	Subtract line 56 from line 46. If line 56 is more than line 46, enter -0- . . . . . ▶	57	

Other Taxes	58	Self-employment tax. Attach Schedule SE	58	
	59	Social security and Medicare tax on tip income not reported to employer. Attach Form 4137 .	59	
	60	Additional tax on IRAs, other qualified retirement plans, etc. Attach Form 5329 if required .	60	
	61	Advance earned income credit payments from Form(s) W-2	61	
	62	Household employment taxes. Attach Schedule H	62	
	63	Add lines 57 through 62. This is your **total tax** . . . . ▶	63	

Payments	64	Federal income tax withheld from Forms W-2 and 1099 . .	64	
	65	2005 estimated tax payments and amount applied from 2004 return	65	

If you have a qualifying child, attach Schedule EIC.

66a	**Earned income credit (EIC)**	66a	
b	Nontaxable combat pay election ▶	66b	
67	Excess social security and tier 1 RRTA tax withheld (see page 59)	67	
68	Additional child tax credit. Attach Form 8812	68	
69	Amount paid with request for extension to file (see page 59)	69	
70	Payments from: **a** ☐ Form 2439 **b** ☐ Form 4136 **c** ☐ Form 8885 .	70	
71	Add lines 64, 65, 66a, and 67 through 70. These are your **total payments** . . . . . ▶	71	

Refund	72	If line 71 is more than line 63, subtract line 63 from line 71. This is the amount you **overpaid**	72	
Direct deposit?	73a	Amount of line 72 you want **refunded to you** . . . . ▶	73a	

See page 59 and fill in 73b, 73c, and 73d.

▶ b Routing number [ ] ▶ c Type: ☐ Checking ☐ Savings
▶ d Account number [ ]

74	Amount of line 72 you want **applied to your 2006 estimated tax** ▶	74	

Amount You Owe	75	**Amount you owe.** Subtract line 71 from line 63. For details on how to pay, see page 60 ▶	75	
	76	Estimated tax penalty (see page 60)	76	

Third Party Designee

Do you want to allow another person to discuss this return with the IRS (see page 61)? ☐ **Yes.** Complete the following. ☐ **No**

Designee's name ▶	Phone no. ▶ ( )	Personal identification number (PIN) ▶ [ ]

Sign Here

Under penalties of perjury, I declare that I have examined this return and accompanying schedules and statements, and to the best of my knowledge and belief, they are true, correct, and complete. Declaration of preparer (other than taxpayer) is based on all information of which preparer has any knowledge.

Joint return? See page 17.

Keep a copy for your records.

Your signature	Date	Your occupation	Daytime phone number ( )
Spouse's signature. If a joint return, **both** must sign.	Date	Spouse's occupation	

Paid Preparer's Use Only

Preparer's signature ▶	Date	Check if self-employed ☐	Preparer's SSN or PTIN
Firm's name (or yours if self-employed), address, and ZIP code ▶		EIN	
		Phone no. ( )	

Form **1040** (2005)

♻ Printed on recycled paper

GROSS INCOME

gross income
All reportable income from any source, including salary, interest income, dividend income, and capital gains received during the tax year.

To calculate your federal income tax, first determine your gross income. **Gross income** consists of all reportable income from any source. It includes your salary, interest income, dividend income, and capital gains received during the tax year. It also includes income from your own business, as well as from tips, prizes and awards, rental property, and scholarships that exceed tuition fees and book costs. Some types of income are not taxed, including health and casualty insurance reimbursements, child support payments received, reimbursements of moving expenses and other expenses by an employer, veteran's benefits, and welfare benefits.

Wages and Salaries

If you work full-time, your main source of gross income is probably your salary. Wages and salaries, along with any bonuses, are subject to federal income taxes. Contributions to your employer-sponsored retirement account, whether made by you or your employer, are not subject to income taxes until those funds are withdrawn from the account. Consequently, they are not subject to immediate taxation. Many employees take advantage of their employer-sponsored retirement plans to reduce their current income taxes and obtain tax-deferred growth of their retirement fund.

Interest Income

interest income
Interest earned from investments in various types of savings accounts at financial institutions, from investments in debt securities such as Treasury bonds, or from providing loans to other individuals.

Individuals can earn **interest income** from investments in various types of savings accounts at financial institutions. They can also earn interest income from investing in debt securities such as Treasury bonds or from providing loans to other individuals. Note that interest income earned from investments in municipal bonds issued by state and local government agencies is normally excluded from federal taxation. Any tax-exempt interest income is not included when determining taxes.

Dividend Income

dividend income
Income received in the form of dividends paid on shares of stock or mutual funds.

Individual taxpayers can earn **dividend income** by investing in stocks or mutual funds. Some firms pay dividends to their shareholders quarterly. Other firms elect not to pay dividends to their shareholders and instead reinvest all of their earnings to finance their existing operations. This can benefit shareholders because a firm's share price is more likely to appreciate over time if the firm reinvests all of its earnings.

The worksheet for adding your interest income and dividend income—Schedule B of Form 1040—is shown in Exhibit 4.2.

Capital Gains

capital gain
Income earned when an asset is sold at a higher price than was paid for the asset.

You can purchase securities (also called financial assets) such as stocks or debt instruments (such as bonds) that are issued by firms to raise capital. You can also invest in other income-producing assets such as rental properties. When you sell these types of assets at a higher price than you paid, you earn a **capital gain**. If you sell the assets for a lower price than you paid, you sustain a capital loss.

short-term capital gain
A gain on assets that were held less than 12 months.

A **short-term capital gain** is a gain on assets that were held 12 months or less. A **long-term capital gain** is a gain on assets that were held for longer than 12 months. The **capital gains tax**, the tax that is paid on short-term capital gains, is based on your marginal tax rate, as if it were additional income. The capital gains tax on a long-term capital gain is restricted to a 15-percent maximum, and is usually lower than the tax on short-term gains. Net short-term gains and long-term gains are reported on Form 1040 in the section on gross income.

long-term capital gain
A gain on assets that were held for 12 months or longer.

capital gains tax
The tax that is paid on a gain earned as a result of selling an asset for more than the purchase price.

The capital gains tax is a maximum of 15 percent of the long-term capital gain and is even lower for individuals in very low ordinary income tax brackets. For example, an individual in the 15 percent marginal income tax bracket will pay a 5 percent capital gains tax. The tax benefits are larger for individuals in higher tax brackets. An individual in the 35 percent tax bracket will pay only a 15 percent tax on long-term capital gains.

Exhibit 4.2 Schedule B of Form 1040

Schedules A&B (Form 1040) 2005   OMB No. 1545-0074   Page **2**

Name(s) shown on Form 1040. Do not enter name and social security number if shown on other side. | **Your social security number**

Schedule B—Interest and Ordinary Dividends

Attachment
Sequence No. **08**

			Amount	
Part I **Interest** (See page B-1 and the instructions for Form 1040, line 8a.)	**1**	List name of payer. If any interest is from a seller-financed mortgage and the buyer used the property as a personal residence, see page B-1 and list this interest first. Also, show that buyer's social security number and address ▶	**1**	

Note. If you received a Form 1099-INT, Form 1099-OID, or substitute statement from a brokerage firm, list the firm's name as the payer and enter the total interest shown on that form.

	2	Add the amounts on line 1	**2**	
	3	Excludable interest on series EE and I U.S. savings bonds issued after 1989. Attach Form 8815	**3**	
	4	Subtract line 3 from line 2. Enter the result here and on Form 1040, line 8a ▶	**4**	

Note. If line 4 is over $1,500, you must complete Part III.

			Amount	
Part II **Ordinary** **Dividends** (See page B-1 and the instructions for Form 1040, line 9a.)	**5**	List name of payer ▶	**5**	

Note. If you received a Form 1099-DIV or substitute statement from a brokerage firm, list the firm's name as the payer and enter the ordinary dividends shown on that form.

	6	Add the amounts on line 5. Enter the total here and on Form 1040, line 9a . ▶	**6**	

Note. If line 6 is over $1,500, you must complete Part III.

		Yes	No
Part III **Foreign** **Accounts** **and Trusts** (See page B-2.)	You must complete this part if you **(a)** had over $1,500 of taxable interest or ordinary dividends; or **(b)** had a foreign account; or **(c)** received a distribution from, or were a grantor of, or a transferor to, a foreign trust.		
	7a At any time during 2005, did you have an interest in or a signature or other authority over a financial account in a foreign country, such as a bank account, securities account, or other financial account? See page B-2 for exceptions and filing requirements for Form TD F 90-22.1.		
	b If "Yes," enter the name of the foreign country ▶		
	8 During 2005, did you receive a distribution from, or were you the grantor of, or transferor to, a foreign trust? If "Yes," you may have to file Form 3520. See page B-2		

For Paperwork Reduction Act Notice, see Form 1040 instructions.   Schedule B (Form 1040) 2005

EXAMPLE

Suppose your current income is high. You are subject to a 28 percent marginal tax rate, so you must pay a tax of 28 percent on any additional income that you earn. Stock that you purchased 11 months ago has increased in value by $20,000. If you sell the stock today, your capital gain will be classified as "short term," and you will pay a tax rate of 28 percent on that gain, or $5,600. If you hold the stock for another month, your capital gain will be classified as "long term," therefore subjecting it to a 15 percent maximum tax rate. If the value of the stock is the same in a month, your tax on a long-term gain will be $3,000. Thus, holding the stock for one more month cuts your taxes by $2,600.

Use the worksheet labeled Schedule D of Form 1040, shown in Exhibit 4.3, to determine your capital gains taxes.

gross income
All reportable income from any source, including salary, interest income, dividend income, and capital gains received during the tax year.

Determining Gross Income

Gross income is determined by adding your salary, interest income, dividend income, and capital gains.

EXAMPLE

Stephanie Spratt earned a salary of $38,000 over the most recent year. She earned no income from interest, dividends, or short-term capital gains. Her gross income over the year is:

Salary	$38,000
+ Interest Income	0
+ Dividend Income	0
+ Capital Gain	0
= Gross Income	$38,000

adjusted gross income (AGI)
Adjusts gross income for contributions to IRAs, alimony payments, interest paid on student loans, and other special circumstances.

Adjusted Gross Income

Your **adjusted gross income (AGI)** is calculated by adjusting your gross income for contributions to individual retirement accounts (IRAs), alimony payments, interest paid on student loans, and other special circumstances. Notice that student loan interest up to $2,500 is deductible whether or not you elect to itemize and is not included as one of your itemized deductions. If you do not have any special adjustments, your adjusted gross income is the same as your gross income.

EXAMPLE

Stephanie Spratt did not contribute any of her salary to an IRA this year. She also does not qualify for any other special adjustments to her gross income. Therefore, her adjusted gross income is $38,000, the same as her gross income.

DEDUCTIONS AND EXEMPTIONS

You may be able to claim deductions and exemptions, which reduce the amount of your gross income subject to taxation.

standard deduction
A fixed amount that can be deducted from adjusted gross income to determine taxable income.

Standard Deduction

The **standard deduction** is a fixed amount deducted from adjusted gross income to determine taxable income. The amount of the standard deduction is not affected by the

Exhibit 4.3 Schedule D of Form 1040

SCHEDULE D (Form 1040) Department of the Treasury Internal Revenue Service (99)	**Capital Gains and Losses** ▶ Attach to Form 1040. ▶ See Instructions for Schedule D (Form 1040). ▶ Use Schedule D-1 to list additional transactions for lines 1 and 8.	OMB No. 1545-0074 2005 Attachment Sequence No. **12**
Name(s) shown on Form 1040		Your social security number

Part I   Short-Term Capital Gains and Losses—Assets Held One Year or Less

(a) Description of property (Example: 100 sh. XYZ Co.)	(b) Date acquired (Mo., day, yr.)	(c) Date sold (Mo., day, yr.)	(d) Sales price (see page D-6 of the instructions)	(e) Cost or other basis (see page D-6 of the instructions)	(f) Gain or (loss) Subtract (e) from (d)
1					

2 Enter your short-term totals, if any, from Schedule D-1, line 2	**2**		
3 **Total short-term sales price amounts.** Add lines 1 and 2 in column (d)	**3**		
4 Short-term gain from Form 6252 and short-term gain or (loss) from Forms 4684, 6781, and 8824	**4**		
5 Net short-term gain or (loss) from partnerships, S corporations, estates, and trusts from Schedule(s) K-1	**5**		
6 Short-term capital loss carryover. Enter the amount, if any, from line 8 of your **Capital Loss Carryover Worksheet** on page D-6 of the instructions	**6**	(	)
7 **Net short-term capital gain or (loss).** Combine lines 1 through 6 in column (f)	**7**		

Part II   Long-Term Capital Gains and Losses—Assets Held More Than One Year

(a) Description of property (Example: 100 sh. XYZ Co.)	(b) Date acquired (Mo., day, yr.)	(c) Date sold (Mo., day, yr.)	(d) Sales price (see page D-6 of the instructions)	(e) Cost or other basis (see page D-6 of the instructions)	(f) Gain or (loss) Subtract (e) from (d)
8					

9 Enter your long-term totals, if any, from Schedule D-1, line 9	**9**		
10 **Total long-term sales price amounts.** Add lines 8 and 9 in column (d)	**10**		
11 Gain from Form 4797, Part I; long-term gain from Forms 2439 and 6252; and long-term gain or (loss) from Forms 4684, 6781, and 8824	**11**		
12 Net long-term gain or (loss) from partnerships, S corporations, estates, and trusts from Schedule(s) K-1	**12**		
13 Capital gain distributions. See page D-1 of the instructions	**13**		
14 Long-term capital loss carryover. Enter the amount, if any, from line 13 of your **Capital Loss Carryover Worksheet** on page D-6 of the instructions	**14**	(	)
15 **Net long-term capital gain or (loss).** Combine lines 8 through 14 in column (f). Then go to Part III on the back	**15**		

For Paperwork Reduction Act Notice, see Form 1040 instructions.   Cat. No. 11338H   Schedule D (Form 1040) 2005

Exhibit 4.3 Schedule D of Form 1040 (*continued*)

Part III	Summary

16   Combine lines 7 and 15 and enter the result. If line 16 is a loss, skip lines 17 through 20, and go to line 21. If a gain, enter the gain on Form 1040, line 13, and then go to line 17 below . .   **16**

17   Are lines 15 and 16 **both** gains?
☐ **Yes.** Go to line 18.
☐ **No.** Skip lines 18 through 21, and go to line 22.

18   Enter the amount, if any, from line 7 of the **28% Rate Gain Worksheet** on page D-7 of the instructions . . . . ▶   **18**

19   Enter the amount, if any, from line 18 of the **Unrecaptured Section 1250 Gain Worksheet** on page D-8 of the instructions . . . . ▶   **19**

20   Are lines 18 and 19 **both** zero or blank?
☐ **Yes.** Complete Form 1040 through line 43, and then complete the **Qualified Dividends and Capital Gain Tax Worksheet** on page 38 of the Instructions for Form 1040. **Do not** complete lines 21 and 22 below.

☐ **No.** Complete Form 1040 through line 43, and then complete the **Schedule D Tax Worksheet** on page D-9 of the instructions. **Do not** complete lines 21 and 22 below.

21   If line 16 is a loss, enter here and on Form 1040, line 13, the **smaller** of:

- The loss on line 16 or
- ($3,000), or if married filing separately, ($1,500)

  . . . .   **21**   (   )

Note. When figuring which amount is smaller, treat both amounts as positive numbers.

22   Do you have qualified dividends on Form 1040, line 9b?
☐ **Yes.** Complete Form 1040 through line 43, and then complete the **Qualified Dividends and Capital Gain Tax Worksheet** on page 38 of the Instructions for Form 1040.
☐ **No.** Complete the rest of Form 1040.

amount of income you earned during the year; instead it varies according to your filing status and whether you are over age 65. Each year the IRS adjusts the amount of the standard deduction to keep pace with inflation. The Tax Relief Act of 2003 addressed the so-called **marriage penalty** in the tax code that caused many two-income married people to pay more in taxes than if they were single. Starting in 2004, the standard deduction for married couples was increased to twice the deduction for single taxpayers. Exhibit 4.4 lists the standard deduction amounts for the 2005 tax year. An additional deduction amount in the last column of Exhibit 4.4 is allowed for taxpayers who are age 65 and older or blind.

marriage penalty
Term used to describe the fact that many two-income married people pay more in taxes than if they were single.

EXAMPLE

Stephanie Spratt's tax filing status is single. Therefore, she can take a standard deduction of $5,000 from her adjusted gross income. Alternatively, she can itemize her deductions (as explained next). She will take the standard deduction unless her itemized deductions exceed the standard deduction.

itemized deductions
Specific expenses that can be deducted to reduce taxable income.

Itemized Deductions

Itemized deductions are specific expenses that can be deducted to reduce taxable income. Congress has approved these itemized deductions as tax preference items to encourage certain behavior such as home ownership and support of not-for-profit organizations. We examine several of the more common itemized deductions below.

Interest Expense. When people borrow funds to purchase a home, they pay interest expense, or interest on the money that they borrow. The annual interest payments made on such a loan are an itemized deduction. Interest payments made on car loans or personal loans, annual credit card fees, and loan fees are not tax-deductible. Itemized deductions are subject to a phase-out based on the taxpayer's income. Itemized deductions are reduced by 3 percent of the amount of the taxpayer's AGI that exceeds $145,950 (in 2005) and cannot be reduced by more than 80 percent.

state income tax
An income tax imposed by some states on people who receive income from employers in that state.

State and Local Taxes. Many states impose a **state income tax** (between 3 and 10 percent) on people who receive income from employers in that state. Local municipalities such as large cities or counties may also impose an income tax. These state and local taxes are deductible as itemized deductions. Deductible state and local taxes for a tax year include any amounts withheld by the taxpayer's employer and amounts paid within the calendar year for a previous tax year.

real estate tax
A tax imposed on a home or other real estate in the county where the property is located.

Real Estate Taxes. Owners of homes or other real estate are subject to a **real estate tax** imposed by the county where the property is located. Real estate tax can be deducted as an itemized deduction.

Exhibit 4.4 Standard Deduction Amounts for the 2005 Tax Year

Status	Under Age 65	Over Age 65 or Blind
Married, filing jointly	$10,000	$1,000
Head of household	7,300	1,250
Single	5,000	1,250
Married, filing separately	5,000	1,000

Medical Expenses. People who incur a large amount of unreimbursed medical expenses may deduct the following expenses:

- Amounts paid for prevention, diagnosis, or alleviation of physical or mental defects or illness

- Amounts paid to affect any structure or function of the body

- Expenses for transportation primarily for and essential to medical care

- Accident and health insurance premiums (such as for health care and prescription drugs)

People with medical expenses that exceed 7.5 percent of adjusted gross income may deduct that excess amount as an itemized deduction. Notice that the amount of medical expenses that is equal to or less than 7.5 percent of the taxpayer's AGI is not deductible. This deduction is specifically for people who incur an unusually high level of medical expenses in relation to their income in a particular year.

Charitable Gifts. People who make charitable gifts to qualified organizations (such as the Humane Society) can deduct their contribution as an itemized deduction. You should keep track of all of your charitable contributions throughout the year whether you paid by cash or check. For large contributions, you will need a receipt from the charitable organization and many organizations, such as churches, will send a confirmation of all donations as a matter of policy. You may deduct the value of property donated to charitable organizations but be careful not to overstate the value of the donated property. If it is a large amount, you should probably get a professional appraisal.

Other Expenses. It may be possible to deduct a portion of losses due to casualties or theft and major job-related expenses that are not reimbursed by employers. However, these expenses are deductible only if they are substantial, as they must be in excess of specified minimum levels (based on a percentage of adjusted gross income). Note that qualified higher education expenses (other than room and board) may also be deducted.

4.2 Financial Planning Online: State Income Tax Rates

Go to
http://taxes.yahoo.com/
statereport.html

This Web site provides income tax rates and information on personal exemptions for each state.

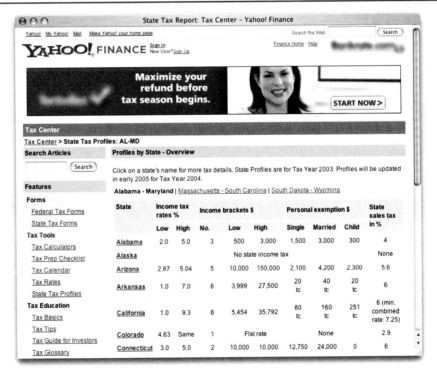

Summary of Deductible Expenses. Taxpayers sum up their deductions to determine whether to itemize or use the standard deduction. If a taxpayer's itemized deductions exceed his or her standard deduction, the taxpayer should take the itemized deduction in lieu of the standard deduction.

EXAMPLE

Stephanie Spratt does not own a home; therefore, she pays no interest expense on a mortgage and pays no real estate taxes. She does not pay state income taxes in her state of Texas. She made charitable contributions amounting to $200. Her total eligible itemized deductions are:

Deductions

Interest Expense	$0
State Income Taxes	0
Real Estate Taxes	0
Unreimbursed Medical	0
Charity	200
Total	$200

If Stephanie decides to take the standard deduction, she can deduct $5,000 from her gross income instead of the itemized deductions described above. Since the standard deduction far exceeds her itemized deductions of $200, she decides to take the standard deduction.

The worksheet for itemized deductions is Schedule A of Form 1040 for individuals. An example of Schedule A is shown in Exhibit 4.5.

Exemptions

personal exemption
An allowable amount by which taxable income is reduced for each person supported by income reported on a tax return.

A **personal exemption** is permitted for each person who is supported by the income reported on a tax return. For example, children in a household are claimed as exemptions by their parents. Exemptions reduce taxable income even if the taxpayer decides to take the standard deduction rather than itemizing. A personal exemption can be claimed for the person filing a tax return, for a spouse, and for each dependent. Each year the amount of the exemption is adjusted for inflation. In the 2005 calendar year, each personal exemption is $3,200. The total amount of exemptions is deducted from gross income to determine taxable income. Similar to itemized deductions, personal exemptions are subject to a phase-out for higher income taxpayers. In 2005 the phase-out begins at an income threshold of $145,950 for single individuals and $218,950 for married taxpayers filing jointly. Phasing out the personal exemption reduces the exemption's value by 2 percent for each $2,500 of AGI above the income threshold.

EXAMPLE

Stephanie Spratt is single and has no children living in her household. She can claim one exemption for herself, which allows her to deduct $3,200 from her adjusted gross income.

TAXABLE INCOME AND TAXES

Before calculating the taxes that you owe, you need to determine your taxable income, as explained next.

Taxable Income

Taxable income is equal to adjusted gross income (AGI) minus deductions and exemptions.

Exhibit 4.5 Schedule A of Form 1040

SCHEDULES A&B
(Form 1040)

Department of the Treasury
Internal Revenue Service   (99)

Schedule A—Itemized Deductions

(Schedule B is on back)

► **Attach to Form 1040.**   ► **See Instructions for Schedules A&B (Form 1040).**

OMB No. 1545-0074

2005

Attachment
Sequence No. **07**

Name(s) shown on Form 1040 | Your social security number

Medical and Dental Expenses

Caution. Do not include expenses reimbursed or paid by others.
1 Medical and dental expenses (see page A-2) . . .   **1**
2 Enter amount from Form 1040, line 38 **2**
3 Multiply line 2 by 7.5% (.075). **3**
4 Subtract line 3 from line 1. If line 3 is more than line 1, enter -0- **4**

Taxes You Paid

(See page A-2.)

5 State and local **(check only one box):**
   a ☐ Income taxes, **or**
   b ☐ General sales taxes (see page A-3)   **5**
6 Real estate taxes (see page A-5) **6**
7 Personal property taxes **7**
8 Other taxes. List type and amount ►--------------   **8**
9 Add lines 5 through 8 . . . .   **9**

Interest You Paid

(See page A-5.)

Note.
Personal interest is not deductible.

10 Home mortgage interest and points reported to you on Form 1098   **10**
11 Home mortgage interest not reported to you on Form 1098. If paid to the person from whom you bought the home, see page A-6 and show that person's name, identifying no., and address ►   **11**
12 Points not reported to you on Form 1098. See page A-6 for special rules **12**
13 Investment interest. Attach Form 4952 if required. (See page A-6.) **13**
14 Add lines 10 through 13 . . . .   **14**

Gifts to Charity

If you made a gift and got a benefit for it, see page A-7.

15a Total gifts by cash or check. If you made any gift of $250 or more, see page A-7 . . . .   **15a**
  b Gifts by cash or check after August 27, 2005, that you elect to treat as qualified contributions (see page A-7) **15b**
16 Other than by cash or check. If any gift of $250 or more, see page A-7. You **must** attach Form 8283 if over $500   **16**
17 Carryover from prior year **17**
18 Add lines 15a, 16, and 17 . . . .   **18**

Casualty and Theft Losses

19 Casualty or theft loss(es). Attach Form 4684. (See page A-8.) **19**

Job Expenses and Certain Miscellaneous Deductions

(See page A-8.)

20 Unreimbursed employee expenses—job travel, union dues, job education, etc. Attach Form 2106 or 2106-EZ if required. (See page A-8.) ►--------------   **20**
21 Tax preparation fees. **21**
22 Other expenses—investment, safe deposit box, etc. List type and amount ►--------------   **22**
23 Add lines 20 through 22 . . . .   **23**
24 Enter amount from Form 1040, line 38 **24**
25 Multiply line 24 by 2% (.02) **25**
26 Subtract line 25 from line 23. If line 25 is more than line 23, enter -0- **26**

Other Miscellaneous Deductions

27 Other—from list on page A-9. List type and amount ►--------------   **27**

Total Itemized Deductions

28 Is Form 1040, line 38, over $145,950 (over $72,975 if married filing separately)?
   ☐ **No.** Your deduction is not limited. Add the amounts in the far right column for lines 4 through 27. Also, enter this amount on Form 1040, line 40.
   ☐ **Yes.** Your deduction may be limited. See page A-9 for the amount to enter.   ►   **28**
29 If you elect to itemize deductions even though they are less than your standard deduction, check here ► ☐

For Paperwork Reduction Act Notice, see Form 1040 instructions.   Cat. No. 11330X   Schedule A (Form 1040) 2005

EXAMPLE

Recall that Stephanie Spratt's adjusted gross income is $38,000, her standard deduction is $5,000, and her exemptions are $3,200. Therefore, her taxable income for the year is:

Adjusted Gross Income	$38,000
– Deductions	5,000
– Exemptions	3,200
= Taxable Income	$29,800

Calculating Taxes

Once you know what your taxable income is, you can use a table such as Exhibit 4.6 to determine the taxes that you owe. Taxes are dependent not only on your taxable income, but also on your filing status. Exhibit 4.6 shows the tax schedules for different filing statuses for the 2005 tax year. Notice that the income tax system in the United States is progressive. That is, the higher an individual's income, the higher the percentage of income paid in taxes.

The Tax Relief Act of 2001 created a new 10 percent bracket that applied to the first $6,000 of income for single taxpayers and $12,000 of income for married couples filing jointly in 2001. The income ranges were increased to $7,000 and $14,000 respectively in 2004 as a result of the Tax Relief Act of 2003. In addition, the income tax rates above 15 percent were reduced in 2003 so that the 27 percent tax rate fell to 25 percent, the 30 percent tax rate fell to 28 percent, the 35 percent tax rate fell to 33 percent, and the 38.6 percent tax rate fell to 35 percent. Furthermore, as mentioned earlier, the income level subject to the 15 percent tax rate for married people filing jointly was increased to twice that of the single taxpayer bracket to eliminate the marriage penalty.

Determining Your Tax Liability. To determine your tax liability, simply refer to your filing status and follow the instructions at the top of the columns of the tax schedule. Converting the instructions into a formula gives the following equation for the tax liability:

$$\text{Tax Liability} = \text{Tax on base} + [\text{Percentage on Excess over the Base} \times (\text{Taxable Income} - \text{Base})]$$

EXAMPLE

marginal tax bracket
The tax rate imposed on any additional (marginal) income earned.

Stephanie Spratt's taxable income is $29,800. Her filing status is single.

Stephanie uses the following steps to determine her taxes:

- Her income falls within the third bracket in Panel A, from $29,700 to $71,950.

- The base of that bracket is $29,700. The tax on the base is $4,090.00, as shown in the second column of Panel A.

- The tax rate applied to the excess income over the base is 25 percent, as shown in the third column of Panel A. This means that Stephanie's **marginal tax bracket** is 25 percent, so any additional (marginal) income that she earns is subject to a 25 percent tax.

- Stephanie's excess income over the base is $100 (computed as $29,800 − $29,700). Thus, the tax on the excess over the base is $25.00 (computed as $100 × 25%).

In summary, her tax liability is:

Tax Liability	=	Tax on Base + [Percentage on Excess over the Base × (Taxable Income − Base)]
	=	$4,090.00 + [25% × ($29,800 − $29,700)]
	=	$4,090.00 + [25% × ($100)]
	=	$4,090.00 + $25.00
	=	$4,115.00.

This tax liability represents about 11 percent of her income. However, recall that she also paid $2,907 in FICA taxes. Thus, Stephanie's total taxes are $7,022.00 (calculated as $4,115 + $2,907).

Tax Credits

tax credits
Specific amounts used to directly reduce tax liability.

You may be able to reduce your tax liability if you are eligible for tax credits. **Tax credits** offset taxes, as the full amount of the tax credit is subtracted from taxes owed: A tax credit of $1,000 will reduce your taxes by $1,000. Compare this result with the

Exhibit 4.6 Individual Tax Rates for 2005

If Your Taxable Income Is	You Pay This Amount on the Base of the Bracket	Plus This Percentage on the Excess over the Base
Panel A. Single Individuals		
Up to $7,300	$0	10.0%
$7,300–$29,700	$730.00	15.0%
$29,700–$71,950	$4,090.00	25.0%
$71,950–$150,150	$14,652.50	28.0%
$150,150–$326,450	$36,548.50	33.0%
Over $326,450	$94,727.50	35.0%
Panel B. Married Couples Filing Jointly or Qualifying Widow(er)		
Up to $14,600	$0	10.0%
$14,600–$59,400	$1,460.00	15.0%
$59,400–$119,950	$8,181.00	25.0%
$119,950–$182,800	$23,317.50	28.0%
$182,800–$326,450	$40,915.50	33.0%
Over $326,450	$88,320.00	35.0%
Panel C. Married Couples Filing Separately		
Up to $7,300	$0	10.0%
$7,300–$29,700	$730.00	15.0%
$29,700–$59,975	$4,090.00	25.0%
$59,975–$91,400	$11,658.75	28.0%
$91,400–$163,225	$20,457.75	33.0%
Over $163,225	$44,160.00	35.0%
Panel D. Head of Household		
Up to $10,450	$0	10.0%
$10,450–$39,800	$1,045.00	15.0%
$39,800–$102,800	$5,447.50	25.0%
$102,800–$166,450	$21,197.50	28.0%
$166,450–$326,450	$39,019.50	33.0%
Over $326,450	$91,819.50	35.0%

effect of a $1,000 deduction. The deduction reduces your taxable income by $1,000, but reduces your taxes by only a proportion of that amount. For this reason, a dollar's worth of tax credits is more valuable than a dollar's worth of deductions.

child tax credit
A tax credit allowed for each child in a household.

Child Credits. A **child tax credit** is a tax credit allowed for each child in a household who is less than 17 years old at the end of the tax year. The child must be either a U.S. citizen or a resident alien. As a result of the Tax Relief Act of 2001, the child tax credit (originally $500 per child) was increased to $600 in 2001 and was increased to $1,000 in 2003–2004. Current tax law provides that the child tax credit will remain at $1,000 per child through 2010. The child tax credit is not available to households above certain income levels. A key provision of the child tax credit is that it is available as a refund to low-income workers who owe no income tax.

college expense credits
A tax credit allowed to those who contribute toward their dependents' college expenses.

College Expense Credits. Some **college expense credits** are also allowed. Parents receive a tax credit equal to $1,000 for the first $1,000 that they provide to each dependent for college expenses in each of the first two years of college. They also receive a 50 percent tax credit on the next $1,000 spent on college (or up to $500) for each child in each of the first two years of college. If you pay $1,800 in the first or second year of college, you receive a tax credit of $1,400 (computed as a $1,000 credit for the first $1,000 paid and a 50 percent credit on the additional $800 paid). Self-supporting students can use the tax credits to reduce their own taxes. There are limits (increased by the Tax Relief Act of 2001) imposed on the amount of expense credits allowed. Furthermore, the tax credit for college expenses is reduced or eliminated for taxpayers with high income levels.

Coverdell Savings Accounts
Tax-free accounts that can be used for a variety of school expenses.

Coverdell Savings Accounts. As a result of the Tax Relief Act of 2001, **Coverdell Savings Accounts** (previously called Education IRAs) allow contributions of up to $2,000 per year (the previous limit was $500 per year). Once used solely to save for college expenses, these accounts can now be used for a wide variety of elementary and high school expenses including tuition, fees, academic tutoring, books, supplies, equipment, and "special needs services" for special needs students. Contributions are in after-tax dollars, but become tax-free if withdrawals are used for appropriate education expenses. The 2001 Tax Relief Act also extended the contribution deadline from December 31 to April 15 to resemble other IRA accounts.

Section 529 College Savings Plan. State and private universities can also offer prepaid tuition programs with tax benefits. In 2001, the tax laws were changed to allow substantial tax benefits for parents who wish to set aside money for their children's future college expenses. When parents invest funds in the Section 529 college savings plan, any income or gains from the investment will not be taxed at the federal level as long as the funds are ultimately used to pay for college expenses. Some states impose a state tax when funds are withdrawn and used to pay college expenses.

All parents are eligible for the 529 plan, regardless of their income. They can contribute up to $200,0000 or more in the account, depending on the state's requirements. If the parents decide not to use the funds to pay for the designated child's college expenses, they can withdraw the funds but are subject to significant penalties.

There are expenses associated with college savings plans. Advisers who help parents establish the accounts and investment firms that manage the accounts charge fees. Each state has its own specific investment manager and investment options. Parents can request that the money be invested in a specific portfolio by the designated investment firm for that state. The performance of the money contributed by the parents will match the growth or decline of the portfolio value.

earned income credit
A credit used to reduce tax liability for low-income taxpayers.

Earned Income Credit. The **earned income credit** is a special credit for low-income taxpayers that reduces the amount of taxes owed, if any. To qualify, you must work, have earned income, and have investment income of less than $2,700. Adjusted gross income in 2005 for single taxpayers must be less than $11,750 for taxpayers without a qualifying child, less than $31,030 for those with one qualifying child, and less than $35,263 for those with more than one qualifying child. The income limits for married taxpayers is slightly higher.

Other Tax Credits. Other tax credits may also be available. For example, there are tax credits for child care and adoptions. The tax credit amount is dependent on the expenses incurred and may be reduced due to income limits.

COMPREHENSIVE TAX EXAMPLE

To reinforce your understanding of the tax concepts discussed in this chapter we will examine a complex tax example. Ken Hein's compensation from his employer was $44,000 in 2005. He also had $1,500 of interest income and $2,500 of dividend income this year. He contributed $4,000 toward his employer-sponsored retirement account. Ken incurred various deductible expenses that will be mentioned shortly. He also had a short-term capital gain of $2,000 and a long-term capital gain of $1,000 this year.

Ken's contribution to his employer-sponsored retirement plan does not count as salary for federal income tax purposes. However, he will still pay FICA taxes on that amount. Ken's FICA taxes, personal income taxes, and capital gain taxes are determined here.

Ken's FICA Taxes
The FICA taxes on Ken Hein's $44,000 salary are as follows:

	Social Security Tax	Medicare Tax
Tax rate	6.2% (up to a salary of $90,000)	1.45%
Tax amount	.062 × $44,000 = $2,728	.0145 × $44,000 = $638

Thus, Ken's total FICA taxes are $2,728 + $638 = $3,366.

Ken's Personal Taxes
Ken's personal taxes are determined by computing his gross income, his adjusted gross income, his deductions, and his exemptions.

Gross Income.   Ken's gross income is:

Salary (after retirement contribution)	$40,000
+ Interest Income	1,500
+ Dividend Income	2,500
+ Long-Term Capital Gain	1,000
+ Short-Term Capital Gain	2,000
= Gross Income	$47,000

Adjusted Gross Income. Ken does not have any special adjustments, so his adjusted gross income is the same as his gross income ($47,000).

Standard Deduction. Ken Hein is married and files his tax return jointly; he is under age 65. Per Exhibit 4.4, his standard deduction is $10,000, which he can deduct from his adjusted gross income to determine his taxable income. Alternatively, he can itemize deductions instead of using the standard deduction. He will choose the option that minimizes his tax liability.

Itemized Deductions. Ken's itemized deductions for this year include $7,000 of mortgage interest, $2,000 in state income taxes, and $3,000 of real estate taxes. In addition, Ken incurred medical expenses of $8,450. Since his adjusted gross income is $47,000, the first $3,525 (computed as .075 × $47,000) of his medical expenses are not deductible. Since his medical expenses exceed 7.5 percent of his adjusted gross income by $4,925, he can deduct $4,925 of medical expenses as an itemized deduction.

Medical Expenses	$8,450	
Amount That Is Not Deductible	− 3,525	(computed as .075 × $47,000)
Amount That Is Deductible	$4,925	

Ken contributed $1,000 to a local animal shelter. Therefore, he can deduct $1,000 as an itemized deduction.

Total Deductions. Ken Hein's deductions from his adjusted gross income are summarized here:

Deductions	
Interest Expense	$7,000
State Income Taxes	2,000
Real Estate Taxes	3,000
Medical	4,925
Charity	1,000
Total	$17,925

Ken Hein can deduct $17,925 as a result of his itemized deductions, versus only $10,000 if he uses the standard deduction. Thus, he is better off itemizing than taking the standard deduction.

Exemptions. Ken Hein has a wife and an 18-year-old daughter that he supports in his household. He can claim his personal exemption and one exemption each for his wife and daughter. Thus, the total amount of exemptions he can claim for the 2005 tax year is:

Personal Exemption	$3,200
Exemptions for Wife and	
One Dependent (2 × $3,200)	$6,400
Total	$9,600

Taxable Income. Recall that Ken Hein's adjusted gross income is $47,000, his itemized deductions amount to $17,925, and his exemptions amount to $9,600. Thus, Ken Hein's taxable income is determined as:

Adjusted Gross Income		$47,000
Deductions	$17,925	
Exemptions	9,600	
Total	$27,525	
Taxable Income		$19,475

Therefore, Ken's taxable income is $19,475. This includes a $1,000 long-term capital gain, which will be discussed in the next section. The following calculations apply to the taxable income, excluding the long-term capital gain, or $19,475 − $1,000 = $18,475. Ken's filing status is "married, filing jointly." Thus, his applicable tax rates are in Panel B of Exhibit 4.6.

Ken uses the following steps to determine his taxes:

- His income falls within the second bracket in Panel B, from $14,600 to $59,400.

- The base of that bracket is $14,600.

- The tax rate applied to the excess income over the base is 15 percent, as shown in the third column of Panel B.

- Ken's excess income over the base is $18,475 − $14,600 = $3,875. Thus, the tax on the excess over the base is 15 percent of $3,875, or $581.25.

In summary, his tax liability prior to adding his capital gain tax is on the following page.

4.3 Financial Planning Online: Estimating Your Taxes

Go to
http://www.turbotax.com/
taxcenter/yahoo/
estimator.html

This Web site provides an estimate of your tax liability for the year and the tax refund that you will receive (if you already paid in more taxes than your tax liability), based on your income, filing status, exemptions, and deductions.

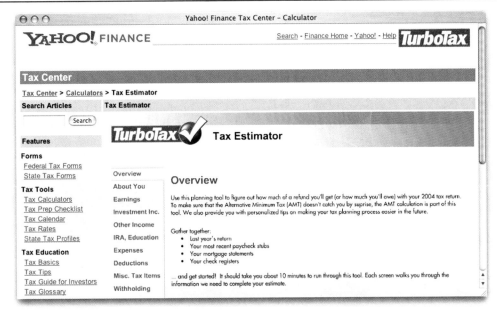

$$
\begin{aligned}
\text{Tax Liability} &= \text{Tax on Base} + [\text{Percentage on Excess over the Base} \\
&\quad \times (\text{Taxable Income} - \text{Base})] \\
&= \$1,460 + [15\% \times (\$18,475 - \$14,600)] \\
&= \$1,460 + [15\% \times (\$3,875)] \\
&= \$1,460 + \$581.25 \\
&= \$2,041.25.
\end{aligned}
$$

Ken's Capital Gain Tax

Recall that Ken had a long-term capital gain of $1,000. Reviewing Exhibit 4.3, based on his taxable income of $19,475, he is subject to a long-term capital gain tax rate of 5 percent (note that the tax rate can be as high as 15 percent for some individuals). Ken's long-term capital gain tax is:

$$
\begin{aligned}
\text{Capital Gain Tax} &= \text{Long-Term Capital Gain} \\
&\quad \times \text{Long-Term Capital Gain Tax Rate} \\
&= \$1,000 \times .05 \\
&= \$50
\end{aligned}
$$

Ken's total tax liability is therefore $2,091.25 ($2,041.25 as computed on the $18,475 + $50 on the long-term capital gain).

FOCUS ON ETHICS: REDUCING YOUR TAXES

Do you know anyone who likes to pay taxes? Odds are you don't. Most people dislike paying taxes and put much effort into reducing their tax liability. It can be tempting to report a lower salary than you earned when filing your tax return. Or self-employed individuals may consider reporting a lower level of income than they actually earned. The IRS monitors tax returns to detect underestimated returns, so there is a strong likelihood that the IRS will uncover any fraudulent behavior. And there are large fines for illegally reducing taxes.

Fortunately, there are many legal ways to reduce your taxes. Organize records for things like your charitable donations and medical expenses in a tax-planning folder so you will not overlook a potential deduction. Prepare your return early in the year, so that you won't make a careless mistake in the rush to meet the April 15 deadline. Make sure that you have included all the tax exemptions and deductions that you qualify for

CLAIM FALSE DEPENDENTS? HA! WHO WOULD DO SUCH A THING?

MARK PARISI 4-15

comics.com   MarkParisi@aol.com ©2004 MARK PARISI DIST. BY UFS, INC.

http://www.comics.com

on your return and that you haven't made any miscalculations. You may even seek advice from an accountant to ensure that you did not overlook any deductible expense.

HOW TAX PLANNING FITS WITHIN YOUR FINANCIAL PLAN

Tax planning involves taking actions throughout the year in order to be able to pay the least amount of taxes allowed by law. The key tax planning decisions for building your financial plan are:

- What tax savings are currently available to you?
- How can you increase your tax savings in the future?
- Should you increase or decrease the amount of your withholding?
- What records should you keep?

If you are about to file your taxes, it is generally too late to take steps to lower your taxes other than to make sure that you include all of the exemptions and deductions for which you are eligible.

Tax planning is more effective when done in advance of the tax year and throughout the tax year. When you are considering whether or not to make a donation to a charitable organization, you should recognize that contributing a larger amount may increase your itemized deductions, but will be totally ineffective as a tax reduction strategy if the total of your itemized deductions fails to exceed the standard deduction amount. If you own stocks, bonds, or mutual funds that are valued at less than their purchase price, you may want to sell the losers this year in order to apply the capital loss (up to $3,000) against ordinary income. Likewise, you can delay selling winners until after December 31 in order to push the taxable income into the next tax year. If, like the couple in the chapter opener, you find yourself with a large medical bill, it is beneficial to pay the entire amount in one tax year, if possible, to enhance your itemized deduction.

Because individuals who earn a high level of income can be exposed to very high tax rates, they should consider ways to reduce their tax liability. Some of the most useful strategies to reduce taxes are having a mortgage (because interest payments are tax-deductible), investing in retirement accounts that offer tax advantages, investing in stocks that pay no dividends, and investing in municipal bonds whose interest is exempt from federal taxes. These strategies are discussed in more detail later in the text.

You may be one of those taxpayers who enjoys getting a large tax refund each year, but in reality that is not an efficient use of your capital. If you have too much withheld in taxes, you are in effect making an interest free loan to the government while foregoing the use of that cash to pay off credit cards or make investments. However, if withholding too much helps to ensure that you do not have to scramble to make your tax payment on April 15, then consider doing so. Some taxpayers use their tax refund to pay for upcoming summer vacations or large consumer purchases for which they may not have the self-discipline to save.

Some actions that you take now will make tax filing easier in the future. For example, if you buy stock within the year but expect to retain the stock for several years, you should maintain a record of the purchase transaction so that you will be able to calculate the gain or loss when you eventually sell the stock. You need to retain a copy of your tax return for at least seven years and retain your supporting documents as well.

An example of how the tax concepts apply to Stephanie Spratt's financial plan is provided in Exhibit 4.7.

Exhibit 4.7 Application of Tax Concepts to Stephanie Spratt's Financial Plan

GOALS FOR TAX PLANNING

1. *Reduce taxable income (thereby reducing taxes paid) to the extent allowable by the IRS.*
2. *Reduce taxes paid by deferring income.*

ANALYSIS

Present Situation:

Annual Salary = *$38,000*

Federal Income Taxes = *$4,115.00*

Taxes (excluding FICA) as a Percentage of Salary = *10.83%*

Reduce Taxes by:	Comment
Increasing deductions?	*The only qualified deduction I had was for a charitable contribution of $200, so this is not an option for me this year.*
Reducing gross income?	*I did not contribute any portion of my income to an individual retirement account or a qualified retirement plan; therefore, this option is not available.*
Total tax savings?	*$0 per year*

Long-Term Tax Plan:

Reduce Taxes by:	Comment
Increasing deductions?	*If I purchase a home, the interest expense on my mortgage loan, as well as the real estate taxes I will pay, both qualify as itemized deductions. These deductions will likely be higher than the standard deduction to which I would be entitled. I can therefore reduce my taxable income and taxes paid.*
Reducing gross income?	*I can also consider a contribution to an IRA or to my employer's qualified pension plan. If I can afford to contribute $3,000 of my salary to either the IRA or the qualified plan, I will reduce my gross income and defer taxes paid on that portion of my income.*
Tax savings (computed below)	*$610.00*

To compute my estimated tax savings, I will compare the taxes paid under my current situation to what I would pay if I bought a home and paid $6,000 in interest and real estate taxes and contributed $3,000 to an IRA.

Category	Current Situation	Long-Term Plan
Gross Income	*$38,000*	*$38,000*
− IRA contribution	*0*	*3,000*
= Adjusted gross income	*38,000*	*35,000*
− Deductions	*5,000*	*6,000*
− Exemptions	*3,200*	*3,200*
= Taxable income	*29,800*	*25,800*
Tax liability (based on applying tax rates to the taxable income)	*4,115.00*	*3,505.00*

Total Tax Savings = *$610.00 per year*

DECISIONS

Decisions Regarding Tax Savings for This Year:

I currently qualify for no tax savings.

19. What is the difference between the tax consequences for short-term and long-term capital gains?

20. What form must be filed with the IRS for itemized deductions?

21. What is the purpose of income tax? Who administers the federal tax system?

FINANCIAL PLANNING PROBLEMS

1. Janet makes $450 per week. How much will be withheld from her weekly check for Social Security tax? Medicare tax? Total FICA taxes?

2. Avery makes $27,000 per year. How much can he expect to contribute to FICA taxes this year? How much will his employer contribute?

3. Nolan is self-employed as a carpenter. He made $42,000 last year. How much did he contribute to FICA taxes last year?

4. Larry is in a 15 percent marginal tax bracket. Last year, he sold stock that he had held for nine months for a gain of $1,900. How much tax must he pay on this capital gain? How much would the tax be if he had held the stock for 13 months?

5. Stuart is in the 25 percent tax bracket. Recently, he sold stock that he had held longer than a year for a gain of $20,000. How much tax will Stuart pay on this gain?

6. Jim sold a stock that he held for 11 months at a capital gain of $10,000. He is in the 25 percent marginal tax bracket. What taxes will he pay on this gain?

7. Teresa and Marvin are married and file a joint return. The standard deduction for their filing status is $10,000. They have the following itemized deductions:

Medical bills above the 7.5% limit	$400
Interest expense	3,500
State income taxes	1,500
Miscellaneous deductions	250

Should Teresa and Marvin itemize their deductions or use the standard deduction?

8. Martha's adjusted gross income is $24,200. She has $1,800 in unreimbursed medical expenses. How much in medical expenses can Martha claim as an itemized deduction?

9. Jerry's adjusted gross income is $16,700. Jerry has $1,800 in unreimbursed medical expenses. How much can Jerry claim as an itemized deduction?

10. Nick is married and has three children in college. His wife is a homemaker. Nick has an adjusted gross income of $37,400. If Nick's standard deduction is $10,000, his itemized deductions are $11,200, and he gets an exemption of $3,200 per dependent, what is his taxable income?

11. Using the information in problem 10, if Nick's itemized deductions increase by $2,000, how will his taxable income be impacted?

12. Martin has a marginal tax rate of 25 percent. He suddenly realizes that he neglected to include a $1,000 tax deduction. How will this oversight affect his taxes?

13. If Martin (from problem 12) had forgotten a $1,000 tax credit (instead of a $1,000 tax deduction), how would his taxes be affected?

14. Tracy is single and has an adjusted gross income of $37,000 this year. Tracy is gathering information for her current year's tax return and has the following items:

Unreimbursed medical expenses	$3,000
State income tax	1,850
Interest expense (first mortgage)	3,040
Interest expense (second mortgage)	1,200
Real estate tax	700
Interest expense—car loan	550
Interest expense—credit card	125
Gifts to charity	300

How much may Tracy claim as itemized deductions?

15. Using the information in problem 14, if Tracy's standard deduction is $5,000 and her exemption is $3,200, what is her taxable income?

Ethical Dilemma

16. The IRS Code allows for the deduction of expenses incurred in traveling to a job interview. Fritz, Erica, and their two children have used this deduction to fund their vacations for the last eight years. Each year, several months prior to their vacation, Fritz and Erica begin reviewing the want ads in newspapers in the city or cities they plan to visit. They each apply for several jobs for which they are qualified. Any applications that result in interviews are scheduled during their vacation. They are careful to deduct only those expenses allowed under the IRS Tax Code, such as mileage, meals (not the children's), and hotel and motel expenses (not their children's). This plan has resulted in between $300 and $500 in allowable tax deductions each year. Fritz and Erica have determined that in most cases they would not accept the jobs if offered; however, if the perfect offer presents, they would give it serious consideration.

    a. Discuss whether you think Fritz and Erica are being ethical in using the IRS Code to fund part of the expenses of their family vacation.

b. Do you see other areas of the tax code discussed in this chapter that could be subject to abuses?

FINANCIAL PLANNING ONLINE EXERCISES

1. Go to http://taxes.yahoo.com/calculators/.

   a. Using the Refund Estimator for the current year, input the following information and calculate the estimated taxes:

Filing status:	Single
Exemptions:	Yourself
Income:	$50,000
Adjustments:	IRA contribution $3,000
Deductions:	Standard deduction
Credits:	Zero
Other taxes:	Zero

   b. Estimate the taxes using all the above information except the $3,000 IRA contribution.

   c. You can input your personal tax information to estimate your taxes. Calculate your taxes with and without a $3,000 IRA contribution to assess the impact of IRA contributions on taxes.

2. Go to http://taxes.yahoo.com.

   a. Click on Tax Prep Checklist and view the data. What documents do you need to prepare a tax return?

   b. Find the "Tax Tips" section. Under "Charitable Contributions," review the recommendations. How can you use this information to save on taxes?

   c. Under "Education," look up the allowable credits and deductions for educational expenses. What information could you use in preparing your tax return?

   d. Click on "Retirement Planning" and read the tips for saving on taxes while saving for retirement. How can you use this information to lower your taxes?

   e. Click on "Tax Calendar" and review the important tax dates for the current year's tax return. Can you make use of this information in your tax planning?

BUILDING YOUR OWN FINANCIAL PLAN

By properly managing your tax situation, you can significantly improve your annual cash flow situation and enhance your ability to achieve your goals in a timely fashion.

This case will give you some insights into what employee benefits you should look for from a prospective employer. Talk to friends and relatives and find out how they reduce their taxes and achieve financial goals.

Another crucial element of proper tax management is the selection of an appropriate tax preparer. Your options vary from doing your own tax return to engaging the services of a certified public accountant. When you begin your search for a tax preparer, you will find some questions in the template for this chapter that should aid your selection. Once you have selected a tax preparer whom you trust, it is really not necessary to periodically review this decision. You should, however, remember that as your personal financial situation becomes more complex (e.g., you have a home, you itemize, your portfolio grows to include international stocks), you may need a tax preparer with more advanced skills. Be sure that the skills of your tax preparer are a match for the sophistication level of your personal financial situation.

Go to the worksheets at the end of this chapter, and to the CD-ROM accompanying this text, to continue building your own financial plan.

THE SAMPSONS—A CONTINUING CASE

Dave and Sharon Sampson want to determine their taxes for the current year. Dave will earn $48,000 this year, while Sharon's earnings from her part-time job will be $12,000. Neither Dave nor Sharon contributes to a retirement plan at this time. Recall that they have two children. Assume child tax credits are currently $1,000 per child. The Sampsons will pay $6,300 in home mortgage interest and $1,200 in real estate taxes this year, and they will make charitable contributions of $600 for the year. The Sampsons are filing jointly.

Go to the worksheets at the end of this chapter, and to the CD-ROM accompanying this text, to continue this case.

Enter the Larger of the Total Itemized Deductions or Standard Deduction		$
Exemptions	$3,200 × _____ (number of exemptions)	$
Taxable Income (Gross Income – Deductions and Exemptions)		$
Tax Liability (Refer to Exhibit 4.6 in text)		
Capital Gains Tax		
Long-Term Capital Gains	$	
Long-Term Capital Gains Tax Rate (From Exhibit 4.3)	%	
Capital Gains Tax		$
Your Total Tax Liability (capital gains tax plus tax liability)		$

2. For each of the goals you established in Chapter 1, indicate tax advantage options that may enable you to increase your deductions and/or reduce your gross income.

Personal Financial Goals

Financial Goal	Dollar Amount	Rate of Return	Priority (Low, Medium, High)	Tax Advantage Options
Short-Term Goals				
1.				
2.				
3.				
Intermediate-Term Goals				
1.				
2.				
3.				
Long-Term Goals				
1.				
2.				
3.				

3. If you are considering hiring a tax preparer, use the following questions as an interview guide to screen candidates.

	Answers
1. How long have you been preparing tax returns?	
2. What training have you had preparing tax returns?	
■ College degrees earned:	
■ Tax training courses:	
■ Certifications:	
3. How long have you worked for this organization?	
4. Do you carry professional liability insurance?	
5. Is this your full-time job?	
6. If I am audited, are you authorized to represent me before the IRS?	
7. How many hours of continuing professional education are you required to have each year to maintain your employment?	
8. How many tax returns do you prepare per year?	
9. What type of software does your firm use to prepare returns?	
10. What percentage of the returns done by you have been audited?	

DECISIONS

1. Describe the actions you will take (i.e., increasing deductions or reducing gross income) to achieve tax savings in the present year.

_____

_____

_____

_____

2. Detail the means by which you will reduce your tax liability in the future (i.e., increasing deductions or reducing gross income).

_____

_____

_____

_____

Chapter 4: The Sampsons—A Continuing Case

CASE QUESTIONS

1. Help the Sampsons estimate their federal income taxes for this year by filling in the following worksheet.

Gross Income _____

Retirement Plan Contribution _____

Adjusted Gross Income _____

Deductions

    Interest Expense _____

    Real Estate Taxes _____

    Contributions _____

Exemptions ($3,200 each) _____

Taxable Income _____

Tax Liability before Tax Credits (use 15 percent tax bracket) _____

Child Tax Credit(s) _____

Tax Liability _____

2. The Sampsons think that it will be very difficult for them to pay the full amount of their taxes at this time. Consequently, they are thinking about underreporting their actual income on their tax return. What would you tell the Sampsons in response to this idea?

_____

_____

_____

_____

_____

_____

_____

_____

Part 1: Brad Brooks—A Continuing Case

CASE QUESTIONS

1a. Prepare personal financial statements for Brad, including a personal cash flow statement and personal balance sheet.

Personal Cash Flow Statement

Cash Inflows   **This Month**

Total Cash Inflows

Cash Outflows

Total Cash Outflows

Net Cash Flows

Personal Balance Sheet

Assets

Liquid Assets

Cash	
Checking account	
Savings account	
Other liquid assets	
Total liquid assets	

Household Assets

Home	
Car	
Furniture	
Other household assets	
Total household assets	

Investment Assets

Stocks	
Bonds	
Mutual funds	
Other investments	
Total investment assets	

Total Assets

Liabilities and Net Worth

Current Liabilities

Loans	
Credit card balance	
Other current liabilities	
Total current liabilities	

Long-Term Liabilities

Mortgage	
Car loan	
Other long-term liabilities	
Total long-term liabilities	

Total Liabilities

Net Worth

b. Based on these statements, make specific recommendations to Brad about what he needs to do to achieve his goals of paying off his credit card balance and saving for retirement.

_____

_____

_____

c. What additional goals could you recommend to Brad for the short and long term?

_____

_____

_____

2. Consider Brad's goal to retire in 20 years by saving $4,000 per year starting five years from now.

a. Based on your analysis of Brad's cash flow and your recommendations, is saving $4,000 per year a realistic goal? If not, what other goal would you advise?

_____

_____

_____

b. In order for Brad to know what his $4,000 per year will accumulate to in 20 years, what additional assumption (or piece of information) must he make (or have)?

_____

_____

_____

c. Assuming that Brad invests the $4,000 per year for 20 years, starting five years from now and achieves a return of 12 percent per year, how much will he accumulate in 25 years?

Future Value of an Annuity

Payment per Period	$4,000
Number of Periods	20
Interest Rate per Period	12%
Future Value	

d. Compare the alternative of investing $4,000 every year for 25 years beginning today with Brad's plan to invest $4,000 every year for 20 years beginning five years from now. How much additional funds will Brad have to save each year to accumulate the same amount that he would have in 25 years if he started saving now instead of five years from now? (Again, assume a 12 percent annual return.)

Future Value of an Annuity

Payment per Period	$4,000
Number of Periods	15
Interest Rate per Period	12%
Future Value	

3. Develop three or four suggestions that could help Brad reduce his income tax exposure.

Suggestions to Reduce Taxes	**Pros**	**Cons**

4. Would any of your recommendations in questions 1 through 3 change if Brad were 45? If he were 60? Why or why not?

5. After you informed Brad of his negative monthly net cash flow, Brad indicated that he may delay paying his credit card bills for a couple of months to reduce his cash outflows. What is your response to his idea?

PART 2

Managing Your Liquidity

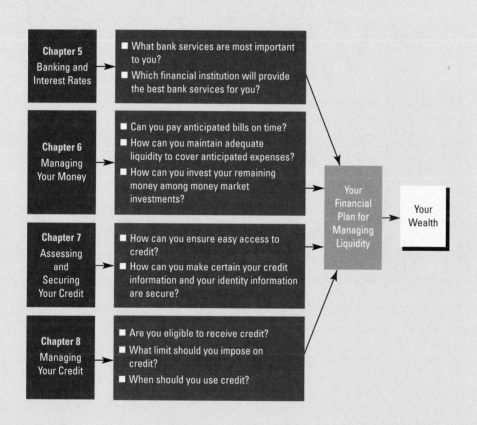

Chapter 5
Banking and
Interest Rates

- What bank services are most important to you?
- Which financial institution will provide the best bank services for you?

Chapter 6
Managing
Your Money

- Can you pay anticipated bills on time?
- How can you maintain adequate liquidity to cover anticipated expenses?
- How can you invest your remaining money among money market investments?

Chapter 7
Assessing
and
Securing
Your Credit

- How can you ensure easy access to credit?
- How can you make certain your credit information and your identity information are secure?

Chapter 8
Managing
Your Credit

- Are you eligible to receive credit?
- What limit should you impose on credit?
- When should you use credit?

Your Financial Plan for Managing Liquidity

Your Wealth

THE CHAPTERS IN THIS PART EXPLAIN THE KEY DECISIONS YOU CAN make to ensure adequate liquidity. Chapter 5 describes how to select a financial institution for your banking needs. Chapter 6 details how you can manage your money to prepare for future expenses. Chapter 7 explains how you can assess your credit situation and Chapter 8 explains how to manage your credit. Your selection of a financial institution, money management, and credit management will influence your liquidity and therefore affect your cash flows and wealth.

Chapter 5

Banking and Interest Rates

When Shawna arrived on campus for her first year of college, she relied on an Automated Teller Machine (ATM) to obtain cash for the many little necessities of college life (food, movies, video rentals, and more food).

It was only on a weekend trip back home, where she reviewed her latest bank statement, that Shawna became aware of a problem. Her bank statement showed 34 separate charges for ATM fees. She had been charged $1.00 for each trip to an "out-of-network" ATM not owned by her bank. There was another $1.50 fee charged by the bank that owned the ATM, so each ATM visit created two charges. In addition, Shawna discovered that she had made five balance inquiries on "out-of-network" ATMs and her bank charged $0.50 for each of them. Altogether, for her 17 visits to the ATM, Shawna had accrued $42.50 in ATM fees and $2.50 in inquiry fees for a total of $45.00. Shocked at this discovery, Shawna found a bank that had a branch on campus and several ATM locations that were convenient for her to use.

This chapter explains how to use a financial institution. A good bank is an essential ingredient of liquidity, whether you are depositing funds in an interest-earning account or are in need of a loan. You may choose a commercial bank, a credit union, or an online bank. In each case it is important to know how well your money is secured. You should also be interested in knowing how the bank sets its interest rates on your deposits and on any loan you might take out. Interest rates fluctuate frequently and are dependent upon several factors, as you will find out later in this chapter.

The objectives of this chapter are to:

- Describe the functions of financial institutions
- Identify the components of interest rates
- Clarify the relationship between the maturity and interest rate of an investment

TYPES OF FINANCIAL INSTITUTIONS

Individuals rely on financial institutions when they wish to invest or borrow funds. In this chapter we'll examine the two major types of financial institutions: depository institutions and nondepository institutions.

Depository Institutions

depository institutions
Financial institutions that accept deposits (which are insured up to a maximum level) from individuals and provide loans.

Depository institutions are financial institutions that offer traditional checking and savings accounts for individuals or firms and also provide loans. They pay interest on savings deposits and charge interest on loans. The interest rate charged on loans exceeds the interest rate paid on deposits. The institutions use the difference to cover expenses and to generate some earnings for their stockholders.

Depository institutions are skilled in assessing the ability of prospective borrowers to repay loans. This is a critical part of their business, since the interest from loans is a key source of their revenue.

There are three types of depository institutions: commercial banks, savings institutions, and credit unions.

commercial banks
Financial institutions that accept deposits and use the funds to provide commercial (business) and personal loans.

Commercial Banks. **Commercial banks** are financial institutions that accept deposits in checking and savings accounts and use the funds to provide commercial (business) and personal loans. The checking accounts normally do not pay interest. The savings accounts pay interest, while certain other accounts pay interest and can be used to write checks. These accounts are described in more detail in the next chapter. Deposits at commercial banks are insured up to $100,000 per depositor by the Federal Deposit Insurance Corporation (FDIC), a government-owned insurance agency that ensures the safety of bank deposits.

You can look to a commercial bank to provide a personal loan for the purchase of a car or other big-ticket items. They also offer mortgage loans for purchasing a home. Some commercial banks own other types of financial institutions (such as those described next) that provide additional services to individuals.

savings institutions (or thrift institutions)
Financial institutions that accept deposits and provide mortgage and personal loans to individuals.

Savings Institutions. **Savings institutions** (also referred to as thrift institutions) accept deposits and provide mortgage and personal loans to individuals. They differ from commercial banks in that they tend to focus less on providing commercial loans. They typically offer the same types of checking and savings deposits as banks, and these deposits are also insured up to $100,000 per depositor by the FDIC.

credit unions
Nonprofit depository institutions that serve members who have a common affiliation (such as the same employer or the same community).

Credit Unions. **Credit unions** are nonprofit depository institutions that serve members who have a common affiliation (such as the same employer or the same community). Credit unions have been created to serve the employees of specific hospitals, universities, and even some corporations. They offer their members deposit accounts that are similar to the accounts offered by commercial banks and savings institutions; the accounts are insured by the National Credit Union Share Insurance Fund (NCUSIF) for up to $100,000 per member. Credit unions also provide mortgage and personal loans to their members.

Focus on Ethics: Special Rates on Deposits

As mentioned earlier, depository institutions pay interest on savings deposits. Some institutions have catchy advertisements stating that they will pay a higher annual interest on new deposits than other depository institutions. Are these offers a sure thing? Probably not. Before making any deposit, you need to check the fine print and ask important questions. How long is the rate for? If it is for a short term, what will it be lowered to? How long must you maintain the deposit before you can withdraw your funds?

Usually the fine print in newspaper or Internet offers indicates that the rate will be lowered after the first month. The deposit is risky if it is not insured, and the rate may be lower than other banks' deposit rates after the first month. Either of these conditions could cause the return on this deposit to be less than that offered by other depository institutions. Carefully research advertised offers.

Nondepository Institutions

nondepository institutions
Financial institutions that do not offer federally insured deposit accounts, but provide various other financial services.

Nondepository institutions are financial institutions that provide various financial services, but their deposits are not federally insured. The main types of nondepository institutions that serve individuals are finance companies, securities firms, insurance companies, and investment companies.

finance companies
Nondepository institutions that specialize in providing personal loans to individuals.

Finance Companies. **Finance companies** specialize in providing personal loans to individuals. These loans may be used for various purposes such as purchasing a car or other products or adding a room to a home. Finance companies tend to charge relatively high rates on loans because they lend to individuals who they perceive to have a higher risk of defaulting on the loans. When the economy weakens, borrowers may have more difficulty repaying loans, causing finance companies to be subject to even higher levels of loan defaults.

securities firms
Nondepository institutions that facilitate the purchase or sale of securities by firms or individuals by providing investment banking services and brokerage services.

Securities Firms. **Securities firms** facilitate the purchase or sale of securities (such as stocks or bonds) by firms or individuals by offering investment banking services and brokerage services. Investment banking services include: (1) placing securities that are issued by firms, meaning that the securities firm finds investors who wish to purchase those securities; (2) advising firms regarding the sale of securities, which involves determining the price at which the securities may be sold and the quantity of securities that should be sold; and (3) advising firms that are considering mergers about the valuation of a firm, the potential benefits of being acquired or of acquiring another firm, and the financing necessary for the merger to occur.

In addition to offering investment banking services, securities firms also provide brokerage services, which facilitate the trading of existing securities. That is, the firms execute trades of securities for their customers. One customer may desire to sell a specific stock while another may want to buy that stock. Brokerage firms make a market for stocks and bonds by matching up willing buyers and sellers.

insurance companies
Nondepository institutions that provide insurance to protect individuals or firms from possible adverse events.

Insurance Companies. **Insurance companies** sell insurance to protect individuals or firms. Specifically, life insurance companies provide insurance in the event of a person's death. Property and casualty companies provide insurance against damage to property, including automobiles and homes. Health insurance companies insure against specific types of health care costs. Insurance serves a crucial function for individuals because it compensates them (or their beneficiaries) in the event of adverse conditions that could otherwise ruin their financial situation. Chapters 11–13 discuss insurance options in detail.

investment companies
Nondepository institutions that sell shares to individuals and use the proceeds to invest in securities to create mutual funds.

Investment Companies. **Investment companies** use money provided by individuals to invest in securities to create mutual funds. The minimum amount an individual can invest in a mutual fund is typically between $500 and $3,000. Since the investment company pools the money it receives from individuals and invests in a portfolio of securities, an individual who invests in a mutual fund is part owner of that portfolio. Thus, mutual funds provide a means by which investors with a small amount of money can invest in a portfolio of securities. More than 8,000 mutual funds are available to individual investors. More details on mutual funds are provided in Chapter 18.

financial conglomerates
Financial institutions that offer a diverse set of financial services to individuals or firms.

Financial Conglomerates

Financial conglomerates offer a diverse set of financial services to individuals or firms. Examples of financial conglomerates include Citigroup, Bank of America, and Merrill

Lynch. In addition to accepting deposits and providing personal loans, a financial conglomerate may also offer credit cards. It may have a brokerage subsidiary that can execute stock transactions for individuals. It may also have an insurance subsidiary that offers insurance services. It may even have an investment company subsidiary that offers mutual funds containing stocks or bonds. Exhibit 5.1 shows the types of services offered by a typical financial conglomerate. By offering all types of financial services, the financial conglomerate aims to serve as a one-stop shop where individuals can conduct all of their financial services.

BANKING SERVICES OFFERED BY FINANCIAL INSTITUTIONS

A depository institution may offer you a wide variety of banking services. While a nondepository institution does not offer banking services, it may own a subsidiary that can provide banking services. Some of the more important banking services offered to individuals are described here.

Checking Services

You use a checking account to draw on funds by writing checks against your account. Most individuals maintain a checking account so that they do not have to carry much cash when making purchases. In addition, it is safer to mail payments by check than by cash. To illustrate how your checking account works, assume that you pay a phone bill of $60 to your phone company today. The phone company provides the check to the bank where it has an account. The bank electronically increases the phone company's account balance by $60. At the same time, the bank reduces your account balance by $60 if your checking account is at that bank, or electronically signals to the bank where your account is to reduce your balance by $60.

Monitoring Your Account Balance. As you write checks, you should record them in your checkbook so that you can always determine how much money is in your account. By keeping track of your account balance, you can make sure that you stay within your limit when writing checks. This is very important because you are charged fees when you write a check that bounces. In addition, you might lose some credibility when writing bad checks, even if it is unintentional.

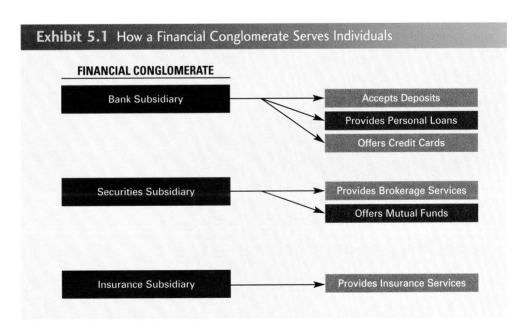

Exhibit 5.1 How a Financial Conglomerate Serves Individuals

Reconciling Your Account Balance. Financial institutions normally send a checking account statement once a month. When you receive your bank statement, you should make sure that the statement reconciles (agrees) with your record of transactions in your check register. Mark off on your register the checks that the statement indicates have cleared. The account balance changes from one month to another for three reasons: depositing or withdrawing funds from your account, cleared checks, and monthly fees related to the checking account.

EXAMPLE   Last month the balance in your checking account was $600. This month you deposited $100 to your account. You wrote four checks that cleared, totaling $400. You did not withdraw any funds from your account. There were no fees charged this month. Your balance for this month is:

Last month's balance	$600
+ Deposits	+ $100
− Checks that cleared	− $400
= New balance	= $300

In a month in which you had no fees, no deposits, no withdrawals, and did not deposit funds, the balance from the statement should be the same as the balance on your register as long as all checks that you wrote cleared. But if some checks have not yet cleared, the balance on your statement will exceed the balance on your register by the dollar amount of the checks that have not yet cleared. If you write additional checks, you may have a negative balance once all the checks clear. For this reason, you should not rely on the monthly statement to determine your balance.

EXAMPLE   Your most recent checking account statement shows that you have a balance of $300. However, yesterday you wrote checks totaling $250 to pay bills. When these checks clear, your balance will be $50. Today you received a credit card bill for $200. Even though this amount is less than the balance shown on your most recent statement, you do not have sufficient funds in your checking account to pay this bill.

If you write a check to cover the credit card bill, it will bounce, because you really only have a $50 account balance. By using the register to keep track of the checks that you write, you will know the amount of funds available in your account.

Many banks provide a worksheet that can be used to reconcile your checkbook balance with the bank's statement of your account. An example of a reconciliation worksheet is shown in Exhibit 5.2. Based on the cleared checks, deposits, and withdrawals, the balance on your bank statement should be $500. This balance can be compared to the balance shown on the bank statement. If there is a discrepancy, your balance may be wrong or the bank's statement could be incorrect. The first step is to verify your math in your checkbook register and then double-check the math on the reconciliation worksheet. If you still cannot resolve the discrepancy, contact the bank.

Accessing Your Account Balance. You can verify your checking account balance with many financial institutions by calling an automated phone service or by going to the institution's Web site and logging in with a password. However, you should not use this balance to determine your spending limit, as some checks you wrote may not yet have cleared.

Check Float

When you write a check, your checking account balance is not reduced until the time at which the check is cashed by the recipient and the check clears. The time from when you

Exhibit 5.2 Example of a Worksheet to Reconcile Your Bank Statement

Beginning balance			**= $1,000**
Deposits	$100		
	$400		
	$500	→	+ $500
Withdrawals	$50		
	$150		
	$200	→	− $200
Checks that have cleared	$25		
	$75		
	$700		
	$800	→	− $800
Bank fees	$0		− $0
Balance Shown on Bank Statement			**$500**
Checks that have not yet cleared	$100		
	$60		
	$40		
	$200	→	− $200
Adjusted bank balance (your prevailing bank balance)			**$300**

write a check until your checking account balance is reduced is referred to as the float. The float is partially due to the time it takes for the bank where the check was deposited to contact your bank. Some individuals do not have sufficient funds in their account when they write a check and they expect that the float will take a few days. This allows them time to deposit enough funds in their checking account before the check clears.

However, in October 2004, The Check Clearing for the 21st Century Act (referred to as Check 21) was implemented. This act allows banks to transmit electronic images of checks. Thus, if you make a payment to a person or company by check, the check may clear the same day. The float may be virtually eliminated, which means you should always make sure you have sufficient funds in your checking account before you write a check.

Another effect of Check 21 is that you may not receive the original canceled checks that you previously wrote. Because the banks that receive the checks may transmit electronic images of them to your bank, you may receive a copy of the electronic image (called a substitute check) instead of the original check with your statement.

Electronic checking deters fraud. When you write a check to a retail store for a purchase, the funds are electronically transferred from your account to the retail store's account. The cashier at the store stamps the back of the check, gives it back to you, and the check clears immediately.

This system reduces fraud because the payee knows if there are sufficient funds in the customer's account to make a purchase. If there are not enough funds, the electronic transfer does not occur, and the check writer cannot make the purchase. Reducing fraud saves the retail stores money and makes them more willing to accept checks.

Credit Card Financing

Individuals use credit cards to purchase products and services on credit. At the end of each billing cycle, you receive a bill for the credit you used over that period. MasterCard and Visa credit cards allow you to finance your purchases through various financial institutions. Thus, if you are able to pay only the minimum balance on your card, the financial institution will finance the outstanding balance and charge interest for the credit that it provides to you.

Debit Cards

You can use a **debit card** to make purchases that are charged against an existing checking account. If you use a debit card to pay $100 for a car repair, your checking account balance is reduced by $100. Thus, using a debit card has the same result as writing a check from your checking account. Many financial institutions offer debit cards for individuals who find using a debit card more convenient than carrying their checkbook with them. In addition, some merchants will accept a debit card but not a check because they are concerned that the check may bounce.

    A debit card differs from a credit card in that it does not provide credit. With a debit card, individuals cannot spend more than they have in their checking account.

Safety Deposit Boxes

Many financial institutions offer access to a **safety deposit box**, where a customer can store valuable documents, certificates, jewelry, or other items. Customers are charged an annual fee for access to a safety deposit box.

Automated Teller Machines (ATMs)

Bank customers are likely to deposit and withdraw funds at an **automated teller machine (ATM)** by using their ATM card and entering their personal identification number (PIN). Located in numerous convenient locations, these machines allow customers access to their funds 24 hours a day, any day of the year. Some financial institutions have ATMs throughout the United States and in foreign countries. You can usually use ATMs from financial institutions other than your own, but you may be charged a service fee, such as $1 per transaction.

Cashier's Checks

A **cashier's check** is a check that is written on behalf of a person to a specific payee and will be charged against a financial institution's account. It is especially useful when the payee is concerned that a personal check may bounce.

debit card
A card that is used to make purchases that are charged against a checking account.

safety deposit box
A box at a financial institution where a customer can store documents, jewelry, or other valuables.

automated teller machine (ATM)
A machine where individuals can deposit and withdraw funds any time of the day.

cashier's check
A check that is written on behalf of a person to a specific payee and will be charged against a financial institution's account.

http://www.cartoonstock.com

"It says, all our accounts have been frozen!"

EXAMPLE   You wish to buy a used car for $2,000 from Rod Simpkins, who is concerned that you may not have sufficient funds in your account. So you go to Lakeside Bank, where you have your checking account. You overcome Rod's concern by obtaining a cashier's check from Lakeside Bank made out to Rod Simpkins. After verifying your account balance, the bank complies with your request and reduces your checking account balance by $2,000. It will likely charge you a small fee such as $10 or $15 for this service. Rod accepts the cashier's check from you because he knows that this check is backed by Lakeside Bank and will not bounce.

money order
A check that is written on behalf of a person and will be charged against an account.

Money Orders

A **money order** is a check that is written on behalf of a person and will be charged against an account. The U.S. Post Office and some financial institutions provide this service for a fee. They are a better alternative to cash when you need to mail funds.

traveler's check
A check that is written on behalf of an individual and will be charged against a large well-known financial institution or credit card sponsor's account.

Traveler's Checks

A **traveler's check** is a check that is written on behalf of an individual and will be charged against a large well-known financial institution or credit card sponsor's account. It is similar to a cashier's check, except that no payee is designated on the check. Traveler's checks are accepted around the world. If they are lost or stolen, the issuer will usually replace them without charge. The fee for a traveler's check varies among financial institutions.

SELECTING A FINANCIAL INSTITUTION

Your choice of a financial institution should be based on convenience, deposit rates and deposit insurance, and fees.

- **Convenience.** You should be able to deposit and withdraw funds easily, which means the financial institution should be located close to where you live or work. You may also benefit if it has ATMs in convenient locations. In addition, a financial institution should offer most or all of the services you might need. Many financial institutions offer Internet banking, which allows you to keep track of your deposit accounts and even apply for loans online.

  Many financial institutions also allow online bill paying. On the Web site, you indicate the payee and amount and the financial institution electronically transfers the funds. There is usually a small fee for this service, but the fee is probably less than the cost of a stamp if you mail the bill yourself.

  Some Web-based financial institutions do not have physical branches. For example, NetBank (http://www.netbank.com) is a Web-based bank. While Web-based banks allow you to keep track of your deposits online, they might not be appropriate for customers who prefer to deposit funds directly at a branch. For customers who prefer to make deposits at a branch but also want easy online access to their account information, the most convenient financial institutions are those with multiple branches and online access.

- **Deposit Rates and Insurance.** The interest rates offered on deposits vary among financial institutions. You should comparison shop by checking the rates on the types of deposits that you might make. Financial institutions also vary on the minimum required balance. A lower minimum balance on savings accounts is preferable because it gives you more flexibility if you do not want to tie up your funds. Make sure that any deposits are insured by the FDIC or NCUSIF.

  Web-based financial institutions tend to pay a higher interest rate on deposits than institutions with physical branches because they have lower expenses and can afford to pay higher deposit rates. Customers must weigh the tradeoff of the higher deposit rates against the lack of access to branches.

  Customers who prefer to make deposits through the mail may want to capitalize on the higher rates at Web-based financial institutions.

- **Fees.** Many financial institutions charge fees for various services. Determine any fees for writing checks or using ATMs. Avoid financial institutions that charge high fees on services you will use frequently, even if the institutions offer relatively high rates on deposits.

5.1 Financial Planning Online: Internet Banking

Go to

http://www.chicagofed.org/
consumer_information/
what_you_should_know_
about_internet_banking.cfm

This Web site provides
information that can help
you decide whether an
Internet bank suits your
needs.

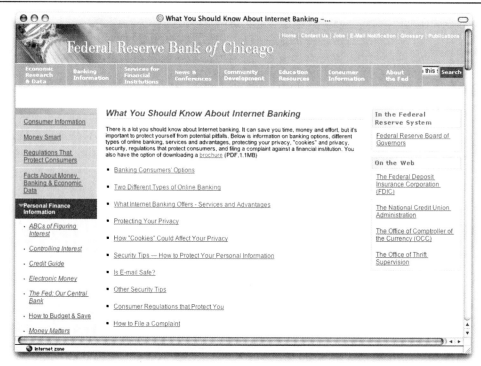

INTEREST RATES ON DEPOSITS AND LOANS

So far, this chapter has focused on financial institutions and their services, such as accepting deposits and providing loans. The return you receive from your deposits in a financial institution and the cost of borrowing money from a financial institution are dependent on the interest rates. Therefore, your cash inflows and outflows are affected by the interest rates at the time of your transactions with the institution.

certificate of deposit (CD)
An instrument that is issued by a depository institution and specifies a minimum investment, an interest rate, and a maturity.

Most depository institutions issue **certificates of deposit (CDs),** which specify a minimum investment, an interest rate, and a maturity. For example, a bank may require a $500 minimum investment on all the CDs it offers. The maturities may include one month, three months, six months, one year, and five years. The money invested in a particular CD cannot be withdrawn until the maturity date, or it will be subject to a penalty for early withdrawal.

The interest rate offered varies among maturities. Interest rates on CDs are commonly stated on an annualized basis so that they can be compared among deposits. An annual interest rate of 6 percent on your deposit means that at the end of one year, you will receive interest equal to 6 percent of the amount that you originally deposited.

Risk-Free Rate

risk-free rate
A return on an investment that is guaranteed for a specified period.

A **risk-free rate** is a return on an investment that is guaranteed for a specified period. As an example, at a commercial bank you can invest in a CD with a maturity that matches your desired investment horizon. When you invest in a CD that has a maturity of one year, you are guaranteed the interest rate offered on that CD. Even if the bank goes bankrupt, the CD is insured for its full value up to $100,000 per customer by the federal government, so you will receive your deposit back at the time of maturity.

Risk Premium

Rather than investing in risk-free deposits that are backed by the federal government, you could invest in deposits of some financial firms that offer a higher interest rate. These deposits are sometimes called certificates, but should not be confused with the CDs that

5.2 Financial Planning Online: Financial Institutions That Can Serve Your Needs

Go to

http://dir.yahoo.com/
business_and_economy/
finance_and_investment/
banking/

This Web site provides information about individual financial institutions (including Internet banks), such as the services they offer and the interest rates they pay on deposits or charge on loans.

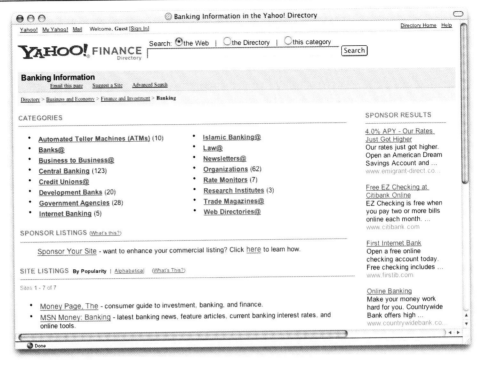

are backed by government insurance. These certificates are subject to default risk, meaning that you may receive a lower return than you expected if the firm goes bankrupt.

If you have accumulated only a small amount of savings, you should maintain all of your savings in a financial institution where deposits are guaranteed by the government. It is not worthwhile to strive for a higher return because you could lose a portion or all of your savings.

If you have a substantial amount of money, however, you may consider investing a portion of it in riskier deposits or certificates, but you should expect to be compensated for the risk. Your potential return should contain a **risk premium**, or an additional return beyond the risk-free rate that you could earn from a deposit guaranteed by the government. The higher the potential default risk of an investment, the higher the risk premium that you should expect.

risk premium
An additional return beyond the risk-free rate that can be earned from a deposit guaranteed by the government.

If a particular risky deposit is supposed to offer a specific return (R) over a period and you know the risk-free rate (R_f) offered on a deposit backed by the government, you can determine the risk premium (RP) offered on the risky deposit:

$$RP = R - R_f$$

EXAMPLE   Today, your local commercial bank is offering a one-year CD with an interest rate of 6 percent, so the existing one-year risk-free rate is 6 percent. You notice that Metallica Financial Company offers an interest rate of 10 percent on one-year certificates. The risk premium offered by this certificate is:

$$RP = R - R_f$$
$$= 10\% - 6\%$$
$$= 4\%.$$

You need to decide whether receiving the extra 4 percentage points in the annual return is worth the default risk. As you have a moderate amount of savings accumulated, you determine that the risk is not worth taking.

Loan Rate

Financial institutions obtain many of their funds by accepting deposits from individuals. They use the money to provide loans to other individuals and firms. In this way, by depositing funds, investors provide credit to financial markets. Financial institutions must charge a higher interest rate on the loans than they pay on the deposits so that they can have sufficient funds to pay their other expenses and earn a profit. Therefore, to borrow funds, you normally must pay a higher interest rate on the loan than the prevailing rate offered on deposits. The annual interest rate on loans to individuals is often 3 to 7 percentage points above the annual rate offered on deposits. For example, if the prevailing annual interest rate on various deposits is 6 percent, the prevailing annual interest rate on loans to individuals may be 9 to 13 percent.

Exhibit 5.3 shows the relationship between the one-year CD rate and the average one-year rate on loans to individuals. Notice how the loan rate rises when the financial institutions must pay a higher rate of interest on the CDs that they offer.

The interest rate a financial institution charges for a loan often varies among individuals. Higher rates of interest are charged on loans that are exposed to higher default risk. So, individuals with poor credit histories or low incomes will likely be charged higher interest rates.

Comparing Interest Rates and Risk

When considering investments that have different degrees of risk, your choice depends on your risk tolerance. If you plan to use all of your invested funds for necessities one year from now, you may need to avoid risk completely. In this case, you should choose a risk-free investment because other investments could be worth less in one year than they are worth today. The tradeoff is that you will receive a relatively low rate of interest on your investment.

If you will need only a portion of your initial investment at the time the investment matures, you may be willing to take some risk. In this case, you may prefer an investment

5.3 Financial Planning Online: Current Interest Rate Quotations

Go to
http://www.bloomberg.com/markets/rates/index.html

This Web site provides updated quotations on key interest rates and charts showing recent movements in these rates. It also illustrates how bank deposit rates and loan rates have changed over time.

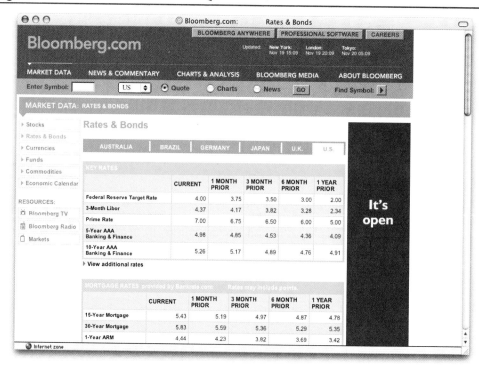

that offers a higher interest rate than the risk-free rate, but is exposed to the possibility of a loss. You can afford to take some risk, since you would still have sufficient funds to pay for your necessities even if the investment results in a loss. However, you should still consider a risky investment only if the risk premium on the investment compensates you for the risk.

No single choice is optimal for all investors, as the proper choice varies with the investor's situation and willingness to tolerate risk. Some individuals are more willing to accept risk than others. The investment decision is based on your risk tolerance, which in turn is influenced by your financial situation.

Exhibit 5.3 Impact of Deposit Rates on Loan Rates

	One-Year CD Rate	Estimated One-Year Loan Rate for Individuals
1993	2.5%	7.5%
1994	3.0%	8.0%
1995	5.0%	10.0%
1996	4.5%	9.5%
1997	4.3%	9.3%
1998	4.2%	9.2%
1999	4.0%	9.0%
2000	5.5%	10.5%
2001	2.5%	8.0%
2002	3.0%	8.5%
2003	3.5%	8.5%
2004	3.9%	8.9%
2005	4.4%	9.4%

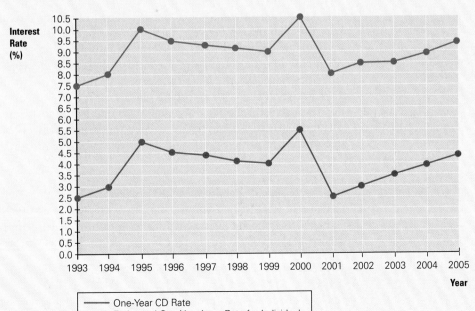

EXAMPLE

Stephanie Spratt plans to invest $2,000. She will use these funds in one year as part of a down payment if she purchases a home. She is considering the following alternatives for investing the $2,000 over the next year:

1. A bank CD that offers a return of 6 percent (the risk-free rate) over the next year and is backed by government insurance.

2. An investment in a deposit at a financial firm that offers an interest rate of 9 percent this year but is not backed by a government guarantee.

Stephanie evaluates her possible investments. The 6 percent return from investing in the CD would result in an accumulated amount of:

$$\text{Accumulated Amount} = \text{Initial Investment} \times (1 + \text{Return})$$
$$= \$2,000 \times (1 + .06)$$
$$= \$2,120.$$

The accumulated amount if Stephanie invests in the risky deposit is:

$$\text{Accumulated Amount} = \text{Initial Investment} \times (1 + \text{Return})$$
$$= \$2,000 \times (1 + .09)$$
$$= \$2,180.$$

Comparing the two accumulated amounts, Stephanie sees that she would earn an extra $60 from the risky deposit if the firm performs well over the next year. There is a risk that the return from the risky deposit could be poorer, however. If the risky deposit pays her only what she originally invested, she would earn zero interest. If the firm goes bankrupt, it might not have any funds at all to pay her. Although the chances that this firm will go bankrupt are low, Stephanie decides that the possibility of losing her entire investment is not worth the extra $60 in interest. She decides to invest in the bank CD.

TERM STRUCTURE OF INTEREST RATES

term structure of interest rates
The relationship between the maturities of risk-free debt securities and the annualized yields offered on those securities.

When considering investing in bank deposits or other debt securities, you must first determine your timeline for investing. When investors provide credit to financial markets, the relationship between the maturity of an investment and the interest rate on the investment is referred to as the **term structure of interest rates**. The term structure is often based on rates of return (or yields) offered by Treasury securities (which are debt securities issued by the U.S. Treasury) with different maturities. The rates of CDs and Treasury securities with a specific maturity are very similar at a given point in time, so this term structure looks very similar to one for deposit rates of financial institutions. The term structure is important to investors and borrowers because it provides the risk-free interest rates that you could earn for various maturities.

EXAMPLE

You are considering depositing $500 in a financial institution. You do not expect to need the funds for at least three years. You want to assess the term structure of interest rates so that you know the interest rate quoted for each maturity. The institution's rates as of today are shown in Exhibit 5.4.

The relationship between the maturities and annualized yields in Exhibit 5.4 is graphed in Exhibit 5.5. The term structure shown here for one specific point in time illustrates that annualized interest rates are higher on investments with longer terms to maturity. Thus, the longer the investment horizon you choose, the higher the annualized interest rate you receive.

You should not invest in a deposit that has a longer term to maturity than the three years in which you will need the funds because you will be subject to a penalty if you withdraw the funds before that date.

Exhibit 5.4 Annualized Deposit Rates Offered on Deposits with Various Maturities	
Maturity	**Annualized Deposit Rate (%)**
1 month	4.0
3 months	4.3
6 months	4.7
1 year	5.0
2 years	5.2
3 years	5.4
4 years	5.5
5 years	5.7
10 years	6.0

Exhibit 5.5 Comparison of Interest Rates among Maturities

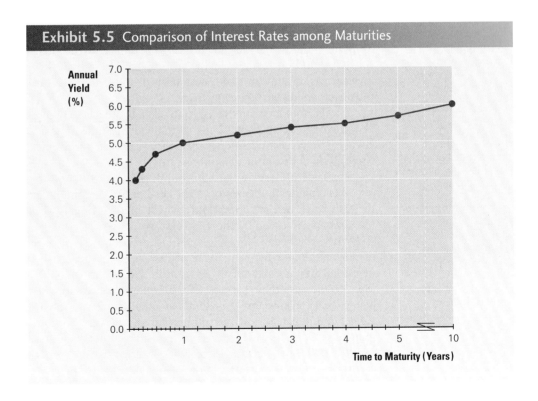

Shifts in the Yield Curve

The yield curve derived from annualized Treasury security yields appears every day in *The Wall Street Journal*, as shown in Exhibit 5.6. The current day's yield curve is compared to the curve from one week ago and four weeks ago. This allows you to easily see how the returns from investing in debt securities with different maturities have changed over time.

Exhibit 5.6 Treasury Security Yields

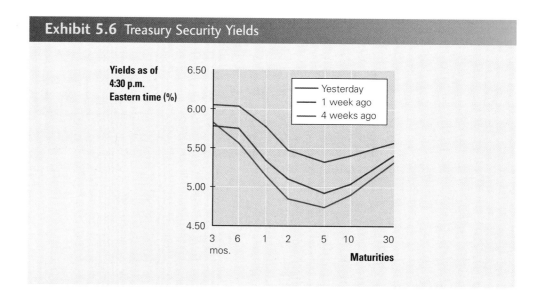

Why Interest Rates Change

A change in the risk-free interest rate causes other interest rates to change. Therefore, understanding why the risk-free interest rate changes allows you to understand why other interest rates change. Because the interest rate is influenced by the interaction between the supply and the demand for funds, a shift in supply or demand will cause a shift in the interest rate.

money supply
Demand deposits (checking accounts) and currency held by the public.

Shift in Monetary Policy. The **money supply** consists of demand deposits (checking accounts) and currency held by the public. The money supply is commonly used by investors as an indicator of the amount of funds that financial institutions can provide to consumers or businesses as loans.

The U.S. money supply is controlled by the Federal Reserve System (called "the Fed"), which is the central bank of the United States. The act of controlling the money supply is referred to as **monetary policy**. The Fed's monetary policy affects the money supply, which can influence interest rates.

monetary policy
The actions taken by the Federal Reserve to control the money supply.

open market operations
The Fed's buying and selling of Treasury securities.

The Federal Reserve Bank has funds that are not deposited in any commercial bank or other financial institution. The Fed most commonly conducts monetary policy through **open market operations**, which involve buying or selling Treasury securities (debt securities issued by the Treasury).

When the Fed wishes to reduce interest rates, it increases the amount of funds at commercial banks by using some of its reserves to purchase Treasury securities held by investors. Investors suddenly have more cash than they did before, which may cause them to increase their savings. The amount of funds supplied to the market increases. The increase in the supply of funds available increases the amount of funds that banks can lend, and places downward pressure on the equilibrium interest rate. Consequently, interest rates decline in response to the Fed's monetary policy.

When the Fed wishes to increase interest rates, it sells to investors some of the Treasury securities that it had previously purchased. The payments made by investors to the Fed for these transactions reduce the amount of funds that investors have for savings. The reduction in the supply of funds available at commercial banks reduces the amount of funds that banks can lend and causes interest rates to increase.

Shift in the Government Demand for Funds. The U.S. government frequently borrows substantial amounts of funds. Any shift in the government's borrowing behavior can affect the aggregate demand for funds and affect the interest rate.

5.4 Financial Planning Online: Updated Treasury Yields

Go to
http://www.bloomberg.com/
markets/rates/index.html

This Web site provides
yields of Treasury securities with various maturities. This information is useful for determining how your return from investing funds in Treasury securities or bank deposits could vary with the maturity you choose.

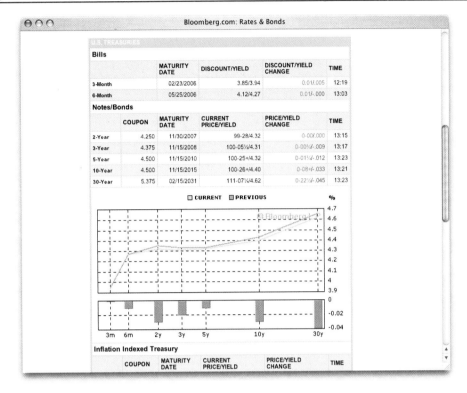

EXAMPLE Assume that the U.S. government suddenly needs to borrow more funds than it normally borrows. The total amount of funds demanded will now be larger which results in a shortage of funds at the original interest rate. This places upward pressure on the interest rate.

If the government reduces (instead of increases) the amount that it borrows, there would be a surplus of funds at the original interest rate which would result in a lower interest rate.

Shift in the Business Demand for Funds. Firms are also common borrowers of funds. When economic conditions change, businesses review their spending plans and adjust their demand for funds. This shift in demand affects the interest rate.

EXAMPLE Assume that businesses have just become more optimistic about the economy and expect an increase in consumer demand for the products they produce. Consequently, they are more willing to expand and must borrow more funds to support their expansion. Their actions result in an increase in the aggregate demand for funds, similar to the effect of increased government borrowing. The shift results in a higher interest rate.

If the businesses had suddenly expected a weaker (instead of a stronger) economy, the opposite effects would occur. Firms tend to reduce their expansion plans when they expect a weak economy. Therefore, they reduce the amount of funds borrowed. This decreases the aggregate demand for funds and results in a lower interest rate.

5.5 Financial Planning Online: Fed's Upcoming Meetings

Go to
http://www.bloomberg.com/
news/economy/
fedwatch.html

This Web site provides updated information about the Fed's recent actions and upcoming meetings, as well as forecasts of future policy decisions and the potential impact of these decisions.

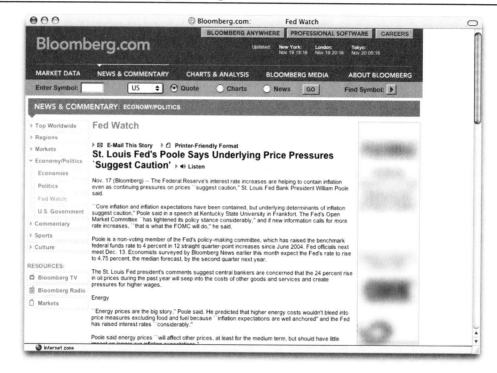

HOW BANKING SERVICES FIT WITHIN YOUR FINANCIAL PLAN

The key banking decisions for your financial plan are:

- What banking service characteristics are most important to you?
- What financial institution provides the best banking service characteristics for you?

Interest rates will play a role in your decisions because you can compare rates among financial institutions to determine where you would earn the highest return on your deposits or pay the lowest rate on your loans. By making informed banking decisions, you can ensure that you receive the banking services that you need to conduct your financial transactions and that have the convenience that you desire, while at the same time reducing your fees. As an example, Exhibit 5.7 shows how banking service decisions apply to Stephanie Spratt's financial plan.

Exhibit 5.7 How Banking Services Fit within Stephanie Spratt's Financial Plan

GOALS FOR BANKING SERVICES

1. *Identify the most important banking services.*
2. *Determine which financial institution will provide me with the best banking services.*

ANALYSIS

Characteristic	How It Affects Me
Interest rate offered on deposits	*This will affect the amount of interest income I earn on deposits.*
Interest rate charged on mortgages	*I could use the same financial institution if I buy a home in the future.*

Interest rate charged on personal loans	*I could use the same financial institution if I obtain a personal loan in the future.*
Fees charged for checking services	*I will be writing many checks, so fees are important.*
Location	*The ideal financial institution would have a branch near my apartment building and near where I work.*
Online services available	*This would make my banking more convenient.*
ATMs	*Check locations for convenience and whether any fees are charged for using ATMs.*

DECISIONS

Decision Regarding Important Characteristics of a Financial Institution:

My most important banking service is the checking account because I will write many checks every month. I prefer a bank that does not charge fees for check writing. I also value convenience, which I measure by the location of the financial institution's branches, and its online services. I would prefer a financial institution that offers reasonable rates on its deposit accounts, but convenience is more important to me than the deposit rate.

Decision Regarding the Optimal Financial Institution:

After screening financial institutions according to my criteria, I found three financial institutions that are desirable. I selected Quality Savings, Inc. because it does not charge for check writing, has branches in convenient locations, and offers online banking. It also pays relatively high interest rates on its deposits and charges relatively low interest rates (compared to other financial institutions) on its loans. I may consider obtaining a mortgage there someday if I buy a home, as its mortgage rate was comparable to those of other financial institutions.

DISCUSSION QUESTIONS

1. How would Stephanie's banking service decisions be different if she were a single mother of two children?

2. How would Stephanie's banking service decisions be affected if she were 35 years old? If she were 50 years old?

SUMMARY

Depository institutions (commercial banks, savings institutions, and credit unions) accept deposits and provide loans. Nondepository institutions include insurance companies (which provide insurance), securities firms (which provide brokerage and other services), and investment companies (which offer mutual funds). Financial conglomerates offer a wide variety of these financial services so that individuals can obtain all their financial services from a single firm.

An interest rate is composed of the risk-free rate and the risk premium. The risk-free rate is the rate of interest paid on an investment that has no risk over a specific investment period (such as a bank deposit backed by government insurance).

Risky investments offer a return that exceeds the risk-free rate. The risk premium is the additional amount above the risk-free rate that risky investments offer. The higher an investment's risk, the higher the risk premium it must offer to entice investors.

The term structure of interest rates is the relationship between interest rates and maturities. It is measured by the yield curve, which shows the interest rate offered at each maturity level. The yield curve is typically upward sloping, meaning that the annualized interest rate is higher for debt securities with longer terms to maturity.

2. Use the following worksheet as a guide for reconciling your checking account balance by entering data from your bank statement and checkbook register. If the two balances do not match, carefully check your math and records. If there is still a discrepancy, contact the financial institution.

Bank Statement Balance	$	Checkbook Register Balance	$
Plus Deposits in Transit *(Total of deposits that appear in your checkbook but do not appear on the bank statement)*	$	Plus Interest	$
Subtotal	$	Subtotal	$
Minus Outstanding Checks *(Total of any checks that you have written that do not appear on the bank statement; use the following worksheet to aid your computations)*	$	Minus Service Charge	$
Subtotal	$	Subtotal	$
Plus—Other *(Any items that appear in your checkbook but do not appear on the bank statement as well as any error that the bank has made)** Description:	$	Plus—Other *(Including errors in your checkbook)* Description:	$
Minus—Other* Description:	$	Minus—Other *(Including errors in your checkbook)* Description:	$
Reconciled Balance	$	Reconciled Balance	$

* Example: If you have ordered new checks and deducted the amount from your checkbook but the bank has not yet deducted the amount from your account.

Outstanding Checks

CK#	$
CK#	$
CK#	$
CK#	$
CK#	$
Total	**$**

DECISIONS

1. Describe the services and characteristics that are of prime importance to you in a financial institution.

_____

_____

_____

_____

_____

_____

_____

2. Which of the financial institutions you evaluated is most optimal for your needs? Why?

_____

_____

_____

_____

_____

_____

_____

Chapter 5: The Sampsons—A Continuing Case

CASE QUESTIONS

1. Advise the Sampsons on the maturity to select when investing their savings in a CD for a down payment on a car. What are the advantages or disadvantages of the relatively short-term maturities versus the longer-term maturities?

2. Advise the Sampsons on the maturity to select when investing their savings for their children's education. Describe any advantages or disadvantages of the relatively short-term maturities versus the longer-term maturities.

3. If you thought that interest rates were going to rise in the next few months, how might this affect the advice that you give the Sampsons?

Managing Your Money

J ared lives from paycheck to paycheck. His checkbook register showed that he had a balance of $110, so he wrote seven checks totaling $90.

Unfortunately, Jared made a math error in entering one of the checks into his checkbook register. Instead of $110 available, his real balance was $10. In addition, he was charged $15 for each bounced check, which resulted in penalty fees of $105.

This expensive lesson for Jared could have been avoided if he had requested overdraft protection on his account or used a debit card. The overdraft protection would have saved him from penalty fees, albeit at the cost of interest charged on the overdraft loan. A debit card would have protected him from bouncing checks by alerting him to the actual status of his checking account balance.

This chapter describes techniques for managing your checking account. It also identifies various types of money market investments and explains how the use of cash management can lead to increased liquidity within your financial plan.

The objectives of this chapter are to:

- Provide a background on money management
- Describe the most popular money market investments
- Identify the risk associated with money market investments
- Explain how to manage the risk of your money market investments

BACKGROUND ON MONEY MANAGEMENT

money management
A series of decisions made over a short-term period regarding cash inflows and outflows.

liquidity
Your ability to cover any cash deficiencies that you may experience.

Money management describes the decisions you make over a short-term period regarding your cash inflows and outflows. It is separate from decisions on investing funds for a long-term period (such as several years) or borrowing funds for a long-term period. Instead, it focuses on maintaining short-term investments to achieve both liquidity and an adequate return on your investments, as explained next.

Liquidity

As discussed in Chapter 1, **liquidity** refers to your ability to cover any short-term cash deficiencies. Recall that the personal cash flow statement determines the amount of excess or deficient funds that you have at the end of a period, such as one month from now. Money management is related to the personal cash flow statement because it determines how to use excess funds, or how to obtain funds if your cash inflows are insufficient. You should strive to maintain a sufficient amount of funds in liquid assets such as a checking account or savings account to draw on when your cash outflows exceed your cash inflows. In this way, you maintain adequate liquidity.

Some individuals rely on a credit card (to be discussed in detail in Chapter 7) as a source of liquidity rather than maintaining liquid investments. Many credit cards provide temporary free financing from the time you make purchases until the date when your payment is due. If you have insufficient funds to pay the entire credit card balance when the bill is due, you may pay only a portion of your balance and finance the rest of the payment. The interest rate is usually quite high, commonly ranging from 8 to 20 percent. Maintaining liquid assets that you can easily access when you need funds allows you to avoid using credit and paying high finance charges.

Liquidity is necessary because there will be periods when your cash inflows are not adequate to cover your cash outflows. But there are opportunity costs when you maintain an excessive amount of liquid funds. A portion of those funds could have been invested in less liquid assets that could earn a higher return than, say, a savings account. In general, the more liquid an investment, the lower its return, so you forgo higher returns when maintaining a high degree of liquidity.

EXAMPLE

Stephanie Spratt's cash inflows are $2,500 per month after taxes. Her cash outflows are normally about $2,100 per month, leaving her with $400 in cash each month. This month she expects that she will have an extra expense of $600; therefore, her cash outflows will exceed her cash inflows by $200. She needs a convenient source of funds to cover the extra expense.

Adequate Return

When you maintain short-term investments, you should strive to achieve the highest possible return. The return on your short-term investments is dependent on the prevailing risk-free rate and the level of risk you are willing to tolerate. Some assets that satisfy your liquidity needs may not necessarily achieve the return that you expect. For example, you could maintain a large amount of cash in your wallet as a source of liquidity, but it would earn a zero rate of return. Other investments may provide an adequate return, but are not liquid. To achieve both liquidity and an adequate return, you should consider investing in multiple money market investments with varied returns and levels of liquidity.

MONEY MARKET INVESTMENTS

Common investments for short-term funds include the following money market investments:

- Checking account
- NOW account
- Savings deposit
- Certificate of deposit
- Money market deposit account (MMDA)
- Treasury bills
- Money market fund
- Asset management account

All of these investments except Treasury bills and money market funds are offered by depository institutions and are insured for up to $100,000 in the event of default by the institution. In this section, we'll examine each of these investments in turn, and focus on their liquidity and typical return.

Checking Account

Individuals deposit funds in a checking account at a depository institution to write checks or use their debit card to pay for various products and services. A checking account is a very liquid investment because you can access the funds (by withdrawing funds or writing checks) at any time.

overdraft protection
An arrangement that protects a customer who writes a check for an amount that exceeds the checking account balance; it is a short-term loan from the depository institution where the checking account is maintained.

Overdraft Protection. Some depository institutions offer **overdraft protection**, which protects a customer who writes a check for an amount that exceeds the checking account balance. The protection is essentially a short-term loan. For example, if you write a check for $300 but have a checking account balance of only $100, the depository institution will provide overdraft protection by making a loan of $200 to make up the difference. Without overdraft protection, checks written against an insufficient account balance bounce, meaning that they are not honored by the depository institution. In addition, a customer who writes a check that bounces may be charged a penalty fee by the financial institution. Overdraft protection's cost is the high interest rate charged on the loan.

stop payment
A financial institution's notice that it will not honor a check if someone tries to cash it; usually occurs in response to a request by the writer of the check.

Stop Payment. If you write a check but believe that it was lost and never received by the payee, you may request that the financial institution **stop payment**, which means that the institution will not honor the check if someone tries to cash it. In some cases, a customer may even stop payment to prevent the recipient from cashing a check. For example, if you write a check to pay for home repairs, but the job is not completed, you may decide to stop payment on the check. Normally, a fee is charged for a stop payment service.

Fees. Depository institutions may charge a monthly fee such as $15 per month for providing checking services unless the depositor maintains a minimum balance in the checking account or a minimum aggregate balance in other accounts at that institution. Some financial institutions charge a fee per check written instead of a monthly fee. The spe-

"Your pot o' gold is doing nothing for you sitting at the end of the rainbow. At the very least, you should put it in a no—risk interest-bearing account."

cific fee structure and the rules for waiving the fee vary among financial institutions, so you should compare fees before you decide where to set up your checking account.

No Interest. A disadvantage of investing funds in a checking account is that the funds do not earn any interest. For this reason, you should keep only enough funds in your checking account to cover anticipated expenses and a small excess amount in case unanticipated expenses arise. You should not deposit more funds in your checking account than you think you may need because you can earn interest by investing in other money market investments.

NOW Account

Another deposit offered by depository institutions is a **negotiable order of withdrawal (NOW)**

NOW (negotiable order of withdrawal) account
A type of deposit offered by depository institutions that provides checking services and pays interest.

account. An advantage of a NOW account over a traditional checking account is that it pays interest, although the interest is relatively low compared with many other bank deposits. The depositor is required to maintain a minimum balance in a NOW account, so the account is not as liquid as a traditional checking account.

EXAMPLE

Stephanie Spratt has a checking account with no minimum balance; she is considering opening a NOW account that requires a minimum balance of $500 and offers an interest rate of 3 percent. She has an extra $800 in her checking account that she could transfer to the NOW account. How much interest would she earn over one year in the NOW account?

Interest Earned = Deposit Amount × Interest Rate

= $800 × .03

= $24.

Stephanie would earn $24 in annual interest from the NOW account, versus zero interest from her traditional checking account. She would need to maintain the $500 minimum balance in the NOW account, whereas she has the use of all of the funds in her checking account. She decides to leave the funds in the checking account, as the extra liquidity is worth more to her than the $24 she could earn from the NOW account.

Savings Deposit

Traditional savings accounts offered by a depository institution pay a higher interest rate on deposits than that offered on a NOW account. In addition, funds can normally be withdrawn from a savings account at any time. A savings account does not provide checking services. It is less liquid than a checking account or a NOW account because you have to go to the institution or to an ATM to access funds, which is less convenient than writing a check. The interest rate offered on savings deposits varies among depository institutions. Many institutions quote their rates on their Web sites.

EXAMPLE

Stephanie Spratt wants to determine the amount of interest that she would earn over one year if she deposits $1,000 in a savings account that pays 4 percent interest.

Interest Earned = Deposit Amount × Interest Rate

= $1,000 × .04

= $40.

Although the interest income is attractive, she cannot write checks on a savings account. As she expects to need the funds in her checking account to pay bills in the near future, she decides not to switch those funds to a savings account at this time.

Certificate of Deposit

As mentioned in Chapter 5, a certificate of deposit (CD) offered by a depository institution specifies a minimum amount that must be invested, a maturity date on which the deposit matures, and an annualized interest rate. Common maturity dates of CDs are one month, three months, six months, one year, three years, and five years. CDs can be purchased by both firms and individuals. CDs that have small denominations (such as $5,000 or $10,000) are sometimes referred to as **retail CDs** because they are more attractive to individuals than to firms.

retail CDs
Certificates of deposit that have small denominations (such as $5,000 or $10,000).

Return. Depository institutions offer higher interest rates on CDs than on savings deposits. The higher return is compensation for being willing to maintain the investment until maturity. Interest rates are quoted on an annualized (yearly) basis. The interest to be generated by your investment in a CD is based on the annualized interest rate and the amount of time until maturity. The interest rates offered on CDs vary among depository institutions.

EXAMPLE

A three-month (90-day) CD offers an annualized interest rate of 6 percent and requires a $5,000 minimum deposit. You want to determine the amount of interest you would earn if you invested $5,000 in the CD. Since the interest rate is annualized, you will receive only a fraction of the 6 percent rate because your investment is for a fraction of the year:

$$
\begin{aligned}
\text{Interest Earned} \quad &= \quad \text{Deposit Amount} \times \text{Interest Rate} \\
&\qquad \times \text{Adjustment for Investment Period} \\
&= \quad \$5,000 \times .06 \times 90/365
\end{aligned}
$$

This process can be more easily understood by noting that the interest rate is applied for only 90 days, whereas the annual interest rate reflects 365 days. The interest rate that applies to your 90-day investment is for about one-fourth (90/365) of the year, so the applicable interest rate is:

$$
\begin{aligned}
\text{Interest Rate} \quad &= \quad .06 \times 90/365 \\
&= \quad .0148 \text{ or } 1.48\%.
\end{aligned}
$$

The 1.48 percent represents the actual return on your investment.

Now the interest can be determined by simply applying this return to the deposit amount:

$$
\begin{aligned}
\text{Interest Earned} \quad &= \quad \text{Deposit Amount} \times \text{Interest Rate} \\
&= \quad \$5,000 \times .0148 \\
&= \quad \$73.97.
\end{aligned}
$$

Liquidity. A penalty is imposed for early withdrawal from CDs, so these deposits are less liquid than funds deposited in a savings account. You should consider a CD only if you are certain that you will not need the funds until after it matures. You may decide to invest some of your funds in a CD and other funds in more liquid assets.

Choice among CD Maturities. CDs with longer terms to maturity typically offer higher annualized interest rates. However, CDs with longer maturities tie up your funds for a longer period of time and are therefore less liquid. Your choice of a maturity for a CD may depend on your need for liquidity. For example, if you know that you may need your funds in four months, you could invest in a three-month CD and then place the funds in a more liquid asset (such as your checking account or savings account) when the CD matures. If you do not expect to need the funds for one year, you may consider a one-year CD.

Focus on Ethics: Risky Deposits

Consider the case of a financial institution that promises an annual rate of interest to depositors that is 4 percent higher than the certificate of deposit rates offered by local banks.

While this certificate sounds appealing, it is probably much riskier than you think. A firm is not going to offer an interest rate of 4 percent more than other interest-bearing investments unless it needs to pay such a high return in order to compensate for risk. Inquire if the deposit is insured by the FDIC. While you might possibly earn 4 percent more on this investment than by depositing the funds at a bank, you might also lose 100 percent of your money if the financial institution goes bankrupt. There are many investment companies that prey on individuals (especially the elderly) who presume that because an investment sounds like a bank deposit, it is insured and safe. If an investment sounds too good to be true, it probably is.

Money Market Deposit Account (MMDA)

money market deposit account (MMDA)
A deposit offered by a depository institution that requires a minimum balance, has no maturity date, pays interest, and allows a limited number of checks to be written each month.

A **money market deposit account (MMDA)** is a deposit account offered by a depository institution that requires a minimum balance to be maintained, has no maturity date, pays interest, and allows a limited number of checks to be written each month. The specific details vary among financial institutions. For example, an account might require that a minimum balance of $2,500 be maintained over the month and charge a $15 per month fee in any month when the minimum balance falls below that level.

An MMDA differs from a NOW account in that it provides only limited checking services while paying a higher interest rate than that offered on NOW accounts. Many individuals maintain a checking account or NOW account to cover most of their day-to-day transactions and an MMDA to capitalize on the higher interest rate. Thus, they may maintain a larger amount of funds in the MMDA and use this account to write a large check for an unexpected expense. The MMDA is not as liquid as a checking account because it limits the amount of checks that can be written.

Treasury Bills

Treasury securities
Debt securities issued by the U.S. Treasury.

As mentioned in Chapter 5, **Treasury securities** are debt securities issued by the U.S. Treasury. When the U.S. government needs to spend more money than it has received in taxes, it borrows funds by issuing Treasury securities. Individuals can purchase Treasury securities through a brokerage firm. Treasury securities are offered with various maturities, such as three months, six months, one year, 10 years, and 30 years. For money management purposes, individuals tend to focus on **Treasury bills (T-bills)**, which are Treasury securities that will mature in one year or less. T-bills are available with a minimum value at maturity (called the par value) of $10,000 and are denominated in multiples of $5,000 above that minimum.

Treasury bills (T-bills)
Treasury securities with maturities of one year or less.

Return. Treasury bills are purchased at a discount from par value. If you invest in a T-bill and hold it until maturity, you earn a capital gain, which is the difference between the par value of the T-bill at maturity and the amount you paid for the T-bill. Your return on the T-bill is the capital gain as a percentage of your initial investment.

EXAMPLE An investor pays $9,400 to purchase a T-bill that has a par value of $10,000 and a one-year maturity. When the T-bill matures, she receives $10,000. The return from investing in the T-bill is:

$$\text{Return on T-Bill} = \frac{\$10,000 - \$9,400}{\$9,400}$$

$$= 6.38\%.$$

When measuring returns on investments, you should annualize the returns so that you can compare returns on various investments with different maturities. An investment over a one-month period will likely generate a smaller dollar amount of return than a one-year investment. To compare the one-month and one-year investments, you need to determine the annualized yield (or percentage return) on each investment.

For an investment that lasts three months (one-fourth of a year), multiply by 4 to determine the annualized return. For an investment that lasts six months (one-half of a year), multiply by 2 to determine the annualized return. The most precise method of annualizing a return is to multiply the return by 365/N, where N is the number of days the investment existed.

EXAMPLE

An investor pays $9,700 to purchase a T-bill with a par value of $10,000 and a maturity of 182 days. The annualized return from investing in the T-bill is:

$$\text{Return on T-Bill} = \frac{\$10,000 - \$9,700}{\$9,700} \times \frac{365}{182}$$

$$= 6.20\%.$$

secondary market
A market where existing securities such as Treasury bills can be purchased or sold.

Secondary Market. There is a **secondary market** for T-bills where they can be sold before their maturity with the help of a brokerage firm. This secondary market also allows individuals to purchase T-bills that were previously owned by someone else. The return on a T-bill is usually slightly lower than the return on a CD with the same maturity, but T-bills are more liquid because they have a secondary market, whereas CDs must be held until maturity. If you sell a T-bill in the secondary market, your capital gain is the difference between what you sold the T-bill for and what you paid for the T-bill. Your return is this capital gain as a percentage of your initial investment.

Quotations. The prices of various T-bills and the returns they offer for holding them until maturity are quoted in financial newspapers and online.

6.1 Financial Planning Online: Deposit Rates Offered by Banks

Go to
http://www.bankrate.com/
brm/rate/dep_home.asp

This Web site provides information on the highest interest rates offered on deposits by banks across the United States as well as in your specific city.

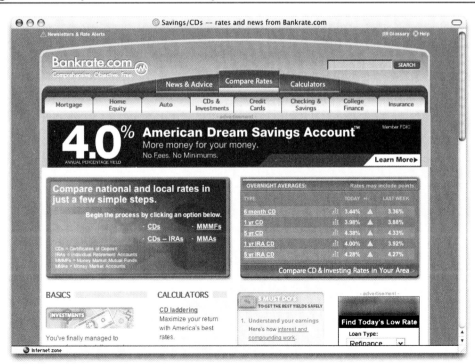

EXAMPLE

An investor purchases a T-bill for $9,700 and sells the T-bill in the secondary market 60 days later for a price of $9,820. The annualized return is:

$$\text{Return on T-Bill} = \frac{\$9,820 - \$9,700}{\$9,700} \times \frac{365}{60}$$

$$= 7.53\%.$$

Money Market Funds (MMFs)

money market funds (MMFs)
Accounts that pool money from individuals and invest in securities that have a short-term maturity, such as one year or less.

commercial paper
Short-term debt securities issued by large corporations that typically offer a slightly higher return than Treasury bills.

Money market funds (MMFs) pool money from individuals to invest in securities that have a short-term maturity, such as one year or less. In fact, the average time remaining to maturity of debt securities held in an MMF is typically less than 90 days. Many MMFs invest in short-term Treasury securities or in wholesale CDs (in denominations of $100,000 or more). Investors can invest in MMFs by sending a check for the amount they wish to have invested for them. Some MMFs invest mainly in **commercial paper**, which consists of short-term debt securities issued by large corporations. Commercial paper typically generates a slightly higher interest rate than T-bills. Money market funds are not insured, but most of them invest in very safe investments and have a very low risk of default.

MMFs offer some liquidity in that individuals can write a limited number of checks on their accounts each month. Often the checks must exceed a minimum amount (such as $250). Individuals may use the checking account associated with an MMF to cover large expenditures, while maintaining a regular checking account to cover smaller purchases. Many individuals invest in an MMF so that they can earn interest until the money is needed. Some MMFs are linked with other accounts so that the money can earn interest until it is transferred to another account. For example, many brokerage accounts allow investors to place any unused funds in an MMF until the funds are used to purchase stock.

EXAMPLE

Assume that you set up an account with $9,000 to purchase stock at a brokerage firm on May 1. On that day, you purchase 100 shares of a stock priced at $50. To cover the purchase, the brokerage firm withdraws $5,000 (computed as $50 × 100 shares) from your account. You still have $4,000 that you have not used, which is placed in a specific MMF account at the brokerage firm. This MMF offers the same limited check-writing services as other MMFs. The money will sit in that account until you use it to purchase stock or write checks against the account. Assuming that the interest rate earned on the MMF is 6 percent annually (.5 percent per month), and you do not purchase any more stock until June 1, you will earn interest on that account over the month when the funds were not used:

$$\text{Amount Invested in MMF} \times \text{Interest Rate per Month} = \text{Interest Earned in 1 Month}$$

$$\$4,000 \times .005 = \$20.$$

Therefore, the MMF account balance increases by $20 to $4,020 because the funds earned interest. Any unused balance will continue to earn interest until you use it to purchase stock or write checks against the account.

Money Market Fund Quotations. Every Thursday the *Wall Street Journal* publishes the yields provided by various money market funds, as shown in Exhibit 6.1. The first column lists the name of the MMF; the second column, the average maturity of the investments of that fund; the third column, the annualized yield generated by the fund; and the fourth column, the size of the fund (measured in millions of dollars). As an example, review the information listed for Janus fund (highlighted in Exhibit 6.1), which invests in government securities. This fund's investments have an average time to maturity of 30 days. The fund generated an annual yield of 4.17 percent for its investors over the last seven days. The fund presently has $180 million in assets.

Exhibit 6.1 Weekly Money Market Fund Yields

FUND	AVG. MAT.	7 DAY YIELD	ASSETS	FUND	AVG. MAT.	7 DAY YIELD	ASSETS	FUND	AVG. MAT.	7 DAY YIELD	ASSETS	FUND	AVG. MAT.	7 DAY YIELD	ASSETS
CNIGvtMMS p	37	3.14	239	FThirdPr I	34	3.79	905	InvNJMuniCsh p	12	2.40	14	PhoenixMM A	47	3.46	105
CNI GvtMMI	37	3.56	39	FThirdTI	29	3.64	394	IvyMnyA	47	3.38	44	PiInsMM 1	27	4.47	97
CNIPrMMA p	26	3.48	423	FBR FdGvInv	44	3.20	241	IvyMnyA	48	2.99	3	PiInsMM 3	27	3.98	52
CNIPrMMS p	26	3.28	224	FIMMDom I	26	4.16	9808	JHanUS	42	3.50	41	PiInsMM 2	27	4.25	147
CNIPrimeInst	26	3.70	334	FIMMDomII	26	4.01	931	JPMGvMMAg	31	4.09	2832	TreasResA	35	2.95	51
ColTRInvA	6	3.14	777	FIMMDomIII	26	3.91	2467	JPMLqAsB	52	3.35	21	TreasResY	35	3.17	69
CS CashResMM	31	3.74	53	FIMMGov I	24	4.16	6222	JPMLqAsR	52	3.62	3881	PionrCs	47	3.54	577
CAMuniC	33	3.09	203	FIMMGovII	24	4.01	507	JPMGvPrem	31	3.94	1751	PipJafGvOb	28	3.46	282
CA MunCS p	33	2.39	182	FIMMGovIII	24	3.91	784	JPMGvCap	31	4.19	10729	PipJafPrOb	33	3.44	3031
CalvCshRInstPr	27	4.09	188	FIMMMMkt I	31	4.18	15675	JPMTrPlInv	14	3.30	2024	PipJafTrOb	7	3.08	33
CalvFtGv	31	3.39	165	FIMMMMktII	31	4.03	316	JPMTrPlRs	14	3.11	1636	PotomacGvt	1	3.18	22
CalvSoc	28	3.52	164	FIMMMMktIII	31	3.93	1088	JPMorg100 Agcy	49	3.68	593	Preferred	62	3.83	259
CashAcctIns	40	4.09	93	FIMMTrOnlyII p	46	3.60	155	JPMorgan100	49	3.33	1842	PremGvtMP	29	4.09	29
CashAcct Prem	40	3.35	3815	FIMMTrOnly3	46	3.50	162	JPMorganFed	30	3.66	205	PremierGvtSecs	30	3.31	1908
CashMgtA	25	3.80	7868	FIMMTrOnly I	46	3.75	1055	JPMorFedAgcy	30	3.99	134	PremierPort	35	4.20	455
CashMgtB t	25	2.96	116	FIMMTry I	5	3.67	4549	JPMorgFedPr	30	3.80	1190	PremierTre p	27	2.95	97
CshTrGv	33	3.24	603	FIMMTryII	5	3.52	279	JPMPrCshMgt	45	3.39	86	PremiumRes	40	3.79	418
CshTrPr	32	3.34	4242	FIMMTryIII	5	3.42	3574	JPMorgPrm	45	3.84	3809	PrmMnObIS	26	4.21	1501
CshTrTreas	14	2.82	325	FLMunIncB	22	2.61	61	JPMorgPrmPr	45	3.90	7093	PrmCshObI	30	4.18	6838
CshTrIl	16	3.04	235	FedTreasObSS	13	3.39	5183	JPMLqAsInv	52	3.81	1689	PrmCshObIC	30	4.11	775
CentnGv	20	3.50	1229	FdShtUS	32	3.83	211	JPMFedInst	30	4.05	2808	PrmCshObSS	30	3.93	1664
Centen	37	3.65	22054	FedMstr	32	3.87	193	JPMPrInst	45	4.15	20530	PrmManObSS	26	3.96	973
CitiFndPUST	52	3.39	296	FedMIMuCshIS	53	3.10	49	JPMPrRsv	45	3.65	419	PrmManObC	26	4.11	849
CitFInsCshRsS p	42	3.96	452	FidAdvTreasC	5	2.43	96	JanusGovt	30	3.72	180	PrimeObTR	32	3.64	15
CitFInsCashRs	42	4.11	686	FidAdvTreasC	5	2.43	92	JanusGvtInst	30	4.17	517	PrimeOb IS	32	4.14	16598
CitFCashRs	65	3.66	1567	FidCashRes	33	3.96	65669	JansInstCshRs	36	4.21	1708	PrimeOb SS	32	3.89	5160
CitFInstLiq	65	4.22	22952	FidGvRes	25	4.00	2530					PrmVluObSS	30	3.98	1421

Asset Management Account

asset management account
An account that combines deposit accounts with a brokerage account and provides a single consolidated statement.

An **asset management account** combines deposit accounts with a brokerage account that is used to buy or sell stocks. The advantage of an asset management account is that it provides a single consolidated statement showing the ending balances and activity of all the accounts. Asset management accounts are available at some depository institutions and brokerage services. The financial institutions that offer these accounts require that the sum of all the accounts in the asset management account exceed some minimum amount, such as $15,000. A special type of asset management account is the **sweep account** that sweeps any unused balance in the brokerage account into a money market investment at the end of each business day. Any unused balance earns interest and remains available for writing checks.

sweep account
An asset management account that sweeps any unused balance in the brokerage account into a money market investment at the end of each business day.

Comparison of Money Market Investments

The various money market investments are compared in Exhibit 6.2. Notice that money market investments that offer a higher return tend to have less liquidity.

Exhibit 6.2 Comparison of Money Market Investments

Money Market Investment	Advantages	Disadvantages
Checking account	Very liquid	No interest
NOW account	Very liquid	Low interest rate; minimum balance required
MMDA	Liquid	Low interest rate
Savings account	Liquid	Low interest rate
Certificate of deposit (CD)	Relatively high interest rate	Less liquid
Treasury bill	Relatively high interest rate	High minimum purchase
Money market fund (MMF)	Liquid	Not as liquid as checking or NOW accounts
Asset management account	Convenient	High minimum balance required

The relationship between the returns and the liquidity of money market investments is illustrated graphically in Exhibit 6.3. Checking accounts offer the most liquidity but provide no return. At the other extreme, a one-year CD provides the highest return but has less liquidity than the other money market instruments.

RISK OF MONEY MARKET INVESTMENTS

Before you consider investing short-term funds in various money market instruments, you must factor in your exposure to risk, or the uncertainty surrounding the potential return. Money market investments are vulnerable to three types of risk: (1) credit risk, (2) interest rate risk, and (3) liquidity risk.

Credit Risk

credit risk (or default risk)
The risk that a borrower may not repay on a timely basis.

When you invest in money market securities, you may be exposed to **credit risk** (also referred to as **default risk**), which is the risk that the borrower will not repay on a timely basis. The borrower may make late payments or may even default on the credit; in that event, you will receive only a portion (or none) of the money you invested. MMFs that invest in large deposits of financial institutions that are insured only up to $100,000 and in short-term securities issued by firms are exposed to credit risk.

Other money market investments are insulated from credit risk. For example, deposits at commercial banks and savings institutions are insured up to $100,000 by the Federal Deposit Insurance Corporation (FDIC). Treasury securities are backed by the federal government.

Interest Rate Risk

interest rate risk
The risk that the value of an investment could decline as a result of a change in interest rates.

Interest rate risk is the risk that the value of an investment could decline as a result of a change in interest rates. Investors who wish to limit their exposure to interest rate risk can invest in debt securities that fit the time frame within which they will need funds. That is, if you need funds in 3 months, you should consider an investment that has a maturity of 3 months, so that you do not have to worry about changes in interest rates. The example on the following page illustrates how the value of an investment can be affected by interest rate movements.

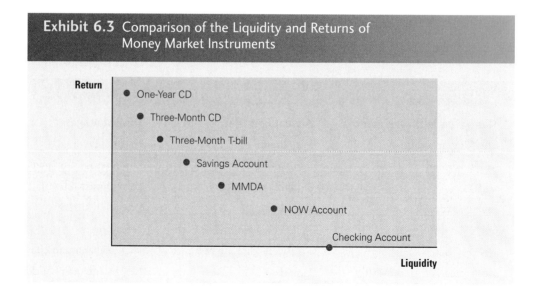

Exhibit 6.3 Comparison of the Liquidity and Returns of Money Market Instruments

6.2 Financial Planning Online: Impact of Different Deposit Rates on Your Wealth

Go to
http://cgi.money.cnn.com/
tools/savingscalc/
savingscalc.html

This Web site provides estimates of future savings that you will accumulate over time at different interest rates in taxable or nontaxable accounts adjusted for inflation.

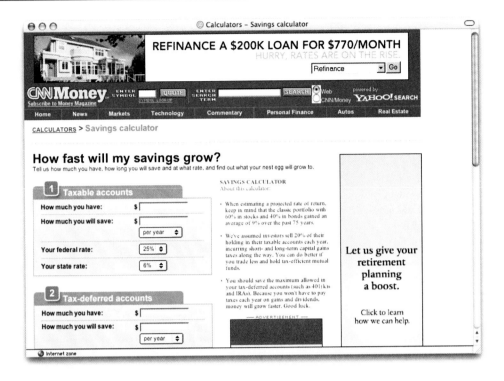

EXAMPLE

Suppose that three months ago you purchased a one-year T-bill that offered a return of 5 percent. Interest rates have recently risen and you are disappointed that you locked in your investment at 5 percent while more recently issued investments (including one-year T-bills) are now offering an annualized return of about 6 percent. You can sell your T-bill in the secondary market, but investors will pay a relatively low price for it because they can buy new securities that offer an annualized return of 6 percent. This explains why the value of a debt security decreases in response to an increase in interest rates.

Rather than selling your T-bill at a discounted price, you can simply hold it to maturity. However, the return on your investment over the entire one-year period will be only 5 percent even though recently issued T-bills are offering higher returns. Neither of your two options is desirable.

Liquidity Risk

liquidity risk
The potential loss that could occur as a result of converting an investment into cash.

Recall that liquidity represents your ability to cover any short-term cash deficiencies. To be liquid, an investment should be easily converted to cash. **Liquidity risk** is the potential loss that could occur as a result of converting an investment to cash. For example, a retail CD has liquidity risk because it cannot be sold in the secondary market. You would suffer a penalty if you tried to redeem it before maturity at the financial institution where you invested in the CD.

The liquidity risk of an investment is influenced by its secondary market. If a particular debt security has a strong secondary market, it can usually be sold quickly and at less of a discount than a debt security with an inactive secondary market. For example, you can easily sell a T-bill in a secondary market, which is why T-bills are more liquid than CDs.

6.3 Financial Planning Online: Identifying Insured Investments

Go to
http://www.chicagofed.org/
consumer_information/
what_you_should_know_
about_internet_banking.cfm

Click on
"Banking Consumers'
Options"

This Web site provides
a comparison of the different methods of investing
your money in a bank and
identifies the investments
that are backed by the U.S.
government.

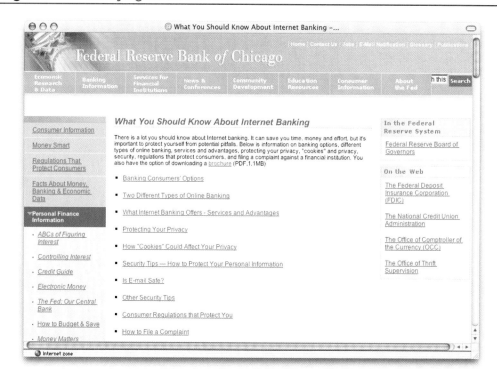

RISK MANAGEMENT OF MONEY MARKET INVESTMENTS

Risk management of money market investments involves (1) assessing the risk exhibited by the investments and (2) using your assessment of risk and your unique financial situation to determine the optimal allocation of your short-term funds among money market investments.

Risk Assessment of Money Market Investments

You must consider the risk-return tradeoff before making investment decisions. The money market securities described in this chapter tend to be insulated from credit risk because they are insured or backed by the government. Treasury securities and small bank deposits are largely free from credit risk. One exception is MMFs that invest in commercial paper. If the commercial paper held by a particular MMF defaults, the return generated by the MMF will be adversely affected, and so will the return to investors who invested in that MMF.

As mentioned earlier, money market investments that have shorter maturities have less interest rate risk. In addition, investments in MMFs tend to have the least liquidity risk, especially when their investments focus on securities that will mature within the next month. Treasury securities that will mature in the next month or so also have very little liquidity risk.

Would you invest in a high-risk security if a lower-risk security offered the same yield? Probably not. Securities that are exposed to risk have to offer higher yields than less risky investments to attract funds from investors. The prospect of a higher return compensates investors for taking on a higher level of risk. Investors can earn a higher return by investing in MMFs that hold investments subject to credit risk and for securities that are particularly vulnerable to interest rate risk. Recall that debt securities with shorter maturities offer lower annualized yields. A three-month debt security typically offers a slightly lower annualized yield than a one-year security. However, the debt securities with longer maturities are more exposed to interest rate movements.

Yields are also higher for securities that are more exposed to liquidity risk. A retail CD must offer a slightly higher yield than a Treasury security with the same maturity because the Treasury security is more liquid.

Determining the Optimal Allocation of Money Market Investments

In general, your money management should be guided by the following steps:

1. Anticipate your upcoming bills and ensure that you have sufficient funds in your checking account.

2. Estimate the additional funds that you might need in the near future and consider investing them in an investment that offers sufficient liquidity (such as an MMF). You may even keep a little extra in reserve here for unanticipated expenses.

3. Use the remaining funds in a manner that will earn you a higher return, within your level of risk tolerance.

The optimal allocation for you will likely be different from the optimal allocation for another individual. If your future net cash flows will be far short of upcoming expenses, you will need to keep a relatively large proportion of funds in a liquid investment (such as a checking account or a NOW account). Another person who has sufficient cash flows to cover expenses will not need much liquidity. The difference is illustrated in Exhibit 6.4. Even though the two individuals have the same level of net cash flows, one person must maintain more liquidity than the other.

Your decision on how to invest your short-term funds (after determining how much money to maintain in your checking account) should account for your willingness to tolerate risk. If you want to minimize all forms of risk, you may simply consider investing all of your funds in an MMF that always focuses on Treasury securities maturing within a month or less. However, you will likely improve on the yield if you are willing to accept some degree of risk. For example, if you know that you will not need your funds for at least six months and do not expect interest rates to rise substantially over that period, you might consider investing your funds in a six-month retail CD. A compromise would be to invest a portion of your short-term funds in the six-month retail CD and the remaining funds in the MMF that focuses on Treasury securities. The CD offers you a higher expected return (although less liquidity), while the MMF offers you liquidity in case you need funds immediately.

Exhibit 6.4 How Liquidity Is Affected by Anticipated Expenses

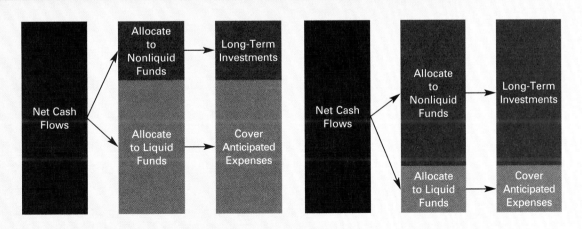

EXAMPLE

Stephanie Spratt has $2,000 available to allocate to money market investments. She knows that she will need $400 to cover several small bills in the next week and may also need $600 in a month or so to pay for repairs on her car engine. She does not expect to need the other funds for at least six months. Her financial institution offers the following annualized yields on various money market instruments:

	Annualized Yield (%)
Checking account	0
NOW account ($500 minimum balance)	2.0
Savings deposit	3.0
MMDA ($2,500 minimum balance)	4.0
MMF ($300 minimum balance)	4.0
Three-month CD	4.5
Six-month CD	5.2
One-year CD	6.0

Stephanie's existing checking account has a balance close to zero. She also has a MMF with a balance of $300, which she must maintain to meet the minimum balance. She will first focus on meeting her liquidity needs and then decide how to invest the remaining funds that are not needed to cover possible expenses. She decides to allocate $400 to her checking account so that she can write several checks to cover her upcoming bills. It is not worthwhile to invest these funds elsewhere as she will need the funds soon, and the checking account is the only investment that will allow her to write several small checks.

She knows that she might need another $600 in the near future for car repairs, but wants to earn as high a return as possible until she needs the money. She immediately eliminates the MMDA from consideration because it would require a minimum balance of $2,500. She decides to invest the $600 in her MMF. She can write a check from this account to cover the car repairs; meanwhile, the funds invested in the MMF will earn 4 percent interest on an annualized basis.

Stephanie now has $1,000 remaining to allocate and anticipates that she will not need the money for at least six months. She does not consider investing the $1,000 in a one-year CD, even though it offers a relatively high interest rate, because she may need the funds in six months. She decides to invest the $1,000 in a six-month CD, so that she can increase liquidity while still earning a relatively high return.

If Stephanie had excess funds that she would not need for a few years, she would consider investing the residual in other investments (such as stocks) that offer a higher potential return. The potential return and risk of these other investments are discussed in Part 5.

HOW MONEY MANAGEMENT FITS WITHIN YOUR FINANCIAL PLAN

The following are the key money management decisions that you should include in your financial plan:

- How can you ensure that you can pay your anticipated bills on time?

- How can you maintain adequate liquidity in case you incur unanticipated expenses?

- How should you invest any remaining funds among money market investments?

By making proper decisions, you can minimize your use of credit and can maximize the return on your liquid assets. As an example, Exhibit 6.5 shows how money market decisions apply to Stephanie Spratt's financial plan.

Exhibit 6.5 How Money Management Fits within Stephanie Spratt's Financial Plan

GOALS FOR MONEY MANAGEMENT

1. *Maintain sufficient liquidity to ensure that all anticipated bills are paid on time.*
2. *Maintain sufficient liquidity in case I incur unanticipated expenses.*
3. *Invest any excess funds in deposits that offer the highest return while ensuring adequate liquidity.*

ANALYSIS

	Amount	Payment Method
Monthly cash inflows	$2,500	*Direct deposited into checking account.*
Typical monthly expenses	1,400	*Write checks to pay these bills.*
Other expenses for clothing or recreation	700	*Use credit cards and then pay the credit card balance by check once a month.*

DECISIONS

**Decision on How to Ensure Adequate Liquidity
to Cover Anticipated Expenses:**

The two paychecks I receive each month amounting to $2,500 after taxes are direct deposited into my check-ing account. I can use this account to cover the $1,400 in anticipated bills each month. I can also use this account to write a check for the monthly credit card bill. I will attempt to leave about $400 extra in the checking account because my expenses may vary from month to month.

**Decision on How to Ensure Liquidity
to Cover Unanticipated Expenses:**

I will also attempt to maintain about $2,500 in a money market fund or a money market deposit account in case I need additional funds. I can earn interest on this money while ensuring liquidity.

**Decision on How to Invest Remaining Funds
to Achieve the Highest Return While Enhancing Liquidity:**

As I accumulate additional savings, I will invest in certificates of deposit with short terms to maturity (such as one month). This money will not be as liquid as the MMF or MMDA, but it will be accessible when the CD matures. The interest rate on the CD will be higher than the interest I can earn on my MMF or MMDA.

DISCUSSION QUESTIONS

1. How would Stephanie's money management decisions be different if she were a single mother of two children?

2. How would Stephanie's money management decisions be affected if she were 35 years old? If she were 50 years old?

SUMMARY

Money management involves the selection of short-term investments that satisfy your liquidity needs and also pro-vide you with an adequate return on your investment. It is challenging because the short-term investments that offer relatively high returns tend to have less liquidity.

Popular short-term investments considered for money management include checking accounts, NOW accounts, savings accounts, CDs, MMDAs, Treasury bills, money mar-ket funds, and asset management accounts. Checking accounts and NOW accounts offer the most liquidity. CDs and T-bills offer the highest return.

The risks related to money market investments are credit (default) risk, interest rate risk, and liquidity risk. The money market investments offered by depository institu-tions are insured and insulate you from the risk that the institution could default. Investments in T-bills have no default risk because they are backed by the federal government. Money market securities tend to have a low level of interest rate risk because they have short-term maturities. They also have relatively low liquidity risk because of the short-term maturities of their assets.

When applying money management, you should first anticipate your expenses in the next month and maintain enough funds in your checking account to cover those expenses. In addition, you should estimate the potential level of unanticipated expenses (such as possible car repairs) and maintain enough funds in a short-term investment such as a money market fund to cover these expenses. Finally, invest the remaining funds to earn a high return within your level of risk tolerance.

INTEGRATING THE KEY CONCEPTS

Your money management decisions determine your level of liquidity and also affect other parts of your financial plan. If your money market investments have a high degree of liquidity, you have more funds that you can use. The amount of liquidity that you maintain is partly determined by your budgeting decisions (Part 1) because you will need more liquidity if your cash outflows are expected to exceed your cash inflows.

The decision to maintain a high degree of liquidity can affect your financing decisions (Part 3) because the more of your cash that you can use, the less you will need to rely on loans. Your money management will also affect your investment decisions (Part 5) because you can focus on investments that are not liquid if you already have sufficient liquidity from your money market investments.

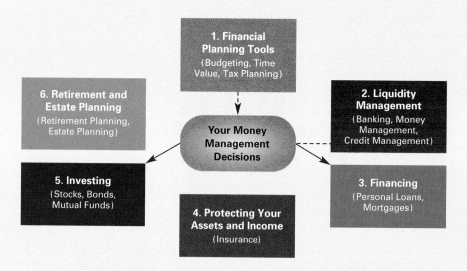

REVIEW QUESTIONS

1. Define money management. How does it differ from long-term investment or long-term borrowing decisions?

2. What is liquidity? How is your personal cash flow statement used to help manage your liquidity? How does money management relate to the cash flow statement?

3. Name some ways an individual might handle a cash flow deficiency. Which way would be preferable? Why?

4. What is the opportunity cost of having excessive amounts of liquid funds?

5. What two factors affect the return on short-term investments? What investments should you consider to achieve liquidity and an adequate return?

6. Why do individuals use checking accounts? What is the disadvantage of having funds in a checking account? Explain overdraft protection and stop payment orders. Are all bank fee structures the same?

7. What is a NOW account? How is it different from a regular checking account? How does a savings account compare with a NOW account?

8. What terms does a financial institution specify for certificates of deposit? Why are rates on CDs higher than those on savings accounts? What factor would most affect your choice of maturity date on a CD?

9. How does a money market deposit account (MMDA) differ from a NOW account? When might a depositor use an MMDA?

10. What are Treasury securities? What is a T-bill? How is it denominated? How do you earn a return on a T-bill? How is the return calculated?

11. Compare the interest rates offered on T-bills and CDs. Which type of investment is more liquid? Why?

12. What are money market funds (MMFs)? What types of securities do they invest in? What is commercial paper? Are MMFs risky investments? Are MMFs liquid?

13. What is an asset management account? Discuss the advantages of such an account as well as its requirements.

14. Compare the return and liquidity of the various money market investments. Give specific examples.

15. What are the three types of risk money market investments are vulnerable to?

16. Generally compare the money market investments described in this chapter in terms of their vulnerability to credit risk, interest rate risk, and liquidity risk. Provide some examples of specific securities. What is the risk-return tradeoff for these investments?

17. What steps should you take to determine the best allocation of your money market investments? What factors should you consider in determining your allocation?

FINANCIAL PLANNING PROBLEMS

1. Teresa has just opened a NOW account that pays 3.5 percent interest. If she maintains a minimum balance of $500 for the next 12 months, how much interest will she earn?

2. Nancy is depositing $2,500 in a six-month CD that pays 4.25 percent interest. How much interest will she accrue if she holds the CD until maturity?

3. Travis has invested $3,000 in a three-month CD at 4 percent. How much will Travis have when the CD matures?

4. Akida has invested $10,000 in an 18-month CD that pays 6.25 percent. How much interest will Akida receive at maturity?

5. Troy paid $9,600 for a T-bill with a face value of $10,000. What is Troy's return if he holds the T-bill to maturity?

6. Bart is a college student who has never invested his funds. He has saved $1,000 and has decided to invest the funds in a money market fund with an expected return of 2.0 percent. Bart will need the funds in one year. The fund imposes fees that will cost Bart $20 at the time he withdraws the funds in one year. How much money will Bart have in one year as a result of this investment?

7. Davis has $20,000 excess cash to invest. He can purchase a $20,000 T-bill for $19,400 or two $10,000 T-bills for $9,600 each. Which will give him the better return?

8. Stacy purchased a $40,000 T-bill for $38,400. A few months later, Stacy sold the T-bill for $39,000. What was Stacy's return on the T-bill?

9. Brenda purchased a $30,000, 90-day T-bill for $29,550. What will Brenda's return be when the T-bill matures? What will her annualized rate be?

10. On June 1, Mia deposited $4,000 in an MMDA that pays 5 percent interest. On October 31, Mia invested $2,000 in a three-month CD that pays 6 percent. At the end of the year, how much interest will Mia have earned, assuming she hasn't taken anything out of the money market deposit account?

11. Thomas can invest $10,000 by purchasing a 1-year T-bill for $9,275, or he can place the $10,000 in a 12-month CD paying 8 percent. Which investment will provide the higher return? In addition to return, what else should Thomas consider when making his investment decision?

Ethical Dilemma

12. Ernie is in his mid 50s and was raised by parents of the Depression era. As a result, he is very risk adverse. Ernie recently came into a very large amount of money and he wants to put it where it will be safe, but where it will earn him some return. His banker tells him that he should put the money in a five-year CD. Ernie asks if there is any way he can lose his money and he is told that the federal government insures the deposit and will give him a higher return than a passbook savings account. Ernie purchases a CD and goes home happy knowing that his money is safe and available whenever he needs it.

Four months later, the roof on Ernie's barn collapses and he needs the money to make repairs, but finds that he can only withdraw it at a substantial penalty.

a. Comment on the ethics of the banker in not fully discussing all risks of money market investments.

b. Is Ernie correct in his thinking that he can find a totally risk-free investment?

FINANCIAL PLANNING ONLINE EXERCISES

1. Go to http://www.calcbuilder.com/cgi-bin/calcs/ SAV2.cgi/FinanCenter. Using this site, you can find the answer to the question, "How Much Will My Savings Be Worth?"

a. By inputting an investment amount, the monthly deposit, the return, the period of investment, the tax rate, and the inflation rate, you can calculate the value of your investment. Input $5,000 as the initial investment, $100 for the monthly deposit,

6 percent for the return, 25 percent for the federal tax rate, 6 percent for the state tax rate and 3 percent for the inflation rate. How much will your investment be worth in 20 years? Click on the Graphs option to view the results graphically.

b. Now change the monthly deposit to $300. How much will your investment be worth in 20 years?

c. Now change the period of investment to 30 years. How much more money will you be able to accumulate in 30 years as opposed to 20, using the original $100 monthly deposit amount?

d. Now change the rate you can earn on your investment from 6 to 8 percent and evaluate the results and graph using the original inputs.

2. Go to http://www.calcbuilder.com/cgi-bin/calcs/SAV3.cgi/FinanCenter.

a. Determine how much you need to save for a major purchase. The amount you need is $8,000.

$1,000 is what you will invest now. You will make $100 monthly deposits for 3 years. You expect a 6 percent return, 25 percent federal tax rate, and a 6 percent state tax rate. Click "results." Will your investing plan allow you to achieve your goal? If not, how should you revise your plan? Click the "graphs" option to view the results graphically.

b. To accumulate $15,000 for a down payment on a house, you plan to save $200 per month over a five-year period at a 6 percent return. Will your plan work? If not, how should you revise it? Assume the same tax rates as in part a.

c. So, you want to be a millionaire. Can you accumulate $1 million to use for your retirement with an initial investment of $25,000, monthly investments of $1000, and a 7 percent return over a 30-year period? If not, what adjustments can you make? Assume the same tax rates as in part a.

BUILDING YOUR OWN FINANCIAL PLAN

Money market investments provide vehicles to assist you in accomplishing your short-term financial goals. Refer to the three short-term goals you established in Chapter 1. Then turn to the worksheets at the end of this chapter, and to the CD-ROM accompanying this text, to continue building your financial plan.

Note: You may find it necessary to revisit some of the financial institutions involved in your Chapter 5 analysis to gather the information necessary to select the most appropriate money market investment for each short-term goal.

THE SAMPSONS—A CONTINUING CASE

Recall from Chapter 2 that the Sampsons currently have about $300 in cash and $1,700 in their checking account. This amount should be enough to cover upcoming bills. The Sampsons have just started saving $800 per month. This money will be placed in CDs every month, which they chose in Chapter 5. These funds, earmarked for a down payment on a car and their children's college education, are not available to the Sampsons for the maturity of the CD. Review the Sampsons' recent cash flow statement and personal balance sheet. The monthly savings of $800 are not included in the cash flow statement.

The Sampsons' Personal Cash Flow Statement

Cash Inflows (Monthly)	$4,000
Cash Outflows (Monthly)	
Rent	$900
Cable TV	60
Electricity and water	80
Telephone	70
Groceries	500

Health care insurance and expenses	160		
Clothing	280		
Car expenses (insurance, maintenance, and gas)	400		
School expenses	100		
Partial payment of credit card balance	20		
Recreation	700		
Total Cash Outflows	**$3,270**		
Net Cash Flows (Monthly)	**+ $730**		

Investment Assets

Stocks	0
Total investment assets	**0**
Total Assets	**$144,000**

The Sampsons' Personal Balance Sheet

Assets

Liquid Assets

Cash	$300
Checking account	1,700
Savings account	0
Total liquid assets	**$2,000**

Household Assets

Home	$130,000
Cars	9,000
Furniture	3,000
Total household assets	**$142,000**

Liabilities and Net Worth

Current Liabilities

Credit card balance	$2,000
Total current liabilities	$2,000

Long-Term Liabilities

Mortgage	$100,000
Car loan	0
Total long-term liabilities	$100,000
Total Liabilities	$102,000
Net Worth	$42,000

Go to the worksheets at the end of this chapter, and to the CD-ROM accompanying this text, to continue this case.

Chapter 6: Building Your Own Financial Plan

GOALS

1. Maintain sufficient liquidity to ensure that all your anticipated bills are paid on time.
2. Maintain sufficient liquidity so that you can cover unanticipated expenses.
3. Invest any excess funds in deposits that offer the highest return while ensuring liquidity.

ANALYSIS

1. Review the cash flow statement you prepared in Chapter 3 and assess your liquidity.
2. Evaluate the short-term goals you created in Chapter 1 as high, medium, or low with respect to liquidity, risk, fees/minimum balance, and return.

Short-Term Goal Prioritization of Factors

Short-Term Goal	Liquidity	Risk	Fees/ Minimum Balance	Return

3. Rank each of the money market investments as good, fair, or poor with respect to liquidity, risk, fees/minimum balance, and return.

Money Market Investment	Liquidity	Risk	Fees/ Minimum Balance	Return
Checking Account				
Now Account				
Savings Account				
Money Market Deposit Account (MMDA)				
Certificate of Deposit				
Treasury Bill				
Money Market Fund				
Asset Management Account				

DECISIONS

1. Describe how you will ensure adequate liquidity to cover anticipated expenses.

   _____
   _____
   _____
   _____
   _____
   _____
   _____

2. Detail how you will ensure liquidity to meet unanticipated expenses.

   _____
   _____
   _____
   _____
   _____
   _____
   _____

3. Explain which money market investments will be most effective in reaching your short-term goals.

   _____
   _____
   _____
   _____
   _____
   _____
   _____

Chapter 6: The Sampsons—A Continuing Case

CASE QUESTIONS

1. Based on the cash flow statement and personal balance sheet, do the Sampsons have adequate liquidity to cover their recurring cash flows and planned monthly savings in the long-run? If not, what level of savings should they maintain for liquidity purposes?

2. Advise the Sampsons on money market investments they should consider to provide them with adequate liquidity.

Exhibit 7.2 A Sample Credit Report

Credit Bureau

Report Number 716-80
08/28/06

Please address all future correspondence to:

Credit Bureau
P.O. Box 0000
City, State, Zip Code
(888) 000–0000

Personal Information

Cynthia Zubicki
120 Greenmeadow Drive
Durham, NC 27704

Social Security Number: 000-00-0000

Previous Addresses:
264 Concord Road
Gilbert, AZ 85296

Last Reported Employment: Architect

401 Brownell Road
Chandler, AZ 85226

Public Record Information

Bankruptcy filed 04/04; Durham District Court; Case Number 873JM34; Liabilities: $56,987; Assets: $672

Collection Agency Account Information

North Shore Collection Agency (888) 000–0000

Collection Reported 11/02; Assigned 1/03 to North Shore Collection Agency; Client: Gilbert Medical Center; Amount: $1,267; Paid Collection Account

Credit Account Information

Company Name	Account Number	Date Opened	Individual or Joint	Months Review	Date of Last Activity	High Credit	Terms	Balance	Past Due	Status	Date Reported
Durham Savings Bank	8762096	02/05	I	6	11/05	$4,897		$2,958		Paid as Agreed	04/06
Macy's	109–82–43176	06/03	I	36	01/06	$2,000		$0		Paid as Agreed	02/06
Chester Auto Finance	873092851	03/04	I	27	02/06	$2,400	$50	$300	$200	Paid 120 days past due date	03/06

Previous Payment History: 2 times 30 days late; 2 times 60 days late

Inquiries

05/27/04 Citibank; 10/15/06 Bloomingdale's; 03/21/06 Home Depot

The credit bureaus rely on a model created by the Fair Isaac Corporation (FICO) for credit scoring. The most important factor used in FICO credit scoring is your credit payment history, which makes up 35 percent of the score. If you have paid your bills on time over the last seven years, you will receive a high rating on that portion of your credit score.

7.2 Financial Planning Online: Obtaining a Free Credit Report

Go to
http://www.ftc.gov/bcp/
conline/pubs/credit/
freereports.htm

This web site provides
information on obtaining a
free credit report.

Credit utilization, the amount of your available credit that you use each month, makes up 30 percent of the credit score. If you continue to rely on most of the credit that you were granted, you will receive a lower score. Put another way, if you have a high credit limit, but do not rely on much of the credit, you will receive a higher score. This situation suggests that you have access to credit, but you have enough discipline not to use it.

Your score is also affected by the length of your relationship with your creditors. You will receive a higher score if you maintain longer relationships with creditors.

Finally, your score is affected by recent credit inquiries. A larger number of credit inquiries may indicate that you are desperately seeking a creditor that will provide you with a loan. Therefore, you will receive a higher score if the number of inquiries is relatively low.

Overall, if you make your credit payments on time, maintain a low level of debt, and have demonstrated your ability to make timely credit payments for many years, you are likely to receive a very high credit score. The credit score is not allowed to reflect your gender, race, religion, natural origin, or marital status.

Differing Scores among Bureaus. While each of the three credit bureaus mentioned earlier rely on FICO to determine your credit score, you may be given a different score from each bureau. The reason for differing scores is that the information that each bureau receives about you is not exactly the same. Assume that Equifax received information from a utility company that you made a payment one month late, while that information was not made available to Experian and TransUnion. In this case, your credit score at Equifax would likely be lower than your credit score assigned by Experian and TransUnion. A recent study by the Consumer Federation of America and the National Credit Reporting Agency found that the range from the lowest credit score to the highest credit score for a given person among the three credit bureaus was 41 points on average. That difference may easily be sufficient to cause some individuals to be approved for a loan based on the credit bureau that provided the highest credit score,

- Examine your health insurance card. If it uses your Social Security number as an identifier discuss the matter with your Human Resource Department to determine if an alternative number can be used.

- Have a discussion with your employer's Human Resource Department about the security measures in place to safeguard your records. Some questions you might consider asking are:

  - What personal data is maintained online?

  - Who has access to the personnel records?

  - Where are the hard copies of personnel records maintained?

  - How secure is the area where records are maintained?

  - Are temporary workers employed in the Human Resource Department and, if so, how are they monitored and their access to files limited?

  - Is a record of personnel who have accessed files maintained?

Also you need to determine that your personal information is being properly safeguarded at you health care providers. Some of the same questions that you should address to your Human Resource Department concerning the handling of your records should be asked of your health care providers. Safe record disposal, which you ask of your credit card issuer and banks, should also be expected of your health care providers.

Identity-Theft Insurance

Identity-theft insurance can be obtained as part of your homeowner or renter policies or as a stand-alone policy. Some credit card issuers add identity-theft insurance as a cardholder benefit.

When obtaining identity-theft insurance, low deductibles, reimbursement for lost wages, coverage for legal fees, and the cost associated with the denial of credit are items to consider in your policy selection. Some critics of identity-theft insurance point out that the associated losses are seldom catastrophic, which is the reason we typically buy insurance. Still, for $25 to $50 per year (the typical cost of a $15,000 to $25,000 policy) a person may be able to obtain peace of mind in dealing with the cost of identity theft.

RESPONSE TO IDENTITY THEFT

If you are a victim of identity theft, you must take action immediately to clean up your credit report. When doing so, it is essential to maintain a record of who you talk to and correspond with, the organization with which they are affiliated, the date of the conversation or correspondence, the phone number and/or address, and if it is a verbal conversation, notes on the nature of that conversation. If your communication is by mail, fax, or e-mail, keep a copy of the correspondence. If your correspondence is by certified mail, attach the verification of the receipt to the correspondence. Also, keep all correspondences and reports (credit, police) that you receive. You will be talking and corresponding with a large number of people, and it will be necessary to refer to previous conversations or correspondences to expedite the process. Maintaining a log will prove a most helpful organizer during this stressful period.

Contact your local police department or sheriff's department and insist that a report be written. Be sure to obtain a copy of the report for your files.

Contact the FTC which, as a result of Congress's passage in October 1998 of the Identity Theft and Assumption Deterrence Act, has been designated to function as a central clearinghouse for all identity-theft complaints.

The Fair and Accurate Credit Transactions Act (FACTA), enacted in December 2003, requires the FTC to issue a standard form and procedures for use by consumers in informing creditors and credit bureaus that they are credit theft victims. Both are available on the FTC's Web site, at http://www.ftc.gov.

7.3 Financial Planning Online: Identity Theft

Notify the major credit reporting companies. Request that a fraud alert be placed in your file. An initial fraud alert will stay on your report for up to 90 days. An extended alert will remain on your credit report for seven years if you provide the credit bureau with an identity theft report. This report consists of a copy of the report filed with your law enforcement agency when you initially reported the theft and any documentation beyond that verifying your identity to the satisfaction of the credit bureau. This alert will enable the company to contact you if there is any attempt to establish credit in your name. Also, request a credit report for your review.

Contact all of your creditors and any creditors in which unauthorized accounts have been opened in your name. This notification will be facilitated by the list you created in the previous section including all creditors and contact information. Many may request a copy of the police report that you obtained from your local law enforcement agency.

While contacting your credit card companies and financial institutions, take the opportunity to change all your passwords. Do not use your mother's maiden name, the last four digits of your Social Security number, your birthday, street address, wedding anniversary or any other readily available information that the identity thief may obtain.

When the identity thief has gained access to your bank accounts or created accounts in your name, you should also contact check verification companies. These companies maintain a database of individuals who have written bad checks and of accounts where there have been excessive or unusual transactions.

If you believe the identity thief has in any way obtained your data or illegally used your personal information involving the U.S. Postal Service, you should contact your local Post Office to make an appointment with the Postal Inspection Service. If the identity thief has compromised your Social Security number, immediately contact the Social Security Administration. It may be necessary that they issue you a new Social Security number.

You may be notified of pending lawsuits against you as a result of the identity theft. If this is the case, immediately seek the services of an attorney.

In some cases of identity theft, the Federal Bureau of Investigation and the Secret Service may also need to be notified. Your local law enforcement agency should be able to advise you if these agencies need to be involved in your particular case.

This list of notifications is by no means exhaustive. Some cases of identity theft may necessitate the notification of your employer's Human Resources Department, while others may involve corresponding with your health care providers and medical insurance companies. For victims who have extensive stock, bond, and mutual fund holdings, notification to brokers, mutual fund companies, and 401(k) administrator may also be advisable.

Exhibit 7.4 provides important contact information that you can use to prevent identity theft, report identity theft, or report related criminal activity.

EXAMPLE

Recently, Stephanie Spratt was shocked to find a statement from Visa indicating that her credit card had been charged to its $5,000 limit. (The statement showed 18 unauthorized purchases, totaling $4,903.88, all made within a two-day time span.) Stephanie paid the balance in full last month, and the only thing she bought with the card this month was a pair of running shoes. Thinking she must have lost her Visa card, Stephanie quickly checked her wallet but it was in its usual compartment.

Stephanie keeps a list of all of her credit card numbers and toll-free phone numbers for the credit card companies in a fireproof box. She retrieves the information she needs and calls customer service at Visa to report the unauthorized charges, close the account, and request a new card. The customer service representative explains to Stephanie that had her card actually been stolen, she would have been liable under federal law for $50 of the $4,903.88 in charges. But, because the thief stole Stepanie's credit card number, she is not liable for unauthorized use.

Stephanie is relieved that she won't be held accountable for the charges, but she is also puzzled about how the thief accessed her credit card number. Also, she is worried that maybe the thief stole more than that. She recalls a recent e-mail from a popular online store, saying that her account would be terminated if she didn't update her credit information. A quick e-mail to the store confirms that no such e-mail was sent—Stephanie is a victim of a phishing scam.

As best she can recall, the information Stephanie provided to the phisher was her Visa account number, her name, and her address. To be safe, Stephanie's next step is to put an alert on her credit report. She decides to check her report in one month, and if there is fraudulent information, she will request corrections and fill out an identity theft report.

HOW CREDIT ASSESSMENT AND SECURITY FITS WITHIN YOUR FINANCIAL PLAN

The following are the key credit assessment and security decisions that should be included within your financial plan:

1. Is your credit standing adequate so that you can use credit?

2. Is your credit and personal identity information secure?

By making proper decisions, you can ensure that you access credit only when your credit standing is adequate, and prevent others from using your credit or identity information. Exhibit 7.5 shows how credit standing and security apply to Stephanie Spratt's financial plan.

Exhibit 7.4 Useful Sources of Information to Protect against Identity Theft

Check Verification Companies

CheckRite	(800) 299-4892
ChexSystems	(800) 428-9623
CrossCheck	(800) 552-1900
Equifax	(800) 685-5000
National Processing Company (NPC)	(800) 526-5380
Telecheck	(800) 710-9898
Scan	(800) 262-7771

How to Prevent Unsolicited Mail and Phone Calls

Pre-approved credit card offers

The following number can be used to notify all three major credit card
bureaus that you wish to opt out of pre-approved credit card offers.
(888) 5optout • (888) 567–8688

Mail solicitations—write to:

Mail Preference Service
P.O. Box 7130
Boulder, CO 80306-7130

Telephone solicitations—write to:

Telephone Preference Service
Direct Marketing Association
P.O. Box 1559
Carmel, NY 105122

Contacts if You Are Subjected to Identity Theft

Major National Credit Bureaus

Equifax Credit Information Services
Consumer Fraud Division
P.O. Box 740256
Atlanta, GA 30374
(800) 525-6285
http://www.credit.equifax.com

Experian
National Consumer Assistance
P.O. Box 9530
Allen, TX 75013
(888) 397-3742
http://www.experian.com

TransUnion Fraud Victim Assistance
Department
P.O. Box 6790
Fullerton, CA 92834
(800) 680-7289
http://www.transunion.com

Governmental Agencies

Federal Trade Commission
Consumer Response Center, Room 130
600 Pennsylvania Avenue, NW
Washington, DC 20580
1-877-FTC-HELP

Social Security Administration
(800) 269-0271
TTY (800) 325-0778
http://www.socialsecurity.gov

Internal Revenue Service
(800) 829-0433

U.S. State Department
Attn: Passport Services
1111 19th Street, NW, Ste. 500
Washington, DC 20522
(To determine if a fraudulent passport has been
issued in your name.)

U.S Postal Inspection Service
(Contact your local Post Office)

United States Secret Service
(Contact the local field office, a list of which can be
found at
http://www.secretservice.gov/field_offices.shtml)

Exhibit 7.5 How Credit Standing and Security Fit within Stephanie Spratt's Financial Plan

GOALS

1. *Ensure that I always have easy access to credit, so that I can obtain personal loans or use credit cards whenever I desire.*
2. *Ensure that my credit and identity information is secure.*

DECISIONS
Decision Regarding My Credit Report

Contact the credit bureaus to request a copy of my credit report and ensure that my credit report is accurate. If there are any deficiencies listed on my report, correct them so that I can ensure easy access to credit in the future.

Decision Regarding the Security of My Credit and Identity

Leave most of my personal information at home. Carry only my Visa and MasterCard, and driver's license with me. Shred any documents I plan to discard that contain personal information.

SUMMARY

Credit, which are funds provided to a borrower that will be repaid in the future, has advantages and disadvantages. An advantage is the convenience that credit provides in making day-to-day purchases without the necessity of carrying large amounts of cash. A disadvantage is that if not used properly, credit can result in bankruptcy or cause a significant reduction in the money you can save.

Non-installment credit is normally issued for a very short period, and is typically provided for specific purchases by some department stores. Installment credit is also provided for specific purchases, but the borrower has a longer time (such as a few years) to repay the amount borrowed. Revolving open-end credit is used for credit cards. Consumers can repay the entire balance at the end of the month, or repay a portion of the balance and interest will be charged on the remaining balance.

Good credit is easy to create by paying utility bills promptly and limiting the use of credit cards. A complete history of your credit transactions is maintained by credit bureaus that numerically rate your credit score and report this information to interested parties.

Lenders commonly access the credit payment history provided by one or more credit bureaus when deciding whether to extend a personal loan. You can obtain a free credit report from any one of the three credit bureaus to ensure that the report is accurate. The credit report contains potentially negative information from public records, such as bankruptcy filings. It also offers information about late payments, accounts in good standing, inquiries made about your credit history, and personal information.

Not all threats to your credit score are the result of your actions. Identity theft, which involves the use of your personal identifying information without your permission, is one of the fastest growing crimes in our country. An identity thief may use your personal information to obtain goods, services, money, or to create a new identity. All of these actions can have a negative effect on your credit history. Protecting your identity against actions such as shoulder surfing, dumpster diving, skimming, and pretexting is everyone's responsibility. Inventorying your wallet, purchasing and using a shredder, mailing checks only in the U.S. Post Office mailbox, and picking up bank statements or new checks at the Post Office or financial institution are all actions that will help safeguard your identity.

Take precautions where you work, bank, and receive medical care. Requesting the elimination of your Social Security number on health care insurance cards, identity badges, and paychecks is a necessary step in safeguarding your identity.

Obtain a copy of your credit report at least twice a year. Carefully review your credit report for unusual account activity and the existence of accounts of which you are not aware.

Should your identity be stolen, notify the police and request a written report. Notify the FTC, credit bureaus, credit card companies, financial institutions, and, when appropriate, the FBI and Secret Service.

INTEGRATING THE KEY CONCEPTS

Your credit decisions affect not only your liquidity, but also other parts of your financial plan. If you use excessive credit, you will restrict your ability for additional financing (Part 3) because lenders will be less likely to lend you additional funds. You will also restrict your ability to invest

(Part 5) because of the need to repay excessive debt. Protecting your identity is crucial to protecting your assets and income (Part 4) and financing because if your credit history has been damaged by identity theft, it may be difficult to borrow money in the future.

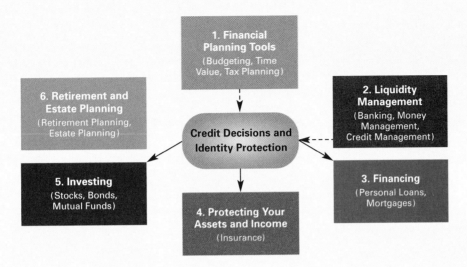

REVIEW QUESTIONS

1. Explain the three types of credit. Under what conditions might a consumer find each type useful?

2. What are the advantages and disadvantages of using credit?

3. The Equal Credit Opportunity Act prohibits creditors from denying credit for what reasons? If you are denied credit, do you have the right to know the reason for the denial?

4. How do utilities extend credit and how can this credit help you establish a credit history?

5. What three types of information do creditors use to determine a prospective borrower's creditworthiness? What specifically are they looking for in each area?

6. Name the three major credit bureaus. How do they score your credit rating? Will all three major credit bureaus always produce the same credit score?

7. What are the six major areas of information that may be included on your credit report?

8. What factors determine your credit score and how are these factors weighted by FICO?

9. How can your improve your credit score and how long can it take to erase a poor credit history?

10. How often should you review your credit report from each of the three major credit bureaus. Why is this review beneficial?

11. What constitutes identity theft?

12. Is identity theft only perpetrated to acquire money, goods, or services?

13. Aside from the financial losses, what other negative impacts might a victim of identity theft encounter?

14. Name and explain at least three tactics used by identity thieves to obtain information.

15. Can identity theft occur through legitimate access to your personal information? Explain.

16. Discuss steps you can take to safeguard your personal information.

17. What steps should you take if you become a victim of identity theft?

VIDEO QUESTIONS

1. Who evaluates the information in your credit report? What must you do regularly to ensure that your credit report is an accurate reflection of your finances?

2. List and explain the negative information that can appear on your credit report.

3. What resources did the segment mention for those whose credit situation is in poor shape?

FINANCIAL PLANNING PROBLEM
Ethical Dilemma

1. Rita is the office manager of a three-doctor practice. Her brother, Juan, a recent college graduate, has recently begun work for a large insurance company that specializes in health insurance. In attempting to build a client base, Juan asks Rita if she will provide him with a list of all the doctors' patients who do not currently have health insurance. Wishing to help her brother be successful in his new job, she runs the list that includes names, addresses, telephone numbers, Social Security numbers, and brief medical histories.

   a. Is Rita acting ethically? Explain.

   b. What problems could Rita be creating for the practice's patients?

FINANCIAL PLANNING ONLINE EXERCISES

1. Go to http://qspace.iplace.com/cobrands/444/quick_rater.asp?sc=6151LPCC

   a. Take the quiz to determine your approximate credit rating.

   b. Is your credit rating higher or lower than you anticipated?

   c. If your credit rating is lower than you anticipated, which of the questions do you believe had a negative impact on your score?

   d. Devise a plan to raise your credit score if it is low, or, if it is high, list what you need to do to maintain your high score.

2. Go to http://www.privacyrights.org/itrc-quiz1.htm

   a. Take the quiz to assess your level of preparedness to defend against identity theft.

   b. Make a list of those areas where the quiz indicates that you are unprepared.

   c. Develop a written plan to address those areas and increase your level of preparedness.

BUILDING YOUR OWN FINANCIAL PLAN

 Credit is one of the most useful and dangerous elements of a personal financial plan. This case will assist you in reviewing your credit and safeguarding it from identity theft.

In the first part of the exercise, you will determine whether your credit history is being properly and accurately reported in the credit reports that banks and other lending institutions use to evaluate your creditworthiness.

Then, you will determine your overall creditworthiness. Finally, you will establish practices that will help safeguard you from identity theft.

Go to the worksheets at the end of this chapter, and to the CD-ROM accompanying this text, to continue building your financial plan.

THE SAMPSONS—A CONTINUING CASE

 The $2,000 credit card balance that the Sampsons are carrying and currently making the minimum payment due, has a credit limit of $10,000. The Sampsons have just received a letter from the credit card company offering to increase their credit limit to $20,000. The Sampsons have also read several articles on identity theft and are concerned with protecting themselves from this fast-growing crime. They currently receive their mail in a curbside mailbox and they dispose of all junk mail in the trash.

Go to the worksheets at the end of this chapter, and to the CD-ROM accompanying this text, to continue this case.

Chapter 7: Building Your Own Financial Plan

GOALS

1. Evaluate your credit report.
2. Determine your overall creditworthiness.
3. Establish practices that will safeguard you from identity theft.

ANALYSIS

1. Obtain a copy of your credit report from http://www.annualcreditreport.com, scrutinize the report, and report any inaccuracies to the credit bureaus.
2. Using the MSN homepage, determine your overall creditworthiness. At http://www.msn.com, click on the tab entitled "Money," and then click on "Planning." When the "Savings and Debt Management" page comes up, go to the section entitled "Debt Evaluator" and follow the instructions.
3. Inventory your wallet/purse to determine if you can reduce your risk of identity theft by selectively removing certain items.

Item Description	Identity Theft Risk (High/Low)	Necessary to Carry? (Yes/No)	If Previous Column Is Marked "No," Where Should Item Be Stored?

DECISIONS

1. Are there any errors on your credit report you must correct? How can you improve your credit-worthiness?

_____

_____

_____

_____

_____

_____

_____

2. In addition to inventorying your wallet/purse and removing items, what other steps can you take in your life to reduce your exposure to identity theft?

_____

_____

_____

_____

_____

_____

_____

_____

Chapter 7: The Sampsons—A Continuing Case

CASE QUESTIONS

1. Should the Sampsons accept the increase in the limit on their credit card even if they do not anticipate using it?

2. Advise the Sampsons on steps that they can take to reduce their exposure to identity theft.

Managing Your Credit

When Tara arrived for her freshman year at college, she was on a tight budget. While the tuition, room, and board were covered by a scholarship, she was on her own for buying books and paying for extras such as entertainment. She calculated that the income she would receive through her job at the campus library would just about cover her expenses, if she limited her spending. Tara decided to apply for a credit card, so that she would be able to make emergency purchases, if necessary. Applying was easy, as a credit card company in the student union offered gifts to anyone who filled out an application form. When Tara received her card with a credit limit of $1,000, she promised herself she would use it only for emergency purchases between paychecks, and she would pay the balance in full every month.

Three years and two additional credit cards later, Tara is graduating with $4,000 of debt. She frequently used her credit cards for unnecessary purchases. She believed that as long as she made a payment each month, it didn't matter that she quickly charged her card to the maximum limit. She didn't realize that the interest charged on unpaid balances was 18.5 percent, or that there was a fee and substantially higher interest associated with cash advances, or that she would be charged $35 for every late payment. The consequences of credit card debt are severe. Now Tara has a poor credit rating, which will affect her ability to get a loan for a large purchase such as a car. In addition, it may take several years for her to pay off her debt.

This chapter focuses on obtaining and effectively using credit. You'll see that a good credit history is built by the proper use and control of credit, not by the absence of credit.

The objectives of this chapter are to:

- Provide a background on credit
- Explain the key characteristics of credit cards
- Offer tips on using credit cards

CREDIT CARDS

The easiest way to establish credit is to apply for a credit card. There is no shortage of credit card companies eager to extend credit to you. A credit card allows you to purchase products on credit wherever that card is honored. You receive a monthly statement that identifies the purchases you made with the credit card during that period. Normally, credit cards are not used for very large expenditures such as cars or homes, but they are very convenient for smaller purchases, such as meals at restaurants, gasoline, clothing, car repairs, and even groceries.

Credit cards offer three advantages. First, you can purchase products and services without carrying a large amount of cash or a checkbook. Second, as long as you pay off your balance each month, you receive free financing until the due date on your credit card statement. Third, you receive a monthly statement that contains a consolidated list of the purchases you made with the credit card, which enables you to keep track of your spending. In some cases, you receive an annual statement as well, detailing expenses by category, which can be useful in preparing your income tax return.

Applying for a Credit Card

When you apply for a credit card, potential creditors obtain information from you, from credit bureaus, so that they can assess your ability to repay credit.

Personal Information. When you apply for credit, you are asked to complete an application that typically requests the following information:

- Cash inflows: What is your monthly income?
- Cash outflows: How much do you spend per month?
- Credit history: Have you borrowed funds in the past? Did you repay any previous loans in a timely manner?
- Capital: Do you have any funds in the form of savings or stocks that can be used if necessary to cover future debt payments?
- Collateral: Do you have any assets that can be used as collateral to secure the borrowed funds? (If you could not repay your debt, you could sell these assets to obtain the funds needed to repay the loans.)

Creditors generally prefer that you have a high level of cash inflows, a low level of cash outflows, a large amount of capital and collateral, and a good credit history. Nevertheless, they commonly extend credit to individuals who do not have all of these attributes. For example, although creditors recognize that college students may not earn much income, they may still provide a limited amount of credit if they believe that the students are likely to repay it. Some creditors also extend credit at higher interest rates to individuals who have a higher risk of defaulting.

Credit Check. When you apply for credit, a credit card issuer typically conducts a credit check as part of the application review process. It can obtain a credit report, discussed in the previous chapter, that indicates your creditworthiness based on information such as whether you have made late payments, and any unpaid current bills. A credit report summarizes credit repayment with banks, retailers, credit card issuers, and other lenders. Recall that credit problems remain on a credit bureau's report for seven years. If you claim bankruptcy, this information normally remains on a credit bureau's report for ten years.

Other Information that Creditors Evaluate. Some creditors also request that the applicant disclose income and existing debt level so that they can assess the existing debt level as a percentage of income. If an applicant's debt level is only a small fraction of his or her income, creditors are more willing to provide credit.

In addition to information about the applicant, creditors also consider existing economic conditions when they evaluate credit applications. If economic conditions weaken, and you lose your job, you may be unable to repay your loan. Thus, creditors are less willing to extend credit when the economy is weak.

Types of Credit Cards

The most popular credit cards are MasterCard, Visa, and American Express. MasterCard and Visa allow your payments to be financed, but American Express requires that the balance be paid in full each month. These three types of cards are especially convenient because they are accepted by most merchants. The merchants honor credit cards because they recognize that many consumers will make purchases only if they can use their credit cards. A credit card company receives a percentage (commonly between 2 and 4 percent) of the payments made to merchants with its credit card. For example, when you use your MasterCard to pay for a $100 car repair at a Shell Oil station, Shell will pay MasterCard a percentage, perhaps $3.

Many financial institutions issue MasterCard and Visa credit cards to individuals. Each financial institution makes its own arrangements with credit card companies to do the billing and financing when necessary. The institution provides financing for individuals who choose not to pay their balance in full when they receive a billing statement. The financial institutions benefit by providing financing because they typically earn a high rate of interest on the credit extended. Some universities and charitable organizations also issue MasterCard and Visa credit cards and provide financing if needed.

8.1 Financial Planning Online: Your Credit Card Report

Go to
http://finance.yahoo.com/creditreports

This Web site provides a credit report that assesses your creditworthiness. The report is available to you online for a small fee.

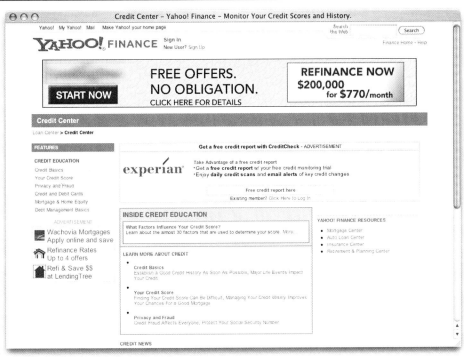

retail (or proprietary) credit card
A credit card that is honored only by a specific retail establishment.

Retail Credit Cards. An alternative to MasterCard, Visa, and American Express credit cards is a **retail** (or **proprietary**) **credit card** that is issued for use at a specific retail establishment. For example, many retail stores (such as J.C. Penney and Macy's) and gas stations (such as Shell Oil and Exxon Mobil) issue their own credit card. If you use a Shell Oil credit card to pay for gas at a Shell station, Shell does not have to pay a small percentage of the proceeds to MasterCard or any other credit card company. You can usually obtain an application for a proprietary card when you are paying for products or services. You may be given instant credit when you complete the application. With most retail credit cards, you can pay a small portion of the balance owed each month, which means that the merchant finances your purchase. The interest rate you are charged when financing with retail credit cards is normally 18 percent or higher.

One disadvantage of a proprietary credit card is that it limits your purchases to a single merchant. You may find that the limit is an advantage if you are trying to restrict your use of credit so that you do not spend beyond your means. For example, you could use a Shell credit card to pay for gasoline and car repairs, but not to buy CDs, clothing, and many other products. Another disadvantage is that using many proprietary cards means you will have several credit card bills to pay each month; using one card for all purchases allows you to write only one check to cover all your credit card payments.

Credit Limit

Credit card companies set a credit limit, which specifies the maximum amount of credit allowed. The credit limit varies among individuals. It may be a relatively small amount (such as $300) for individuals who have a low income. The credit limit can usually be increased for individuals who prove that they are creditworthy by paying their credit card bills on time. Some credit card companies may allow a large limit (such as $10,000 or more) to households that have made their credit payments consistently and have higher incomes.

1-26   © LaughingStock International Inc./dist. by United Media, 2004

"We were wondering if we could extend the maximum limit on our charge account."

Overdraft Protection

Some credit cards provide overdraft protection, which allows you to make purchases beyond your stated credit limit. This is similar to the overdraft protection that is provided on some checking accounts at financial institutions, in which checks can be written and will clear even if there are not enough funds in the checking account. The overdraft protection on credit cards prevents a situation in which you try to use your credit card, but it is rejected because you are over your credit limit.

Fees are charged, however, whenever overdraft protection is needed. The fees vary among credit card issuers, but can be as high as $30 or more each time the protection is needed. Thus, a person who made five transactions in a particular month after reaching the credit limit may incur overdraft protection fees of $150 (computed as five transactions × $30 fee per transaction) in that month.

Some people prefer to have overdraft protection to avoid the embarrassment of having their credit card rejected when making purchases, and to have the flexibility to spend beyond the credit limit when necessary. Other people prefer no overdraft protection, so that they cannot spend beyond their credit limit and will not be charged overdraft protection fees.

Annual Fee

Many credit card companies charge an annual fee, such as $50 or $70, for the privilege of using their card. The fee is sometimes waived for individuals who use their credit cards frequently and pay their credit card bills in a timely manner.

Incentives to Use the Card

Some credit card companies offer a bonus to cardholders. For example, they may award a point toward a free trip on an airline for every dollar spent. After accumulating 20,000 points, you receive a coupon for a free flight anywhere in the United States. If you spend $20,000 over the year on purchases and use this particular credit card for all of them, you will accumulate enough points by the end of the year to earn a free round-trip on a designated airline to any destination in the United States. Some airlines issue their own credit cards, which provide similar benefits.

Prestige Cards

prestige cards
Credit cards, such as gold cards or platinum cards, issued by a financial institution to individuals who have an exceptional credit standing.

Financial institutions may issue **prestige cards** to individuals who have an exceptional credit standing. These cards, sometimes referred to as gold cards or platinum cards, provide extra benefits to cardholders. For example, the card may provide insurance on rental cars and special warranties on purchases. Many cardholders receive an upgrade to a gold card or platinum card after they prove that they are creditworthy by making their payments on time.

Grace Period

Credit cards typically allow a grace period in which you are not charged any interest on your purchases. The grace period is usually about 20 days from the time the credit card statement is "closed" (any purchases after that date are put on the next month's bill) and the time the bill is due. The credit card issuer essentially provides you with free credit from the time you made the purchase until the bill is due.

8.2 Financial Planning Online: Eliminating Credit Card Debt

Go to
http://cgi.money.cnn.com/tools/debtplanner/debtplanner.jsp

This Web site provides estimates of your future credit card payments based on your credit card balance, the interest rate you are charged, and the desired time in which you want it paid.

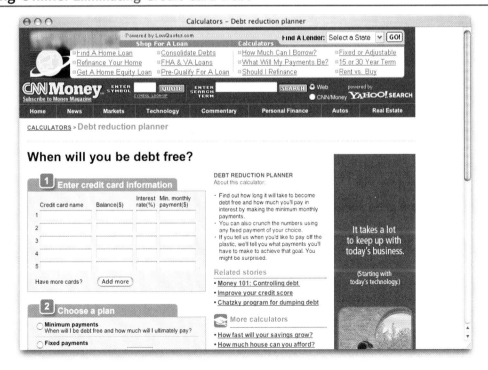

EXAMPLE

On June 1, Stephanie Spratt paid a car repair bill of $200 with her credit card. The closing date for that month's billing statement is June 30, and the bill is due around July 20. In this case, Stephanie receives about 50 days of free credit. On June 20, she purchased some clothing with her credit card. For that purchase, which is also on the billing statement, she receives about 30 days of free credit. On July 10, she purchased concert tickets with her credit card. This purchase occurs after the closing date of the billing statement and therefore will be listed on the next billing statement, which is due on about August 20. For this purchase, credit is extended for about 40 days.

Cash Advances

Many credit cards also allow cash advances at automated teller machines (ATMs). Since a cash advance represents credit extended by the sponsoring financial institution, interest is charged on this transaction. A transaction fee of 1 or 2 percent of the advance may also be charged. Credit card companies also provide checks that you can use to make purchases that cannot be made by credit card. The interest rate applied to cash advances is often higher than the interest rate charged on credit extended for specific credit card purchases. The interest rate is applied at the time of the cash advance; the grace period that applies to purchases with a credit card does not apply to cash advances. So, although cash advances are convenient, they can also be extremely costly.

Financing

Some individuals use credit cards as a means of financing their purchases. That is, they pay only a portion of the credit card bill at the end of the month, and the sponsoring financial institution extends credit for the remainder and charges an interest rate. The interest rate charged on credit is commonly between 15 and 20 percent on an annualized basis and does not vary much over time. Although financing is convenient for individuals who are short of funds, it is expensive and should be avoided if possible.

Credit cards can offer a variable rate, a fixed rate, or a tiered rate. A variable rate adjusts in response to a specified market interest rate, such as a one-year Treasury bill rate, or the federal funds rate. For example, the credit card interest rate could be set equal to the one-year Treasury bill rate + 6 percent. The bank that provides financing on a credit card can change the fixed interest rate that it charges, but it must notify you if it does so.

Some banks offer a tiered interest rate on their credit cards, in which cardholders who make late payments are charged a higher rate. Banks that offer a tiered interest rate are expected to inform their cardholders.

Many credit cards advertise a very low "teaser" interest rate, which is normally applicable for the first three or six months. Some people transfer their balances from one credit card to another as soon as the period of low interest rates has ended. The issuer of the first credit card may charge a fee when transferring the balance to a new credit card with the low teaser rate.

finance charge
The interest that you must pay as a result of using credit

The **finance charge** represents the interest that you must pay as a result of using credit. Purchases after the statement closing date are not normally considered when determining the finance charge because of the grace period, as they will appear on your next monthly statement. The finance charge applies only to balances that were not paid in full before their due date in the current billing period. However, some credit card companies add any new purchases when determining the average daily balance if there is an outstanding balance in the previous period.

The following three methods are commonly used to calculate finance charges on outstanding credit card balances:

Previous Balance Method. Under the previous balance method, interest is charged on the balance at the beginning of the new billing period. This method is the least favorable of the three to the cardholder because finance charges are applied even if part of the outstanding balance is paid off during the billing period.

Average Daily Balance Method. The most frequently used method is the average daily balance method. For each day in the billing period, the credit card company takes your beginning balance at the start of the day and then subtracts any payments made by you on that day in order to determine the balance at the end of the day. Then, it determines the average daily balance at the end of the day for every day in the billing period. This method takes into account the time when you pay off any part of the outstanding balance. Thus, if you pay off part of the outstanding balance during the billing period, your finance charges will be lower under this method than under the previous balance method. There are variations of this method. The method may be adjusted to exclude any new purchases or to compute the average over two billing periods instead of one period.

Adjusted Balance Method. Under the adjusted balance method, interest is charged based on the balance at the end of the new billing period. This method is most favorable for you because it applies finance charges only to the outstanding balance that was not paid off during the billing period.

The following example illustrates the three methods for determining finance charges.

EXAMPLE   Assume that as of June 10, you have an outstanding credit card balance of $700 from purchases made over the last month. The new billing period begins on June 11. Assume that your outstanding balance for the first 15 days of this new billing period (from June 11 to June 25) is $700. Then, on June 25, the financial institution receives a payment of $200 from you, reducing the balance to $500. This is the balance for the remaining 15 days of the billing period.

- Previous Balance Method. Under this method you will be subject to a finance charge that is calculated by applying the monthly interest rate to the $700 outstanding at the beginning of the new billing period. Using a monthly interest rate of 1.5 percent, your finance charge is:

  $700 × .015 = $10.50.

- Average Daily Balance Method. Under this method the monthly interest rate is applied to the average daily balance. Since your daily balance was $700 over the first 15 days and $500 over the last 15 days, your average daily balance was $600 over the 30-day billing period. Using a monthly interest rate of 1.5 percent, your finance charge is:

  $600 × .015 = $9.00.

- Adjusted Balance Method. Under this method you will be subject to a finance charge that is calculated by applying the monthly interest rate to the $500 outstanding at the end of the new billing period. Using a monthly interest rate of 1.5 percent, your finance charge is:

  $500 × .015 = $7.50.

Notice from this example that the finance charge is lower if the credit card company uses the adjusted balance method. Individuals who frequently have financing charges can save a substantial amount of money over time by relying on a credit card that uses this method. The best way to reduce financing charges, however, is still to pay the entire credit card bill before the due date every month.

simple interest rate
The percentage of credit that must be paid as interest on an annual basis.

Impact of the Interest Rate on Credit Payments
When you borrow funds, you are charged an interest rate. The **simple interest rate** is the percentage of the credit that you must pay as interest on an annual basis.

8.3 Financial Planning Online: Your Rights When Using Credit

Go to
http/www.chicagofed.com/
consumer_information/
personal_finance_
information.cfm

Click on
"Credit Guide"

This Web site provides
information about various
laws that protect your
rights when using credit.

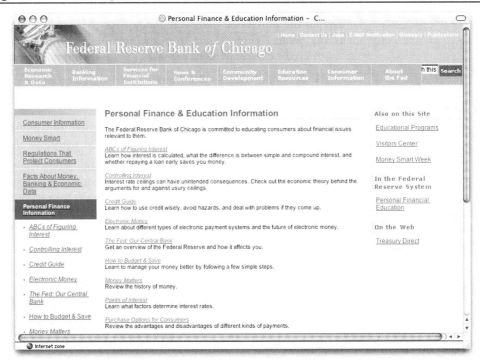

When you receive your account statement, you should always scrutinize it for errors. There may be a math error, a double charge for a purchase, or an incorrect amount on a purchase. Under consumer protection laws, you have the right to dispute possible errors.

Comparing Credit Cards

Some individuals have numerous credit cards, which can complicate record keeping and increase the probability of losing one or more credit cards. You can consolidate your bills by using just one credit card to cover your purchases. If you decide to use only one credit card, the following criteria will help you determine which card is most desirable.

Acceptance by Merchants. You should make sure that your card is accepted by the types of merchants where you typically make your purchases. MasterCard and Visa are accepted by more merchants than other credit cards.

Annual Fee. Shop around for a credit card that does not charge an annual fee.

Interest Rate. The interest rate varies among financial institutions that provide financing on credit cards. Shop around for the lowest rate.

The interest rate may be a key factor that determines the credit card that is appropriate for you if you plan to carry over part of your balance each month. A card with a higher interest rate can result in substantially higher interest expenses.

EXAMPLE   You plan to pursue credit card X because it has no annual fee, while credit car Y has an annual fee of $30. You typically have an outstanding credit balance of $3,000 each month. Credit card X charges an annual interest rate of 18 percent on balances carried forward, while credit card Y charges an interest rate of 12 percent on balances carried forward. The difference in the expenses associated with each credit card are shown here:

	Credit Card X	Credit Card Y
Average monthly balance	$3,000	$3,000
Annual interest rate	18%	12%
Annual interest expenses	18% × $3,000 = $540	12% × $3,000 = $360
Annual fee	$0	$30
Total annual expenses	**$540**	**$390**

The annual interest expenses can be determined from knowing the average monthly balance over the year. The higher the average monthly balance, the higher your interest expenses because you will have to pay interest on the balance.

Notice that credit card X results in $540 in annual interest expenses, which is $180 more than the annual interest expenses from credit card Y. Thus, while credit card X does not charge the annual fee, your interest expenses from using credit card X could be very high. The high interest expenses more than offset the advantage of no annual fee.

If you have always paid off your balance in the month that it occurred, you would not have any interest expenses. In this case, the interest rate on the credit card would not be important, and you may prefer credit card X because it does not have an annual fee. That is, you would benefit from no annual fee, and would not be adversely affected by the high interest rate.

As mentioned earlier, some credit cards offer a low "teaser rate" to entice you to apply for that card. Be aware, however, that this rate is likely to be available only for a short time before the normal interest rate is charged.

Maximum Limit. Some credit cards allow a higher maximum limit on monthly purchases than others. A very high maximum may not be necessary, and may tempt you to spend excessively. Make sure that the maximum limit is high enough to cover any nec-

8.4 Financial Planning Online: The Best Credit Card for You

Go to
http://www.bankrate.com/brm/rate/cc_home.asp

This Web site provides links to help you get the best overall credit card rate, the lowest introductory rate, frequent flier credit cards, and other special features.

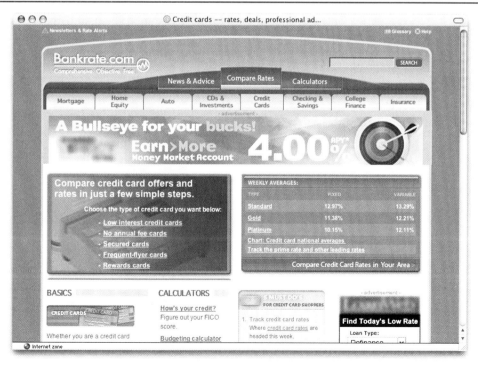

Some individuals use their money to invest in risky investments (such as stocks) rather than pay off their credit card bills. They apparently believe that their return from the investments will be higher than the cost of financing. Although some investments have generated large returns in specific years, it is difficult to earn returns that consistently exceed the high costs of financing with credit cards. If the thrill of a good return on your investment makes you think about delaying your credit card payment, consider the following logic. When you use money to pay your credit card bill immediately, you are preventing a charge of about 20 percent interest. Therefore, you have effectively increased your savings by 20 percent by using these funds to pay off the credit card debt.

EXAMPLE

Stephanie Spratt just received a credit card bill for $700. The sponsoring financial institution charges a 20 percent annual interest rate on the outstanding balance. Stephanie has sufficient funds in her checking account to pay the credit card bill, but she is considering financing her payment. If she pays $100 toward the credit card bill and finances the remaining $600 for one year, she will incur interest expenses of:

$$\text{Interest} = \text{Loan Amount} \times \text{Interest Rate}$$

$$= \$600 \times .20$$

$$= \$120.$$

She could use the $600 to invest in savings rather than pay off her credit card bill. After one year, the $600 in a savings account will accumulate to $618 based on a 3 percent annual interest rate, as shown here:

$$\text{Interest Earned on Deposit} = \text{Initial Deposit} \times \text{Interest Rate}$$

$$= \$600 \times .03$$

$$= 18.$$

Her interest owed on the credit card loan ($120) exceeds the interest earned on the deposit ($18) in one year by $102. Stephanie decides that she would be better off using her cash to pay off the credit card bill immediately. By using her money to cover the credit card bill, she gives up the opportunity to earn 3 percent on that money, but she also avoids the 20 percent rate charged on the credit card loan. Thus, her wealth is $102 higher as a result of using funds to pay off the credit card bill rather than investing in a bank deposit. Although she could have used the funds to invest in a high-risk investment that might achieve a greater return, paying off the credit card guarantees that she can avoid a 20 percent financing rate.

Use Savings if Necessary to Pay the Credit Card Bill on Time

If your cash inflows are not sufficient to cover your credit card bill, you should pull funds from savings (if there is no penalty for withdrawal) to cover the payment.

If You Cannot Avoid Credit Card Debt, Pay It Off before Other Debt

If you cannot pay off your credit card balance in full each month with income or with savings, at least pay off this balance as soon as possible and cut back your discretionary spending. If you have other debt outstanding, you should pay off credit card debt first (assuming that the credit card debt has a higher interest rate). Even if you cannot pay your bill in full, you should still attempt to pay as much as possible so that you can minimize finance charges.

If possible, you may even consider taking out a home equity loan (discussed in the next chapter) to pay any credit card bills so that you can avoid the high interest expenses. This strategy makes sense only if your credit card debt is substantial (such as several thousand dollars), and the interest rate on the home equity loan is less than that on your credit card.

8.6 Financial Planning Online: Estimating the Time Necessary to Pay Off Your Balance

Go to
http://www.free-financial-advice.net/time-to-pay-debt.html

This Web site provides estimates of the time it will take to pay off your credit cards utilizing different monthly payments.

Avoid Credit Repair Services

Companies that offer credit repair services claim to be able to solve your credit problems. For example, they may help you fix a mistake on your credit report. However, you could have done this yourself, without paying for the service. If you have made late credit payments or have defaulted on a loan, a credit repair service does not have the power to remove such credit information from your report.

DEALING WITH CREDIT DEBT

If you find yourself with an excessive credit balance, there are several steps you can take. First, spend as little as possible. Then, consider how you can obtain funds to meet your monthly payment or to pay off your balance. Get a job if you don't have one, or work more hours at your current job. However, for students, additional work could disrupt your school schedule. An alternative solution is to borrow funds from a family member. You will now have a monthly loan payment to a family member rather than credit card balances, but the payments may be lower. Another possibility is a debt consolidation loan from a financial institution. The structured schedule for paying off the loan in a set time period will instill more discipline in you than meeting a low minimum monthly payment on a credit card. If you do not choose to get a loan, you should still discipline yourself to make more than the minimum payment on your credit card.

You might even consider selling some assets to obtain cash, such as trading in a relatively new car for an old car. Also consider ways of reducing your everyday expenses. For example, if you have large monthly payments due to your cell phone, you could discontinue the use of a cell phone. If you have your own apartment, you may consider getting a roommate.

personal bankruptcy
a plan to the court in which you repay at least a portion of your debt and pay attorney and filing fees.

If all else fails, you may need to file for **personal bankruptcy**. In this case, you propose a plan to the court for repaying at least a portion of your debt and pay attorney and court filing fees. The two types of personal bankruptcy plans are known as Chapter 7 and Chapter 13. Chapter 7 allows the discharge of almost all debts, but you may also

How do credit and retail cards generate revenue? What is the biggest disadvantage of a proprietary card?

5. What is a credit limit? How can you increase your credit limit?

6. How might you eliminate the annual fees that are charged by some credit cards?

7. Discuss how credit cards offer incentives to use the cards. How else might credit card companies reward cardholders with excellent credit ratings?

8. What is a grace period? How can you use it to your advantage?

9. When is a finance charge applied to credit purchases? What are teaser rates? What is the common range of interest rates on credit cards?

10. What is a cash advance? How are they commonly obtained? Discuss interest rates and grace periods with regard to cash advances.

11. List some items that appear on the credit card statement. What accounts for the difference between your previous balance and your new balance?

12. What should you consider when comparing credit cards?

13. List five tips for using credit cards wisely.

14. Should you view credit cards as a source of funds? Why or why not? Why should you self-impose a tight credit limit?

15. Why is paying your credit card balance in full so important? What should you do if you can't avoid credit card debt? Explain.

16. What credit management decisions should be included in your financial plan?

17. Discuss some ways that charging large amounts on your credit cards might affect your overall financial planning.

18. What are the three methods used by financial institutions to calculate finance charges on outstanding credit card balances? Briefly describe how interest is computed under each method.

VIDEO QUESTIONS

1. If you cannot immediately get rid of your credit card debt, what steps should you take?

2. Credit cards are a big part of everyday life in the U.S. How does Sarah Rose of *Money Magazine* suggest avoiding credit card problems?

3. Eric Tyson, one of the personal finance advisers in the segment, explained how to calculate consumer debt level. According to Mr. Tyson, what is an acceptable percentage of consumer debt?

FINANCIAL PLANNING PROBLEMS

1. You just borrowed $7,500 and are charged a simple interest rate of 8 percent. How much interest do you pay each year?

2. Jarrod has narrowed his choice to two credit cards that may meet his needs. Card A has an APR of 21 percent. Card B has an APR of 14 percent, but also charges a $25 annual fee. Jarrod will not pay off his balance each month, but will carry a balance forward of about $400 each month. Which credit card should he choose?

3. Paul's credit card closes on the 9th of the month, and his payment is due on the 30th. If Paul purchases a stereo for $300 on June 12, how many interest-free days will he have? When will he have to pay for the stereo in full in order to avoid finance charges?

4. Chrissy currently has a credit card that charges 15 percent interest. She usually carries a balance of about $500. Chrissy has received an offer for a new credit card with a teaser rate of 3 percent for the first three months; after that, the rate goes to 19.5 percent. What will her total annual interest be with her current card? What will her interest be the first year after she switches? Should she switch?

5. Margie has had a tough month. First, she had dental work that cost $700. Next, she had her car transmission rebuilt, which cost $1,400. She put both of these unexpected expenses on her credit card. If she does not pay her credit card balance when due, she will be charged 15 percent interest. Margie has $15,000 in a money market account that pays 5 percent interest. How much interest would she pay (annualized) if she does not pay off her credit card balance? How much interest will she lose if she writes the check out of her money market account? Should she write the check?

6. Troy has a credit card that charges 18 percent on outstanding balances and on cash advances. The closing date on the credit card is the first of each month. Last month Troy left a balance on his credit card of $200. This month Troy took out a cash advance of $150 and made $325 in purchases. Troy made a payment of $220. What will the total of Troy's new balance be on his next credit card statement, taking into account finance charges?

7. Eileen is a college student who consistently uses her credit card as a source of funds. She has maxed out her credit card at the $6,000 limit. Eileen does not plan on increasing her credit card balance any further, but has already been declined for a car loan on a badly needed vehicle due to her existing credit card debt. Her credit card charges her 20 percent annually on outstanding balances. If Eileen does not reduce her credit card debt, how much will she pay annually to her credit card company?

Question 8 requires a financial calculator.

8. Eileen (from question 7) desires a car that costs $12,000. How long would it have taken Eileen to save for the outright purchase of the car if she did not have any credit card debt and used the interest payments to save for the purchase of the car? Eileen can invest funds in an account paying 8 percent interest.

Ethical Dilemma

9. Chen recently graduated from college and accepted a job in a new city. Furnishing his apartment has proven more costly than he anticipated. To assist him with making purchases, he applied for and received a credit card with a $5,000 credit limit. Chen planned to pay off the balance over six months.

   Six months later Chen finds that other expenses incurred in starting a new career have restricted him to making only minimum payments. Not only that, he has borrowed on his card to the full extent of its credit limit. Upon returning from work today, Chen finds a letter from the credit card company offering to increase his limit to $10,000 because he has been a good customer and has not missed a payment.

   a. Discuss the ethics of credit card companies that offer to increase credit limits to individuals who make only minimum payments and who have maxed out their card.

   b. Should Chen accept the credit card company's offer?

FINANCIAL PLANNING ONLINE EXERCISES

1. Go to http://banking.yahoo.com. Under "Tools" click on "Rates."

   a. Check the rates on savings deposits, personal loans, auto loans, and 30-year mortgages. What are the most attractive rates for each category?

   b. Go back to the previous page. Under "Banking Education" click on "Managing Credit Cards." Review the information about credit cards. What are some common factors that may your ability to qualify for a credit card?

   c. Under "Banking Education" click on "Bank Accounts & Services." Then click on "Setting Up Direct Deposit" under "Managing Your Checking Account." What are some of the benefits of direct deposit? Are there risks?

2. Go to http://www.calcbuilder.com/cgi-bin/calcs/ CRE1.cgi/yahoo_banking

   a. Input $2,000 as the amount owed on your credit card, $150 future monthly charges, $350 future monthly payments, 19 percent annual interest rate, and zero as the annual fee. Click on "graphs."

   b. Click on "inputs." Change the annual interest rate to 7 percent. Click on "graphs." How do the time to pay off the debt and the total interest expenses change?

   c. Click on "inputs." Using the same interest rate of 7 percent, increase the future monthly payments to $450. Click on "graphs." What is the effect on interest expense and the time to pay off the debt?

   d. Click on "inputs." Using the interest rate of 7 percent and payments of $350, reduce future monthly charges to $100. How does this alter the interest expense and the time to pay off the debt?

BUILDING YOUR OWN FINANCIAL PLAN

Good credit decisions involve using credit properly and selecting the best sources of credit. The exercises in this case will assist you in the decisions regarding the use and selection of credit cards. They will help you determine how long it will take to pay off credit card debt you might have accrued and help you evaluate the many credit cards currently on the market.

Go to the worksheets at the end of this chapter, and to the CD-ROM accompanying this text, to continue building your financial plan.

THE SAMPSONS—A CONTINUING CASE

The Sampsons have been carrying a balance of about $2,000 on their credit card. They have been paying the minimum amount due and have been using any excess net cash flows to implement their new savings plan for a new car and their children's college education. To date, they have saved $2,000; they are currently earning 5 percent on the savings. Meanwhile, their credit card is charging them 18 percent. Dave and Sharon want to evaluate the return they are receiving from their savings versus the interest expenses they are accruing on their credit card.

Go to the worksheets at the end of this chapter, and to the CD-ROM accompanying this text, to continue this case.

PART 2: BRAD BROOKS—A CONTINUING CASE

Brad Brooks is pleased with your assistance in preparing his personal financial statements and your suggestions for improving his personal financial situation. He has called you for guidance on questions that have come to mind after reviewing the information you have given him to date.

First, he wants to know what bank and brokerage firm he should move his accounts to. He is mostly interested in financial institutions that will assist him in making investment and money management decisions. He finds savings accounts boring and has no desire to have one because the interest rate is so low.

Brad is also concerned about his liquidity. His credit card (with a $35 annual fee and 18 percent interest rate) is nearing its credit limit of $10,000. He is reluctant to sell his stocks to get cash to pay off part of the credit balance; he thinks they could double in value over the next five years.

Brad is questioning whether to pay off his credit card. He can easily afford the $200 monthly payment and sees no reason to pay off the balance.

Go to the worksheets at the end of this chapter, and to the CD-ROM accompanying this text, to continue this case.

Chapter 8: Building Your Own Financial Plan

GOALS

1. Establish a credit limit that will enable you to pay credit card balances in full each month.
2. Select credit cards that will provide the most favorable terms at the lowest cost.

ANALYSIS

1. Referring to your personal cash flow statement, determine how much excess cash inflows you have each month. Based on this amount, set a self-imposed credit limit each month so that you can pay off your balance in full. if you have existing credit card debt, use the worksheet below to determine how many months it will take you to pay off your balance at three different monthly payment amounts. (The Excel worksheet will perform the calculations for you.) Revise your cash flow statement based on your decisions.

	Alternative 1	Alternative 2	Alternative 3
Credit Card Debt			
Monthly Payment			
Interest Rate per Year			
Months to Pay Off Debt			

2. Use the following worksheet to select a credit card with favorable terms. Rate the cards from 5 being the best in a category to 1 being the worst.

Bank Credit Card Scorecard

Question	Credit Card Issuer				
	1	2	3	4	5
1. Annual fee					
2. Interest rate on purchases					
3. Interest rate on cash advances					
4. Transaction fee for cash advances					
5. Insurance on purchases					
6. Credit earned toward purchases at selected businesses					
7. Frequent flyer miles					
8. Free delivery on mail order purchases					
9. Phone card capability					
10. Credit limit available					
Total					

DECISIONS

1. What is your self-imposed credit limit each month for future credit card purchases? How much of your cash inflows do you need to allot each month to paying off existing credit card debt?

_____

_____

_____

_____

_____

_____

_____

_____

_____

_____

_____

_____

_____

_____

_____

2. What credit cards offer the most favorable terms for your needs?

_____

_____

_____

_____

_____

_____

_____

_____

_____

_____

_____

_____

_____

Chapter 8: The Sampsons—A Continuing Case

CASE QUESTIONS

1. Compare the amount of interest that the Sampsons are earning on their savings and paying on their credit card debt by completing the following worksheet.

Savings

Interest rate earned on savings	5%
Savings balance	
Annual interest earned on savings	

Paying Off Credit Balance

Interest rate paid on credit	18%
Credit balance	
Annual interest paid on credit	

2. Advise the Sampsons on whether they should continue making minimum payments on their credit card or use money from their savings to pay off the credit balance.

_____

_____

_____

_____

_____

_____

_____

3. Explain how the Sampsons' credit card decisions are related to their budget.

_____

_____

_____

_____

_____

_____

Part 2: Brad Brooks—A Continuing Case

CASE QUESTIONS

1. Assuming that you could convince Brad to maintain checking, savings, and retirement accounts, discuss the pros and cons of various types of financial institutions where Brad could maintain his
   a. checking account
   b. savings account
   c. retirement accounts

   Be sure to comment on Brad's idea to find financial institutions that can give him advice on his financial decisions.

   _____

   _____

   _____

   _____

   _____

   _____

2. If Brad's stocks double in value over the next five years, what annual return would he realize? (Hint: Use the future value table.) Based on his projected annualized return, would it be advisable to sell the stocks to pay off his credit card? Should Brad consider shopping for a new credit card?

   _____

   _____

   _____

   _____

   _____

   _____

3. How would you address Brad's reluctance to pay off his credit card balance? Show him what he could earn in five years if he paid it off and invested the interest saved at 6 percent.

   Future Value of a Lump Sum

Yearly Savings	
Number of Periods	
Interest Rate per Period	
Future Value	

4. Would your advice change if Brad were:

   a. 45 years old?

   b. 60 years old?

5. In talking to Brad, you mentioned the increasing threat of identify theft. Brad seems concerned and after asking him several questions, you determine the following:

   a. For convenience, Brad has his driver's license number printed on his checks. He also uses checks to make virtually all payments, including transactions with local merchants. Brad has a debit card, but seldom uses it.

   b. Since Brad drives past the Post Office to and from work each day, he maintains a Post Office box and mails all letters and payments at the Post Office.

   c. Brad has several credit cards in his wallet, but uses only one regularly. He also carries his Social Security card, as he can never remember the number.

   d. Brad recycles, including old invoices, credit card statements, and bank statements after retaining them for the appropriate legal time period.

   e. Brad uses his cell phone for virtually all his telephone calls, including ordering merchandise and paying by credit card.

   Comment on each of the above in terms of the risk of identity theft and make recommendations to Brad for appropriate changes that will reduce his risk of exposure to identity theft.

6. Prepare a written or oral report on your findings and recommendations for Brad.

_____

_____

_____

_____

_____

_____

_____

_____

_____

_____

_____

_____

_____

_____

_____

_____

_____

_____

_____

_____

_____

_____

_____

_____

_____

_____

_____

Personal Financing

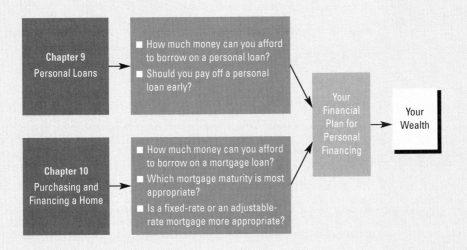

THE CHAPTERS IN THIS PART EXPLAIN HOW YOU CAN USE CREDIT TO obtain funds to support your spending. Chapter 9 describes the process of obtaining a personal loan for a large purchase such as a car and the types of decisions that you need to make when considering a personal loan. Chapter 10 describes the process of obtaining a mortgage and the types of decisions that you need to make when considering a mortgage loan. Your decisions regarding whether to borrow, how much to borrow, and how to borrow will affect your cash flows and wealth.

Chapter 9

Personal Loans

Karen realized that her car was facing some serious mainte-nance issues, and decided to lease a new car. The monthly lease was $499.35 and she was allowed to drive 15,000 miles per year with extra miles charged at $0.25 per mile. After 18 months, however, Karen began to tire of the large monthly payments. She went back to the auto dealer to explore ending the lease early. The dealership told her that in order to end the lease, she must pay $7,350. Karen only had two real choices: buying the car outright or continuing the lease to its three-year term. Ending the lease was not a financially attractive option.

You may be faced with a similar decision in your future. The time to make a "lease versus buy" decision is before the lease is signed or before the car is purchased. Once committed to either action, you most likely will need to remain committed to your course.

This chapter focuses on your use of personal loans to finance large purchases. Proper decisions on whether to obtain a personal loan, which source to use for a personal loan, how much to borrow, and what terms to arrange can have a significant impact on your finan-cial situation.

The objectives of this chapter are to:

- Provide a background on personal loans

- Outline the types of interest rates that are charged on personal loans

- Describe home equity loans

- Discuss car loans

- Explain how to decide between financing the purchase of a car and leasing a car

- Describe the key features of student loans

BACKGROUND ON PERSONAL LOANS

Consumers commonly obtain a personal loan to finance a large purchase such as a car. A personal loan is different from access to credit (from a credit card) in that it is normally used to finance one large purchase and has a specific repayment schedule. The loan is provided at the time of your purchase and is used along with your cash down payment to cover the entire purchase price. You can pay off the personal loan on an installment basis, for example, by making a payment each month for the next 48 months.

The first step in obtaining a personal loan is to identify possible sources of financing and evaluate the possible loan terms.

Sources of Loans

The most common source of financing is a personal loan from a financial institution. Commercial banks, savings institutions, finance companies, and credit unions all provide personal loans. Some finance companies are subsidiaries of automobile manufacturers that finance car purchases. For example, GMAC Financial Services is a finance company that is owned by General Motors. Savings institutions are the primary lenders to individuals who need mortgage loans, the subject of Chapter 10.

An alternative source of financing is one or more family members or friends. If they trust that you will repay the loan on time and in full, they may be willing to provide you with a loan that earns the same interest rate as their savings account. You could also offer to pay an interest rate on the loan that is a few percentage points above the savings rate. By borrowing funds from family and friends, you can often get a more favorable rate than financial institutions offer. The loan agreement should be in writing and signed by all parties to avoid any possible misinterpretations.

The Personal Loan Process

The process of applying for a personal loan from a financial institution involves filling out the application, negotiating the loan contract, and negotiating the interest rate. A sample loan application is shown in Exhibit 9.1.

Application Process. When applying for a loan, you need to provide information from your personal balance sheet and personal cash flow statement to document your ability to repay the loan.

- **Personal Balance Sheet.** Recall from Chapter 2 that your financial condition is partially measured by a personal balance sheet. The personal balance sheet indicates your assets, liabilities, and net worth at a specific point in time. The assets are relevant because they may serve as possible collateral to back a loan. The liabilities are relevant because they represent your existing debts.

- **Personal Cash Flow Statement.** Your financial condition is also represented by your personal cash flow statement, as discussed in Chapter 2. This statement indicates your cash inflows and cash outflows and therefore suggests how much free cash flow you have on a periodic basis. Lenders use this cash flow information to determine whether you qualify for a loan and, if so, the maximum size of

Exhibit 9.1 An Example of a Loan Application

DCU Digital Federal Credit Union
141 PARKER STREET • PO BOX 125 • MAYNARD, MA 01754-0125
800-328-8797 • WEB SITE: www.dcu.org • E-MAIL: dcu@dcu.org

Loan application

Vehicle: ☐ Purchasing   ☐ RV/Boat
☐ Refinance   ☐ Motorcycle

Loan Amount or monthly payment amount $_____   Loan Term_____ months

BORROWER

Member #	SS#
Name	Date of Birth
Home Address	
City	State Zip
Home Phone #	Work Phone #
# of Dependents/Ages	
Own / Rent / Board (circle one) Payment Amount	How Long?
Mortgage/Landlord Name	
Employer Name	Date of Hire
Previous Employer From	To
Checking Account Institution	

CO-BORROWER/COSIGNER

Member #	SS#
Name	Date of Birth
Home Address	
City	State Zip
Home Phone #	Work Phone #
# of Dependents/Ages	
Employer Name	Date of Hire

M730A (3/2000)

Monthly Gross Income (please attach verification of income). Alimony, child support, or separate maintenance income need not be revealed if you do not wish to have it considered as a basis for repaying this obligation.

	Gross Income	Overtime	Other
Borrower	$	$	$
Co-Borrower	$	$	$

Are you obligated to pay alimony, child support, separate maintenance? If yes, amount $_____ per_____

SIGNATURES REQUIRED BELOW

Subject to Digital Federal Credit Union (DCU) Loan Underwriting Guidelines.

BY SIGNING THIS APPLICATION YOU AGREE TO THE FOLLOWING: You agree that we may obtain and use consumer credit reports and exchange credit and employment information in connection with this application and any update, renewal, or extension of credit we may extend to you. You agree, upon approval of this loan, that you will ensure DCU is properly listed as lienholder on the vehicle title as: Digital Federal Credit Union, 141 Parker Street, Maynard, MA 01754. You agree that your account will be subject to the terms and conditions of all applicable Loan Agreements and Disclosure Statements. You agree that a photocopy or facsimile of this application shall be as binding as the original. You understand that we will retain this application whether or not it is approved. Everything you have stated in this application is correct.

Borrower's Signature _____ Date _____

Co-Borrower's/Cosigner's Signature _____ Date _____

CREDIT LIFE/DISABILITY INSURANCE

☐ I am interested in obtaining Credit Life and/or Disability Insurance. Please send me more information.

ELECTRONIC PAYMENT METHOD

By selecting one of the two electronic payment methods below, you agree to the following as applicable:

DCU Initiated Automatic Transfer: You authorize us to initiate a transfer of sufficient funds from the DCU account indicated to pay all amounts due monthly. The transfers will be made as indicated below. You agree you are responsible for maintaining a sufficient balance to cover the amount of the payment and that the funds will be available to transfer as of the start of business on the scheduled transfer date. We will only transfer from the available balance in the account you have designated. If there are insufficient funds, the available funds will be transferred but your payment may be considered late.

Member Initiated Loan Payment Via PC Branch or Easy Touch Telephone Teller: You agree to initiate and complete one or more loan payment transactions via either the "Account Transfer" or "Automatic Transfer" PC Branch option or the "Loan Payment Transaction" Easy Touch Telephone Teller option each month on or before the loan payment due date. You understand that you will not receive a coupon book or monthly bill. You accept responsibility and agree that you will have paid no less than the Monthly Payment Due to your loan by 5:00 p.m. on the payment due date each month.

PLEASE SELECT ONE OF THE FOLLOWING:

☐ **DCU Initiated Automatic Transfer**
Frequency:
☐ Weekly (Friday)   ☐ Monthly (On the payment due date or business day closest to but not before)

Transfer From:
☐ DCU Primary Savings   ☐ DCU Checking
Member #_____   Account #_____

☐ **Member Initiated PC Branch or Easy Touch Telephone Teller**

☐ **Coupon Book** (non-Electronic)

You understand that direct deposit and use of an Electronic Payment Method is voluntary and is not a factor in whether the loan will be granted. However, both are required to obtain the reduced interest rate.

We reserve the right to terminate this payment method and adjust the annual percentage rate if the privilege is abused. Termination will not affect prior transactions nor your responsibility to repay the entire amount.

Borrower's Signature _____ Date _____

Co-Borrower's/Cosigner's Signature _____ Date _____

Internal Use Only
Member #_____, Loan#_____
Processed By #_____, Date____/____/____

the loan that you deserve. An individual with existing loans or credit card debt may have insufficient cash flows to cover the payments on any additional loans.

The key component of the personal cash flow statement of most prospective borrowers is their income. Lenders require income documentation, such as a Form W-2, which indicates annual earnings, or pay stubs, which indicate recent salary.

loan contract
A contract that specifies the terms of a loan, as agreed to by the borrower and the lender.

Loan Contract. If the lender approves your loan application, it will work with you to develop a **loan contract**, which specifies the terms of the loan, as agreed to by the borrower and the lender. Specifically, the loan contract identifies the amount of the loan, interest rate, repayment schedule, maturity, and collateral.

- **Amount of the Loan.** The amount of the loan is based on how much the lender believes you can pay back in the future. You should borrow only the amount of funds that you will need because you will be charged interest on the entire amount that you borrow.

- **Interest Rate.** The interest rate is critical because it determines the cost incurred on a personal loan. It must be specified in a loan contract. More information about interest rates is provided in a later section.

amortize
To repay the principal of a loan (the original amount loaned out) through a series of equal payments. A loan repaid in this manner is said to be amortized.

- **Loan Repayment Schedule.** Personal loans are usually **amortized**, which means that the principal (original amount loaned out) is repaid through a series of equal payments. Each loan repayment includes both interest owed and a portion of the principal. As more of the principal is paid down, the amount of interest is reduced, and a larger portion of the payment is used to repay principal.

maturity
With respect to a loan, the life or duration of the loan.

- **Maturity.** A loan contract specifies the **maturity**, or life of the loan. A longer maturity for a loan results in lower monthly payments and therefore makes it easier to cover the payments each month. For example, the monthly payment on a five-year loan for $16,000 may be $100 less than the payment on a four-year loan for the same amount. With the five-year loan, however, you are in debt for an additional year, and you pay more interest over the life of the loan than you would on the four-year loan. In general, you should select a maturity on personal loans that is as short as possible, as long as you allow yourself sufficient liquidity. If you have extra funds during the time you have a loan, you should consider paying off the loan early for two reasons. First, you can reduce the total amount of interest by paying off the loan early. Second, you will be able to save the money that you would otherwise have used to make the loan payments.

collateral
Assets of a borrower that back a secured loan in the event that the borrower defaults.

- **Collateral.** A loan agreement also describes the **collateral**, or assets of the borrower (if any) that back the loan in the event that the borrower defaults. When a loan is used to purchase a specific asset, that asset is commonly used as collateral. For example, if your purchase of a boat is partly financed, the boat would serve as collateral. That is, the lender could repossess the boat if you were unable to make the loan payments. Some loans are backed by assets other than those purchased with the loan. For example, a boat loan could be backed by stocks that you own.

secured loan
A loan that is backed or secured by collateral.

unsecured loan
A loan that is not backed by collateral.

A loan that is backed or secured by collateral is referred to as a **secured loan**; a loan that is not backed by collateral is an **unsecured loan**. In general, you will receive more favorable terms (such as a lower interest rate) on a secured loan because the lender has less to lose in the event that the loan is not repaid.

payday loan
A short-term loan provided in advance of a paycheck.

A **payday loan** is a short-term loan provided to you if you need funds in advance of receiving your paycheck. To obtain a payday loan, you write a check to the lender for the amount of the loan plus the interest. You date the check for the date in the future when you will receive your paycheck. The payday loan firm will hold the check until that time and will cash it then because your checking account will have sufficient funds. After you provide this check to the payday loan firm, it provides you with your loan in cash or by transmitting funds into your checking account.

As an example, assume that you need $400 for some immediate purpose, but will not have any money until you receive your paycheck one week from today. You provide the payday loan firm a check dated one week from today. Be aware that firms such as Cash King, Cash One, CheckMate, and EZLoans, which provide payday loans, charge a high rate of interest on these short-term loans. The payday loan firm may request that your payment be $440, which reflects the loan of $400 and $40 interest and/or fees. You are paying $40 more than the loan you received, which reflects 10 percent of the loan amount. The cost of financing a payday loan is shown below.

"A high-five isn't binding, sir. You still have to sign a loan agreement."

http://www.cartoonstock.com

$$\text{Cost of Financing} = 10 \text{ percent} \times (\text{number of days in a year/number of days in which you have the loan})$$
$$= 10\% \times (365/7)$$
$$= 521\%.$$

9.1 Financial Planning Online: Loan Request Online

This is not a misprint. It is within the typical range of the cost of financing charged for payday loans.

While states have usury laws that place a limit on the maximum interest rate that can be charged, the payday loan firms have circumvented that limit by referring to the interest as fees. Some states recognize that the fees are really interest payments and prevent payday firms from establishing businesses. However, payday loan firms can reside in the states that allow them and still reach residents in any state via the Internet.

You should avoid payday loans for the following reasons. First, by using your next paycheck to cover a loan payment, you may not have sufficient cash available to make normal purchases after covering the loan. Thus, you may need another loan to cover your purchases in that period, and this can create a continual cycle in which your paycheck is always needed to repay short-term loans.

Second, as we have seen, the cost of financing with a payday loan is outrageous. Consider how much you would have paid in interest on $400 if you were able to get a loan that charged you a more reasonable rate such as 10 percent annually.

$$\text{Interest rate for a 7-day period} = 10\% \times (7/365)$$
$$= .192\%.$$

The interest to be paid = $400 \times .192$ percent = $0.76. Thus, you would pay less than $1 interest on a seven-day loan if you were charged a 10 percent annualized interest rate. This is substantially less than the interest you would be charged by a payday loan firm. The payday loan firms are able to charge excessive rates because some people who need money quickly may not be creditworthy and therefore have difficulty obtaining funds from other sources. Alternatively, some borrowers do not realize how high the cost of financing is when they borrow money from a payday loan firm.

The simple solution is to avoid borrowing money until you have the funds to spend. But if you have to borrow, there are alternative ways of financing that are not as expensive. For example, perhaps you can borrow funds from a friend or family member for a week. Or you may be able to obtain credit through your credit card. While relying on credit card financing is not recommended, it is substantially wiser than financing through a payday loan. To illustrate, assume that you could have used a credit card to make your $400 purchase. Also assume that the rate on your credit card is 18 percent annually, or 1.5 percent over one month. In this case, your cost of financing would be 400×1.5percent = $6. This financing cost for one month is much lower than the cost of financing when using a payday loan, and in this example the credit card financing lasts three weeks longer than the payday financing period.

Cosigning. Some borrowers are only able to obtain a personal loan if someone with a stronger credit history cosigns. The cosigner is responsible for any unpaid balance if the borrower does not repay the loan. If the borrower defaults and the cosigner does not repay the loan, the lender has the right to sue the cosigner or to try to seize his assets, just as if he were the borrower. In addition, cosigning on a loan can restrict the amount that the cosigner is able to borrow. Therefore, you should only be willing to consign a loan if you trust the borrower and will not need to borrow funds for yourself in the near future.

Focus on Ethics: Predatory Lending
Watch out for dishonest predatory lenders who use illegal practices. Several of the more common predatory lending practices are listed here:

- A lender charges high loan fees, which cause the financing cost to be much higher than the quoted interest rate.

- A lender provides a home equity loan with the expectation that the loan will not be repaid because the lender wants to take ownership of the collateral backing the loan.

- A lender stipulates that a loan will only be provided if the borrower purchases insurance or other financial services.

- A lender includes a large balloon payment at the end of a loan that will require additional financing to pay off.

- A loan agreement includes confusing information that does not clearly disclose the borrower's obligations.

Borrowers who accept these kinds of terms often think they have no alternative, but shopping around for the best loan terms and interest rates is always the best option. There are several other steps you can take to protect yourself. Be wary of any lenders who pursue you with high-pressure tactics. Short-term offers and up-front application fees also indicate a disreputable lender. Always make sure you understand the loan terms before signing a loan agreement. If you cannot obtain reasonable loan terms, reconsider whether you truly need a loan at this time.

INTEREST RATES ON PERSONAL LOANS

The three most common types of interest rates financial institutions use to measure the interest due on personal loans are the annual percentage rate, simple interest, and add-on interest.

Annual Percentage Rate

annual percentage rate (APR)
A rate that measures the finance expenses (including interest and other expenses) on a loan annually.

As a result of the Truth-in-Lending Act (1969), lenders are required to disclose a standardized loan rate with directly comparable interest expenses over the life of the loan. This makes it easier for you to compare loans offered by different lenders and select the best loan. The **annual percentage rate (APR)** measures the finance expenses (including interest and all other expenses) on a loan annually.

EXAMPLE   Suppose that you have a choice of borrowing $2,000 over the next year from Bank A, Bank B, or Bank C. Bank A offers an interest rate of 10 percent on its loan. Bank B offers an interest rate of 8 percent, but also charges a fee of $100 at the time the loan is granted. Bank C offers an interest rate of 6 percent, but charges a loan fee of $200 at the time the loan is granted. Exhibit 9.2 shows the APRs.

In this example, Bank A offers the lowest APR for a one-year loan. Even though its interest rate is higher, its total financing costs are lower than those charged by the other banks because it does not have any fees. Thus, the APR on its loan is equal to the interest rate charged on the loan. In contrast, the APRs on the loans provided by Banks B and C are much higher than the interest rate charged on their loans because of the fees.

Simple Interest

simple interest
Interest on a loan computed as a percentage of the existing loan amount (or principal).

Simple interest is the interest computed as a percentage of the existing loan amount (or principal). It is measured using the principal, the interest rate applied to the principal, and the loan's time to maturity (in years). The loan repayment schedule is easily determined by a computer or a calculator or even on various Web sites. If you input the loan amount, the interest rate, and the loan maturity, the loan repayment schedule will provide you with the following information:

- The monthly payment.

- The amount of each monthly payment applied to pay interest.

- The amount of each monthly payment applied to pay down the loan principal.

- The outstanding loan balance that remains after each monthly payment.

The size of the monthly payment is dependent on the size of the loan, the interest rate, and the maturity. The larger the loan amount, the larger the monthly payment. The higher the interest rate, the larger the monthly payment. For a given loan amount and interest rate, the longer the period over which the loan is repaid (e.g., 36 months versus 24 months), the smaller the monthly payment. As mentioned earlier, however, the longer the maturity, the more you will pay in interest expenses.

EXAMPLE   You obtain a loan of $2,000 that is based on the simple interest method with an annual interest rate of 12 percent (1 percent per month) and 12 equal monthly payments. Given this information, a computer generates the loan repayment schedule in Exhibit 9.3. Notice at the top of the exhibit that each monthly payment is $177.70. Each payment consists of an interest payment and a portion that goes to repay the loan principal. At the end of the first month, the interest owed on $2,000 based on a monthly interest rate of 1 percent is:

Exhibit 9.2 Measurement of the Annual Percentage Rate

	Interest Expenses	Other Finance Expenses	Total Finance Expenses	Number of Years	Average Annual Finance Expenses	Annual Percentage Rate (APR)*
Bank A	$200	0	$200	1	$200	$200/$2,000 = 10%
Bank B	160	$100	260	1	260	$260/$2,000 = 13%
Bank C	120	200	320	1	320	$320/$2,000 = 16%

*The APR is calculated by dividing the average annual finance expenses by the average annual loan balance.

Exhibit 9.3 Example of Loan Repayment Schedule: One-Year Loan, 12 Percent Interest Rate (Monthly Payment = $177.70)

Month	Interest Payment	Payment of Principal	Outstanding Loan Balance
			$2,000.00
1	$20.00	$157.70	1,842.30
2	18.42	159.28	1,683.02
3	16.83	160.87	1,522.16
4	15.22	162.48	1,359.68
5	13.60	164.10	1,195.58
6	11.96	165.74	1,029.84
7	10.30	167.40	862.44
8	8.63	169.07	693.37
9	6.94	170.76	522.61
10	5.23	172.47	350.13
11	3.50	174.20	175.94
12	1.76	175.94	0

$$\text{Interest Owed} = \text{Outstanding Loan Balance} \times \text{Interest Rate}$$
$$= \$2,000 \times .01$$
$$= \$20.$$

Since the total payment is $177.70, and the interest payment is $20, the remainder ($157.70) is applied to pay down the principal. The outstanding loan balance after one month is:

$$\text{Outstanding Loan Balance} = \text{Previous Balance} - \text{Principal Payment}$$
$$= \$2,000 - \$157.70$$
$$= \$1,842.30.$$

At the end of the second month, the interest rate of 1 percent is applied to the outstanding balance to determine the interest payment:

$$\text{Interest Owed} = \$1,842.30 \times .01$$
$$= \$18.42.$$

This same process is followed to determine the amount of interest that is paid each month. The remainder of each payment is applied to pay off the principal. As each month passes, the outstanding loan balance is reduced, so the interest payment in the following month is reduced. The total monthly payment remains the same for all months, so the principal payment increases over time.

add-on interest method
A method of determining the monthly payment on a loan; involves calculating interest that must be paid on the loan amount, adding together interest and loan principal, and dividing by the number of payments.

Add-On Interest

With the **add-on interest method,** the amount of the monthly payment is determined by calculating the interest that must be paid on the loan amount, adding the interest and loan principal together, and dividing by the number of payments.

EXAMPLE   Reconsider the example in which you receive a loan of $2,000 to be repaid over one year, but assume that you are charged 12 percent interest based on the add-on method. You would first determine the amount of interest that is owed by applying the annual interest rate to the loan amount:

Interest Owed   = $2,000 × .12

= $240.

Next, determine the total payment owed by adding the interest to the loan amount:

Total Payment   = $2,000 + $240

= $2,240.

Finally, divide the total payment by the number of monthly payments:

Monthly payment = $2,240/12

= $186.67.

Notice that your monthly payment with the add-on method is about $9 per month more than your payment with the simple interest method. Even though the same interest rate is used for both methods, the add-on method is more costly. The reason is that the interest payment is not reduced over time as you pay off the loan.

HOME EQUITY LOAN

home equity loan
A loan where the equity in a home serves as collateral for the loan.

equity of a home
The market value of a home minus the debt owed on the home.

One of the most popular types of personal loans is a **home equity loan**, which allows homeowners to borrow against the equity in their home. The home serves as collateral to back the loan. The borrowed funds can be used for any purpose, including a vacation, tuition payments, or health care expenses.

The **equity of a home** is determined by subtracting the amount owed on the home from its market value. If a home has a market value of $100,000 and the homeowner has a mortgage loan (discussed in the next chapter) with a balance of $60,000, the equity value is $40,000. A home equity loan essentially provides you with a line of credit. That is, it allows you to borrow the amount that you need up to a specific credit limit. You pay interest only on the amount of funds that you borrow. You can typically pay the interest owed per month on the amount you borrow and then pay the principal at a specified maturity date. You may also be allowed to pay off the principal at any point prior to maturity and still have access to the funds if you need them in the future.

Credit Limit on a Home Equity Loan

Financial institutions provide home equity loans of up to 80 percent (or more in some cases) of the value of the equity in a home.

Financial institutions define the market value of your equity as the market value of your home minus the mortgage balance (amount still owed on the home). When the market value of a home rises, they are willing to provide more credit than if the market value remains the same.

If you default on a home equity loan, the lender can claim your home, use a portion of the proceeds to pay off the mortgage, and use the remainder to cover your home equity loan. If the market price of the home declines, the equity that you invested is reduced. For this reason, lenders do not like to lend the full amount of the equity when extending a home equity loan.

The following example illustrates how to determine the maximum amount of credit that can be provided on a home equity loan.

9.2 Financial Planning Online: Applying for a Home Equity Loan

Go to
http://www.ditech.com

Click on
"Apply Now," then click on
"Home Equity," then apply

This Web site provides
access to home equity loan
applications.

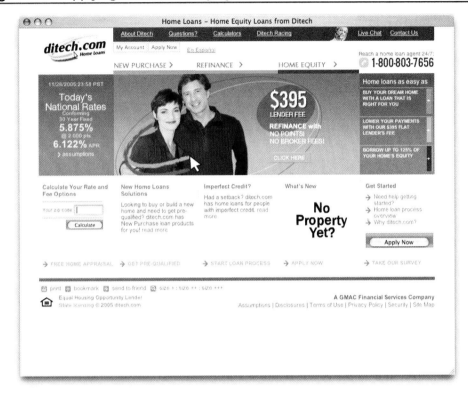

EXAMPLE

Suppose that you own a home worth $100,000 that you purchased four years ago. You initially made a down payment of $20,000 and took out an $80,000 mortgage. Over the last four years, your mortgage payments have added $10,000 in equity. Thus, you have invested $30,000 in the home, including your $20,000 down payment. Assume that the home's market value has not changed. Also, assume that a creditor is willing to provide you with a home equity loan of 70 percent based on the market value of equity in the home. In this example, the market value of equity is equal to the amount of equity you invested in the home.

$$\text{Maximum Amount of Credit Provided} = \text{Market Value of Equity in Home} \times .70$$
$$= \$30,000 \times .70$$
$$= \$21,000.$$

EXAMPLE

Use the information in the previous example, except now assume that the market value of your home has risen from $100,000 to $120,000 since you purchased it. Recall that you paid off $10,000 of the $80,000 mortgage loan, so your mortgage balance is $70,000. The market value of the equity in the home is:

$$\text{Market Value of Equity in Home} = \text{Market Value of Home} - \text{Mortgage Balance}$$
$$= \$120,000 - \$70,000$$
$$= \$50,000.$$

The market value of the equity is $50,000, while the amount of equity that you invested in the home is $30,000. The difference between these two amounts is the $20,000 increase in the value of the home since you purchased it. The credit limit based on the market value of the equity is:

$$\text{Maximum Amount of Credit Provided} = \text{Market Value of Equity in Home} \times .70$$
$$= \$50,000 \times .70$$
$$= \$35,000.$$

Interest Rate

A home equity loan typically uses a variable interest rate that is tied to a specified interest rate index that changes periodically (such as every six months). The loan contract specifies how the interest rate will be determined. For example, it may be set equal to the average deposit rates across financial institutions within a particular district plus 3 percentage points. Because the home serves as collateral for a home equity loan, the lender faces less risk than with an unsecured loan and the interest rate is lower.

Tax-Deductible Interest. Interest that is paid on a home equity loan of up to $100,000 is tax-deductible. Borrowers can therefore reduce their taxes by using a home equity loan instead of other types of loans or credit cards.

EXAMPLE   You borrow $10,000 with a home equity loan and pay $1,000 in interest on the home equity loan in a particular year. Assuming that you can deduct this amount from your taxable income and that your marginal income tax rate is 25 percent, your tax savings in that year are:

$$\begin{aligned}\text{Tax Savings in One Year} & \\ \text{from Home Equity Loan} &= \text{Amount of Interest Paid} \times \text{Marginal Tax Rate} \\ &= \$1,000 \times .25 \\ &= \$250.\end{aligned}$$

Thus, when you use a home equity loan, not only do you benefit from a relatively low interest rate, but also you generate tax savings.

CAR LOANS

Another common type of personal loan is a car loan. When you decide to buy a car, you must select the car, negotiate the price, and determine whether to finance the purchase of the car or lease the car.

Selecting the Car

Before making any car-buying decisions, you should take into account the following points.

Personal Preferences. First, determine the type of car that you need. Keep in mind that the car that you want can be different from the car that you need. Reduce the list of available cars by deciding on the size of the car that you need. Do you want a small car that is easy to park and gets good gas mileage? Or do you need a minivan to fit your children and their sports equipment? You can always screen the cars on your list further by deciding on the size of the engine. Do you want a car with a large engine that has fast acceleration or a car with a small engine that is less expensive?

Price. Stay within your budget. Avoid purchasing a car that will require you to obtain a second job or establish an unrealistic monthly budget to afford the car payments.

9.3 Financial Planning Online: Prices of New Cars

Go to
http://autos.yahoo.com/

Click on
"New Cars"

This Web site provides estimates of what you should pay for any new car based on the car's features and options that you specify.

Some college students are on a tight budget, and would only have sufficient funds to purchase a very inexpensive car that is likely to require more maintenance in the near future. Newer cars require less maintenance but are much more expensive. A compromise is a car that is a few years old. While its price may exceed the amount of cash that many college students have, financing can be arranged. No matter what your budget is, you should not consider purchasing the most expensive car that financing will allow because the finance payments will absorb much of your income for the next several years.

Condition. When buying a used car, be sure to assess the condition of your car beginning with the exterior. Has some of the paint worn off? Is there rust? Are the tires in good shape? Are the tires worn on one side (which may indicate that a wheel alignment is needed)? Next, check the interior. Are the seats worn? Do the electric devices work? Now look under the hood. Is there any sign of leaks? If you are still seriously considering the vehicle, ask the car owner for repair and maintenance records. Has the car been properly maintained and serviced over time? Has the oil been changed periodically?

All of these checks can help you assess a car's condition, but none replaces the expertise of a qualified mechanic. The cost of having a mechanic evaluate the car is worthwhile, because it may enable you to avoid buying a car that will ultimately result in large repair expenses.

Insurance. Some cars are subject to significantly higher insurance costs because they are more difficult to repair after accidents, are higher priced, or are common theft targets. Obtain insurance estimates on any car before making the purchase.

Resale Value. Some cars have a much higher resale value than others. For example, you can expect that an Acura will have a higher resale value than a Hyundai. Although you cannot perfectly predict the future resale value of a car, you can look at today's resale value of similar cars that were sold years ago. Numerous sites on the Internet, such as

Using the Internet, Stephanie easily obtains the information shown in Exhibit 9.4. Car A has a relatively low resale value after two years. Car D has relatively high repair expenses and service maintenance. Cars A and C have relatively high insurance rates. Therefore, she eliminates Cars A, C, and D. She will choose between Cars B and E.

Negotiating the Price

When shopping for a car, you have a choice between dealers that negotiate and dealers that offer one set price for a specific car to all customers. Any dealer that negotiates will purposely price its cars well above the price for which it is willing to sell the car. For example, the dealer may initially quote a price that represents the manufacturer's suggested retail price (MSRP). This price is also referred to as the sticker price. The strategy of some dealers is to make you think that you are getting a great deal as a result of the negotiations. If any customer is naïve enough to pay the full price, the car dealer earns a much larger profit at the customer's expense.

The salespeople are trained to act as if they are almost giving the car away to the customer by reducing the price by 5 to 20 percent. During the negotiations, they will say that they must discuss the price you offer with the sales manager. They already know the price at which they can sell the car to you, but this creates the appearance that they are pleading with the sales manager. During the negotiations, the dealer may offer you "free" rustproofing, a CD system, floor mats, or other features. These features are usually priced very high to make you believe that you are getting a good deal.

Negotiating by Phone. When purchasing a new car, it may be beneficial to negotiate by phone. After deciding on the type of car that you want, call a dealer and describe the car and options you desire. Explain that you plan to call other local car dealers, and that you will select the dealer that offers the lowest price. You may also want to emphasize that you will only call each dealer once.

Some dealers may not have the exact car that you want, so you may still have to compare features. For example, one dealer may quote a price that is $200 lower than the next-lowest quote, but the car may not be the specific color you requested. Nevertheless, the process described here can at least minimize the negotiation process.

Trade-In Tactics. If you are trading a car in, some dealers will pay a relatively high price for your trade-in, but charge a high price for the new car. For example, they may pay you $500 more than your used car is worth, but then charge you at least $500 more than they would have charged for the new car if you did not have a car to trade in. Attempt to negotiate the price on the new car first, before even mentioning that you have a car to trade in.

Exhibit 9.4 Stephanie Spratt's Car Analysis

Car	Expected Resale Value after Two Years (as a proportion of original sales price)	Repair Expenses and Service Maintenance	Insurance
A	Low	Moderate	High
B	Moderate	Low	Low
C	Moderate	Moderate	High
D	Moderate	High	Moderate
E	Moderate	Low	Moderate

9.6 Financial Planning Online: Prevailing Car Loan Interest Rates

Go to
http://biz.yahoo.com/b/r/a.html

This Web site provides average car loan interest rates across regions of the U.S. and in specific states, which provide a useful benchmark for you to consider before obtaining a car loan.

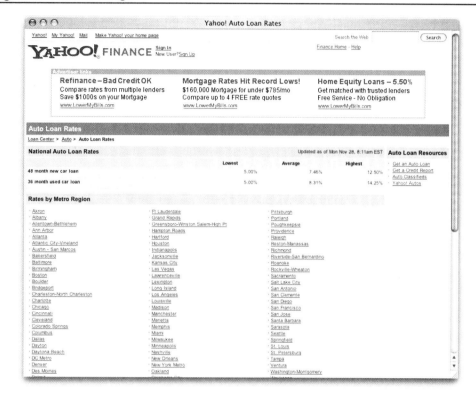

If you purchase a car from a typical dealer, many of the salespeople will congratulate you as if you had just won the lottery. This is also part of their strategy to make you feel that you got a great deal.

No-Haggle Dealers. Recently, many car dealerships have been created that do not haggle on the price. Buying a car from these dealers is not only less stressful but far less time-consuming. They set one price for a car, so you do not have to prepare for a negotiating battle. Some of these car dealerships still negotiate, however, so before you buy the car, you should make sure the price is no higher than that quoted by other dealers.

The Value of Information. Some car dealers attempt to make a higher profit from customers who are not well informed about the price that they should pay for a car. One way to avoid being taken when purchasing a car is to become informed. Shop around and make sure that you know the typical sales price for your car. You can obtain this information from *Consumer Reports* and other consumer magazines. Some Web sites will provide you with a quote based on the car model and features you want. You can do all of your shopping from your computer. For example, you may be able to obtain the dealer invoice price, which represents the price that the dealer pays the manufacturer for the car. The difference between the price quoted by the dealer and the invoice price represents the dealer markup. Be aware that manufacturers commonly provide dealers a rebate (referred to as a hold back), but dealers do not normally provide this information to their customers. A dealer could possibly charge a price that is only $200 above its dealer invoice, but if it received an $800 rebate from the manufacturer, the price is really marked up $1,000.

Purchasing a Car Online. You can buy a car online directly from some car manufacturers or from car referral services such as Autobytel Inc. or Carpoint. Car referral ser-vices forward your price quotation request to specific dealerships, which then respond by sending you a quote. http://www.carsdirect.com provides you with quotes based on deals it has made with various dealerships. That is, it receives guarantees from some dealerships on the prices for various types of cars. When a customer requests a quote, the car-buying service provides quotations that include a markup for its service. In other words, it is serving as the middleman between you and the dealership. If a customer agrees to the price, the car-buying service informs one of its dealerships to deliver the car.

Buying a new car online is not as efficient as buying an airline ticket or a book online. A car is not as standardized as a book, and the personal options can make the online correspondence more difficult. At a dealership, a customer can see the actual difference in the design of the two models of a particular car. It is not as easy to detect the differences on a Web site. Unlike a Web site, a dealership can anticipate your questions and arrange for a test drive. It is also more difficult to force an online service to meet its delivery promise to you. For example, an online car seller may guarantee you a price for a specific car, but not necessarily meet the delivery date. You have limited ability to enforce the deal because you may only be able to reach them by e-mail or voice mail. You can place more pressure on a local dealership to meet its promise by showing up at the dealership and expressing your concerns.

You can also buy used cars online, through eBay. However, the purchase of a used car online is subject to the same limitations as the purchase of a new car online. Given the limitations of buying a car online, many customers still prefer to buy a car at a dealership.

EXAMPLE

Stephanie Spratt has decided to use the Internet to shop for her car. Several Web sites state the price for each of the two new cars she is considering (Cars B and E from the previous example). She reviews specific details about each car, including which car has more value relative to its price, the options, available colors, and the delivery dates. She believes that while Car B is cheaper, its value will depreciate more quickly than Car E's. In addition, she can get the exact options and color she desires for Car E, and it can be delivered soon. She is almost ready to purchase Car E, which is priced at $18,000 including taxes. But first, she wants to consider the financing costs per month and whether to lease the car or purchase it.

Financing Decisions

If you consider purchasing a new car and plan to finance the purchase, you should estimate the dollar amount of the monthly payment. By evaluating your typical monthly cash inflows and outflows, you can determine whether you can afford to make the required payments to finance the car. You should conduct the estimate before shopping for a car so that you know how much you can afford. The more money needed to cover the car payments, the less you can add to your savings or other investments.

EXAMPLE

Stephanie Spratt wants to compare her monthly car payments if she borrows $15,000 versus $17,000 to buy a car. She must also decide whether to repay the loan over three years, four years, or five years. The larger the down payment she makes, the less she will need to borrow. However, she wants to retain some of her savings to maintain liquidity and to use for a future down payment on a house.

Stephanie goes to a car-financing Web site where she is asked to input the approximate amount she will borrow. The Web site then provides the available interest rate and shows the payments for each alternative loan amount and repayment period, as shown in Exhibit 9.5. The interest rate of 7.6 percent at the top of the exhibit is a fixed rate that Stephanie can lock

Exhibit 9.5 Stephanie's Possible Monthly Loan Payments (7.6 Percent Interest Rate)

	Loan Amount	
Loan Maturity	$15,000	$17,000
36 months (3 years)	$467	$530
48 months (4 years)	363	412
60 months (5 years)	301	341

in for the loan period. The possible loan amounts are shown at the top of the columns and each row shows a different loan repayment period.

Notice how the payment decreases if Stephanie extends the loan period. If she borrows $17,000, her payment would be $530 for a three-year loan, $412 for a four-year loan, or $341 for a five-year loan. Alternatively, she can lower her monthly payments by reducing her loan amount from $17,000 to $15,000. Notice that if she takes out a four-year loan for $15,000, her monthly payment is less than if she borrows $17,000.

Stephanie selects the $17,000 loan with a four-year term and a $412 monthly payment. The four-year term is preferable because the monthly loan payment for a three-year term is higher than she wants to pay. Since the purchase price of the car is $18,000, she will use the proceeds from selling her old car to cover the $1,000 down payment.

9.7 Financial Planning Online: What Is the Optimal Loan Maturity?

Go to
http://www.bankrate.com/brm/auto-loan-calculator.asp

This Web site provides a comparison of what your car loan payments will be depending on whether you obtain a loan with a relatively short maturity or a loan with a longer maturity.

PURCHASE VERSUS LEASE DECISION

A popular alternative to buying a car is leasing one. An advantage of leasing is that you do not need a substantial down payment. In addition, you return the car to the car dealer at the end of the lease period, so you do not need to worry about finding a buyer for the car.

Leasing a car also has disadvantages. Since you do not own the car, you have no equity investment in it, even though the car still has value. You are also responsible for maintenance costs while you are leasing it. Keep in mind that you will be charged for any damage to the car over the lease period.

Some car dealers impose additional charges beyond the monthly lease payments. You will be charged if you drive more than the maximum number of miles specified in the lease agreement. You may be assessed a fee if you end the lease before the period specified in the contract. You may also have to purchase more car insurance than you already have. Some of these charges may be hidden within the lease agreement. Thousands of customers have filed legal claims, alleging that they were not informed of all possible charges when they leased a car. If you ever seriously consider leasing, make sure that you read and understand the entire lease agreement.

EXAMPLE

Stephanie Spratt now wonders if she should lease the car she selected, rather than purchasing it for $18,000. If she purchases the car, she can invest $1,000 as a down payment today, and the remaining $17,000 will be financed by a car loan. She will pay $412 per month over four years to cover the financing. She expects that the car will be worth $10,000 at the end of four years. By purchasing instead of leasing, she forgoes interest that she could have earned from investing the $1,000 down payment over the next four years. If she invests the funds in a bank, she would earn 4 percent annually after considering taxes paid on the interest.

Alternatively, she could lease the same car for $300 per month over the four-year period. The lease would require an $800 security deposit, which she would receive back at the end of the four-year period. However, she would forgo interest she could have earned if she had invested the $800 instead. And, at the end of a lease, she would have no equity and no car.

Stephanie's comparison of the cost of purchasing versus leasing is shown in Exhibit 9.6. Stephanie estimates the total cost of purchasing the car to be $10,936 while the total cost of leasing is $14,528. Therefore, she decides to purchase the car.

The decision to purchase versus lease a car is highly dependent on the estimated market value of the car at the end of the lease period. If the expected value of the car in the previous example were $6,000 instead of $10,000 after four years, the total cost of purchasing the car would have been $4,000 more. Substitute $6,000 for $10,000 in Exhibit 9.6 and recalculate the cost of purchasing to verify this. With an expected market value of $6,000, the total cost of purchasing the car would have been higher than the total cost of leasing, so leasing would have been preferable. Remember that some dealers may impose additional charges for leasing, such as a charge for driving more than the maximum miles allowed. Include any of these expenses in your estimate of the leasing expenses.

STUDENT LOANS

student loan
A loan provided to finance part of the expenses a student incurs while pursuing a degree.

Another popular type of personal loan is a **student loan,** which is a loan to finance a portion of a student's expenses while pursuing an undergraduate or graduate degree. One of the best sources of information about student loans is your school's financial aid office. Some student loans are provided directly to the student, while others are provided to the student's parents.

Exhibit 9.6 Stephanie's Comparison of the Cost of Purchasing versus Leasing

Cost of Purchasing the Car

	Cost
1. Down payment	$1,000

2. Down payment of $1,000 results in forgone interest income:

Forgone Interest

Income per Year = Down Payment × Annual Interest Rate

= $1,000 × .04

= $40

Forgone Interest over Four Years = $40 × 4	
= $160	160

3. Total monthly payments are:

Total Monthly Payments = Monthly Payment × Number of Months

= $412 × 48

= $19,776	19,776
Total	$20,936
Minus: Expected amount to be received when car is sold in four years	– 10,000
Total cost	$10,936

Cost of Leasing the Car for Four Years

	Cost

1. Security deposit of $800 results in forgone interest income
(although she will receive her deposit back in four years):

Forgone Interest

Income per Year = Down Payment × Annual Interest Rate

= $800 × .04

= $32

Forgone Interest over Four Years = $32 × 4	
= $128	$128

2. Total monthly payments are:

Total Monthly Payments = Monthly Payment × Number of Months

= $300 × 48

= $14,400	14,400
Total cost	$14,528

9.8 Financial Planning Online: Should You Lease or Buy?

Go to
http://www.bloomberg.com/
analysis/calculators/
leasebuy.html

This Web site provides
a comparison of the cost
of leasing versus purchasing a car.

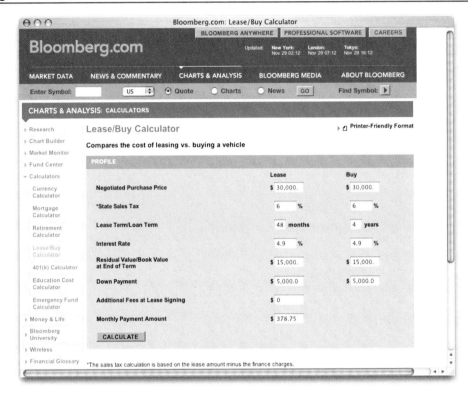

The lender may be the federal government or one of many financial institutions that participate in student loan programs. For example, the Federal Direct Loan Program provides government loans to students through schools' financial aid offices. In addition, the Stafford loan program extends loans from financial institutions directly to students. There are set limits on how much a student can borrow each year that increase as students progress. Loan limits are lower for students who are dependents. The repayment schedule is deferred, so students do not begin to repay the loans until they have completed their degrees and entered the workforce.

Even if you don't complete your education, you still have to pay back your student loans. Failure to do so will damage your credit history. The interest is tax-deductible up to a maximum of $2,500, which reduces the financing costs even more. The tax benefits are phased out for individuals who are in high tax brackets.

HOW PERSONAL LOANS FIT WITHIN YOUR FINANCIAL PLAN

The following are the key personal loan decisions that should be included within your financial plan:

1. How much money can you afford to borrow on a personal loan?

2. If you obtain a personal loan, should you pay it off early?

By making sound decisions, you can avoid accumulating an excessive amount of debt. Exhibit 9.7 provides an example of how personal loan decisions apply to Stephanie Spratt's financial plan. The exhibit shows how Stephanie reviews her typical monthly cash flows to determine whether she can cover her monthly loan payments.

Exhibit 9.7 How Personal Loan Management Fits within Stephanie Spratt's Financial Plan

GOALS FOR PERSONAL FINANCING

1. Limit the amount of financing to a level and maturity that I can pay back on a timely basis.

2. For any personal loan, I will consider paying off the loan balance as soon as possible.

ANALYSIS

Monthly Cash Inflows	$2,500
− Typical Monthly Expenses	1,400
− Monthly Car Loan Payment	412
= Amount of Funds Available	**$688**

DECISIONS

Decision on Affording a Personal Loan:

The financing of my new car requires a payment of $412 per month. This leaves me with $688 per month after paying typical monthly expenses. I can afford to make the payments. I will not need additional personal loans for any other purpose.

Decision on Paying Off Personal Loan Balances:

The car loan has an interest rate of 7.6 percent. I expect that my stock investment will earn a higher rate of return than this interest rate. Once I have accumulated more savings, however, I will seriously consider using my savings and invested funds to pay off the balance of the loan early.

DISCUSSION QUESTIONS

1. How would Stephanie's personal loan decisions be different if she were a single mother of two children?

2. How would Stephanie's personal loan decisions be affected if she were 35 years old? If she were 50 years old?

SUMMARY

When applying for a personal loan, you need to disclose your personal balance sheet and cash flow statement so that the lender can evaluate your ability to repay a loan. A loan contract specifies the amount of the loan, interest rate, maturity, and collateral.

The common types of interest rates charged on personal loans are the annual percentage rate (APR), simple interest, and add-on interest. The APR measures the interest and other expenses as a percentage of the loan amount on an annualized basis. Simple interest measures the interest as a percentage of the existing loan amount. Add-on interest calculates interest on the loan amount, adds the interest and principal, and divides by the number of payments.

A home equity loan commonly has more favorable terms than other personal loans. It has a relatively low interest

rate because of the collateral (the home) that backs the loan. In addition, the interest paid on a home equity loan is tax-deductible up to a limit.

Your decision to purchase a car may require financing. You can reduce your monthly payments on the car loan if you make a higher down payment, but doing this may reduce your liquidity. Alternatively, you can reduce your monthly payments by extending the loan period.

The decision of whether to purchase a car with a car loan or lease a car requires an estimation of the total cost of each alternative. The total cost of purchasing a car consists of the down payment, the forgone interest income from the down payment, and the total monthly loan payments. The total cost of leasing consists of the forgone interest income from the security deposit and the total monthly lease payments.

INTEGRATING THE KEY CONCEPTS

Your personal loan decisions not only determine how much money you can spend, but also affect other parts of your financial plan. Your decision to obtain a personal loan can affect your liquidity management (Part 2) because an existing personal loan may reduce the amount of credit you can obtain with credit cards. A personal loan also places some pressure on your liquidity needs because you will need to ensure sufficient funds to cover your monthly loan payment. Personal loans can affect insurance planning (Part 4), as additional life insurance would be needed to

cover these loans. If your personal loan decision results in the purchase of a new car, you will also have to obtain insurance (Part 4) because you will need to protect the value of the car and be insured against any liability resulting from the car. Personal loans can also affect your investment decisions (Part 5) because it may be wise to avoid investments until the personal loan is paid off. Once you have a personal loan, the decision to invest makes sense only if the return on the investment will exceed the interest rate on the personal loan. Otherwise, you would benefit from using your money to pay off the loan rather than make investments.

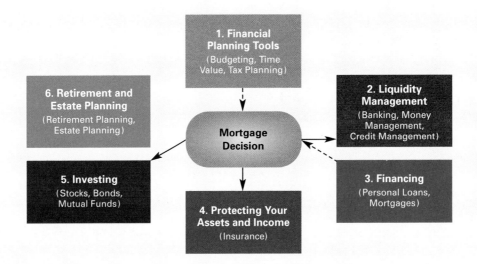

REVIEW QUESTIONS

1. List some possible sources of personal loans. What precautions should be taken with loans from family members or friends?

2. What does the personal loan process involve?

3. What does it mean if a loan is amortized? What do the loan payments represent?

4. What information must borrowers supply to lenders in the loan application process? Why is this information important to lenders?

5. What information is included in a loan contract? How is the amount of the loan determined?

6. Explain how collateral works. Do all loans have collateral? What is the relationship between collateral and interest rates?

7. How does the maturity of a loan affect the monthly payments? What should you consider when selecting the maturity?

8. Explain the difference between a 10% rate charged on a payday loan and a 10% rate charged by a bank on a personal loan.

9. What are your responsibilities if you cosign a loan? What are the potential consequences of failing to live up to your responsibilities as a cosigner?

10. What is the purpose of the annual percentage rate measurement? Could lenders with the same interest rates report different APRs?

11. What is simple interest? What information is needed to compute it? What information is contained in a loan repayment schedule?

12. How are payments calculated under the add-on interest method?

13. Why are loan payments under the simple interest method usually lower than loan payments under the add-on interest method?

14. What is home equity? Describe how a home equity loan works.

15. Discuss the two ways financial institutions might define equity to set credit limits. What happens if you default on a home equity loan?

16. How are interest rates calculated for home equity loans? Why do borrowers prefer home equity loans to other loans?

17. How can borrowers enjoy tax savings by using a home equity loan? How are these tax savings computed?

18. List the steps in buying a car. What financial criteria should be considered? Discuss each briefly.

19. Why is purchasing a new car online not as efficient as buying a new car at a dealership?

20. Describe some techniques that car salespeople might use in negotiating the price of the car. What should you be aware of at "no-haggle" dealerships?

21. What should be the first step in financing a purchase? Aside from the interest rate, what two factors will have the largest impact on the size of your monthly payment?

22. What are the advantages and disadvantages of leasing? Give some advice for someone considering leasing.

23. Who extends student loans? What are the characteristics of student loans?

VIDEO QUESTIONS

1. If you are looking for a new car, the segment highlights several points to keep in mind. List and explain each point.

2. What advice did the experts offer to those considering trading in a car?

3. Car commercials and dealers encourage leasing as an option. How did the experts weigh in on the decision to buy or lease a car?

FINANCIAL PLANNING PROBLEMS

1. Jack needs to borrow $1,000 for the next year. Bank South will give him the loan at 9 percent. SunCoast Bank will give him the loan at 7 percent with a $50 loan origination fee. First National will give him the loan at 6 percent with a $25 loan origination fee. Determine the total interest and fees Jack will be charged in each case. Which loan should Jack choose?

2. Beth has just borrowed $5,000 on a four-year loan at 8 percent simple interest. Complete the amortization table below for the first five months of the loan.

3. What if Beth had made the same loan as an add-on interest loan? How would her payments differ? Why is there a difference?

4. Tracy is borrowing $8,000 on a six-year, 11 percent, add-on interest loan. What will Tracy's payments be?

5. Mary and Marty are interested in obtaining a home equity loan. They purchased their house five years for $125,000 and it now has a market value of $156,000. Originally, Mary and Marty paid $25,000 down on the house and took out a $100,000 mortgage. The current balance on their mortgage is $72,000. The bank uses 70 percent of equity in determining the credit limit. What will their credit limit be if the bank bases their credit limit on equity invested and will loan them 70 percent of the equity?

6. Refer to question 5. What will Mary and Marty's credit limit be if the bank uses the market value of equity to determine their credit limit and will loan them 70 percent of the equity?

7. John and Cheryl just borrowed $30,000 on a home equity line of credit. The interest rate for the loan is 6.75 percent for the entire year, and they took out the loan on May 1. John and Cheryl are in the 28 percent tax bracket. What will be their tax savings for the first year ending December 31?

Payment Number	Beginning Balance	Payment Amount	Applied to Interest	Applied to Principal	New Balance
1	$5,000.00	$122	$33.33	$88.67	$4,911.33
2	a	122	32.74	b	4,822.07
3	4,822.07	c	d	89.85	4,732.22
4	4,732.22	122	e	90.45	f
5	4,641.77	122	30.95	g	h

8. Noel has a 15 percent marginal tax rate. If he pays $1,400 in interest on a home equity loan in the first year, what will his tax savings be?

9. Sharon is considering the purchase of a car. After making the down payment, she will finance $15,500. Sharon is offered three maturities. On a four-year loan, Sharon will pay $371.17 per month. On a five-year loan, Sharon's monthly payments will be $306.99. On a six-year loan, they will be $264.26. Sharon rejects the four-year loan, as it is not within her budget. How much interest will Sharon pay over the life of the loan on the five-year loan? On the six-year loan? Which should she choose if she bases her decision solely on total interest paid?

10. Refer to question 9. If Sharon had been able to afford the four-year loan, how much interest would she have saved compared to the five-year loan?

11. Bill wants to purchase a new car for $45,000. Bill has no savings, so he needs to finance the entire purchase amount. With no down payment, the interest rate on the loan is 13 percent and the maturity of the loan is six years. His monthly payments will be $903.33. Bill's monthly net cash flows are $583.00. Bill also has a credit card with a $10,000 limit and an interest rate of 18 percent. If Bill uses all of his net cash flows to make the monthly payments on the car, how much will he add each month to his credit card balance if he uses it to finance the remainder of the car? What will the finance charges be on his credit card for the first two months that finance charges apply? (Assume that Bill makes no payments on his credit card.)

Ethical Dilemma

12. Fritz and Helga work for a local manufacturing company. Since their marriage five years ago, they have been working extensive overtime, including Sundays and holidays. Fritz and Helga have established a lifestyle based on their overtime earnings. Recently, the company lost two major contracts and all overtime has been eliminated. As a result, Fritz and Helga are having difficulty paying their bills. Several months ago they began using a local payday loan company to pay their bills on time. The first week they borrowed only a small amount to cover some past due bills. The next week, however, in order to pay back the loan plus interest, they were left with an even smaller amount to pay bills resulting in a higher payday loan the second week. In paying back the second week's loan, their remaining available funds were fur-

ther reduced. This cycle continued until they were no longer able to borrow because the repayment plus interest would have exceeded their paychecks. Fritz and Helga have had their cars repossessed, their home foreclosed on, and they are preparing to file for bankruptcy.

a. Is the payday loan company being ethical in continuing to loan more and more to Fritz and Helga each week?

b. What could Fritz and Helga have done to avoid ultimate financial ruin?

FINANCIAL PLANNING ONLINE EXERCISES

1. Go to http://www.kbb.com.

a. Click on "Used Car Values By Make & Model." In the fields provided, select "1995" for year, "Ford" for make, and "Taurus" for model. Click "Go," then click on "Retail Value." Click on "GL Sedan 4D". Assume a 3.0 liter V6 engine, mileage of 85,000, standard equipment, and enter your ZIP Code. Click "Continue." What is the retail value if the car is in excellent condition?

b. Click on "Trade-In Value." What is the trade-in price? How does it differ from the retail price?

c. Click on the "Reviews & Ratings" tab, then click on "Previews: Check Out New and Future Models" and "Auto Show Coverage." Look for information on a car for which the have been major revisions.

d. Click on "New Cars" tab. Select a make and model that interests you. You will find useful information about the new model.

2. Go to http://loan.yahoo.com/a/autocalc.html.

a. In the Auto Loan Calculators section, click on "Loan vs. Lease Calculator." Input $12,000 price, 6 percent sales tax, 48-month term of loan and lease, 8 percent interest rate, $6,000 residual value at end of lease, and a $3,500 down payment. How do payments for borrowing and leasing and the total cost for each option compare?

b. Use the Back option on your browser to go back to the previous page. Choose a shorter-term lease of 36 months. With the shorter maturity, what is the change in the lease payments and the total cost of leasing?

BUILDING YOUR OWN FINANCIAL PLAN

Loans to finance purchases such as automobiles and homes may be obtained from a variety of sources, each of which has advantages and disadvantages. For example, automobile purchases may be financed through the dealer, a local bank, a credit union, or a finance company. Review all loans that you currently have or anticipate having upon graduation and identify as many sources of these loans as possible. Evaluate the advantages and disadvantages of each source to assist you in determining where to best meet your various borrowing needs.

Go to the worksheets at the end of this chapter, and to the CD-ROM accompanying this text, to continue building your financial plan.

THE SAMPSONS—A CONTINUING CASE

After about 10 months of saving $500 a month, the Sampsons have achieved their goal of saving $5,000 that they will use as a down payment on a new car. (They have also been saving an additional $300 per month over the last year for their children's college education.) Sharon's new car is priced at $25,000 plus 5 percent sales tax. She will receive a $1,000 trade-in credit on her existing car and will make a $5,000 down payment on the new car. The Sampsons would like to allocate a maximum of $500 per month to the loan payments on Sharon's new car. The annual interest rate on a car loan is currently 7 percent. They would prefer to have a relatively short loan maturity, but cannot afford a monthly payment higher than $500.

Go to the worksheets at the end of this chapter, and to the CD-ROM accompanying this text, to continue this case.

Chapter 9: Building Your Own Financial Plan

GOALS

1. Limit your personal financing to a level and maturity that you can pay back on time.
2. For loans you anticipate needing in the future, evaluate the advantages and disadvantages of lenders.
3. Compare the cost of buying and leasing a car.

ANALYSIS

1. Review your personal cash flow statement. How much can you afford to pay each month for personal loans?
2. Identify several prospective lenders for personal loans you may need in the future. What are the advantages and disadvantages of each source with respect to the interest rates offered, method of calculating interest, and other criteria of importance to you?

Loan Evaluation

Loan One

Description of Loan	Sources for Loan	Advantages of Source	Disadvantages of Source
	1.		
	2.		
	3.		

Loan Two

Description of Loan	Sources for Loan	Advantages of Source	Disadvantages of Source
	1.		
	2.		
	3.		

Loan Three

Description of Loan	Sources for Loan	Advantages of Source	Disadvantages of Source
	1.		
	2.		
	3.		

3. Compare the cost of purchasing a car versus leasing a car over a four-year period.

Cost of Purchasing versus Leasing a Car

Cost of Purchasing a Car

Down payment	
Interest rate	
Number of months	
Annual forgone interest on down payment	
Monthly payment on car loan	
Total monthly payments	
Total cost of purchasing	
Expected amount to be received when car is sold	
Total cost of purchasing	

Cost of Leasing a Car

Security deposit	
Forgone interest	
Monthly lease payments	
Total monthly payments	
Total cost of leasing	

If you enter this information in the Excel worksheet, the software will create a graphical comparison of purchasing versus leasing.

DECISIONS

1. Report how much you can afford to spend each month on personal loans.

_____

_____

_____

_____

_____

_____

2. Report which lenders you may consider using in the future and why.

_____

_____

_____

_____

_____

_____

_____

3. Is purchasing or leasing a vehicle a better choice for your needs?

_____

_____

_____

_____

_____

_____

_____

Chapter 9: The Sampsons—A Continuing Case

CASE QUESTIONS

1. Advise the Sampsons on possible loan maturities. Go to http://loan.yahoo.com/a/autocalc.html and click on "Loan Payment Calculator." Input information to determine the possible monthly car payments for a three-year (36-month) payment period, a four-year (48-month) payment period, and a five-year (60-month) period. Enter the results in the following table:

	Three-Year (36-month) Periods	Four-Year (48-month) Periods	Five-Year (60-month) Periods
Interest rate	7%	7%	7%
Monthly payment			
Total finance payments			
Total payments including the down payment and the trade-in			

2. What are the tradeoffs among the three alternative loan maturities?

_____

_____

_____

_____

_____

3. Based on the information on finance payments that you retrieved from the loan payment Web site, advise the Sampsons on the best loan maturity for their needs.

_____

_____

_____

_____

_____

Purchasing and Financing a Home

T wo years ago, Brian Menke purchased a small home that he could easily afford near the firm where he works. His co-worker, Tim Remington, also bought a home. Unlike Brian, Tim would need most of his paycheck to cover the mortgage and expenses of his home, but he thought the purchase would make a good investment.

Because his mortgage payment was relatively low, Brian was able to save money during the next year. Tim, however, was unable to save any money, and also had large credit card bills on which he was paying only the minimum amount. Tim suddenly realized he could not afford his home. Because the demand for homes had weakened, housing prices had declined since Tim purchased his home. Tim sold his home, but for $20,000 less than he paid for it. He also had to pay the real estate broker a commission of $16,000. Thus, Tim received $36,000 less from the sale of his home than his purchase price in the previous year.

During the following year, the economy improved and home prices increased. Brian's home was now worth $12,000 more than he paid for it. But the improved economy did not help Tim, who no longer owned a home and was still paying off the debt that he accumulated.

Financial planning made the difference. Brian's strategy was more conservative, which allowed for the possibility that the economy and market conditions could weaken temporarily. Conversely, Tim did not properly estimate how much money he would need to cover expenses of a home, and also wrongly assumed that home prices would never decline.

Buying your first home is an important personal financial decision due to the long-term and costly nature of the investment. Your decision on how much to spend and how much to finance will affect your cash flows for years. This chapter describes the fundamentals of purchasing a home and will help you evaluate your first home purchase.

The objectives of this chapter are to:

- Explain how to select a home to purchase

- Explain how to conduct a valuation of a home

- Describe the transaction costs of purchasing a home

- Describe the characteristics of a fixed-rate mortgage

- Describe the characteristics of an adjustable-rate mortgage

- Show how to compare the costs of purchasing versus renting a home

- Explain the mortgage refinancing decision

SELECTING A HOME

Buying a home may be the single biggest investment you will ever make, so the decision should be taken very seriously. You should carefully consider several factors. Evaluate the homes for sale in your target area to determine the typical price range and features. Once you decide on a realistic price range, identify a specific home that you desire. You can compare the cost of buying that home to the cost of renting. This way, you can weigh the extra costs against the benefits of home ownership.

An alternative to purchasing a house is to purchase a condominium. In a condominium, individuals own units of a housing complex, but jointly own the surrounding land and common areas (such as parking lots) and amenities (such as a swimming pool). The benefits of a condominium are somewhat different from those of a house. Whereas a house is detached, units in a condominium are typically attached, so there is less privacy. Condominium expenses are shared among unit owners, while the owners of a house pay for expenses on their own. Nevertheless, the factors to be considered when selecting or financing a house are also relevant when purchasing a condominium. Thus, the following discussion will use *home* rather than *house* to indicate that it also applies to a condominium.

Relying on a Realtor

You may consider advice from a real estate broker when you assess homes, decide whether to buy a home, or determine which home to purchase. Yet you should not rely completely on the advice of real estate brokers because they have a vested interest: they earn a commission only if you purchase a home through them. You should consider their input, but make decisions that meet your needs and preferences. A good real estate broker will ask you about your preferences and suggest appropriate homes.

Using Online Realtor Services

Increasingly, online services are being used to facilitate home purchases. Web sites such as http://www.ziprealty.com allow sellers to present detailed information about their home in a database that is made accessible to potential home buyers. These types of Web sites are sometimes limited to particular cities. The realty company sponsoring the Web site may provide services to complete a contract, and the commission for using the online service is less than the traditional commission charged by real estate agents.

Other online services allow sellers to list their home in a database, without providing other real estate–related services. The contract would have to be completed by the buyer and seller without the help of a realtor. The advantage of this type of service is that it charges lower commissions than a traditional full-service real estate company. Some of these online services are actually subsidiaries of the traditional full-service real estate companies. For example, Blue Edge Realty (http://blueedge.com) is a subsidiary of

Coldwell Banker Real Estate Corporation. Customers who want full-service real estate services can rely on Coldwell Banker, while customers who primarily want to list their home for potential buyers can use Blue Edge Realty.

HOW MUCH CAN YOU AFFORD?

When selecting a home, you should first determine how much money you can afford to pay per month for a mortgage based on your budget. Once you remove homes from consideration that are too expensive, you should use various criteria to evaluate the homes that you are still considering.

Most individuals pay for a home with a down payment (perhaps 10 to 20 percent of the purchase price) and obtain a mortgage loan to finance the rest. You will pay monthly mortgage payments over the life of the loan. Mortgage loan lenders determine how much money they will lend you based on your financial situation and credit history. Various Web sites can estimate the maximum value of a home you can afford based on your financial situation (such as your income and your net worth).

Financial planners suggest that a home price should be no more than two times the total gross annual household income and that all of the monthly household debt payments (including the mortgage loan) should be no more than about 40 percent of the total monthly gross income. However, these generalizations do not apply to everyone, as other financial information and spending habits of the homeowners should also be considered.

"You see that dark, spooky image on the screen? That's your credit history coming back to haunt you."

Affordable Down Payment

You can determine your maximum down payment by estimating the market value of the assets that you are willing to convert to cash for a down payment and for transaction costs (such as closing costs) when obtaining a mortgage. Be sure to maintain some funds for liquidity purposes to cover unanticipated bills.

Affordable Monthly Mortgage Payments

How large a mortgage payment can you afford? Refer to your cash flow statement to determine how much net cash flow you have to make a mortgage payment. If you purchase a home, you will no longer have a rent payment, so that money can be used as part of the mortgage payment. You should also be aware, however, that owning a home entails some periodic expenses (such as property taxes, homeowner's insurance, and home repairs). You should not plan to purchase a home that will absorb all your current excess cash inflows. The larger your mortgage payments, the less you can add to your savings or other investments.

EXAMPLE

Stephanie Spratt just received an unexpected bonus and a promotion from her employer. After assessing her financial situation, she decides that she may want to purchase a home in the near future. She has about $15,000 in liquid assets for use toward a down payment and transaction costs. She evaluates her personal cash flows. Since she would no longer need to pay rent for her apartment, she can afford to allocate $900 a month to monthly mortgage payments. She begins to look at homes for sale in the range of $70,000 to $85,000. Once she identifies a home that she may want to purchase, she will obtain estimates of the required down payment, the transaction costs, and the mortgage payment.

10.1 Financial Planning Online: How Much Money Can You Borrow?

Go to
http://www.calcbuilder.com/
cgi-bin/calcs/HOM1.cgi/
excite

This Web site provides
an estimate of how much
money you could borrow
to finance a home, based
on your income and other
financial information.

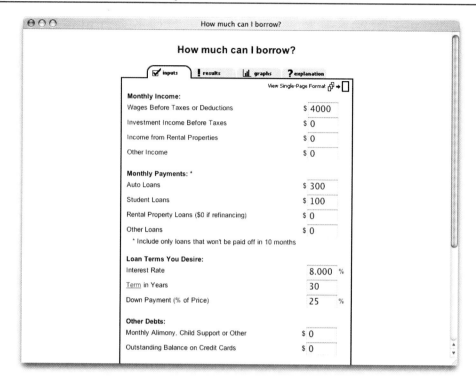

Criteria Used to Select a Home

The most important factors to consider when selecting a home are identified here:

- **Price.** Stay within your budget. Avoid purchasing a home that you cannot afford. Although your favorite home may have ample space and a large yard, it may not be worth the stress of struggling to make the mortgage payments.

- **Convenient Location.** Focus on homes in a convenient area so that you can minimize commuting time to work or travel time to other activities. You may save 10 or more hours of travel time a week.

- **Maintenance.** Some homes built by well-known construction companies have lower repair bills than others. In addition, newer homes tend to need fewer repairs than older homes. A home with a large yard requires more maintenance.

  In condominiums, residents share common areas, such as a swimming pool or tennis court. The residents normally pay a fixed monthly fee to cover the costs of maintaining the common areas. In addition, they may be assessed an extra fee to maintain the structure of the condominium, such as a new roof or other repairs.

- **School System.** If you have children, the reputation of the school system is very important. Even if you do not have children, the resale value of your house benefits from a good school system.

- **Insurance.** When you own a home, you need to purchase homeowner's insurance, which covers the home in case of burglary or damage. The cost of insurance varies among homes. It is higher for more expensive homes and for homes in high-risk areas (such as flood zones) because it costs the insurer more to replace parts of the home that are damaged.

- **Taxes.** Taxes are imposed on homes to pay for local services, such as the local school system and the local park system. Taxes vary substantially among loca-

10.2 Financial Planning Online: Recent Sales Prices of Nearby Homes

Go to
http://realestate.yahoo.com/
re/homevalues/

This Web site provides sales prices of homes on a street in a city that you specify over a recent period. It can also provide a list of homes in the city you specify that sold within a certain price range.

tions. Annual property taxes are often between 1 and 2 percent of the market value of the home. Thus, the tax on a $100,000 home is typically between $1,000 and $2,000 per year. Property taxes are tax-deductible if you itemize deductions on your income tax return. You can deduct them from your income when determining your federal income tax.

- **Homeowner's Association.** Some homes are connected with homeowner's associations, which set guidelines for the homes and may even assess fees that are used to hire security guards or to maintain common grounds within the area. The monthly fees charged by some homeowner's associations are very high and should be considered when buying a home.

- **Resale Value.** The resale value of a home is highly dependent on its location. Most homes with similar features within a specific subdivision or neighborhood are in the same range. Although home prices in a given subdivision tend to move in the same direction, the price movements can vary substantially among homes. For example, homes in a subdivision that are within walking distance of a school may be worth more than comparable houses several miles from the school.

    You cannot perfectly predict the future resale value of a home, but you can evaluate today's resale value of similar homes in that location that were sold years ago. Information about home prices is provided on numerous Web sites. Be aware, however, that the rate of increase in home prices in previous years does not necessarily serve as a good predictor of the future.

    Keep in mind that when you use a realtor to sell a home (as most people do), you will pay the realtor a commission that is usually about 6 percent of the selling price. Thus, if you resell your home for $100,000, you will probably pay a commission of about $6,000 and therefore receive $94,000. The buyer of a home does not pay a commission.

10.3 Financial Planning Online: Listing of Homes Nearby for Sale

Go to

http://www.realtor.com

This Web site provides a listing of homes for sale in an area that you specify and homes in the price and size range that you specify.

- **Personal Preferences.** In addition to the general criteria described above, you will have your own personal preferences regarding features such as the number of bedrooms, size of the kitchen, and size of the yard.

Focus On Ethics: Disclosing Defects

For both the buyer and seller, the sale of a home is stressful due to the large amount of money involved. Concerns about unethical behavior only add to the tension. For example, there are many cases of sellers of homes who did not disclose problems (such as a leaky roof or cracked foundation).

As a seller, by law most states require that you fully disclose any defect that may affect the value of the home. In addition to being the legal thing to do, disclosure is the moral thing to do. You would hope that a seller would be completely honest with you, so you should treat the potential buyer in the manner that you wish to be treated. And if any problem arises shortly after you sell a house, the buyer can sue you for any misrepresentations.

VALUATION OF A HOME

You should use the criteria described previously to screen your list of desirable homes so that you can spend time analyzing the advantages and disadvantages of three or four particular homes. You will probably find some homes that meet all your criteria, but are simply overpriced and therefore should not be considered.

Market Analysis

market analysis
An estimate of the price of a home based on the prices of similar homes in the area.

You can conduct a **market analysis**, in which you estimate the price of a home based on the prices of similar homes in the area. The market value can be estimated by multiplying the number of square feet in a home by the average price per square foot of similar homes in the area. A real estate broker or appraiser may also provide you with a valuation.

EXAMPLE

Stephanie Spratt finds the selling prices of three other homes in the same area, with a similar lot size, and about the same age as the home that she wants to purchase. The purchase prices are shown in the second column of Exhibit 10.1.

She recognizes that homes in an area vary in price due to their size. She determines the price per square foot by dividing each home's price by the square feet, as shown in the third column. Then she determines that the average price per square foot of the three homes is $64, as shown at the bottom of the exhibit.

Since the home that Stephanie wants to purchase has 1,300 square feet, she estimates its market value to be:

$$
\begin{aligned}
\text{Market Value of Home} \; &= \; \text{Average Price per Square Foot} \times \text{Square Feet of Home} \\
&= \; \$64 \times 1{,}300 \\
&= \; \$83{,}200.
\end{aligned}
$$

She estimates the price of this home at $83,200. Although she will consider other factors, this initial analysis gives her some insight into what the home is worth. For example, the real estate broker told her that the owner of the home has already moved and wants to sell it quickly. Stephanie considers making an offer of $80,000, but she first needs to determine the costs that she will incur as a result of purchasing the home.

Effects of Business Activity and Zoning Laws

The value of a home is also dependent on the demand for homes in that area or subdivision, which can vary in response to business activity or zoning laws.

Business Activity Nearby. When a large firm moves into an area, people hired for jobs at that firm search for homes nearby. As a result, demand for homes in the area increases, and home prices may rise as well. Conversely, when a large firm closes its facilities, home prices in that area may decline as homeowners who worked there attempt to sell their homes. The large supply of homes for sale relative to demand may cause homeowners to lower their price in order to find a willing buyer.

Zoning Laws. Locations are zoned for industrial use or residential use. When zoning laws for a location change, its desirability may be affected. Homes near areas that have just been zoned for industrial use become less desirable. Therefore, the demand for homes in these areas may decline, causing prices of homes to decline as well.

Zoning laws also change for school systems. The value of a subdivision can change substantially in response to a change in the public schools that the resident children would attend. Proximity to schools can increase home values, while increased distance from schools often lowers home values.

Exhibit 10.1 Using a Market Analysis to Purchase a Home

House Size	Price	Price per Square Foot
1,200 square feet	$78,000	$78,000/1,200 = $65
1,300 square feet	$87,100	$87,100/1,300 = $67
1,100 square feet	$66,000	$66,000/1,100 = $60

Average price per square foot = ($65 + $67 + $60)/3 = $64

Obtaining a Second Opinion on Your Valuation

If your valuation leads you to believe that a particular home is undervalued, you may want to get a second opinion before you try to purchase that home. If you are using a real estate broker to help you find a home, that broker may conduct a valuation of the home and offer suggestions about the price that you should be willing to offer. Be aware, however, although brokers are experienced at valuing homes, some brokers provide a valuation that is intended to serve the seller rather than the buyer. That is, they may overestimate the value so that potential buyers are convinced that the home is worth buying. In this way, the brokers can ensure that a home will sell and that they will receive a commission. Although many real estate brokers are honest and will provide an unbiased estimate, you should always conduct your own valuation and carefully assess the broker's valuation.

Negotiating a Price

Once you have finished your valuation and are convinced that you should buy a particular home, you need to negotiate a price with the seller of the home by making an offer. Some homes are initially priced above the price that the seller will accept. As with any investment, you want to make sure that you do not pay more than you have to for a home.

You may consider the advice of your real estate broker on the offer that you should make. Most sellers are willing to accept less than their original asking price. Once you decide on an offering price, you can submit an offer in the form of a contract to buy the home, which must be approved by the seller. Your real estate broker takes the contract to the seller and serves as the intermediary between you and the seller during the negotiation process.

The seller may accept your offer, reject it, or suggest that you revise it. If the asking price is $100,000, and you offer $90,000, the seller may reject that offer but indicate a willingness to accept an offer of, say, $96,000. Then the decision reverts back to you. You can agree, reject that offer, or revise the contract again. For example, you may counter by offering $94,000. The contract can go back and forth until the buyer and seller either come to an agreement or decide that it is no longer worthwhile to pursue a possible agreement. The contract stipulates not only the price, but also other conditions that are requested by the buyer, such as repairs to be completed by the seller and the date when the buyer will be able to move into the home.

TRANSACTION COSTS OF PURCHASING A HOME

Once you have started the offer process, you should begin applying for a mortgage from a financial institution. The loan application process requires that you summarize your financial condition, including your income, your assets, and your liabilities. You will need to provide proof of income, such as recent paycheck stubs and bank statements. The lender will check your financial condition by contacting your employer to verify your employment and to learn your present salary.

In addition to applying for a mortgage, you will need to plan to cover the transaction costs of purchasing the home. These include the down payment and closing costs.

Down Payment

When you purchase a home, you use your money to make a down payment and pay the remaining amount owed with financing. Your down payment represents your equity investment in the home.

For a conventional mortgage, a lender typically requires a down payment of 10 to 20 percent of the home's selling price. The lender expects you to cover a portion of the purchase price with your own money because the home serves as collateral to back the loan. The lending institution bears the risk that you may possibly default on the loan. If you are unable to make your mortgage payments, the lender can take ownership of the home and sell it to obtain the funds that you owe.

10.4 Financial Planning Online: Applying for a Mortgage

Go to
http://www.loanweb.com

Click on
"Loan Type" under "Start Here" and complete area code and state.

This Web site provides access to mortgage applications and a guide for assessing whether to refinance a mortgage.

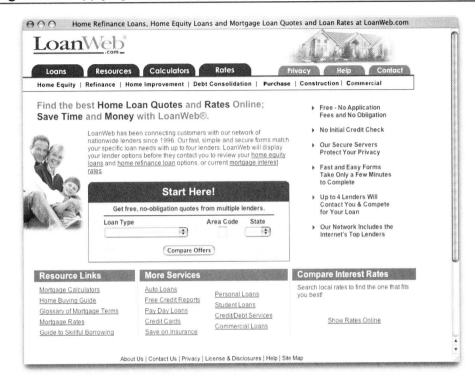

If the home's value declines over time, however, a creditor may not obtain all the funds that it initially lent. Your down payment provides a cushion in case the value of the home declines. The lender could sell the home for less than the original purchase price and still recover all of the mortgage loan.

With government-backed loans, a traditional lender extends the loan, but the government insures it in the event of default. Government-backed mortgages may require lower down payments and may even specify lower interest rates than conventional mortgages. Government-backed mortgages are often backed by the Federal Housing Administration (FHA) or the Veterans Administration (VA). To qualify for federally insured mortgages, borrowers must satisfy various requirements imposed by the guarantors. The FHA loans enable low- or middle-income individuals to obtain mortgage financing. The VA loans are extended to military veterans. Both FHA and VA loans are assumable in the event that the homeowner who initially qualified for the mortgage loan decides to sell the home.

Closing Costs

A borrower incurs various fees in the mortgage loan application process. These fees are often referred to as closing costs. The most important fees are identified here.

Loan Application Fee. When applying for a mortgage loan, you may be charged an application fee by the lender. The fee typically ranges from $100 to $500.

points
A fee charged by the lender when a mortgage loan is provided; stated as a percentage of the purchase price.

Points. Lenders often charge a fee that is commonly referred to as **points**. Points are stated as a percentage of the loan amount. Many lenders charge between 1 and 2 percent of the mortgage loan. If you are charged 2 points when you obtain a mortgage in the amount of $100,000, a fee of $2,000 (computed as 2% × 100,000) is charged at the time the loan is granted. Points are tax-deductible, so the expense can be deducted from your income when determining your taxable income.

Loan Origination Fee. Lenders may also charge a loan origination fee, which is usually 1 percent of the mortgage amount. If you are charged a 1 percent origination fee on a $100,000 mortgage, the fee is $1,000 (computed as 1% × $100,000). Many lenders allow homeowners to select among different fee structures, so you may be able to pay a lower loan origination fee if you accept a slightly higher interest rate. Some lenders may not charge an origination fee, but they charge a higher interest rate on the mortgage instead.

Appraisal Fee. An appraisal is used to estimate the market value of the home and thus protects the financial institution's interests. If you are unable to make your monthly payments, the financial institution can sell the home to recoup the mortgage loan that it provided. The appraisal fee commonly ranges between $200 and $500.

Title Search and Insurance. An agreement to purchase a home from a current owner (as opposed to a new home from a developer) typically involves various transaction costs for a title search and insurance. A title search is conducted by the mortgage company to ensure that the home or property is owned by the seller. Title insurance provides you with protection in the event that persons other than the seller show evidence that they hold the actual deed of ownership to the property. It also protects you in the event that there are other liabilities attached to the home that were not discovered during the title search.

Both the closing costs and the down payment are due after the offer for the home has been accepted at the time of the closing. During the closing, the title for the home is transferred to the buyer, the seller is paid in full, and the buyer takes possession of the home.

EXAMPLE

Recall that Stephanie Spratt is considering making an offer of $80,000 on a house. She wants to determine what her transaction costs would be. She is planning to make a down payment of $8,000 and borrow $72,000. She called York Financial Institution for information about obtaining a mortgage loan. She learned that if she applied for a $72,000 mortgage, York would charge the following:

- 1 point
- 1 percent origination fee
- $300 for an appraisal
- $200 application fee
- $400 for a title search and title insurance
- $200 for other fees

Thus, the total closing costs would be:

Points	(1% × $72,000)	$720
Origination Fee	(1% × $72,000)	720
Appraisal Fee		300
Application Fee		200
Title Search and Insurance		400
Other Fees		200
Total		**$2,540**

Stephanie will need a down payment of $8,000 and $2,540 in closing costs to purchase the home.

CHARACTERISTICS OF A FIXED-RATE MORTGAGE

fixed-rate mortgage
A mortgage in which a fixed interest rate is specified until maturity.

A mortgage loan is most likely the biggest loan you will ever obtain in your lifetime. The terms for mortgages vary. You will need to decide whether to obtain a fixed-rate or adjustable-rate mortgage and what the maturity of the mortgage should be. Traditionally, mortgages had a fixed interest rate and a maturity of 30 years. A **fixed-rate mortgage** specifies a fixed interest rate that is constant for the life of the mortgage. When homeowners expect that interest rates will rise, they tend to prefer fixed-rate mortgages because their mortgage payments will be sheltered from the rising market interest rates. Many other types of mortgages are available, but the traditional fixed-rate 30-year mortgage is still popular. You can access various Web sites to obtain a general summary of prevailing mortgage rates, but rates vary among financial institutions. If you sell a home before the mortgage is paid off, you can use a portion of the proceeds from selling the home to pay off the mortgage. Alternatively, it may be possible for the buyer to assume your mortgage under some conditions.

Amortization Table

Your monthly mortgage payment for a fixed-rate mortgage is based on an amortization schedule. This schedule discloses the monthly payment that you will make, based on a specific mortgage amount, a fixed interest rate level, and a maturity.

Allocation of the Mortgage Payment. Each monthly mortgage payment represents a partial equity payment that pays a portion of the principal of the loan and an interest payment.

10.5 Financial Planning Online: Mortgage Rates

Go to
http://biz.yahoo.com/b/r/m.html

Click on
"Mortgage" under "Today's Rates"

This Web site provides national averages for mortgage rates, as well as average mortgage rates for specific regions and states.

EXAMPLE

Stephanie Spratt decides to review mortgage Web sites to estimate her monthly mortgage payments. One Web site asks her to input the mortgage amount she desires and the interest rate that she expects to pay on a 30-year mortgage. She inputs $72,000 as the amount and 8 percent as the interest rate. The Web site then provides her with an amortization schedule, which is summarized in Exhibit 10.2. This exhibit shows how her mortgage payments would be allocated to paying off principal versus interest. Notice how the initial payments are allocated mostly to interest, with a relatively small amount used to pay off the principal. For example, for month 2, $49 of her payment is applied to the principal, while $479 goes to pay the interest expense. Initially, when the amount of principal is large, most of her payment is needed to cover the interest owed. As time passes, the proportion of the payment allocated to equity increases. Notice that by month 360, $525 of the payment is applied to principal and $3 to interest.

Notice, too, that her balance after 100 months is $65,163. This means that over a period of more than eight years, Stephanie would pay off less than $7,000 of the equity in her home, or less than 10 percent of the original mortgage amount. After 200 months (two-thirds of the life of the 30-year mortgage), her mortgage balance would be almost $52,000, which means she would have paid off about $20,000 of the $72,000 mortgage.

The amount of Stephanie's annual mortgage payments that would be allocated to paying off the principal is shown in Exhibit 10.3. In the first year, she would pay off only $601 of the principal, while the rest of her mortgage payments ($5,738) in the first year would be used to pay interest. This information is very surprising to Stephanie, so she reviews the mortgage situation further to determine if it is possible to build equity more quickly.

Exhibit 10.2 Amortization Schedule for a 30-Year (360-Month) Fixed-Rate Mortgage for $72,000 at an 8 Percent Interest Rate

Month	Payment	Principal	Interest	Balance
1	$528	$48	$480	$71,952
2	528	49	479	71,903
10 • • •	528	51	477	71,502
25 • • •	528	57	472	70,691
49 • • •	528	66	462	69,211
100 • • •	528	93	435	65,163
200 • • •	528	181	347	51,877
360	528	525	3	0

Note: Numbers are rounded to the nearest dollar.

Exhibit 10.3 Allocation of Principal versus Interest Paid per Year on a $72,000 Mortgage

Year	Principal Paid in That Year	Interest Paid in That Year
1	$601	$5,738
2	651	5,688
3	705	5,634
4	764	5,576
6	896	5,444
8	1,051	5,289
10	1,233	5,107
12	1,446	4,894
15	1,836	4,503
17	2,154	4,186
20	2,736	3,603
22	3,209	3,131
24	3,764	2,576
26	4,415	1,925
28	5,178	1,161
30	6,073	266

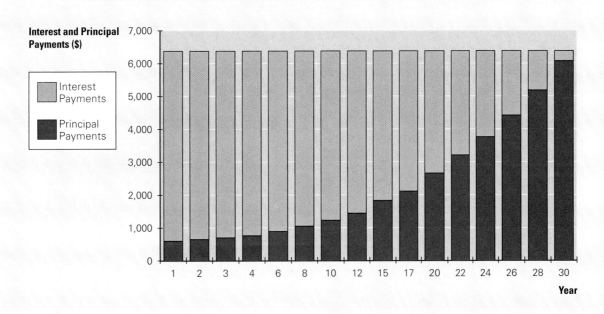

Impact of the Mortgage Amount on the Monthly Payment

The larger the mortgage amount, the larger your monthly payments will be for a given interest rate and maturity. Exhibit 10.4 shows the monthly payment based on a 30-year mortgage and an 8 percent interest rate for different mortgage amounts. Notice the change in the mortgage payment for larger mortgage amounts. For example, the monthly mortgage payment for a $90,000 mortgage is $660, while the monthly payment for a $100,000 mortgage is $734.

Exhibit 10.4 Monthly Mortgage Payments Based on Different Mortgage Amounts (30-Year Fixed-Rate Mortgage; 8 Percent Interest Rate)

Mortgage Amount	Monthly Mortgage Payment
$60,000	$440
70,000	513
80,000	587
90,000	660
100,000	734
110,000	807
120,000	880

Impact of the Interest Rate on the Monthly Payment

Given the large amount of funds that you may borrow to finance a home, you should make every effort to obtain a mortgage loan that has a low interest rate. The lower the interest rate on the mortgage, the smaller the monthly mortgage payment. Even a slight increase (such as 0.5 percent) in the interest rate increases your monthly mortgage payment.

In the last decade, the 15-year mortgage has become very popular as an alternative to the 30-year mortgage. The interest rate charged on 15-year and 30-year fixed-rate mortgages is typically related to other long-term interest rates (such as the 30-year Treasury bond rate) at the time that the mortgage is created. For this reason, homeowners seek a fixed-rate mortgage when they believe that interest rates will rise in the future.

10.6 Financial Planning Online: Estimating Mortgage Payments

Go to
http://www.bloomberg.com/ analysis/calculators/ mortgage.html

This Web site provides the monthly payment on a mortgage based on the loan amount, interest rate, and the loan maturity.

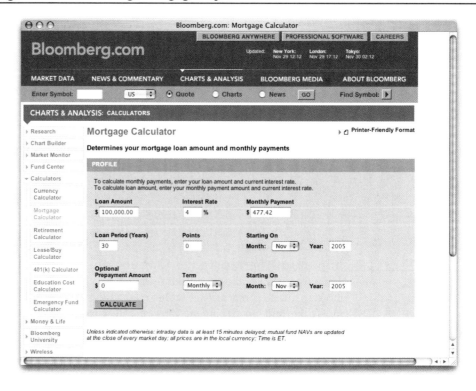

Impact of the Mortgage Maturity on the Monthly Payment

The maturity of the mortgage indicates how long you will take to complete your financing payments and pay off the mortgage. At that point, you own the home outright. The advantage of a 15-year mortgage is that you will have paid off your mortgage after 15 years, whereas a 30-year mortgage requires payments for an additional 15 years. Monthly payments on a 15-year mortgage are typically higher, but you pay less interest over the life of the loan and build equity at a faster pace.

The advantage of a 30-year mortgage is that you have smaller monthly payments for a given mortgage loan amount than you would for a 15-year mortgage. The monthly payments may be more affordable, and you may have more liquidity.

Estimating the Monthly Mortgage Payment

You can use mortgage loan Web sites to obtain estimates of your monthly payments based on a specific mortgage amount and maturity.

EXAMPLE

Stephanie Spratt wants to estimate her monthly mortgage payment on a $72,000 fixed-rate mortgage, based on several interest rate scenarios for 15- and 30-year maturities, as shown in Exhibit 10.5. At an interest rate of 7 percent, the monthly payment on the 30-year mortgage would be $479. At an interest rate of 9 percent, the monthly payment on the 30-year mortgage would be $579, or $100 more. Next, Stephanie evaluates the payments for a 15-year term. She believes she can obtain a loan at an 8 percent interest rate on either maturity, so she focuses on the difference in monthly payments pertaining to that rate.

Although the monthly payment is more for the 15-year mortgage, the difference is not as large as Stephanie expected. Given the interest rate of 8 percent, the 15-year mortgage requires a monthly payment of $688, which is $160 more than the $528 payment on the 30-year mortgage. This is the obvious disadvantage of a 15-year mortgage.

The advantage is that she would pay down the mortgage sooner, meaning that she would more quickly accumulate a larger equity investment in the home. To gain more insight on this advantage, she reviews a Web site to compare the remaining loan balance for each of the two mortgage maturities on a year-by-year basis. This comparison is summarized in Exhibit 10.6. Notice that after six years, she would still owe $67,554 on the 30-year mortgage, versus

Exhibit 10.5 Comparison of Monthly Payments for a 30-Year versus a 15-Year Mortgage of $72,000 Based on Different Interest Rates

	Monthly Payment on a:	
Interest Rate	**30-Year Mortgage**	**15-Year Mortgage**
7.0%	$479	$647
7.5	503	667
8.0	528	688
8.5	554	709
9.0	579	730
9.5	605	752
10.0	632	774

Note: Payments are rounded to the nearest dollar.

Exhibit 10.6 Comparison of Mortgage Balance for a 30-Year versus a 15-Year Mortgage ($72,000 Initial Mortgage Amount; 8 Percent Interest Rate)

End of Year	Balance on 30-Year Mortgage	Balance on 15-Year Mortgage
1	$71,399	$69,410
2	70,747	66,604
3	70,042	63,566
4	69,278	60,275
5	68,450	56,712
6	67,554	52,852
7	66,583	48,672
8	65,533	44,146
9	64,395	39,244
10	63,162	33,934
11	61,826	28,185
12	60,381	21,957
13	58,815	15,213
14	57,119	7,910
15	55,283	0

Note: Balances are rounded to the nearest dollar.

$52,852 (almost $15,000 less) on the 15-year mortgage. After 10 years, she would owe almost $30,000 more on the 30-year mortgage than on the 15-year mortgage. After 15 years, she would still owe about $55,000 on the 30-year mortgage, while the 15-year mortgage would be paid off.

The Web site also shows the total payments over the life of the mortgage for both types of mortgages if the mortgage is not paid off until maturity.

	30-Year Mortgage	15-Year Mortgage
Total Principal Payments	$72,000	$72,000
Total Interest Payments	118,192	51,852
Total Payments	$190,192	$123,852

Stephanie would pay about $66,000 more in interest with the 30-year mortgage than with the 15-year mortgage. The total interest payments on the 30-year mortgage are much larger than the total principal payments that would be made over the life of the 15-year mortgage.

Weighing the advantages of the 15-year mortgage against the disadvantage of paying the extra $160 per month, Stephanie decides she prefers the 15-year mortgage. Even if she decides to sell this home before she pays off the 15-year mortgage, she will have paid down a larger amount of the mortgage. Since she will have a larger equity investment (from paying off more of the principal) with the 15-year mortgage, she will increase her net worth to a greater degree.

CHARACTERISTICS OF AN ADJUSTABLE-RATE MORTGAGE

adjustable-rate mortgage (ARM)
A mortgage where the interest owed changes in response to movements in a specific market-determined interest rate.

An alternative to a fixed-rate mortgage is an **adjustable-rate mortgage (ARM)**, in which the interest owed changes in response to movements in a specific market-determined interest rate. An ARM is sometimes referred to as a variable-rate mortgage. ARMs should definitely be considered along with fixed-rate mortgages. Like a fixed-rate mortgage, an ARM can be obtained for a 15-year or a 30-year maturity. ARMs have various characteristics that must be stated in the mortgage contract.

In 2003, adjustable-rate mortgages made up about 28 percent of all mortgages. As interest rates increased during 2004 and 2005, more home buyers preferred to avoid fixed-rate mortgages because they expected that interest rates would decline over time. By 2005, the proportion of adjustable-rate morgages increased to about 35 percent.

Initial Rate

Many ARMs specify a relatively low initial mortgage rate over the first year or so. This initial rate is beneficial to homeowners in that it results in a low monthly mortgage payment over the first year. Recognize, however, that this rate is only temporary, as the mortgage rate will be adjusted.

Interest Rate Index

The initial mortgage rate will be adjusted after a period (such as one year) in line with a specified interest rate index. The interest rate index to which the mortgage rate is tied must be included in the mortgage contract. Many ARMs use a rate that is tied to the average cost of deposits of financial institutions. For example, the interest rate charged on an ARM might be set at 3 percentage points above that benchmark. Thus, if the benchmark is 4 percent in a given year, the ARM will apply an interest rate of 7 percent (computed as 4% + 3%). If the interest rate index has risen to 5 percent by the time of the next mortgage rate adjustment, the new mortgage rate will be 8 percent (computed as 5% + 3%).

10.7 Financial Planning Online: Should You Obtain a Fixed- or an Adjustable-Rate Mortgage?

Go to
http://www.federalreserve.gov/pubs/arms/arms_english.htm

This Web site provides valuable information regarding adjustable-rate mortgages that may be useful when deciding whether to finance your home with a fixed- or adjustable-rate mortgage.

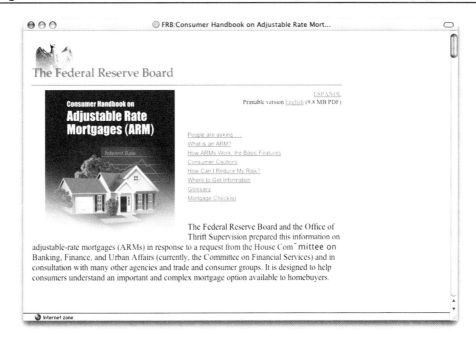

Frequency of Rate Adjustments

The mortgage contract also specifies how frequently the mortgage rate will be adjusted. Many ARMs specify that the rate will be adjusted once a year. Thus, the mortgage rate is set based on the specified interest rate index and then remains the same for the next 12 months. This means that the monthly payments will be constant for the next 12 months. At the end of the 12-month period, the mortgage rate is revised based on the prevailing interest rate index and is held constant for the following 12 months.

Some mortgages allow for less frequent adjustments, such as every three years or every five years. Others allow a single adjustment at the end of the fifth year, and the adjusted rate is then held constant over the next 25 years of a 30-year mortgage.

Other ARMs offer the following alternatives:

- An interest rate that adjusts every five years.

- An interest rate that is fixed for the first three years, but converts to an ARM (and adjusts annually) after three years.

- An interest rate that is fixed for the first five years, but converts to an ARM (and adjusts annually) after five years.

- An interest rate that adjusts for the first five years and then is fixed (based on an interest rate index at that time) for the next 25 years.

With so many alternatives available, you can easily find a mortgage that fits your preferences. For example, if you expect that interest rates will decline consistently over time, you may prefer an ARM that is adjusted every year. If your expectations are correct, your mortgage rate will decline over time with the decline in market interest rates. It is difficult to forecast the direction of interest rates accurately, however, which means that your future mortgage payments are uncertain.

CAPS ON ADJUSTABLE-RATE MORTGAGES

caps
Maximum and minimum fluctuations in the interest rate on an adjustable-rate mortgage.

The mortgage contract also typically specifies **caps**, or a maximum and minimum fluctuation in the interest rate. For example, an ARM may have a cap of 2 percent per year, which prevents the mortgage rate from being adjusted upward by more than 2 percentage points from its existing level in each year. Assume the market interest rate increases by 3 percentage points from one year to the next. Without a cap, the mortgage rate on the ARM would increase by 3 percentage points. With a 2 percent cap, however, only an increase of 2 percentage points is allowed in that year. This cap is useful because it limits the potential increase in the mortgage payments that may result from an increase in interest rates.

In addition to a cap on the annual increase in the mortgage rate, there is usually a lifetime cap, which represents the maximum amount of the increase in the mortgage rate over the life of the mortgage. A lifetime cap of 5 percent is commonly used. Thus, if an ARM has an initial mortgage rate of 7 percent and a 5 percent cap, the maximum mortgage rate over the life of the mortgage would be 12 percent.

Financing with a Fixed- versus an Adjustable-Rate Mortgage

Your decision to use a fixed- versus an adjustable-rate mortgage to finance the purchase of a home is dependent on your expectations of future interest rates. The primary advantage of an ARM is that the initial interest rate is lower than that of a fixed-rate mortgage. Yet, if interest rates rise, you may end up paying a higher interest rate on your mortgage than if you had obtained a fixed-rate mortgage.

EXAMPLE

Stephanie Spratt has already determined that if she finances with a 15-year fixed-rate mortgage, she would pay an 8 percent interest rate. Alternatively, she could obtain an adjustable-rate mortgage that specifies an initial rate of 6 percent, with the interest rate adjusted each year to an index reflecting the average cost of bank funds plus 3 percentage points. Assuming the index rate is 5 percent next year, the rate applied to her mortgage would be 8 percent for the following year.

Stephanie notices that financial experts have predicted an increase in interest rates in the near future. She is uncomfortable with the uncertainty surrounding her mortgage rate and therefore surrounding her mortgage payment. Although an ARM would result in a lower mortgage payment in the first year, it would result in a higher mortgage payment in the following years if interest rates increase. Thus, Stephanie decides to choose a fixed-rate mortgage instead of an ARM.

DECISION TO OWN VERSUS RENT A HOME

When considering the purchase (and therefore ownership) of a home, you should compare the cost of purchasing a home with the cost of renting. People attribute different advantages and disadvantages to owning a home versus renting because preferences are subjective. Some individuals value the privacy of a home, while others value the flexibility of an apartment, which allows them to move without much cost or difficulty. The financial assessment of owning a home versus renting can be performed objectively. Once the financial assessment is conducted, personal preferences can also be considered.

Estimating the Total Cost of Renting and Owning

The main cost of renting a home is the monthly rent payment. There is also an opportunity cost of tying up funds in a security deposit. Those funds could have been invested if you did not need to provide the security deposit. Another possible cost of renting is the purchase of renter's insurance.

The primary costs of purchasing a home are the down payment and the monthly mortgage payment. The down payment has an opportunity cost because the funds could have been invested to earn interest if they were not tied up in the purchase of the home. Closing costs are incurred at the time the home is purchased, although a portion of these costs is tax-deductible. Owning a home also involves some additional costs, such as maintenance and repair. Property taxes are assessed annually as a percentage of the home's value. Homeowner's insurance is paid annually and is primarily based on the value of the home.

EXAMPLE

Stephanie Spratt has found a home she desires and has obtained financing. Before making a final decision, she wants to compare the cost of the home to the cost of remaining in her apartment. Although she would prefer a home, she wants to determine how much more expensive the home is compared to the apartment. If she purchases the home, she expects to live in it for at least three years. Therefore, she decides to compare the cost of owning a home to the cost of renting over the next three years. First, Stephanie calculates the cost of renting:

- **Cost of Rent.** Her estimated cost of renting is shown in the top panel of Exhibit 10.7. Her rent is currently $600 per month, so her annual rent is $7,200 (computed as $600 × 12). She does not expect a rent increase over the next three years and therefore estimates her cost of renting over this period to be $7,200 × 3 = $21,600. (If she had expected an increase in rent, she would have simply added the extra cost to the estimated rent over the next three years.)

- **Cost of Renter's Insurance.** She does not have renter's insurance at this time, as the value of her household assets is low.

- **Opportunity Cost of Security Deposit.** She provided a security deposit of $1,000 to the apartment complex. While she expects to get this deposit back when she stops renting, there is an opportunity cost associated with it. She could have invested those funds in a tax-free money market fund earning 4 percent annually, which would have generated annual interest of $40 (computed as $1,000 × .04). The opportunity cost over three years is three times the annual cost, or $120.

- **Total Cost of Renting.** Stephanie estimates the total cost of renting as $7,240 per year and $21,720 over the next three years, as shown in Exhibit 10.7.

Stephanie determines the total cost of purchasing a home by adding up expenses, subtracting any tax savings, and subtracting the value of the equity:

- **Mortgage Payment.** The primary cost of buying a home is the mortgage payment, which she expects to be $688 per month or $8,256 per year (not including payments for property taxes or house insurance).

- **Down Payment.** Stephanie would make a down payment of $8,000 to buy the home.

- **Opportunity Cost of the Down Payment.** If Stephanie did not buy a house, she could have invested the $8,000 in a tax-free security and earned 4 percent per year. Therefore, the annual opportunity cost (what she could have earned if she invested the funds) is $320 (computed as $8,000 × .04).

Exhibit 10.7 Comparing the Total Cost of Renting versus Buying a Home over a Three-Year Period

Cost of Renting

	Amount per Year	Total over Next Three Years
Rent ($600 per month)	$7,200	$21,600
Renter's insurance	0	0
Opportunity cost of security deposit	40	120
Total cost of renting	$7,240	$21,720

Cost of Purchasing

	Amount per Year	Total over Next Three Years
Mortgage payment ($688 per month)	$8,256	$24,768
Down payment	8,000	8,000 (first year only)
Opportunity cost of down payment	320	960
Property taxes	1,000	3,000
Home insurance	600	1,800
Closing costs	2,540	2,540 (first year only)
Maintenance costs	1,000	3,000
Total costs before tax benefits		**$44,068**
Total tax savings		$1,180
Equity investment		$16,434
Increase in home value		0
Value of equity		$16,434
Cost of purchasing home over three years		**$26,454**

- **Property Taxes.** Stephanie assumes that the annual property tax will be $1,000 based on last year's property tax paid by the current owner of the home.

- **Home Insurance.** Insurance on this home will cost $600 per year (this estimate is based on the home insurance premium paid by the current owner of the home).

- **Closing Costs.** Closing costs (transaction costs) associated with buying a home must be included, although those costs are incurred only in the first year for a mortgage. The closing costs are estimated to be $2,540, as shown earlier.

- **Maintenance Costs.** Stephanie expects maintenance costs on the home to be $1,000 per year.

- **Utilities.** She will pay for utilities such as water and electricity and will incur a cable TV bill if she buys the home. She already incurs those costs while renting an apartment, so she does not need to include them in her analysis.

- **Tax Savings.** Stephanie must also consider the tax savings that a home provides. Since the home mortgage interest is tax-deductible, she estimates that her taxes will be reduced by 25 percent of the amount by which her taxable income is reduced. The amount of mortgage interest changes every year, and therefore so does her tax savings from interest expenses. She can estimate her interest expenses over three years by using an amortization table based on her mortgage amount, mortgage maturity, and mortgage rate. She estimates that her interest expense over the next three years will be about $16,000.

Note that Stephanie will generate tax savings from property taxes because they are tax-deductible. Given an annual property tax of $1,000, she will have a $3,000 tax deduction over the next three years. Stephanie will also generate tax savings from the points that she would pay (a one-time fee of $720) as part of the closing costs, because the points are tax-deductible.

The total itemized deductions resulting from the purchase of the house over the next three years are:

	Deduction
Interest	$16,000
Property Taxes	$3,000
Points	$720
Total	$19,720

However, keep in mind that individuals without significant tax deductions can receive their standard deduction. Recall from Chapter 4 that Stephanie can take a standard deduction of $5,000 each year if she does not itemize her deductions. If she does not buy the home, she would take the standard deduction each year, which would be worth $15,000 over three years ($5,000 × 3 years).

The tax savings from buying the home occur because the value of itemized deductions exceeds the value of standard deductions by $4,720 ($19,720 − $15,000) over the three-year period. When considering Stephanie's marginal tax rate, extra deductions result in a tax savings of:

Tax Savings	=	Value of Extra Deductions × Marginal Tax Rate
	=	$4,720 × .25
	=	$1,180.

- **Value of the Equity Investment.** Another advantage of owning a home is that Stephanie will have an equity investment in it. Her down payment will be $8,000, and she will pay about $8,434 in principal on her mortgage over the three-year period.

The value of this equity investment could be higher in three years if the market value of the home increases. If Stephanie assumes that the home's value will not change, the value of the equity investment will be $16,434 (computed as $8,000 + $8,434).

- **Total Cost of Purchasing a Home.** The total cost of purchasing a home is determined by adding all the expenses, subtracting the tax savings, and then subtracting the equity investment. As shown in Exhibit 10.7, Stephanie estimates that the total cost of purchasing the home over the three-year period will be $26,454.

The total cost of purchasing a home over three years is about $4,734 more than the cost of renting. Stephanie decides that she wants to buy the home, mainly because she would rather live in a home than an apartment. She also believes that the home's value may rise over time, a factor that was not part of her analysis. If the value of the home increased by 2 percent a year, the market value of her equity in the home would increase by about $5,000.

Now that Stephanie has decided that she wants to purchase a home and can afford it, she submits her offer of $80,000, which is accepted by the seller.

SPECIAL TYPES OF MORTGAGES

In some cases, prospective buyers do not qualify for a traditional fixed-rate mortgage or an adjustable-rate mortgage. Some special types of mortgages are available that can make a home more affordable.

Graduated Payment Mortgage

graduated payment mortgage
A mortgage where the payments are low in the early years and then rise to a higher level over time.

A **graduated payment mortgage** sets relatively low monthly mortgage payments when the mortgage is first created and then gradually increases the payments over the first five or so years. The payments level off after that time. This type of mortgage may be useful for someone whose income will increase over time, since the mortgage payments will increase as the homeowner's income increases. A graduated payment mortgage would not be desirable for people who are not certain that their income will rise.

Balloon Payment Mortgage

balloon payment mortgage
A mortgage where the monthly payments are relatively low, but one large payment is required after a specified period to pay off the mortgage loan.

A **balloon payment mortgage** sets relatively low monthly payments and then requires one large payment (called a balloon payment) after a specified period (such as five years) to pay off the remainder of the mortgage loan. A balloon payment mortgage is sometimes offered by the seller of a home to the buyer, especially when the buyer cannot afford to make large monthly payments and does not qualify for a more traditional mortgage. In this situation, the seller might provide a mortgage for five years. The expectation is that the buyer's income will rise, enabling the buyer to obtain a traditional mortgage from a financial institution before the end of the five-year period. Then, the buyer will have enough cash to make the balloon payment to the seller.

Interest-only Mortgage

Interest-only mortgages are adjustable-rate mortgages that allow home buyers to pay only interest on the mortgage during the first few years. These mortgages have become very popular in recent years because no principal is paid in this period and mortgage payments are more affordable. However, the disadvantage is that the mortgage payment increases abruptly at the time that the homeowner must begin to make principal payments. The mortgage payment may be 30 percent higher at this point, and some homeowners may not be able to make a mortgage payment that is substantially higher than their previous payments.

10.8 Financial Planning Online: Should You Rent or Buy?

Go to
http://realestate.yahoo.com/
calculators/
rent_vs_own.html

This Web site provides a recommendation on whether you should buy a home, based on your rent versus the expenses of the home you are considering.

⊖ ○ ○ Find Rent vs Own Calculators, Mortgage Calculators, Refinance Loans and Home Equity Loans on Yahoo! Real Estate
• Home Equity Loans & Rates

Rent vs. Own Calculator

This calculator lets you calculate the difference between renting a property and buying a home.

Monthly Rental Payment:	$
Annual Rent Increase Rate:	%
Purchase Price of Home:	$
Anticipated Home Price Increment:	(% of Home Price)
Anticipated Down Payment:	10 (% of Purchase Price)
Other Loan Cost:	$
Mortgage Interest Rate:	5.5 %
Term in Years:	30
Your State + Federal Tax Rate:	28 %
Selling Cost:	6 (% of Selling Price)
Property Tax:	1 (% of Home Price)
Yearly Homeowners Insurance:	$

See more calculators   (Calculate)

Sponsored Links

Visit our partners' sites

Countrywide
Free, no obligation loan consultation
Expert advice: 888-536-0529

Quicken Loans
America's Home Loan Experts™
$200K home loan for only $875/mo.
Click here or call 800-719-1533

LendingTree
When Banks Compete You Win
Æ
Low rates from 5.74% Start Now

MORTGAGE REFINANCING

mortgage refinancing
Paying off an existing mortgage with a new mortgage that has a lower interest rate.

Mortgage refinancing involves paying off an existing mortgage with a new mortgage that has a lower interest rate. You may use mortgage refinancing to obtain a new mortgage if market interest rates (and therefore mortgage rates) decline. One disadvantage of mortgage refinancing is that you will incur closing costs again. Nevertheless, it may still be advantageous to refinance because the savings on your monthly mortgage payments (even after considering tax effects) may exceed the new closing costs. Mortgage refinancing is more likely to be worthwhile when the prevailing mortgage interest rate is substantially below the interest rate on your existing mortgage. It is also more likely to be worthwhile when you expect to be living in the home for a long time because you will reap greater benefits from the lower monthly mortgage payments that result from refinancing.

Rate Modification

When interest rates decline, some mortgage lenders may be willing to allow a "rate modification" to existing mortgage holders with a fixed-rate mortgage. They may charge a one-time fee that is typically between $500 and $1,500. Your fixed-rate mortgage may be revised to reflect the prevailing mortgage rate. You can benefit because you receive the lower interest rate. You would not need to go through the process of refinancing through another mortgage lender, or incur costs associated with a new mortgage application. Some mortgage lenders are willing to allow rate modifications because they realize that if they do not provide you with an opportunity to pay the lower interest rate, you will likely obtain a new mortgage from another lender and will pay off your existing mortgage. In this case, you will no longer make payments at the high interest rate and your existing mortgage lender will lose you as a customer. By allowing a rate modification, your existing mortgage lender retains you as a customer by offering you a mortgage that is similar to what it is presently offering to other new customers, and it earns a one-time fee from you for modifying the mortgage rate that you are charged.

Refinancing Analysis

To determine whether you should refinance, you can compare the advantage of monthly savings of interest expenses to the cost of refinancing. If the benefits from reducing your interest expenses exceed the closing costs incurred from refinancing, the refinancing is feasible.

The advantages of refinancing (lower interest payments) occur each year, while the disadvantage (closing costs) occurs only at the time of refinancing. Therefore, refinancing tends to be more beneficial when a homeowner plans to own the home for a longer period. The savings from a lower interest payment can accumulate over each additional year the mortgage exists.

EXAMPLE

Stephanie Spratt decides that if interest rates decline in the future, she may refinance. If interest rates decline to 7 percent a year from now, Stephanie would save about $40 on her monthly mortgage payment by refinancing. Stephanie needs to determine the potential savings in the monthly interest payments over the time that she expects to remain in the home.

A monthly reduction in interest payments of $40 reflects an annual reduction of $480 (computed as $40 × 12). But because interest on the mortgage is tax-deductible, the reduction in interest payments by $480 interest means that her taxable income would be $480 higher. Since her marginal tax rate is 25 percent, her taxes would increase:

$$\text{Annual Increase in Taxes} = \text{Annual Increase in Taxable Income} \times \text{Marginal Tax Rate}$$
$$= \$480 \times .25$$
$$= \$120.$$

Her annual savings due to refinancing at a lower interest rate would be:

$$\$480 - \$120 = \$360.$$

Assuming that she plans to remain in the home for two more years from the time of refinancing, her total savings would be:

$$\$360 \times 2 = \$720.$$

The disadvantage of refinancing is that Stephanie may once again incur the same closing costs ($2,540). Before comparing this cost to the benefits of refinancing, she accounts for the tax savings. Since the points are tax-deductible, she determines the tax savings from these costs:

$$\text{Tax Savings on Points} = \text{Cost of Points} \times \text{Marginal Tax Rate}$$
$$= \$720 \times .25$$
$$= \$180.$$

$$\text{After-tax Closing Costs} = \text{Closing Costs} - \text{Tax Savings}$$
$$= \$2,540 - \$180$$
$$= \$2,360.$$

The after-tax closing costs ($2,360) due to refinancing would exceed the savings on the interest payments ($720) over the next two years. Stephanie is now aware that if interest rates decrease by 1 percent over the next year, it would not be worthwhile for her to refinance her home.

HOW A MORTGAGE FITS WITHIN YOUR FINANCIAL PLAN

The following are the key mortgage loan decisions that should be included within your financial plan:

- What mortgage amount can you afford?

- What maturity should you select?

- Should you consider a fixed-rate or an adjustable-rate mortgage?

By making informed decisions, you can avoid accumulating an excessive amount of debt. Exhibit 10.8 provides a summary of how Stephanie Spratt's mortgage loan decisions apply to her financial plan.

Exhibit 10.8 How Mortgage Financing Fits within Stephanie's Financial Plan

---

GOALS FOR MORTGAGE FINANCING

1. Limit the amount of mortgage financing to a level that is affordable.
2. Select a short loan maturity if possible, assuming that the payments are affordable.
3. Select the type of mortgage loan (fixed- or adjustable-rate) that is more likely to result in lower interest expenses.

ANALYSIS

	15-Year Mortgage (8% interest rate)	30-Year Mortgage (8% interest rate)
Monthly payment	$688	$528
Total interest payments	$51,852	$118,192
Advantages	Pay off mortgage in half the time of a 30-year mortgage; pay lower interest expenses on the loan	Smaller monthly payment
Difference between mortgage payment and rent payment	$688 – $600 = $88	$528 – $600 = –$72

DECISIONS

Decision on Affording a Mortgage:

The monthly interest payment on a $72,000 mortgage loan with a 15-year maturity is $688. My rent is $600 per month, so the difference is $88 per month. Since my monthly cash flows (from my salary) exceed my typical monthly expenses (including my car loan payment) and my purchases of clothes by almost $600, I can afford that difference. I will not save as much money as I planned if I buy a home, but I will be building equity.

Decision on the Mortgage Maturity:

I prefer the 15-year mortgage because I will pay off a larger portion of the principal each year.

Decision on the Type of Mortgage Loan:

I prefer the fixed-rate mortgage because I know with certainty that the monthly payments will not increase. I am worried that interest rates may increase in the future, which would cause interest expenses to be higher on the adjustable-rate mortgage.

DISCUSSION QUESTIONS

1. How would Stephanie's mortgage financing decisions be different if she were a single mother of two children?

2. How would Stephanie's mortgage financing decisions be affected if she were 35 years old? If she were 50 years old?

SUMMARY

When considering the purchase of a home, you should evaluate your financial situation to determine how much you can afford. Some of the key criteria used in the selection process are price, convenience of the location, quality, the school system, and the potential resale value.

You can conduct a valuation of a home with a market analysis. Homes in the same area that were recently sold can be used to determine the average price per square foot. Then this price per square foot can be applied to the square footage of the home you wish to value.

The transaction costs of purchasing a home include the down payment and closing costs. The key closing costs are points and the origination fee.

A fixed-rate mortgage specifies a fixed interest rate to be paid over the life of the mortgage. Since most of the monthly mortgage payment on a 30-year mortgage is allocated to cover the interest expense in the early years, a relatively small amount of principal is paid off in those years. A 15-year fixed-rate mortgage is a popular alternative to the 30-year mortgage. It requires a larger monthly pay-

ment, but a larger proportion of the payment is allocated to principal in the early years.

An adjustable-rate mortgage (ARM) ties the interest rate to an interest rate index, so the mortgage interest rate changes over time with the index. Homeowners who expect interest rates to decline in the future are especially likely to choose ARMs.

Before making a final decision to buy a home, you can compare the total cost of owning a home versus renting over a particular period to determine which choice will enhance your financial position more. The total cost of owning a home is estimated by adding up the expenses associated with the home, subtracting the tax savings from owning the home, and subtracting the expected value of the equity of the home at the end of the period.

You may consider mortgage refinancing when quoted interest rates on new mortgages decline. When refinancing, you will incur closing costs. Thus, you should consider refinancing only if the benefits (expected reduction in interest expenses over time) exceed the closing costs.

INTEGRATING THE KEY CONCEPTS

Your mortgage decision affects your ability to purchase a home, as well as other parts of your financial plan. You will need to maintain more liquidity (Part 2) than before to ensure that you will have sufficient funds each month to make your mortgage payment. Your decision to buy a home means that you will have to obtain insurance (Part 4) to protect the home and be insured against any liability resulting from the home. You will likely have less funds for

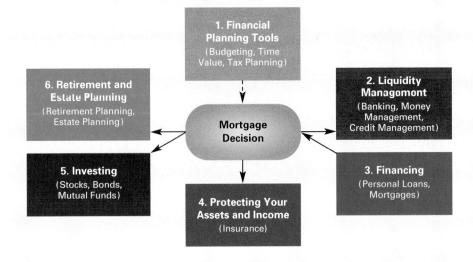

investments (Part 5) and may even have to sell some of your investments to have sufficient cash to make a down payment or monthly mortgage payments.

REVIEW QUESTIONS

1. What is your first task when considering buying a home? Why is this step important? How can a real estate broker help you?

2. What are the two financial components you must consider before purchasing a home? Why should you consider them?

3. What should you consider when determining an affordable down payment and monthly mortgage payments?

4. List the criteria you should use when selecting a home.

5. How do price, convenience of the location, and maintenance affect your home-buying decisions?

6. Why is the reputation of the school system in the area of the home you are buying important?

7. Why do insurance costs and taxes vary among homes?

8. What is the main factor in determining a home's resale value? How can you predict a home's resale value? Who pays commissions when a home is sold?

9. Once you have reduced your list of three or four homes down to one home, what is your next step? Should you offer the price the seller is asking? Describe how you would conduct a market analysis of the home.

10. Why does the value of a home depend on the demand for homes? What factors influence the demand for homes?

11. How do lenders protect their interest in a home? Describe two government-backed home loan programs.

12. What are closing costs? List and briefly describe the different closing costs you might incur when applying for a mortgage.

13. Describe the characteristics of a fixed-rate mortgage. Why do certain homeowners prefer a fixed-rate mortgage to an adjustable-rate mortgage?

14. What is an amortization table? What does each mortgage payment represent?

15. List the three things that determine the amount of the monthly mortgage payment. Explain how each affects the payment.

16. Discuss the characteristics of an adjustable-rate mortgage. What influences your choice of a fixed- or adjustable-rate mortgage?

17. What are the costs of renting a home?

18. Describe some of the costs of buying a home. Are there potential tax savings associated with buying a home?

19. Describe the features of graduated payment and balloon payment mortgages.

20. What is mortgage refinancing? Are there any disadvantages to refinancing?

VIDEO QUESTIONS

1. A home is the single biggest purchase most of us will ever make. On top of the cost of a home, you need to budget for furnishings, maintenance, and home improvement. Per the advice of the experts in the segment, how can you make an informed decision?

2. According to expert John Guyton, what are two common trigger points for deciding to rent versus buy?

3. What are three major reasons why Terri Foley could not buy a home despite the fact that she needed more space?

FINANCIAL PLANNING PROBLEMS

1. Dorothy and Matt are ready to purchase their first home. Their current monthly cash inflows are $4,900, and their current monthly cash outflows are $3,650. Their rent makes up $650 of their cash flows. They would like to put 10 percent of their cash inflows in savings and leave another $200 in their checking account for emergencies. How much of a mortgage payment can they manage under these conditions?

2. Denise and Kenny are ready to make an offer on an 1,800-square-foot home that is priced at $135,000. They investigate other homes on lots of similar size and find the following information:

   - 2,400-square-foot home sold for $168,000.
   - 1,500-square-foot home sold for $106,500.
   - 1,100-square-foot home sold for $79,000.

   What offer should they make on the home?

3. Larry and Laurie have found a home and made a $125,000 offer that has been accepted. They make a down payment of 10 percent. Their bank charges a loan origination fee of 1 percent of the loan and points of 1.5 percent (both are applied to the loan amount). Other fees include a $25 loan application fee, a $250 appraisal fee, and $350 for title search and insurance. How much cash will Larry and Laurie need at closing?

4. This month you made a mortgage payment of $700, of which $600 was an interest payment and $100 is a payment of the loan principal. You are in the 25 percent marginal tax bracket. What is the tax savings as a result of this payment?

5. Lloyd and Jean are considering purchasing a home requiring a $75,000 mortgage. The payment on a 30-year mortgage for this amount is $498.97. The payment for a 15-year maturity is $674.12. What is the difference in the total interest paid between the two different maturities?

6. Teresa rents her apartment for $650 per month, utilities not included. When she moved in, she paid a $700 security deposit using money from her savings account that was paying 3 percent interest. Her renter's insurance costs her $60 per year. What are Teresa's total annual costs of renting?

7. Matt has found a condominium in an area where he would enjoy living. He would need a $5,000 down payment from his savings and would have to pay closing costs of $2,500 to purchase the condo. His monthly mortgage payments would be $520 including property taxes and insurance. The condominium's homeowner's association charges maintenance fees of $400 per year. Calculate the cost of Matt's condo during the first year if he currently has the $5,000 down payment invested in an account earning 5 percent interest.

8. Matt (from problem 7) paid mortgage interest of $4,330 during his first year in the condo. His property taxes were $600, and his homeowner's insurance was $460. If Matt is in a 25 percent marginal tax rate bracket, what were his tax savings for his first year?

9. Doug and Lynn bought their home three years ago. They have a mortgage payment of $601.69. Interest rates have recently fallen, and they can lower their mortgage payments to $491.31 if they refinance. What would their annual savings be if they refinance? They are in a 15 percent marginal tax rate bracket. (Hint: Consider the reduction in tax savings.)

10. If the cost of refinancing their house is $3,860, how long would Doug and Lynn (from problem 9) have to remain in their home in order to recover the cost? (Ignore any interest on the savings in answering this question.)

Questions 11 and 12 require a financial calculator.

11. Paul really wants to purchase his own home. He currently lives in an apartment, and his rent is being paid by his parents. Paul's parents have informed him that they would not pay his mortgage payments. Paul has no savings, but can save $400 per month. The

home he desires costs $100,000, and his real estate broker informs him that a down payment of 20 percent would be required. If Paul can earn 8 percent on his savings, how long will it take him to accumulate the required down payment?

12. Paul (from problem 11) will be able to save $400 per month (which can be used for mortgage payments) for the indefinite future. If Paul finances the remaining cost of the home (after making the $20,000 down payment) at a rate of 9 percent over 30 years, what are his resulting monthly mortgage payments? Can he afford the mortgage?

Ethical Dilemma

13. Sarah and Joe own a small home that they would like to sell in order to build their dream home. Their current home has a mortgage and needs extensive repairs to make it marketable. A local loan company is offering home equity loans equal to 125% of the home's value. Since Sarah and Joe have good jobs and can make the additional home equity loan payments, they easily qualify for the 125% equity home loan. It takes the entire home equity loan to complete the repairs and upgrades to the home.

To their shock, they find that even after the upgrades they are unable to sell the home for enough to repay the mortgage and the home equity loan. In other words, they have negative equity in the home.

a. Comment on the finance company's ethics in making loans in excess of a home's appraised value.

b. What are Sarah and Joe's options in their current situation? Is there a way they can proceed with building their dream home?

FINANCIAL PLANNING ONLINE EXERCISES

1. Go to http://www.calcbuilder.com/cgi-bin/calcs/ HOM1.cgi/excite and click on "How much can I borrow?"

a. Input $3,000 wages, $500 in other income, $300 in auto loans, $100 for student loans, $125 for other loans, a desired interest rate of 9 percent, a 15-year loan term, a 5 percent down payment, no other debts, a $200 monthly credit card payment, $1,500 property tax, and $300 property insurance. What are the conservative estimates and aggressive estimates of what you can afford to borrow to finance the purchase of a home?

b. Now change the interest rate to 10 percent. What is the difference in monthly payments on the loan?

c. Now change the loan term to 30 years. What is the difference in monthly payments on the loan?

2. Go to http://biz.yahoo.com/b/r/m.html.

   a. What are the average national mortgage rates for 30-year fixed, 15-year fixed, and adjustable-rate mortgages?

   b. What mortgage rates are available in your nearest metro region? What mortgage rates are available in your state?

   c. Compare the mortgage rates available in New York and in Utah. Which is higher? Why?

3. Go to http://loan.yahoo.com/m/.

   a. Click on "More" and go to the "Starting the Loan Process" section. Click on "Am I Better Off Renting?" Values are already input for the monthly rent, price of home, taxes, etc. Find out if renting is better than buying for the scenario presented on the Web site or for your own situation.

   b. Now change the amount of monthly rent to $500 and see how that affects the recommendation on buying or renting.

4. Go to http://www.calcbuilder.com/cgi-bin/calcs/custom/HOM6.cgi/navyfederal and click on "Which is better: 15 or 30 year term?" Use the values already input for the 15- and 30-year mortgage terms. Obtain a comparison on the monthly payments and the total cost of each option by clicking the "Results" tab. What is the difference between the monthly payments for the two loan options? How much less will the 15-year loan cost over the life of the loan than the 30-year loan?

5. Go to http://loan.yahoo.com/m/mortcalc.html. Click on "Payment Calculator."

   a. Input a $100,000 mortgage amount, 8 percent interest rate, and 30-year term. What are the monthly payments?

   b. Click on "Amortization Calculator." Input the same information as in (a) without any extra payments for both 15-year and 30-year terms. Compare the total amount of money paid in principal and interest for the two maturities.

BUILDING YOUR OWN FINANCIAL PLAN

The purchase of a home is the largest expenditure that most individuals will make in their lifetime. For this reason, you should approach this decision with as much information as possible. This exercise will familiarize you with various information sources and will alert you to what you can and cannot expect from a realtor.

Go to the worksheets at the end of this chapter, and to the CD-ROM accompanying this text, to continue to build your financial plan.

THE SAMPSONS—A CONTINUING CASE

The Sampsons purchased a home last year. They have a 30-year mortgage with a fixed interest rate of 8.6 percent. Their monthly mortgage payment (excluding property taxes and insurance) is about $700 per month. In the last year, interest rates have declined. A 30-year mortgage now has an interest rate of 8 percent. Dave and Sharon want to determine how much they can lower their monthly payments by refinancing. By refinancing, they would incur transaction fees of $1,400 after considering any tax effects. The Sampsons are in the 25 percent tax bracket.

Go to the worksheets at the end of this chapter, and to the CD-ROM accompanying this text, to continue this case.

PART 3: BRAD BROOKS—A CONTINUING CASE

Brad Brooks decides it is time to upgrade his car and housing situations. Brad has more closely monitored his entertainment expenses, reducing them by $207. As a result, his monthly cash inflows now exceed his outflows by approximately $350 per month. Brad is interested in purchasing an SUV for $35,000. He still owes $10,000 on his two-year-old sedan (which has 57,000 miles) and has found a buyer who will pay him $15,000 cash. This would enable him to pay off his current car loan and still have $5,000 for a down payment on the SUV. He would finance the remainder of the purchase price for four years at 8 percent. Anticipating your objections to purchasing the SUV, Brad has an alternative plan to lease the SUV for three years. The terms of the lease are $600 per month, a 20¢ charge per mile over 15,000 miles annually, and $1,200 due upon signing for the first month's lease payment and security deposit.

Brad would also like to purchase his condo. He knows that he will enjoy tax advantages with ownership and is eager to reduce his tax burden. He can make the purchase with 10 percent down; the total purchase price is $90,000. A 30-year mortgage is available with an 8 percent rate. Closing costs due at signing will total $3,100. The property taxes on his condo will be $1,800 per year, his Property Owners' Association (POA) fee is $70 per month, and his household insurance will increase by $240 a year if he buys the condo.

Turn to the worksheets at the end of this chapter, and to the CD-ROM accompanying this text, to continue this case.

Chapter 10: Building Your Own Financial Plan

GOALS

1. Limit the amount of mortgage financing to an affordable level; determine if homeownership or renting is better financially.
2. Select the shortest loan maturity with affordable monthly payments.
3. Select the mortgage loan type (fixed or adjustable rate) that is most likely to result in the lowest interest expenses.

ANALYSIS

1. The amount of home that a person can afford is affected by many factors. The following worksheets will help you to determine the impact of interest rates, term of loan, and loan type (i.e., fixed or adjustable rate) on this process. Go to http://www.lendingtree.com. Click on "Knowledge Center," then on "Calculators." Referring to the personal cash flow statement developed in Chapter 2, use the amount that you determined is available for rent as the basis for the amount of home payment that you can afford each month. By using trial and error on the adjustable and fixed mortgage loan calculators, adjust the amount of mortgage either up or down until the "monthly payment" approximately equals the amount you determined for rent in your cash flow statement. Enter the amount of the mortgage that you can afford in the worksheets below as well as the amount of the down payment that you have or expect to have when you purchase a home. Repeat the process using the other interest rates and mortgage terms indicated in the worksheets. Remember: Maintain the same "number of months between adjustments," "expected adjustments," and "interest rate cap" for each of the adjustable-rate calculations.

Fixed Rate

Interest Rate	6%
Term	30 Years
Amount of Down Payment	$
Amount of Mortgage	$
Total Price of Home (Down Payment Plus Mortgage)	$

Interest Rate	8%
Term	30 Years
Amount of Down Payment	$
Amount of Mortgage	$
Total Price of Home (Down Payment Plus Mortgage)	$

Interest Rate	6%
Term	15 Years
Amount of Down Payment	$
Amount of Mortgage	$
Total Price of Home (Down Payment Plus Mortgage)	$

Interest Rate	8%
Term	15 Years
Amount of Down Payment	$
Amount of Mortgage	$
Total Price of Home (Down Payment Plus Mortgage)	$

Adjustable Rate

Starting Interest Rate	6%
Term	15 Years
Months between Adjustments (not to exceed 12 months)	
Expected Adjustment	
Interest Rate Cap	
Amount of Down Payment	$
Amount of Mortgage	$
Total Price of Home (Down Payment Plus Mortgage)	$

Starting Interest Rate	8%
Term	15 Years
Months between Adjustments (not to exceed 12 months)	
Expected Adjustment	
Interest Rate Cap	
Amount of Down Payment	$
Amount of Mortgage	$
Total Price of Home (Down Payment Plus Mortgage)	$

Starting Interest Rate	6%
Term	30 Years
Months between Adjustments (not to exceed 12 months)	
Expected Adjustment	
Interest Rate Cap	
Amount of Down Payment	$
Amount of Mortgage	$
Total Price of Home (Down Payment Plus Mortgage)	$

Starting Interest Rate	8%
Term	30 Years
Months between Adjustments (not to exceed 12 months)	
Expected Adjustment	
Interest Rate Cap	
Amount of Down Payment	$
Amount of Mortgage	$
Total Price of Home (Down Payment Plus Mortgage)	$

2. At http://www.msn.com, search listings of homes for sale in your price range by clicking on "Shop," then "Buying a House." Complete the information requested under "Compare and Find Homes" to research cities and neighborhoods that you are interested in. Record information on homes of interest below.

	From	To
Price Range:		
Zip Code:		

Potential Homes

Address	List Price	MSN Price Estimate	Monthly Payment	Realtor

3. Referring to your cash flow statement and personal balance sheet, compare the monthly payment estimates to the rent you are currently paying. Determine the amount of a down payment you can afford to make.

Down payment $ _____

4. At http://www.msn.com, click on "House and Home," then on "Loans and Financing." Gather current information on loan rates and record it below.

Mortgage Type	Rate

5. Create an amortization table for the fixed-rate mortgage that is most affordable. (The Excel worksheet will calculate the monthly payment based on your input and create the amortization table.)

Loan Amount   _____

Number of Years   _____

Annual Interest Rate _____

Monthly Payment   _____

Amortization Schedule for Year 1

Monthly Payment	Payment	Principal	Interest	Balance

Compare the allocation of principal versus interest paid per year on the loan. (The Excel worksheet will create a bar graph based on your input.)

Amortization Schedule (Annual Totals)

Year	Annual Payments	Principal	Interest	Balance
1				
2				
3				
4				
5				
6				
7				
8				
9				
10				
11				
12				
13				
14				
15				
16				
17				
18				
19				
20				
21				
22				
23				
24				
25				
26				
27				
28				
29				
30				

6. Select the mortgage with the best terms. Compare the cost of purchasing a home with these mortgage terms to renting over a three-year period.

Renting versus Owning a Home

Cost of Renting	Per Month	Amount per Year	Total over Three Years
Rent			
Renter's Insurance			
Opportunity cost of security deposit			
Total cost of renting			

Cost of Purchasing	Per Month	Amount per Year	Total over Three Years
Mortgage payment			
Down payment			
Opportunity cost of down payment			
Property taxes			
Home insurance			
Closing costs			
Maintenance costs			
Total costs before tax benefits			
Total tax savings			
Equity investment			
Increase in home value			
Value of equity			
Cost of purchasing home over three years			

If you enter this information on the Excel worksheet, the software will create a chart comparing the cost of renting versus purchasing.

DECISIONS

1. What is the mortgage amount and down payment that you can afford?

   _____
   _____
   _____
   _____
   _____
   _____
   _____

2. Is a fixed-rate or adjustable-rate mortgage better suited to your financial situation? What maturity, interest rate, and monthly payment can you afford?

   _____
   _____
   _____
   _____
   _____
   _____
   _____

3. Describe whether homeownership or renting is preferable for you.

   _____
   _____
   _____
   _____
   _____
   _____

Chapter 10: The Sampsons—A Continuing Case

CASE QUESTIONS

1. Use a Web site or a financial calculator to determine the monthly mortgage payment (excluding property taxes and insurance) on a $90,000 mortgage if the Sampsons obtain a new 30-year mortgage at the 8 percent interest rate. (One Web site that can be used for this purpose is http://loan.yahoo.com/m/mortcalc.html.)

Mortgage loan	$90,000
Interest rate	8%
Years	30
Loan payment	

2. The Sampsons expect that they will not move for at least three years. Advise the Sampsons on whether they should refinance their mortgage by comparing the savings of refinancing with the costs.

Current mortgage payment	
New mortgage payment	
Monthly savings	
Annual savings	
Marginal tax rate	
Increase in taxes	
Annual savings after tax	
Years in house after refinancing	
Total savings	

3. Why might your advice about refinancing change in the future?

_____

_____

_____

_____

_____

_____

Part 3: Brad Brooks—A Continuing Case

CASE QUESTIONS

1. Refer to Brad's personal cash flow statement that you developed in Part 1. Recompute his expenses to determine if Brad can afford to
   a. Purchase the new car
   b. Lease the new car
   c. Purchase the condo
   d. Purchase the car and the condo
   e. Lease the car and purchase the condo

Personal Cash Flow Statement

Cash Inflows	**This Month**
Total Cash Inflows

Cash Outflows |
--- | ---
 |
 |
 |
 |
Total Cash Outflows |
Net Cash Flows |

2. Brad's uncle has offered to provide him with a loan for the closing costs and the down payment needed to purchase the condo. Brad exclaims, "This is great. I don't even need a loan contract!" Advise Brad on the situation.

3. What are the advantages and disadvantages to Brad of leasing rather than purchasing the car?

_____

_____

_____

_____

_____

_____

4. Based on the information you provided, Brad decides not to buy the condo at this time. How can he save the necessary funds to purchase a condo or house in the future? Be specific in your recommendations.

Future Value of an Annuity

Payment per Period	
Number of Periods	
Interest Rate per Period	
Future Value	

_____

_____

_____

_____

_____

_____

5. How would your advice to Brad differ if he were

a. 45 years old?

_____

_____

_____

b. 60 years old?

_____

_____

_____

6. Prepare a written or oral report on your findings and recommendations to Brad.

Protecting Your Wealth

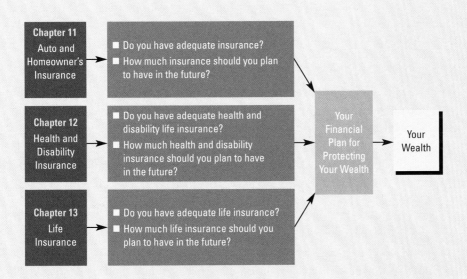

THE CHAPTERS IN THIS PART FOCUS ON INSURANCE, WHICH IS critical for protecting you and your personal assets against damages and liability. Chapter 11 focuses on decisions about auto and homeowner's insurance. Chapter 12 presents key considerations regarding health and disability insurance, and Chapter 13 explains the provisions of life insurance.

Auto and Homeowner's Insurance

Matt was recently in a major accident that caused extensive damage to his eight-year-old sedan. When his insurance company asked Matt to get an estimate of the cost of repairs, he took it to a well-respected repair shop. They quoted a total repair bill of $5,250.

Matt was prepared to pay his $250 deductible as long as the insurance company paid the rest. Since the book value of a car of his make and model, in good condition, is only $3,240, the insurance company "totaled" his car, declaring it a total loss and reimbursing him only to the extent of the book value. Matt must either repair the car using the insurance company reimbursement plus over $2,000 out of his own pocket or accept the loss and buy another car.

Understanding your insurance needs is important in determining the type and amount of coverage you need to shield you from financial loss and protect you against liability.

The objectives of this chapter are to:

- Explain the role of risk management
- Outline typical provisions of auto insurance
- Describe financial coverage provided by homeowner's insurance

BACKGROUND ON INSURANCE

Property insurance ensures that any damages to your auto and home are covered, and that your personal assets are protected from any liability. In the context of insurance, the term *liability* is used to mean that you may be required to pay someone for damages that you caused. Health insurance can ensure that most of your medical bills will be covered, and therefore can also protect your personal assets from any liability. Life insurance can ensure financial support for your dependents, other individuals, or charities when you die.

The primary function of insurance is to maintain your existing level of wealth by protecting you against potential financial losses or liability as a result of unexpected events. It can ensure that your income continues if an accident or illness prevents you from working, or it can prevent others from taking away your personal assets.

You benefit from having insurance even when you do not receive any payments from the insurance company because you have the peace of mind of knowing that your assets are protected if you are in a collision. Insurance may seem costly, but it is well worth the cost to ensure that your wealth will not be taken away from you.

MANAGING RISK

risk
Exposure to events or perils that can cause a financial loss.

risk management
Decisions about whether and how to protect against risk.

In the context of insurance, the term **risk** can be defined as exposure to events (or perils) that can cause a financial loss. **Risk management** represents decisions about whether and how to protect against risk. The first step in risk management is to recognize the risks to which you are exposed. Then you must decide whether to protect against risk. Once you decide whether to obtain a particular type of insurance, you must decide on the amount of coverage and policy provisions. When deciding whether to protect against risk, your alternatives include avoiding risk, reducing risk, and insuring against risk. If you decide to insure against risk, you must decide on the amount of coverage as well as policy provisions.

Avoid Risk

Consider your actions that expose you to a financial loss. Owners are exposed to a financial loss if their property is damaged. You can avoid the risk of property damage if you do not own any property. However, you cannot completely avoid risk by avoiding ownership of property. If you lease a car, you are still exposed to liability and financial loss if the car is in an accident. Other types of risk are unrelated to property. For example, you are exposed to a financial loss if you require medical attention or become disabled.

Reduce Risk

One method of managing risk is to reduce your exposure to financial loss. For example, you can purchase a small home rather than a large home in order to reduce the maximum possible financial loss due to property damage. You can purchase an inexpensive car in order to limit the possible financial loss due to property damage. You may be able to reduce your exposure to an illness or a disability by getting periodic health checkups.

Yet these steps do not fully block your exposure to financial loss. If you drive a car, you are not only subject to property damage, but also liability. Your financial loss could be large even if the car you drive has little value.

Accept Risk

A third alternative when managing risk is to accept risk by not seeking to limit your exposure to a financial loss. This alternative may be feasible when the likelihood of an event that could cause a financial loss is very low and the potential financial loss due to the event is small. For example, if you seldom drive your car and live in a town with little traffic, you are relatively unlikely to get into an accident. You are also more likely to accept risk when the possible financial loss resulting from the event is limited. For example, if you drive an inexpensive and old car, you may be willing to accept your exposure to financial loss due to property damage. However, you are still subject to liability, which could put all of your personal assets in jeopardy.

Insure against Risk

A final alternative is to insure against risk. If you cannot avoid a specific type of risk, and you cannot reduce that risk, and you do not wish to be exposed to financial loss as a result of the risk, you should consider insurance.

premium
The cost of obtaining insurance.

The decision to obtain insurance is determined by weighing the costs and the benefits. The cost of obtaining insurance is the **premium** that is paid for a policy each year. The benefit of obtaining insurance is that it can protect your assets or your income from events that otherwise might cause a financial loss. Consequently, you protect your existing net worth and also increase the likelihood that you will be able to increase your net worth in the future. Without insurance, you could lose all of your assets if you are involved in an accident that caused major repair expenses or liability.

You cannot insure against all types of risk, as some types of insurance are either unavailable or too expensive. Your risk management will determine which types of risk you wish to insure against. When there is a high likelihood that an event will cause a financial loss, and the potential financial loss from that event is large, insurance should be considered. You may choose to accept the types of risk that might only result in small financial losses. In this chapter and the following two, you will learn the key provisions of auto, homeowner's, health, disability, and life insurance. With this background, you can determine your own risk management plan.

Your risk management decisions are also affected by your degree of risk tolerance. For example, you and your neighbor could be in the same financial position and have the same exposure to various types of risk. Yet, you may obtain more insurance than your neighbor because you are more concerned about exposure to financial loss. While you incur annual insurance expenses from insurance premiums, you are protected from financial losses resulting from covered perils.

ROLE OF INSURANCE COMPANIES

Insurance companies offer insurance policies that can protect you against financial loss. Since there are many different types of risk that could cause financial losses, there are many different types of insurance that can protect you from those risks. Exhibit 11.1 describes the common events that can cause a major financial loss and the related insurance that can protect you from these events. The most popular forms of insurance for individuals are property and casualty insurance, life insurance, and health insurance. Property and casualty insurance is used to insure property and therefore consists of auto insurance and home insurance. Some insurance companies specialize in a particular type of insurance, while others offer all types of insurance for individuals. Companies that offer the same type of insurance vary in terms of the specific policies that they offer.

In recent years, commercial banks, savings institutions, securities firms, and other types of financial institutions have established insurance businesses. Some financial institutions have an insurance center within their branches. This enables customers to take care of their insurance needs where they receive other financial services.

Exhibit 11.1 Common Events That Could Cause a Financial Loss

Event	Financial loss	Protection
You have a car accident and damage your car	Car repairs	Auto insurance
You have a car accident in which another person in your car is injured	Medical bills and liability	Auto insurance
You have a car accident in which another person in the other driver's car is injured	Medical bills and liability	Auto insurance
Your home is damaged by a fire	Home repairs	Homeowner's insurance
Your neighbor is injured while in your home	Medical bills and liability	Homeowner's insurance
You become ill and need medical attention	Medical bills	Health insurance
You develop an illness that requires long-term care	Medical bills	Long-term care insurance
You become disabled	Loss of income	Disability insurance
You die while family members rely on your income	Loss of income	Life insurance

Insurance Company Operations

When an insurance company sells an insurance policy to you, it is obliged to cover claims as described in the insurance policy. For example, if your car is insured by a policy, the insurance company is obligated to protect you from financial loss due to an accident. If you are in a car accident while driving that car, the insurance company provides payments (subject to limits specified in the contract) to cover any liability to passengers and to repair property damage resulting from the accident.

In general, insurance companies generate their revenue from receiving payments for policies, and from earning a return from investing the proceeds until the funds are needed to cover claims. They incur costs from making payments to cover policyholder claims. The majority of policyholders do not need to file claims during the coverage period. When an insurance company makes payments due to a claim, the payments are commonly more than the annual premium that was received by the policyholder. For example, consider a policyholder who pays $1,000 in auto insurance for the year. Assume that he is in an accident, and the insurance company has to pay $20,000 to cover liability and to repair the car. The payout by the insurance company is 20 times the premium received. In other words, it would take a total of 20 auto insurance policy premiums to generate enough revenue to cover the cost of the one claim.

Relationship between Insurance Company Claims and Premiums. Since insurance companies rely mostly on their premiums to cover claims, they price their insurance policies to reflect the probability of a claim and the size of the claim. For an event that is very unlikely and could cause minor damage, the premium would be relatively low. For an event that is more likely and could cause major damage, the insurance premium would be relatively high.

Insurance Underwriters. An insurance company relies on **underwriters**, who calculate the risk of specific insurance policies, to decide what insurance policies to offer and what

underwriters
From an insurance perspective, are hired to calculate the risk of specific insurance policies, decide what policies to offer, and what premiums to charge.

premiums to charge. Underwriters recognize that their insurance company must generate revenue that is greater than its expenses to be profitable, so they set premiums that are aligned with anticipated payouts.

Insurance Company Credit Ratings and Service

An initial step in finding the right insurance policy is to contact several insurance companies to determine the types of policies that are offered. Also, check with your employer. Some employers obtain discounts on insurance for their employees, especially for health insurance and disability insurance.

It is important to select an insurance company that is in good financial condition. You are relying on the insurance company to provide you with adequate coverage over the policy period. If the company has financial problems, it may not be able to cover a claim against you, which means that you could be held liable. If the insurance company goes bankrupt, you would need to get another policy and would probably lose the premium that you had already paid. There are several services that rate insurance companies, including A.M. Best (http://www.ambest.com), Demotech, Inc. (http://www.demotech.com), Moody's Investor Services (http://www.moodys.com), and Standard & Poor's Corporation (http://www.standardandpoors.com/ratings).

The level of service among insurance companies varies. The best insurance companies provide quick and thorough claims service. Sources of information on service by insurance companies include the Better Business Bureau, *Consumer Reports* magazine, and state insurance agencies.

insurance agent
Recommends insurance policies for customers.

captive (or exclusive) insurance agent
Works for one particular insurance company.

Role of Insurance Agents and Brokers

When contacting an insurance company, it is likely that you will communicate with an insurance agent or broker. An **insurance agent** represents one or more insurance companies and recommends an insurance policy that fits the customer's needs. **Captive** (or **exclusive**) **insurance agents** work for one particular insurance company, whereas

11.1 Financial Planning Online: Reviews of Insurance Companies

Go to
http://www.ambest.com/ratings/guide.asp

This Web site provides information on how insurance companies are rated.

independent insurance agent
Represents many different insurance companies.

independent insurance agents (also called insurance brokers) represent many different insurance companies. They are linked online to various insurance companies and therefore can quickly obtain quotations for different policies. In addition to helping customers with various types of insurance, insurance agents may also offer financial planning services, such as retirement planning and estate planning. Some insurance agents are also certified to serve as a broker for mutual funds or other financial products.

AUTO INSURANCE

Auto insurance insures against damage to an automobile and expenses associated with accidents. In this way, it protects one of your main assets (your car) and also limits your potential liabilities (expenses due to an accident). If you own or drive a car, you need auto insurance. Policies are purchased for a year or six months at property and casualty insurance companies. Your policy specifies the amount of coverage if you are legally liable for bodily injury, if you and your passengers incur medical bills, and if your car is damaged as the result of an accident or some other event (such as a tree falling on the car).

The average amount spent on auto insurance per year is shown in the first bar chart in Exhibit 11.2. Notice how expenditures for auto insurance have increased over time. The expenditures also vary among states within a given time, as you can see from the second bar chart. They are much larger in the highly populated states with much traffic, such as New York and New Jersey, and relatively small in states with less traffic, such as North Dakota and South Dakota.

Auto Insurance Policy Provisions

insurance policy
Contract between an insurance company and the policyholder.

auto insurance policy
Specifies the coverage provided by the insurance company for a particular individual and vehicle.

An **insurance policy** is a contract between the insurance company and the policyholder. An **auto insurance policy** specifies the coverage (including dollar limits) provided by an insurance company for a particular individual and vehicle. The contract identifies the policyholder and family members who are also insured if they use the insured vehicle. You should have insurance information such as your policy number and the name of a contact person at the insurance company with you when you drive. If you are in an accident, exchange your insurance information with that of the other driver and also fill out a police report.

Every auto insurance policy explains what is covered in detail. Review your own auto insurance policy as you read on, so that you understand your coverage.

Coverage A: Liability Coverage

bodily injury liability coverage
Protects against liability associated with injuries caused by the policyholder.

Liability coverage consists of two key components: (1) bodily injury liability and (2) property damage liability. **Bodily injury liability coverage** protects you against liability associated with injuries that you (or family members listed on the policy) cause. You or your family members are also covered if you cause injuries to others while driving someone else's car with their permission. Bodily injury expenses include medical bills and lost wages as a result of an accident that you cause. The coverage is designed to protect you if you cause an accident and the driver of the other car sues you.

Given the large awards granted in lawsuits in the United States, it is critical to have adequate liability coverage. Any legal expenses incurred by an insurance company when defending you against a lawsuit are not considered when determining the limits on liability coverage. For example, if a person sues you and is awarded an amount that is less than the liability limit in your contract, it is covered by your policy regardless of the legal expenses incurred by the insurance company. If the award granted in a lawsuit against you exceeds the limit on your policy's liability coverage, you will be required to pay the difference and therefore could lose your other assets. At a minimum, you should have coverage of $50,000 for any individual and $100,000 to cover all persons who are injured. A more common recommendation is $100,000 for any individual and $300,000 to $400,000 to cover all injured persons.

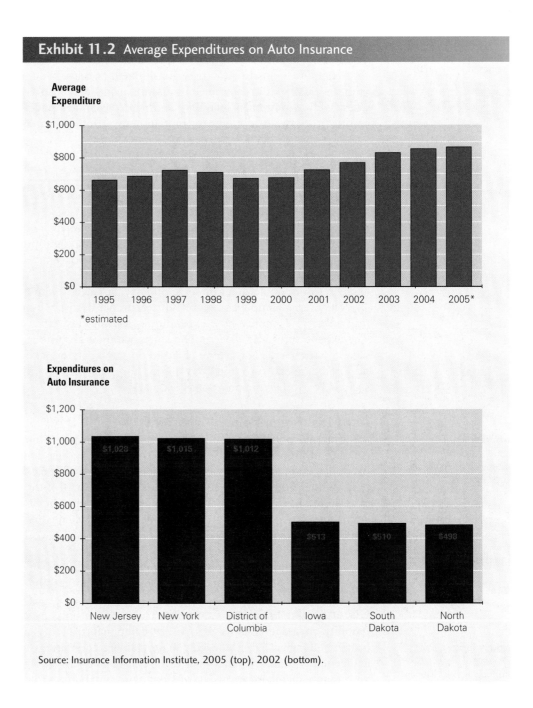

Exhibit 11.2 Average Expenditures on Auto Insurance

Average Expenditure

*estimated

Expenditures on Auto Insurance

Source: Insurance Information Institute, 2005 (top), 2002 (bottom).

property damage liability coverage
Protects against losses that result when the policyholder damages another person's property with his car.

Property damage liability coverage protects you from losses that result when you damage another person's property with your car. Examples include damage to a car, a fence, a lamppost, or a building. Note that property damage liability does not cover your own car or other property that you own. A common recommendation for property damage liability coverage is between $40,000 and $50,000.

Policy Limits. The auto insurance policy specifies monetary limits on the coverage of the bodily injury per person, bodily injury for all people who are injured, and property damage. The policy's limits are often presented as a set of three numbers, split by slashes that are referred to as split liability limits. For example, the split liability limit of 100/300/50 means that the coverage is limited to $100,000 per person injured in an accident, $300,000 for all people combined, and $50,000 to cover damage to the car or other property. If one person suffers bodily injury that results in a liability of $80,000, the entire amount of the liability is covered. If one person's bodily injury results in a liability of $120,000, the coverage is limited to $100,000. If four people suffer bodily injuries amounting to a total of $400,000, $300,000 of that amount is covered.

financial responsibility laws
Laws that require individuals who drive cars to purchase a minimum amount of liability insurance.

Most states have **financial responsibility laws** that require individuals who drive cars to purchase a minimum amount of liability insurance. State governments recognize that if an uninsured driver causes an accident, he or she would avoid financial responsibility for any individuals harmed in the accident. These important state laws tend to require a very low level of insurance, which would not cover the liability in many accidents.

There are two types of financial responsibility laws. The first type requires that drivers show proof of auto insurance when they register the car in order to receive their license plates. This law is not always effective because some drivers obtain insurance and then cancel it after they receive their license plates. The second type of financial responsibility law requires that drivers show proof of their auto insurance when they are in an accident. If they are caught without insurance, they may lose their driver's license. Yet the uninsured driver still escapes his financial responsibility at the expense of other individuals who are harmed in the accident.

The minimum liability coverage varies by state, but is usually at least $10,000 to cover each person injured in an accident, $30,000 to cover all persons injured in an accident, and at least $10,000 to cover property damage to the car. Exhibit 11.3 shows the minimum insurance required by many states. Look at the minimum level for your state. Because there are drivers in your state who are underinsured, you will need adequate insurance in case you are in an accident with a driver who has minimal auto insurance, even if the accident is their fault.

Exhibit 11.3 Minimum Auto Insurance Liability Limits

State	Liability Limits	State	Liability Limits	State	Liability Limits
Alabama	20/40/10	Kentucky	25/50/10	North Dakota	25/50/25
Alaska	50/100/25	Louisiana	10/20/10	Ohio	12.5/25/7.5
Arizona	15/30/10	Maine	50/100/25	Oklahoma	25/50/25
Arkansas	25/50/25	Maryland	20/40/15	Oregon	25/50/10
California	15/30/5	Massachusetts	20/40/5	Pennsylvania	15/30/5
Colorado	25/50/15	Michigan	20/40/10	Rhode Island	25/50/25
Connecticut	20/40/10	Minnesota	30/60/10	South Carolina	15/30/10
Delaware	15/30/5	Mississippi	25/50/25	South Dakota	25/50/25
D.C.	25/50/10	Missouri	25/50/10	Tennessee	25/50/10
Florida	10/20/10	Montana	25/50/10	Texas	20/40/15
Georgia	25/50/25	Nebraska	25/50/25	Utah	25/50/15
Hawaii	20/40/10	Nevada	15/30/10	Vermont	25/50/10
Idaho	25/50/15	New Hampshire	25/50/25	Virginia	25/50/20
Illinois	20/40/15	New Jersey	15/30/5	Washington	25/50/10
Indiana	25/50/10	New Mexico	25/50/10	West Virginia	20/40/10
Iowa	20/40/15	New York	25/50/10	Wisconsin	25/50/10
Kansas	25/50/10	North Carolina	30/60/25	Wyoming	25/50/20

Source: Insurance Information Institute.

medical payments coverage
Insures against the cost of medical care for you and other passengers in your car when you are at fault in an accident.

Coverage B: Medical Payments Coverage

Medical payments coverage insures against the cost of medical care for you and other passengers in your car when you are at fault in an accident. The medical coverage applies only to the insured car. If you were driving someone else's car, the owner of that car would be responsible for the medical coverage for passengers in that car. You can also obtain medical insurance that covers you if you ride in a car driven by an uninsured driver.

Some advisers may suggest that a minimal amount of medical payments coverage is adequate for your car if you have a good health insurance plan. However, medical payments coverage can be valuable even if you have health insurance, because your health insurance policy would not cover non-family passengers in your car who could be injured. The coverage may even include funeral expenses.

If the driver of the other car in the accident is determined to be at fault, the medical payments may be covered by that driver's policy. However, if that driver's insurance provides insufficient coverage, your policy can be applied. Some states require that drivers obtain a minimal amount of medical payments coverage, such as $1,000 per person. However, insurance professionals recommend a higher level of coverage, such as $10,000 per person.

uninsured motorist coverage
Insures against the cost of bodily injury when an accident is caused by another driver who is not insured.

underinsured motorist coverage
Insures against bodily injury and drivers who have insufficient coverage.

Coverage C: Uninsured or Underinsured Motorist Coverage

Uninsured motorist coverage insures against the cost of bodily injury when an accident is caused by another driver who is not insured. Given the large number of uninsured drivers, this coverage is needed.

The coverage also applies if you are in an accident caused by a hit-and-run driver or by a driver who is at fault but whose insurance company goes bankrupt. This coverage applies to bodily injury when you are not at fault, while the liability coverage from Part A applies to bodily injury when you are at fault. Like the insurance on bodily injury in Part A, there are policy limits that you specify, such as $100,000 per person and $300,000 for all persons. The higher the limits, the higher the insurance premium. At a minimum, you should have coverage of $40,000 per accident. Some financial planners recommend coverage of $300,000 per accident.

You can also obtain **underinsured motorist coverage** to insure you against bodily injury and drivers who have insufficient coverage. Suppose that there is bodily injury to you as a result of an accident caused by an underinsured driver. If the damages to you are $40,000 and the insurance policy of the underinsured driver only covers $30,000, your insurance company will provide the difference of $10,000.

collision insurance
Insures against costs of damage to your car resulting from an accident in which the policyholder is at fault.

comprehensive coverage
Insures you against damage to your car that results from floods, theft, fire, hail, explosions, riots, and various other events.

Coverage D: Collision and Comprehensive Coverage

Collision and comprehensive coverage insure against damage to your car. **Collision insurance** insures you against costs of damage to your car resulting from an accident in which you are at fault. **Comprehensive coverage** insures you against damage to your car that results from floods, theft, fire, hail, explosions, riots, vandalism, or various other events.

Collision and comprehensive coverage is optional in most states. Yet, car loan providers may require the borrower to maintain insurance that will cover any property damage to the car to protect the lender in the event that the car owner has an accident and stops making the loan payments on the car loan. The car that serves as collateral on the loan may be worthless if it is damaged in an accident.

Collision and comprehensive coverage is especially valuable if you have a new car that you would likely repair if it were damaged. The coverage may not be so valuable if you have an old car because you may not feel the need to repair damage as long as the car can still be driven. Note that the coverage is limited to the cash value of the car. For example, if your car was worth $2,000 before the accident and $1,200 after the accident, your insurance company will pay no more than $800. The insurance company will not incur extremely high repair expenses to replace cars that have little value.

Collision coverage can be valuable even if you do not believe you were at fault in an accident. If the other driver claims that you were at fault, you and your insurance company may need to take the matter to court. Meanwhile, you can use the collision coverage to have the car repaired. If your insurance company wins the lawsuit, the other driver's insurance company will be required to pay the expenses associated with repairing your car.

Collision coverage is normally limited to the car itself and not to items that were damaged while in the car. For example, if you were transporting a new computer at the time of an accident, the damage to the computer would not be protected by comprehensive coverage.

deductible
A set dollar amount that you are responsible for paying before any coverage is provided by your insurer.

Deductible. The **deductible** is the amount of damage that you are responsible for paying before any coverage is provided by the insurance company. For example, a deductible of $250 means that you must pay the first $250 in damages due to an accident. The insurance company pays any additional expenses beyond the deductible. The deductible is normally between $250 and $1,000.

Other Provisions

You can elect coverage for expenses not covered in the standard policy. Specifically, a policy can cover the cost of a rental car while your car is being repaired after an accident. You can also elect coverage for towing, even if the problems are not the result of an accident. Your premium will increase slightly for these provisions.

You can also include a provision on your auto insurance policy to cover any car that you rent. If you do not have such a provision, the rental car agency will typically offer to sell you collision damage coverage, liability insurance, medical coverage, and even coverage for theft of personal belongings from the car. If rent-a-car insurance is not covered by your policy, some credit cards provide you with collision and comprehensive insurance benefits when you use that card to pay for the rental services.

11.2 Financial Planning Online: How Much Car Insurance Coverage Do You Need?

Go to
http://insurance.yahoo.com/auto.html

Click on
"Auto Coverage Analyzer"

This Web site provides a recommendation on the amount of car insurance coverage that is appropriate for you.

An auto insurance policy also specifies exclusions and limitations of the coverage. For example, coverage may not apply if you intentionally damage a car, if you drive a car that is not yours without the permission of the owner, or if you drive a car that you own but that is not listed on your insurance policy. It also explains how you should comply with procedures if you are in an accident.

Summary of Auto Insurance Provisions

The most important types of coverage identified above are included in a standard insurance policy. They are summarized in Exhibit 11.4. Notice that the exhibit classifies the potential financial damages as: (1) related to your car in an accident, (2) related to the other car or other property in an accident, and (3) related to your car when not in an accident.

Auto Insurance Policy. An insurance policy describes the insurance coverage and shows how the premium was determined. Rates vary substantially among locations, among insurance companies, and even among all the policyholders who use the same insurance company in the same location.

In general, the liability coverage is the most expensive and represents about 60 percent of the total premium on average. Notice that the limits for bodily injury are specified. The cost of collision and comprehensive insurance commonly represents about 30 percent of the total premium, but it varies with the car. The cost of collision insurance represents a higher proportion of the total premium for new cars than for older cars.

Expenses Incurred by Auto Insurance Companies. The allocation of expenses by auto insurance companies is shown in Exhibit 11.5. Notice that claims on collision and property damage account for about 34 percent of the expenses. Twelve percent of the total expenses goes to pay lawyers' fees.

Exhibit 11.4 Summary of Auto Insurance Provisions

Financial Damages Related to Your Car in an Accident	Auto Insurance Provision
Liability due to passengers in your car when you are at fault	Bodily injury liability
Liability due to passengers in your car when you are not at fault but driver of other car is uninsured or underinsured	Uninsured/Underinsured Motorist Coverage
Damage to your own car	Collision
Treatment of injuries to driver and passengers of your car	Medical

Financial Damages Related to the Other Car or Other Property in an Accident	
Liability due to passengers in the other car	Bodily injury liability
Liability due to damage to the other car	Property damage liability
Liability due to damage to other property	Property damage liability

Financial Damages Related to Your Car When Not in an Accident	
Damage to your car as a result of theft, fire, vandalism, or other non-accident events	Comprehensive

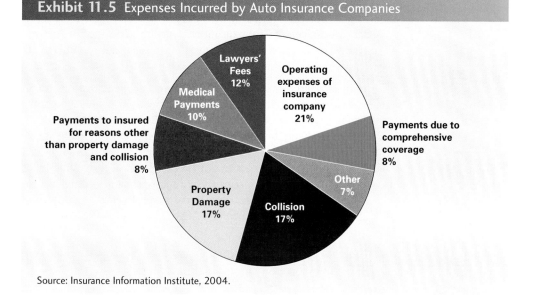

Exhibit 11.5 Expenses Incurred by Auto Insurance Companies

Lawyers' Fees 12%

Medical Payments 10%

Operating expenses of insurance company 21%

Payments to insured for reasons other than property damage and collision 8%

Payments due to comprehensive coverage 8%

Other 7%

Property Damage 17%

Collision 17%

Source: Insurance Information Institute, 2004.

FACTORS THAT AFFECT YOUR AUTO INSURANCE PREMIUMS

Your insurance premium is influenced by the likelihood that you will submit claims to the insurance company and the cost to the insurance company for covering those claims. As explained earlier, your auto insurance premium will be higher for a policy that specifies a greater amount of liability coverage and a lower deductible. However, there are other factors that can also affect your premium.

Characteristics of Your Car
The type of car you drive and the amount of coverage provided by your insurance policy affect the premium that you pay.

Value of Car. Insurance premiums are high when the potential financial loss is high. The collision and comprehensive insurance premiums are high for new cars. In addition, the premium is normally higher for an expensive car than an inexpensive car of the same age. The insurance on a new Mercedes is higher than the insurance on a new Saturn.

Repair Record of Your Car. Some car models require more repair work for the same type of damage. For example, replacing a door on a Toyota may be easier than on some other cars, which reduces the repair bill. When a car can be repaired easily and inexpensively, its insurance premium is lower.

Your Personal Characteristics
Other factors that characterize you personally affect your insurance premium.

Your Age. Insurance companies often base their premiums on personal profiles, and age is one of the most important characteristics. Younger drivers are more likely to get into accidents, and therefore they pay higher insurance premiums. In particular, drivers between the ages of 16 and 25 are considered to be high risk. Insurance companies incur higher expenses from covering their claims and offset the higher expenses by charging higher premiums. Another important characteristic is gender, as male drivers tend to get into more accidents than female drivers. For these reasons, male teenagers are charged very high auto insurance premiums.

Your Mileage. You are more likely to get into an accident the more miles you drive. Thus, your premium will be higher if you drive more miles. Many insurance companies classify drivers in two or more mileage groups. For example, if you drive less than 10,000 miles per year, you may qualify for the low-mileage group, which entitles you to a lower premium.

Your Driving Record. If you have an excellent driving record, including no accidents and no traffic tickets for a year or longer, you may be charged a lower premium than other drivers. No one purposely creates a bad driving record, but some drivers do not realize how much their insurance premium will increase if they establish a poor driving record. Since most insurance companies attempt to avoid drivers with a history of causing accidents, these drivers cannot comparison shop effectively. They may have to accept the premium of any insurance company that is willing to insure their car. Once drivers are labeled as high risk, it will take several years of safe driving to prove that they have improved their driving habits. Thus, they will pay relatively high insurance premiums for several years.

Your Location. Auto insurance is more expensive in large cities, where the probability of being involved in an accident is higher.

Your Driver Training. Insurance companies recognize that driver training can improve driver performance, and can reduce the likelihood of accidents in the future. They encourage drivers to take driver training programs. If you have completed a driver training program, you may qualify for a discount.

Your School Performance. Insurance companies recognize that good students also appear to be safer drivers. Therefore, they may charge good students lower premiums.

Comparing Premiums among Insurance Companies

One final factor that affects your auto insurance premium is the insurance company that you select. You may be able to reduce your auto insurance premium by obtaining quotations from various insurance companies. Auto insurance premiums can vary substantially among insurance companies, so always obtain several quotes before you select an insurance company. Several Web sites (such as http://www.insweb.com and http://www.esurance.com) provide auto insurance quotes online. Some Web sites even allow you to buy insurance online.

If you have specific questions about the coverage and want to speak to an insurance salesperson, you can call some insurance companies directly. A comparison of quotes online might at least help you determine which insurance companies to call for more information. Alternatively, you can call an independent insurance agent, who can help you purchase insurance from one of several insurance companies.

When comparing prices, recognize that the price comparison may vary with the type of policy desired. For example, an insurance company may have relatively low premiums compared to its competitors for a policy involving substantial coverage for bodily injury liability, but relatively high premiums for a policy involving collision coverage. Therefore, you should not select a company based on advice you receive from a friend or family member. If their policy is different from the policy you desire, another company may offer a better deal. In addition, companies change their premiums over time, so a company may charge relatively low premiums in one period, but relatively high premiums in the following period for the same policy.

Comparing Prices at the Time of Renewal. Once an auto insurance policy has been in effect for 60 days, an insurance company can only cancel your policy if you provided fraudulent information on your application, if your driver's license is suspended, or if you do not pay your insurance premium. However, an insurance company may decide not to renew your policy when it expires if you had a poor driving record over the recent policy period. For example, it is unlikely to renew your contract if you caused an accident as a result of drunk driving.

If an insurance company is willing to renew your policy, it may raise the premium in the renewal period even if your driving record has been good. You can switch to a different insurance company when the policy expires if you are not satisfied with your present insurance company or think that the premium is too high. You should compare auto insurance prices among companies before renewing your policy. However, recognize that your driving record will follow you. If you recently caused one or more accidents, you will likely be charged a higher premium whether you continue with your existing insurance company or switch to a new company.

EXAMPLE

Stephanie Spratt is about to renew her car insurance policy. She is considering two policies. Policy A is 100/300/40, which means that the liability coverage is limited to $100,000 per person injured in an accident, $300,000 maximum per accident, and $50,000 to cover damage to the other vehicle or other property. The policy has collision and comprehensive coverage with a deductible of $200. The annual premium for this policy is $1,240. Policy B has liability coverage of 60/100/20 and an annual premium of $800. Stephanie prefers the first policy, because the alternative policy subjects her to a high level of risk due to liability. While Policy B is less expensive, the potential savings is not worth the extra risk that would result from having lower liability coverage.

Stephanie's insurance agent advises her that raising her deductible from $250 to $400 will result in a premium of $1,100. This premium is $140 less than the $1,240 premium quoted for a policy with a $200 deductible. She decides to raise her deductible so that she can reduce next year's premium by $140. The policy Stephanie chose is shown in Exhibit 11.6.

Exhibit 11.6 Stephanie Spratt's Auto Insurance Policy

Insured Policyholder:	Stephanie Spratt
Policy Number:	WW77-QG22-999
Coverage Begins On:	April 6 for one year
Insured Car:	Honda Accord
Due Date:	April 6
License Number:	ZZ QQZZ
Amount Due:	$1,100
Drivers of Car in Your Household:	One driver, age 25.
Ordinary Use of Car:	Less than 10,000 miles per year.

COVERAGE

Liability	
Bodily Injury ($100,000/$300,000 limit)	
Property Damage ($50,000 limit)	
Total Liability	$480
Medical Expenses and Income Loss	$170
Uninsured/Underinsured Motorist ($100,000/$300,000 limit)	$210
Collision ($400 Deductible)	$270
Comprehensive ($400 Deductible)	$86
Emergency Road Service	$4
Total	**$1,220**

Discounts in the Premium	
Antilock Brakes	$30
Accident-free last seven years	$90
Total Discounts	$120
Amount Due	**$1,100**

Focus on Ethics: Impact of Lawsuits and Fraud on Premiums

According to the Insurance Information Institute, the average cost of insuring a car in 2004 was $857, a $23 increase from 2003. One reason for the premium increase is fraud, which occurs when an insurance company pays an unmerited claim. Common forms of fraud include faking an accident, injury, theft, or arson to collect money illegally. While there are many legitimate personal injury lawsuits resulting from car accidents, there are also many frivolous lawsuits. The U.S. court system rarely penalizes individuals who fake or exaggerate injuries in their attempt to win big awards. The Rand Institute of Civil Justice estimates that one-third of all people injured in accidents exaggerate their injuries, which results in an additional 13 to 18 billion dollars per year in insurance expenses.

To the policyholder, some insurance abuse may seem like an innocent white lie. For example, you may consider misrepresenting the extent of the damage to your car or your medical condition after an accident to make sure that your costs will be covered. Much insurance abuse stems from attorneys who aggressively seek out anyone who has been in an accident. Personal injury attorneys may encourage accident victims to embellish their condition to create grounds for a lawsuit, since the attorneys could receive a third or more of the award. The awards granted by the courts for "pain and suffering" combined with the attorney's fees represent more than half of the insurance premiums received by insurance companies. That is, more than half of every dollar of auto insurance premiums received by insurance is used to cover costs associated with lawsuits.

Insurance companies pass along the costs of insurance fraud to policyholders. The costs include attorney fees for fighting false claims and lawsuits as well as expenses for anti-fraud units within insurance companies. The state and federal government are also involved in fighting insurance fraud. Forty-five states have anti-fraud bureaus, and tougher state and federal laws are being created. Until insurance fraud is defeated, you and all other policyholders will continue to pay indirectly for the large awards from lawsuits.

no-fault insurance programs
Do not hold a specific driver liable for causing the accident.

Some states have implemented **no-fault insurance programs**, which do not hold a specific driver liable for causing the accident. The intent is to avoid costly court battles in which each driver attempts to blame the other.

No-fault provisions vary among the states that have imposed no-fault laws. In general, the insurance companies in these states provide coverage (up to specified limits) to their respective policyholders for direct costs incurred due to bodily injury, medical bills, replacement of lost income due to the insured's inability to work, and funeral expenses. However, they do not pay for indirect expenses such as emotional distress or pain and suffering due to an accident.

If you suffer emotional distress from an accident that you believe was caused by the other driver in a no-fault state, you would have to sue the other driver to be compensated. Yet, this is typically only allowed if there is some evidence that the other driver was at fault. For example, if the accident was caused by the other driver running a red light and that driver received a ticket, there may be justification to initiate a lawsuit. The specific restrictions on lawsuits vary among the no-fault states. The no-fault laws have been successful in reducing the costs to insurance companies, which results in lower premiums for policyholders.

A disadvantage of the insurance system in no-fault states is that drivers who cause accidents are not penalized to the degree that they should be. Since the fault is not placed on either driver, the driver who did not cause the accident essentially subsidizes the driver that caused the accident. A driver could conceivably be in multiple accidents that were all caused by other drivers, but the fault is not assigned to the other drivers in a no-fault state.

Insurance companies in some no-fault states have been subjected to fraud, especially in New York and New Jersey. A common example of fraud is when a person files a phony claim for medical care as a result of an accident. Some medical professionals charge individuals in accidents for more medical care than is really provided or necessary, knowing that the insurance company will cover the bill. According to the Insurance Research Council, one in four claims for medical payments in New York is at least partially fraudulent.

IF YOU ARE IN AN AUTO ACCIDENT

If you are in an auto accident, contact the police immediately. Request information from the other driver(s) in the accident, including their insurance information. You may also obtain contact information (including license plate numbers) from witnesses, just in case they leave before the police arrive. Make sure that you can validate whatever information other drivers provide. Some drivers who believe they are at fault and without insurance may attempt to give you a fake name and leave before police arrive. Take pictures of any evidence that may prove that you were not at fault. Write down the details of how the accident happened while they are fresh in your mind. Ask for a copy of the police report.

File a claim with your insurance company immediately. Your insurance company will review the police report and may contact witnesses. It will also verify that your insurance policy is still in effect, and determine whether the repairs and medical treatment will be covered based on your policy's provisions. The insurance policy may specify some guidelines for having your car repaired, such as obtaining at least two estimates before you have repairs done. A claims adjuster employed by the insurance company may investigate the accident details, and attempt to determine how much you should be paid.

Once you incur expenses, such as car repair or medical expenses, send this information along with receipts to the insurance company. The insurance company will respond by reimbursing you for the portion of the expenses that are based on your policy. It may provide full or partial reimbursement. Alternatively, it may state that some or all of your expenses are not covered by your policy.

If your insurance company believes that the other driver is at fault, it should seek damages from the other driver's insurance company. If the other driver is not insured, your insurance company will pay your claim if you have uninsured or underinsured motorist insurance. If your claim is denied by your insurance company and you still believe that the other driver is at fault, you may need to file a claim against the other driver or the other driver's insurance company. This is also the case when an injured party seeks damages greater than those offered by his or her policy.

HOMEOWNER'S INSURANCE

homeowner's insurance
Provides insurance in the event of property damage, theft, or personal liability relating to your home.

Homeowner's insurance provides insurance in the event of property damage, theft, or personal liability relating to home ownership. It not only protects the most valuable asset for many individuals, but also limits their potential liabilities (expenses) associated with the home. Premiums on homeowner's insurance are commonly paid yearly or may be included in your mortgage payment.

Types of Perils Covered by Homeowner's Insurance
Financial loss due to the ownership of a home could occur from a wide variety of adverse events, ranging from a flood to burglary. Homeowner's insurance is structured in six different packages, distinguished by the degree of coverage. After selecting the package that you prefer, you can request additional provisions for the policy to fit your particular needs. The six packages are summarized in Exhibit 11.7. Notice that HO-1, HO-2, HO-3, and HO-5 focus on insurance for the home. The higher the number, the greater the coverage, and the higher the premium that would be paid for a given home. The other two packages, HO-4 and HO-6, provide renter's insurance, and insurance for condominium owners respectively.

HOMEOWNER'S INSURANCE POLICY PROVISIONS

A homeowner's insurance policy typically provides coverage of property damage and protection from personal liability. As shown in Exhibit 11.7, the specific details regard-

Exhibit 11.7 Types of Perils Protected by Homeowner's (HO) Insurance Policies

HO-1: Protects against fire, lightning, explosions, hail, riots, vehicles, aircraft, smoke, vandalism, theft, malicious mischief, glass breakage.

HO-2: Protects against the events identified in HO-1, along with falling objects, the weight of ice, snow, or sleet, the collapse of buildings, overflow of water or steam, power surges, and the explosion of steam or hot-water systems, frozen plumbing, heating units, air-conditioning systems, and domestic appliances.

HO-3: Protects the home and any other structures on the property against all events except those that are specifically excluded by the homeowner's policy. The events that are typically not covered by this insurance are earthquakes, floods, termites, war, and nuclear accidents. It may be possible to obtain additional insurance to protect against floods or earthquakes. This policy also protects personal assets against the events that are listed in HO-2.

HO-4: Renter's insurance. Protects personal assets from events such as theft, fire, vandalism, and smoke.

HO-5: Protects the home, other structures on the property, and personal assets against all events except those that are excluded by the specific homeowner's policy. This policy provides coverage of the home similar to that provided by HO-3, but slightly more coverage of personal assets.

HO-6: Condominium owner's insurance. Protects personal assets from events such as theft, fire, vandalism, and smoke (review the specific policy to determine which events are covered).

HO-8: Protects the home from the same events identified in HO-1, except that it is based on repairs or cash values, not replacement costs.

ing the coverage vary among homeowner's insurance policies. Most homeowner's insurance policies focus on the following types of coverage.

Property Damage

cash-value policy
Pays you for the value of the damaged property after considering its depreciation.

replacement cost policy
Pays you for the actual cost of replacing the damaged property.

The homeowner's policy covers damage to the home. The specific provisions of the policy explain the degree of coverage. A **cash value policy** pays you for the value of the damaged property after considering its depreciation (wear and tear). A **replacement cost policy** pays you for the actual cost of replacing the damaged property. A replacement cost policy is preferable because the actual cost of replacing damaged property is normally higher than the assessed value of property. For example, assume a home is completely destroyed and was valued at $90,000 just before it was destroyed. A cash value policy would provide insurance coverage of $90,000, even though the cost of rebuilding (replacing) the home could be $100,000 or more. In contrast, the replacement cost policy would insure the home for its replacement cost, and therefore would cover the entire cost of repairing the damage up to a limit specified in the homeowner's policy. A policy typically specifies a deductible, or an amount that you would need to pay for damage before the insurance coverage is applied.

Minimum Limit. Many insurers require that your homeowner's insurance policy cover at least 80 percent of the full replacement cost. The financial institution that provides your mortgage loan will likely require homeowner's insurance coverage that would at least cover your mortgage. In most cases, you would want more insurance than is required by the mortgage lender. You should have sufficient insurance not only to cover the mortgage loan balance, but also to replace the property and all personal assets that are damaged.

Other Structures on Property

The homeowner's insurance policy also specifies whether separate structures such as a garage, shed, or swimming pool are covered, and the maximum amount of coverage. Trees and shrubs are usually included with a specified maximum amount of coverage. A deductible may be applied to these other structures.

Personal Property

A policy normally covers personal assets such as furniture, computers, or clothing up to some specified maximum amount. For example, a policy may specify that all personal assets such as furniture and clothing are covered up to $40,000. Standard homeowner's insurance policies limit the coverage of personal property to no more than one-half of the coverage of the dwelling. A deductible may also be applied to the personal property.

home inventory
Contains detailed information about your personal property that can be used when filing a claim.

A **home inventory** includes detailed information about your personal property that can be used when filing a claim. Create a list of all your personal assets and estimate the market value of each of them. Use a video camera to film your personal assets in your home for proof of their existence. Keep the list and the video in a safe place outside of your home, so that you have access to them even if your home is destroyed.

2-20   © Jim Unger/dist. by United Media, 2001

"Whaddya mean, we've only got fire insurance!"

personal property floater
An extension of the homeowner's insurance policy that allows you to itemize your valuables.

Personal Property Replacement Cost Coverage. Many homeowner's policies cover personal property for their cash value. For example, if a home entertainment system priced at $2,500 three years ago is assumed to have a life of five years, it would have used up three-fifths of its life. Based on this amount of depreciation, the insurer will pay you the cash value of $1,000. Yet, if this home entertainment system was destroyed in a fire, you might need to spend $3,000 to replace it.

Just as the dwelling can be insured at replacement cost rather than cash value, so can personal assets. This provision will increase your insurance premium slightly, but it may be worthwhile if you have personal assets that have a high replacement cost.

Personal Property Floater. Some personal assets are very valuable, and are not fully covered by your homeowner's policy. You may need to obtain a **personal property floater** (also called personal articles floater), which is an extension of the homeowner's insurance policy that allows you to itemize your valuables. For example, if you have very expensive computer equipment or jewelry in your home, you may purchase this additional insurance to protect those specific assets. An alternative type is an unscheduled personal property floater, which provides protection for all of your personal property.

Home Office Provision. Assets in a home office such as a personal computer are not covered in many standard homeowner's policies. You can request a home office provision, which will require a higher premium. Alternatively, you could purchase a separate policy to cover the home office.

Liability

The policy specifies coverage in the event that you are sued as the result of an event that occurs in your home or on your property. Normally, you are responsible for an injury to another person while they are on your property. For example, if a neighbor falls down the steps of your home and sues you, your policy would likely cover you. Your exposure to liability is not tied to the value of your home. Even if you have a small home with a low value, you need to protect against liability. Some insurance companies provide minimum coverage of $100,000 against liability. However, a higher level of coverage, such as $300,000, is commonly recommended. The coverage includes the court costs and awards granted as a result of lawsuits against you due to injuries on your property.

Other Types of Expenses

There are many other possible provisions that could be included in a policy to cover a wide variety of circumstances. For example, if an event such as a fire forces you to live away from home, you will incur additional living expenses. A loss-of-use provision specifies whether your policy covers these expenses and the maximum amount of coverage.

Expenses Incurred by Homeowner's Insurance Companies

The allocation of expenses incurred by homeowner's insurance companies is displayed in Exhibit 11.8. Overall, claims paid represent 62 percent of the total expenses. The cost of settling claims represents 9 percent of the total expenses.

HOMEOWNER'S INSURANCE PREMIUMS

The annual cost of insuring a home can be substantial over time, as shown in Exhibit 11.9. The premium has risen in recent years and is expected to rise in the future. This section describes the factors that influence the premium charged, and explains how you can reduce your premium. Your homeowner's insurance premium is influenced by the likelihood that you will submit claims to the insurance company and the cost to the insurance company of covering those claims.

Factors That Affect Homeowner's Insurance Premiums

The premium you pay for homeowner's insurance is primarily dependent on the following factors.

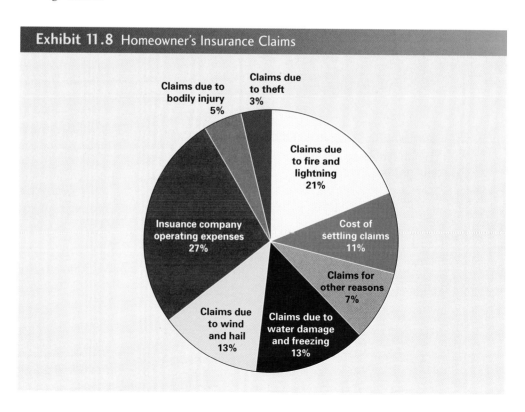

Exhibit 11.8 Homeowner's Insurance Claims

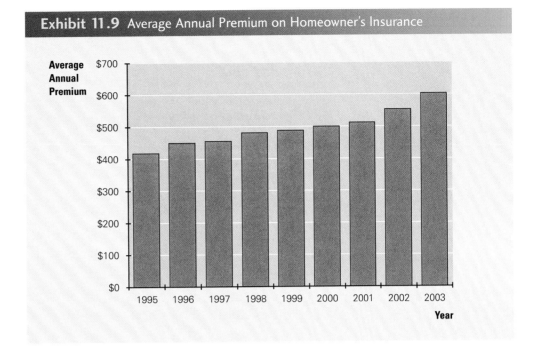

Exhibit 11.9 Average Annual Premium on Homeowner's Insurance

- **Value of Insured Home.** Insurance premiums reflect the value of the insured home and therefore are higher for more expensive homes.

- **Deductible.** A higher deductible reduces the amount of coverage provided by the homeowner's insurance, and therefore results in a lower insurance premium.

- **Location.** The potential for damage is greater in some areas, and therefore the premiums are higher as well. For example, homes along the Gulf Coast are more likely to be damaged by a hurricane than homes located 40 miles inland. Home insurance rates are therefore much higher along the coast. Similarly, premiums will be higher for homes in locations prone to tornadoes, floods, or earthquakes.

- **Degree of Protection.** If you want protection against an earthquake on a home in California, you must pay a higher premium. If you want protection against a flood, you may need to buy an additional insurance policy.

- **Discounts.** You may obtain discounts on your insurance by maintaining a smoke detector system in your home, paying for your insurance in one lump sum, or purchasing multiple types of insurance (such as auto, health, and life) from the same insurer.

Reducing Your Homeowner's Insurance Premium
Consider the following actions you can take to reduce your homeowner's insurance premium.

Increase Your Deductible. If you are willing to pay a higher deductible, you can reduce your premium. For example, if you use a deductible of $1,000 instead of $100, you may be able to reduce your premium by about 20 percent or more.

Improve Protection. If you improve the protection of your home, your insurance premium will decline. For example, you could install storm shutters to protect against bad weather or a security system to protect against burglary.

Use One Insurer for All Types of Insurance. Some insurance companies offer lower premiums to customers who purchase more than one type of insurance from them.

11.3 Financial Planning Online: Purchasing Homeowner's Insurance

Go to
http://www.insurance.com/
FAQs/HomeFAQs.aspx/

This Web site provides
answers to many important
questions concerning
homeowner insurance.

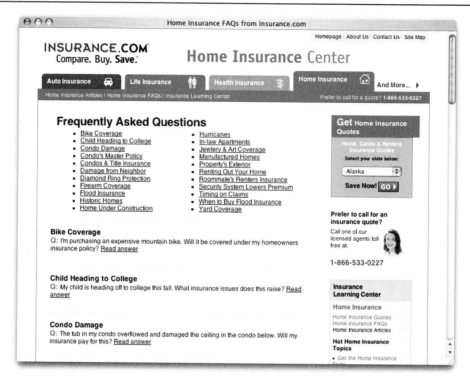

Stay with the Same Insurance Company. When you stay with the same insurance company, you may be rewarded with a lower insurance premium.

Shop Around. As with auto insurance, you may be able to reduce your homeowner's insurance premium by obtaining quotations from various insurance companies. The insurance premium can vary substantially among insurers.

EXAMPLE

Stephanie Spratt is reviewing her homeowner's insurance policy, which is shown in Exhibit 11.10, to determine whether she should change her homeowner's insurance policy once her existing policy expires. She is considering increasing her deductible from $500 to $1,000 and using the same insurance company that insures her car. She calls an insurance agent from her current homeowner's insurer to request a quote based on a $1,000 deductible. Then she calls her auto insurance company to request a quote on homeowner's insurance with the same coverage and deductibles. Her current homeowner's insurance company quotes a premium of $300, which is $30 less than her present premium. Her current auto insurance company quotes a homeowner's premium of $280, which includes a discount reflecting multiple policies with the same insurance company. Stephanie decides to switch companies to gain a package discount once her present homeowner's policy expires.

FILING A CLAIM

If your property is damaged, you should contact your insurance company immediately. A claims adjuster from your insurance company will come to estimate the damage. Present your home inventory to the adjuster. Her estimate will include the cost of repairing the damage done to your home and compensation for damaged property. The company may be willing to issue a check so that you can hire someone to do the repairs. You should consider obtaining an independent estimate on the repairs to ensure that the

Exhibit 11.10 Stephanie Spratt's Homeowner's Insurance Policy

Coverages and Limits

Dwelling	$70,000
Personal Property ($500 deductible)	$25,000
Personal Liability	$100,000
Damage to Property of Others	$500
Medical Payments to Others (per person)	$1,000
Discounts	$25 for House Alarm
Annual Premium	$330

amount the insurance company offers you is sufficient. If the insurance company's estimate is too low, you can appeal it.

RENTER'S INSURANCE

renter's insurance
An insurance policy that protects your possessions within a house, condo, or apartment that you are renting.

Renter's insurance insures your possessions within a house, condo, or apartment that you are renting. It does not insure the structure itself because the insurance is for the renter only, not the owner of the property. It covers personal assets such as furniture, a television, computer equipment, and stereo equipment. The insurance protects against damage due to weather or the loss of personal assets due to burglary. It can cover living expenses while the rental property is being repaired. It also covers liability in the event that a friend or neighbor is injured while on the rental property.

11.4 Financial Planning Online: Renter's Insurance Quotation

Go to
http://insurance.com/
Home.aspx

This Web site provides online quotes for renter's insurance.

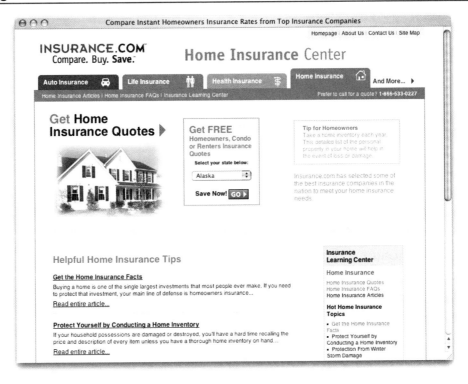

Renters whose personal assets have a high market value need renter's insurance to protect those assets. Even renters without valuable personal assets may desire renter's insurance to protect against liability.

Renter's Insurance Policy Provisions

Renter's insurance specifies the maximum amount of coverage for your personal assets. It may also specify maximum coverage for specific items such as jewelry. The insurance premium is dependent on the amount of coverage you desire. Your renter's insurance may also cover liability resulting from injury to a person while on your premises. For example, if your pet injures a neighbor in your yard, your renter's insurance may cover your liability up to a limit. Because renter's insurance policies vary, you should closely review any policy to ensure that the insurance coverage is appropriate.

UMBRELLA PERSONAL LIABILITY POLICY

umbrella personal liability policy
A supplement to auto and homeowner's insurance that provides additional personal liability coverage.

You can supplement your auto and homeowner's insurance with an **umbrella personal liability policy**, which provides additional personal liability coverage.

This type of policy is intended to provide additional insurance, not to replace the other policies. In fact, the insurance will not be provided unless you show proof of existing insurance coverage. Umbrella policies are especially useful when you have personal assets beyond a car and home that you wish to protect from liability. You may be able to purchase an umbrella policy for about $200 per year for coverage of $1 million.

HOW HOME AND AUTO INSURANCE FIT WITHIN YOUR FINANCIAL PLAN

The following are the key decisions about car and homeowner's insurance that should be included within your financial plan:

- Do you have adequate insurance to protect your wealth?

- How much insurance should you plan to have in the future?

Exhibit 11.11 provides an example of how auto and homeowner's insurance decisions apply to Stephanie Spratt's financial plan.

Exhibit 11.11　How Auto and Homeowner's Insurance Fit within Stephanie Spratt's Financial Plan

GOALS FOR AUTO AND HOMEOWNER'S INSURANCE PLANNING

1. Maintain adequate insurance for my car and my home.
2. Determine whether I should increase my auto and homeowner's insurance levels in the future.

ANALYSIS

Type of Insurance	Protection	Status
Auto	Protects one of my main assets and limits my potential liabilities.	Already have insurance, but I'm considering more liability coverage.
Homeowner's	Protects my largest asset and limits my potential liabilities.	Recently purchased homeowner's insurance as a result of buying a home.

DECISIONS

Decision on Whether My Present Insurance Coverage Is Adequate:

I will increase my auto insurance liability coverage to 100/300/40. While more costly, the increased liability coverage is worthwhile. I will also raise my deductible from $250 to $400, which will reduce the insurance premium.

I currently have sufficient homeowner's insurance, but I will switch my policy over to my auto insurance company when the present policy expires. I will receive a discount in the insurance premium as a result of having multiple insurance contracts with the same insurance company. In the meantime, I will create a home inventory.

Decision on Insurance Coverage in the Future:

If I buy a more expensive car, I will need additional insurance. However, I will not be buying a new car in the near future. If I buy a more expensive home or if the value of my existing home rises substantially, I will need more insurance.

DISCUSSION QUESTIONS

1. How would Stephanie's auto and homeowner's insurance purchasing decisions be different if she were a single mother of two children?

2. How would Stephanie's auto and homeowner's insurance purchasing decisions be affected if she were 35 years old? If she were 50 years old?

SUMMARY

The term *risk* can be defined as exposure to events (or perils) that can cause a financial loss. Your risk management decisions determine whether and how to protect against risk. Your alternatives are to avoid risk, reduce risk, accept risk, or insure against risk. There are some types of risk that are difficult to avoid and dangerous to accept. For these types of risk, insurance is needed. Once you decide whether to obtain a particular type of insurance, you must decide on the amount of coverage, and on where to purchase the insurance.

Automobile insurance insures against damage to your automobile and expenses associated with an accident. The premium paid for auto insurance is dependent on the automobile's value and type, as well as the insurance deductible.

Homeowner's insurance provides insurance in the event of property damage or personal liability. The premium paid for homeowner's insurance is dependent on the home's value, the deductible, and the likelihood of damage to the home.

INTEGRATING THE KEY CONCEPTS

Your decisions regarding auto and homeowner's insurance affect other parts of your financial plan. Auto and home insurance not only protect specific assets, but also limit your liability. Such protection gives you more flexibility on

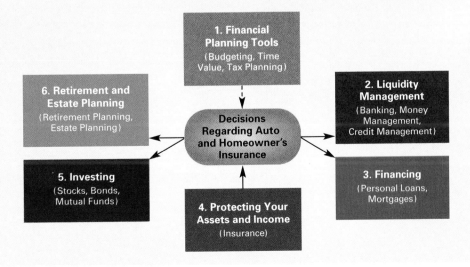

your other financial planning decisions. For example, it allows you to maintain a smaller amount of liquidity (Part 2) because you do not have to accumulate the large amount of funds that would be needed to insure yourself. Insurance makes purchasing a home possible because financing (Part 3) is available only if you insure your home. It also allows you to maintain a smaller amount of investments (Part 5) because you do not have to accumulate a large amount of investments to insure yourself. Finally, it allows you to contribute extra savings toward retirement (Part 6) rather than maintain the funds to cover any liability due to an accident or other unexpected event.

REVIEW QUESTIONS

1. What is the purpose of insurance? What is meant by the term *liability*? How can individuals benefit from insurance?

2. What is risk? What is risk management? How does insurance fit into risk management?

3. What is the responsibility of the insurance company that sells you a policy? What is the relationship between insurance company claims and premiums paid by policyholders?

4. What is the role of insurance underwriters? What is the role of insurance agents? Define the two different types of insurance agents.

5. Describe the two components of liability coverage in an auto insurance policy.

6. What do policy limits of 25/50/25 mean? Do you think the minimum amounts of liability insurance required by your state are suitable for all drivers? Explain your answer.

7. Describe the two types of financial responsibility laws most states have. Are these laws always effective?

8. How does medical payments coverage under an auto insurance policy work? Why is medical payments coverage valuable even if you have a good health insurance plan?

9. Describe collision and comprehensive coverage. Is this type of coverage required by most states? Who may require this type of coverage?

10. List and briefly discuss factors that will affect your auto insurance premium.

11. What steps should you take if you are in a car accident?

12. What is the intent of no-fault insurance? How does no-fault insurance generally work? What is a disadvantage of no-fault insurance?

13. What is homeowner's insurance? How are the premiums normally paid?

14. List and briefly describe the four packages of homeowner's insurance that focus on insurance for the home.

15. What is a "cash value" homeowner's policy? What is a "replacement cost" homeowner's policy?

16. Is personal property typically insured under a homeowner's insurance policy? If so, are there limits to the coverage of personal property? What is a home inventory?

17. What is a personal property floater? What is the difference between scheduled and unscheduled floaters?

18. List and briefly describe some of the factors that affect homeowner's insurance premiums.

19. What are some steps you could take to reduce your homeowner's insurance premium?

20. Describe the steps you would take to file a claim on your homeowner's insurance.

21. How is renter's insurance different from homeowner's insurance? Who should consider purchasing renter's insurance? Briefly describe some of the provisions of a renter's insurance policy.

22. What is the purpose of an umbrella personal liability policy? Who might need one?

VIDEO QUESTIONS

1. In the segment there was a dispute between the insurance company and the contractor that delayed the rebuilding of the family's home. What advice is offered to remedy such a dispute?

2. In the video segment, Janet Bamford explains the differences between guaranteed replacement cost and actual cost value coverage. Explain the differences between these two coverage types using a specific example.

3. Janet Bamford explains some factors that may help to lower a homeowner's insurance premium. List and explain each factor.

FINANCIAL PLANNING PROBLEM

Ethical Dilemma

1. You teach Personal Finance at a local community college. The state in which you teach requires proof of liability insurance in order to renew your license plates.

During the discussion of this topic in class, several students admit that they obtain a liability policy just prior to the renewal of their license plates and then cancel it immediately thereafter. They do this because they know that the state has no system for following up on the cancellation of the liability policies once the license plates are issued. These students, who are out of work as a result of a local plant shutdown, indicate that they cannot afford to maintain the insurance, but they must have access to cars for transportation.

a. Discuss whether you consider the conduct of the students to be unethical.

b. How does the conduct of these students potentially impact other members of the class who maintain liability insurance on their vehicles?

FINANCIAL PLANNING ONLINE EXERCISE

1. Go to http://insurance.yahoo.com/auto.html.

a. Click on "Auto Coverage Analyzer" and enter the requested information. Click "View your results." The screen will display recommendations for coverage under an auto insurance plan.

b. Click on "Get Quotes from InsWeb." Enter your ZIP Code, answer the questions, and click "Start Saving Now!" Complete the forms provided and obtain an auto insurance quote.

c. Now obtain an auto insurance quote from another provider. How do the quotes compare. Why do you think the quotes are different?

BUILDING YOUR OWN FINANCIAL PLAN

Referring to the balance sheet that you prepared in Chapter 2, identify assets that you believe require insurance coverage from an auto or homeowner's policy. Do not overlook risk exposures that can be covered by insurance for less obvious items such as clothing and other personal property.

Go to the worksheets at the end of this chapter, and to the CD-ROM accompanying this text, to continue building your financial plan.

THE SAMPSONS—A CONTINUING CASE

As the next step in reviewing their finances, the Sampsons are taking stock of their insurance needs related to their vehicles and home. They indicated the amount of money they spend on insurance on their personal balance sheet in Chapter 2.

They currently have auto insurance on their two cars. Each insurance policy has a $1,000 deductible and specifies limits of 100/200/20 ($100,000 per person injured in an accident, $200,000 for all people combined, and $20,000 to cover other damage to the car or to other property). Dave and Sharon live in a no-fault state.

Their homeowner's insurance covers the market value of their home and has a deductible of $3,000. Their policy does not cover floods, which periodically occur in their area. Their house has never been flooded, though, so Dave and Sharon are not concerned.

Go to the worksheets at the end of this chapter, and to the CD-ROM accompanying this text, to complete this case.

Chapter 11: Building Your Own Financial Plan

GOALS

1. Ensure that your car and dwelling are adequately insured.
2. Prepare a home inventory.
3. Determine whether you should increase your auto and homeowner's or renter's insurance in the future.

ANALYSIS

1. Review the personal balance sheet you created in Chapter 2. Which assets require coverage from an auto or homeowner's/renter's policy? What risks should you insure against?

_____

_____

_____

_____

_____

2. Using Web sites such as http://www.insurance.com and http://www.insweb.com, obtain two quotes from two different companies for auto insurance. Have information on hand for the year, make, and model of your vehicle and estimates for how many miles you drive per year. Base the quotations on the limits of liability listed (e.g., bodily injury limit of $100,000/$300,000 limit). Insert the deductible you desire in the respective blanks on the form (and be sure to maintain the same deductible for all quotes). Input the information from each quote in the following worksheets to aid your comparison of the various policies.

Company A: _____

Coverage

Liability

Bodily Injury ($100,000/$300,000 limit)	$	
Property Damage ($50,000 limit)	$	
Subtotal Liability		$
No-Fault Medical Expenses and Income Loss	$	
Uninsured/Underinsured Motorist ($100,000/$300,000 limit)	$	
Collision ($ _____ Deductible)	$	
Comprehensive ($ _____ Deductible)	$	
Emergency Road Service	$	
Subtotal		$

Additional Charges (List):	$	
	$	
	$	
	$	
	$	
	$	
	$	
Subtotal		$

Discounts in the Premium

Anti-Lock Brakes	$	
Accident-Free Last Seven Years	$	
Other Discounts (List):	$	
	$	
	$	
	$	
	$	
Minus Total Discounts		$
Total Amount Due		$

Company B: _____

Coverage

Liability

Bodily Injury ($100,000/$300,000 limit)	$	
Property Damage ($50,000 limit)	$	
Subtotal Liability		$
No-Fault Medical Expenses and Income Loss	$	
Uninsured/Underinsured Motorist ($100,000/$300,000 limit)	$	
Collision ($ _____ Deductible)	$	
Comprehensive ($ _____ Deductible)	$	
Emergency Road Service		
Subtotal		$

Additional Charges (List):	$	
	$	
	$	
	$	
	$	
	$	
	$	
Subtotal		$

Discounts in the Premium

Anti-Lock Brakes	$	
Accident-Free Last Seven Years	$	
Other Discounts (List):	$	
	$	
	$	
	$	
	$	
Minus Total Discounts		$
Total Amount Due		$

3. Complete your home inventory using the following worksheet. If you input this information in the Excel worksheet, the software will perform calculations and present pie charts showing the purchase cost of your property versus the replacement cost. Based on your inventory, how much personal property coverage should you have? Is replacement cost or cash value a better policy option? Do you need a personal property floater for any high-ticket items?

In addition to facilitating the process of settling insurance claims and verifying losses, a home inventory helps you determine the amount of insurance you need. The complexity of your inventory depends on your stage in life and family situation. It's a good idea to include copies of sales receipts and purchase contracts with your inventory. After completing your home inventory, print multiple copies and file them in secure locations (safety deposit box, fireproof box, at your parent's home, and so on). You should also consider taking pictures of individual items or videotaping entire rooms as further documentation.

Home Inventory

	Item Description	Make and Model	Date Acquired	Estimated Purchase Cost	Estimated Replacement Cost
Electronics					
Computer Equipment					
Television					
Stereo Equipment					
DVD/VCR					
Cellular Phone/Pager					
Camera/Video Camera					
Major Appliances					
Refrigerator/Freezer					
Stove					
Dishwasher					
Washer/Dryer					
Microwave					
Coffee Maker					
Vacuum					
Blender/Food Processor					
Clothing and Accessories					
Pants					
Shirts					
Sweaters					
Coats					
Dresses					
Skirts					
Shoes					
Accessories (Belts, Ties, etc.)					
Watches					

Home Inventory (continued)

	Item Description	Make and Model	Date Acquired	Estimated Purchase Cost	Estimated Replacement Cost
Clothing and Accessories (continued)					
Rings					
Earrings					
Necklaces					
Bracelets					
Cufflinks					
Linens					
Towels					
Bedding					
Furniture					
Living Room Set					
Dining Room Set					
Bedroom Sets					
Kitchen Set					
Bookshelves					
Lamps					
Rugs					
Patio Set					
Art and Music					
Books					
CDs/Records/ Audio Tapes					
DVD/VCR Tapes					
Artwork					

Home Inventory (continued)

	Item Description	Make and Model	Date Acquired	Estimated Purchase Cost	Estimated Replacement Cost
Kitchen Equipment					
Dishes					
Glassware					
Silverware					
Pots and Pans					
Utensils					
Athletic Equipment					
Collectibles					
Other					

4. Using the following Web sites, obtain quotes for your homeowner's/renter's insurance policy. After obtaining the quotes, complete the worksheets below to aid your comparison of policies. Note: Some of these Web sites will provide you with a quote online while others will indicate that a quote will be sent to you via U.S. mail or other medium. Insert the deductible you desire on the form (and be sure to maintain the same deductible for all quotes).

Web sites:

http://www.amica.com
http://www.val-u-web.com/house.htm
http://www.savvy-bargains.com
http://www.homeownerswiz.com/

Company A: _____

Coverage and Limits

Dwelling	$
Personal Property ($_____ Deductible)	$
Personal Liability	$
Damage to Property of Others	$
Medical Payments to Others (per Person)	$
Discounts	$
Annual Premium	$

Company B: _____

Coverage and Limits

Dwelling	$
Personal Property ($_____ Deductible)	$
Personal Liability	$
Damage to Property of Others	$
Medical Payments to Others (per Person)	$
Discounts	$
Annual Premium	$

DECISIONS

1. What are the key risks related to auto and homeowner's/renter's insurance that you will insure against?

_____

_____

_____

_____

_____

2. What coverage levels will you maintain for your auto policy? Which of the policy quotes you requested is most attractive? What actions can you take to receive policy discounts in the future?

_____

_____

_____

_____

_____

_____

_____

3. What coverage levels will you maintain for your homeowner's/renter's policy? Which of the policy quotes you requested is most attractive? What actions can you take to receive policy discounts in the future?

_____

_____

_____

_____

_____

_____

_____

_____

Chapter 11: The Sampsons—A Continuing Case

CASE QUESTIONS

1. Advise the Sampsons regarding their car insurance. Do they have enough insurance? Do they have too much insurance? How might they be able to reduce their premium?

2. Sharon has recently been in an accident that was caused by a drunk driver. The other driver did not receive a ticket for driving while intoxicated. Sharon is considering suing the other driver for emotional distress. Do you think the lawsuit will be successful?

3. Consider the Sampsons' homeowner's insurance. Do they have enough insurance? Do they have too much insurance? Is increasing their deductible well advised?

Health and Disability Insurance

W hile out of town, Ruby felt chest pains, so she went to the nearest hospital, and was required to stay the night for tests. One week later, Ruby received a bill of $15,000 from the hospital. Even though she had medical insurance, she would have to pay over $5,000 out of pocket. It could have been worse. Had Ruby not had insurance, the entire $15,000 bill would have been hers to pay.

Health care can be very expensive. The health insurance policy that you select will determine how much of your health care expenses are covered. Proper health insurance decisions can protect your net worth.

The objectives of this chapter are to:

- Identify and compare the types of private health care plans

- Explain the use of government health care plans

- Describe long-term care insurance

- Explain the benefits of disability insurance

HEALTH INSURANCE

health insurance
A type of insurance offered by private insurance companies or the government that covers health care expenses incurred by policyholders for necessary medical care.

Health insurance covers health care expenses incurred by policyholders. It limits your potential liabilities and ensures that you will receive necessary medical care. Many more options are available for health insurance than for auto or homeowner's insurance. Health insurance is offered by private insurance companies and by the government. The nation's largest health care insurer, Blue Cross and Blue Shield, serves many employers with a group participation plan. Blue Cross and Blue Shield makes agreements with doctors and hospitals on the types of services it will cover and the amount it will pay for each service. Individuals insured by Blue Cross and Blue Shield are then covered up to the agreed-on specific dollar amount for each service. Policyholders are responsible for any additional costs beyond the set limit. Some private insurance companies provide only health insurance, while other companies offer it along with other types of insurance.

Without health insurance, the high expenses of health care could quickly eliminate most of your wealth. Therefore, health insurance is a critical component of your financial planning.

Health insurance has received much attention in recent years because it has become so expensive. The need for health care is greater for individuals who are older, and the average age of the population has increased in recent years. Since older individuals require more health care, the cost of providing health care is rising. People are living longer, partly due to effective health care, and therefore require medical attention for a longer period of time. The health insurance industry relies on technology for improvements, which can be very expensive. Technological advances have been achieved that can save or extend lives, but they are costly. The health care industry relies on bureaucratic procedures that result in higher costs. The process used by insurers to reimburse individuals or to pay health care providers can be confusing. Consequently, fraudulent claims made by patients or health care providers sometimes slip through and are reimbursed. All these factors are increasing the cost of health care.

While health insurance is expensive, it is necessary. Your health insurance decision is not whether to obtain it, but which health plan to purchase and how much coverage to purchase. By closely assessing your health insurance options, you can select health insurance that is within your budget and offers adequate protection.

PRIVATE HEALTH INSURANCE

private health insurance
Health insurance that can be purchased from private insurance companies to provide coverage for health care expenses.

Private health insurance refers to health insurance that can be purchased from private insurance companies to provide coverage for health care expenses.

Types of Private Health Insurance Coverage
Private health insurance plans include hospitalization insurance, surgical insurance, and physician insurance.

hospitalization insurance
Insurance that covers the cost of many hospital facility and service fees.

Hospitalization Insurance. **Hospitalization insurance** policies provide reimbursement for the cost of a hospital room, including meals, pharmaceuticals, and nursing services, and the use of hospital facilities such as operating rooms, labs, and x-rays while you are in the hospital. It may also provide reimbursement for rehabilitation services at home and ambulance services.

The policy may specify the maximum number of days in which hospitalization costs will be covered. Alternatively, it may specify the maximum based on a multiple of the daily room rate charged by the hospital. Because hospitalization insurance only covers up to a specified maximum, insured policyholders may have to pay some of the expenses.

surgical expense insurance
Insurance that covers the cost of some surgeries.

Surgical Expense Insurance. **Surgical expense insurance** policies provide reimbursement for the cost of surgery, including anesthetics, lab fees, and x-rays. The policy may specify a maximum reimbursement per surgical procedure, and most policies do not cover elective cosmetic surgeries. Policies vary in their coverage of surgeries that are viewed as experimental. For example, a specific procedure may have a low probability of curing a specific illness, but be the only possible cure available. Policies that offer more coverage for experimental surgeries are typically more expensive.

physician expense insurance
Insurance that covers the cost of many nonsurgical physician fees.

Physician Expense Insurance. **Physician expense insurance** covers the physician fees for nonsurgical health care in the hospital or lab tests and x-rays outside the hospital. There may be a deductible applied to the first few appointments for any particular cause.

major medical insurance
Insurance used as a backup to basic health insurance, covering major medical expenses that are beyond the scope of the basic policy.

Major Medical Insurance. Because basic health insurance does not cover all health care expenses, **major medical insurance** serves as a valuable backup. It provides reimbursement for major medical expenses beyond those covered by basic health insurance. It may involve a deductible, and pay only a portion of the expenses that were not covered by basic insurance. The policy has a lower premium if it specifies a large deductible before expenses are reimbursed. Lifetime maximum limits may be imposed.

Options for Purchasing Private Health Insurance

You can purchase this insurance directly from private health insurance companies or through your employer. Most large employers offer their employees the opportunity to participate in a health insurance plan as part of their benefits package. The employer and employee typically share the cost of the health insurance. The employees' portion of the premium is deducted from their pay, and the employer pays the remainder. Some employers pay a large portion of the premium in order to attract and retain good employees. Employers tend to obtain all their health insurance from one company.

Private insurance is usually less expensive when provided under an employer's plan. Information about health insurance premiums is available at http://www.insweb.com and http://www.insure.com.

Private Health Care Plans

Private health care plans are commonly classified as indemnity plans or managed health care plans.

indemnity plan
Health insurance that reimburses individuals for part or all of the expenses they incur from health care providers; individuals are free to decide whether to seek care from a primary care physician or a specialist.

Indemnity Plans. An **indemnity plan** reimburses individuals for part or all of the health care expenses they incur from health care providers (such as doctors or hospitals). Individuals have the freedom to decide whether to seek care from a primary care physician or a specialist. They are billed directly by the health care providers and then must complete and submit forms to request reimbursement for the services rendered and prescriptions. Many indemnity plans have a coinsurance provision in which the insurance company pays a percentage of the bill. For example, a provision may specify that the insurance company pays 80 percent of the bill and that you pay the remaining 20 percent. After you reach the policy's out-of-pocket limit, the insurance company pays 100 percent of covered medical expenses.

The advantage of an indemnity plan is that you can choose your own health care provider. The disadvantage is that you must deal with a bureaucracy to get reimbursement for your health care bills. Although indemnity plans offer more flexibility than managed care plans, they also charge higher premiums. Normally you must pay a deductible, although most of the bill will be reimbursed by the insurer.

managed health care plan
A health insurance policy under which individuals receive services from specific doctors or hospitals that are part of the plan.

Managed Health Care Plans. **Managed health care plans** allow individuals to receive health care services from specific doctors or hospitals that are part of the plan. When you receive services, you are billed only for any amounts not covered by your insurance. Therefore, you do not have to pay the full cost and then wait to be reimbursed, as is typically the process for indemnity plans. Managed health care plans charge lower premiums than indemnity plans, but impose more restrictions on the specific health care providers (doctors, hospitals) that individuals can use. Managed health care plans are normally classified as health maintenance organizations or preferred provider organizations.

health maintenance organization (HMO)
A health insurance plan that covers health care services approved by doctors; a primary care physician provides general health services and refers patients to a specialist as necessary.

Health Maintenance Organizations. A **health maintenance organization (HMO)** provides insurance for health care services approved by doctors. The HMO is self-administered and offers health care services to customers who want to participate in exchange for health insurance premiums. Normally, premiums are withheld from the insured individual's paychecks and paid to the HMO by the employer. For this reason, an HMO is sometimes referred to as a prepaid health plan. You pay the same premium whether you use the plan's services or not.

The HMO establishes an agreement with select health care providers (such as doctors and hospitals) that are obligated to provide services to the HMO customers. The health care providers involved in the agreement are paid a predetermined amount of compensation per month. Their compensation is referred to as per member per month (PMPM) for each patient who participates in the plan. Even though the fee is prearranged, the cost to the health care provider varies with the demand for services. For example, if the patients of a particular plan require minimal health care, a hospital will incur limited costs to pay its nurses and for medical supplies. Yet, if the patients of a particular plan require substantial health care, a hospital will incur higher costs to pay some of its nurses for overtime work and to maintain adequate medical supplies. The hospital is more profitable when the demand for health care services by the HMO participants is relatively low.

Individuals choose a primary care physician who is part of the HMO. The primary care physician provides general health services, such as checkups and treatment of minor illnesses, and refers patients to a specialist as necessary. Individuals are directed to the appropriate specialist, rather than deciding on their own which type of specialist they need. If they see a specialist without being referred by the primary care physician, the related expenses may not be covered by the HMO. By restricting access to specialists, HMOs also seek to control costs.

An advantage of HMOs is that they offer health care services at a low cost. Since HMOs emphasize the early detection and treatment of illnesses, they can keep the premiums relatively low. Individuals also typically pay a small fee (such as $10) for a visit to a physician who participates in an HMO or for a prescription. An HMO also typically covers a portion of prescription expenses.

A disadvantage, however, is that individuals must choose among the primary care physicians and specialists who participate in the plan. Thus, they cannot select a physician who is not approved by the HMO. HMO members pay lower premiums in exchange for less flexibility.

preferred provider organization (PPO)
A health insurance plan that allows individuals to select a health care provider and covers most of the fees for services; a referral from a doctor is not required to visit a specialist.

Preferred Provider Organizations. A **preferred provider organization (PPO)** allows individuals to select their health care providers and have most of the fee covered. A PPO also uses a primary care physician, but there are more physicians available for each area of specialization than in an HMO. The premiums and fees for health care services are higher in a PPO than an HMO, however. For example, individuals may be charged 20 percent of the bill for certain health care services provided by a PPO versus a small flat fee such as $15 for the same services provided by an HMO.

discount on charge arrangement
An arrangement in which the preferred provider organization (PPO) agrees to pay a specific percentage of the health care provider's charges.

A common payment arrangement between health care providers and PPOs is the **discount on charge arrangement**, in which the PPO agrees to pay a specific percentage

"Isn't it nice to find out right away if insurance will cover the procedure?"

per diem rate arrangement
An arrangement in which the preferred provider organization (PPO) pays the provider a specific sum for each day a patient is hospitalized.

of the provider's charges. For example, if the provider charged $1,000, the PPO would pay a total of $700 (70 percent of $1,000). Under this arrangement, the provider receives $300 less than what it normally charges for this type of service. A portion of the $700 payment to the provider would be made by the patient and the rest of the payment would be made by the PPO. The specific breakdown of the payments is dictated by the contract between the PPO and the patient.

A second type of arrangement between the PPO and the provider is the **per diem rate arrangement**, in which the provider is paid a specific amount for each day the patient is hospitalized. Suppose a hospital charges $1,000 for a one-day stay in the hospital, but its PPO arrangement specifies a $650 per diem rate. The total amount owed to the hospital would be $650. The payment by the patient to the hospital is determined by the contract between the patient and the PPO.

A patient's contract with the PPO typically specifies that the PPO pays 80 percent of the amount owed, and the patient pays the remaining 20 percent. If the total amount owed to the provider is $700, the PPO would pay 80 percent of the $700, or $560. The patient would be required to pay 20 percent of $700, or $140. The patient's payment is often referred to as a co-payment. Patients receive an Explanation of Benefits (EOB) form from the PPO after receiving health care services. The EOB lists the total charges, the total amount that is owed to the provider, and the amount owed by the patient.

Individuals who are unemployed or whose employer does not offer a health plan can obtain managed care or other types of health insurance directly from private insurance companies. However, the insurance premiums are normally higher if insurance is purchased individually rather than through an employer-sponsored plan.

Premiums for Private Health Care Insurance

Employers may offer individual coverage or family coverage. Higher premiums are charged for family coverage. A married couple without children should compare the premiums if each of them purchases individual insurance versus if one person buys family insurance. Individuals or couples who have children or plan to have children in the near future need a family plan.

You can obtain insurance quotes and go through the application process online. Some Web sites provide general quotes on the premiums charged by various insurance companies for health care. The quotes may also include information on the deductible, the coinsurance rate, and the fee you would pay for a visit to a doctor. If you want to obtain more information about any specific quote, the Web site provides a link to the insurance company providing that quote. When you submit an application online, the initial quote of the premium may be changed after you provide information such as your medical history and present health condition.

Comparison of Private Health Insurance Plans

A comparison of private health insurance plans is provided in Exhibit 12.1. This exhibit illustrates the tradeoff between the flexibility that individuals have in selecting their physician and the premium that they are charged for health insurance.

HMOs and PPOs offer brochures that provide the comparative information you need before you decide which plan to select. Exhibit 12.2 lists the questions that you should ask before you make your selection. If these questions cannot be answered by the brochure, contact a representative who can provide the answers.

Exhibit 12.1 Comparison of Private Health Insurance Plans

Type of Private Health Plan	Premium	Selection of Physician
Indemnity Plan	High	Flexibility to select physician or specialist
Managed Care: HMOs	Relatively low	Primary care physician refers patients to specialist
Managed Care: PPOs	Low, but usually higher than HMOs	There is a greater number of physicians to choose from in PPOs than HMOs.

Exhibit 12.2 Questions to Ask When Considering a Particular HMO or PPO

Questions Regarding Your Cost

1. Monthly premium?
2. Deductible?
3. Coinsurance/Co-Pay amounts?
4. Limits on coverage?
5. Maximum out-of-pocket expenses per year?

Questions Regarding the Doctors/Health Care Providers

1. How many doctors are in the plan?
2. Who are the doctors in the plan?
3. Which doctors are accepting new patients?
4. How long in advance must you schedule a routine visit to the doctor?
5. Where are the doctors located?
6. What health care services do the doctors provide?
7. What hospitals/labs/diagnostic centers are in the plan?

General Questions

1. Is access to specialists only allowed with a referral from a primary care physician?
2. What coverage is provided if the patient receives services out of the primary network (for example, a visit to an emergency room while out of town)?
3. If a physician is accessed outside of the plan, are there out-of-network benefits?

EXAMPLE

When Stephanie Spratt started working for her present employer, she was offered the opportunity to participate in an HMO or an indemnity plan, in which she would be able to seek whatever health care provider she preferred. She is now reviewing her health care choice. The premium for the indemnity plan is $100 higher per month than her HMO. She also has the opportunity to switch to a PPO, but her premium would be $75 per month higher than her HMO. An advantage of this PPO over her HMO is that there are more physicians available in each health care specialization. At this time, Stephanie does not have a need for any specialists. She decides that she will continue to participate in the HMO because she does not think that the advantages of the indemnity plan or the PPO are worth the extra premium.

12.1 Financial Planning Online: Should You Enroll in an HMO or a PPO?

Go to
http://www.individual-health-plans.com

Click on
"PPO Plans" and "HMO Plans" under "Types of Plans"

This Web site provides information on different types of plans including PPOs and HMOs.

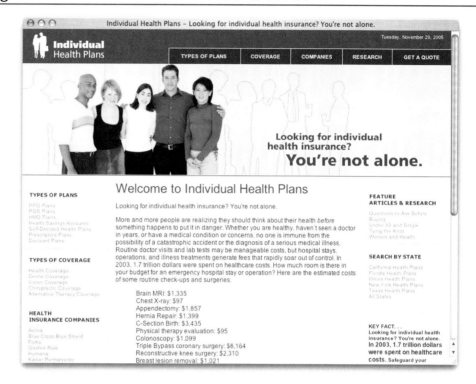

Individual Insurance

Some people cannot participate in a group plan, either because they are self-employed or because their employer does not provide health insurance. They must purchase individual health insurance coverage. The insurance may be purchased through an association. If you need individual insurance, make sure that it provides broad coverage of major medical expenses. Some policies focus on coverage for a single disease, and will not cover most health care services.

Short-term medical insurance is available to individuals who are presently not in a group health insurance plan but hope to be in the future. It provides protection while you are waiting for employer group coverage. It typically offers coverage for a period of one to six months.

CONTENTS OF HEALTH CARE INSURANCE POLICIES

Health care insurance policies contain the following information.

Identification of Insured Persons

A health insurance contract identifies the persons who are covered. It may be an individual or a family.

Location

Some U.S. insurance companies provide coverage for health care in the United States only, while others provide coverage in non-U.S. countries. Typically, full health insurance benefits are confined to the local area of the beneficiary. Benefits are reduced or eliminated for non-emergency health care received out of the area.

Preexisting Conditions

A policy may exclude coverage for preexisting conditions, which are health conditions that existed before your policy was granted. For example, if you had torn ligaments when you applied for the health care policy, you may not be allowed coverage for surgery to repair the ligaments. The preexisting conditions clause prevents people from buying insurance just to treat existing illnesses or injuries.

Cancellation Options

A health insurance contract may allow the insurance company to cancel the contract at any time. Other contracts guarantee continuous coverage as long as the policyholders pay the premiums on time.

Determinants of Unreimbursed Medical Expenses

For a given health care service, the insurance policy specifies the means by which you can determine the amount of the bill that you must pay. This amount is determined by the deductible, coinsurance, stop-loss provision coverage limits, and coordination of benefits, as explained next.

Deductible. A deductible requires that the insured bear the cost of the health care up to a level that is specified in the policy. If a policy specifies a deductible of $500 for specific health care, and the bill is $475, you will have to pay the entire amount. If the bill is $900, you will pay the first $500, and the policy will cover the remaining $400. The deductible in health care is similar to the deductible in auto insurance, in that it reduces the potential liability to the insurance company. Therefore, the premiums charged for a particular policy are generally lower when the deductible is higher.

Coinsurance. A coinsurance clause specifies the proportion of health care expenses that will be paid by the insurance company. For example, for a $1,000 bill that is subject to a 20% copay, you will pay $200 (20% of $1,000).

Stop Loss Provision. A stop loss provision sets a maximum amount that you must pay for one or more health care services.

Coverage Limits. Many policies have limits on the amount of coverage that the insurance company will provide for particular health care services. The limits may be applied to hospital expenses, surgery procedures, and nursing services. Thus, if policyholders select health care services costing more than what is covered by the policy, they will have the pay the difference themselves. These limits may be imposed even if the total health care expenses due to a specific illness or injury are not subject to a maximum limit. This policy is intended to discourage excessive charges by the health care providers for any particular health care service. Consider an injury that resulted in charges for labs, x-rays, doctor fees, and surgery that add up to $10,000. Each charge is compared to the usual maximum allowable limit for that type of health care to determine the amount that is paid.

Coordination of Benefits. When a policy has a coordination of benefits provision, it means that the benefits are dependent on what benefits would be paid by other policies that you have. The benefits that would be paid by multiple policies could possibly overlap, but this provision limits the total reimbursement to no more than your expenses. This provision can be beneficial to you because your insurance premiums and coinsurance will be lower if the insurance benefits are coordinated amoong policies to limit the reimbursement amount.

Rehabilitation

Some health insurance policies provide coverage for rehabilitation, which may include physical therapy sessions and counseling.

Mental Illness

Health insurance policies vary in terms of their coverage for mental illness. Because mental illness is not necessarily cured by a hospital visit or surgery, it is not always covered under traditional health insurance. Some policies cover mental illness to a limited degree. They may provide partial reimbursement for expenses associated with the treatment of mental disorders. They may also specify a maximum period or lifetime amount in which such treatments are covered.

Pregnancy

Some health insurance policies offer no coverage for expenses associated with pregnancy, while others provide coverage of direct expenses, and may even pay for sick leave during the last weeks of pregnancy.

Renewability Option

Your health insurance contract should specify if you are given the option to renew your contract up to a specified age level. If you renew the contract, the insurance company can charge you a higher premium if your health conditions diminished since you last applied for health insurance.

Maintaining Private Health Care Insurance Coverage

Federal regulations ensure that individuals can maintain continuous health care coverage, despite their employment status. In particular, the following acts have played a major role.

COBRA. As a result of the Consolidated Omnibus Budget Reconciliation Act (COBRA) of 1986, you can continue your health insurance provided through an employer's plan for 18 months after you stop working for the employer. The act applies to private firms and state government agencies, but not to federal government agencies. If you retire, COBRA allows you to continue your health insurance (within the 18-month maximum period) up to the point at which you qualify for government health care.

HIPAA. The Health Insurance Portability and Accounting Act (HIPAA) of 1996 ensures that workers can continue their health insurance coverage even if they have switched jobs. Specifically, the act prohibits insurance companies from denying health insurance coverage based on an applicant's health status, medical condition or history, previous health insurance claims, or disability. The act is especially important for workers who have preexisting medical problems. For example, consider a woman employed by a firm in Kansas who has an existing medical condition. She wants to move to Dallas and is searching for work with a new employer there. Before HIPAA, she may not have been able to obtain health insurance in Texas because the insurance company would have been concerned that she might need to file many claims given her existing medical condition. Yet, as a result of HIPAA, she cannot be denied health insurance because of her existing medical condition.

To remain eligible for protection under HIPAA, a person must maintain continuous enrollment in a health care plan. This provision is intended to prevent individuals from participating in a health insurance plan only when they have a medical condition or illness for which they want treatment.

Expenses Not Covered by Private Insurance Plans

Regardless of the private health insurance plan used, there will likely be some health care expenses that are not covered. You should budget for the possibility of some health care expenses that may not be included in your coverage.

A **flexible spending account** is an account established by an employer for employees to use pretax income to pay for medical expenses. The amount that you set aside each pay period for your flexible spending account is not subject to federal, state, and local income taxes, or to FICA taxes. If you have unreimbursed medical or dental expenses, you can draw from this account to pay these expenses. By using this account, you are not taxed on the income that you used to pay these health care expenses.

flexible spending account
Account established by the employer for the employee to use pretax income to pay for medical expenses.

One disadvantage of the flexible spending account is that the funds allocated to the account cannot roll over into the next year. Thus, you need to use all the funds that are allocated to the account within the same year. For this reason, some individuals allocate a minimal amount to the account.

GOVERNMENT HEALTH CARE PLANS

The government-sponsored health care plans are Medicare and Medicaid.

Medicare

Recall from Chapter 4 that the Medicare program provides health insurance to individuals who are 65 years of age or older and qualify for Social Security benefits, or who are disabled. Medicare also provides payments to health care providers in the case of illness. Medicare is composed of two parts, called Part A and Part B. Part A consists of hospital insurance and is used to cover expenses associated with inpatient care (including surgeries) in hospitals or nursing facilities, and a limited amount of home health care. There is no additional premium required for Part A coverage for individuals who qualify because they (or their spouse) paid sufficient Medicare taxes while working. Part B represents optional medical insurance and covers some expenses that are not covered by Part A, such as outpatient hospital care, physical therapy, and some home health services. You must pay a monthly premium to receive Part B coverage.

medigap insurance
Insurance provided by private insurance companies to cover medical expenses that are not covered by Medicare.

Medigap Insurance. Some individuals want supplemental insurance that offers more coverage than Medicare provides. **Medigap insurance** is provided by private insurance companies to cover medical expenses that are not covered by Medicare. There are various types of Medigap policies. In most states, there are 10 standardized policies, which are classified as Medigap plans A through J. Plan A is the most basic and includes coverage of hospitalization expenses that are not covered by Medicare. The other plans provide additional coverage beyond Plan A, each differentiated by the amount of medical care covered. Plan J offers the most comprehensive coverage. Insurance companies can select whatever plans they wish to offer to individuals. The premiums that they charge are higher for the policies that provide more coverage.

Medicare Prescription Act. The Medicare Prescription Drug Improvement and Modernization Act of 2003 allows coverage for senior citizens and people with disabilities. Medicare now covers some prescription drugs that were not covered before, which may prevent some illnesses and therefore eliminate the need for other high cost health care services.

The act allows seniors to purchase various forms of coverage for prescription drugs. The coverage is provided through private firms, either by itself or as a part of managed care plans. As of 2006, the standard coverage requires a premium of about $35 per month, and an annual deductible of $250. The premium and the deductible will change over time to reflect costs.

The standard coverage is 75 percent of prescription expenses for the first $2,000 spent after the $250 deductible for the year. Thus, an individual would have to pay the entire cost of the first $250 that was spent, and would then pay only 25% of the next $2,000 in prescription expenses, after accounting for the coverage. Additional coverage is provided only if a senior's expenses exceed $3,600 for the year. Low-income seniors are not charged a premium and are not subject to a deductible.

health savings account
An account that shelters income from taxes and that can be used to pay health care expenses.

The act also allows individuals to establish a **health savings account**, which shelters income from taxes and can be used to pay health care expenses. The health savings account is set up with pre-tax dollars, similar to a tax-sheltered annuity plan. Federal income taxes are not paid on the amount paid into this account. A maximum of $4,500 of income can be deposited in the account each year. Because this money is not taxed, individuals have an incentive to create an account and thus reduce their taxes. The tax

12.2 Financial Planning Online: Medicare Coverage

Go to

http://www.medicare.gov

This Web site provides:
an overview of services offered by Medicare, including the specific benefits that are available.

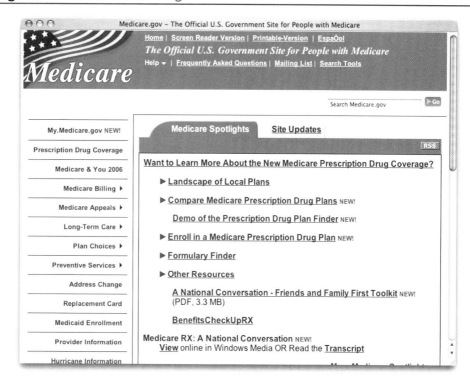

saving incentive of the health savings account is similar to some college savings accounts and retirement accounts that have been created by the U.S. government to encourage saving. It differs from those accounts in that it is designed to ensure that individuals save sufficient money to cover their annual health care expenses. If individuals have more money in their account than they need in a given year, the money remains in the account and can be used in the following year. In addition, money in the account earns interest until it is spent on health care.

Businesses can set up health savings accounts for their employees, and can contribute to their accounts (up to the $4,500 maximum). People must be under age 65 to qualify for the plan and have a high-deductible health plan, which is defined as a minimum $1,000 deductible for individuals and $2,000 deductible for family plans.

Medicaid

Medicaid
A federal program that provides health care to the aged, blind, disabled, and needy families with dependent children.

The **Medicaid** program provides health insurance for individuals with low incomes and those in need of public assistance. It is intended to provide health care to the aged, blind, disabled, and needy families with dependent children. To qualify, individuals must meet some federal guidelines, but the program is administered on a state-by-state basis. Individuals who qualify for Medicare may also be eligible for Medicaid if they need public assistance; in this case, they will receive more health benefits.

LONG-TERM CARE INSURANCE

Many people who are elderly or have long-term illnesses need some assistance with everyday tasks such as eating or dressing. Others need around-the-clock medical assistance. According to the Americans for Long-term Care Security (ALTCS), 20 percent of individuals in the United States aged 50 and older will need long-term care services. In addition, more than half of all individuals in the United States will need long-term care at some period during their life, and long-term care can be very expensive. The cost of having an aide provide basic care at home such as feeding or dressing each day can easily exceed $1,000 per week. The cost of care by a nurse is higher. For individuals who enter a nursing home, the cost is about $55,000 per year on average.

Government health care plans offer little assistance. Medicare does not cover the costs of long-term care. While Medicaid might cover some of these expenses for qualifying individuals, the coverage is limited.

long-term care insurance
Covers expenses associated with long-term health conditions that cause individuals to need help with everyday tasks.

Long-term care insurance covers expenses associated with long-term health conditions that cause individuals to need help with everyday tasks. It is provided by many private insurance companies, and typically covers care in a nursing home, assisted living facility, or at home. However, given the high expenses associated with long-term care, the premiums for long-term care insurance are very high. Premiums of $3,000 or more per year for long-term care are quite common.

Long-Term Care Insurance Provisions

Like other insurance policies, you can design a long-term care policy that fits your needs. Some of the more common provisions are listed here.

Eligibility to Receive Benefits. Policies include the range of benefits for which policyholders can file claims. For example, a policy may specify that the long-term care be restricted to medical health care services, while a more flexible policy may also allow other care such as feeding or dressing.

Types of Services. Long-term care insurance policies specify the types of medical care services that are covered. A policy that covers nursing home care or assisted living will have higher premiums than a policy that only covers nursing home care. For individuals who prefer a more flexible long-term care policy that covers the cost of home health aides, premiums will be higher.

Amount of Coverage. Policies also specify the maximum amount of coverage provided per day. If you want the maximum amount of coverage that a company will provide, you will pay a high premium. If you are willing to accept a lower maximum amount of daily coverage, your premium can be reduced. A policy with less coverage may not completely cover the daily costs that you could incur. In that case, you would need to cover a portion of your expenses.

A policy can contain a coinsurance provision that requires the policyholder to incur a portion of the health care expense. For example, a policyholder can select a policy in which the insurance company pays 80 percent of the health care expenses specified in the policy, while the policyholder pays the remaining 20 percent. Since the potential expense to the insurance company is lower as a result of the coinsurance provision, the premium will be lower.

Elimination Period to Receive Benefits. A policy may specify an elimination (or waiting) period before policyholders are eligible to have their long-term care costs covered. An elimination period of between 60 and 90 days is common. The policyholder is responsible for covering expenses until the elimination period is completed. If the health care is needed over a period that is shorter than the elimination period, it will not be covered by the long-term care insurance.

Maximum Period to Receive Benefits. You can choose to receive insurance benefits for the entire period in which you need long-term care, even if the period is 30 years or longer. If you choose to receive insurance benefits for a limited period, you would be charged a lower premium. For example, your long-term care could be covered for up to three years.

Continued Coverage. A policy may contain a *waiver of policy premium* provision that allows you to stop paying premiums once you need long-term care. There are some alternative provisions that may also allow a limited amount of coverage after you have a policy for a specified number of years, without having to pay any more premiums. In general, any provision that provides additional benefits in the future will require higher premiums today.

Inflation Adjustment. Some policies allow for the coverage to increase in line with inflation over time. Thus, the maximum benefits will rise each year with the increase in an inflation index. You will pay a higher premium for a long-term health care policy that contains this provision.

Stop-Loss Provision. The insurance covering a long-term illness may also specify a stop-loss provision, which sets a maximum limit on the health care expense to be incurred by the policyholder. Reconsider the previous example in which the policyholder was required to pay 20 percent of expenses associated with his long-term illness. If the related health care expenses are $600,000 over time, the policyholder would have to pay $120,000 (20 percent of $600,000). However, if the policyholder has a stop-loss provision specifying a $30,000 limit, the policyholder would only owe $30,000. The lower the stop-loss limit, the higher the premium.

Other Factors That Affect Long-Term Care Insurance Premiums

The insurance premium charged for long-term care insurance is influenced by the likelihood that the insurance company will have to cover claims, and the size of those claims. Since the long-term care policy provisions described above affect the likelihood and size of claims, they affect the premiums on long-term care insurance. In addition to the provisions of the policy, the following characteristics of the policyholder also affect the premiums on long-term care insurance.

Age. Individuals who are older are more likely to need long-term care insurance, so they are charged higher premiums. Policy premiums are especially high for individuals who are 60 years of age or older.

Health Condition. Individuals who have an existing long-term illness are more likely to need to file a claim, so they are charged higher premiums.

Reducing Your Cost of Long-Term Care Insurance

When comparing long-term care insurance offered by insurance companies, recognize that a higher premium will be charged for various provisions that provide more comprehensive coverage. You can save money by selecting a policy that is only flexible on the provisions that are most important to you. For example, if you can tolerate a longer elimination period before the policy goes into effect, you can reduce your premium. If you think the continued coverage or the inflation-adjustment provisions are not very beneficial to you, select a policy that does not contain these provisions.

Insurance companies charge varying premiums for long-term care insurance policies. You should shop around and compare premiums. Internet quotes are one option. Also, review how insurance premiums charged by the insurance companies have changed over time, since they may serve as an indication of future premiums.

Determining the Amount of Coverage

To determine whether you need long-term care insurance, consider your family's health history. If there is a history of long-term illnesses, then you are more likely to need coverage. In addition, consider your financial situation. If you can afford substantial coverage for long-term insurance, it may be worthwhile. Individuals who are under age 60 and have no serious illnesses can obtain long-term care insurance at reasonable rates.

ADDITIONAL TYPES OF HEALTH CARE PLANS

Other types of health insurance commonly offered through employers include dental and vision insurance. You should consider participating in these plans if your employer offers them as part of your benefits package.

Dental Insurance

dental insurance
Covers part or all of the fees imposed for dental services, including annual checkups, orthodontics, and oral surgery.

Dental insurance covers part or all of the fees imposed for dental services, including annual checkups, orthodontics, and oral surgery. Dental insurance, like other types of private insurance, can be offered as an indemnity or a managed care plan.

Vision Insurance

vision insurance
Covers part or all of the fees imposed for optician and optometrist services, including annual checkups, glasses, contact lenses, and surgery.

Vision insurance covers part or all of the fees imposed for optician and optometrist services, including annual checkups, glasses, contact lenses, and surgery. The specific premiums and benefits of vision insurance vary among plans.

DISABILITY INSURANCE

disability income insurance
Insurance that provides income to policyholders in the event that they become disabled.

Disability income insurance provides income to policyholders in the event that they become disabled. The probability of becoming disabled in a given year is less than 4 percent for individuals under age 40 and less than 8 percent for individuals under age 50. However, the probability is about 15 percent at age 60, and it increases with age. Thus, disability insurance is especially important for older individuals who rely on their income. However, younger individuals should also consider disability insurance because it provides peace of mind and the premiums are low. Disability insurance can ensure that you will still be able to support yourself and your dependents if you become disabled.

One of the most important aspects of disability insurance is the definition of disability. Benefits are paid to you only if you meet the definition of disability as defined by your policy. The most liberal definition (easiest to qualify for) of disability is the "own occupation" definition. The disability insurance policy will provide benefits if you are unable to do the duties required of your occupation. A more restrictive definition of disability is the "any occupation" definition. The "any occupation" coverage will only provide benefits if you cannot do the duties of any job that fits your education and experience. Since the coverage provided by this type of policy is more restrictive, it has a lower premium than "own occupation" policies. Some policies offer coverage if you are unable to do your job in your own occupation for an initial period, such as two years. After that point, they only offer coverage if you are unable to do the duties of any job that fits your education and experience. The Social Security Administration will consider you disabled only if you are disabled for a period of at least 5 months with the expectation that the disability will last at least 12 months or is likely to result in death.

Sources of Disability Income Insurance

Some of the more common sources of disability income insurance are discussed here.

Individual Disability Insurance. You can purchase individual disability insurance and specify the amount of coverage that you desire. The insurance premium varies with your type of job. For example, workers in a steel plant are more at risk than workers in an office building.

Employer Disability Insurance. About half of all large and medium-sized firms offer an optional disability plan through an insurance company. Employees at some firms either are provided the insurance at no cost or participate in a plan by paying for the coverage. The premiums charged through group plans are normally low. A typical disability policy offered through employers covers about 60 percent of the employee's salary. The maximum time that disability benefits are provided varies substantially among policies.

Insurance from Social Security. If you are disabled, you may receive some income from the Social Security Administration. The income is determined by the amount of Social Security contributions you have made over time. The guidelines to qualify for disability benefits from Social Security are strict, meaning that you may not necessarily receive benefits even if you believe that you are disabled. In addition, the income provided by Social Security may not be sufficient to maintain your lifestyle. Therefore, you will probably need disability income insurance to supplement the possible disability benefits that you would receive from Social Security.

Insurance from Worker's Compensation. If you become disabled at your workplace, you may receive some income through worker's compensation from the state where you reside. The income you receive is influenced by your prevailing salary level. Disability income insurance may supplement any benefits that you would receive from worker's compensation.

Disability Insurance Provisions
The specific characteristics of disability insurance vary among insurance companies, as explained here.

Amount of Coverage. The disability insurance contract specifies the amount of income that will be provided if you become disabled. The amount may be specified as a maximum dollar amount or as a percentage of the income that you were earning before being disabled. The higher your coverage, the more you will pay for disability insurance.

You should have enough coverage so that you can maintain your lifestyle and still support your dependents if you become disabled. You can determine the disposable (after-tax) income that you would normally need to support your lifestyle and your dependents.

E X A M P L E

Stephanie Spratt receives some disability insurance coverage from her employer, but she is considering purchasing additional disability insurance. She wants to determine how much more coverage she would need to cover her typical expenses. She normally needs about $2,100 per month to cover her typical expenses. About $100 of those monthly expenses are attributed to work, such as clothing and commuting expenses. Since Stephanie would not be going to work if she were disabled, she need not consider those expenses. Her normal monthly expenses when excluding work-related expenses are $2,000 per month, as shown in Panel A of Exhibit 12.3. This is the amount of disability coverage that she would need.

The next step is to determine how much disability coverage she already has. To be conservative, she assumes that there will be no Social Security benefits, as she may have a disability that is not covered by its guidelines. Her employer-provided disability policy's coverage is $800 per month. She presumes that any disability that she might have someday will not result from her work, so that worker's compensation does not apply.

The final step is comparing the coverage that she needs (Panel A of Exhibit 12.3) with the coverage that she has from sources other than her individual disability insurance. In this example, the difference is: $2,000 − $800 = $1,200. If she buys additional disability insurance, she will purchase coverage of $1,200 per month. Since her present salary is $38,000, the amount of extra coverage reflects about 32 percent of her salary ($1,200/$3,800 = .32). The disability income that she would receive is normally not subject to federal tax. Disability

Exhibit 12.3 Determining Stephanie Spratt's Disability Insurance Needs

Panel A: Total Coverage Needed

Typical monthly expenses	$2,100
– Expenses related to work	–100
= Typical monthly expenses after excluding work expenses	$2,000

Panel B: Coverage That You Expect to Receive from:

Employer Disability Insurance	$800
Social Security	$0
Worker's Compensation	$0
Total	$800
Amount Needed from Individual Disability Insurance	$1,200

income is subject to a state income tax, but this tax does not apply to Stephanie since she resides in a state in which taxes are not imposed.

Stephanie decides that she will buy the extra $1,200 disability insurance coverage through her employer. At $10 per month, the premium is affordable.

probationary period
The period extending from the time your disability income application is approved until your coverage goes into effect.

Probationary Period. You may be subject to a **probationary period**, which extends from the time your application is approved until your coverage goes into effect. A common probationary period is one month.

waiting period
The period from the time you are disabled until you begin to receive disability income benefits.

Waiting Period. The disability insurance contract should specify if there is a **waiting period** (such as three months or six months) before you would begin to receive any income benefits. You would have to cover your expenses during the waiting period. For example, if you become disabled today, and your policy specifies a three-month waiting period, you will receive benefits only if your disability lasts beyond the three-month period. One reason for the waiting period is that it eliminates many claims that would occur if people could receive benefits when they were disabled for just a few days or weeks because of a sore neck or back. The premiums for disability insurance would be higher if there were no waiting period or a very short waiting period.

Length of Time for Disability Benefits. Disability benefits may be limited to a few years or may last for the policyholder's lifetime. The longer the period in which your policy provides disability income, the more you will pay for disability insurance.

Non-Cancelable Provision. A non-cancelable provision gives you the right to renew the policy each year at the same premium, with no change in the benefits. In exchange, you pay a higher premium now to ensure that it will not be increased in the future.

Renewable Provision. A renewable provision gives you the right to renew the policy, with the same benefits. The insurance company can increase your premium if it is increasing the premium for all of its insured customers with the same profile.

Deciding on Disability Insurance
You can contact insurance companies about disability insurance rates or ask your employer's benefits department whether the insurance is available.

HOW HEALTH AND DISABILITY INSURANCE FIT WITHIN YOUR FINANCIAL PLAN

The following are the key decisions about health and disability insurance that should be included within your financial plan:

- Do you have adequate insurance to protect your wealth?

- How much insurance should you plan to have in the future?

Exhibit 12.4 provides an example of how health and disability decisions apply to Stephanie Spratt's plan.

Exhibit 12.4 How Health and Disability Insurance Fit within Stephanie Spratt's Financial Plan

GOALS FOR HEALTH AND DISABILITY INSURANCE PLANNING

1. *Ensure that my exposure to health problems or a disability is covered by insurance.*
2. *Determine whether I should increase my health and disability insurance in the future.*

ANALYSIS

Type of Insurance	Protection	Status
Health	*Protects my assets and wealth.*	*I have a good health insurance plan through work.*
Disability	*Protects my income if I become disabled.*	*My employer-provided disability policy offers some coverage, but I am buying a policy that offers additional coverage.*

DECISIONS

Decision on Whether My Present Health and Disability Insurance Coverage Is Adequate:

I presently rely on the HMO offered through my employer. This plan offers adequate insurance at an affordable premium. Because I am in my twenties and in good health, I do not need long-term care insurance at this time.

I presently have $800 of disability insurance coverage per month that is provided by my employer. I have decided to purchase a policy specifying an additional $1,200 of coverage per month to cover my monthly expenses of $2,000 if I'm disabled. The insurance will provide adequate coverage for me if I become disabled.

Decision on Health and Disability Insurance Coverage for the Future:

I may switch to a PPO someday if I want more flexibility to select specialists. I will consider long-term care insurance in the future. I will also increase my disability insurance if my income or expenses increase over time.

DISCUSSION QUESTIONS

1. How would Stephanie's health and disability insurance purchasing decisions be different if she were a single mother of two children?

2. How would Stephanie's health and disability insurance purchasing decisions be affected if she were 35 years old? If she were 50 years old?

SUMMARY

Health insurance covers health care expenses incurred by policyholders. Health care plans can be classified as private plans or managed care plans. Private plans allow much flexibility in your choice of the health care provider, but require a reimbursement process. Managed care plans include health maintenance organizations (HMOs) and preferred provider organizations (PPOs), which bill only the amount that is not covered by the plan. This avoids the reimbursement process. HMOs require the use of a specified primary care physician who refers the individual to a specialist when necessary; PPOs allow more flexibility in the choice of the health care provider, but require much higher premiums. There are also government health plans. The Medicare program provides health insurance to individuals who are over 65 years of age and qualify for Social Security, or are disabled. The Medicaid program provides health insurance to individuals with low incomes.

Long-term care insurance covers expenses associated with long-term illnesses, including care by a nursing home, assisted living facility, or at home. The premium for long-term care insurance is very high but can be reduced by accepting a longer elimination period.

Disability insurance provides income to you if you become disabled. It can replace a portion of the income that you would have received had you been able to continue working.

INTEGRATING THE KEY CONCEPTS

Your decisions regarding health and disability insurance affect the other parts of your financial plan. With health and disability insurance, you may not need to rely on your savings or other assets to cover your health care expenses. In addition, you should not need to borrow funds to cover insurance expenses. The decision to purchase adequate health and disability insurance can affect other financial decisions. You may be able to save more money (Part 2). You have more capacity to finance the purchase of a car or a home (Part 3). In addition, you are more capable of investing in stocks (Part 5) and in your retirement (Part 6).

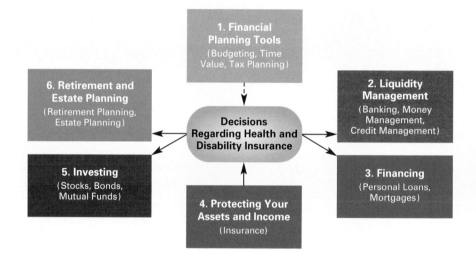

REVIEW QUESTIONS

1. How do individuals benefit from having health insurance? Why has health insurance received a lot of attention recently?

2. What is private health insurance? Briefly describe some types of private health insurance coverage.

3. Who offers health insurance? Do employers offer health insurance?

4. Compare and contrast private health care indemnity plans and managed health care plans.

5. Describe how an HMO works. What are the advantages and disadvantages of this type of health care coverage?

6. What questions should you ask when considering an HMO or PPO?

7. What is a preferred provider organization (PPO)? How does it operate?

8. Compare and contrast the discount on charge arrangement and the per diem arrangement associated with PPOs.

9. Briefly describe two federal regulations intended to ensure that individuals can maintain continuous health care coverage if their employment status changes.

10. What is a flexible spending account? Why do some individuals allocate a minimal amount to this account?

11. What is Medicare? Describe Parts A and B of Medicare.

12. Briefly describe the provisions of the Medicare Prescription Act.

13. What is Medigap insurance?

14. What is Medicaid? How do individuals qualify for Medicaid?

15. What is the purpose of long-term care insurance? What factors influence long-term care insurance premiums? What factors should be considered when purchasing long-term care insurance?

16. What are some other types of health insurance that might be offered by an employer?

17. What is the purpose of disability income insurance? Why might younger individuals consider purchasing disability insurance?

18. Briefly describe some of the sources of disability income insurance.

19. Briefly describe some of the provisions of disability income insurance.

FINANCIAL PLANNING PROBLEMS

1. Pete's health insurance policy specifies that he should pay 30 percent of expenses associated with a long-term illness. Furthermore, he has a stop-loss provision of $35,000 in his policy. If Pete incurs expenses of $70,000, how much would he owe?

2. A PPO uses a discount on charge arrangement. Marie incurred total charges by a hospital of $20,000, and the percentage paid to the provider is 70 percent. Marie's contract with the PPO specifies her co-pay as 20 percent. How much does Marie have to pay?

3. Christine's total monthly expenses typically amount to $1,800. About $50 of these expenses are work related. Christine's employer provides disability insurance coverage of $500 per month. How much individual disability insurance should Christine purchase?

Ethical Dilemma

4. Vera is an 85-year-old widow and retiree from a large corporation. Her former employer recently changed the health care coverage for retirees to an HMO. Vera is having difficulty with her knees and has requested a referral to an orthopedist. After ordering x-rays, her primary care physician informs her that her knees are not serious enough to warrant knee replacement and he gives her a prescription to alleviate the pain. Several weeks later Vera reads an article that doctors in her HMO are rewarded for keeping utilization costs down.

   a. Discuss the ethics of HMOs rewarding physicians for keeping utilization costs down.

   b. Does Vera have any options?

FINANCIAL PLANNING ONLINE EXERCISES

1. Go to http://ehealthinsurance.com/.

   a. Obtain medical insurance estimates for yourself by providing your birthdate and some personal information. How do the resulting plans differ? Which plan do you find most attractive? Why?

   b. Now obtain dental insurance estimates by providing some personal information. Which plan do you find most attractive? Why?

2. Go to http://www.medicare.gov/basics/overview.asp.

   a. Describe some choices for Medicare plans. Which plan do you find the most attractive? Why?

   b. Go to "Search Tools" and click on "Participating Physician Directory." Enter your zip code and select a speciality. How many physicians in that specialty are listed in the directory?

   c. Click on "Plan Choices" and access "Medigap (Supplemental Insurance)." Describe Medigap. How many policies are available.

BUILDING YOUR OWN FINANCIAL PLAN

Health and disability income insurance do not depend on tangible assets but rather on your perceived need for this type of insurance and your general well-being.

Health insurance has become quite expensive in recent years. The first step in researching health insurance options is to evaluate offerings from your employer.

Go to the worksheets at the end of this chapter, and to the CD-ROM accompanying this text, to continue building your financial plan.

THE SAMPSONS—A CONTINUING CASE

Dave and Sharon Sampson are happy with their auto and homeowner's insurance coverage. As a next step in determining their insurance-related needs, they are assessing the amount of health insurance and disability income insurance they have.

The Sampsons' health insurance is provided by a health maintenance organization (HMO). Recently, Dave and Sharon have heard about preferred provider organizations (PPOs) and are wondering whether they should switch to a PPO. Upon hearing that PPOs are more expensive than HMOs, Dave and Sharon are hesitant to switch, but they have not yet made up their minds. Dave and Sharon are both

happy with their primary care physician and any specialists they need to consult under the HMO plan.

Dave and Sharon currently do not have disability income insurance because they both have office jobs and do not believe that they are at risk of becoming disabled. Recall from Chapter 2 that Dave and Sharon have about $3,400 a month in expenses, none of which are work related. Their net cash flow is about $600 a month. Dave's employer provides $200 in disability insurance coverage.

The Sampsons have also recently heard about long-term care insurance and are wondering whether they should purchase this type of insurance.

Go to the worksheets at the end of this chapter, and to the CD-ROM accompanying this text, to continue this case.

Chapter 12: Building Your Own Financial Plan

GOALS

1. Ensure that your health and disability insurance adequately protects your wealth.
2. Develop a plan for your future health insurance needs, including long-term care.

ANALYSIS

1. Complete the following worksheet to aid your evaluation of information provided by your employer for your health insurance options. Which type of policy (indemnity plan, HMO, or PPO) is best suited to your needs and budget?

Health Insurance Coverage Comparison

Indemnity Plan

Premium Co-Pay	☐ Yes	☐ No	
If Yes, Amount of Premium Co-Pay	$		
Coverage Eligibility	☐ Self	☐ Two-person	☐ Family
Coverage:			
In State	☐ Yes	☐ No	
Out of State	☐ Yes	☐ No	
Out of the Country	☐ Yes	☐ No	
Prescription Coverage	☐ Yes	☐ No	
If Yes, Amount of Co-Pay	$		
Office Visits:			
Co-Pay Amount	$		
Annual Deductible	☐ Yes	☐ No	
If Yes, Amount of Deductible	$		
Hospital Benefits:			
Maximum Days of Hospital Care		Days	
Maximum Days for Mental Health or Substance Abuse		Days	
Co-Pay	☐ Yes	☐ No	
If Yes, Amount of Co-Pay	$		
Annual Deductible	☐ Yes	☐ No	
If Yes, Amount of Deductible	$		

Outpatient Care:

Emergency Room Care	☐ Yes	☐ No
Physical Therapy	☐ Yes	☐ No
Occupational Therapy	☐ Yes	☐ No
Speech Therapy	☐ Yes	☐ No

Dental Coverage:

Dental Coverage:	☐ Yes	☐ No
If Yes, Co-Pay for Regular Checkups	☐ Yes	☐ No
If Yes, Amount of Co-Pay	$	

Orthodontic Coverage:

Orthodontic Coverage:	☐ Yes	☐ No
If Yes, Co-Pay for Regular Checkups	☐ Yes	☐ No
If Yes, Amount of Co-Pay	$	

Vision Coverage:

Vision Coverage:	☐ Yes	☐ No
Frequency of Regular Eye Exams		
Co-Pay for Regular Eye Exams	$	
Frequency for New Lenses		
Co-Pay for New Lenses	$	
Frequency for New Frames		
Co-Pay for New Frames	$	

HMO

Premium Co-Pay	☐ Yes	☐ No	
If Yes, Amount of Premium Co-Pay	$		
Coverage Eligibility	☐ Self	☐ Two-person	☐ Family
Coverage:			
In State	☐ Yes	☐ No	
Out of State	☐ Yes	☐ No	
Out of the Country	☐ Yes	☐ No	
Prescription Coverage	☐ Yes	☐ No	
If Yes, Amount of Co-Pay	$		

Office Visits:

Co-Pay Amount	$
Annual Deductible	☐ Yes ☐ No
If Yes, Amount of Deductible	$

Hospital Benefits:

Maximum Days of Hospital Care	Days
Maximum Days for Mental Health or Substance Abuse	Days
Co-Pay	☐ Yes ☐ No
If Yes, Amount of Co-Pay	$
Annual Deductible	☐ Yes ☐ No
If Yes, Amount of Deductible	$

Outpatient Care:

Emergency Room Care	☐ Yes ☐ No
Physical Therapy	☐ Yes ☐ No
Occupational Therapy	☐ Yes ☐ No
Speech Therapy	☐ Yes ☐ No

Dental Coverage: ☐ Yes   ☐ No

If Yes, Co-Pay for Regular Checkups	☐ Yes ☐ No
If Yes, Amount of Co-Pay	$

Orthodontic Coverage: ☐ Yes   ☐ No

If Yes, Co-Pay for Regular Checkups	☐ Yes ☐ No
If Yes, Amount of Co-Pay	$

Vision Coverage: ☐ Yes   ☐ No

Frequency of Regular Eye Exams	
Co-Pay for Regular Eye Exams	$
Frequency for New Lenses	
Co-Pay for New Lenses	$
Frequency for New Frames	
Co-Pay for New Frames	$

PPO

Premium Co-Pay	☐ Yes	☐ No
If Yes, Amount of Premium Co-Pay	$	
Coverage Eligibility	☐ Self	☐ Two-person ☐ Family
Coverage:		
In State	☐ Yes	☐ No
Out of State	☐ Yes	☐ No
Out of the Country	☐ Yes	☐ No
Prescription Coverage	☐ Yes	☐ No
If Yes, Amount of Co-Pay	$	
Office Visits:		
Co-Pay Amount	$	
Annual Deductible	☐ Yes	☐ No
If Yes, Amount of Deductible	$	
Hospital Benefits:		
Maximum Days of Hospital Care	Days	
Maximum Days for Mental Health or Substance Abuse	Days	
Co-Pay	☐ Yes	☐ No
If Yes, Amount of Co-Pay	$	
Annual Deductible	☐ Yes	☐ No
If Yes, Amount of Deductible	$	
Outpatient Care:		
Emergency Room Care	☐ Yes	☐ No
Physical Therapy	☐ Yes	☐ No
Occupational Therapy	☐ Yes	☐ No
Speech Therapy	☐ Yes	☐ No
Dental Coverage:	☐ Yes	☐ No
If Yes, Co-Pay for Regular Checkups	☐ Yes	☐ No
If Yes, Amount of Co-Pay	$	

Orthodontic Coverage:	☐ Yes	☐ No
If Yes, Co-Pay for Regular Checkups	☐ Yes	☐ No
If Yes, Amount of Co-Pay	$	
Vision Coverage:	☐ Yes	☐ No
Frequency of Regular Eye Exams		
Co-Pay for Regular Eye Exams	$	
Frequency for New Lenses		
Co-Pay for New Lenses	$	
Frequency for New Frames		
Co-Pay for New Frames	$	

2. If you are under age 60, long-term care insurance has probably not been a major concern to date. Based on your family health history, your financial situation, and any long-term illnesses that you have, should you look into getting a policy? Why or why not?

_____

_____

_____

_____

_____

_____

3. Referring to the personal cash flow statement you developed in Chapter 2, complete the following worksheet to determine your disability insurance needs. If you input this information in the Excel worksheet, the software will create a chart showing your sources of disability income.

_____

_____

_____

_____

_____

_____

Disability Insurance Needs

Cash Inflows	$	
Minus Work-Related Cash Inflows*	$	
Cash Inflows if Disabled		$
Total Cash Outflows	$	
Minus Work-Related Cash Outflows*	$	
Cash Outflows if Disabled		$
Cash Inflows Minus Outflows Net Cash Flows if Disabled		$
Employer Disability Insurance	$	
Social Security	$	
Workmen's Compensation	$	
Total Insurance Cash Inflows		$
Net Cash Flows if Disabled Minus Total Insurance Cash Inflows**		$

*   Cash flows that will discontinue if you are not working.

** A negative number indicates the amount of disability insurance coverage that you need per month. However, if the number is positive it indicates that you have no need for disability insurance.

DECISIONS

1. What steps have you taken or will you take to ensure that your health insurance needs are being met? Which type of health insurance plan will you seek from your employer?

    _____

    _____

    _____

    _____

    _____

    _____

    _____

    _____

    _____

2. Does your age, personal health history, or family health history indicate that you should consider long-term care insurance?

_____

_____

_____

_____

_____

_____

_____

_____

_____

3. What are your disability insurance needs? What amount of additional coverage, if any, do you require?

_____

_____

_____

_____

_____

_____

_____

_____

_____

_____

Chapter 12: The Sampsons—A Continuing Case

CASE QUESTIONS

1. Make suggestions to the Sampsons regarding their health insurance. Do you think they should switch from the HMO to a PPO? Why or why not?

2. Do you think the Sampsons should purchase disability insurance? Why or why not?

3. Should the Sampsons purchase long-term care insurance? Why or why not?

Life Insurance

Maria quit her job to care for her young children. Shortly after she stopped working, her husband Diego was killed in an auto accident. It was only then that Maria fully appreciated the benefit of a $400,000 life insurance policy. Shortly after their first child was born, their neighbor, an insurance agent, approached Maria and Diego. The agent convinced them that because he was the sole provider for the family, Diego needed a sizable insurance policy to replace his income in the event of his death. The insurance is enough to cover expenses until well after the children are in school and Maria reenters the workforce.

Without life insurance, the death of a breadwinner eliminates some or all of the household's employment income forever. Life insurance can provide financial protection for members of a household.

The objectives of this chapter are to:

- Describe the types of life insurance that are available

- Identify the factors that influence insurance needs

- Review the factors that affect life insurance premiums

- Examine the decision of whether to purchase life insurance

- Explain the settlement options that are available for beneficiary payments

BACKGROUND ON LIFE INSURANCE

life insurance
Insurance that provides a payment to a specified beneficiary when the policyholder dies.

Life insurance provides a payment to a specified beneficiary when the policyholder dies. Therefore, it allows you to provide financial support to specified beneficiaries in the event of your death. A $100,000 policy means that in the event that you die, the beneficiary named in the policy will receive $100,000. The amount received by the beneficiary is not taxed.

Life insurance is provided by life insurance companies, which may be independent firms or subsidiaries of financial conglomerates. Many financial institutions that provide banking and brokerage services also have a subsidiary that provides life insurance. You pay a premium on a periodic (such as quarterly) basis for life insurance.

Role of Life Insurance

Before deciding whether to buy life insurance or how much life insurance to buy, you need to consider your financial goals. The most common financial goal related to life insurance is to maintain financial support for your dependents. Life insurance is critical to protect a family's financial situation in the event that a breadwinner dies. Life insurance provides the family with financial support to cover burial expenses or medical expenses not covered by health insurance. Life insurance can also maintain the family's future lifestyle even without the breadwinner's income. In addition, life insurance may help the dependents pay off any accumulated debt. If you are the breadwinner and have others who rely on your income, you should have life insurance.

If no one else relies on your income, life insurance may not be necessary. For example, if you and your spouse both work full-time and your spouse could be self-sufficient without your income, life insurance is not as important. If you are single and are not providing financial support to anyone, life insurance may not be needed.

However, many individuals without dependents still want to leave money to their heirs. For example, you may decide that you want to finance your nephew's college education. If you die before your nephew attends college, a life insurance policy can achieve your goal. Alternatively, you may want to provide financial support for your parents. In this case, you can designate your parents as the beneficiaries in a life insurance policy. You can even set up a life insurance policy that designates your favorite charity as the beneficiary.

As time passes, rethink your life insurance decisions. Even if you decide not to purchase life insurance now, you may require life insurance in the future. If you already have a life insurance policy, you may need to increase the coverage or add a beneficiary at a future point in time.

Role of Life Insurance Companies

Many insurance companies can provide you with life insurance coverage. They can explain the different types of life insurance that are available and help you determine the type of life insurance that would satisfy your needs. They can also help you determine the amount of life insurance coverage that you need. Many people who purchase life insurance will be alive 40 or more years after they purchase the policy, and they rely on the life insurance company to provide the benefits upon their death in the future. Thus, it is important that the life insurance company is financially sound so that it will continue to exist and fulfill its insurance contracts for its policyholders in the distant future.

TYPES OF LIFE INSURANCE

While the needs for life insurance are straightforward, there are many options for policies. Term insurance, whole life insurance, and universal life insurance are the most popular types of life insurance.

Term Insurance

term insurance
Life insurance that is provided over a specified time period and does not build a cash value.

Term insurance is life insurance provided over a specified time period. The term is typically from 5 to 20 years. Term insurance does not build a cash value, meaning that the policy does not serve as an investment. It is intended strictly to provide insurance to a beneficiary in the event of death. If the insured person remains alive over the term, the policy expires at the end of the term and has no value.

Consider the case of a single mother with three young children. She plans to provide financial support for her children until they complete their college education. While her income is sufficient to provide that support, she wants back-up support if she dies. She decides to purchase 20-year term insurance. If she dies during this period, her children will receive the coverage specified in the policy. If she is still living at the end of the term, the policy will expire. Even under these conditions, the policy would have served its purpose, giving her peace of mind over the period by ensuring sufficient financial support for her children. Once the term expires, the children will be old enough to support themselves financially.

Premiums on Term Insurance. Insurance companies may require that the premium on term insurance be paid monthly, quarterly, semi-annually, or annually. If the premium is not paid by the due date, the policyholder is given a grace period. If the premium is not paid during the grace period, the policy will be terminated.

Reviewing Premiums on Term Insurance Using the Internet. Some life insurance companies provide quotes for term insurance on the Web sites. You need to provide information such as your date of birth, your state of residency, the amount of coverage, the length of the term of insurance, and answer some general questions about your health. Within a minute of providing this information, you will receive quotes. You can even adjust the amount of insurance coverage if you want to determine how the premium is affected by alternative levels of coverage.

Some Web sites such as http://www.insure.com, http://www.insweb.com, and http://finance.yahoo.com/insurance provide quotes from various life insurance companies based on your specified needs and link you directly to those companies. First they request some information as described above, and then they list various quotes on term insurance by different companies. This allows you to select the company that you believe would accommodate your needs. You can link to the policy contract of that company and may be able to access the name and phone number of a company representative. The value of this type of Web site is that it may help you obtain quotes without being subjected to a sales pitch. Yet, once you have screened the list of possible insurance companies, you can speak to an insurance agent before you select a company. Of course, you should also assess the financial soundness of the company that you select.

Why Premiums for Term Insurance Vary. The annual insurance premiums for term insurance vary. First, the longer the term of the policy, the longer the period in which the insurance company must provide coverage and the higher the annual premium.

Second, the older the policyholder, the higher the policy premium. Older people are more likely to die within a given term. Exhibit 13.1 provides a sampling of quoted annual premiums (based on no unusual medical problems of the policyholder). The actual premiums will vary among life insurance companies, but the general comparison described here still holds. Notice from Exhibit 13.1 that the annual premium for a 45-year-old is more than twice that of a 25-year-old. In addition, the annual premium for a 60-year-old is more than four times that of a 45-year-old.

Third, the greater the insurance coverage (benefits upon death), the higher the insurance premiums. Exhibit 13.2 illustrates the annual premiums for two profiles based on various coverage levels. Notice that the annual premium for a $500,000 policy is more than twice that of a $100,000 policy.

Fourth, the annual premium is higher for a male than for a female of the same age. Because females tend to live longer than males, the probability of a male dying during a specified term is higher than that of a female of the same age. Exhibit 13.3 shows the difference in quoted annual premiums between males and females for various levels of insurance coverage. In general, the quoted annual premiums for males are between 10 and 25 percent higher than for females.

Fifth, the annual premium is substantially larger for smokers than for nonsmokers. Exhibit 13.4 shows the difference in annual premiums of male smokers versus male nonsmokers for various coverage levels. The annual premiums for smokers are more than twice that of nonsmokers, regardless of the coverage level. This general relationship holds regardless of the age or gender of the applicant.

Sixth, the annual premium may be much larger for policyholders whose family members have a history of medical problems. For example, the annual premium quoted

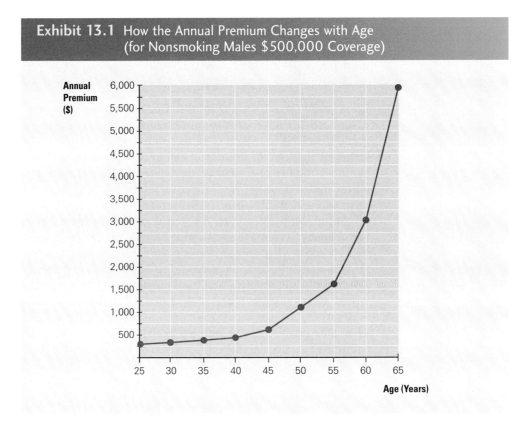

Exhibit 13.1 How the Annual Premium Changes with Age (for Nonsmoking Males $500,000 Coverage)

Exhibit 13.2 How Annual Premiums Differ Across Coverage Levels

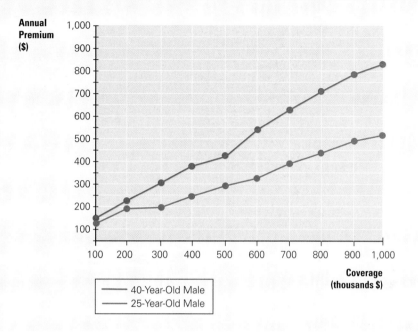

Exhibit 13.3 How Annual Premiums Differ for Males versus Females
(for 25-year-old Nonsmoking Males and Females)

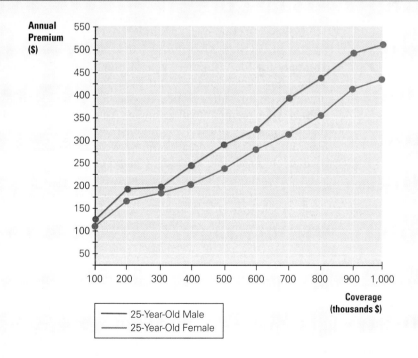

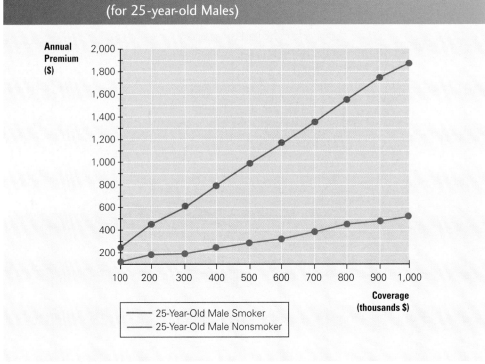

Exhibit 13.4 How Annual Premiums Differ for Smokers versus Nonsmokers (for 25-year-old Males)

may be more than doubled if members of the applicant's immediate family have diabetes, heart disease, or kidney disease prior to age 60.

The size of the premium on term insurance is dependent on the likelihood of death over the specified term and the length of the term in which insurance is desired. The likelihood of death is affected by health, age, and gender. A term insurance premium for a given person will vary among life insurance companies.

Focus on Ethics: Applying for Life Insurance

To apply for life insurance, you fill out a detailed application form with information about your medical history and lifestyle that is used to determine your eligibility and premium. If you suffer from a chronic illness such as diabetes or heart disease or are a smoker, your premium will be higher. You may be tempted to omit some information so that you can pay a lower premium. As part of the application process, you will most likely go through a medical exam. Between the exam and information available from the Medical Information Bureau, a clearinghouse of medical information that insurers share, the insurer will most likely uncover any inaccuracies in your application.

If your application does slip through with inaccuracies, your insurance benefits could be eliminated. The policy is a legal contract between you and the insurance company, so you must be truthful. It is not worth jeopardizing the peace of mind that life insurance brings by trying to save a relatively small amount on premiums.

decreasing-term insurance
A form of term insurance in which the benefits that will be paid to the beneficiary are reduced over time and the premium remains constant.

Decreasing-Term Insurance. A common type of term insurance is **decreasing-term insurance**, in which the insurance benefits to the beneficiary are reduced over time. The premium paid for the insurance remains constant over the term. This type of insurance is popular for families because it provides a relatively high level of insurance in the earlier years when it is most needed. As time passes, a family can accumulate savings, pay off part of a mortgage, and increase their investments, so smaller life insurance benefits are needed. Several forms of decreasing-term insurance are available, with different terms and different degrees to which the insurance benefits decrease over the term. The

13.1 Financial Planning Online: Buying Term Life Insurance

Go to
http://moneycentral.msn.com/

Click on
"Insurance" under "Planning,"
then click "Quotes for Life"
under "Insurance"

This Web site provides
access to online life
insurance quotes.

same factors that affect the premium of term insurance also affect the premium of decreasing-term insurance.

mortgage life insurance
Life insurance that pays off a mortgage in the event of the policyholder's death.

Mortgage Life Insurance. Mortgage life insurance pays off a policyholder's mortgage in the event of his death. It is commonly purchased to ensure that a family can afford to continue living in their home even if the breadwinner dies. Mortgage insurance is a special form of decreasing-term insurance. In fact, individuals can achieve the same goal (and possibly save money) by purchasing a term insurance policy that provides benefits large enough to pay off the mortgage.

group term insurance
Term insurance with generally lower than typical premiums that is available to people within a defined group.

Group Term Insurance. Group term insurance is term insurance provided to a designated group of people with a common bond, such as the same employer. Group term premiums are usually lower than the typical premiums an individual would pay because the insured receive a group discount. Some companies that have a group plan may pay for term insurance for its employees as a benefit.

Whole Life Insurance

whole life insurance (permanent insurance)
Life insurance that continues to provide insurance as long as premiums are paid; not only provides benefits to the beneficiary but also has a cash value.

Whole life insurance (sometimes referred to as **permanent insurance**) continues to provide insurance as long as premiums are paid; the policy accumulates savings for the policyholder over time. In this way, it not only provides benefits to a beneficiary if the policyholder dies, but also creates a form of savings with a cash value. For this reason, whole life insurance is sometimes referred to as cash-value life insurance.

The cash value is typically specified on a schedule. Your whole life insurance premium is a fixed amount that is used for two purposes: life insurance and savings. A portion of the premium pays for the life insurance provided by the policy, so that the beneficiaries you identify in the policy will be covered if you die. The remainder of the premium is invested for you as a form of savings that builds a cash value over time. If you withdraw the cash, the amount by which the cash value exceeds the premiums that were paid is subject to taxes.

You can change your policy by using your cash value to make a one-time payment for a new policy. The death benefit of the new policy is dependent on the cash value amount of the policy that you exchange.

A whole life insurance policy can serve as a source of liquidity. You can borrow against the cash value at an interest rate specified in the policy. However, recognize that this type of loan reduces the cash value of your insurance policy.

Whole Life Premiums. Many insurance policies allow the premium to be paid on a monthly, quarterly, or annually. The premium on whole life insurance is constant for the duration of the policy. In the earlier years, a portion of the premium paid for the insurance reflects the potential payout to a beneficiary someday, and the remainder is invested by the insurance company as a form of savings. The portion of the premium dedicated to savings is high in the earlier years when the policyholder is young because the portion of the premium needed to insure against the possibility of death is relatively low. In the later years, the premium required to insure against possible death is relatively high, as the likelihood of death is greater. Because the insurance premium is constant, it is not sufficient to cover the amount needed to insure against possible death in the later years. Thus, a portion of the policy's cash value is used to supplement the premium paid in these years.

If you do not pay a premium on a whole life policy, the insurance company will (with your consent) draw from the cash value of your policy to cover the premium.

The premiums among whole life policies can vary substantially. Because a whole life policy provides life insurance coverage, the annual premiums are also influenced by the same factors that affect the size of term insurance premiums. In particular, the quoted annual premiums are higher when the applicant is a male who smokes, is over 60 years old, and who requires a larger amount of insurance coverage.

13.2 Financial Planning Online: Should You Buy Whole Life or Term Insurance?

Go to
http://www.calcbuilder.com/
cgi-bin/calcs/INS5.cgi/
yahoo_insurance

This Web site provides an opinion on whether you should purchase whole life insurance or term insurance based on the premiums and other information.

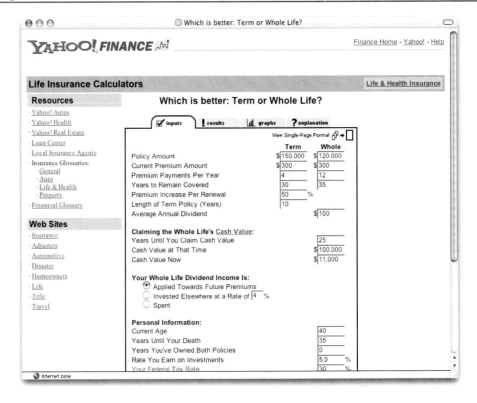

Forms of Whole Life Insurance. Many alternative forms of whole life insurance are available, so you can structure the premium payments in a manner that fits your needs. One such policy is a **limited payment policy** that allows you to pay premiums over a specified period but remain insured for life. For example, you could make payments until you retire, but continue to be insured after retirement. If you are 45 years old and plan to retire at age 65, this means you would request a payment period of 20 years. The insurance premiums are larger than if you were required to pay premiums continuously, but you build a large cash value during the payment period. Once the payment period ends, your savings accumulated within the whole life policy are used to cover your future premiums.

limited payment policy
Allows you to pay premiums over a specified period but remain insured for life

Alternatively, a whole life policy can be structured to provide a higher level of death benefits to the beneficiaries in the earlier years of the policy. For example, it may specify insurance coverage of $300,000 over the next 10 years, and $100,000 of coverage after 10 years. This type of policy may be useful for policyholders who have young children. The coverage is higher in the years when the children are young and unable to take care of themselves.

Comparison to Term Insurance. Premiums for whole life insurance are higher than premiums for term insurance. The advantage of whole life insurance over term insurance is that it not only provides insurance against possible death, but also accumulates savings over time. However, you can accumulate savings on your own by purchasing term insurance with lower premiums and then investing the difference.

Some people may prefer whole life insurance because it forces them to save money and accumulate funds. However, it is an inefficient way to save money. They may be better off if they establish a routine in which they automatically deposit a portion of their paychecks in a bank account to force some level of saving over time.

The choice of term insurance versus whole life insurance is dependent on your particular needs. If you only have life insurance to insure beneficiaries in the event of your death, term insurance is probably more appropriate.

If you live beyond the term stated in a term insurance policy, you would have to pay a higher annual premium when establishing a new term insurance policy. Conversely, the premium for the basic whole life policy remains constant. Nevertheless, term insurance is typically a less expensive way to meet your life insurance needs.

EXAMPLE

Stephanie Spratt has a close relationship with her two young nieces, who come from a broken home. While Stephanie is presently focused on building her own wealth, she hopes that someday she will have sufficient funds to pay for her nieces' college education. She is considering purchasing life insurance that would provide benefits of $100,000 and naming her nieces as beneficiaries. She will either invest in a 20-year term life insurance policy for $120 per year or in a whole life policy for $500 per year.

The whole life premium is higher, but the policy builds a cash value over time. If she buys a term insurance policy for $120 per year, she could invest the difference on her own. If she invests the money in a manner similar to the whole life policy, she will likely be able to accumulate savings more quickly on her own. A whole life insurance policy generally generates low returns on the cash that is invested because part of the premium is used to cover administrative fees. Stephanie decides to purchase the term life policy.

Universal Life Insurance

Universal life insurance provides insurance over a specified term and accumulates savings for policyholders over this time. It is a combination term insurance and a savings plan. Because it allows policyholders to build savings, it is classified as a cash-value life insurance policy.

universal life insurance
Life insurance that provides insurance over a specified term and accumulates savings for the policyholder over this time.

Universal life insurance policies allow "term-riders" so you can temporarily increase the level of insurance for a particular period. For example, if you needed an extra $100,000 of insurance ccoverage over the next five years, you could purchase a term-rider to provide the additional coverage.

Universal life insurance allows policyholders to alter their payments over time. It specifies the premium needed to cover the term insurance portion. When policyholders pay more than that amount, the extra amount is invested in savings on which policyholders earn interest.

Unlike whole life insurance policies where the insurance company makes the investment decisions, policyholders are given a set of alternative investments that are administered by the insurance company and can decide how the savings plan funds are to be invested. If policyholders skip premium payments, the amount needed to cover the term insurance portion or any administrative expenses will be withdrawn from their savings plan.

variable life insurance
Life insurance that provides insurance over a specified term and allows policyholders to invest residual funds, after the premium on the term portion is paid, in various types of investments.

Variable Life Insurance. One type of universal life insurance called **variable life insurance** allows policyholders to invest the residual funds, after the premium payment on the term portion is paid, in various types of investments, some of which are similar to mutual funds. Variable life insurance differs from whole life insurance in that it allows policyholders to make their own investment decisions.

An advantage of variable life insurance is that it provides policyholders with some flexibility in making their payments and in deciding how the savings should be invested. However, the fees on variable life insurance can be high. You can achieve the same benefits by simply purchasing term insurance and investing other money in the manner you prefer, without incurring the high administrative fees that you pay for variable life insurance.

Since variable life policyholders can choose to have their savings plan invested in stocks, their cash value can rise substantially during favorable stock market conditions. In the late 1990s, variable life insurance became very popular, as the stock market performed well. However, in the 2000–2002 period stock market conditions were very poor, causing major reductions in the cash values of individual policies.

DETERMINING THE AMOUNT OF LIFE INSURANCE NEEDED

Once you identify the policy type that best suits your needs, your next decision is the policy amount. You can determine the amount of life insurance you need by applying the income method or the budget method, as explained next.

Income Method

income method
A method that determines how much life insurance is needed based on the policyholder's annual income.

The **income method** is a general formula for determining how much life insurance you should maintain based on your income. This method normally specifies the life insurance amount as a multiple of your annual income, such as 10 times your annual income. For example, if you have an annual income of $40,000, this formula would suggest that you need $400,000 in life insurance. This method is very easy to use. The disadvantage is that it does not consider your age and your household situation (including your annual household expenses). Thus, it does not differentiate between a household with no children and one with children, which will likely need more life insurance because its expenses will be higher.

EXAMPLE   The Trent household earns $50,000 per year. The Carlin household also earns $50,000. Both households rely on a neighbor who sells insurance for advice, and were told that they should have coverage of 10 times their annual income. However, the Trent household financial situation is completely different from that of the Carlin household. The Trents are in their early 30s. They have two very young children. Daren Trent is the present breadwinner and Rita Trent plans to stay at home for several more years. The Trents have even discussed having more children. They have large credit card balances, two car loans, and a mortgage loan. Their $50,000 income barely covers their existing expenses and they have very little savings. They tend to overspend on their children, and will likely continue to do so. They have a goal of sending their children to private universities and they would like to purchase a bigger home in the future.

The Carlins do not have any children. They are in their late 50s and both work part time. They have established a very large amount of savings and a substantial retirement account, so that they could retire now if they had to. They have completely paid off their mortgage, and do not have any other debt.

Given the distinct differences in their financial conditions, the insurance coverage should not be the same for both households. The Trents should apply a higher multiple of their annual income, while the Carlins should apply a lower multiple. Some insurance agents would likely suggest that the Trents use a multiple such as 20, so that their life insurance would be 20 × $50,000 = $1,000,000. The Carlins may use a much smaller multiple such as 6 so that their life insurance coverage would be 6 × $50,000 = $300,000.

The difference in the appropriate amount of coverage in the example above is due to the difference in future funds that would be needed in the event of death. However, the adjustments here are arbitrary and may not provide proper coverage. Thus, the income method is limited, even if it allows for some adjustments to account for differences in financial situations.

Budget Method

budget method (needs method)
A method that determines how much life insurance is needed based on the household's future expected expenses.

An alternative method is the **budget method** (also referred to as the **needs method**), which determines your life insurance needs by considering your future budget based on your household's future expected expenses and your current financial situation. This method requires a little more effort than the income method to determine the necessary insurance coverage. However, it provides a better estimate than the income method. The main reason for having life insurance is to ensure that a household's needs are covered in the event of death, not just to replace lost income. The budget method estimates the amount of future funds that will be needed, so that the insurance coverage will be adequate. Some important factors that should be considered when determining needs follow:

- **Annual Living Expenses.** You should have sufficient insurance so that your family can live comfortably without your income. Your family's future expenses will be higher if you have children. Younger children will need financial support for a longer period of time.

- **Special Future Expenses.** If you want to ensure a college education for your children, you need adequate life insurance to cover the expected future expenses.

- **Debt.** If your family relies on your income to cover debt, you may want to ensure that your life insurance can pay off credit card bills and even a mortgage.

- **Job Marketability of Spouse.** If your spouse has very limited job marketability, you may need more life insurance so that your spouse can receive job training.

- **Value of Existing Savings.** If you have accumulated a large amount of savings, your family may possibly draw interest or dividends from these savings to cover a portion of their periodic expenses. The more savings your household has accumulated, the less life insurance you need.

EXAMPLE   You wish to purchase a life insurance policy that generates a pre-tax income of at least $30,000 per year for the next 20 years to cover living expenses (excluding the mortgage payment) for your spouse and two children in the event that you die. You have just enough savings to cover burial expenses, and you anticipate no unusual expenses for the household in the future.

To determine your insurance needs, you must estimate the amount of insurance today that will cover your household's future living expenses. You can use the time value of money concepts from Chapter 3 to determine the amount of funds today that can provide an annuity equal to $30,000 over each of the next 20 years. First, assume that you expect that your spouse will be able to earn at least 6 percent annually by investing the money received from the life insurance policy. Next, estimate the present value of an annuity (see the Table B-4 in Appendix B) that can provide your household with a $30,000 annuity over 20 years if it generates an annual return of 6 percent:

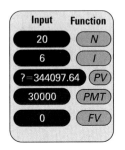

$$
\begin{aligned}
\text{Amount of Insurance Needed} \;&=\; \text{Annuity Amount} \times \textit{PVIFA} \; (i = 6\%, \, n = 20) \\
&=\; \$30,000 \times 11.47 \\
&=\; \$344,100.
\end{aligned}
$$

Based on the following additional information about your household, you then adjust the amount of insurance needed:

- **Other Special Future Expenses.** You also want to allocate an extra $50,000 in life insurance to pay for your two children's college expenses. Although college expenses will rise in the future, the money set aside will accumulate interest over time, so it should be sufficient.

- **Job Training.** You want to have additional insurance of $20,000 to ensure that your spouse can pay for job training in the event of your death.

- **Debt.** You have a $60,000 mortgage and no other loans or credit card debt outstanding. You decide to increase the life insurance amount so that the mortgage can be paid off in the event that you die. Therefore, you specify an extra $60,000 in life insurance.

By summing up your preferences, you determine you need a total of $474,100 in life insurance. You round off the number, and obtain quotes for policies with coverage of $475,000 or $500,000.

Using the Internet to Determine Your Insurance Coverage. Some insurance companies' Web sites allow you to determine your beneficiary's needs, so that you can decide on the amount of insurance coverage that is necessary. The Web sites ask you to provide basic information such as your total amount of debt, how much annual income you want your family to receive upon your death, and how many years you want the income to last. These sites may even allow you to specify the amount of funds that you wish to provide for the education of your family members.

Limitations in Estimating Needs. When using the budget method to decide needs, keep in mind that the amount of funds that you will need is subject to much uncertainty. Here are some common reasons why you may underestimate the life insurance coverage that you need:

- Someone within your household could experience an unanticipated major illness or disability.

- The income level of your household may not rise over time as expected. It could even decline due to layoffs.

- Inflation could cause you to underestimate the cost of some needs. For example, you may have identified a home as one of your future needs and estimated that the home would cost $120,000 based on existing home prices. However, the price of a home could possibly double within 10–20 years. If the insurance policy only allowed for $120,000 for a home, it might not be sufficient to purchase the kind of home that you desire.

- The insurance policy that you purchase today may not provide coverage until many years from now. For households that save money between purchasing a policy and the death of the policyholder, the funding needed from an insurance policy is reduced. However, for households that accumulate more debt every year, the funding needed from an insurance policy increases. Households should consider the potential change in their debt level over time so that they can more accurately estimate the insurance coverage they will need.

As you attempt to determine your needs, account for the uncertainty by recognizing how the values of these needs may be higher under some conditions. For example, allow for the possibility of higher home prices or tuition when you estimate the values of these needs.

Overestimating your future needs means that you will have more insurance benefits than you really need. You may pay an extra $50 or so in annual premiums for the extra coverage. Underestimating your future needs means you will have less insurance than you really need. The insurance benefits would not be adequate to provide the desired standard of living for your family. When accounting for the uncertainty about your family's future needs, it is better to overestimate your future needs than to underestimate them.

Distinguishing between Needs and Dreams. Before you estimate your needs, distinguish between needs and dreams. To illustrate, consider a young couple that presently has no savings, but has dreams that the breadwinner's career path will generate a substantial amount of income and savings over the years, so that they can retire by age 55 and live in a large home in a mountain resort town. To achieve their dreams, they will likely need about $3 million by the time they are 55 years old. However, if the breadwinner dies, the spouse's life and aspirations may change completely. The dream of a large home in a mountain resort may no longer exist if the couple cannot live there together. The needs to be covered by life insurance should be separated from dreams.

To guide a household in determining needs, the following logic may be applied. First, decide what necessities must be covered for the household to survive and continue its normal standard of living if the breadwinner dies. This exercise can help to determine the minimal life insurance coverage.

Next, the household may wish to consider some additional preferences beyond necessities, such as having enough money to ensure that the children's college education is covered. There is an obvious tradeoff. The greater the total value of needs if the breadwinner dies, the greater the necessary life insurance coverage, and the higher the life insurance premiums. A higher level of life insurance premiums today results in a smaller amount of funds that could be used for other purposes. In general, households attempt to strike a compromise when identifying their life insurance needs. The breadwinner may desire that the family could enjoy an even higher standard of living than is possible today. However, life insurance is not normally viewed as a means by which the surviving family members can suddenly become rich. Ideally, life insurance can provide the financial support so that the family members can continue with their lives and pursuit of goals, just as if the breadwinner were still alive.

CONTENTS OF A LIFE INSURANCE POLICY

A life insurance policy contains the following information.

Beneficiary

The named **beneficiary** receives the benefits when the policyholder dies. When you name a beneficiary on your life insurance policy, keep the following points in mind. First, you can name multiple beneficiaries and specify how you want the death benefits to be divided. You can also name a contingent beneficiary who would receive the benefits in the event that your primary beneficiary is no longer living. You can change the beneficiary any time you wish, but until you do, the existing contract will be enforced. If you name a person rather than your estate as your beneficiary, the benefits can be paid to the person directly and avoid probate and related expenses.

Grace Period

The insurance policy specifies the grace period allowed beyond the date when payment is due. The typical grace period is 30 days.

Living Benefits

Some whole life insurance policies allow **living benefits** (also referred to as **accelerated death benefits**), in which policyholders can receive a portion of the death benefits under special circumstances including terminal illness or long-term care needs of the insured.

Nonforfeiture Clause

A key provision of the whole life policy is a **nonforfeiture clause**, which allows you to use the accumulated cash value if you terminate your whole life policy. You can elect to receive the cash or may be able to direct the funds to purchase a term life insurance contract with a one-time payment. The coverage of the new policy is dependent on the amount of cash value available.

Loans

You can borrow cash from your whole life policy once it has accumulated cash value. The loan rates are usually lower than rates offered on personal loans and interest is paid back into the cash value of the policy.

Incontestability Date

Policies specify a date after which the provisions are incontestable. Until that date, an insurance company can cancel a policy if it determines that some of the information provided by the policyholder is inaccurate.

Renewability Option

A **renewability option** allows you to renew your term insurance policy for another term (up to an age limit specified in the policy) once the existing term expires. The premium for the next term will be higher than that for the prevailing term, since you will be older. In addition, the premium charged in the next term can increase to reflect any change in your health. The advantage of the renewability option is that your renewal is guaranteed. Without a renewability option, you may not be able to renew your insurance if your health has deteriorated. Many term insurance policies include the renewability option at no extra charge. Make sure that this option is available in any term insurance policy that you consider.

Conversion Option

A **conversion option** allows you to convert your term insurance policy into a whole life policy that will be in effect the rest of your life. An insurance policy with a conversion option specifies the period in which the conversion can occur. At the time of this conversion, the premium will be increased, but it will then stay constant for the rest of your life.

beneficiary
Person named to receive the benefits of an insurance policy.

living benefits (accelerated death benefits)
Benefits that allow the policyholder to receive a portion of death benefits prior to death.

nonforfeiture clause
Allows you to receive the savings you accumulated if you terminated your whole life policy.

renewability option
Allows you to renew your policy for another term once an existing policy expires.

conversion option
Allows you to convert your term insurance policy into a different type of policy (called a whole life policy) that will be in effect the rest of your life.

settlement options
The alternative ways a beneficiary can receive life insurance benefits in the event that the insured person dies.

lump-sum settlement
A single payment of all the benefits owed to a beneficiary under a life insurance policy.

installment payments settlement
The payment of life insurance benefits owed to a beneficiary as a stream of equal payments over a specified number of years.

interest payments settlement
A method of paying life insurance benefits in which the company retains the amount owed for a specified number of years and pays interest to the beneficiary.

Settlement Options

Settlement options are the alternative ways beneficiaries can receive life insurance benefits in the event that the insured person dies. Normally, the benefits are not taxed, although there are some exceptions beyond the scope of this text. When you purchase a life insurance policy, you select the settlement option that is most appropriate for your beneficiaries. The appropriate option is dependent on the needs and other characteristics of the beneficiaries. Some of the common options are identified next.

Lump Sum. A **lump-sum settlement** provides all the benefits to the beneficiary in a single payment upon the death of the insured. A $250,000 life insurance policy would provide $250,000 to the beneficiary in a lump sum. This settlement is often used if the beneficiary is disciplined and will use the proceeds wisely. If the beneficiary does not have sufficient discipline, however, an alternative settlement option may be more appropriate.

Installment Payments. The policyholder can elect to use an **installment payments settlement**, which means that the beneficiary will receive a stream of equal payments over a specified number of years. For example, instead of paying $300,000 to the beneficiary in a lump sum, the policy may specify that the beneficiary will receive annual payments starting at the time of the policyholder's death and lasting for 10 years. By spreading the amount over time, this settlement option ensures that the beneficiary will not immediately spend the total amount to be received.

Interest Payments. The policyholder can also elect to use an **interest payments settlement**, which means that the amount owed to the beneficiary will be held by the life insurance company for a specified number of years. Until the amount is distributed, the beneficiary will receive periodic interest payments on the amount. Like the installment payments option, this settlement option prevents the beneficiary from quickly spending all of the policy proceeds.

13.3 Financial Planning Online: How Much Life Insurance Do You Need?

Go to
http://moneycentral.msn.com/
investor/calcs/n_life/main.asp

This Web site provides a recommendation for the amount of life insurance that you should have, based on your financial situation.

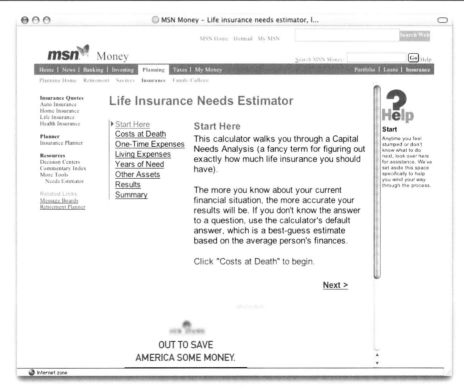

SELECTING A LIFE INSURANCE COMPANY

All life insurance companies are not the same. For this reason, you should research multiple life insurance companies before you select one. Keep the following criteria in mind when you choose a life insurance company.

Other Types of Insurance

Some life insurance companies offer all types of insurance, including liability insurance and health insurance. You may want to select a life insurance company that can also provide these other types of insurance, assuming that this company satisfies all other criteria. It is more convenient to have all types of insurance at one company. In addition, you may receive a discount on your life insurance premium if you purchase other types of insurance from the same company.

The Specific Policy That You Want

While all life insurance companies offer some forms of term insurance and whole life insurance, make sure the company offers the specific policy that you want. For example, you may want a 10-year term policy with a settlement option that provides installment payments.

Services

Make sure that the insurance company will provide you with the type of service that you can expect. For example, you may want to ensure that the insurance company can supply convenient online services. If you want to discuss possible changes to your life insurance policy in person, you may consider choosing an insurance company that has a branch close to your residence. You may want to make sure that you are comfortable with the agent employed by the insurance company. Some agents receive certifications when they have completed specialized training, such as the Chartered Life Underwriter (CLU) certificate. However, keep in mind that while your policy may be in place at a specific company for many years, the agent may leave the company tomorrow. Your policy does not leave with the agent.

Relatively Low Insurance Premiums

The cost of insurance is an important factor to consider when selecting a particular life insurance policy. As you compare the premiums across insurance companies, make sure that the quotes you receive are for comparable policies.

Strong Financial Condition

As mentioned earlier, policyholders rely on a life insurance company to survive in the long run so that it can serve them upon their death. If a life insurance company fails, it will not pay the benefits of its policyholders in the future. People who paid life insurance premiums in the past will not receive the benefits that they deserve. Thus, it is important to assess the financial condition of the life insurance company before you purchase an insurance policy.

Some people believe that insurance companies that focus only on life insurance coverage are safer because they would not be exposed to potential liability resulting from health insurance or liability claims. For example, assume that you have a life insurance policy with a small company that also provides liability coverage. Assume that one of its customers is sued and the court system awards $50 million to the plaintiff. Consequently, the insurance company may go bankrupt because it cannot afford to cover the claim, and therefore cannot provide any life insurance benefits in the future. Companies that focus only on life insurance can avoid this type of exposure. The future life insurance benefits that must be paid are more predictable than future benefits that must be paid for liability or health insurance claims.

Many people who are not qualified to judge the financial condition of an insurance company rely on ratings assigned by rating services such as A.M. Best, Moodys, and Standard & Poors. The Web site http://www.insure.com provides ratings of many insurance companies at no charge. Only consider insurance companies that are rated highly.

HOW LIFE INSURANCE FITS WITHIN YOUR FINANCIAL PLAN

The following are the key decisions about life insurance that should be included within your financial plan:

- Do you need life insurance?

- What type of life insurance is most appropriate for you?

- How much life insurance should you plan for in the future?

Exhibit 13.5 provides an example of how life insurance decisions apply to Stephanie Spratt's financial plan.

Exhibit 13.5 How Life Insurance Fits within Stephanie Spratt's Financial Plan

GOALS FOR LIFE INSURANCE PLANNING

1. Determine whether I need to purchase life insurance.
2. Determine whether I should purchase or add to my life insurance in the future.

ANALYSIS

Type of Insurance Plan	Benefits	Status
Term insurance	Insurance benefits provided to beneficiary.	Not needed at this time since I do not have a spouse or dependents.
Whole life insurance	Insurance benefits provided to beneficiary, and policy builds a cash value over time.	Not needed at this time.
Universal life insurance	Insurance benefits provided to beneficiary, and policy builds a cash value over time.	Not needed at this time.

DECISIONS

Decision on Whether I Need Life Insurance:

I decided to purchase term life insurance to provide my two nieces with a college education if I die. My reason for buying life insurance is simply to have insurance, not to build a cash value. Term insurance serves my purpose and is much cheaper than whole or universal policies.

Decision on Insurance Coverage in the Future:

In the future, I will need to ensure proper life insurance coverage if I have a family. I would want to ensure that my children have sufficient funds to support them and possibly even pay for their college education if I die. If I have a child, I will obtain a 20-year term life insurance policy for $300,000.

DISCUSSION QUESTIONS

1. How would Stephanie's decisions regarding purchasing life insurance be different if she were a single mother of two children?

2. How would Stephanie's decisions regarding purchasing life insurance be affected if she were 35 years old? If she were 50 years old?

SUMMARY

Life insurance provides payments to specified beneficiaries if the policyholder dies. Term insurance is strictly intended to provide insurance in the event of the death of the policyholder, while whole life insurance and universal life insurance use a portion of the premium to build a cash value. The premiums for whole life and universal life insurance are higher to account for the portion distributed into a savings plan and for the administrative fees.

The amount of life insurance that you need can be measured by the income method, in which you attempt to replace the income that would be discontinued due to death. The amount of life insurance can be more precisely measured by the budget method, which considers factors such as your household's future annual living expenses and existing debt.

The life insurance premium is dependent on the amount of life insurance coverage, on whether the life insurance policy has a cash value, and on personal characteristics such as age and health.

The decision to purchase life insurance is partially dependent on whether family members are currently relying on your income. If you decide to purchase insurance, a related decision is the choice of the insurance company. Since the payment from the insurance company to your beneficiaries may not occur until the distant future, you should select an insurance company that you believe will definitely be in service at that time. You can review life insurance company ratings to assess their financial condition, which may indicate whether they will survive over time.

A life insurance policy can be set up to pay beneficiaries a lump-sum payment, installment payments over a specified period, or interest payments over a specified period with a lump sum at the end of the period. The installment option or interest payment option may be most appropriate for ensuring that beneficiaries do not squander the entire life insurance coverage.

INTEGRATING THE KEY CONCEPTS

Your decisions regarding life insurance affect other parts of your financial plan. Because life insurance provides income to your beneficiaries in the event of your death, you are not forced to create a level of wealth that will support your dependents. Instead, you can make investment and borrowing decisions without focusing on the future support of your dependents. This allows you to use a more conservative and long-term approach for your investing and borrowing decisions. You may maintain a larger amount of liquidity (Part 2) because there is no pressure to achieve the very highest returns on your money. You can finance a car or a home if you wish (Part 3) because you can more easily afford to make periodic loan payments. Finally, you can contribute extra savings to retirement (Part 6).

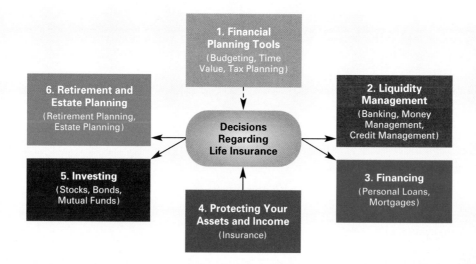

REVIEW QUESTIONS

1. What is the purpose of life insurance? Do you think everyone needs life insurance? Explain.

2. What is term insurance? What factors determine the premium for term insurance? What is decreasing-term insurance?

3. What is mortgage life insurance? Is mortgage life insurance a good buy? Why or why not?

4. Briefly describe some of the term insurance options.

5. What is whole life insurance? What benefit does it provide that term life insurance does not?

6. Describe the nonforfeiture and loan clauses of whole life insurance policies.

7. Why is the premium paid for whole life higher than the premium for term life? What alternative approach to purchasing life insurance might provide the same benefits as whole life?

8. What is universal life insurance? How does it differ from term life and whole life?

9. What is variable life insurance? What are the advantages and disadvantages of variable life policies? How can individuals avoid the high fees of variable life insurance?

10. Describe the income method of determining the amount of life insurance needed. What is the disadvantage of this method?

11. Discuss why life insurance needs should not be based on a family's dreams for the future.

12. Describe the budget method of determining the amount of life insurance needed. What elements must be considered in making this calculation?

13. List and briefly discuss the factors that affect an individual's life insurance premium.

14. Explain how the Internet can expedite the purchase of life insurance. Why do many customers prefer this method?

15. What are settlement options? Which option should you choose?

16. What is a lump-sum settlement? What kind of beneficiary would benefit the most from this option?

17. What is an installment payments settlement? When would an insured individual choose this option?

18. What is the interest payments option? How does it differ from the installment payments option?

FINANCIAL PLANNING PROBLEMS

1. Nancy is a widow with two teenage children. Nancy's gross income is $3,000 per month, and taxes take about 30 percent of her income. Using the income method, Nancy calculates she will need to purchase about eight times her disposable income in life insurance to meet her needs. How much insurance should Nancy purchase?

2. Nancy's employer provides her with two times her annual gross salary in life insurance. How much additional insurance should Nancy purchase based on the information in the previous problem?

3. Peter is married and has two children. He wants to be sure that he has sufficient life insurance to take care of his family if he dies. Peter's wife is a homemaker but attends college part-time pursuing a law degree. It will cost approximately $40,000 for her to finish her education. Since the children are teenagers, Peter feels he will only need to provide the family with income for the next 10 years. He further calculates that the household expenses run approximately $35,000 per year. The balance on the home mortgage is $30,000. Peter set up a college fund for his children when they were babies, and it currently contains sufficient funds for them to attend college. Assuming that Peter's wife can invest the insurance proceeds at 8 percent, calculate the amount of insurance Peter needs to purchase.

4. Marty and Mary have jobs and contribute to the household expenses according to their income. Marty contributes 75 percent of the expenses and Mary contributes 25 percent. Currently, their household expenses are $30,000 annually. Marty and Mary have three children. The youngest child is 12, so they would like to ensure that they could maintain their current standard of living for at least the next eight years. They feel that the insurance proceeds could be invested at 6 percent. In addition to covering the annual expenses, they would like to make sure that each of their children has $25,000 available for college. If Marty were to die, Mary would go back to school part-time to upgrade her training as a nurse. This would cost $20,000. They have a mortgage on their home with a balance of $55,000. How much life insurance should they purchase for Marty?

5. Considering the information in the previous problem, how much life insurance should they purchase for Mary?

6. Bart is a college student. Since his plan is to get a job immediately after graduation, he determines that he will need about $250,000 in life insurance to provide for his future wife (Bart is not married yet) and future children (Bart does not have any children yet). Bart has obtained a quote over the Internet that would require him to pay $200 annually in life insurance premiums. As a college student, this is a significant expense for Bart, and he would likely have to borrow the money necessary to pay for the insurance premiums. Advise Bart on the timing of his life insurance purchase.

Ethical Dilemma

7. Shortly after Steve graduated from college, he considers a whole life insurance policy that would provide $10,000 in life insurance protection and accumulate a cash value of twice his current annual income by age 65. Two years later, after Steve's marriage, he bought a second policy. Through his working years he paid the $280 annual premium per policy. Steve kept remembering what the agent had told him many years before about each policy having a cash value double his annual income.

   Steve was nearing age 65 and dug out the policies from his safety deposit box so that he could begin to put numbers together to plan his retirement. As he opened the two policies, he was appalled to see that the cash value on the older policy was $17,000 and on the newer policy was only $15,000. The two policies together amounted to only one-third his current annual earnings, far from the figure promised him by the agent.

   a. Was the agent being unethical in now showing Steve the potential impact of inflation on the policies' cash value?

   b. Taking just the first policy, would Steve have been better off to invest the $280 annual premium in a mutual fund that would have given an annual return of 8 percent per year (assume a 30-year investment period).

FINANCIAL PLANNING ONLINE EXERCISES

1. Go to http://www.calcbuilder.com/cgi-bin/calcs/INS5.cgi/yahoo_insurance.

   a. View the findings on the screen based on the default information. Click on "graphs" to see a graphical presentation of the results. By clicking on the "explanation" tab, you will get additional information on the calculations.

   b. Now change the policy amount to $500,000 for term and $250,000 for whole life. Change both premiums to $500. Keep other values the same, and check information displayed when you click "results," "graph," and "explanation."

2. Go to http://moneycentral.msn.com/investor/calcs/n_life/main.asp. The "Life Insurance Needs Estimator" walks you through a series of steps to determine your insurance requirements. After you input amounts in each step, the estimator will provide you with the results.

3. Go to http://www.insurance.com/life.aspx.

   a. Select a coverage amount and click "Go." Answer the questions based on your personal information to obtain a life insurance quote.

   b. Now reduce your estimated monthly after-tax income by 10 percent. How does this change affect the life insurance quote?

   c. Now reduce your estimated monthly expenses by 10 percent. How does this change affect your life insurance quote?

4. Go to http://insurance.yahoo.com.

   a. Click on "Life Insurance Calculators." Using your personal information, how much life insurance do you need? To determine some of the required inputs (such as the inflation rate) you will need to research other Web sites.

   b. What is the return on a universal policy based on your personal information?

5. Go to http://insurance.yahoo.com. Under "Insurance Education" click on "General Insurance." Review the section on choosing a type of insurer and comment on this information. Is it good advice? On the same page, read about buying insurance without an agent. What are the pros and cons?

BUILDING YOUR OWN FINANCIAL PLAN

Life insurance is the most controversial and hard-to-select form of insurance. It is controversial because no external source requires that you have life insurance in the way that you are required to insure an auto or home. It is also the one form of insurance for which you, the policyholder, will not be the one to file the claim. Selection is difficult because the insurance industry has numerous policy options for term and whole life insurance.

Insurance needs should be reviewed when major changes occur in your life. Specifically, this review should be done if you marry, divorce, or become a parent.

Go to the worksheets at the end of this chapter, and to the CD-ROM accompanying this text, to continue building your financial plan.

THE SAMPSONS—A CONTINUING CASE

The Sampsons have one remaining insurance need: life insurance. They have decided to purchase term life insurance. They want a life insurance policy that will provide for the family in the event of Dave's death, since he is the breadwinner. The Sampsons do not know how much insurance to purchase, but their goal is to have enough money for general expenses over the next 15 years.

Recall that Dave's salary after taxes is about $40,000. He wants to ensure that the family would have insurance benefits that could provide $40,000 for the next 15 years. By the end of this period, the children would have completed college. Dave also wants to add an additional $330,000 of insurance coverage to provide support for Sharon through her retirement years, since they have not saved much money for retirement.

Go to the worksheets at the end of this chapter, and to the CD-ROM accompanying this text, to continue this case.

PART 4: BRAD BROOKS—A CONTINUING CASE

Brad tells you about his plans to upgrade his auto insurance. Specifically, he would like to add several types of coverage to his policy, such as uninsured motorist coverage and rental car coverage. Recall that Brad is 30 years old. Brad also has a driving record that contains several speeding tickets and two accidents (one of which he caused). He realizes that adding coverage will increase the cost of his insurance. Therefore, he is thinking about switching insurance companies to a more inexpensive carrier.

When you ask Brad whether he has renter's insurance, it is obvious that Brad does not know what renter's insurance is.

Brad mentions that he is generally happy with the HMO he is insured with through the technology company he works for. However, Brad also mentions that he does not particularly like to see his primary care physician each time he requires a consultation with a specialist. Brad tells you that his company also offers a PPO, but that he did not choose that plan because he knows little about it.

Brad is trying to decide between term life insurance and whole life insurance. Brad likes whole life insurance, as he believes that the loan feature on that policy will give him an option for meeting his liquidity needs.

Go to the worksheets at the end of this chapter, and to the CD-ROM accompanying this text, to continue this case.

Chapter 13: Building Your Own Financial Plan

GOALS

1. Determine whether you need to purchase life insurance and if so, how much.
2. Determine the most appropriate types of life insurance.
3. Decide whether you should purchase or add to your life insurance in the future.

ANALYSIS

1. Your life insurance needs are dependent on several factors. The worksheet below employs the budget method discussed in the text to determine the amount of insurance that you need. Complete the worksheet by filling in the appropriate information to determine your life insurance needs.

1. Annual living expenses *(Refer to your personal cash flow statement developed in Chapter 2 to determine this figure.)*	$		
2. Minus spouse's disposable "after-tax" income	$		
3. Minus interest or dividends from savings*	$		
4. Minus other income	$		
5. Annual living expenses to be replaced by insurance (line 1 minus lines 2, 3, and 4)		$	
6. Assuming a 6 percent rate of return and the number of years of expenses for which you will need coverage, determine the present value (line 5 times *PVIFA* for _____ years at 6 percent)		×	
7. Insurance needs for annual living expenses (line 5 times line 6)			$
8. Special future expenses		$	
9. The number of years until line 8 occurs and multiply by the present value of a dollar assuming 6 percent (line 8 times *PVIF* _____ years at 6 percent)		×	
10. Insurance needs for special future expenses (line 8 times line 9)			$
11. Current debt to be repaid by insurance proceeds			$

12. Educational/training expenses for spouse to be paid by insurance proceeds		$
13. Value of existing savings		$
14. Final expenses *(Funeral and other related items)*		$
15. Life insurance provided by employer		$
Total Insurance Needs (Add lines 7, 10, 11, 12, and 14 and subtract lines 13 and 15)		$

* This number should be adjusted if savings are to be liquidated and included in line 13. Only the interest and dividends from those savings not counted in line 13 should be included here.

2. Review the following information about types of life insurance plans. Indicate how suitable each type is for your situation in the third column.

Type of Insurance Plan	Benefits	Suitability
Term Insurance	Insurance benefits provided to beneficiary	
Whole-Life Insurance	Insurance benefits provided to beneficiary and policy builds a cash value over time	
Universal Insurance	Insurance benefits provided to beneficiary and policy builds a cash value over time	

3. If you have determined that you need life insurance, obtain premiums for the policy type and amount you desire at http://www.prudential.com. Click on the "Products & Services" tab. At the "Calculators & Guides" section, click on "Life Insurance Quotes," and enter the premiums in the following worksheet.

Policy Type			
Name of Insurance Company			
Total Premium	$	$	$

4. Make any necessary changes to your personal cash flow statement to reflect premiums for life insurance.

Personal Cash Flow Statement

Cash Inflows | This Month

Cash Inflows	This Month
Disposable (after-tax) income	
Interest on deposits	
Dividend payments	
Other	
Total Cash Inflows	

Cash Outflows

Cash Outflows	
Rent	
Cable TV	
Electricity and water	
Telephone	
Groceries	
Health care insurance and expenses	
Clothing	
Car expenses (insurance, maintenance, and gas)	
Recreation	
Other	
Total Cash Outflows	
Net Cash Flows	

DECISIONS

1. Do you need life insurance? If so, how much and what type of policy will suit your needs?

_____

_____

_____

_____

_____

2. What do you anticipate your life insurance coverage needs to be in the future?

_____

_____

_____

_____

_____

Chapter 13: The Sampsons—A Continuing Case

CASE QUESTIONS

1. Determine the present value of the insurance benefits that could provide $40,000 over the next 15 years for the Sampson family. Assume that the insurance payment could be invested to earn 6 percent interest over time.

Annual Amount	$40,000
Number of Years	15
Annual Interest Rate	6%
Present Value	$

2. Considering the insurance benefits needed to provide $40,000 over the next 15 years, plus the additional $330,000 of insurance coverage, what amount of insurance coverage is needed?

3. Given the total amount of insurance coverage needed and Dave's present age (30 years old), estimate the premium that the Sampsons would pay using one of the insurance Web sites mentioned in the chapter (http://www.insure.com or http://finance.yahoo.com/insurance).

4. Dave Sampson is a social smoker. Since he only smokes occasionally, he would like to omit this information from his life insurance application. Advise Dave on this course of action.

Part 4: Brad Brooks—A Continuing Case

CASE QUESTIONS

1. Regarding Brad's auto insurance decision, comment on

   a. His plan to add different types of coverage to his auto insurance policy

   _____

   _____

   _____

   b. The associated costs of adding different types of coverage to his auto insurance policy

   _____

   _____

   _____

   c. Any resulting negative consequences of switching to a more inexpensive auto insurance company

   _____

   _____

   _____

   d. Any other factors Brad should consider before switching insurance companies

   _____

   _____

   _____

2. Describe renter's insurance to Brad. What determines whether renter's insurance is appropriate for Brad?

   _____

   _____

3. Describe to Brad how he could benefit from a PPO. Are there any negative factors Brad needs to know about if he seriously considers switching to a PPO? Consider Brad's cash flow situation from the previous parts when answering this question.

   _____

   _____

   _____

4. Concerning Brad's life insurance decision, comment on

a. His need for life insurance

_____

_____

_____

b. If you think he needs life insurance, is whole life his best choice?

_____

_____

_____

c. His plan to use the whole life policy's loan feature as a means for maintaining liquidity

_____

_____

_____

Personal Investing

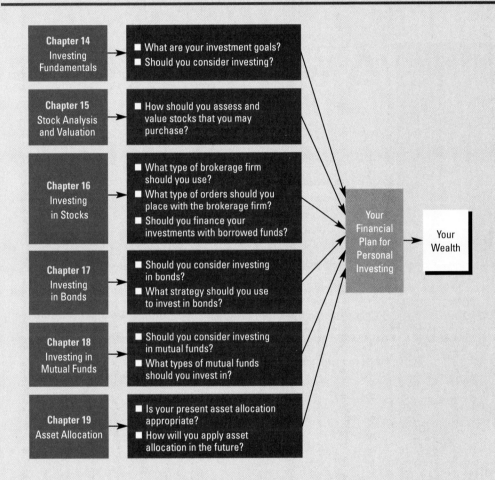

Chapter 14 Investing Fundamentals	■ What are your investment goals? ■ Should you consider investing?
Chapter 15 Stock Analysis and Valuation	■ How should you assess and value stocks that you may purchase?
Chapter 16 Investing in Stocks	■ What type of brokerage firm should you use? ■ What type of orders should you place with the brokerage firm? ■ Should you finance your investments with borrowed funds?
Chapter 17 Investing in Bonds	■ Should you consider investing in bonds? ■ What strategy should you use to invest in bonds?
Chapter 18 Investing in Mutual Funds	■ Should you consider investing in mutual funds? ■ What types of mutual funds should you invest in?
Chapter 19 Asset Allocation	■ Is your present asset allocation appropriate? ■ How will you apply asset allocation in the future?

Your Financial Plan for Personal Investing → Your Wealth

THE CHAPTERS IN THIS PART EXPLAIN THE VARIOUS TYPES OF investments that are available, how to value investments, and how to determine which investments to select. Chapter 14 provides a background on investing, and Chapters 15 and 16 explain how to decide which stocks to buy. Chapter 17 focuses on investing in bonds. Chapter 18 on mutual funds explains the advantages and disadvantages of investing in a portfolio of securities rather than individual stocks and bonds. Chapter 19 stresses the importance of allocating your money across various types of investments. Your decisions regarding whether to invest, how much to invest, and how to invest will affect your cash flows and wealth.

Chapter 14

Investing Fundamentals

Anita is a patient investor. In 1995 she invested $3,000 in stocks of well-known companies. By 2006, her original investment was worth $8,000.

Meanwhile, Lisa invested $3,000 in stock of Zyko Co. because Zyko suggested its technology would change the world. Lisa wanted to earn higher returns on her investment than she might earn on stock of well-established firms. Zyko's technology failed, and in 2006, Zyko went bankrupt. Consequently, Lisa's stock was worthless.

These examples demonstrate that the same type of investment can have entirely different outcomes. As you will learn in this chapter, there are a variety of investments, and the risk and return of these different investments vary widely. Your ability to analyze investments can enhance your investment income and increase your net worth.

The objectives of this chapter are to:

- Describe the common types of investments
- Explain how to measure the return on investments
- Identify the risks of investments
- Explain the tradeoff between the return and risk of investments
- Describe common investment mistakes that should be avoided

TYPES OF INVESTMENTS

If you have money to invest, your first priority should be to ensure adequate liquidity. You can satisfy your liquidity needs by placing deposits in financial institutions or by investing in money market securities such as certificates of deposit. Since these types of investments are primarily focused on providing liquidity, they offer a relatively low return. If you have additional funds beyond your liquidity needs, you have a wide variety of investments to consider.

Money Market Securities

Recall from Chapter 6 that there are several different money market securities available, including certificates of deposit, money market deposit accounts, and money market funds. Most money market securities provide interest income. Even if your liquidity needs are covered, you may invest in these securities to maintain a low level of risk. Yet, you can also consider some alternative securities that typically provide a higher rate of return but are more risky.

Stocks

primary market
A market in which newly issued securities are traded.

initial public offering (IPO)
The first offering of a firm's stock to the public.

secondary market
A market in which existing securities are traded.

institutional investors
Professionals responsible for managing money on behalf of the clients they serve.

As defined in Chapter 2, stocks are certificates representing partial ownership of a firm. Stock investors become shareholders of the firm. Firms issue stocks to obtain funds to expand their business operations. Investors invest in stock when they believe that they may earn a higher return than alternative investments offer. Since stocks are a popular type of investment for individuals, they are the focus of Chapters 15 and 16.

Primary and Secondary Stock Markets. Stocks can be traded in a primary or a secondary market. The **primary market** is a market in which newly issued securities are traded. Firms can raise funds by issuing new stock in the primary market. The first offering of a firm's stock to the public is referred to as an **initial public offering (IPO)**. A **secondary market** facilitates the trading of existing securities by enabling investors to sell their shares at any time. These shares are purchased by other investors who wish to invest in that stock. Thus, even if a firm is not issuing new shares of stock, investors can easily obtain shares of that firm's stock by purchasing them in the secondary market. On a typical day, more than 1 million shares of any large firm's stock are traded in the secondary market. The price of the stock changes each day in response to changes in supply and demand.

portfolio managers
Employees of financial institutions who make investment decisions.

individual investors
Individuals who invest funds in securities.

Types of Stock Investors. Stock investors can be classified as institutional investors or individual investors. **Institutional investors** are professionals employed by a financial institution who are responsible for managing money on behalf of the clients they serve. They attempt to select stocks or other securities that will provide a reasonable return on investment. The employees of financial institutions who make investment decisions are referred to as **portfolio managers** because they manage a portfolio of securities (including stocks). More than half of all trading in financial markets is attributable to institutional investors.

    Individual investors commonly invest a portion of the money earned from their jobs. Like institutional investors, they invest in stocks to earn a reasonable return on their

14.1 Financial Planning Online: IPOs

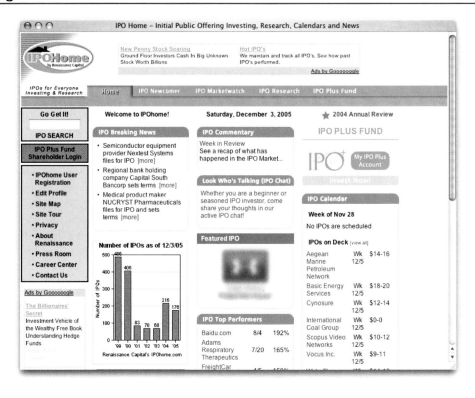

investment. In this way, their money can grow by the time they wish to use it to make purchases. The number of individual investors has increased substantially in the last 20 years.

Many individual investors hold their stocks for periods beyond one year. In contrast, some individual investors called **day traders** buy stocks and then sell them on the same day. They hope to capitalize on very short-term movements in security prices. In many cases, their investments last for only a few minutes. Many day traders conduct their investing as a career, relying on their returns from investing as their main source of income. This type of investing is very risky because the stock prices of even the best-managed firms periodically decline. Day trading is not recommended for most investors.

day traders
Investors who buy stocks and then sell them on the same day.

Return from Investing in Stock. Stocks can offer a return on investment through dividends and stock price appreciation. Some firms distribute quarterly income to their shareholders in the form of dividends rather than reinvest the earnings in the firm's operations. They tend to keep the dollar amount of the dividends per share fixed from one quarter to the next, but may periodically increase the amount. They rarely reduce the dividend amount unless they experience relatively weak performance and cannot afford to make their dividend payment. The amount of dividends paid out per year is usually between 1 and 3 percent of the stock's price.

A firm's decision to distribute earnings as dividends, rather than reinvesting all of its earnings to support future growth, may depend on the opportunities that are available to the firm. In general, firms that pay high dividends tend to be older, established firms that have less chance for substantial growth. Conversely, firms that pay low dividends tend to be younger firms that have more growth opportunities. The stocks of firms with substantial growth opportunities are often referred to as **growth stocks**. An investment in these younger firms offers the prospect of a very large return because they have not reached their full potential. At the same time, an investment in these firms is exposed to much higher uncertainty because young firms are more likely to fail or experience very weak performance than mature firms.

growth stocks
Stocks of firms with substantial growth opportunities.

The higher the dividend paid by a firm, the lower its potential stock price appreciation. When a firm distributes a large proportion of its earnings to investors as dividends, it limits its potential growth and the potential degree to which its value (and stock price) may increase. Stocks that provide investors with periodic income in the form of large dividends are referred to as **income stocks**.

income stocks
Stocks that provide investors with periodic income in the form of large dividends.

Shareholders can also earn a return if the price of the stock increases by the time they sell it. The market value of a firm is based on the number of shares of stock outstanding multiplied by the price of the stock. The price of a share of stock is determined by dividing the market value of the firm by the number of shares of stock outstanding. Thus, a firm that has a market value of $600 million and 10 million shares of stock outstanding has a value per share of:

$$
\begin{aligned}
\text{Value of Stock per Share} &= \text{Market Value of Firm/} \\
&\qquad \text{Number of Shares Outstanding} \\
&= \$600,000,000/10,000,000 \\
&= \$60.
\end{aligned}
$$

The market price of a stock is dependent on the number of investors who are willing to purchase the stock (the demand for the stock) and the number of investors who wish to sell their holdings of the stock (the supply of stock for sale). There is no limit to how high a stock's price can rise. The demand for the stock and the supply of stock for sale are influenced by the respective firm's business performance, as measured by its earnings and other characteristics. When the firm performs well, its stock becomes more desirable to investors, who demand more shares of that stock. In addition, investors holding shares of this stock are less willing to sell it. The increase in the demand for the stock and the reduction in the number of shares of stock for sale by investors results in a higher stock price.

14.2 Financial Planning Online: Price Trends of Your Stocks

Go to
http://finance.yahoo.com/

Click on
"GO" after you type in the symbol for your stock. To view charts showing the stock's price movements over time, click the links displayed under the chart shown. Using these charts, you can assess the price movements of the stock you specify for today, for the last year, or even for the last five years

This Web site provides
historical price movements for stock that you specify. shown.

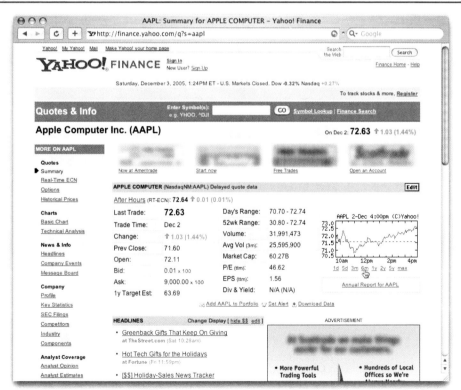

Conversely, when a firm performs poorly (has low or negative earnings), its market value declines. The demand for shares of its stock also declines. In addition, some investors who had been holding the stock will decide to sell their shares, thereby increasing the supply of stock for sale and resulting in a lower stock price. The performance of the firm depends on how well it is managed.

Investors benefit when they invest in a well-managed firm because the firm's earnings usually will increase, and so will its stock price. Under these conditions, investors may generate a capital gain, which represents the difference between their selling price and their purchase price. In contrast, a poorly managed firm may have lower earnings than expected, which could cause its stock price to decline.

Common versus Preferred Stock. Stock can be classified as common stock or preferred stock. **Common stock** is a certificate issued by a firm to raise funds that represents partial ownership in the firm. Investors who hold common stock normally have the right to vote on key issues such as the sale of a company. They elect the board of directors, which is responsible for ensuring that the firm's managers serve the interests of its shareholders. **Preferred stock** is a certificate issued by a firm to raise funds that entitles shareholders to first priority (ahead of common stockholders) to receive dividends. Corporations issue common stock more frequently than preferred stock. The price of preferred stock is not as volatile as the price of common stock and does not have as much potential to increase substantially. For this reason, investors who strive for high returns typically invest in common stock.

common stock
A certificate issued by a firm to raise funds that represents partial ownership in the firm.

preferred stock
A certificate issued by a firm to raise funds that entitles shareholders to first priority to receive dividends.

Bonds

Recall that bonds are long-term debt securities issued by government agencies or corporations. Treasury bonds are issued by the Treasury and backed by the U.S. government. Corporate bonds are issued by corporations.

Return from Investing in Bonds. Bonds offer a return to investors in the form of coupon payments and bond price appreciation. They pay periodic interest (coupon) payments, and therefore can provide a fixed amount of interest income per year. Thus, they are desirable for investors who want to have their investments generate a specific amount of interest income each year.

A bond's price can increase over time and therefore may provide investors with a capital gain, representing the difference between the price at which it was sold by an investor versus the price at which it was purchased. However, a bond's price may decline, which could cause investors to experience a capital loss. Even the prices of Treasury bonds decline in some periods. More details about bonds are provided in Chapter 17.

Mutual Funds

Recall that mutual funds sell shares to individuals and invest the proceeds in a portfolio of investments such as bonds or stocks. They are managed by experienced portfolio managers. They are attractive to investors who have limited funds and want to invest in a diversified portfolio. Because a stock mutual fund typically invests in numerous stocks, it enables investors to achieve broad diversification with an investment as low as $500. There are thousands of mutual funds to choose from.

Return from Investing in Mutual Funds. The coupon or dividend payment generated by the mutual fund's portfolio of securities is passed on to the individual investor. Since a mutual fund represents a portfolio of securities, its value changes over time in response to changes in the values of those securities. Therefore, the price at which an investor purchases shares of a mutual fund changes over time. A mutual fund can generate a capital gain for individual investors, since the price at which investors sell their shares of the fund may be higher than the price at which they purchased the shares. However, the price of the mutual fund's shares may also decline over time, which would result in a capital loss. Mutual funds are discussed in more detail in Chapter 18.

Publicly Traded Indexes. Another option for investors who want a diversified portfolio of stocks is to invest in **publicly traded stock indexes**, which are securities whose values move in tandem with a particular stock index representing a set of stocks.

Much research has shown that sophisticated investors (such as well-paid portfolio managers of financial institutions) are unable to outperform various stock indexes on average. Thus, by investing in an index, individual investors can ensure that their performance will match that index.

One of the most popular publicly traded indexes is the Standard & Poor's Depository Receipt (S.P.D.R., also called Spider), which is a basket of stocks that matches the S&P 500 index and is traded on the American Stock Exchange. You can buy Spiders through a broker, just like stocks. When investors expect that the large U.S. stocks represented by the S&P 500 will experience strong performance, they can capitalize on their expectations by purchasing shares of Spiders. Spiders provide investors with a return not only in the form of potential share price appreciation, but also dividends in the form of additional shares to the investors. Any expenses incurred by the Spiders from creating the index are deducted from the dividends.

Investors can also invest in specific sector indexes as well as in market indexes. There are publicly traded indexes that represent a variety of specific sectors, including the Internet, energy, technology, and financial sectors. Because an index represents several stocks, you can achieve some degree of diversification by investing in an index.

> **publicly traded stock indexes**
> Securities whose values move in tandem with a particular stock index representing a set of stocks.

Real Estate

One way of investing in real estate is by buying a home. The value of a home changes over time, in response to supply and demand. When the demand for homes in your area increases, home values tend to rise. The return that you earn on your home is difficult to measure because you must take into account the financing, real estate agent commissions, and tax effects. However, a few generalizations are worth mentioning. For a given amount invested in the home, your return is dependent on how the value of your home changes over the time that you own it. Your return is also dependent on your original down payment on the home. The return will be higher if you made a smaller down payment when purchasing the home. Since the value of a home can decline over time, there is the risk of a loss (a negative return) on your investment. If you are in a hurry to sell your home, you may have to lower your selling price to attract potential buyers, which will result in a lower return on your investment.

You can also invest in real estate by purchasing rental property or land. The price of land is based on supply and demand. There is little open land and dense populations along the coasts of the United States, so open land along the coasts typically has a high price.

Return from Investing in Real Estate. Real estate that can be rented (such as office buildings and apartments) generates income in the form of rent payments. In addition, investors may earn a capital gain if they sell the property for a higher price than they paid for it. Alternatively, they may sustain a capital loss if they sell the property for a lower price than they paid for it.

The price of land changes over time in response to real estate development. Many individuals may purchase land as an investment, hoping that they will be able to sell it in the future for a higher price than they paid for it.

INVESTMENT RETURN AND RISK

When individuals consider any particular investment, they typically attempt to assess two characteristics: (1) the potential return that will be earned on the investment, and (2) the risk of the investment.

Measuring the Return on Your Investment

For investments that do not provide any periodic income (such as dividends or coupon payments), the return can be measured as the percentage change in the price (P) from the time the investment was purchased (time $t-1$) until the time at which it is sold (time t):

$$R = \frac{P_t - P_{t-1}}{P_{t-1}}$$

For example, if you pay $1,000 to make an investment and receive $1,100 when you sell the investment in one year, you earn a return of:

$$R = \frac{\$1,100 - \$1,000}{\$1,000}$$

$$= .10, \text{ or } 10\%.$$

Incorporating Dividend or Coupon Payments. If you also earned dividend or coupon payments over this period, your return would be even higher. For a short-term period such as one year or less, the return on a security that pays dividends or interest can be estimated by adjusting the equation above. Add the dividend or coupon amount to the numerator. The return on your investment in stocks accounts for any dividends or coupon payments you received as well as the change in the investment value over your investment period. For stocks that pay dividends, the return is:

$$R = \frac{(P_t - P_{t-1}) + D}{P_{t-1}}$$

where R is the return, P_{t-1} is the price of the stock at the time of the investment, P_t is the price of the stock at the end of the investment horizon, and D is the dividends earned over the investment horizon.

EXAMPLE   You purchased 100 shares of Wax, Inc., stock for $50 per share one year ago. During the year, the firm experienced strong earnings. It paid dividends of $1 per share over the year, and you sold the stock for $58 at the end of the year. Your return on your investment was:

$$R = \frac{(P_t - P_{t-1}) + D}{P_{t-1}}$$

$$= \frac{(\$58 - \$50) + \$1}{\$50}$$

$$= .18, \text{ or } 18\%.$$

Differing Tax Rates on Returns. Income received as a result of interest payments or bond coupon payments is classified as ordinary income for tax purposes. In addition, capital gains resulting from the sale of investments held for one year or less are classified as ordinary income. Capital gains resulting from the sale of investments held more than one year are subject to a long-term capital gains tax. Given the difference in tax rates applied to short- and long-term capital gains, some investors may achieve a higher after-tax return by holding on to investments for more than one year.

EXAMPLE   As in the previous example, you purchased 100 shares of Wax stock, except that instead of selling the stock after one year, you sell the stock after 366 days (one day beyond a year). Because you have held the stock for one more day, your capital gain shifts from a short-term gain to a long-term gain (taxed at 15 percent). Assume that your marginal tax rate (tax rate charged on any additional ordinary income) is 35 percent. The tax effects of the previous example involving a short-term capital gain are shown in the second column of Exhibit 14.1, while the tax effects of the long-term capital gain are shown in the third column. The taxes on dividends are as follows:

$$\text{Tax on Dividends Received} = \text{Amount of Dividend} \times \text{Dividend Tax Rate}$$
$$= \$100 \times .15$$
$$= \$15.$$

The tax on capital gains depends on whether the gain is short term or long term. The short-term capital gains tax is:

$$\text{Tax on Short-Term Capital Gain} = \text{Amount of Short-Term Capital Gain} \times \text{Marginal Income Tax Rate}$$
$$= \$800 \times .35$$
$$= \$280.$$

The long-term capital gains tax is:

$$\text{Tax on Long-Term Capital Gain} = \text{Amount of Long-Term Capital Gain} \times \text{Long-Term Capital Gain Tax Rate}$$
$$= \$800 \times .15$$
$$= \$120.$$

The long-term capital gains tax is $160 lower than the short-term capital gains tax. Thus, your after-tax income from holding the stock one extra day is $160 higher.

How Wealth Is Influenced by Your Return on Investment

When an investment provides income to you, any portion of that income that you save will increase the value of your assets. For example, if you receive a coupon payment of $100 this month as a result of holding a bond and deposit the check in your savings

Exhibit 14.1 Comparing the Tax Effects on Short- and Long-Term Capital Gains

	If Stock Is Held for One Year	If Stock Is Held for More Than One Year
Dividends	$100	$100
Short-term capital gain	800	0
Long-term capital gain	0	800
Total income	$900	$900
Tax on dividends (15%)	$15	$15
Short-term capital gains tax (35%)	280	0
Long-term capital gains tax (15%)	0	120
Total taxes	$295	$135
After-tax income	$605	$765

account, your assets will increase by $100. If the value of your investments increases and your liabilities do not increase, your wealth increases.

The degree to which you can accumulate wealth is partially dependent on your investment decisions. You can estimate the amount by which your wealth will increase from an investment based on some assumed rate of return. If you invest the same amount at the end of each year, the future value (*FV*) of this investment can be measured applying the time value of money to the future value interest factors for an annuity:

$$FV \text{ of Investment} = \text{Investment} \times FVIF_{i,n}$$

where *i* is the annual return on the investment and *n* is the number of years until the end of the investment period.

E X A M P L E

Stephanie Spratt hopes to invest $4,000 at the end of the year. If her investments appreciate by 6 percent annually, the value of her investment will be $7,163 in 10 years. If she earns an annual return of 10 percent, the value of those investments will be $10,375 in 10 years. If she can earn an annual return of 20 percent, the value of her investment will be $24,767 in 10 years. The higher the rate of return, the higher the future value interest factor (*FVIF*), and the larger the amount of funds that she will accumulate.

If you can invest a specific amount in the stock market every year, the future value of these annual investments can be estimated as:

$$FV \text{ of Annual Stock Investments} = \text{Annual Investment} \times FVIFA_{i,n}$$

E X A M P L E

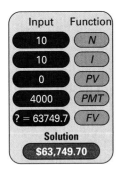

Input	Function
10	N
10	I
0	PV
4000	PMT
? = 63749.7	FV

Solution

$63,749.70

Stephanie Spratt believes that she can save $4,000 to invest in stocks at the end of each year for the next 10 years. If she expects the investment value to increase by 10 percent annually, she can use the future value interest factor of an annuity at 10 percent over 10 years, which is 15.937 (see Table B-3 in Appendix B). Based on her annual investment of $4,000 and the future value interest factor of an annuity (*FVIFA*), she will accumulate:

$$
\begin{aligned}
FV \text{ of Annual Stock Investments} &= \text{Annual Investment} \times FVIFA_{i,n} \\
&= \$4,000 \times 15.937 \\
&= \$63,748.
\end{aligned}
$$

The input for the financial calculator is shown at the left.

If Stephanie's investment value increases by 20 percent per year, the *FVIFA* is 25.959, and the value of her annual investments in 10 years will be:

Input	Function
10	N
20	I
0	PV
4000	PMT
? = 103834.73	FV

Solution

$103,834.73

$$
\begin{aligned}
FV \text{ of Annual Stock Investments} &= \text{Annual Investment} \times FVIFA_{i,n} \\
&= \$4,000 \times 25.959 \\
&= \$103,836.
\end{aligned}
$$

The input for the financial calculator is shown at the left.

Notice how the increase in Stephanie's wealth is sensitive to the rate of return earned on her annual investment. An annual increase in investment value of 20 percent would allow her to accumulate $40,088 more than if the annual increase is 10 percent.

The example shows how your investment decisions and the performance of your investments can affect your future wealth.

Risk from Investing

The risk of an investment comes from the uncertainty surrounding its return. The return that you will earn on a specific stock is uncertain because its future dividend payments are not guaranteed, and its future price (when you sell the stock) is uncertain. The return that you will earn on a bond is uncertain because its coupon payments are not guaranteed, and its future price (when you sell the bond) is uncertain. The return that you will earn from investing in real estate is uncertain because its value when you sell it is uncertain. Chapters 15, 16, 17, and 18 discuss specific risks that stock, bond, and mutual fund investments are subject to.

The future values of investments are dependent on the demand by investors. When economic conditions are favorable, the income levels of investors are high, the earnings levels of firms are high, and there is a strong demand for most types of investments. When economic conditions are weak, the income levels of investors are low, the earnings levels of firms are low, and there is a weak demand for most types of investments. However, future economic conditions are uncertain, so it is difficult to predict the level of demand for various investments, and therefore the future values of these investments.

EXAMPLE   You are considering purchasing the stock of Cerro Inc. The future value of Cerro's stock is dependent on the future performance of Cerro Inc. If the economy strengthens, Cerro Inc. should perform well, and the value of its stock may increase by more than 9 percent. However, if the economy weakens, Cerro Inc. will perform poorly, and the stock could decline by 30 percent or more.

It is easy to find examples to illustrate the risk from investing. Many firms went bankrupt in the 2001–2002 period, including large firms such as Enron, Global Crossing, and WorldCom. Numerous investors who invested in these stocks lost 100 percent of their investment. Even firms that have normally performed well over time can experience weak performance in particular periods. Thus, it is not unusual for the stock or bond prices of even the most well-known firms to decline by more than 10 percent within a particular month or year. Stocks and bonds of smaller firms tend to be even more risky, as they commonly experience pronounced fluctuations in their performance level. Some firms are more stable than others and are therefore less likely to experience a major decline in their performance. Nevertheless, some investors prefer investments that have a higher growth potential, and they tolerate the higher level of risk. Before you select an investment, you should assess the risk.

Measuring an Investment's Risk. Investors measure the risk of investments to determine the degree of uncertainty surrounding their future returns. Two common measures of an investment's risk are its range of returns and the standard deviation of its returns. These measures can be applied to investments whose prices are frequently quoted over time.

Range of Returns. By reviewing the monthly returns of a specific investment over a given period, you can determine the **range of returns**, from the smallest (most negative) to the largest return. Compare an investment that has a range of monthly returns from .2 percent to 1.4 percent over the last year with another investment that has a range of −3.0 percent to 4.3 percent. The first investment is less risky because its range of returns is smaller and therefore it is more stable. Investments with a wide range have more risk because they have a higher probability of experiencing a large decline in price.

range of returns
Returns of a specific investment over a given period.

standard deviation
The degree of volatility in the stock's returns over time.

Standard Deviation of Returns. A second measure of risk is the **standard deviation** of a stock's monthly returns, which measures the degree of volatility in the stock's returns over time. A large standard deviation means that the returns deviate substantially from the mean over time. The more volatile the returns, the greater the chance that the stock could deviate far from its mean in a given period. Thus, an investment with a high standard deviation is more likely to experience a large gain or a large loss in a given period.

The investment's return is subject to greater uncertainty, and for this reason, it is perceived as more risky.

Although these two measures differ, they tend to rank the risk levels of stocks rather consistently. That is, a very risky stock will normally have a relatively wide range of returns and a high standard deviation of returns.

Subjective Measures of Risk. The use of the range and standard deviation is limited because these measures of risk are not always accurate predictors of the future. For example, an investment that had stable returns in the past could experience a substantial decline in price in the future in response to poor economic conditions. Because of this limitation, the risk of some investments is commonly measured subjectively. For example, the risk of a bond may be measured by a subjective assessment of the issuing firm's ability to repay its debt. The assessment may include an estimate of the firm's future monthly revenue to determine whether the firm will have sufficient funds to cover its interest and other expenses. Investors may rely on experts to offer their risk assessment of a particular type of investment. Bond rating agencies offer risk assessments of various bonds, as explained in Chapter 17.

TRADEOFF BETWEEN RETURN AND RISK

Every individual investor would like investments that offer a very high return and have no risk. However, such investments do not exist. Investors must weigh the tradeoff between the potential return of an investment and the risk. If you want an investment that may generate a higher return, you have to tolerate the higher degree of uncertainty (risk) associated with that investment.

E X A M P L E

Stephanie Spratt has $1,000 that she could invest for the next three months in a three-month bank CD or in a stock. The bank CD offers a guaranteed return of 2 percent over the three-month period. Alternatively, she thinks the price of the stock will rise by 5 percent over the next three months. Yet, since the future price of the stock is uncertain, her return from investing in this stock is also uncertain. The return could be less than 5 percent, and might even be negative. Stephanie decides to invest in the CD rather than the stock.

The example above illustrates the tradeoff between a risk-free investment and a risky investment. There are also tradeoffs between assets with varying degrees of risk, as explained below for each type of investment.

Return-Risk Tradeoff among Stocks

Some firms have the potential to achieve a much higher performance level than others. But to do so, they take on more risk than other firms. That is, they may try to operate with less funding and pursue long-shot opportunities. Investors who invest in one of these firms may earn very high returns if the firm's strategies are successful. However, they could lose most or all of their investment if the firm's strategies fail.

In general, smaller firms have more potential for fast growth and their stocks have the potential to increase in value to greater degree. Yet, their stocks are risky because many small firms never reach their potential. The more mature firms that have already achieved high growth have less potential for future growth. However, these firms tend to be less risky because their business is more stable.

Initial public offerings (IPOs) are another stock investment option. You may have heard that IPO returns often exceed 20 percent over the first day. However, there is much risk to this type of investment. Individual investors rarely have access to these IPOs at the initial price. Institutional investors (such as mutual funds or insurance companies with large amounts of money to invest) normally have the first shot at purchasing shares of an IPO. Most individual investors can invest (if there are any shares left) only after the institutional investors have had a chance to purchase shares. By the time individual investors are able to invest in a newly issued stock, the price has already risen. Thus, individual investors commonly obtain the shares only after the price has reached its peak, and incur large losses as the stock price declines over the next several months.

Many IPOs have performed poorly. On average, the long-term return on IPOs is weak compared to typical returns of other stocks in aggregate. Many firms (such as pets.com) that engaged in IPOs failed within a few years, causing investors to lose all of their investment.

Return-Risk Tradeoff among Bonds

You may invest in a bond issued by a firm to earn the high coupon payment. The risk of your investment is that the firm may be unable to pay its coupon payment if its financial condition deteriorates. If you purchase a bond of a large, well-known, and successful firm, there is minimal risk that the firm will default on its payments. If you purchase a bond issued by a firm that is struggling financially, there is more risk that this firm will default on its payments. If this firm defaults on the bond, your return will be very poor.

High-risk bonds tend to offer higher coupon payments. Thus, you must weigh the tradeoff between the potential return and the risk. If you are willing to tolerate the higher risk, you may consider investing in the bond issued by a weak firm. Alternatively, if you prefer less risk, you can purchase a bond issued by a successful and established firm, as long as you are willing to accept a lower return on your investment.

Return-Risk Tradeoff among Mutual Funds

When you invest in a mutual fund composed of stocks, you earn a return from the dividend payments and the increase in the prices of stocks held by the mutual fund. The risk of a stock mutual fund is that the prices of stocks can decline in any particular period. Since the mutual fund is composed of numerous stocks, the adverse impact caused by any single stock is reduced. However, when economic conditions weaken, most stocks tend to perform poorly. Just as smaller stocks tend to be more risky than larger stocks, mutual funds that contain mostly small stocks are more risky than mutual funds that contain larger stocks. Yet, some investors still prefer mutual funds that contain small stocks because they expect a higher return from these stocks.

When you invest in a mutual fund composed of bonds, your primary risk is that the bonds held by the mutual fund could default. Since a bond mutual fund contains numerous bonds, the adverse effect of a single bond default within a mutual fund is reduced. Yet, when economic conditions deteriorate, many firms that issued bonds could experience financial problems and have difficulty making their coupon payments. Some bond mutual funds are not highly exposed to risk because they invest only in corporate bonds issued by the most creditworthy corporations. Others are highly exposed because they invest in bonds issued by relatively weak corporations that pay high coupon rates. Investors who prefer risky bond mutual funds because of their potential to offer a high return must tolerate the high level of risk.

"Good news! I held my IPO at recess and now I'm the 12th richest man in America."

Return-Risk Tradeoff among Real Estate Investments

When you invest in real estate, your risk depends on your particular investment. If you buy rental property, it may not generate your anticipated periodic income if you cannot find renters or if your renters default on their rent payment. In addition, there is a risk that the property's value will decline over time. The degree of risk varies with the type of real estate investment. If you purchase an office building that is fully occupied, the risk is relatively low. Conversely, if you purchase a piece of open land in New Mexico because you hope that you will someday discover oil on the land, there is much risk in this investment.

Comparing Different Types of Investments

As a prudent investor, you must choose investments that suit your personal objectives. If you want to achieve a fixed return over a short-term period without any risk, you should consider investing in a certificate of deposit. The disadvantage of this investment is that it offers a relatively low return. If you want to achieve a stable return over a long-term period, you should consider Treasury bonds, or mutual funds that contain Treasury bonds. At the other extreme, if you desire a very high return, you could consider investing in land or in some small stocks.

Many investors fall in between these two extremes. They prefer a higher return than is offered by CDs or Treasury bonds but want to limit their risk. There is no formula that can determine your ideal investment because the choice depends on how much risk you want to take, and on your financial situation.

To illustrate, consider the following situations and the possible solutions shown in Exhibit 14.2. In general, you are in a better position to take some risk when you know that you will not need to sell the investment in the near future. Even if the value of the investment declines, you have the flexibility to hold on to the investment until the value increases. Conversely, individuals investing for the short term should play it safe. Since the prices of risky investments fluctuate substantially, it is dangerous to invest in a risky investment when you know that you will be selling that investment in the near future. You could be forced to sell it when the investment has a low value. Investors who decide to pursue higher potential returns must be willing to accept the high risk associated with these investments.

By having a variety of investments, you can find a tolerable risk level. You can diversify your investments among many different stocks, thereby reducing your exposure to any particular investment. If you divide your money equally among five investments and one investment performs poorly, your exposure is limited.

Exhibit 14.2 How Investment Decisions Vary with Your Situation

Situation	Decision
You have $1,000 to invest but will need the funds in one month to pay bills.	You need liquidity. You should only consider money market securities.
You have $3,000 to invest but will need the funds in a year to make a tuition payment.	You should consider safe money market securities such as a 1-year insured CD.
You have $5,000 to invest, and will likely use the funds in about 3 years when you buy a home.	Consider a 3-year insured CD, or stocks of relatively stable firms that have relatively low risk.
You have $10,000 to invest, and have no funds set aside for retirement in 20 years.	Consider investing in a diversified stock mutual fund.
You have $5,000 to invest. You expect that you will be laid off from your job within the next year.	You should probably invest the funds in money market securities so that you will have easy access to the funds if you lose your job.

Even if you diversify your portfolio among various investments, you are still exposed to general economic conditions, as the values of all investments can decline during periods in which economic conditions are weak. For this reason, you should consider diversifying among various types of investments that are not equally sensitive to economic conditions. The strategy of diversification is crucial for investors, and is given more attention in Chapter 19.

LEARNING FROM THE INVESTMENT MISTAKES OF OTHERS

Many individual investors learn from their own mistakes or the mistakes of others. Consider the following investment mistakes, so that you can avoid them.

Making Decisions Based on Unrealistic Goals

One of the most common mistakes is letting unrealistic goals dictate your investment decisions. These goals may force you to take more risk than you should, and can result in major losses.

EXAMPLE Laurie Chen has $4,000, which should cover her school expenses next year. She is considering investing the money in a one-year CD that would earn about 6 percent, or about $240 in interest before next year. However, she would like to earn a higher return on her money within the next year, so that she can buy a used car. She decides to invest in a small stock that earned a return of 50 percent last year. If the stock's value increases by 50 percent again, her investment would generate a gain of $2,000, which would allow her to buy a used car. Unfortunately, the stock's value declines by 30 percent over the year. At the end of the year, her investment is worth $2,800, a $1,200 loss. She does not have sufficient funds to buy the car or cover her school expenses. She did not view her investment as a gamble, as the money was invested in the stock of a firm. However, her investment in one small stock was just as risky as gambling, especially since she had no information to support her decision except for the fact that the stock performed well in the previous year.

Borrowing to Invest

Another common mistake is to invest money that could have been used to pay off an existing loan. The potential to earn a high return on an investment can tempt individuals to take more risk than they should.

EXAMPLE Charles Krenshaw recently took out a $5,000 loan to cover this year's college expenses. His parents gave him $5,000 so that he could pay off the loan. Rather than pay off the loan, Charles invested the $5,000 from his parents in a stock. He had hoped that he could earn a large return on the $5,000, so that he could sell the investment at the end of the year, pay off the loan, and have enough funds to travel through Europe during the summer. During the year, he had to make interest payments on the existing loan. The stock that he purchased declined in value by 90 percent, leaving him with just $500 at the end of the year. He now has insufficient funds to take a vacation, or to pay off the loan.

Taking Risks to Recover Losses from Previous Investments

Another common mistake is taking excessive risks to recover your losses. This can lead to additional losses, and may even push individuals toward bankruptcy.

E X A M P L E   Sarah Barnes lost 10 percent of her investment in the last year from investing in a diversified mutual fund. She needs the money before next winter to purchase a new furnace for her home. Yet, she wants to make up for her loss, and has shifted her money into a risky mutual fund that will likely generate a higher return if economic conditions are favorable but will perform poorly if economic conditions are unfavorable. She experiences a 20 percent loss on this investment because economic conditions weakened. She no longer has a sufficient amount of funds to pay for the furnace.

During the late 1990s, many investors bid up the prices of stocks because of their unrealistic expectations about how well these stocks would perform in the future. The media hype added to the investors' irrational exuberance. These actions created a so-called speculative bubble, meaning that once the prices are blown up to a certain level, the speculative bubble will burst, and stock prices will decline to where they should be. One reason for the generally poor stock performance in 2000–2002 was that the speculative bubble burst. In addition, economic conditions weakened. Stock prices of Motorola, Oracle, Cisco, and many other firms declined substantially in the 2000–2002 period.

While there may someday be another period in which stocks or other investments earn abnormally high returns, you should be realistic when making investment decisions. An investment that has the potential to rise substantially in value also has the potential to decline substantially in value. If you cannot afford the possible loss, you should not make that investment.

Focus on Ethics: Falling Prey to Online Investment Fraud

The Internet is a remarkably easy and inexpensive means of obtaining investment advice and researching investment opportunities. Hundreds of online newsletters recommend investments, such as specific stocks or bonds. Investors can use online bulletin boards to share information. Advice is also distributed in the form of spam, or junk e-mail.

With all of these sources at hand, it can be tough to tell the difference between legitimate and fraudulent opportunities. The recommendations could be provided by unqualified individuals or people paid by the companies to recommend their stocks or bonds. In some cases individuals send out millions of e-mails and set up Web sites to push a particular firm's stock. Others push specific investments that they already own, hoping to create more demand to drive the price higher. For some small stocks that have less than 1,000 shares traded per day, orders instigated by Internet rumors could easily push the stock price higher, at least temporarily.

To protect against this type of fraud, avoid making any investment decisions until you have the facts at hand. Obtain the annual report of the firm to review general background information. Check credible news sources such as the *Wall Street Journal*. If you would rather not wait a day to read a financial newspaper, use trustworthy online services such as Bloomberg.com (http://www.bloomberg.com). However, be careful how you interpret news about a rumor. The news source may repeat a rumor, but will not necessarily confirm that the rumor is true. Another option is to check with a trusted financial adviser. As a general rule, be wary about promises of quick profits, "guaranteed" or limited-time opportunities, or investments that are in foreign countries.

HOW INVESTMENTS FIT WITHIN YOUR FINANCIAL PLAN

The following are the key investment decisions that should be included within your financial plan:

- What are your investment goals?

- Given your existing budget, should you make investments?
- Based on your risk tolerance, how should you invest funds?

Exhibit 14.3 provides an example of how these decisions apply to Stephanie Spratt's financial plan.

Exhibit 14.3 How Investments Fit within Stephanie Spratt's Financial Plan

GOALS FOR INVESTING

1. *Determine my investment goals.*
2. *Determine whether to make investments.*
3. *Determine the types of investments that would achieve my investment goals.*

ANALYSIS OF FUNDING

Monthly Cash Inflows	*$2,500*
– Typical Monthly Expenses	*1,488*
– Monthly Car Loan Payment	*412*
= Amount of Funds Available	*$600*

ANALYSIS OF POSSIBLE INVESTMENTS

Type of Investment	Assessment
1. CDs and Other Money Market Securities	*Many money market securities provide good liquidity and are safe, but they typically offer low returns.*
2. Stocks	*Can provide high returns, but are risky given the limited amount of funds I anticipate I will have for investing.*
3. Bonds	*Some bonds have low risk, but they offer lower potential returns than stocks.*
4. Real Estate	*The value of my home may increase over time. Additional real estate investments can generate high returns but are usually risky.*
5. Stock Mutual Funds	*Can provide high returns, and offer more diversification than investing in individual stocks, but can generate losses if stock market conditions are weak.*
6. Bond Mutual Funds	*Offer more diversification than investing in individual bonds, but can generate losses if bond market conditions are weak.*

DECISION

My primary investment goal is to maintain sufficient liquidity in any funds that I invest to cover any unanticipated expenses. However, I would like to earn a return on any funds that I have until they are needed to cover expenses.

After paying for my typical monthly expenses (not including recreation), I have $600 left each month. I am not in a financial position to make long-term investments at this time because I will use some of these funds each month for recreation and will deposit the remaining funds in liquid accounts such as a money market fund. I need to increase my liquidity since I might incur unexpected home repair expenses periodically. Beyond maintaining liquidity, I hope to save enough money to pay off my car loan early. Once I pay off that loan, I will reconsider whether to invest in riskier investments that have the potential to offer a higher return. My salary should also increase over time, which will make investments more affordable.

When I start long-term investing, I will consider stock mutual funds and bond mutual funds rather than individual stocks or bonds. I can periodically invest in mutual funds with small amounts of money and achieve diversification benefits. Since I already own a home, I do not want to invest in additional real estate.

DISCUSSION QUESTIONS

1. How would Stephanie's investing decisions be different if she were a single mother of two children?

2. How would Stephanie's investing decisions be affected if she were 35 years old? If she were 50 years old?

SUMMARY

Common types of investments include money market securities, stocks, bonds, mutual funds, and real estate. Each type of investment is unique in terms of how it provides a return to its investors.

The return on an investment is determined by the income that the investment generates and the capital gain of the investment over the investment horizon. Some stocks offer periodic income in the form of dividends, while bonds offer periodic income in the form of coupon payments.

The risk from making an investment varies among types of investments. In particular, money market securities tend to have low risk, while many stocks and real estate investments have high risk. However, the risk also varies within a particular type of investment. Some money market securities have more risk than others. Some stocks have more risk than others.

Investors weigh the tradeoff between return and risk when making investments. When they select investments that have the potential to offer high returns, they must accept a higher degree of risk. Alternatively, they can select invest-

ments that have lower risk, but they must accept a relatively low return. The proper choice is dependent on the investor's willingness to accept risk, which is influenced by the investor's financial position. Some investors are not in a financial position in which they can afford to take much risk, and should therefore select investments that have little or no risk.

You can learn from investment mistakes made by others. In particular, do not make investments that are driven by unrealistic goals. Do not invest when the funds could be more properly used to pay off existing debt. Do not attempt high-risk investments as a means of recovering recent losses. Recognize the risk of making investments that may be experiencing a speculative bubble.

INTEGRATING THE KEY CONCEPTS

Your investment decisions can affect your income (dividends and capital gains). Since these decisions can affect your cash inflows over time, they may also affect your liquidity (Part 2). They may also affect the amount of financing you need (Part 3), the amount of insurance you need (Part 4), and your retirement planning (Part 6).

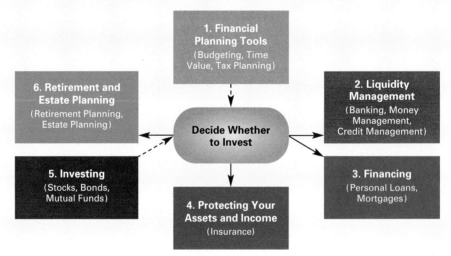

REVIEW QUESTIONS

1. What should your first priority of investing be? What is the disadvantage of investments that satisfy that priority?

2. What are stocks? How are stocks beneficial to corporations? Why do investors invest in stocks?

3. Distinguish between the primary and secondary stock markets. Why does the price of a stock change each day in the secondary market?

4. Classify and describe the two types of investors. What are day traders?

5. How do shareholders earn returns from investing in stocks? How is the market value of a firm determined? What determines the market price of a stock?

6. What type of firm typically pays dividends? What are growth stocks? What are income stocks?

7. What are dividends? Do all firms pay them?

8. Discuss the differences between common stock and preferred stock.

9. What are bonds? How do bonds provide a return to investors?

10. How do mutual funds operate? Who manages mutual funds? How are coupon or dividend payments handled by the mutual fund? Can investors incur capital losses with mutual funds?

11. In what geographic areas is the price of land relatively high? What components make up the return from investing in real estate?

12. What is the formula for estimating returns on dividend-paying stocks? Describe each element of the formula. How do you calculate the dollar amount of your returns?

13. What is the difference in tax rates on long-term versus short-term capital gains?

14. How can investments in stock increase your wealth? How would you calculate the value of a stock investment of a single sum over time? How would you calculate the value of a stock investment of a specific amount over several periods?

15. Define the risk of an investment. What types of firms are particularly risky?

16. Why do investors measure risk? Describe the two common measures of risk.

17. What is the return-risk tradeoff? What types of stock investments are particularly tempting for stock investors? What other factors must individual investors consider before making this type of investment?

18. Describe the return-risk tradeoffs among bonds, mutual funds, and real estate investments.

19. How can you limit your risk through diversification?

20. Describe common investment mistakes made by individuals.

FINANCIAL PLANNING PROBLEMS

1. Joel purchased 100 shares of stock for $20 per share. During the year, he received dividend checks amounting to $150. Joel recently sold the stock for $32 per share. What was Joel's return on the stock?

2. What is the dollar amount of Joel's return (see question 1)?

3. Joel (from question 1) is in a 25 percent tax bracket. What amount of taxes will he pay on his capital gain if he held the stock for less than a year?

4. How much would Joel (from question 1) save in taxes if he held the stock for more than a year, assuming he sold it for the same amount?

5. Emma bought a stock a year ago for $53 per share. She received no dividends on the stock and sold the stock today for $38 per share. What is Emma's return on the stock?

6. Tammy has $3,500 that she wants to invest in stock. She believes she can earn a 12 percent annual return. What would be the value of Tammy's investment in 10 years if she is able to achieve her goal?

7. Dawn decides to invest $2,000 each year in stock at the end of each of the next five years. She believes she can earn a 9 percent return over that time period. How much will Dawn's investment be worth at the end of five years?

8. Bob purchased a dot-com stock, which was heavily advertised on the Internet for $40 per share shortly after the stock's IPO. Over the next three years, the stock price declined by 15 percent each year. What is the company's stock price after three years?

9. Floyd wants to invest the $15,000 he received from his grandfather's estate. He wants to use the money to finance his education when he pursues his doctorate in five years. What amount will he have in five years if he earns a 9 percent return? If he receives a 10 percent return? If he receives a 12 percent return?

10. Morris will start investing $1,500 a year in stocks. He feels he can average a 12 percent return. If he follows this plan, how much will he accumulate in 5 years? In 10 years? In 20 years?

11. Thomas purchased 400 shares of stock A for $23 a share and sold them more than a year later for $20 per share. He purchased 500 shares of stock B for $40 per share and sold them for $53 per share after holding them for more than a year. Both of the sales were in the same year. If Thomas is in a 25 percent tax bracket, what will his capital gains tax be for the year?

12. Charles just sold 500 shares of stock A for $12,000. In addition, he just sold 600 shares of stock A for $6,000. Charles had paid $20 per share for all his shares of stock A. What amount of loss will he have, assuming both sales were on stocks held for more than one year?

Ethical Dilemma

13. Carlo and Rita's daughter just celebrated her 16th birthday and Carlo and Rita realize they have accumulated only half the money they will need for their daughter's college education. With college just two years away, they are concerned about how they will save the remaining amount in such a short time.

    Carlo regularly has lunch with Sam, a co-worker. While discussing his dilemma of financing his daughter's education, Sam tells Carlo about an investment that he made based on a tip from his cousin, Leo, that doubled his money in just over one year. Sam tells Carlo that Leo assured him that there was very little risk involved. Carlo asks Sam if he will contact Leo to see if he has any additional hot tips that could double his daughter's college savings in two years with virtually no risk.

    The next day at lunch Sam gives Carlo the name of a stock that Leo recommended. It is a small startup company that Leo believes will double within the next 24 months with virtually no risk. Carlo immediately invests his daughter's college fund into the stock of the company. Six months later, Carlo receives a letter from the company announcing they are out of business and closing their doors. Upon calling his broker, Carlo finds the stock is now worthless.

    a. Comment on Leo's ethics of assuring his friends and relatives that the investments he recommends can produce major rewards with virtually no risk.

    b. What basic investing principle did Carlo forget in his desire to fund his daughter's college education?

FINANCIAL PLANNING ONLINE EXERCISES

1. Go to http://www.quicken.com/taxes/capgains. The purpose of this exercise is to estimate the capital gains taxes that you might owe on a stock investment if you held it for 12 months or less, versus more than 12 months.

    a. Input the following information in the online calculator: $1600 for initial investment, $2300 for current value, 15 percent federal tax rate. Select "12 months or less" for the holding period. Click "Calculate." Make a note of the taxes you would owe (displayed in the text box).

    b. Now select "More than 12 months" for the holding period. Click "Calculate" again. Under which holding period do you pay the least taxes?

    c. What effect does the holding period have on your return on investment?

    d. What effect does the tax rate have on the return for each option? What role should taxes play in making investment decisions?

2. Go to http://www.bankofamerica.com. Under "Financial Education & Tools" click on "Investing." Then click the "Planning Tools" tab, and click on "Investing." Under "Stocks" (under "Investing") click "At what price should I sell a stock to achieve my target rate of return?" A calculator page is displayed. The purpose of this exercise is to estimate the price at which you need to sell a stock you own in order to achieve a return that you specify.

    a. Enter a 12 percent annualized return desired, $30 share price at purchase, 200 shares purchased, $100 average quarterly dividend, 60 months owned, 15 percent federal tax rate, and 8 percent state tax rate. The fees at purchase and sale are fixed dollar amounts of $200 each. Enter zeros for "Fees at Sale," "Fees at Purchase," "Percent of Total Amount," and "Dollar Amount per Share." Dividend income is invested elsewhere at a rate of 4 percent. Click the "Results" tab. What is the selling price necessary to achieve your target return? Click "Graphs" to view the results graphically.

    b. Now change the annualized return desired to 30 percent and check the results and graph. What is the selling price necessary to achieve your desired return?

    c. Now change the annualized return desired to 12 percent, federal tax rate to 25 percent, and state tax rate to 8 percent. Check the results and graph. At what price must you sell the stock to achieve your target return?

    d. What impact does a higher desired return have on the selling price? What impact do federal and state taxes have on the necessary selling price for a desired return?

BUILDING YOUR OWN FINANCIAL PLAN

Very likely, some of the goals you established in Chapter 1 can best be met through investing. Before taking the plunge into investing, however, you need to address a few questions.

The first of these is to determine your risk tolerance. Not all investors have the "stomach" for the uncertainty surrounding returns on investments.

The next issue to be addressed is how different investments are suited to different goals. For example, a growth stock might be desirable if your goal is to build savings for a retirement that is 30 years away, while a certificate of deposit might be better suited to provide the down payment for a house within the next five years.

The decision as to what kind of investment is right for a particular goal should be reviewed annualy. The closer a goal comes to fulfillment, the more likely it is that a change in investing strategy will be necessary.

Go to the worksheets at the end of this chapter, and to the CD-ROM accompanying this text, to continue building your financial plan.

THE SAMPSONS—A CONTINUING CASE

Recall that the Sampsons recently started saving about $300 per month ($3,600 per year) for their children's college education. They are currently investing this amount in bank CDs each month, but they are now considering investing in stock instead. Dave and Sharon have never owned stock before. They are currently earning an interest rate of 5 percent on their CDs. If they invest in a specific stock from this point on, they will achieve an annual return ranging from 2 to 9 percent. The stock will generate an annual return of only 2 percent if stock market conditions are weak in the future, but it could generate an annual return of 9 percent if stock market conditions are strong. The Sampsons want to compare the potential returns of investing in stock to the CD.

Go to the worksheets at the end of this chapter, and to the CD-ROM accompanying this text, to continue this case.

Chapter 14: Building Your Own Financial Plan

GOALS

1. Determine whether to invest, given your current cash flows.
2. Determine what kinds of investments you should purchase to meet your financial goals.

ANALYSIS

1. Review your cash flow statement to determine how much you can afford to invest in stocks each month.
2. Evaluate your risk tolerance to see if your temperament is suited to the uncertainty of stock investments.

Risk Tolerance Quiz

Answer True or False by entering an X in the appropriate box.
(The Excel worksheet will offer an assessment based on your input.)

	TRUE	FALSE
1. If I own stock, I will check its price at least daily if not more often.	☐	☐
2. When driving on an interstate, and traffic and weather permit, I never drive in excess of the posted speed limit.	☐	☐
3. If the price of my stock declines, my first reaction is to sell.		
4. Another stock market crash similar to 1929 could occur very unexpectedly.	☐	☐
5. When I fly in less than perfect weather, I tend to get nervous and concerned about my safety.	☐	☐
6. If I sold a stock at a loss of more than 25 percent, it would greatly shake my confidence in my ability to invest.	☐	☐
7. I intensely dislike blind dates.	☐	☐
8. When I travel, I write down a packing list to be sure that I don't forget anything.	☐	☐
9. When traveling with others, I prefer to do the driving.	☐	☐
10. Before buying a bond I would want to talk to at least two other people to confirm my choice.	☐	☐

Results

0–3 True: You have the risk tolerance to invest in individual common stocks.

4–6 True: You would be a nervous investor, but with more knowledge and a few successes, you could probably raise your risk tolerance to a suitable level. Mutual funds might prove a good starting point for your level of risk tolerance.

7–10 True: You are probably a very conservative and risk-intolerant investor who is probably better suited to a bond portfolio.

3. Determine whether investments will help you achieve your short-, intermediate-, and long-term goals. Complete the worksheet below for the short-, intermediate-, and long-term goals that you have established and reviewed throughout the course. In determining whether investing is suitable for each goal, take into consideration the timeline for accomplishing the goal, the critical nature of the goal, and, of course, the results of your risk tolerance test. For those goals that you determine investments are not suitable, enter "No" in column two, and do not complete the rest of the line for that goal. If, however, you enter "Yes" in column two, think about the kind of investment that is appropriate and justify your selection of stocks as a risk-appropriate means to accomplish this goal.

Short-Term Goals	Suitable? Yes or No	Type of Investment	Justification
1.			
2.			
3.			

Intermediate-Term Goals	Suitable? Yes or No	Type of Investment	Justification
1.			
2.			
3.			

Long-Term Goals	Suitable? Yes or No	Type of Investment	Justification
1.			
2.			
3.			

DECISIONS

1. Summarize your reasoning for either investing or not investing to meet your goals.

_____

_____

_____

_____

_____

_____

2. If you decide to invest, how much will you invest each month? What types of investments will you purchase? Why?

Chapter 14: The Sampsons—A Continuing Case

CASE QUESTIONS

1. Compare the returns from investing in bank CDs to the possible returns from stock over the next 12 years by filling in the following worksheet.

Savings Accumulated over the Next 12 Years

	CD: Annual Return = 5%	Weak Stock Market Conditions	Strong Stock Market Conditions
Amount Invested per Year	$3600	$3600	$3600
Annual Return	5%	2%	9%
FVIFA (n = 12 Years)			
Value of Investments in 12 Years			

2. Explain to the Sampsons why there is a tradeoff when investing in bank CDs versus stock to support their children's future college education.

3. Advise the Sampsons on whether they should invest their money each month in bank CDs, in stocks, or in some combination of the two, to save for their children's college education.

4. The Sampsons are considering investing in an IPO of a high-tech firm, since they have heard that the return on IPOs can be very high. Advise the Sampsons on this course of action.

Chapter 15

Stock Analysis and Valuation

B lake thought he had a good strategy for investing. For any company in which he was interested, he carefully read the summary provided by the chief executive in the company's annual report. He also read research reports about those companies, which were provided by investment companies. His confidence in investing grew because each company in which he was interested also had a very optimistic view in its annual report. In addition, the research reports provided about these companies were always very positive. Blake was so confident, he invested all $9,000 of his savings in stocks. After a year, many of the stocks that Blake owned experienced large price declines. Blake could not understand how this could occur, since his own view of the stocks was fully supported by the annual reports and other research reports.

What Blake learned the hard way was that most outlooks by chief executives and research reports by investment companies tend to be overly optimistic. If Blake had relied on a more objective method of stock analysis and valuation, he may have been able to make better investments.

This chapter explains how to conduct stock analysis and valuation so that you can make investment decisions that enhance your wealth.

The objectives of this chapter are to:

- Describe how to interpret stock quotations,

- Illustrate how to conduct an analysis of a firm,

- Describe how to conduct an economic analysis of stocks,

- Show how to conduct an industry analysis of stocks, and

- Explain how to value stocks.

STOCK QUOTATIONS

If you're considering investing in stocks, you will need to learn how to obtain and interpret stock price quotations. Fortunately, price quotations are readily available for actively traded stocks. The most up-to-date quotes can be obtained online. Price information is available from stockbrokers and is widely published by the news media. Popular sources of stock quotations are financial newspapers (such as the *Wall Street Journal*), business sections of many local newspapers, financial news television networks (such as CNBC), and financial Web sites.

Stock quotations provide information about the price of each stock over the previous day or a recent period. An example of stock quotations provided by the *Wall Street Journal* is shown in Exhibit 15.1. Notice that the name of the stock is abbreviated in the third column. To the left (the first and second columns), the high (HI) and low (LO) price of the stock is provided. Those stocks that are subject to much more uncertainty tend to have a wider range in prices over time. Some investors use this range as a simple measure of the firm's risk.

Exhibit 15.1 Daily Stock Quotations

52-WEEK HI	LO	STOCK (DIV)	YLD %	PE	VOL 100s	CLOSE	NET CHG
16.13	8.65	BiminiMtg 1.99e	21.7	5	1575	9.17	0.12
26.06	19.39	BiomdRltyTr 1.08	4.4	55	4250	24.30	-0.10
27.28	13.74	Biovail .50p	...	24	16514	24.83	1.10
16.71	12.44	BisysGp lf	...	26	6970	14.22	0.21
93.71	75.70	BlackDeck 1.12	1.3	13	9554	87.89	0.93
44.63	29.19	BlackHills 1.28	3.6	45	3350	35.25	0.64
113.87	69.38	BlkRk A 1.20	1.1	34	901	109	0.52
30	22.99	BlockHR s .50	2.0	14	31753	24.45	-0.10
10.65	3.19	Blkbstr A .06j	...	dd	16535	3.73	-0.02
10.18	2.96	Blkbstr B .04e	1.2	...	1618	3.39	0.06
19.60	14.60	BlountInt	...	11	1852	16.66	0.73
11.41	8.45	BlSqIsrael .52e	4.7	...	22	10.96	0.62
24.75	12.10	Bluegreen	...	11	3646	16.70	0.90
18.25	8.25	BluelinxHldgs .50	4.4	18	791	11.39	0.14
33.84	17.70♣	Blyth .46f	2.2	11	1848	20.69	-0.26
19.51	17.58	BdwlkPipePtnr n	...	...	2168	18.64	0.66
72.40	49.52	Boeing 1.20f	1.7	25	49135	70.44	0.20
18	11.50	BoisDArcEngy n	...	...	801	16.08	0.22
6.59	2.67	Bombay	...	dd	2577	2.92	-0.04
27.47	18.65	BordersGrp .40f	1.9	16	7639	21.46	-0.21
↓ 61.73	44.85	BorgWarner .64f	1.0	15	3384	61.76	1.13
27.27	19.85	BostBeer	...	23	422	24.95	-0.05
76.67	56.66	BostProp 2.72a	3.6	25	6644	75.36	1.23
35.50	22.80	BosSci	...	36	39666	24.46	-0.03
44.40	24.73	Bowater .80	2.6	dd	10195	30.77	0.05
16.16	11.65♣	Bowne .22	1.5	17	1043	15.14	0.30
59.25	37.34	BoydGaming .50	1.0	24	8633	48.40	0.74
15.48	8.83	BoykinLdg	...	16	478	12.42	0.20
18.50	7.47	BrdleyPharm lf	...	8	1521	9.35	-0.15
39.90	26.30	Brady A s .52	1.4	20	1723	37.06	0.88
33.42	25.88	BrndywnRlty 1.76	6.1	51	4422	28.94	1.03

52-WEEK HI	LO	STOCK (DIV)	YLD %	PE	VOL 100s	CLOSE	NET CHG
49.99	42.91	Citigroup 1.76	3.6	11	152841	49.29	0.76
14.05	12.08	CtznComm 1.00a	8.2	31	24603	12.15	-0.08
7.01	4.74♣	Ctzn A stk	...	27	344	5.48	0.03
76.10	66.39	CityNtl 1.44	2.0	17	2072	73.69	1.25
29.74	19.67	ClairStrs .40a	1.4	18	13078	29.20	-0.02
31.98	24.60	Clarcor s .27	.9	22	2507	30.42	0.71
18.49	12.03	Clark .24	1.8	17	798	13.60	0.35
33.60	27.54	ClearChanl .75	2.4	26	30873	31.85	0.40
20.40	17.75	ClrChOutdrHldg n	...	...	1076	19.59	-0.46
24.36	18.93	CLECO .90	4.2	13	4048	21.36	0.51
99.25	46.80	ClvlndClfs s .80	.9	6	4197	92.58	4.01
66.04	52.50	Clorox 1.16f	2.0	9	7306	57.15	0.26
36.84	24.51	Coach s	...	31	25277	33.30	-0.04
17.49	10.76	Coachmen .24	2.0	dd	369	12.16	0.35
45.26	40.31	CocaCola 1.12	2.7	19	66513	40.90	0.59
29	22.08	CC Femsa ADS .31e	1.1	...	1084	27.38	0.37
23.92	18.52	CocaColaEnt .16	.8	14	20816	19.27	0.10
31.55	23	CocaCola ADS .33e	1.1	...	17	29.45	0.17
4.70	2.70	Coeur dAMn	...	cc	70916	4.28	0.28
↓ 17.49	15.80	CogdellSpncr n 1.40p	...	...	605	17.35	0.46
23.62	14.80	CohenSteers .44	2.3	23	401	19.21	0.58
64.02	52.55	ColesMyer ADS 1.99e	3.3	...	61	60.85	1.31
57.15	48.25	ColgatePalm 1.16	2.1	24	18253	54.91	0.06
26	19.56	ColonlBcgp .61	2.6	16	8206	23.90	0.08
47.90	35.55♣	ColonlProp 2.70	6.2	10	2080	43.22	1.24
16.40	13.65	ColumEqtyTr n .26e	1.6	...	1417	16.20	0.05
63.38	53.17	Comerica 2.20	3.8	11	16453	57.60	0.84
9.95	6.15	CmfrtSysUSA .03p	...	28	1699	9.39	0.19
35.98	26.87	ComrcBcpNJ s .48f	1.4	19	25460	34.33	-0.08
70	53.25	CommrcGpInc 1.52	2.7	8	592	56.77	-0.51
39	22.74	ComrclMtls s .24	.6	8	13337	38.17	0.63

The annual dividends (if any) paid on the stock appear just to the right of the name of the stock. The dividend yield (annual dividends as a percentage of the stock price) is shown in the fourth column. This represents the annual return that you would receive soley from dividends if you purchased the stock today, and if the dividend payments remain unchanged.

In the fifth column is the price-earnings (PE) ratio, which represents the stock price divided by the firm's earnings per share. Some investors closely monitor the PE ratio when attempting to value stocks, as will be discussed in more detail later in this chapter.

The remaining information summarizes the trading of the stock on the previous day. The sixth column shows the volume of trading (in 100s). For some widely traded stocks, a million shares may trade per day, while 20,000 or fewer shares may trade per day for smaller stocks.

The seventh column shows the closing price (CLOSE), which is the price at the end of the day when the stock market closes. The last column discloses the net change (NET CHG) in the price of the stock, which is measured as the change in the closing price from the previous day. Investors review this column to determine how stock prices changed from one day to the next.

Review the stock quotations of Black & Decker in Exhibit 15.1. Its stock price has traded between $75.70 and $93.71 per share over the last year. It pays an annual dividend of $1.12 per share. This annual dividend reflects a dividend yield of 1.3 percent, meaning that investors purchasing the stock at the time of this quotation would earn an annual dividend equal to 1.3 percent of their investment if the annual dividend remains unchanged. The price-earnings ratio is 13, which means that the prevailing stock price of Black & Decker is 13 times its annual earnings per share. Its volume of trading for the day was 955,400 shares. At the close of trading in the stock market, its stock price was $87.89. The net change in the price was up $.93 per share from the day before.

15.1 Financial Planning Online: Stock Information

Go to
http://www.bloomberg.com

This Web site provides stock quotations for the stocks that you specify. It also provides a summary of financial market conditions and links to information about investments.

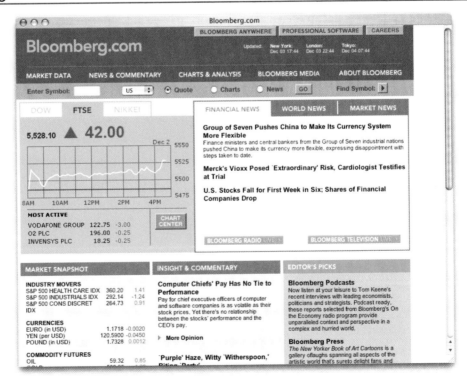

ANALYSIS OF THE FIRM

One firm can outperform another in the same industry because its managers make better decisions about how to finance its business, market its products, and manage its employees. By conducting an analysis of a firm, you can assess its future performance.

Annual Report

Firms that are publicly traded create an annual report that contains standardized financial information. Specifically, the report includes a letter from the firm's chief executive officer (CEO) summarizing recent performance and expected performance in the future. It also contains financial statements measuring the firm's financial condition that you can examine in the same manner that you evaluate your personal financial statements to determine your financial condition. Many annual reports can be downloaded online. Prospective investors typically focus on the balance sheet and income statement.

balance sheet
A financial statement that indicates a firm's sources of funds and how it has invested its funds as of a particular point in time.

Balance Sheet. The firm's **balance sheet** indicates its sources of funds and how it has invested its funds as of a particular point in time. The balance sheet shown in Exhibit 15.2 is segmented into two parts: (1) assets and (2) liabilities and shareholder's equity. These two parts must balance.

The firm's assets indicate how it has invested its funds and what it owns. Assets are often classified as short-term and long-term assets. Short-term assets include cash, securities purchased by the firm, accounts receivable (money owed to the firm for previous sales), and inventories (materials used to produce products and finished products waiting to be sold). Long-term assets (sometimes called fixed assets) include machinery and buildings purchased by the firm.

The liabilities and shareholder's equity indicate how the firm has obtained its funds. Liabilities represent the amount owed to creditors or suppliers and are classified as short term or long term. Shareholder's equity is the net worth of the firm. It represents the investment in the firm by investors.

income statement
A financial statement that measures a firm's revenues, expenses, and earnings over a particular period of time.

Income Statement. The firm's **income statement** measures its revenues, expenses, and earnings over a particular period of time. Investors use it to determine how much income (earnings) the firm generated over a particular period or what expenses the firm incurred. An annual report may include an income statement for the year of concern and for the four quarters within that year.

An example of an income statement is shown in Exhibit 15.3. The income statement starts with revenues generated by the firm over the period of concern. Then the cost of goods sold (which includes the cost of materials used in production) is subtracted to

---

Exhibit 15.2 Balance Sheet for Stewart Corporation (Numbers Are in Millions)

Assets		Liabilities and Shareholder's Equity	
Short-term (current) assets		Short-term liabilities	
Cash and marketable securities	$100	Accounts payable	$300
Accounts receivable	400	Short-term debt	0
Inventories	500	**Total short-term liabilities**	**$300**
Total short-term assets	**$1,000**		
Fixed assets	$400	**Long-term debt**	**$200**
Less depreciation	−100		
Net fixed assets	**$300**	**Shareholder's equity**	800
Total assets	**$1,300**	**Total liabilities and shareholder's equity**	**$1,300**

Exhibit 15.3 Income Statement for Stewart Corporation (Numbers Are in Millions)

Revenue (Sales)	$3,000
Cost of goods sold	1,400
Gross profit	$1,600
Operating expenses	1,130
Earnings before interest and taxes	$470
Interest expense	20
Earnings before taxes	$450
Taxes	150
Earnings after taxes	$300

derive gross profit. Operating expenses (such as salaries) are subtracted from the gross profit to determine earnings before interest and taxes (also referred to as operating profit). Finally, interest payments and taxes are subtracted to determine the earnings after taxes (also referred to as net profit).

Firm-Specific Characteristics

Investors use a firm's balance sheet and income statement to analyze the following characteristics:

- Liquidity

- Financial leverage

- Efficiency

- Profitability

Each of these characteristics is described in turn, and some popular ratios used to measure these characteristics are summarized in Exhibit 15.4 and applied to Stewart Corporation's financial statements.

Liquidity. A firm's assets and liabilities can be assessed to determine its liquidity, or its ability to cover any expenses. A firm has a high degree of liquidity if it has a large amount of assets that can be easily converted to cash and has a relatively small amount of short-term liabilities. You can assess a firm's liquidity by computing its **current ratio**, which is the ratio of its short-term assets to its short-term liabilities. A high ratio relative to the industry norm represents a relatively high degree of liquidity.

Financial Leverage. Investors assess a firm's balance sheet to determine its ability to make debt payments. A firm obtains funds by borrowing funds from suppliers or creditors or by selling shares of its stock (equity) to investors. Many firms prefer to borrow funds rather than issue stock. An excessive amount of stock may spread the shareholder ownership of the firm too thin, placing downward pressure on the stock price. If a firm borrows too much money, however, it may have difficulty making its interest payments on loans. The firm's **financial leverage** indicates its reliance on debt to support its operations.

A firm's financial leverage can be measured by its **debt ratio**, which measures the proportion of total assets financed with debt. A firm with a high debt ratio relative to the industry norm has a high degree of financial leverage and therefore may have a relatively high risk of default on its future debt payments. Some firms with a relatively high

current ratio
The ratio of a firm's short-term assets to its short-term liabilities.

financial leverage
A firm's reliance on debt to support its operations.

debt ratio
A measure of financial leverage that measures the proportion of total assets financed with debt.

Exhibit 15.4 Ratios Used to Analyze Stewart Corporation

Measures of Liquidity

Stewart Corporation (numbers in millions)

$$\text{Current ratio} = \frac{\text{current assets}}{\text{current liabilities}}$$

$$\text{Current ratio} = \frac{\$1,000}{\$300} = 3.33$$

Measures of Financial Leverage

$$\text{Debt ratio} = \frac{\text{total long-term debt}}{\text{total assets}}$$

$$\text{Debt ratio} = \frac{\$200}{\$1,300} = .15$$

$$\text{Times interest earned ratio} = \frac{\text{earnings before interest and taxes}}{\text{interest payments}}$$

$$\text{Times interest earned ratio} = \frac{\$470}{\$20} = 23.5$$

Measures of Efficiency

$$\text{Inventory turnover} = \frac{\text{cost of goods sold}}{\text{average daily inventory}}$$

$$\text{Inventory turnover} = \frac{\$1,400}{\$500^*} = 2.8$$

$$\text{Average collection period} = \frac{\text{average receivables}}{\text{average daily sales}}$$

$$\text{Average collection period} = \frac{\$400}{(\$3,000/365)} = 48.67$$

$$\text{Asset turnover ratio} = \frac{\text{sales}}{\text{average total assets}}$$

$$\text{Asset turnover ratio} = \frac{\$3,000}{\$1,300^\dagger} = 2.31$$

Profitability Ratios

$$\text{Net profit margin} = \frac{\text{earnings}}{\text{sales}}$$

$$\text{Net profit margin} = \frac{\$300}{\$3,000} = 10\%$$

$$\text{Return on assets} = \frac{\text{earnings}}{\text{assets}}$$

$$\text{Return on assets} = \frac{\$300}{\$1,300} = 23\%$$

$$\text{Return on equity} = \frac{\text{earnings}}{\text{equity}}$$

$$\text{Return on equity} = \frac{\$300}{\$800} = 37.5\%$$

*This assumes that the inventory level represents the average level during the year.
†This assumes that the prevailing asset level represents the average level.

times interest earned ratio
A measure of financial leverage that measures the ratio of the firm's earnings before interest and taxes to its total interest payments.

degree of financial leverage can easily cover their debt payments if they generate stable cash inflows over time. The debt ratio focuses just on the firm's level of debt and does not account for its cash flows. Thus, a more appropriate measure of a firm's ability to repay its debt is the **times interest earned ratio**, which measures the ratio of the firm's earnings before interest and taxes to its total interest payments. A high times interest earned ratio (relative to the industry norm) means that the firm should be more capable of covering its debt payments.

Efficiency. The composition of assets can indicate how efficiently a firm uses its funds. If it generates a relatively low level of sales and earnings with a large amount of assets, it is not using its assets efficiently. A firm that invests in assets has to obtain funds to support those assets. The less assets it uses to generate its sales, the less funds it needs to borrow or obtain by issuing stock.

You can use the **inventory turnover** to measure how efficiently a firm manages its inventory. It is calculated as the cost of goods sold divided by average daily inventory. A higher number relative to the industry norm represents relatively high turnover, which is more efficient.

You can use the **average collection period** to determine the average age of accounts receivable. It is measured as accounts receivable divided by average daily sales. A higher number relative to the industry norm means a longer collection period, which is less efficient.

You can use the **asset turnover ratio** to assess how efficiently a firm uses its assets. This ratio is measured as sales divided by average total assets. A higher number relative to the industry norm reflects higher efficiency.

Profitability. You can also use the income statement and balance sheet to assess a firm's profitability. The **operating profit margin** is the operating profit divided by sales, and the **net profit margin** measures net profit as a percentage of sales. The **return on assets** is the net profit divided by total assets. The **return on equity** is measured as net profit divided by the owner's investment in the firm (stockholder's equity). The higher the profitability ratios relative to the industry norm, the higher the firm's profitability.

Information Provided by Value Line

Firm-specific information is also available from Value Line Investment Survey. Each component of Exhibit 15.5 discussed here is designated with a letter code. The name of the firm is shown in the top left corner (a). Along the top of the page, notice the recent stock price (b), the price-earnings (PE) ratio (c), the relative PE ratio comparable to other firms in the industry (d), and the firm's dividend yield, equal to annual dividends divided by the price per share (e).

Just below the firm's name in the upper left corner are Value Line's ratings of the firm (f). The firm's beta (g), which measures the sensitivity of its stock price relative to the market, is shown below those ratings. To the right of the beta is the firm's stock price trend over the last several years (h). The firm's stock trading volume information (i) appears below the stock price trend.

In the middle of the page is a spreadsheet that shows the trends of various financial statistics that are identified in the right margin. The top rows of the spreadsheet (j) show the financial statistics on a per share basis so that they can be compared with those of other firms.

In the middle of the spreadsheet, you will find the trend of the PE ratio (k), the relative PE ratio (l), and the dividend yield (m). Also notice the trends of various profitability ratios, including the net profit margin (n).

The firm's long-term sources of funds are shown in the section called "capital structure" (o) to the left of the bottom part of the spreadsheet. Just below the capital structure is information (p) that can be used to assess the firm's liquidity. Below that information, you will find quarterly data on sales (q), earnings (r), and dividends (s). A general summary of the firm's business (t) appears below the right portion of the spreadsheet and a general analysis of the business (u) appears below the business summary.

inventory turnover
A measure of efficiency; computed as the cost of goods sold divided by average daily inventory.

average collection period
A measure of efficiency; computed as accounts receivable divided by average daily sales.

asset turnover ratio
A measure of efficiency; computed as sales divided by average total assets.

operating profit margin
A firm's operating profit divided by sales.

net profit margin
A measure of profitability that measures net profit as a percentage of sales.

return on assets
A measure of profitability; computed as net profit divided by total assets.

return on equity
A measure of profitability; computed as net profit divided by the owner's investment in the firm (stockholder's equity).

"Remember, the customer always comes first in the billing department."

Exhibit 15.5 An Example from Value Line Investment Survey

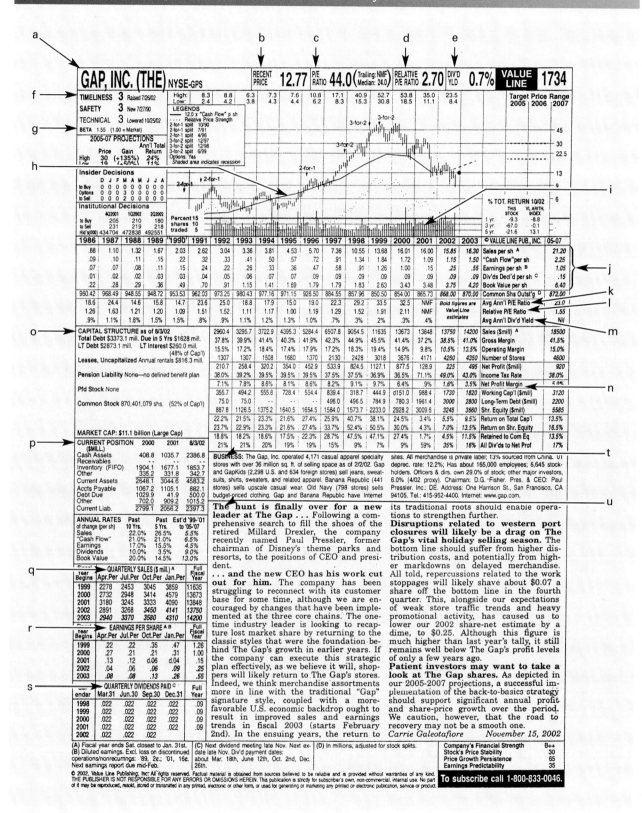

15.2 Financial Planning Online: Determining Industry Norms

Go to
http://biz.yahoo.com/
research/indgrp

This Web site provides
information on various
industry groups and allows
you to obtain financial
information on firms you
specify in any industry. By
reviewing financial information for various firms within
an industry, you can mea-
sure the industry norm.

Focus on Ethics: Accounting Fraud

Recent nationwide scandals have brought attention to the accounting practices of certain firms. These scandals have made investors question whether they can use a firm's
financial statements to assess its performance. Since 2001, many firms have either
acknowledged or have been suspected of overstating their revenue, including Enron,
Xerox, Qwest Communications, Dynegy, Global Crossing, Gemstar, Reliant Resources,
Adelphia Communications, and WorldCom.

Motivation for Fraud. The top managers of a firm are commonly evaluated according
to how the firm's value (as measured by stock price) changes over time. These managers
may receive shares of the firm's stock as part of their compensation. Their goal is to
increase the value of the firm, so that they can sell their shares at a high price and earn
a high level of compensation.

Consequently, they may seek an accounting method that will either inflate their level
of revenue or deflate their reported level of expenses, so that they can boost their
reported earnings. Investors who use those reported earnings to derive the stock value
will buy the stock when they believe that the firm's earnings have risen. Their actions
push the value of the stock higher.

Some accounting methods may only inflate revenue or deflate expenses for a short-
term period, which means that the managers cannot boost their reported earnings indef-
initely. At some point, investors will recognize that the estimates are misleading, and
they will sell their holdings in the firm's stock.

Revenue-Inflating Techniques. The accounting methods used to measure revenue can
vary substantially, which makes it difficult for investors to compare various financial
ratios among firms. Several examples of accounting methods used to inflate revenue are
listed here:

- A service firm may have a five-year contract with a client, in which the client can
cancel the agreement after the first year. The firm records the expected revenue

over the next five years in the first year of the contract, even though it only received payment for the first year.

- A publisher of a magazine receives three-year subscriptions, in which payment is made annually. It reports all of these sales as revenue even when the cash has not been received. The cash flow attributed to the sales will either occur in a future period, or not at all.

- A firm uses a lenient policy that allows customers to cancel their orders. The firm counts all the orders as revenue even though it is likely that many of the orders will be canceled.

The Enron and WorldCom Scandals. The scandals involving Enron in 2001 and WorldCom in 2002 highlight the degree to which revenue, expenses, and earnings can be misstated. Enron was formed in 1985 and grew to become the seventh-largest firm in the United States by 2000. Investors did not recognize that Enron's earnings were distorted until the fall of 2001. Once Enron knew that it was being investigated, it announced that it was restating its earnings for the previous five years, as it had overestimated earnings over that period by about $600 million. The stock price abruptly declined as investors recognized that the stock was overvalued. In December 2001, Enron filed for bankruptcy.

During the year before Enron's financial problems were known by the public, 29 Enron executives sold some of their holdings of Enron stock for more than $1 billion. It appears that these executives knew the stock was overvalued. Many investors who believed that the reported earnings were accurate paid a much higher price for the stock than they should have and lost all or most of their investment.

In June 2002, WorldCom admitted that it had underestimated its expenses by $3.8 billion over the previous five quarters. Once again, there were many investors who had paid a high price for the shares because they trusted the earnings report. Those who owned the shares at the time this news was disclosed lost most or all of their investment.

Preventing Future Accounting Fraud. Publicly traded firms are required to have their financial statements audited by an independent auditor to ensure that the statements are accurate. Yet, auditors did not prevent Enron, WorldCom, or many other firms from issuing inaccurate financial statements. One reason for this type of negligence is that the auditors want to keep their clients. They may worry that if they force a firm to report more accurate earnings, the firm will hire a different auditor in the future. Arthur Andersen was the accounting firm responsible for auditing Enron. In the year 2000, it received $25 million in auditing fees and $27 million in consulting fees from Enron. If it did not sign off on Enron's books, it would have risked losing annual fees of this scale in future years. Investors learned from the Enron scandal that they cannot necessarily trust that a firm or its auditor will provide reliable information about earnings.

The Securities and Exchange Commission (SEC) and the stock exchanges have enforced new rules intended to ensure more accurate disclosure by firms. In particular, the chief executive officer and chief financial officer of a large firm must sign off on reported financial statements to verify that the numbers are accurate.

ECONOMIC ANALYSIS OF STOCKS

A firm's future revenue and earnings are influenced by demand for its products, which is typically influenced by economic and industry conditions. In addition, firm-specific conditions (such as managerial expertise) can influence the firm's revenue or earnings.

An economic analysis involves assessing any economic conditions that can affect a firm's stock price, including economic growth, interest rates, and inflation. Each of these conditions is discussed in turn.

Economic Growth

economic growth
A measure of growth in a country's economy over a particular period.

In the United States, **economic growth** is the growth in the U.S. economy over a particular period. It is commonly measured by the amount of production in the United States, or the **gross domestic product (GDP),** which reflects the total market value of all products and services produced in the United States. The production level of products and services is closely related to the aggregate (overall) demand for products and services. When aggregate demand by consumers rises, firms produce more products to accommodate the increased demand. This higher level of production results in more jobs and higher incomes. Consumers now have more money to spend, which results in additional aggregate demand for products and services. The firms that provide products and services experience higher sales (revenue) and earnings, and their stock prices may rise.

gross domestic product (GDP)
The total market value of all products and services produced in a country.

Weak Economic Conditions. When economic conditions are weak, the aggregate demand for products and services declines. Firms experience a lower level of sales and earnings, and their stock prices may decline as a result. Some firms lay off employees. Consumers have less income and therefore they have less money to spend. This may cause an additional decline in the aggregate demand for products and services, and firms' stock prices may decrease further.

fiscal policy
The means by which the U.S. government imposes taxes on individuals and corporations and by which it spends its money.

Fiscal Policy Effects. Given the potential impact of economic growth on stock prices, investors also monitor the U.S. government's **fiscal policy,** or the means by which the government imposes taxes on individuals and corporations and by which it spends its money. When corporate tax rates are increased, the after-tax earnings of corporations are reduced, which means there is less money for shareholders. When individual tax rates are increased, individuals have less money to spend and therefore consume fewer products. The demand for products and services declines as a result, reducing firms' earnings.

15.3 Financial Planning Online: Information on Economic Conditions

Go to
http://www.oecd.org

Click on
OECD Economic Outlook

This Web site provides information about economic conditions that can affect the values of investments.

Interest Rates

Interest rates can affect economic growth and therefore have an indirect impact on stock prices. In general, stocks perform better when interest rates are low because firms can obtain financing at relatively low rates. Firms tend to be more willing to expand when interest rates are low, and their expansions stimulate the economy. When interest rates are low, investors also tend to shift more of their funds into stock because the interest earned on money market securities is relatively low. The general shift into stocks increases the demand for stocks, which places upward pressure on stock prices.

Lower interest rates may enable more consumers to afford cars or homes. Car manufacturers and homebuilders then experience higher earnings, and their stock prices tend to increase as well.

Financial publications often refer to the Federal Reserve Board ("the Fed") when discussing interest rates because the Fed uses monetary policy to influence interest rates. Through its interest rate policies, the Fed affects the amount of spending by consumers with borrowed funds and therefore influences economic growth.

Inflation

Stock prices are also affected by **inflation**, or the increase in the general level of prices of products and services over a specified period. One of the most common measures of inflation is the **consumer price index (CPI)**, which represents prices of consumer products such as groceries, household products, housing, and gasoline. An alternative measure of inflation is the **producer price index (PPI)**, which represents prices of products such as coal, lumber, and metals, that are used to produce other products. Inflation can cause an increase in the prices that firms pay for materials or equipment.

The main publications providing information about inflation and other economic conditions are listed in Exhibit 15.6. These publications commonly provide historical data for inflation, economic growth, interest rates, and many other economic indicators.

inflation
The increase in the general level of prices of products and services over a specified period.

consumer price index (CPI)
A measure of inflation that represents prices of consumer products such as groceries, household products, housing, and gasoline.

producer price index (PPI)
A measure of inflation that represents prices of products such as coal, lumber, and metals, that are used to produce other products.

Exhibit 15.6 Sources of Economic Information

Published Sources

- **Federal Reserve Bulletin:** provides data on economic conditions, including interest rates, unemployment rates, inflation rates, and the money supply.

- **Federal Reserve District Bank publications:** provide information on national and regional economic conditions.

- **Survey of Current Business:** provides data on various indicators of economic activity, including national income, production levels, and employment levels.

Online Sources

- **Bloomberg (http://www.bloomberg.com):** provides reports on interest rates, other economic conditions, and news announcements about various economic indicators.

- **Yahoo! (http://www.yahoo.com):** provides information and news about economic conditions.

- **Federal Reserve System (http://www.federalreserve.gov):** provides detailed statistics on economic conditions.

- **St. Louis Federal Reserve District (http://www.stlouisfed.org):** provides updated information about U.S. economic conditions.

INDUSTRY ANALYSIS OF STOCKS

A firm's stock price is also susceptible to industry conditions. The demand for products or services within an industry changes over time. For example, the popularity of the Internet increased the demand for computers, disks, printers, and Internet guides in the 1990s. Producers of these products initially benefited from the increased demand. However, as other firms notice the increased demand, they often enter an industry. Competition is another industry factor that frequently affects sales, earnings, and therefore the stock price of a firm. Competition has intensified for many industries as a result of the Internet, which has reduced the costs of marketing and delivering products for some firms.

Industry Indicators

Investors can obtain information about firms and their corresponding industry from various sources, as summarized in Exhibit 15.7. Numerous financial Web sites also provide information on specific industries. Another indicator of industry performance is the industry stock index, which measures how the market value of the firms within the industry has changed over a specific period. The prevailing stock index for a particular industry indicates the expectations of investors in general about that industry.

STOCK VALUATION

Some stocks of high-performing firms are priced high, and therefore may not be good investments for the future. Before investing in a stock, you should estimate its market value just as you would estimate the market value of a car or a home. A stock is different from a car or a home, however, in that it does not serve a physical function such as transportation or housing. A stock is simply intended to generate a return on the money invested.

Exhibit 15.7 Sources of Industry Information

Published Sources

Although some government publications offer industry information, the most popular sources are provided by the private sector.

- **Value Line Industry Survey:** provides an industry outlook, performance levels of various industries, and financial statistics for firms in each industry over time.

- **Standard and Poor's Industry Survey:** provides statistics used to assess industry conditions.

- **Standard and Poor's Analysts Handbook:** provides financial statistics for various industries over time.

Online Sources

- **Bloomberg (http://www.bloomberg.com):** identifies industry stock indexes that have experienced substantial changes.

- **Investorlinks (http://www.investorlinks.com):** contains news articles related to specific industries.

- **Yahoo! (http://www.yahoo.com):** provides financial news and statistics for each industry.

- **CNBC (http://moneycentral.msn.com/investor/market/leading.asp):** provides stock indexes for various industry sectors.

The price of a stock is based on the demand for that stock versus the supply of stock for sale. The demand for shares is determined by the number of investors who wish to purchase shares of the stock. The supply of stock for sale is determined by the number of investors who decide to sell their shares.

The valuation process involves identifying a firm that you think may perform well in the future and determining whether its price is overvalued, undervalued, or on target. You buy a stock when you think that it is undervalued and that you can therefore achieve a high return from investing in it. Yet your purchase of the stock means that some other investor was willing to sell it. So, while you believe the stock is undervalued, others apparently think it is overvalued. This difference in opinion is what causes a high volume of trading. For some stocks, more than 1 million shares are traded each day as a result of these divergent views of the stock's true value. Investors who use specific methods to value a stock may be able to achieve higher returns than others.

When valuing stocks, investors may use technical analysis or fundamental analysis. **Technical analysis** is the valuation of stocks based on historical price patterns. For example, you might purchase a stock whenever its price rises for three consecutive days, because you expect that a trend in prices indicates future price movements. Alternatively, you may decide to sell a stock if its price declines for several consecutive days, because you expect that the trend will continue.

Fundamental analysis is the valuation of stocks based on an examination of fundamental characteristics such as revenue or earnings, or the sensitivity of the firm's performance to economic conditions. There are many different ways to apply fundamental analysis when valuing stocks, including the two popular methods explained below. Although both methods can easily be applied to value a stock, they are subject to limitations that will be addressed.

technical analysis
The valuation of stocks based on historical price patterns.

fundamental analysis
The valuation of stocks based on an examination of fundamental characteristics such as revenue or earnings, or the sensitivity of the firm's performance to economic conditions.

price-earnings (PE) method
A method of valuing stocks in which a specific firm's earnings per share are multiplied by the mean industry price-earnings (PE) ratio.

Price-Earnings (PE) Method

One method for determining the value of a stock is based on the value of the firm's earnings. The higher the earnings, the more funds the firm has to pay dividends to its shareholders or to reinvest for further expansion (which will ultimately generate additional earnings). The most common method of using earnings to value stocks is the **price-earnings (PE) method**, in which a firm's earnings are multiplied by the mean industry PE ratio. A stock's PE ratio is its stock price per share (P) divided by its annual earnings per share (E):

$$\text{Price-Earnings (PE) Ratio} = P/E.$$

You can find the PE ratio of any firm in stock quotations in financial newspapers such as the *Wall Street Journal* and on many financial Web sites. A PE ratio of 10 means that the firm's stock price is 10 times the firm's earnings per share. You can use the PE method to value a firm as follows:

1. Look up the PE ratios of stocks in the firm's industry.

2. Multiply the average industry PE ratio times the firm's earnings per share.

3. Compare your estimated value of the firm's stock to its market value to determine whether the stock is currently undervalued or overvalued.

EXAMPLE

Stephanie Spratt is impressed with Trail.com, an online clothing firm that focuses on the 18–22 age bracket. Their prices are much lower than their competitors', and the quality is high. Reading about the firm on its Web site and in various financial newspapers, Stephanie has learned that it plans to expand its clothing lines. The prevailing price of Trail.com stock is $61 per share.

Stephanie decides to apply the PE method to value Trail.com stock, which has had recent annual earnings of $5 per share. Only three other corporations have very similar businesses to Trail.com and have stock that is traded. Stephanie uses the Stock Quotes section of the

Yahoo! Web site to determine the PE ratios of these firms. One firm has a PE ratio of 10, the second firm has a PE ratio of 12, and the third has a PE ratio of 14.

Stephanie derives a value for Trail.com's stock by multiplying its recent annual earnings per share by the average industry PE ratio:

1. Mean PE Ratio of Industry   =   (10 + 12 + 14)/3

                                 =   12.

2. Valuation of Stock   =   Firm's Earnings per Share × Mean Industry PE Ratio

                         = $5 × 12

                         = $60.

This valuation of $60 is below the prevailing stock price ($61) of Trail.com, indicating that the stock is slightly overvalued. Given this valuation, Stephanie decides not to purchase Trail.com stock at this time.

Deriving an Estimate of Earnings.   Because the stock price of a firm is influenced by expected earnings, investors may prefer to use expected earnings rather than past earnings to value a firm and its corresponding industry. Many investors rely on Value Line, the Institutional Brokerage Estimate System (IBES), and other investment services for earnings forecasts. Some earnings forecasts can be obtained from publications and Web sites. If investors expect no change in earnings from last year to this year, last year's earnings can be used.

Limitations of the PE Method.   Forecasting earnings is difficult. Therefore, valuations of a stock that are based on expected earnings may be unreliable. Investors who overestimate future earnings risk overpaying for a stock.

15.4 Financial Planning Online: Earnings Estimates for Valuing Your Stock

Go to
http://biz.yahoo.com/
research/earncal/
today.html

This Web site provides recent earnings per share estimates of a firm that you specify, which you can use when applying the PE method of valuing stocks.

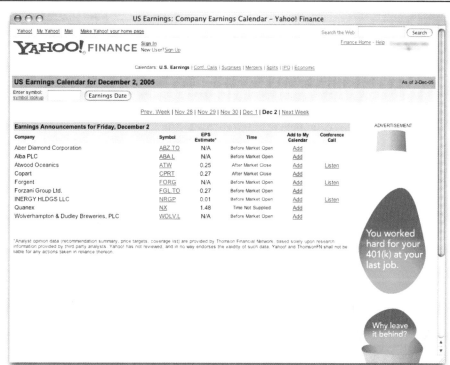

Even if the forecast of earnings is accurate, there is still a question of the proper PE multiple that should be used to value a stock. The firm that you are valuing may deserve to have a lower PE ratio than other firms, if its future performance is subject to more uncertainty. For example, perhaps the firm is using less advanced technology than its competitors, which could adversely affect its performance in a few years. Consequently, its lower PE ratio may not necessarily mean that the firm's stock is undervalued by the market.

Another limitation of the PE method is that the results will vary with the firms selected to derive a mean industry PE ratio. Should this ratio be derived from the three closest competitors (as in the example)? Or from the 10 closest competitors? For firms that conduct several types of business, it is difficult to determine who the closest competitors are. Investors who apply the wrong industry PE ratio will derive an inaccurate valuation, which may cause them to buy stocks that are not really undervalued.

Price-Revenue (PR) Method

price-revenue (PR) method
A method of valuing stocks in which the revenue per share of a specific firm is multiplied by the mean industry ratio of share price to revenue.

A second common valuation method is the **price-revenue (PR) method**, in which the industry's average ratio of share price to revenue is multiplied by revenue per share for a specific firm. When a firm sells its products, it generates revenue. The higher a firm's revenues, the higher its valuation within a specific industry. Since stock prices reflect expectations of future performance, investors should use recently reported revenues only if they believe the reported revenues represent a reasonable forecast of the future. The PR method is especially popular for valuing firms (such as some Internet firms) that cannot be valued with the PE method because they have negative earnings.

E X A M P L E

Stephanie Spratt applies the PR method to value Trail.com's stock. A financial Web site discloses that Trail.com has expected revenues of $29 per share and that the other firms in the same industry have a price-to-revenue (PR) ratio of 2.0 on average. Based on this information, Stephanie estimates the value of Trail.com to be:

$$\text{Valuation of Stock} = \text{Expected Revenues of Firm per Share} \times \text{Mean Industry PR Ratio}$$
$$= \$29 \times 2.0$$
$$= \$58.$$

Since Trail.com stock is currently priced at $61, she decides that the stock is overpriced, so she will not buy it at this time.

Limitations of the PR Method. The *PR* method is subject to error if it is based on an overestimate of revenues or on a set of firms whose operations are not very similar to those of the firm that is being valued. Second, revenues do not indicate how well a firm is managed. If two firms in the same industry have the same revenues, the firm with the lower costs will normally be valued higher. Yet the *PR* method will give these two firms the same value because this method ignores costs incurred by the firms. For this reason, the PE method may be a more appropriate valuation method.

INTEGRATING YOUR ANALYSES

By conducting an analysis of the firm itself, the economy, and the industry, you can assess a firm's future performance. This process enables you to determine whether to purchase the firm's stock. Exhibit 15.8 summarizes the potential impact of economic, industry, and firm-specific conditions on a firm's stock price.

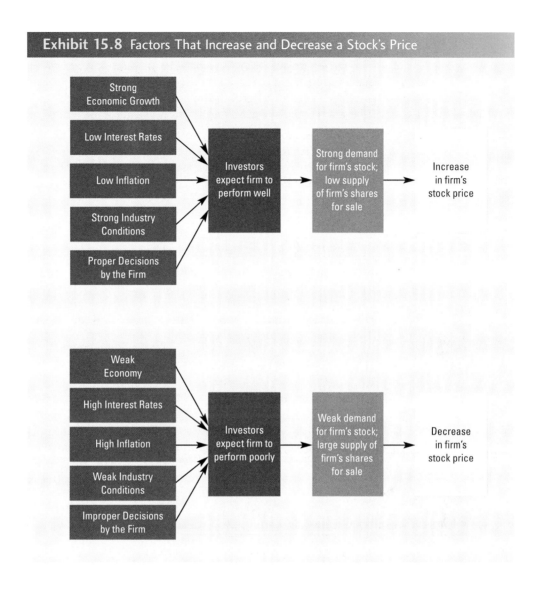

Exhibit 15.8 Factors That Increase and Decrease a Stock's Price

Stephanie Spratt has been monitoring the firm Trail.com, which sells clothing to people in the 18–22 age bracket. Her valuations of the stock indicated that it is overvalued. She decides to conduct an economic and industry analysis in order to make a more informed decision about whether to buy this stock.

First Stephanie reviews various financial Web sites that provide information about future economic growth. Most of these Web sites suggest that economic growth will be strong and that the unemployment rate will be low. She expects that a strong economy will enhance Trail.com's future performance.

Then Stephanie reviews Web sites on the clothing industry for the 18–22 age bracket. She reads that several small clothing firms are expanding rapidly and will be establishing retail stores in malls throughout the country. All of these firms are also establishing Web sites so that they can sell their clothing directly to customers who wish to place orders online. Many of these firms are expected to compete directly with Trail.com because they also sell clothing to customers in the 18–22 age bracket. This industry analysis suggests that Trail.com will face much more competition in the near future.

Stephanie learns from an online news source that Trail.com has announced plans to expand and has recently borrowed a substantial amount of funds to support its growth. Consequently, it has a high debt ratio. She believes there is room for only a limited number of firms to achieve a successful growth strategy in this industry and that Trail.com may not generate sufficient revenue to meet its high debt payments in the future.

Overall, the economic outlook is favorable for Trail.com, but the industry outlook is very unfavorable for the firm, and its high debt level is a concern. She decides not to invest in the stock unless industry conditions become more favorable, and Trail.com proves that it can handle its large amount of debt without experiencing financial problems.

STOCK MARKET EFFICIENCY

Because investors use different methods to value and analyze stocks, they derive different valuations for a stock. Stock market efficiency is relevant for investors who are attempting to achieve abnormally high returns by analyzing financial information or relying on investment advisers. If stock prices fully reflect information that is available to investors, the stock market is said to be **efficient**.

Conversely, the stock market is referred to as **inefficient** if stock prices do not reflect all information. In general, an efficient stock market implies that you and other investors will not be able to identify stocks that are undervalued because stocks are valued properly by the market.

The argument for efficiency is that demand for shares by investors should drive the equilibrium price of a stock toward its proper value. If a stock was really priced below its proper value, the large institutional investors who have more access to information about the stock than individual investors would buy substantial amounts of it. The

efficient stock market
A market in which stock prices fully reflect information that is available to investors.

inefficient stock market
A market in which stock prices do not reflect all information that is available to investors.

15.5 Financial Planning Online: Screening Stocks for Investment Decisions

Go to
http://screen.yahoo.com/
stocks.html

This Web site provides a list of stocks that meet criteria that you specify for performance over the last year, such as a specific price-earnings (PE) ratio and other characteristics.

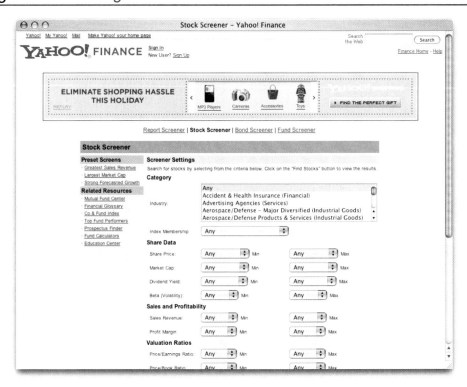

strong demand for shares would force the price of the stock higher, bringing the stock's price close to its proper value. Thus, institutional investors capitalizing on the discrepancy would push the stock price back to its proper value.

Reviewing historical stock prices, investors can identify several stocks that experienced very large returns. Some stocks have doubled in price in a single day. Some stocks will experience very large returns in the future. These performances do not mean the stock market is inefficient, however, unless information that was available to investors should have justified higher valuations of those stocks before their prices increased. It is easy to look back and realize that we would have benefited from purchasing shares of Microsoft or Dell Computer when their stocks first publicly traded. Yet who really knew that these stocks would perform so well at that time? An investor can achieve high returns from a hunch about a specific stock. The concept of market efficiency acknowledges that when you invest in stocks, some of those stocks may outperform the market in general. However, it implies that stock selections by an investor will not consistently beat the market.

HOW STOCK VALUATION FITS WITHIN YOUR FINANCIAL PLAN

Recall the key decisions about stock that should be included within your financial plan:

- Should you consider buying stock?
- How should you value stocks when determining whether to buy them?
- What methods should you use for investing in stocks?

The first decision was discussed in the previous chapter. If you consider buying stock, you need to determine which common stocks are undervalued and deserve to be purchased. This decision requires an analysis of stocks, as discussed in this chapter. Exhibit 15.9 provides an example of how this decision applies to Stephanie Spratt's financial plan. Methods for investing in stock will be discussed in the next chapter.

Exhibit 15.9 How Stock Valuation Fits within Stephanie Spratt's Financial Plan

GOALS FOR INVESTING IN STOCKS

1. *Determine if I could benefit from investing in stocks (discussed in the previous chapter).*
2. *If I consider investing in stocks, decide which stocks to purchase.*

ANALYSIS

Method Used to Assess the Value of Trail.com Stock	Opinion
1. Assessment of the firm, economy, and industry	*These methods provide much valuable information, but they are subjective and do not lead to a precise estimate of the firm's value.*
2. Price-earnings (PE) method	*Can easily be used to value a stock, but is limited because it assumes that the firm has the same PE ratio as its competitors.*
3. Price-revenue (PR) method	*Is more appropriate than the PE method when the firm's earnings are negative. However, it is limited because it assumes the firm has the same PR ratio as its competitors.*

DECISION

Decision Regarding How to Value Stocks:

Although all three methods can be used, each has limitations. I plan to use all three methods when valuing a stock. I will consider purchasing a stock only if all three methods indicate that the stock is undervalued. I may still consider investing in a stock only if other sources of information (such as financial experts) agree with my views. Until I have more cash inflows, I should limit the amount of money that I invest in individual stocks.

DISCUSSION QUESTIONS

1. How would Stephanie's stock investing decisions be different if she were a single mother of two children?

2. How would Stephanie's stock investing decisions be affected if she were 35 years old? If she were 50 years old?

SUMMARY

A stock's price quotations are provided in daily newspapers and online. These quotations should be considered when deciding whether to purchase a stock.

An analysis of a firm involves reviewing the annual report and the financial statements (such as the balance sheet and income statement), along with other financial reports. This analysis includes an assessment of the firm's liquidity, financial leverage, efficiency, and profitability.

Be careful when interpreting financial statements, since accounting guidelines allow firms to use methods that may exaggerate their performance.

An economic analysis involves assessing how a stock's price can be affected by economic conditions. The most closely monitored economic factors that can affect stock prices are economic growth, interest rates, and inflation. In general, stocks are favorably affected by economic growth, a decline in interest rates, and a decline in inflation.

An industry analysis involves assessing how a stock's price can be affected by industry conditions. Two closely monitored industry characteristics are consumer preferences within an industry and industry competition. Stocks are favorably affected when the firms recognize shifts in consumer preferences and when the firms face a relatively low degree of competition.

Stocks can be valued using several methods. The price-earnings (PE) method estimates the stock's value by applying the mean industry PE ratio to the firm's recent or expected annual earnings. The price-revenue (PR) method estimates the stock's value by applying the mean industry PR ratio to the firm's revenue per share.

Stock market efficiency implies that stock prices reflect all public information. If the stock market is efficient, there are no benefits from trying to use public information to achieve unusually high returns. Many investors, however, believe that the stock market is not efficient and therefore attempt to determine whether a specific stock is undervalued.

INTEGRATING THE KEY CONCEPTS

Your decision to invest in specific stocks is not only related to your other investment decisions, but also affects other parts of your financial plan. When buying stocks, you should consider your liquidity (Part 2). If your liquidity is limited, you may desire to achieve some degree of liquidity from any stocks you purchase. The stocks of large firms would be most appropriate because they are more liquid than stocks of small firms. That is, they can be sold more easily in the market because there are more potential buyers who are willing to buy well-known stocks.

Before investing in any stocks, you should reassess your financing (Part 3). Compare your expected return on any specific stock you may purchase with the interest rate incurred on any personal loan that you have. Consider paying off any personal loans before you invest in stocks, unless the return on stocks will exceed the interest rate incurred on personal loans. In addition, make sure your insurance needs are covered (Part 4) before using funds to buy stocks. If you decide to invest in stocks, you need to determine whether the investment should be for your retirement account (Part 6). Your choice of stocks may depend on whether the investment is for your retirement account because those stocks

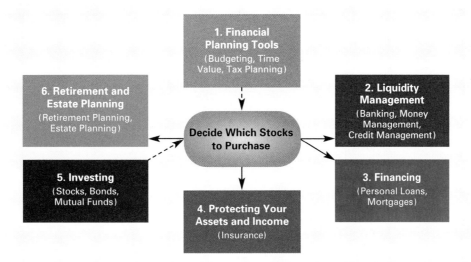

that typically result in more taxes (such as those that pay high dividends) may be more appropriate for a retirement account where the dividend income may be tax-deferred.

REVIEW QUESTIONS

1. Why is it necessary to analyze a firm? What is an annual report? What information does it contain to aid the analysis?

2. List the characteristics of a firm that investors analyze by using the balance sheet and the income statement.

3. What is liquidity? How is it measured?

4. What is financial leverage? Discuss two ways to measure financial leverage.

5. What is an indicator of the efficiency of a firm? How can efficiency be measured?

6. Where can you find the necessary information to determine a firm's profitability? Describe the financial ratios used to measure profitability.

7. List some sources of information about individual firms other than the annual report. Why should you carefully evaluate the information you use?

8. What information is provided by the Value Line Investment Survey?

9. Why may the top managers of a firm be tempted to use misleading estimates of revenues and expenses? How may managers be able to boost the reported earnings of their firm?

10. What are the limitations of measuring financial characteristics using financial ratios?

11. When performing an economic analysis of stocks, what three economic factors are most closely watched?

12. Explain how economic growth is measured. How does economic growth affect stock prices? What are some popular indicators of economic growth? How does the government's fiscal policy affect economic growth?

13. How do interest rates affect economic growth? Why do interest rates affect some stock prices more than others? Which federal agency influences interest rates?

14. What is inflation? How is inflation measured? How does inflation affect stock prices?

15. Why is an industry analysis of stocks important? List some sources of information about firms and their industry.

16. What two basic factors drive the price of a stock? What is the first step in the valuation process for a stock? What are you trying to determine through stock valuation? How do differences in stock valuation affect the volume of trading? Which investors may be able to achieve a high rate of return?

17. How is the price-earnings ratio computed? Describe how you can use the PE method to value a firm. How can you derive an estimate of earnings? What are the limitations of using the PE method?

18. When might you use the price-revenue method rather than the PE method to value a stock? How is the PR ratio calculated? What are some limitations of the PR method?

19. What does the term *efficient market* mean? What is an inefficient market?

20. What is the argument for market efficiency?

21. Historically, some stocks that provide very high returns can be identified. Does this mean the market is inefficient? Why or why not?

VIDEO QUESTIONS

1. What is the price earnings ratio of a stock?

2. What information does a high price earnings ratio indicate?

FINANCIAL PLANNING PROBLEMS

1. Denise has a choice between two stocks. Stock A has a current stock price of $33.50 and earnings per share of $2.23. Stock B has a current stock price of $30.50 and earnings per share of $2.79. Both stocks are in the same industry, and the average PE ratio for the industry is 13. Using the PE ratio, which stock is the better choice? Why?

2. Denise (from problem 1) decides to use the price-revenue method to value the firms. She determines that the industry PR ratio is 1.5. Stock A is reporting revenues at $20 per share. Stock B is reporting revenues at $22 per share. Both stocks are currently trading for $32 per share. Which stock is the better choice?

3. Peter would like to purchase a stock with a current stock price of $30. The three closest competitors of the stock have an average PE ratio of 17, and the firm's most recent earnings per share were $1.70. Using the PE method, determine whether Peter should purchase this stock.

The following information applies to problems 4 through 7.

Balance Sheet for Polly Corporation
(numbers are in millions)

Assets

Cash and marketable securities	$150
Accounts receivable	$320
Inventories	$430
Net fixed assets	$700
Total assets	**$1,600**

Liabilities and Shareholder's Equity

Accounts payable	$350
Short-term debt	$100
Long-term debt	$300
Shareholder's equity	$850
Total liabilities and shareholder's equity	**$1,600**

Income Statement for Polly Corporation
(numbers are in millions)

Revenue	$4,500
Cost of goods sold	$2,800
Gross profit	$1,700
Operating expenses	$1,200
EBIT	$500
Interest	$50
EBT	$450
Taxes	$200
Earnings after taxes	$250

4. What is Polly Corp.'s current ratio? If the current ratio averages 2.5 in Polly's industry, is Polly Corp. liquid?

5. Compute two measures of financial leverage for Polly Corp. and interpret them.

6. What is Polly's average collection period? Other firms in the industry collect their receivables in 25 days, on average. How does Polly compare to other firms in the industry?

7. Use ratios to assess Polly Corp.'s profitability.

8. Amelia Corp. has cost of goods sold of $2.2 million and a current level of inventory of $1 million. The industry inventory turnover is 3. Is Amelia more or less efficient than average firms in the industry?

Ethical Dilemma

9. The management of a publicly traded manufacturing company is reviewing the projected fourth quarter financial results in late November. Based on the projected sales, they will fall short of their yearly profit goals. This will result in the company's executives and managers not receiving their year-end bonuses. A discussion follows as to how sales can be increased sufficiently to produce results that will qualify the executives and managers for year-end bonuses. A decision is made to notify all customers that if they will agree to accept shipments for first quarter orders prior to the end of the fourth quarter, the company will agree to pick up the shipping costs. The company's controller and CFO review the plan and agree that it is within acceptable guidelines of Generally Accepted Accounting Principles (GAAP).

The plan results in a significant increase in both sales and net income despite the company's increased shipping costs. The increase is sufficient to warrant payment of bonuses to the executives and managers and also results in a significant increase in the company's stock price.

a. Was the incentive plan devised by the company's management for the purpose of increasing sales and profits to a level justifying bonuses ethical? Why or why not?

b. Discuss any negative impact that this incentive program could have for the company and its shareholders in the future.

FINANCIAL PLANNING ONLINE EXERCISES

1. Go to http://finance.yahoo.com.

   a. In this exercise, you will examine information on the financial condition of a stock. Under "Yahoo! Finance," enter the stock symbol UNM. You will get information on UnumProvident Corporation. Click on "Profile." Several pages of information will be provided, including a description of the company's businesses addresses, recent events, insider purchases and sales, officers of the company, and price and volume information on the stock. How is this information useful to investors?

   b. In the "Key Statistics" section, review the Book Value per Share, Earnings per Share, Price/Earnings ratio, Profit Margin, Return on Assets, Return on Equity, and Debt/Equity ratio. Do you think UnumProvident shares are a good investment at the current share price?

   c. Now enter the symbol MSFT and obtain information on Microsoft. Click on "Profile." Review the financial ratios. Do you think Microsoft shares are a good investment at the current price? Why or why not?

   d. How do Microsoft and UnumProvident Corporation compare as investments based on the financial information available on this Web site?

2. Go to http://screen.yahoo.com/stocks.html.

   a. This exercise allows you to identify stocks that satisfy your criteria. Under "Category," choose "Any;" for "Share Price" choose $10 for minimum and $100 for maximum; for "Market Cap," choose $100 million to $50 billion; for "Price/Earnings Ratio," choose 5 to 50; for "Est. 1-Yr EPS Growth," choose "Up more than 25%." Click "Find Stocks." What stocks meet the criteria? What are their ticker symbols, PE ratios, returns percentages, prices, and growth rates?

   b. Compare two stocks that meet the criteria. Which is the better investment? Why?

   c. Click "New Screen." Now under "Industry," choose "Any;" for "Share Price" choose $25 for minimum and $100 for maximum; for "Market Cap," choose a minimum of $500 million; for "Price/Earnings Ratio," choose 5 to 50; for "Est. 1-Yr EPS Growth," choose "Up more than 25%," and choose "Buy Rating (1)" for "Avg Analyst Rec." Click "Find Stocks." What stocks meet the selected criteria?

   d. Compare two stocks on this list based on the financial information provided and justify your preference between the two stocks.

BUILDING YOUR OWN FINANCIAL PLAN

One of the best financial instruments to accomplish many intermediate- and long-term goals is investment in stocks. Investment specialists have said that at any given time there are 20 to 50 stocks that could make someone a millionaire within a short time. The secret, of course, is to find just one of those 20 to 50 stocks. In this exercise, you will analyze two or three stocks to determine if they are good investments and, therefore, a suitable means to accomplish some of the intermediate- and long-term goals you established in Chapter 1.

When investing in stocks, it is necessary to monitor happenings in the economy and the market. Events may very quickly have a significant impact—favorable or unfavorable—on the price trends of a stock. How frequently you monitor information depends on market conditions and the volatility of your individual stocks. Web sites such as http://finance.yahoo.com/?u allow you to research financial news about any firm easily.

Go to the worksheets at the end of this chapter, and to the CD-ROM accompanying this text, to continue building your financial plan.

THE SAMPSONS—A CONTINUING CASE

The Sampsons have decided to invest some of their savings in stocks to support their children's future college education. They do not know much about investing in stocks, so they investigate various Web sites that provide information on economic and industry conditions. They learn that the economy is expected to strengthen in the future and that the technology sector is expected to perform particularly well. Dave and Sharon are tempted to invest their entire savings in technology stocks to capitalize on what they have learned.

Go to the worksheets at the end of this chapter, and to the CD-ROM accompanying this text, to continue this case.

Chapter 15: Building Your Own Financial Plan

GOALS

1. Determine how to value a stock based on information about the economy and the firm.

ANALYSIS

1. Select a stock in which you are considering investing.
2. Go to the http://www.federalreserve.gov/FOMC/BeigeBook/2005. Click on the most current report indicated and read the summary. As you do so, keep in mind the product and/or service provided by the company you have selected to analyze. In the space provided below, record your analysis of the Beige Book's economic analysis and its impact on your stock.

_____
_____
_____
_____
_____
_____
_____
_____

3. Go to http://www.smartmoney.com. Click on "Funds" and then roll down to "Fund Snapshots." You will see a box that says "Enter Symbol or Name." Enter the symbol or name of the company you wish to analyze and click on "GO." This will bring up the "Snapshot" tab for your company. Answer the following questions, finding the data in the tab indicated:

Snapshot

a. Is the price of your stock currently close to its 52-week high or 52-week low? _____

b. Does this stock pay a dividend and, if so, how much? _____

Charting

c. What has been the long-term price trend of your company's stock?

_____
_____
_____

News

d. Do you see any significant news events that may favorably or unfavorably affect your stock?

_____

_____

_____

Earnings

e. How well has your company met its earnings estimates?

_____

_____

_____

f. How does your company's estimated growth for the current and next fiscal year compare to industry projections?

_____

_____

_____

g. How does your company's estimated growth for the current and next fiscal year compare to the S&P 500?

_____

_____

_____

h. How does your company's estimated three–five year annual growth compare to the industry projections?

_____

_____

_____

i. How does your company's estimated three–five year annual growth compare to the S&P 500?

_____

_____

_____

Ratings

j. How many Wall Street analysts rate your stock?

_____

k. What has been the net change in recommendation?

_____

l. How many rate your stock as a:

Strong buy _____

Moderate buy _____

Hold _____

Moderate sell _____

Strong sell _____

m. How do the recommendations for your stock compare to others in the industry?

_____

_____

_____

Competition

n. How does your company compare, in terms of market value, of its competition, i.e., is it one of the larger or smaller companies in its industry?

_____

_____

_____

o. How does your company's net profit margin compare to that of its competition, i.e., is it one of the larger or smaller companies in its industry?

_____

_____

_____

Key Ratios

p. How does your company's return on equity compare to that of the industry?

_____

_____

_____

q. How does your company's assets compare to that of the industry?

_____

_____

_____

Financials

r. How does the growth in revenues of your company compare to that of its competition?

_____

_____

_____

s. How does the growth in net earnings of your company compare to that of its competition?

_____

_____

_____

Insiders

t. In analyzing any stock, it is always good to know what the insiders are doing. From the chart, are they buying, selling, intending to buy, or doing nothing?

_____

_____

_____

Summary

u. Based on your analysis of the above, answer the following questions:

1. Would this stock be considered a(n) (enter an X to signify your choice):

Growth stock _____

Income stock _____

Growth/income stock _____

2. For which of the intermediate or long-term goals that you established in Chapter 1 would this stock be a suitable investment, if any?

Intermediate-Term Goals	Suitable? (Yes or No)	Rationale for Selection
1.		
2.		
3.		

Long-Term Goals	Suitable? (Yes or No)	Rationale for Selection
1.		
2.		
3.		

DECISIONS

1. Based on your valuation, will you purchase this stock?

2. If you invest in this particular stock, which of your financial goals will the investment be aimed at achieving?

Chapter 15: The Sampsons—A Continuing Case

CASE QUESTIONS

1. Advise the Sampsons on whether they should put all of their investments in technology stocks.

   _____

   _____

   _____

   _____

2. Should the information the Sampsons read on Web sites affect how they invest in stocks?

   _____

   _____

   _____

   _____

3. Dave Sampson recently received an annual report from a corporation and is very impressed by the optimism expressed in the report about the firm's future. Dave researched the firm and found that the firm has a very low PE ratio relative to other firms in the industry. Therefore he believes the stock to be undervalued and would like to invest in it. What do you think about Dave's plan?

   _____

   _____

   _____

   _____

Chapter 16

Investing in Stocks

*L*ynn owned 500 shares of a stock that she bought at $40 per share. As the price rose steadily over the course of several months to over $48, Lynn decided to implement a sell strategy that would take the uncertainty out of the sales transaction. She called her broker and placed a limit order to sell her stock if and when it reached $50 per share. A $50 per share price would allow Lynn to earn at least a 25 percent return on her investment and result in a $5,000 gain before subtracting the commissions.

Over the next few days the price slipped to the mid-40s and then drifted lower still. Lynn didn't sell because she was sure the dip in price was only temporary. Finally, when the price reached $30 per share, she called her broker and sold all of her shares. Lynn ultimately suffered a $5,000 loss on her investment.

When investing in stocks, your investment decisions depend upon your risk tolerance, investing knowledge, and experience. You should approach any potential stock purchase with an investment strategy that will guide you in your stock selection. That investment strategy is the focus of this chapter.

The objectives of this chapter are to:

- Identify the functions of stock exchanges

- Explain how to execute the purchase or sale of stocks

- Discuss buying stocks on margin

- Explain how to assess your stock portfolio's performance

STOCK EXCHANGES

stock exchanges
Facilities that allow investors to purchase or sell existing stocks.

Now that you understand how to value and evaluate stocks, you can start to make stock investments. **Stock exchanges** are facilities that allow investors to purchase or sell existing stocks. They facilitate trading in the secondary market so that investors can sell stocks that they previously purchased. An organized securities exchange occupies a physical location where trading occurs. A stock has to be listed on a stock exchange to be traded there, meaning that it must fulfill specific requirements of the exchange. For example, to list its stock, a firm may have to be a minimum size and have a minimum number of shares of stock outstanding. The requirements ensure that there will be an active market for stocks in which shares are commonly traded.

New York Stock Exchange

The most popular organized exchange in the United States is the New York Stock Exchange (NYSE), which handles transactions for approximately 2,800 stocks. The transactions are conducted by the traders who own the 1,366 "seats" on the NYSE and are allowed to trade stocks listed on the exchange for themselves or others. A seat essentially represents a license to trade stocks on the exchange. All 1,366 seats are occupied. A would-be trader can obtain a seat only if someone else is willing to sell it. The price of a seat was about $46,000 in 1990, rose to $2.7 million in 2000, tumbled to around $1 million in 2004, and then rebounded to a high of $3 million in August of 2005. The price of a seat is impacted by levels of trading volume and stock market volatility. Some traders (called **floor traders**) execute trades to accommodate requests by other investors (such as yourself) while other traders execute trades for themselves.

floor traders
Traders at a stock exchange who execute trades to fulfill orders placed by other investors.

When floor traders execute trades for other investors they earn a commission in the form of a bid-ask spread, which reflects the difference between the price at which they are willing to buy a stock and the price at which they are willing to sell it. For example, suppose a trader executed an order where one investor bid $20.12 per share to buy a stock while the seller received $20.00 per share. The bid-ask spread of $.12 per share goes to the floor trader. In this example, a trade of 1,000 shares cost $120 because of the bid-ask spread. Some traders, called **specialists**, help to make a market in one or more stocks by taking the position opposite orders placed by clients. That is, they may be willing to buy the stocks that you want to sell or sell holdings of their stocks that you want to buy.

specialists
Traders who help to make a market in one or more stocks by taking the position opposite of orders placed by clients.

A Typical Stock Transaction on the NYSE. To buy a stock that is listed on the NYSE, you tell your brokerage firm the name of the stock and the number of shares you want to purchase. The brokerage firm sends the message electronically to one of the floor traders at the NYSE, who stands at the spot on the trading floor where that stock is traded. The floor trader signals a willingness to buy the shares of that stock and receives a response from another trader there who is trying to sell that stock. The price is negotiated. Once the trade is completed, the floor trader at the NYSE sends confirmation to the brokerage firm that the trade has been made, and the brokerage firm informs you that the trade has been completed.

Other Stock Exchanges

About 800 stocks are listed on the American Stock Exchange (AMEX). These stocks are generally from smaller firms and are less actively traded than those on the NYSE. There are also some regional securities exchanges located in large U.S. cities. These regional exchanges tend to have less stringent listing requirements and therefore list stocks from smaller firms that may be well known in that specific region. Stocks are traded on the AMEX and the regional stock exchanges in much the same way as on the NYSE.

Over-the-Counter (OTC) Market

over-the-counter (OTC) market
An electronic communications network that allows investors to buy or sell securities.

market-makers
Traders who execute trades on the OTC market and earn commissions in the form of a bid-ask spread.

The **over-the-counter (OTC) market** is an electronic communications network that allows investors to buy or sell securities. It is not a visible facility like the organized exchanges. Trades are communicated through a computer network by **market-makers**, who execute the trades on the OTC, and earn commissions in the form of a bid-ask spread. Whereas trades on stock exchanges are between two traders who are standing next to each other, trades in the OTC market are conducted over a computer network between two dealers sitting in their respective offices who may be hundreds or thousands of miles apart.

The listing requirements for the OTC market are generally less stringent than those for the NYSE. More than 4,000 stocks are listed on the OTC market. A key part of the OTC market is the Nasdaq, or the National Association of Securities Dealers Automated Quotation system. The Nasdaq provides continual updated market price information on OTC stocks that meet its requirements on size and trading volume. The Nasdaq and the AMEX merged in 1998, although they still perform separate functions.

Electronic Communication Networks (ECNs)

Electronic Communication Networks (ECNs)
Computer systems that match desired purchases and sales of stocks.

Electronic Communication Networks (ECNs) are computer systems that match desired purchases and sales of stocks. For example, the ECN receives orders from investors to buy shares of a stock at a specified price and matches them with orders from investors to sell the stock at that price. A person is not needed to perform the match. ECNs now make up about 30 percent of all trading of Nasdaq stocks. ECNs enable investors to bypass the market-makers and therefore avoid the transaction costs (bid-ask spread) they charge.

ECNs are also being used to execute some transactions on the NYSE and AMEX. They can match orders any time, so they are especially valuable at night after the exchanges are closed.

At some online brokerage firms, if an order comes in after the stock exchanges are closed (during so-called after-hours trading), the firm will send the order to the ECNs, where the trade will be executed. Yet at night the trading volume may be insufficient. An investor who wants to sell a stock may not be able to find a willing buyer. As more investors learn that they can have orders executed at night by some online brokerage firms, the trading volume will increase, and the ECNs will become even more popular.

Foreign Stock Exchanges

American depository receipts
Certificates representing ownership of foreign stocks.

Foreign stock exchanges facilitate investments in foreign securities. Most countries have at least one stock exchange where local stocks are traded. Investors in the United States can purchase foreign stocks through their brokerage firm. The U.S. brokerage firm electronically transfers the order to a brokerage firm in the foreign country. The foreign brokerage firm then transfers the order to the local stock exchange to complete the trade. The investor sends a check (in dollars) to the U.S. brokerage firm, which converts the money to a foreign currency and makes the payment. Investors' transaction costs for foreign stock trades are higher than for trades that can be completed on a U.S. exchange. Some foreign stocks are traded on U.S. stock exchanges as **American depository receipts**, which are certificates representing ownership of foreign stocks.

PURCHASING OR SELLING STOCKS

The market for a stock is created from the flow of buy and sell orders from investors. Recall from Chapter 14 that the orders to buy a stock are matched with orders to sell that security at a price agreeable to both parties in each transaction. To buy or sell a stock, you establish an account at a brokerage firm.

Relying on Brokerage or Analyst Recommendations

When using a full-service broker, you can receive investment advice. In addition, you also have access to stock ratings that are assigned by stock analysts employed by brokerage firms.

Evaluating Analyst Advice. Recommendations from brokers and analysts have limitations, however. Some brokerage firms may advise you to buy or sell securities frequently, rather than holding on to your investment portfolio over time. For each transaction, however, you must pay a commission to that brokerage firm. In addition, frequent trading may cause you to hold on to stocks less than one year, so the capital gain is treated like ordinary income for federal income tax purposes (unless the gain occurs as a result of trading stocks in your retirement account). If your marginal tax rate on ordinary income is higher than 15 percent (the maximum long-term capital gain tax rate), you will be subject to a higher tax rate because you did not hold the stocks for at least one year. Brokerage firms should remind you of this tax effect before suggesting that you sell stocks that you have held for less than one year.

Many studies have shown that the recommendations by brokers or analysts do not lead to better performance than the stock market in general. Some advisers have very limited experience in analyzing and valuing securities. Even those who are very experienced will not necessarily be able to help you achieve unusually high performance.

Focus on Ethics: Relying on Analyst Recommendations

Brokers and analysts tend to be overly optimistic about stocks. They are generally unwilling to recommend that investors sell stocks because they do not want to offend any firms with which their own investment firm might do business in the future. In 1999, the firm First Call tracked 27,000 recommendations of stocks by analysts, and only 35 of these recommendations were to sell a specific stock. In other words, analysts made about 1 "sell" recommendation for every 770 "buy" recommendations.

In response to much criticism, recently some analysts have been more willing to offer sell recommendations on some stocks. However, there is still a tendency for analysts to be generally optimistic about most stocks and there may be some conflicts of interest. For example, an analyst may own the stock she is recommending, so it is in her best interest to create a demand for the stock so that its price will rise. Today, analysts have to disclose ownership of stocks that they recommend.

How Can You Review Your Broker's History? Go to the Web site http://www.nasd.com, where there is a section called Regulation Public-Disclosure. You can perform a search by typing in a broker's name and the name of the brokerage firm. You can review a broker's job history to determine whether a broker switches jobs excessively. You can also determine whether a broker has been convicted of a felony or filed for bankruptcy by going to the Disclosure Events section. The Web site http://nasd.com provides information regarding brokers who have been subject to disputes with customers that have been resolved through arbitration. In addition, you can go to your state regulator's Web site to find the phone number of the Central Registration Depository (CRD), where you can request a report that discloses whether any disciplinary action has been taken toward a broker.

discount brokerage firm
A brokerage firm that executes your desired transactions but does not offer investment advice.

full-service brokerage firm
A brokerage firm that offers investment advice and executes transactions.

Brokerage Commissions. You can choose a discount or full-service brokerage firm. A **discount brokerage firm** executes your desired transactions but does not offer investment advice. A **full-service brokerage firm** offers investment advice and executes transactions. Full-service brokerage firms tend to charge higher fees for their services than discount brokers. For example, a full-service brokerage firm may charge a commission of between 3 and 8 percent of the transaction, or between $150 and $400 for a $5,000 transaction, whereas a discount brokerage firm will likely charge you between $8 and $60 for the same transaction.

Buying or Selling Stock Online

Individuals who wish to buy or sell stocks are increasingly using online brokerage ser-vices such as Ameritrade and E*Trade. One advantage of placing orders online is that the commission charged per transaction is very low, such as $8 or $20, regardless of the size of the transaction (up to a specified maximum level). A second advantage is the convenience. In addition to accepting orders, online brokers provide real-time stock quotes and financial information. To establish an account with an online brokerage service, you go to its Web site and follow the instructions to set up an account. Then you send the online broker a check, and once the check has cleared, your account will show that you have funds that you can use to invest online.

Recall from Chapter 5 that many online brokerage firms have a money market fund where your cash is deposited until it is used to make transactions. Consequently, you can earn some interest on your funds until you use them to purchase securities. Once you place an order, the online brokerage firm will use the money in your money market fund to pay for the transaction. You may even receive blank checks so that you can write checks against your money market account.

As many investors have shifted to online brokerage, traditional brokerage firms (such as Quick & Reilly and Merrill Lynch), now offer online services. You can place an order from your computer in less than a minute, and the order will be executed within a minute.

Placing an Order

Whenever you place an order to buy or sell a stock, you must specify the following:

- Name of the stock
- Buy or sell
- Number of shares
- Market order or limit order

ticker symbol
The abbreviated term that is used to identify a stock for trading purposes.

Name of the Stock. It is important to know the **ticker symbol** for your stock. The ticker symbol is the abbreviated term that is used to identify a stock for trading purposes. For example, Microsoft's symbol is MSFT, and Nike's symbol is NKE. A symbol is shorter and simpler than the formal name of a firm and easily distinguishes between different firms with similar names.

Buy or Sell. Brokerage firms execute buy and sell transactions. Therefore, it is necessary to specify whether you are buying or selling a security at the time you place the order. Once you place your order and it is executed, you are bound by the instructions you gave.

round lot
Shares bought or sold in multiples of 100.

odd lot
Less than 100 shares of stock.

Number of Shares. Shares are typically sold in multiples of 100, referred to as **round-lot** transactions. An order to buy or sell less than 100 shares is referred to as an **odd-lot** transaction.

16.1 Financial Planning Online: Analyst Recommendations

Go to
http://finance.yahoo.com/?u

Click on
"Research" after you type the symbol of a stock in which you are interested

This Web site provides analyst recommendations about a stock that you specify.

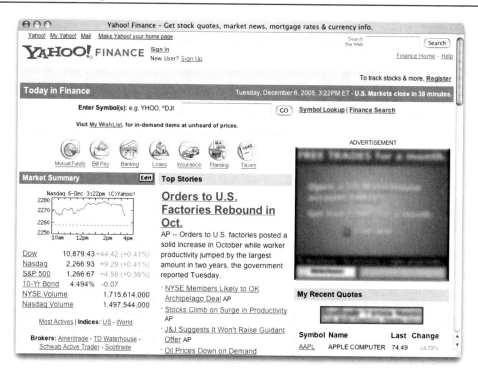

---

market order
An order to buy or sell a stock at its prevailing market price.

Market Order or Limit Order. You can buy or sell a stock by placing a **market order**, which is an order to execute the transaction at the stock's prevailing market price. The advantage of a market order is that you are assured that your order will be executed quickly. A disadvantage is that the stock price could change abruptly just before you place your order, causing you to pay much more for the stock than you expected.

EXAMPLE

You want to buy 100 shares of Trendy stock, which had a closing price of $40. You assume that you will pay about $40 per share when the market opens this morning, or $4,000 ($40 × 100 shares) for the shares ignoring the commission. However, your order is executed at $43, which means that you pay $4,300 ($43 × 100 shares). Unfortunately for you, many other investors wanted to buy Trendy stock this morning, creating increased demand for the stock. The strong demand relative to the small amount of shares available for sale caused the stock price to increase to $43 before your broker could find a willing seller of Trendy stock.

limit order
An order to buy or sell a stock only if the price is within limits that you specify.

Alternatively, you can buy or sell stock by placing a **limit order**, which is an order to execute the transaction only if the price is within the limits that you specify. A limit order sets a maximum price at which the stock can be purchased and can be for the day or good until canceled (normally canceled in six months if a transaction has not been executed by then). Your limit order will specify whether you are willing to accept a portion of the shares desired (normally, in round lots of 100); alternatively, you can specify that you want the full number of shares to be traded or none at all.

EXAMPLE

Using the information in the previous example, you place a limit order on Trendy stock, with a maximum limit of $41, good for the day. When the stock opens at $43 this morning, your order is not executed because the market price exceeds your limit price. Later in the day, the stock price declines to $41, at which time your order is executed.

16.2 Financial Planning Online: Trading Stocks Online

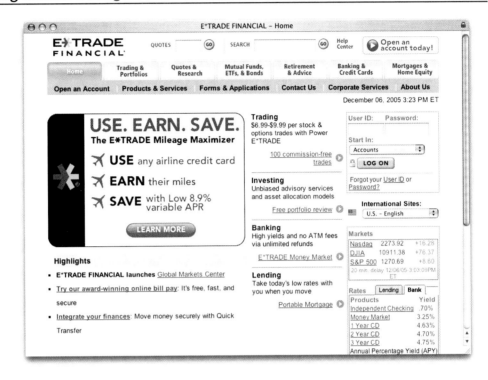

stop order
An order to execute a transaction when the stock price reaches a specified level; a special form of limit order.

The example on the previous page illustrates the advantage of a limit order. However, the disadvantage is that you may miss out on a transaction that you desired. If the price of Trendy stock had continued to rise throughout the day after opening at $43, your order would not have been executed at all.

Limit orders can also be used to sell stocks. In this case, a limit order specifies a minimum price at which the stock should be sold.

EXAMPLE

You own 100 shares of Zina stock, which is currently worth $18 per share. You would be willing to sell it at $20 per share. You do not have time to monitor the market price so that you can sell the stock when its price is at least $20 per share. So you place a limit order to sell 100 shares of Zina stock at a minimum price of $20, good until canceled. A few months later, Zina's price rises to $20 per share. You soon receive confirmation from your brokerage firm that the transaction has been executed.

buy stop order
An order to buy a stock when the price rises to a specified level.

sell stop order
An order to sell a stock when the price falls to a specified level.

Stop Orders. A **stop order** is a special form of limit order; it is an order to execute a transaction when the stock price reaches a specified level. A **buy stop order** is an order for the brokerage firm to buy a stock for the investor when the price rises to a specified level. Conversely, a **sell stop order** is an order for the brokerage firm to sell a stock when the price falls to a specified level.

BUYING STOCK ON MARGIN

on margin
Purchasing a stock with a portion of the funds borrowed from a brokerage firm.

Some investors choose to purchase stock **on margin**, meaning that a portion of their purchase is funded with money borrowed from their brokerage firm. Buying a stock on margin enables you to purchase stocks without having the full amount of cash necessary. Interest rates are sufficiently high so that brokerage firms earn a decent return on their loans.

The Federal Reserve limits the margin to 50 percent, so a maximum of 50 percent of the investment can be borrowed from the brokerage firm. For example, for a $1,500 purchase of stock, you and the brokerage firm would each pay $750. If the value of investments made with partially borrowed funds declines, you may receive a **margin call** from your brokerage firm, meaning that you have to increase the cash in your account to bring the margin back up to the minimum level.

margin call
A request from a brokerage firm for the investor to increase the cash in the account in order to bring the margin back up to the minimum level.

Impact of Margin on Returns

When you buy a stock on margin, the return on your investment is magnified. This effect is favorable if the stock's price increases over the period you hold the stock.

EXAMPLE   You want to buy 100 shares of Lynde stock, which would require $50 per share, or $5,000. You purchase the 100 shares of Lynde stock on margin by paying $3,000 in cash and borrowing $2,000 from the brokerage firm at an annual interest rate of 12 percent. After one year, you sell the stock for $60 per share, or $6,000, and repay the brokerage firm the amount borrowed plus interest. Lynde stock paid dividends of $1 per share, or $100 over the year. The return from buying a stock on margin is:

$$Return = (SP + D - I - LP)/I$$

where SP is the proceeds from selling the stock, D is the dividends received over the investment period, I is the initial cash investment, and LP is the amount paid to the broker to repay the loan after selling the stock at the end of the investment period.

You borrowed $2,000, so your loan repayment is:

$$LP = \$2,000 \times (1 + .12)$$
$$= \$2,240.$$

Thus, the return on your investment is:

$$Return = (SP + D - I - LP)/I$$
$$= (\$6,000 + \$100 - \$3,000 - \$2,240)/\$3,000$$
$$= .2867, \text{ or } 28.67\%.$$

If you had invested $5,000 cash to purchase the Lynde stock instead of relying on borrowed funds, there would have been no loan repayment. Your return would have been:

$$Return = (SP + D - I)/I$$
$$= (\$6,000 + \$100 - \$5,000)/\$5,000$$
$$= .22, \text{ or } 22\%.$$

Notice that the return from buying on margin was 6.67 percentage points higher than when using cash to make the investment.

Impact of Margin on Risk

Margin purchases can amplify stock price movements in a negative way as well. If the price of the stock you buy on margin declines, the negative return from buying on margin will be worse than the return from using all cash.

EXAMPLE   Suppose that Lynde stock declines to $40 per share (instead of increasing to $60 per share) by the end of the year, so you receive $4,000 when you sell the stock. Your return is:

$$Return = (SP + D - I - LP)/I$$
$$= (\$4,000 + \$100 - \$3,000 - \$2,240)/\$3,000$$
$$= -.38, \text{ or } -38\%.$$

If you had used all cash and no borrowed funds to buy Lynde stock, however, your return would be:

Return $= (SP + D - I)/I$

$= (\$4,000 + \$100 - \$5,000)/\$5,000$

$= -.18$, or -18%.

Thus, your return in this case is 20 percentage points worse when buying on margin.

Buying on margin changes the risk-return tradeoff. The higher the proportion of funds borrowed to buy on margin, the higher your potential return and the higher your risk.

ASSESSING PERFORMANCE OF STOCK INVESTMENTS

When investing in a stock, how can you measure the performance of your stock? How can you distinguish between performance due to general market conditions and performance due to the firm itself?

Comparing Returns to an Index

A convenient and effective method of measuring performance is to compare the return on your stock (or stock portfolio) to the return of a stock index representing similar types of stocks. Stock index returns are provided in most business periodicals and on numerous Web sites such as Yahoo!'s site.

EXAMPLE

Stephanie Spratt invested in one stock about one year (or four quarters) ago. The returns on her stock are shown in column 2 in Exhibit 16.1. Her return was lowest in the first quarter, but increased in the next three quarters. Stephanie wants to compare her stock's return to the market in general to get a true assessment of its performance. This comparison will indicate whether her specific selection generated a higher return than she could have earned by simply investing in a stock index. In Exhibit 16.1, the return on a market index over the same quarters is shown in column 3. Given the information in columns 2 and 3, Stephanie determines the excess return on her stock as:

$ER = R - R_i$

where ER is excess return, R is the return of her stock, and R_i is the return of the stock index.

The excess return of the stock was negative in each of the four quarters. Stephanie is disappointed in the performance of the stock, and decides to sell it in the near future if its performance does not improve.

Exhibit 16.1 Stock Performance Evaluation

	Return on Stephanie's Stock	Return on a U.S. Stock Index	Excess Return of Stephanie's Stock (above the market)
Quarter 1	−1%	3%	−4%
Quarter 2	2%	3%	−1%
Quarter 3	2%	4%	−2%
Quarter 4	3%	4%	−1%

Price Quotations for Indexes Used to Measure Stock Performance

Quotations of levels for market and sector indexes are reported in financial newspapers. For example, the *Wall Street Journal* provides stock index quotations, as shown in Exhibit 16.2. The *Wall Street Journal* shows the range of index levels during the previous day. It also provides the percentage change in each stock index over the previous day, the last 12 months, and since the start of the calendar year. Thus, it serves as a useful indicator of the general short-term stock market performance.

Consider the Standard & Poor's MidCap 400 index highlighted in Exhibit 16.2. The index level reached a high of 750.00 and a low of 732.57 for the day. When the market closed for the day, the index level was 749.02, which reflects a net change of 10.97, or an increase of 1.49 percent from the previous day. The index was up by 16.67 over the last year. The percentage change in the index from the beginning of the calendar year is shown in the last column.

Exhibit 16.2 An Example of Stock Index Information

Major Stock Indexes

	DAILY					52-WEEK			YTD
Dow Jones Averages	HIGH	LOW	CLOSE	NET CHG	% CHG	HIGH	LOW	% CHG	% CHG
30 Industrials	10862.78	10684.45	10847.41	+129.91	+1.21	10940.55	10012.36	+ 2.04	+1.21
20 Transportations	4215.15	4101.72	4199.16	+ 3.13	+0.07	4266.75	3382.89	+14.16	+0.07
15 Utilities	413.73	404.54	413.55	+ 8.44	+2.08	437.63	324.68	+25.91	+2.08
65 Composite	3678.66	3605.27	3675.02	+ 36.96	+1.02	3696.50	3211.74	+10.47	+1.02
Dow Jones Indexes									
Wilshire 5000	12727.51	12474.89	12713.88	+196.19	+1.57	12755.58	11217.81	+ 8.66	+1.57
Wilshire 2500	3016.77	2956.30	3013.36	+ 48.14	+1.62	3021.77	2662.75	+ 8.80	+1.62
Wilshire Lrg Gro	2683.52	2625.60	2679.28	+ 42.28	+1.60	2693.93	2289.69	+10.15	+1.60
Wilshire Lrg Val	3001.12	2948.29	2999.05	+ 48.89	+1.66	2999.05	2754.47	+ 7.05	+1.66
Wilshire Sml Gro	3109.89	3035.24	3104.69	+ 46.59	+1.52	3114.08	2546.44	+15.30	+1.52
Wilshire Sml Val	5051.53	4926.20	5045.86	+ 79.47	+1.60	5117.90	4338.99	+ 8.16	+1.60
Wilshire Micro	6939.39	6842.61	6937.68	+ 54.62	+0.79	6965.34	5851.39	+ 3.91	+0.79
Global Titans 50	201.00	196.74	200.62	+ 3.88	+1.97	200.62	188.00	+ 4.35	+2.04
Asian Titans 50	144.80	142.42	144.14	+ 1.64	+1.15	144.19	110.86	+21.74	+1.08
DJ STOXX 50	3399.10	3358.66	3379.72	+ 19.91	+0.59	3379.72	2763.16	+20.66	+0.91
Nasdaq Stock Market									
Nasdaq Comp	2249.68	2189.91	2243.74	+ 38.42	+1.74	2273.37	1904.18	+ 6.45	+1.74
Nasdaq 100	1686.59	1633.62	1679.93	+ 34.73	+2.11	1709.10	1406.85	+ 6.88	+2.11
Biotech	804.87	781.44	800.97	+ 10.66	+1.35	812.65	641.35	+ 8.14	+1.35
Computer	1020.92	988.53	1017.97	+ 26.17	+2.64	1034.43	845.22	+ 9.06	+2.64
Standard & Poor's Indexes									
500 Index	1270.22	1245.74	1268.80	+ 20.51	+1.64	1272.74	1137.50	+ 6.80	+1.64
MidCap 400	750.00	732.57	749.02	+ 10.97	+1.49	749.61	627.38	+16.67	+1.49
SmallCap 600	356.63	347.37	356.02	+ 5.35	+1.53	361.46	301.06	+12.25	+1.53
SuperComp 1500	287.29	281.56	286.95	+ 4.58	+1.62	287.93	255.39	+ 7.82	+1.62
New York Stock Exchange and Others									
NYSE Comp	7916.47	7753.97	7912.41	+158.46	+2.04	7912.41	6935.31	+11.59	+2.04
NYSE Financial	8165.74	7996.93	8160.51	+163.57	+2.05	8160.51	6905.21	+10.74	+2.05
Russell 2000	685.23	666.58	684.05	+ 10.83	+1.61	690.57	575.02	+ 8.83	+1.61
Value Line	418.44	409.57	417.87	+ 5.37	+1.30	420.30	363.98	+ 6.81	+1.30
Amex Comp	1797.76	1757.20	1794.99	+ 35.91	+2.04	1794.99	1385.85	+28.30	+2.04

Source: Reuters

16.3 Financial Planning Online: Stock Market Summary

Go to
http://www.bloomberg.com

Click on
"Market Data"

This Web site provides
a summary of recent stock performance.

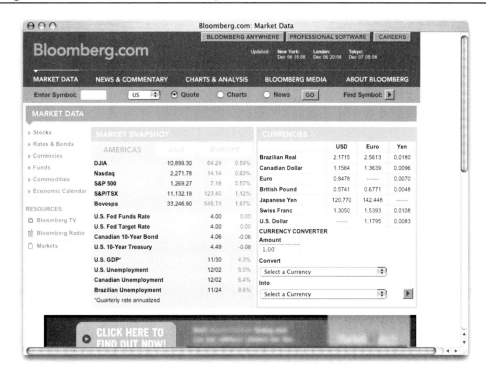

16.4 Financial Planning Online: Stock Index Quotations

Go to
http://finance.yahoo.com/m1?u

Click on
"Charts" to review historical movements in any specific index and assess the general trend in the performance of that index.

This Web site provides
recent quotations of indexes that can be used as benchmarks when assessing your investment portfolio's performance.

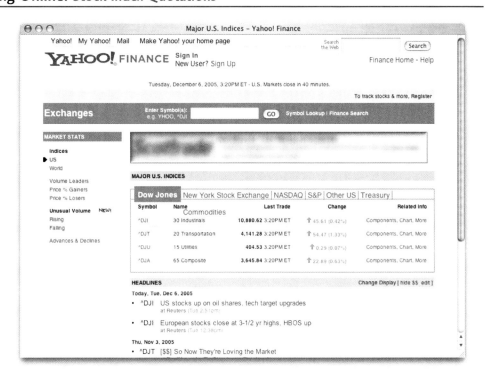

HOW STOCK INVESTMENT METHODS FIT WITHIN YOUR FINANCIAL PLAN

The following are the key decisions about investing in stock that should be included within your financial plan:

- Should you consider buying stock?

- Which stocks should you purchase?

- What methods should you use for investing in stocks?

The first decision was discussed in Chapter 14, while the second decision was considered in Chapter 15. The third decision, about how to conduct stock transactions, has been examined here. Exhibit 16.3 provides an example of how this decision applies to Stephanie Spratt's financial plan.

Exhibit 16.3 How Stock Investment Methods Fit within Stephanie Spratt's Financial Plan

GOALS FOR INVESTING IN STOCK

1. *Determine if I could benefit from investing in common stock (discussed in Chapter 15).*
2. *If I consider investing in stocks, determine which stocks to purchase (discussed in Chapter 15).*
3. *Determine how to execute stock transactions.*

ANALYSIS

Type of Brokerage Firm

Full-service	*Guidance on stock selection; higher commissions charged on transactions.*
Discount	*No guidance on stock selection; lower commissions charged on transactions.*

Type of Order When Purchasing Stock

Market Order	*A buy order is executed at the market price.*
Limit Order	*A buy order is only executed if the price is at or below a price that I may specify.*
Buy Stop Order	*A buy order is executed if the price rises to a price that I may specify.*

Whether to Borrow

Pay with Cash	*Need cash to pay for the entire investment. My return will be equal to the return on the stock itself.*
Buying on Margin	*Can make investment with less money (by borrowing a portion of the funds needed). My return will be larger than the return on the stock itself. My return (whether it is a gain or loss) is more pronounced if I borrow to buy the stock, which increases the risk of my investment.*

DECISION

In the future when I invest in stocks, I will use a discount broker instead of a full-service broker because I prefer to make my own investment decisions and the commissions charged by a discount broker are low. I will use only limit orders to buy stocks, so that I can set the maximum price that I am willing to pay. I will only invest in a stock if I have sufficient funds to cover the entire investment because it is a less risky method of executing a stock transaction. Buying on margin magnifies the return (whether positive or negative) on the stock, and causes the investment to be more risky than I desire.

DISCUSSION QUESTIONS

1. How would Stephanie's decisions concerning conducting stock transactions be different if she were a single mother of two children?

2. How would Stephanie's decisions concerning conducting stock transactions be affected if she were 35 years old? If she were 50 years old?

SUMMARY

Stocks are listed on stock exchanges, where they can be purchased or sold. You can relay your order to a brokerage firm, which sends the order to an exchange where the stock is listed. The order is executed by traders at the exchange. Some orders are executed through Electronic Communication Networks (ECNs), which are computer systems that match desired purchases and sales of stocks.

Once you have decided which stocks to buy or sell, you contact a brokerage firm. You can use an online brokerage firm, which can be more convenient and also less costly than a traditional full-service brokerage firm. Upon receiving your order, the brokerage firm sends your order to the stock exchange where the trade is executed.

When buying a stock on margin, you fund part of the purchase with money borrowed from the brokerage firm. This approach can magnify the returns that you earn from investing in the stock. However, it also magnifies the losses and therefore increases your risk.

After you execute a stock transaction, you should monitor the performance of your investment over time. Compare the return on that stock with an index of stocks that represents similar firms. Several stock market indexes and sector indexes are available to use as benchmarks when assessing a stock's performance.

INTEGRATING THE KEY CONCEPTS

This chapter explains the decisions involved in executing stock transactions. One of the key decisions is whether to buy stock with all cash or to buy stock on margin. This decision is related to the other parts of your financial plan. First, it is related to your liquidity decisions (Part 2), because if you buy on margin, you do not need to withdraw as much funds to make the investment. It is also related to your financing decision (Part 3) because it may limit the amount of additional financing that you can qualify for.

This chapter also explains how to assess the performance from your stock investments. Your investment performance may affect your insurance needs (Part 4) because you may need more liability coverage if your investments perform well and increase your wealth. Your investment performance also affects your retirement planning decisions (Part 6), because you may need to save additional funds for retirement if the return on your investment is low.

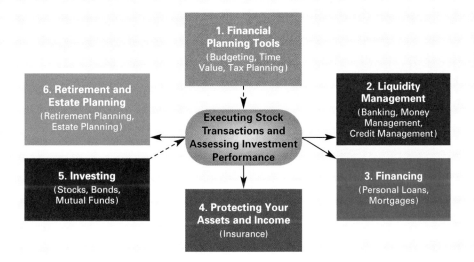

REVIEW QUESTIONS

1. What are stock exchanges? How do they facilitate the trading of stocks?

2. Describe a typical stock transaction at the New York Stock Exchange (NYSE). What are floor traders? What are specialists? What other exchanges trade stock similar to the NYSE?

3. What are Electronic Communication Networks (ECNs)? How are ECNs used?

4. How is the market for a stock created? How do brokerage firms expedite this process? Compare the two types of brokerage services.

5. What are some advantages of using online brokerage services? Describe how an investor would set up and use an online brokerage account.

6. What information must you provide when placing an order to buy or sell stock? What is a ticker symbol, and why is it important?

7. What do the terms *round lot* and *odd lot* mean in stock transactions?

8. Discuss the differences between a market order, a limit order, and a stop order.

9. List some reasons an investor should be cautious about using an adviser's recommendations when purchasing stock. Will investing according to an adviser's recommendations bring a higher return? Why or why not?

10. What is buying a stock on margin? What may happen if the value of the stock bought on margin declines? What are the advantages to investors and brokerage firms when stocks are bought on margin?

11. Discuss the impact of margin on risk and return.

12. Describe an effective method of measuring the performance of a stock.

13. How can market sectors be used to measure the performance of a stock? Give an example.

VIDEO QUESTIONS

1. Per this video segment, what are the four key rules to follow when investing in the stock market?

2. Professor Gary Gray discussed two methods of evaluating a company's stock. Explain these methods.

FINANCIAL PLANNING PROBLEMS

1. A year ago, Rebecca purchased 100 shares of Havad stock for $25 per share. Yesterday, she placed a limit order to sell her stock at a price of $30 per share before the market opened. The stock's price opened at $29 and slowly increased to $32 in the middle of the day, before declining to $28 by the end of the day. The stock did not pay any dividends over the period in which Rebecca held it. What was Rebecca's return on her investment?

2. Explain how the results would be different if Rebecca used a limit order of $33.

3. Trey wants to buy 200 shares of Turner stock that is selling for $40 per share. Trey pays $4,000 in cash and borrows $4,000 from his broker at 11 percent interest to complete the purchase. One year later, Trey sells the stock for $50 per share. What is Trey's return if the stock paid no dividends during the year?

4. What return would Trey (from problem 3) receive if he had purchased the stock without borrowing?

5. Ryan purchased 200 shares of Neptune stock on margin for $7,000. To complete the purchase, Ryan paid $5,000 and borrowed $2,000 from his broker at 13 percent interest. The stock paid $2 per share in dividends during the year, and Ryan sold the stock for $9,000 after one year. What is Ryan's return?

6. What return would Ryan (from problem 5) have received if he had sold the stock for $6,500 after one year?

7. Bill purchased an index mutual fund last year for $21 per share. The fund currently trades for $22.30 per share. Bill is happy with this performance. The S&P 500 index increased from a level of 932 to 967 during the same time period. What is the excess return on Bill's mutual fund?

Ethical Dilemma

8. Nick, a recent college graduate, wishes to begin investing to meet some of his financial goals. His father recommends a stockbroker who he says has always given him good advice. Nick's grandfather has also begun doing business with the same stockbroker as a result of Nick's father's recommendation. Over the next several months, the broker recommends four stocks as a must for Nick's portfolio. Nick buys all four stocks based on his broker's advice. During the family's annual reunion, Nick, his father, and grandfather compare their investing experiences with the same broker. Nick is surprised that the broker recommended the same four stocks to both his father and grandfather. Nick's father defends the broker by saying that if it's a good stock for Nick, why isn't it a good stock for all of them? Besides, his father says,

since the broker's company does all of the investment banking work for the four stocks that he recommended, they undoubtedly know everything there is to know about these four firms.

a. Discuss the ethical issues of the broker's recommending the same four stocks to Nick, his father, and his grandfather.

b. Why could these four stocks be a good investment for Nick, but not his father or grandfather?

FINANCIAL PLANNING ONLINE EXERCISES

1. Go to http://finance.yahoo.com to review analysts' stock recommendations.

a. Enter the stock symbol NOK, for Nokia Corporation. Click on "Analyst Opinion." Information on analysts' recommendations and various earnings-related information will be provided. What is the average broker recommendation? What is your opinion of Nokia after reviewing the analysts' comments and earnings estimates?

b. Now enter the symbol XRX, for Xerox. Click on "Research Reports." What is the average broker recommendation? What is your opinion of Xerox after reviewing the analysts' comments and estimates?

c. What are the major differences between Nokia and Xerox, based on the information on each company provided by analysts?

d. Now enter the symbol "T," for AT&T. Click on "Research Reports." What is the average broker

recommendation? What is your opinion of AT&T after reviewing the analysts' comments and estimates?

2. Go to http://www.bloomberg.com.

a. This site provides a snapshot of the S&P 500 stock index by clicking on "Market Data," then "Stocks," and finally "S & P 500." The best and worst performing stocks for the trading session can be found by clicking on "% Change." A listing of all 500 stocks in the index can be obtained by clicking at the bottom of the page. What categories of stocks did well, and what categories did poorly during this trading session?

b. Review the graphs that show the change in the index for the day and for the year. What does the trend in the yearly graph indicate about the performance of the stock market during the past 12 months?

3. Go to http://finance.yahoo.com/m1?u.

a. This Web site provides recent quotations of indexes such as the Dow Jones Averages, New York Stock Exchange, Nasdaq, and S&P 500. Click on "Chart" for any of the indexes shown and review historical movements of that index. Compare the percentage change in the NYSE Composite and the Nasdaq Composite for the last trading session. Comment on the reasons for any difference in the performance of the indexes.

b. Compare recent performance of the major U.S. indexes. Which index, in your opinion, most closely reflects the U.S. stock market currently? Why? Click on "Chart" for each index shown and review the performance of each one for the last 12 months. How does this information correspond to your choice for the best index?

BUILDING YOUR OWN FINANCIAL PLAN

Selecting the right stock investment method is an important decision for any investor. This case walks you through a list of questions designed to assist you in making the important decision of whether a full-service broker or online/discount broker better suits your needs. Carefully consider the types of investments you will be making, how frequently you will make transactions, and how important one-on-one advice from a broker is to you. When comparing brokerage firms' offerings, be sure to consider at least one online or discount broker.

As you get older and your portfolio grows in size and possibly in complexity, you need to review the suitability of your broker periodically just as you do your tax preparer, as we discussed in Chapter 4.

Go to the worksheets at the end of this chapter, and to the CD-ROM accompanying this text, to continue building your financial plan.

THE SAMPSONS—A CONTINUING CASE

Recall that one of the Sampsons' goals is to invest for their children's future college education. To become more educated investors, they have been reviewing analyst and brokerage firm recommendations on the Web site http://finance. yahoo.com. Dave and Sharon are ready to invest in several firms that this Web site identifies as having BUY recommendations. Before they purchase the stock, they ask you to weigh in with an opinion.

Go to the worksheets at the end of this chapter, and to the CD-ROM accompanying this text, to continue this case.

Chapter 16: Building Your Own Financial Plan

GOALS

1. Determine a method to use for investing in stocks.

ANALYSIS

1. Answer each of the following questions by checking the appropriate box.

	Yes	No
a. I will feel better if I have a specific person to talk to about my account.	☐	☐
b. I will require professional research assistance to make investment decisions.	☐	☐
c. I will utilize banking-type services such as check writing and debit cards.	☐	☐
d. I will feel more comfortable if I have a broker who calls me from time to time with suggestions about how to improve the performance of my portfolio.	☐	☐
e. I will have a relatively complex portfolio that includes an after-tax account, Roth and/or traditional IRAs, and rollover IRAs.	☐	☐
f. I will use my portfolio to meet a variety of goals with varying time horizons (short-, intermediate-, and long-term).	☐	☐
g. I will require advice on the tax implications of my investments.	☐	☐
h. My portfolio is large enough to require an annual review and rebalancing.	☐	☐
i. I will sleep better if I know who is watching my money.	☐	☐
j. I will feel better doing business with people who know my name.	☐	☐

If you answered "Yes" to five or more of the above questions, you should seriously consider a full-service broker. If you answered "Yes" to fewer than five, you should use an online/discount broker.

2. Use the following worksheet as a guide to compare three potential online or discount brokerage companies.

	Company 1	Company 2	Company 3
Cost per Trade	$	$	$
Available Investments:			
Common Stocks	☐Yes ☐No	☐Yes ☐No	☐Yes ☐No
Preferred Stocks	☐Yes ☐No	☐Yes ☐No	☐Yes ☐No
Corporate Bonds	☐Yes ☐No	☐Yes ☐No	☐Yes ☐No
Municipal Bonds	☐Yes ☐No	☐Yes ☐No	☐Yes ☐No
Options	☐Yes ☐No	☐Yes ☐No	☐Yes ☐No
Commodities	☐Yes ☐No	☐Yes ☐No	☐Yes ☐No
Annuities	☐Yes ☐No	☐Yes ☐No	☐Yes ☐No
Mutual Funds (Load)	☐Yes ☐No	☐Yes ☐No	☐Yes ☐No
Mutual Funds (No Load)	☐Yes ☐No	☐Yes ☐No	☐Yes ☐No
Money Markets	☐Yes ☐No	☐Yes ☐No	☐Yes ☐No

(continued)	Company 1	Company 2	Company 3
Navigability of Web Site			
Phone Access to Account Information			
Real-Time Portfolio Updates			
Minimum Initial Investment			
Availability of Banking Features (e.g., Credit Cards and Checks)			
Research Tools Available			
Accounts Available:			
Brokerage Account Maintenance Fee	☐Yes ☐No $_____	☐Yes ☐No $_____	☐Yes ☐No $_____
Traditional IRA Maintenance Fee	☐Yes ☐No $_____	☐Yes ☐No $_____	☐Yes ☐No $_____
Roth IRA Maintenance Fee	☐Yes ☐No $_____	☐Yes ☐No $_____	☐Yes ☐No $_____
Rollover IRA Maintenance Fee	☐Yes ☐No $_____	☐Yes ☐No $_____	☐Yes ☐No $_____
College Savings Accounts Maintenance Fee	☐Yes ☐No $_____	☐Yes ☐No $_____	☐Yes ☐No $_____
Referral Service to Independent Financial Advisers	☐Yes ☐No	☐Yes ☐No	☐Yes ☐No
Record-Keeping Services	☐Yes ☐No	☐Yes ☐No	☐Yes ☐No
Extended Hours Trading Service	☐Yes ☐No	☐Yes ☐No	☐Yes ☐No

3. What type of orders—market, limit, or buy stop—do you intend to use when purchasing stocks? Do you intend to pay with cash or buy on margin? Why?

_____

_____

_____

_____

DECISIONS

1. What type of brokerage firm will you work with—full-service or discount/online? Why?

_____

_____

_____

_____

_____

_____

_____

_____

2. Summarize your decision on the type of orders you will place to purchase stocks and your preference for using cash versus buying on margin.

_____

_____

_____

_____

_____

_____

_____

_____

_____

Chapter 16: The Sampsons—A Continuing Case

CASE QUESTIONS

1. Offer advice to the Sampsons on whether they should buy these stocks based on the information on the Web site.

2. Other Web sites identify firms that were top performers the previous day. Should the Sampsons buy these stocks? Explain.

Chapter 17

Investing in Bonds

Neal wanted to invest in bonds because he knew that they could provide periodic interest payments that would serve as a source of income. He knew that he could buy bonds issued by the U.S. Treasury. However, these bonds only offered a yield of 5 percent. Neal wanted to earn a higher yield. His broker suggested that he invest in junk bonds, which are issued by companies whose financial condition is weak. Neal noticed that some of these bonds offer a yield of 10 percent, double the yield provided by Treasury bonds. He also noticed that these bonds provided very high returns to investors over the previous five years while the economy was strong, much higher than U.S. Treasury bonds. He decided to invest in junk bonds issued by one particular company that were presently offering a yield of 11 percent. During the following year, the U.S. economy weakened and this company could not afford to cover its debt. It filed for bankruptcy and Neal's bonds became worthless. While many other companies also had poorer performance while the U.S. economy was weak, their financial condition was strong enough to cover their debt payments. Neal realized the potential adverse consequence of investing in risky bonds.

Like other investments, bonds have unique characteristics. As with stocks, the return and risk of bonds vary depending on their issuer as well as current and expected economic conditions. Understanding the different types of bonds and various bond investment strategies can help you build your own investment portfolio and enhance your wealth.

The objectives of this chapter are to:

- Identify the different types of bonds

- Explain what affects the return from investing in a bond

- Describe why some bonds are risky

- Identify common bond investment strategies

BACKGROUND ON BONDS

Recall that investors commonly invest some of their funds in **bonds**, which are long-term debt securities issued by government agencies or corporations. Bonds often offer more favorable returns than bank deposits. In addition, they typically provide fixed interest payments that represent additional income each year. The **par value** of a bond is its face value, or the amount returned to the investor at the maturity date when the bond is due.

Most bonds have maturities between 10 and 30 years, although some bonds have longer maturities. Investors provide the issuers of bonds with funds (credit). In return, the issuers are obligated to make interest (or coupon) payments and to pay the par value at maturity. When a bond has a par value of $1,000, a coupon rate of 6 percent means that $60 (.06 × $1,000) is paid annually to investors. The coupon payments are normally paid semiannually (in this example, $30 every six months). Some bonds are sold at a price below par value; in this case, investors who hold the bonds until maturity will earn a return from the difference between par value and what they paid. This income is in addition to the coupon payments earned.

You should consider investing in bonds rather than stock if you wish to receive periodic income from your investments. As explained in Chapter 19, many investors diversify among stocks and bonds to achieve their desired return and risk preferences.

Bond Characteristics

Bonds that are issued by a particular type of issuer can offer various features such as a call feature or convertibility.

Call Feature. A **call feature** on a bond allows the issuer to buy back the bond from the investor before maturity. This feature is desirable for issuers because it allows them to retire existing bonds with coupon rates that are higher than the prevailing interest rates.

Investors are willing to purchase bonds with a call feature only if the bonds offer a slightly higher return than similar bonds without a call feature. This premium compensates the investors for the possibility that the bonds may be called before maturity.

EXAMPLE   Five years ago, Cieplak, Inc., issued 15-year callable bonds with a coupon rate of 9 percent. Interest rates have declined since then. Today, Cieplak could issue new bonds at a rate of 7 percent. It decides to retire the existing bonds by buying them back from investors and to issue new bonds at a 7 percent coupon rate. By calling the old bonds, Cieplak has reduced its cost of financing.

Convertible Feature. A **convertible bond** allows the investor to convert the bond into a stated number of shares of the issuer's stock if the stock price reaches a specified price. This feature enables bond investors to benefit when the issuer's stock price rises. Because convertibility is a desirable feature for investors, convertible bonds tend to offer a lower return than nonconvertible bonds. Consequently, if the stock price does not rise to the specified trigger price, the convertible bond provides a lower return to investors than

bonds
Long-term debt securities issued by government agencies or corporations.

par value
For a bond, its face value, or the amount returned to the investor at the maturity date when the bond is due.

call feature
A feature on a bond that allows the issuer to repurchase the bond from the investor before maturity.

convertible bond
A bond that can be converted into a stated number of shares of the issuer's stock if the stock price reaches a specified price.

alternative bonds without a convertible feature. If the stock price does reach the trigger price, however, investors can convert their bonds into shares of the issuer's stock, thereby earning a higher return than they would have earned on alternative nonconvertible bonds.

A Bond's Yield to Maturity

yield to maturity
The annualized return on a bond if it is held until maturity.

A bond's **yield to maturity** is the annualized return on the bond if it is held until maturity. Consider a bond that is priced at $1,000, has a par value of $1,000, a maturity of 20 years, and a coupon rate of 10 percent. This bond has a yield to maturity of 10 percent, which is the same as its coupon rate, because the price paid for the bond equals the principal.

As an alternative example, if this bond's price were lower than the principal amount, its yield to maturity would exceed the coupon rate of 10 percent. The bond would also generate income in the form of a capital gain because the purchase price would be less than the principal amount to be received at maturity. Conversely, if this bond's price were higher than the principal amount, its yield to maturity would be less than the 10 percent coupon rate because the amount paid for the bond would exceed the principal amount to be received at maturity.

Bond Trading in the Secondary Market

Investors can sell their bonds to other investors in the secondary market before the bonds reach maturity. Bond prices change in response to interest rate movements and other factors. Some bonds are traded on stock exchanges such as the New York Stock Exchange. Other bonds are traded in the over-the-counter market. Many investors sell their bonds in the secondary market to raise funds to cover upcoming expenses or to invest in other more attractive types of securities. Brokerage firms take orders from investors to buy or sell bonds.

17.1 Financial Planning Online: Your Bond's Yield

Go to
http://www.calcbuilder.com/cgi-bin/calcs/BON1.cgi/yahoo_bonds

This Web site provides an estimate of the yield to maturity of your bond based on its present price, its coupon rate, and its maturity. Thus, you can determine the rate of return that the bond will generate for you from today until it matures.

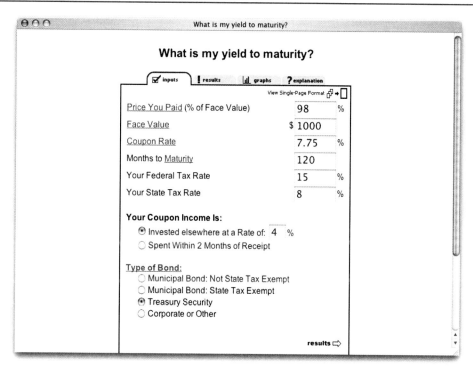

TYPES OF BONDS

Bonds can be classified according to the type of issuer as follows:

- Treasury bonds
- Municipal bonds
- Federal agency bonds
- Corporate bonds

Treasury Bonds

Treasury bonds
Long-term debt securities issued by the U.S. Treasury.

Treasury bonds are long-term debt securities issued by the U.S. Treasury, a branch of the federal government. Because the payments are guaranteed by the federal government, they are not exposed to the risk of default by the issuer. The interest on Treasury bonds is subject to federal income tax, but it is exempt from state and local taxes. Treasury bonds are very liquid because they can easily be sold in the secondary market.

Municipal Bonds

municipal bonds
Long-term debt securities issued by state and local government agencies.

Municipal bonds are long-term debt securities issued by state and local government agencies; they are funded with proceeds from municipal projects such as parks or sewage plants, as well as tax revenues, in some cases. Because a state or local government agency might possibly default on its coupon payments, municipal bonds are not free from the risk of default. Nevertheless, most municipal bonds have a very low default risk. To entice investors, municipal bonds that are issued by a local government with a relatively high level of risk offer a higher yield than other municipal bonds with a lower level of risk.

The interest on municipal bonds is exempt from federal income tax, which is especially beneficial to investors who are in tax brackets of 28 percent or higher. The interest is also exempt from state and local taxes when the investor resides in the same state as the municipality that issued the bonds. Municipal bonds tend to have a lower coupon rate than Treasury bonds issued at the same time. However, the municipal bonds may offer a higher after-tax return to investors.

EXAMPLE

Mike Rivas lives in Florida, where there is no state income tax. For federal income tax, however, he faces a 35 percent marginal rate, meaning that he will pay a tax of 35 percent on any additional income that he earns this year. Last year, Mike invested $100,000 in Treasury bonds with a coupon rate of 8 percent and $100,000 in municipal bonds with a coupon rate of 6 percent. His annual earnings from these two investments are shown here:

	Treasury Bonds		**Municipal Bonds**	
Interest income before taxes	$8,000	(computed as .08 × $100,000)	$6,000	(computed as .06 × $100,000)
Federal taxes owed	2,800	(computed as .35 × $8,000)	0	
Interest income after taxes	**$5,200**		**$6,000**	

Notice that even though Mike received more interest income from the Treasury bonds, he must pay 35 percent of that income to the federal government. Therefore, he keeps only 65 percent of that income, or a total of $5,200. In contrast, none of the interest income of $6,000 from the municipal bonds is taxed. Consequently, every year Mike receives $800 more in after-tax interest income from the municipal bonds with the 6 percent coupon rate than from the Treasury bonds with the 8 percent coupon rate.

Federal Agency Bonds

federal agency bonds
Long-term debt securities issued by federal agencies.

Federal agency bonds are long-term debt securities issued by federal agencies. The Government National Mortgage Association (called Ginnie Mae or abbreviated as GNMA), for example, issues bonds so that it can invest in mortgages that are insured by the Federal Housing Administration (FHA) and by the Veteran's Administration (VA). The Federal Home Loan Mortgage Association (called Freddie Mac) also commonly issues bonds and uses the proceeds to purchase conventional mortgages. A third government agency that commonly issues bonds is the Federal National Mortgage Association (Fannie Mae). Though federally chartered, it is owned by individual shareholders rather than the government. It uses the proceeds from the bonds to purchase residential mortgages.

The bonds issued by these three federal agencies are backed by the mortgages in which the agencies invest. Thus, the bonds have a very low degree of default risk. The income provided by these bonds is subject to state and federal taxes.

Corporate Bonds

corporate bonds
Long-term debt securities issued by large firms.

high-yield (junk) bonds
Bonds issued by smaller, less stable corporations that are subject to a higher degree of default risk.

Corporate bonds are long-term debt securities issued by large firms. The repayment of debt by corporations is not backed by the federal government, so corporate bonds are subject to default risk. At one extreme, bonds issued by corporations such as Coca-Cola and IBM have very low default risk because of the companies' proven ability to generate sufficient cash flows for many years. At the other extreme, bonds issued by smaller, less stable corporations are subject to a higher degree of default risk. These bonds are referred to as **high-yield bonds** or **junk bonds**. Many investors are willing to invest in junk bonds because they offer a relatively high rate of return. However, they are more likely to default than other bonds, especially if economic conditions are poor.

17.2 Financial Planning Online: Municipal Bond Quotations

Go to
http://www.bloomberg.com/markets/rates/index.html

This Web site provides quotations of yields offered by municipal bonds with various terms to maturity. Review this information when considering purchasing municipal bonds.

Corporate Bond Quotations. Corporate bond quotations are provided in the *Wall Street Journal*, as shown in Exhibit 17.1. The quotations include the following information:

- Coupon rate

- Maturity

- Current yield

- Volume

- Closing price

- Net change in the price from the previous trading day

Consider the bonds issued by Hewlett Packard Co. (HPQ). The bonds pay an annual coupon rate of 5.75 percent, which reflects a payment of $57.50 per $1,000 par of value. The maturity date of these bonds is December 15, 2006. The last price at which these bonds were traded on the previous day was 100.865, which means that the bonds are selling at a price just slightly above the par value. The last yield (4.796 percent) represents the yield that will be earned by investors who purchase the bond at the latest price and hold it until maturity. The estimated trading volume of Hewlett Packard bonds is $3,197,000.

RETURN FROM INVESTING IN BONDS

If you purchase a bond and hold it until maturity, you will earn the yield to maturity specified when you purchased the bond. As mentioned earlier, however, many investors sell bonds in the secondary market before they reach maturity. Since a bond's price changes over time, your return from investing in a bond is dependent on the price at the time you sell it.

Impact of Interest Rate Movements on Bond Returns

Your return from investing in a bond can be highly influenced by the interest rate movements over the period you hold the bond. To illustrate, suppose that you purchase a bond at par value that has a coupon rate of 8 percent. After one year, you decide to sell the bond. At this time, new bonds being sold at par value are offering a coupon rate of 9 percent. Since investors can purchase a new bond that offers coupon payments of 9 percent, they will not be willing to buy your bond unless you sell it to them for less than par value. In other words, you must offer a discount on the price to compensate for the bond's lower coupon rate.

If interest rates had declined over the year rather than increased, the opposite effects would have occurred. You could sell your bond for a premium above par value, because the coupon rate of your bond would be higher than the coupon rate offered on newly issued bonds. Thus, interest rate movements and bond prices are inversely related. Your return from investing in bonds will be more favorable if interest rates decline over the period you hold the bonds.

Tax Implications of Investing in Bonds

When determining the return from investing in a bond, you need to account for tax effects. The interest income that you receive from a bond is taxed as ordinary income for federal income tax purposes (except for tax-exempt bonds as explained earlier). Selling bonds in the secondary market at a higher price than the price you originally paid for them results in a capital gain. The capital gain (or loss) is the difference between the price at which you sell the bond and the initial price that you paid for it. Recall from

Exhibit 17.1 An Example of Corporate Bond Quotations

Corporate Bonds

Tuesday, January 3, 2006

Forty most active fixed-coupon corporate bonds

COMPANY (TICKER)	COUPON	MATURITY	LAST PRICE	LAST YIELD	*EST SPREAD	UST†	EST $ VOL (000's)
American General Finance Corp (AIG)	5.400	Dec 01, 2015	99.934	5.408	104	10	162,025
Lehman Brothers Holdings Inc (LEH)	5.000	Jan 14, 2011	99.958	5.008	69	5	67,425
Citigroup Inc (C)	5.300	Jan 07, 2016	101.338	5.126	78	10	63,580
General Electric Capital Corp (GE)	6.000	Jun 15, 2012	105.440	5.001	63	5	56,465
AT&T Inc (SBC)	6.150	Sep 15, 2034	100.473	6.114	156	30	55,558
Cardinal Health Inc (CAH)	5.850	Dec 15, 2017	102.528	5.557	117	10	52,770
Telefonos de Mexico S.A. de C.V. (TFONY)	8.250	Jan 26, 2006	100.240	3.782	n.a.	n.a.	50,400
TXU Electric Delivery Co (TXU)	6.375	May 01, 2012	105.376	5.359	99	5	44,056
Scottish Power PLC (SPW)	4.910	Mar 15, 2010	99.254	5.108	78	5	43,130
Goldman Sachs Capital I (GS)	6.345	Feb 15, 2034	105.636	5.930	135	30	41,933
National Rural Utilities Cooperative Finance Corp (NRUC)	6.000	May 15, 2006	100.451	4.681	n.a.	n.a.	40,096
Morgan Stanley (MWD)	6.600	Apr 01, 2012	107.792	5.123	75	5	37,911
Anheuser-Busch Companies Inc (BUD)	5.000	Mar 01, 2019	97.777	5.235	87	10	37,800
Diageo Investment Corp (DGE)	7.450	Apr 15, 2035	126.706	5.586	103	30	37,800
Simon Property Group, L.P. (SPG)	5.100	Jun 15, 2015	97.550	5.435	107	10	34,190
Credit Suisse First Boston (USA) Inc (CRDSUI)	3.875	Jan 15, 2009	97.133	4.906	59	3	32,056
Hewlett-Packard Co (HPQ)	5.750	Dec 15, 2006	100.865	4.796	n.a.	n.a.	31,970
Comcast Corp (CMCSA)	6.500	Nov 15, 2035	101.878	6.358	182	30	30,900
General Electric Capital Corp (GE)	4.875	Oct 21, 2010	99.859	4.907	58	5	29,966
General Electric Capital Corp (GE)	4.375	Mar 03, 2012	96.819	4.980	61	5	29,700
HSBC Finance Corp (HSBC)	5.750	Jan 30, 2007	100.971	4.801	n.a.	n.a.	29,628
First Data Corp (FDC)	4.700	Aug 01, 2013	93.543	5.764	140	10	28,083
General Electric Co (GE)	5.000	Feb 01, 2013	100.303	4.948	60	10	27,911
Lehman Brothers Holdings Inc (LEH)	4.800	Mar 13, 2014	97.829	5.127	76	10	27,717
John Deere Capital Corp (DE)	7.000	Mar 15, 2012	110.639	4.980	61	5	27,524
General Electric Capital Corp (GE)	5.875	Feb 15, 2012	104.658	4.980	61	5	26,291
Wachovia Corp (WB)	4.950	Nov 01, 2006	100.130	4.778	n.a.	n.a.	26,153
AT&T Inc (SBC)	5.100	Sep 15, 2014	98.014	5.388	102	10	26,068
Anchor Glass Container Corp (AGCC)	11.000	Feb 15, 2013	71.750	17.890	1353	10	25,836
International Lease Finance Corp (AIG)	3.300	Jan 23, 2008	96.892	4.910	57	2	25,780
Albertson's Inc (ABS)	6.950	Aug 01, 2009	101.343	6.520	222	3	25,650
Susa Partnership LP (GE)	8.200	Jun 01, 2017	124.076	5.351	98	10	25,356
Goldman Sachs Group Inc (GS)	5.150	Jan 15, 2014	99.557	5.218	85	10	25,307
Pfizer Inc (PFE)	4.500	Feb 15, 2014	98.329	4.750	40	10	25,302
Albertson's Inc (ABS)	8.350	May 01, 2010	105.904	6.747	242	5	25,270
Coca-Cola Enterprises Inc (CCE)	6.750	Sep 15, 2028	113.875	5.656	110	30	25,204
Enbridge Energy Partners LP (EEP)	4.750	Jun 01, 2013	95.437	5.508	114	10	25,200
Beneficial LLC (LAVORO)	6.330	Jan 14, 2008	102.600	4.963	62	2	25,200
Progressive Corp (PGR)	6.250	Dec 01, 2032	109.803	5.544	103	30	25,200
Pepco Holdings Inc (POM)	4.000	May 15, 2010	95.350	5.205	90	5	25,200
Diageo Capital PLC (DIAG)	4.850	May 15, 2018	96.135	5.279	90	10	25,080

Volume represents total volume for each issue; price/yield data are for trades of $1 million and greater. * Estimated spreads, in basis points (100 basis points is one percentage point), over the 2, 3, 5, 10 or 30-year hot run Treasury note/bond. 2-year: 4.250 11/07; 3-year: 4.375 11/08; 5-year: 4.375 12/10; 10-year: 4.500 11/15; 30-year: 5.375 02/31. †Comparable U.S. Treasury issue.

Source: MarketAxess Corporate BondTicker

Chapter 4 that a capital gain from an asset held one year or less is a short-term capital gain and is taxed as ordinary income. A capital gain from an asset held for more than one year is subject to a long-term capital gains tax.

EXAMPLE   You purchase 10 newly issued bonds for $9,700. The bonds have a total par value of $10,000 and a maturity of 10 years. The bonds pay a coupon rate of 8 percent, or $800 (computed as .08 × $10,000) per year. The coupon payments are made every six months, so each payment is $400. Exhibit 17.2 shows your return and the tax implications for four different scenarios. Notice how taxes incurred from the investment in bonds are dependent on the change in the bond price over time and the length of time the bonds are held.

VALUING A BOND

Before investing in a bond, you may wish to determine its value using time value of money analysis. A bond's value is determined as the present value of the future cash flows to be received by the investor, which are the periodic coupon payments and the principal payment at maturity. The present value of a bond can be computed by discounting the future cash flows (coupon payments and principal payment) to be received from the bond. The discount rate used to discount the cash flows should reflect your required rate of return. The value of a bond can be expressed as:

$$\text{Value of Bond} = \sum_{t=1}^{n} [C_t/(1 + k)^t] + Prin/(1 + k)^n$$

where C_t represents the coupon payments in year t, $Prin$ is the principal payment at the end of year n when the bond matures, and k is the required rate of return. Thus, the value of a bond is composed of the present value of the future coupon payments, along with the present value of the principal payment. If you pay the price that is obtained by this valuation approach and hold the bond to maturity, you will earn the return that you require.

Exhibit 17.2 Potential Tax Implications from Investing in Bonds

Scenario	Implication
1. You sell the bonds after 8 months at a price of $9,800.	You receive one $400 coupon payment 6 months after buying the bond, which is taxed at your ordinary income tax rate; you also earn a short-term capital gain of $100, which is taxed at your ordinary income tax rate.
2. You sell the bonds after 2 years at a price of $10,200.	You receive coupon payments (taxed at your ordinary income tax rate) of $800 in the first year and in the second year; you also earn a long-term capital gain of $500 in the second year, which is subject to the long-term capital gains tax in that year.
3. You sell the bonds after 2 years at a price of $9,500.	You receive coupon payments (taxed at your ordinary income tax rate) of $800 in the first year and in the second year; you also incur a long-term capital loss of $200 in the second year.
4. You hold the bonds until maturity.	You receive coupon payments (taxed at your ordinary income tax rate) in each year over the 10-year life of the bond. You also receive the bond's principal of $10,000 at the end of the 10-year period. This reflects a long-term capital gain of $300, which is subject to a long-term capital gains tax in the year you receive the gain.

17.3 Financial Planning Online: Today's Events That Could Affect Bond Prices

EXAMPLE

Victor is planning to purchase a bond that has seven years remaining until maturity, a par value of $1,000, and a coupon rate of 6 percent (let's assume the coupon payments are paid once annually at the end of the year). He is willing to purchase this bond only if he can earn a return of 8 percent because he knows that he can earn 8 percent on alternative bonds.

The first step in valuing a bond is to identify the coupon payments, principal payment, and required rate of return:

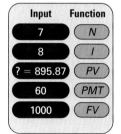

- Future cash flows:

  Coupon payment (C) = .06 × $1,000 = $60

  Principal payment (*Prin*) = $1,000

- Discount rate:

  Required rate of return = 8 percent.

The next step is to use this information to discount the future cash flows of the bond with the help of the present value tables in Appendix B:

$$
\begin{aligned}
\text{Value of Bond} \ &= \ \text{Present Value of Coupon Payments} + \text{Present Value of Principal} \\
&= \ [C \times (PVIFA, 8\%, 7 \text{ yrs})] + [Prin \times (PVIF, 8\%, 7 \text{ yrs})] \\
&= \ [\$60 \times 5.2064] + [\$1,000 \times .5835] \\
&= \ \$312.38 + \$583.50 \\
&= \ \$895.88.
\end{aligned}
$$

When using a financial calculator to determine the value of the bond, the future value will be $1,000 because this is the amount the bondholder will receive at maturity.

Based on this analysis, Victor is willing to pay $895.88 for this bond, which will provide his annualized return of 8 percent. If he can obtain the bond for a lower price, his return will exceed 8 percent. If the price exceeds $895.88, his return would be less than 8 percent, so he would not buy the bond.

The market price of any bond is based on investors' required rate of return, which is influenced by the interest rates that are available on alternative investments at the time. If bond investors require a rate of return of 8 percent as Victor does, the bond will be priced in the bond market at the value derived by Victor. However, if the bond market participants use a different required rate of return than Victor, the market price of the bond will be different. For example, if most investors require a 9 percent return on this bond, the bond will have a market price below the value derived by Victor (conduct your own valuation using a 9 percent discount rate to verify this).

RISK FROM INVESTING IN BONDS

Bond investors are exposed to the risk that the bonds may not provide the expected return. The main sources of risk are default risk, call risk, and interest rate risk.

Default Risk

risk premium
The extra yield required by investors to compensate for the risk of default.

default risk
Risk that the borrower of funds will not repay the creditors.

If the issuer of the bond (a government agency or a firm) defaults on its payments, investors do not receive all of the coupon payments that they are owed and do not receive the principal. Investors will invest in a risky bond only if it offers a higher yield than other bonds to compensate for its risk. The extra yield required by investors to compensate for default risk is referred to as a **risk premium**. Treasury bonds do not contain a risk premium because they are free from **default risk**.

To illustrate how bond prices can change due to the perceived default risk, consider the case of various telecommunications companies that experienced weak performance over the one-year period ending in May 2002. During that year, investors became concerned that some of these companies might not be capable of repaying their debt. Consequently, the price of AT&T bonds declined by 8 percent, the price of Qwest bonds declined by about 24 percent, the price of Sprint bonds declined by 11 percent, the price of WorldCom bonds declined by 53 percent, and the price of Global Crossing bonds declined by 98 percent.

Use of Risk Ratings to Measure the Default Risk. Investors can use ratings (provided by agencies such as Moody's Investor Service or Standard and Poor's) to assess the risk of corporate bonds. The ratings reflect the likelihood that the issuers will repay their debt over time. The ratings are classified as shown in Exhibit 17.3. Investors can select the corporate bonds that fit their degree of risk tolerance by weighing the higher potential return against the higher default risk of lower-grade debt securities.

Relationship of Risk Rating to Risk Premium. The lower (weaker) the risk rating, the higher the risk premium offered on a bond.

Impact of Economic Conditions. Bonds with a high degree of default risk are most susceptible to default when economic conditions are weak. Investors may lose all or most of their initial investment when a bond defaults. They can avoid default risk by investing in Treasury bonds or can at least keep the default risk to a minimum by investing in government agency bonds or AAA-rated corporate bonds. However, they will receive a lower yield on these bonds than investors who are willing to accept a higher degree of default risk.

Exhibit 17.3 Bond Rating Classes

Risk Class	Standard & Poor's	Moody's
Highest quality (least risk)	AAA	Aaa
High quality	AA	Aa
High-medium quality	A	A
Medium quality	BBB	Baa
Medium-low quality	BB	Ba
Low quality	B	B
Poor quality	CCC	Caa
Very poor quality	CC	Ca
Lowest quality	DDD	C

E X A M P L E

Stephanie Spratt reviews today's bond yields as quoted in financial newspapers for bonds with a 10-year maturity, as shown in the second column:

Type of Bond	Bond Yield Offered	Risk Premium Contained within Bond Yield
Treasury bonds	7.0%	0.0%
AAA-rated corporate bonds	7.5	0.5
A-rated corporate bonds	7.8	0.8
BB-rated corporate bonds	8.8	1.8
CCC-rated corporate bonds	9.5	2.5

Based on the bond yields, she derives the risk premium for each type of bond, shown in the third column. Notice that since the Treasury bonds are risk-free, they have no risk premium. However, the other bonds have a risk premium, which is the amount by which their annualized yield exceeds the Treasury bond yield. The premium can change over time.

Stephanie decides that she prefers Treasury bonds or AAA-rated bonds to other types of bonds because she believes the risk premium is not enough compensation for the risk. However, at this time, she cannot afford to buy any type of bond. Some investors would select specific CCC-rated corporate bonds that they believe will not default. If these bonds do not default, they will provide a yield that is 2.0 percentage points above the yield offered on AAA-rated bonds and 2.5 percentage points above the yield offered on Treasury bonds.

Focus on Ethics: Accounting Fraud and Default Risk

If a bond is issued by a firm whose financial statements become questionable, its price can decline quickly. Firms such as Enron, Global Crossing, Qwest Communications, and WorldCom have used misleading accounting techniques to hide their debt or to inflate their revenue. The higher bond rating, which indicates a lower risk to investors, allows the firm to obtain funds at a lower cost when issuing bonds.

Yet once a debt rating agency becomes aware that the financial statements are misleading, it will lower the bond rating and investors will in turn reduce their demand for the bonds. In addition, investors will lose trust in the firm. Even if a bond does not default, its price will decline when the perception of its risk is increased by credit rating agencies and investors. Under these conditions, investors will likely earn a negative return on their investment.

The role of the Securities and Exchange Commission (SEC) is to ensure that firms accurately disclose their financial condition. However, some firms still provide misleading financial statements. Some bondholders who invested in the bonds issued by Enron, WorldCom, and many other firms that recently went bankrupt lost most or all of their investment. Therefore, you need to recognize that a firm may default on its bonds even if its most recent financial statement was very optimistic.

Call Risk

call (prepayment) risk
The risk that a callable bond will be called.

Bonds with a call feature are subject to **call risk** (also called **prepayment risk**), which is the risk that the bond will be called. If issuers of callable bonds call these bonds, the bondholders must sell them back to the issuer.

E X A M P L E   Two years ago, Christine Ramirez purchased 10-year bonds that offered a yield to maturity of 9 percent. She planned to hold the bonds until maturity. Recently, interest rates declined and the issuer called the bonds. Christine could use the proceeds to buy other bonds, but the yield to maturity offered on new bonds is lower because interest rates have declined. The return that Christine will earn from investing in new bonds is likely to be less than the return that she would have earned if she could have retained the 10-year bonds until maturity.

Interest Rate Risk

interest rate risk
The risk that a bond's price will decline in response to an increase in interest rates.

All bonds are subject to **interest rate risk**, which is the risk that the bond's price will decline in response to an increase in interest rates. A bond is valued as the present value of its future expected cash flows. Most bonds pay fixed coupon payments. If interest rates rise, investors will require a higher return on a bond. Consequently, the discount rate applied to value the bond is increased, and the market price of the bond will decline.

E X A M P L E   Three months ago, Rob Suerth paid $10,000 for a 20-year Treasury bond that has a par value of $10,000 and a 7 percent coupon rate. Since then, interest rates have increased. New 20-year Treasury bonds with a par value of $10,000 are priced at $10,000 and offer a coupon rate of 9 percent. Thus, Rob would earn 2 percentage points more in coupon payments from a new bond than from the bond he purchased three months ago. He decides to sell his Treasury bond and use the proceeds to invest in the new bonds. He quickly learns that no one in the secondary market is willing to purchase his bond for the price he paid. These investors avoid his bond for the same reason that he wants to sell it; they would prefer to earn 9 percent on the new bonds rather than earn 7 percent on his bond. The only way that Rob can sell his bond is by lowering the price to compensate for the bond's lower coupon rate (compared to new bonds).

Impact of a Bond's Maturity on Its Interest Rate Risk. Bonds with longer terms to maturity are more sensitive to interest rate movements than bonds that have short terms remaining until maturity. To understand why, consider two bonds. Each has a par value of $1,000 and offers a 9 percent coupon rate, but one bond has 20 years remaining until maturity while the other has only 1 year remaining until maturity. If market interest rates suddenly decline from 9 to 7 percent, which bond would you prefer to own? The bond with 20 years until maturity becomes very attractive because you would be able to receive coupon payments reflecting a 9 percent return for the next 20 years. Conversely, the bond with one year remaining until maturity will provide the 9 percent payment only over the next year. Although the market price of both bonds increases in response to the decline in interest rates, it increases more for the bond with the longer term to maturity.

"Interest rates gyrated wildly today, on rumors that the Federal Reserve Board would be replaced by the cast of 'Saturday Night Live.'"

Now assume that, instead of declining, interest rates have risen from their initial level of 9 percent to 11 percent. Which bond would you prefer? Each bond provides a 9 percent coupon rate, which is less than the prevailing interest rate. The bond with one year until maturity will mature soon, however, so you can reinvest the proceeds at the higher interest rates at that time (assuming the rates are still high). Conversely, you are stuck with the other bond for 20 more years. Although neither bond would be very desirable under these conditions, the bond with the longer term to maturity is less desirable. Therefore, its price in the secondary market will decline more than the price of the bond with a short term to maturity.

Selecting an Appropriate Bond Maturity. Since bond prices change in response to interest rate movements, you may wish to choose maturities on bonds that reflect your expectations of future interest rates. If you prefer to reduce your exposure to interest rate risk, you may consider investing in bonds that have a maturity that matches the time when you will need the funds. If you expect that interest rates will decline over time, you may consider investing in bonds with longer maturities than the time when you will need the funds. In this way, you can sell the bonds in the secondary market at a relatively high price, assuming that your expectations were correct. If interest rates increase instead of declining over this period, however, your return will be reduced.

BOND INVESTMENT STRATEGIES

If you decide to invest in bonds, you need to determine a strategy for selecting them. Most strategies involve investing in a diversified portfolio of bonds rather than in one bond. Diversification reduces your exposure to possible default by a single issuer. If you cannot afford to invest in a diversified portfolio of bonds, you may consider investing in a bond mutual fund with a small minimum investment (such as $1,000). Additional information on bond mutual funds is provided in Chapter 18. Whether you focus on individual bonds or bond mutual funds, the bond investment strategies summarized here apply.

Interest Rate Strategy

interest rate strategy
Selecting bonds for investment based on interest rate expectations.

With an **interest rate strategy**, you select bonds based on interest rate expectations. When you expect interest rates to decline, you invest heavily in long-term bonds whose prices will increase the most if interest rates fall. Conversely, when you expect interest rates to increase, you shift most of your money to bonds with short terms to maturity in order to minimize the adverse impact of the higher interest rates.

Investors who use the interest rate strategy may experience poor performance if their guesses about the future direction of interest rate movements are incorrect. In addition, this strategy requires frequent trading to capitalize on shifts in expectations of interest rates. Some investors who follow this strategy frequently sell their entire portfolio of bonds so that they can shift to bonds with different maturities in response to shifts in interest rate expectations. The frequent trading results in high transaction costs (in the form of commissions to brokerage firms). In addition, the high turnover of bonds may generate more short-term capital gains, which are taxed at the ordinary federal income tax rate. This rate is higher for most investors than the tax on long-term capital gains.

Passive Strategy

passive strategy
Investing in a diversified portfolio of bonds that are held for a long period of time.

With a **passive strategy**, you invest in a diversified portfolio of bonds that are held for a long period of time. The portfolio is simply intended to generate periodic interest income in the form of coupon payments. The passive strategy is especially valuable for investors who want to generate stable interest income over time and do not want to incur costs associated with frequent trading.

A passive strategy does not have to focus on very safe bonds that offer low returns; it may reflect a portfolio of bonds with diversified risk levels. The diversification is intended to reduce the exposure to default from a single issuer of bonds. To reduce exposure to interest rate risk, a portfolio may even attempt to diversify across a wide range of bond maturities.

One disadvantage of this strategy is that it does not capitalize on expectations of interest rate movements. Investors who use a passive strategy, however, are more comfortable matching general bond market movements than trying to beat the bond market and possibly failing.

Maturity Matching Strategy

matching strategy
Investing in bonds that will generate payments to match future expenses.

The **matching strategy** involves selecting bonds that will generate payments to match future expenses. For example, parents of an 8-year-old child may consider investing in a 10-year bond so that the principal can be used to pay for the child's college education. Alternatively, they may invest in a bond portfolio just before retirement so that they will receive annual income (coupon payments) to cover periodic expenses after retirement. The matching strategy is conservative, in that it is simply intended to cover future expenses, rather than to beat the bond market in general.

HOW BOND DECISIONS FIT WITHIN YOUR FINANCIAL PLAN

The following are the key decisions about bonds that should be included within your financial plan:

- Should you consider buying bonds?

- What strategy should you use for investing in bonds?

Exhibit 17.4 provides an example of how bond decisions apply to Stephanie Spratt's financial plan. Stephanie's first concern is maintaining adequate liquidity and making her existing loan payments. She is not in a position to buy bonds right now, but will consider bonds once her financial position improves.

Exhibit 17.4 How Bonds Fit within Stephanie Spratt's Financial Plan

GOALS FOR INVESTING IN BONDS

1. Determine if I could benefit from investing in bonds.

2. If I decide to invest in bonds, determine what strategy to use to invest in bonds.

ANALYSIS

Strategy to Invest in Bonds	Opinion
Interest rate strategy	*I cannot forecast the direction of interest rates (even experts are commonly wrong on their interest rate forecasts), so this strategy could backfire. This strategy would also complicate my tax return.*
Passive strategy	*May be appropriate for me in many situations, and the low transaction costs are appealing.*
Maturity matching strategy	*Not applicable to my situation, since I am not trying to match coupon payments to future expenses.*

DECISIONS

Decision on Whether to Invest in Bonds:

I cannot afford to buy bonds right now, but I will consider purchasing them in the future when my financial position improves. Bonds can generate a decent return, and some bonds are free from default risk. I find Treasury or AAA-rated bonds to be most attractive.

Decision on the Strategy to Use for Investing in Bonds:

I am not attempting to match coupon payments with future anticipated expenses. I may consider expected interest rate movements according to financial experts when I decide which bond fund to invest in, but I will not shift in and out of bond funds frequently to capitalize on expected interest rate movements. I will likely use a passive strategy of investing in bonds and will retain bond investments for a long period of time.

DISCUSSION QUESTIONS

1. How would Stephanie's bond investing decisions be different if she were a single mother of two children?

2. How would Stephanie's bond investing decisions be affected if she were 35 years old? If she were 50 years old?

SUMMARY

Bonds are long-term debt securities. Bonds can be classified by their issuer. The common issuers are the U.S. Treasury, municipalities, federal government agencies, and corporations.

A bond's yield to maturity is the annualized return that is earned by an investor who holds the bond until maturity. This yield is composed of interest (coupon) payments and the difference between the principal value and the price at which the bond was originally purchased.

Bonds can be exposed to default risk, which reflects the possibility that the issuer will default on the bond payments. Some bonds are exposed to call risk, or the risk that the bond will be called before maturity. Bonds are also subject to interest rate risk, or the risk of a decline in price in response to rising interest rates.

A popular bond strategy is the interest rate strategy, where the selection of which bonds to buy is dependent on the expectation of future interest rates. An alternative strategy is a passive strategy, in which a diversified portfolio of bonds is maintained. A third bond strategy is the maturity matching strategy, in which the investor selects bonds that will mature on future dates when funds will be needed.

INTEGRATING THE KEY CONCEPTS

Your decision to invest in bonds is not only related to your other investment decisions, but also affects other parts of your financial plan. Before investing in bonds, you should reassess your liquidity (Part 2). Bonds that provide periodic coupon payments offer some liquidity. However, the value of a bond is subject to an abrupt decline, and you may not want to sell the bond when its price is temporarily depressed.

The bond decision is related to financing (Part 3) because you should consider paying off any personal loans before you invest in bonds. If after considering your liquidity and your financing situation, you still decide to invest in bonds, you need to decide whether the investment should be for

your retirement account (Part 6). There are some tax advantages to that choice, but also some restrictions on when you have access to those funds (as explained in more detail in Chapter 20).

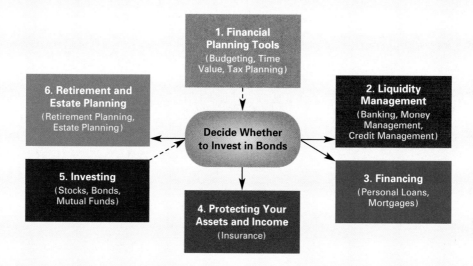

REVIEW QUESTIONS

1. What is a bond? What is a bond's par value? What are coupon payments, and how often are they normally paid? What happens when investors buy a bond below par value? When should you consider investing in bonds?

2. What is a call feature on a bond? How will a call feature affect investor interest in purchasing the bond?

3. What is a convertible bond? How does a bond's convertibility feature affect its return?

4. What is a bond's yield to maturity? How does the price paid for a bond affect its yield to maturity?

5. Discuss how bonds are sold on the secondary market.

6. What are Treasury bonds? Describe their key characteristics.

7. What are municipal bonds? Why are they issued? Are all municipal bonds free from default risk? What characteristic makes municipal bonds especially attractive to high-income investors?

8. What are federal agency bonds? Compare and contrast the three most common federal agency bonds.

9. What are corporate bonds? Are corporate bonds subject to default risk? What are junk bonds? Why would investors purchase junk bonds?

10. List the information provided in corporate bond quotations.

11. When an investor sells a bond in the secondary market before the bond reaches maturity, what determines the return on the bond? How do interest rate movements affect bond returns in general?

12. Discuss the effect of taxes on bond returns.

13. Discuss default risk as it relates to bonds. How may investors use risk ratings? What is the relationship between the risk rating and the risk premium? How do economic conditions affect default risk?

14. What is the risk to investors on bonds that have a call feature?

15. What is interest rate risk? How does a rise in interest rates affect a bond's price?

16. How is interest rate risk affected by a bond's maturity? How can investors use expectations of interest rate movements to their advantage?

17. Describe how the interest rate strategy for bond investment works. What are some of the potential problems with this strategy?

18. How does the passive strategy for bond investment work? What is the main disadvantage of this strategy?

19. Describe the maturity matching strategy of investing in bonds. Give an example. Why is this strategy considered conservative?

20. How is the value of a bond determined? What information is needed to perform the calculation?

VIDEO QUESTIONS

1. How does inflation factor into an investment's return?

2. How does Mr. Westbury explain that a bond can be used to finance a child's education?

FINANCIAL PLANNING PROBLEMS

1. Bernie purchased 20 bonds with par values of $1,000 each. The bonds carry a coupon rate of 9 percent payable semiannually. How much will Bernie receive for his first interest payment?

2. Paul has $10,000 that he wishes to invest in bonds. He can purchase Treasury bonds with a coupon rate of 7 percent or municipal bonds with a coupon rate of 5.5 percent. Paul lives in a state with no state income tax and has a marginal tax rate of 25 percent. Which investment will give Paul the higher annual earnings after taxes are considered?

3. Sandy has a choice between purchasing $5,000 in Treasury bonds paying 7 percent interest or purchasing $5,000 in BB-rated corporate bonds with a coupon rate of 9.2 percent. What is the risk premium on the BB-rated corporate bonds?

4. Bonnie paid $9,500 for corporate bonds that have a par value of $10,000 and a coupon rate of 9 percent, payable annually. Bonnie received her first interest payment after holding the bonds for 12 months and then sold the bonds for $9,700. If Bonnie is in a 35 percent marginal tax bracket for federal income tax purposes, what are the tax consequences of her ownership and sale of the bonds?

5. Katie paid $9,400 for a Ginnie Mae bond with a par value of $10,000 and a coupon rate of 6.5 percent. Two years later, after having received the annual interest payments on the bond, Katie sold the bond for $9,700. What are her total tax consequences if she is in a 25 percent marginal tax bracket?

6. Timothy has an opportunity to buy a $1,000 par value municipal bond with a coupon rate of 7 percent and a maturity of five years. The bond pays interest annually. If Timothy requires a return of 8 percent, what should he pay for the bond?

7. Mia wants to invest in Treasury bonds that have a par value of $20,000 and a coupon rate of 4.5 percent. The bonds have a 10-year maturity, and Mia requires a 6 percent return. How much should Mia pay for her bonds, assuming interest is paid annually?

8. Emma is considering purchasing bonds with a par value of $10,000. The bonds have an annual coupon rate of 8 percent and six years to maturity. The bonds are priced at $9,550. If Emma requires a 10 percent return, should she buy these bonds?

9. Mark has a Treasury bond that has a par value of $30,000 and a coupon rate of 6 percent. The bond has 15 years to maturity. Mark needs to sell the bond and new bonds are currently carrying coupon rates of 8 percent. At what price should Mark sell the bond?

10. What if Mark's Treasury bond in the previous question had a coupon rate of 9 percent and new bonds still had interest rates of 8 percent? What price should Mark sell the bond for in this situation?

Ethical Dilemma

11. John is a relatively conservative investor. He has recently come into a large inheritance and wishes to invest the money were he can get a good return, but not worry about losing his principal. His broker recommends that he buy 20-year corporate bonds in the country's largest automobile company, United General. His broker assures him that the bonds are secured by the assets of the company and the interest payments are contractually set. He explains that although all investments carry some risk, the risk of losing his investment with these bonds is minimal. John buys the bonds and over the next two years enjoys the steady stream of interest payments. During the third year, United General posts the largest quarterly loss in its history. Although the company is far from bankruptcy, the bond rating agencies downgrade the company's bonds to junk status. John is horrified to see the decline in the price in his bonds as he is considering selling a large portion of them to buy a home. When he discusses his dissatisfaction with his broker, his broker tells him that he is still receiving his interest payments and if he holds the bonds until maturity he will not sustain a loss. The broker reiterates that in their initial meeting John's concerns were safety of principal and interest payments and the investment still offers both of these.

a. Was the broker being ethical by not informing John of the other risks involved in the purchase of bonds? Why or why not?

b. What could John have done differently with his bond investments if he anticipated buying a home in the next three to five years?

FINANCIAL PLANNING ONLINE EXERCISES

1. Go to http://screen.yahoo.com/bonds.html.

   a. Under bond type, select "Treasury bonds." For price, select "Prem > 100" and for coupon range," select ">3%." Click "Find Bonds" and review the Treasury bonds that satisfy the criteria. Then go back and add an additional criterion, in which maturity is ">10" years. Click "Find Bonds." What happens to the list of eligible Treasury bonds?

   b. Now go back and change to Corporate bonds instead of Treasury bonds. Click "Find Bonds." Notice the change in the types of bonds that satisfy your criteria.

   c. Now go back and add another criterion, in which the minimum debt rating is "BBB." Notice the change in the types of bonds that satisfy your criteria.

   d. Now go back and change the minimum debt rating to "AA" and click "Find Bonds." What happens to the list of eligible bonds?

   e. Now go back and add another criterion that the bonds be callable and click "Find Bonds." What happens to the list of eligible bonds?

2. Go to http://www.bondsonline.com/ Todays_Market/Composite_Bond_Yields.php, which allows you to monitor the performance of the bond market.

   a. You will see a list of the current yield to maturity for Treasury bonds, agency bonds, and corporate bonds Explain the differences in rates within each category and among the categories.

   b. Now look at the graph entitled "Yield Curve." What does the Yield Curve tell you? Does the Yield Curve look normal? If not, why?

3. Go to http://www.bloomberg.com/markets/rates/ index.html. You will see information on municipal bond yields for various maturities. The yields observed during the last two trading days will be shown along with the percentage change in yields. The yields from a week ago and six months ago will also be provided. The equivalent yield on a taxable bond for an investor with a federal marginal tax rate of 28 percent will be shown for comparison, as the interest received on municipal bonds is exempt from federal income taxes. Why are the yields different for the various maturities?

BUILDING YOUR OWN FINANCIAL PLAN

Based on an investor's risk tolerance and/or timeline for goal achievement, bonds may prove to be a useful investment instrument. Referring to the risk tolerance test that you took in Chapter 14 and the goals that you established in Chapter 1, consider the extent to which bonds may play a role in your overall financial planning. Carefully consider whether any of your financial goals can be met with bond investing; revise your goals and personal cash flow statement to reflect any decision you make.

Bonds, like stocks, need to be reviewed as market conditions change, although bonds are far less volatile than stocks and, therefore, do not require daily monitoring.

Go to the worksheets at the end of this chapter, and to the CD-ROM accompanying this text, to continue building your financial plan.

THE SAMPSONS—A CONTINUING CASE

The Sampsons are considering investing in bonds as a way of saving for their children's college education. They learn that there are bonds with maturities between 12 and 16 years from now, which is exactly when they need the funds for college expenses. Dave and Sharon notice that some highly rated municipal bonds offer a coupon rate of 5 percent, while some highly rated corporate bonds offer a coupon rate of 8 percent. The Sampsons could purchase either type of bond at its par value. The income from the corporate bonds would be subject to tax at their marginal rate of 25 percent. The income on the municipal bonds would not be subject to federal income tax. Dave and Sharon are looking to you for advice on whether bonds are a sound investment and, if so, what type of bond they should purchase.

Go to the worksheets at the end of this chapter, and to the CD-ROM accompanying this text, to continue this case.

Chapter 17: Building Your Own Financial Plan

GOALS

1. Determine if you could benefit from investing in bonds.
2. If you decide to invest in bonds, determine what strategy to use.

ANALYSIS

1. Go to http://www.smartmoney.com and click on "Economy and Bonds." This will bring you to a page that contains numerous articles that you should review to determine if bonds are suitable for your portfolio considering your financial goals. Review these articles in detail, particularly the one entitled A Bond Primer.

2. Go to http://www.investinginbonds.com. Click on "Learn More," then "Buying and Selling Bonds," then "Investor's Checklist." Answer the basic questions and review the perspective of each question.

After completing your review, carefully consider whether any of your financial goals could be met with bond investing. Indicate the bond type (Treasury, corporate, municipal, government agency) and maturity.

Short-Term Goals	Use Bonds? (Yes or No)	Type of Bond	Maturity (Years)	Reasoning (Factoring in Risk Exposure)
1.				
2.				
3.				
Intermediate-Term Goals				
1.				
2.				
3.				
Long-Term Goals				
1.				
2.				
3.				

3. Consider the suitability of the following bond investment strategies for your financial situation. Enter your conclusions in the second column.

Strategy to Invest in Bonds	Opinion
1. Interest Rate Strategy	
2. Passive Strategy	
3. Maturity Matching Strategy	

4. Review your personal cash flow statement. If you decide bonds are a good investment, allocate money for them.

Personal Cash Flow Statement

Cash Inflows	This Month
Disposable (after-tax) income	
Interest on deposits	
Dividend payments	
Other	
Total Cash Inflows	

Cash Outflows	
Rent/Mortgage	
Cable TV	
Electricity and water	
Telephone	
Groceries	
Health care insurance and expenses	
Clothing	
Car expenses (insurance, maintenance, and gas)	
Recreation	
Other	
Total Cash Outflows	
Net Cash Flows	

DECISIONS

1. Describe your rationale for investing or not investing in bonds.

_____

_____

_____

_____

2. If you decide to invest in bonds, what strategy will you use?

_____

_____

_____

_____

Chapter 17: The Sampsons—A Continuing Case

CASE QUESTIONS

1. Should the Sampsons consider investing a portion of their savings in bonds to save for their children's education? Why or why not?

_____

_____

_____

_____

2. If the Sampsons should purchase bonds, what maturities should they consider, keeping in mind their investment goal?

_____

_____

_____

_____

3. If the Sampsons should consider bonds, should they invest in corporate bonds or municipal bonds? Factor into your analysis the return they would receive after tax liabilities, based on the bonds having a $1,000 par value and the Sampsons being in a 25 percent marginal tax bracket.

_____

_____

_____

_____

After-Tax Rate Computation

Corporate Bond Yield	
Marginal Tax Rate	
After-Tax Rate	
Annual After-Tax Interest ($)	

4. The Sampsons learn that many corporate bonds have recently been downgraded due to questionable financial statements. However, the Sampsons are not concerned, since the corporate bond they are considering is highly rated. Explain the possible impact of a downgrade of the corporate bond to the Sampsons, given their financial goals.

_____

_____

_____

_____

_____

_____

_____

_____

Investing in Mutual Funds

Rob bought 200 shares of a mutual fund for $25 per share in late September. By December, his mutual fund shares were priced at $23.50, so he was not terribly disappointed, as this was a long-term investment.

What surprised Rob, however, was the capital gains distribution that he received in December. While the value of his investment was $300 less than the purchase price, the mutual fund distributed $3.95 per share, a total distribution of $790 that Rob must report as taxable income. What Rob failed to realize at the time of his purchase was that the fund he had selected was sitting on accumulated capital gains from stocks that it had purchased in previous years. After five years of good returns, the fund managers had sold some of the stocks within the fund to lock in gains. Rob, as a current shareholder, received his share of the gains. Too late, Rob realized that most mutual funds distribute their gains, as they are required to do so by law, near the end of the year. Rob has more to learn about mutual funds and their tax implications.

This chapter explains how to invest in stock mutual funds and bond mutual funds to diversify your investment portfolio. An understanding of mutual funds can help you make proper investment decisions and can enhance your wealth.

The objectives of this chapter are to:

- Identify the types of stock funds
- Present the types of bond funds
- Explain how to choose among mutual funds
- Describe quotations of mutual funds
- Explain how to diversify among mutual funds

BACKGROUND ON MUTUAL FUNDS

stock mutual funds
Funds that sell shares to individuals and invest the proceeds in stocks.

bond mutual funds
Funds that sell shares to individuals and invest the proceeds in bonds.

Mutual funds can be broadly distinguished according to the securities in which they invest. **Stock mutual funds** sell shares to individuals and invest the proceeds in stocks. **Bond mutual funds** sell shares to individuals and invest the proceeds in bonds. Mutual funds employ portfolio managers who decide what securities to purchase; the individual investors do not have to select stocks themselves. The minimum investment in a mutual fund is usually between $500 and $3,000, depending on the fund. Many mutual funds are subsidiaries of other types of financial institutions.

Motives for Investing in Mutual Funds

By investing in a mutual fund, you can invest in a broadly diversified portfolio with a small initial investment. If you have $1,000 to invest, you (along with other investors) can own a portfolio of 100 or more stocks through a mutual fund. Yet, if you had attempted to buy stocks directly with your $1,000, you might not have enough money to buy even 100 shares of a single stock.

A second motive for investing in mutual funds is the expertise of the portfolio managers. Your investments reflect the decisions of experienced professionals who have access to the best research available.

A third motive for investing in mutual funds is that they can meet specific investment goals. For example, some mutual funds are designed to satisfy investors who desire potential appreciation in their investments, while other mutual funds are designed to provide periodic income to investors.

Net Asset Value

net asset value (NAV)
The market value of the securities that a mutual fund has purchased minus any liabilities owed.

Each mutual fund's value can be determined by its **net asset value (NAV)**, which represents the market value of the securities that it has purchased minus any liabilities owed. For example, suppose that a mutual fund owns 100 different stocks including 10,000 shares of Nike that are currently worth $60 per share. This mutual fund's holdings of Nike are worth $600,000 (computed as $60 × 10,000 shares) as of today. The value of the other 99 stocks owned by the fund is determined in the same manner, and all the values are summed. Then, any liabilities such as expenses owed to the mutual fund's managers are subtracted to determine the NAV.

The NAV is commonly reported on a per-share basis by dividing the NAV by the number of shares in the fund. Each day, the market value of all the mutual fund's assets is determined. Any interest or dividends earned by the fund are added to the market value of the assets, and any expenses (such as mailing, marketing, and portfolio management) that are charged to the fund or any dividends distributed to the fund's shareholders (investors) are deducted. As the value of the mutual fund's portfolio increases, so does the fund's NAV.

Open-End versus Closed-End Funds

open-end mutual funds
Funds that sell shares directly to investors and repurchase those shares whenever investors wish to sell them.

Mutual funds are classified as either open-end funds or closed-end funds.

Open-End Funds. **Open-end mutual funds** sell shares directly to investors and repurchase those shares whenever investors wish to sell them. The funds are managed by investment companies that are commonly subsidiaries of a larger financial conglomer-

family
A group of separately managed open-end mutual funds held by one investment company.

closed-end funds
Funds that sell shares to investors but do not repurchase them; instead fund shares are purchased and sold on stock exchanges.

premium
The amount by which a closed-end fund's share price in the secondary market is above the fund's NAV.

discount
The amount by which a closed-end fund's share price in the secondary market is below the fund's NAV.

no-load mutual funds
Funds that sell directly to investors and do not charge a fee.

load mutual funds
Funds whose shares are sold by a stockbroker who charges a fee (or load) for the transaction.

ate. Merrill Lynch, Citigroup, First Union, and many other financial institutions have investment company subsidiaries that operate open-end mutual funds. Many investment companies operate a **family**, or group of separately managed open-end mutual funds. For example, Fidelity, T. Rowe Price, and Vanguard manage several different open-end funds, each of which has its own investment objective. By offering a diverse set of mutual funds, these investment companies satisfy investors with many different investment preferences.

Consider an open-end stock mutual fund that receives $10 million today as new investors purchase shares of the fund. In addition, today some investors who had previously purchased shares decide to sell those shares back to the fund, resulting in $6 million in redemptions in the fund. In this example, the stock mutual fund has a net difference of $4 million of new money that its portfolio managers will invest.

On some days, the value of redemptions may exceed the value of new shares purchased. Mutual fund managers typically maintain a small portion of the fund's portfolio in the form of cash or marketable securities so that they have sufficient liquidity when redemptions exceed new share purchases. Otherwise, they could sell some stocks in their portfolio to obtain the necessary money for redemptions.

Closed-End Funds. **Closed-end funds** issue shares to investors when the funds are first created, but do not repurchase shares from investors. Unlike an open-end fund, shares of a closed-end fund are purchased and sold on stock exchanges. Thus, the fund does not sell new shares upon demand to investors and does not allow investors to redeem shares. The market price per share is determined by the demand for shares versus the supply of shares that are being sold. The price per share of a closed-end fund can differ from the fund's NAV per share. A closed-end fund's share price may exhibit a **premium** (above the NAV) in some periods and a **discount** (below the NAV) in other periods.

Load versus No-Load Funds

Open-end mutual funds can be either load funds or no-load funds. **No-load mutual funds** sell directly to investors and do not charge a fee. Conversely, **load mutual funds** charge a fee (or load) when you purchase them. In most cases, the fee goes to stockbrokers or other financial service advisers who execute transactions for investors in load mutual funds. Since no-load funds do not pay a fee to brokers, brokers are less likely to recommend them to investors.

Investors should recognize the impact of loads on their investment performance. In some cases, the difference in loads is the reason one mutual fund outperforms another.

EXAMPLE

You have $5,000 to invest in a mutual fund. You have a choice of investing in a no-load fund by sending your investment directly to the fund or purchasing a mutual fund that has a 4 percent load and has been recommended by a broker. Each fund has an NAV of $20 per share, and their stock portfolios are very similar. You expect each fund's NAV will be $22 at the end of the year, which would represent a 10 percent return from the prevailing NAV of $20 per share (assuming there are no dividends or capital gain distributions over the year). You plan to sell the mutual fund in one year. If the NAVs change as expected, your return for each fund will be as shown in Exhibit 18.1.

Notice that you would earn a return of 10 percent on the no-load fund versus 5.6 percent on the load fund. While the load fund's portfolio generated a 10 percent return, your return is less because of the load fee. Based on this analysis, you decide to purchase shares of the no-load fund.

Studies on mutual funds have found that no-load funds perform at least as well as load funds on average, even when ignoring the fees paid on a load fund. When considering the fee paid on load funds, no-load funds have outperformed load funds, on average.

So why do some investors purchase load funds? They may believe that specific load funds will generate high returns and outperform other no-load funds, even after considering the fee that is charged. Or perhaps some investors who rely on their brokers for advice do not consider no-load funds. Some investors may purchase load funds because they do not realize that there are no-load funds or do not know how to invest in them. To invest in no-load funds, you can simply call an 800 number for an application or print it off a fund's Web site.

Expense Ratios

expense ratio
The annual expenses per share divided by the net asset value of a mutual fund.

As mentioned earlier in this chapter, mutual funds incur expenses, including administrative, legal, and clerical expenses and portfolio management fees. Some mutual funds have much higher expenses than others. These expenses are incurred by the fund's shareholders because the fund's NAV (which is what investors receive when redeeming their shares) accounts for the expenses incurred. Investors should review the annual expenses of any mutual funds in which they invest. In particular, they should focus on the fund's **expense ratio**, which measures the annual expenses per share divided by the NAV of the fund. An expense ratio of 1 percent means that shareholders incur annual expenses amounting to 1 percent of the value of the fund. The higher the expense ratio, the lower the return for a given level of portfolio performance. Mutual funds that incur more expenses are worthwhile only if they offer a high enough return to offset the extra expenses.

On average, mutual funds have an expense ratio of about 1.5 percent. The expense ratios of mutual funds can be found in various financial newspapers and on many financial Web sites.

Exhibit 18.1 Comparison of Returns from a No-Load Fund and a Load Fund

No-Load Fund

Invest $5,000 in the mutual fund	$5,000
Your investment converts to 250 shares	− $0
	$5,000
	÷ $20
$5,000/$20 per share = 250 shares	250 shares
End of Year 1: You redeem shares for $22 per share	× $22
Amount received = 250 shares × $22 = $5,500	$5,500
Return = ($5,500 − $5,000)/$5,000 = 10%	10%

Load Fund

Invest $5,000; 4% of $5,000 (or $200) goes to the broker	$5,000
	− $200
The remaining 96% of $5,000 (or $4,800) is used to purchase 240 shares	$4,800 ÷ $20
$4,800/$20 per share = 240 shares	240 shares
You redeem shares for $22 per share	× $22
Amount received = 240 shares × $22 = $5,280	$5,280
Return = ($5,280 − $5,000)/$5,000 = 5.6%	5.6%

Reported Components of Expense Ratios. Many mutual funds break their expense ratios into three categories: management, 12b-1 fee, and other. The management fee represents the fee charged for managing the mutual funds portfolio and is typically the largest component of the expense ratio. It includes the cost of researching various securities and compensating the employees who manage the mutual fund portfolio. The 12b-1 fee is charged by some mutual funds to pay brokers who invest in the mutual fund on behalf of customers. A mutual fund may be called "no-load" but still compensate brokers. Some mutual funds have this arrangement with brokers because it enables them to attract more investors. Yet, the shareholders who invest in the mutual fund incur a higher expense ratio than if the fund did not charge such a fee. The 12b-1 fee can be as high as 1 percent of assets. The third category of the expense ratio ("other" expenses) includes general business expenses such as mailing and customer service.

Some mutual funds do not include the commissions that they pay brokers within their reported expense ratio. This expense may be .5 percent or more for some mutual funds. Thus, the exclusion of the commissions from the expense ratio is misleading and allows some mutual funds to understate the expenses that are charged to shareholders. Until regulators require clearly standardized reporting by mutual funds, investors must recognize the difference in the reporting process among mutual funds.

Relationship between Expense Ratios and Performance. Research has shown that mutual funds with relatively low expenses tend to outperform other funds with similar objectives. This finding suggests that the mutual funds with higher expenses cannot justify them.

TYPES OF MUTUAL FUNDS

Investors can select from a wide array of mutual funds, including stock mutual funds and bond mutual funds. Each category includes many types of funds to suit the preferences of individual investors.

Types of Stock Mutual Funds

Open-end stock mutual funds are commonly classified according to their investment objectives. If you consider investing in a stock mutual fund, you must decide on the type of fund in which you wish to invest. Some of the more common investment objectives are described here.

growth funds
Mutual funds that focus on stocks that have potential for above-average growth.

Growth Funds. Growth funds focus on stocks that have potential for above-average growth.

capital appreciation funds
Mutual funds that focus on stocks that are expected to grow at a very high rate.

Capital Appreciation Funds. Capital appreciation funds focus on stocks that are expected to grow at a very high rate. These firms tend to pay low or no dividends so that they can reinvest all of their earnings to expand.

small capitalization (small-cap) funds
Mutual funds that focus on firms that are relatively small.

Small Capitalization (Small-Cap) Funds. Small capitalization (small-cap) funds focus on firms that are relatively small. Small-cap funds and capital appreciation funds overlap somewhat because smaller firms tend to have more potential for growth than larger firms.

mid-size capitalization (mid cap) funds
Mutual funds that focus on medium-size firms.

Mid-Size Capitalization (Mid-Cap) Funds. Mid-size capitalization (mid-cap) funds focus on medium-size firms. These firms tend to be more established than small-cap firms, but may have less growth potential.

equity income funds
Mutual funds that focus on firms that pay a high level of dividends.

Equity Income Funds. Equity income funds focus on firms that pay a high level of dividends. These firms tend to exhibit less growth because they use a relatively large portion of their earnings to pay dividends rather than reinvesting earnings for expansion. The firms normally have less potential for high returns and exhibit less risk.

balanced growth and income funds
Mutual funds that contain both growth stocks and stocks that pay high dividends.

sector funds
Mutual funds that focus on a specific industry or sector, such as technology stocks.

technology funds
Mutual funds that focus on stocks of Internet-based firms and therefore represent a particular type of sector fund.

index funds
Mutual funds that attempt to mirror the movements of an existing stock index.

Balanced Growth and Income Funds. **Balanced growth and income funds** contain both growth stocks and stocks that pay high dividends. This type of fund distributes dividends periodically, while offering more potential for an increase in the fund's value than an equity income fund.

Sector Funds. **Sector funds** focus on stocks in a specific industry or sector, such as technology stocks. Investors who expect a specific industry to perform well may invest in a sector fund. Sector funds enable investors with a small amount of funds to invest in a diversified portfolio of stocks within a particular sector.

An example of a sector fund is a **technology fund**, which focuses on stocks of Internet-based firms. Most of these firms are relatively young. They have potential for very high returns, but also exhibit a high degree of risk because they do not have a consistent record of strong performance.

Index Funds. **Index funds** are mutual funds that attempt to mirror the movements of an existing stock index. Investors who invest in an index fund should earn returns similar to what they would receive if they actually invested in the index. For example, Vanguard offers a mutual fund containing a set of stocks that moves in the same manner as the S&P 500 index. It may not contain every stock in the index, but it is still able to mimic the index's movement. Since the S&P 500 index includes only very large stocks, an S&P 500 index fund does not necessarily move in tandem with the entire stock market.

Other index funds mimic broader indexes such as the Wilshire 5000 for investors who want an index that represents the entire stock market. In addition, there are small capitalization index funds that are intended to mirror movements in the small-cap index. Other index funds mimic foreign stock indexes, such as a European index and a Pacific Basin index. Investors who want to invest in a particular country, but do not want to incur excessive expenses associated with foreign stock exchanges, can invest in an index fund targeted to that country.

Index funds have become very popular because of their performance relative to other mutual funds. They incur less expenses than a typical mutual fund because they are not actively managed. The index fund does not incur expenses for researching various stocks because it is intended simply to mimic an index. In addition, the fund's portfolio is not frequently revised. Consequently, index funds incur very low transaction costs, which can enhance performance. Some index funds have expense ratios of between 0.20 and 0.30 percent, which is substantially lower than the expense ratios of most other mutual funds.

Index funds can also offer tax advantages. Since they engage in less trading than most other mutual funds, they generate a limited amount of capital gains that must be distributed to shareholders. Those index funds composed of stocks that do not pay dividends are especially valuable because they do not have dividend income that must be distributed to shareholders.

Much research has found that the performance of portfolios managed by portfolio managers is frequently lower than the performance of an existing stock index. Thus, investors may be better off investing in an index fund rather than investing in an actively managed portfolio.

Some index funds have expense ratios that are 1.25 percent or higher, even though their portfolio management expenses are low. You should ensure that the expense ratio is low before selecting a fund.

EXAMPLE   You consider investing in either a no-load mutual fund that focuses on growth stocks or an index mutual fund. When ignoring expenses incurred by the mutual funds, you expect that the growth fund will generate an annual return of 9 percent versus an annual return of 8 percent for the index fund. The growth fund has an expense ratio of 1.5 percent, versus an expense ratio of 0.2 percent for the index fund. Based on your expectations about the portfolio returns, your returns would be:

	Growth Fund	Index Fund
Fund's portfolio return (before expenses)	9.0%	8.0%
Expense ratio	1.5%	0.2%
Your annual return	**7.5%**	**7.8%**

The comparison shows that the index fund can generate a higher return for you than the other fund even if its portfolio return is lower. Based on this analysis, you should invest in the index fund.

international stock funds

Mutual funds that focus on firms that are based outside the United States.

socially responsible stock funds

Mutual funds that screen out firms viewed as offensive by some.

International Stock Funds. **International stock funds** focus on firms that are based outside the United States. Some of these funds focus on firms in a specific country, while others focus on a specific region or continent. Many of these funds require a minimum investment of $1,000 to $2,500, but a few require only $500. Funds with a country or regional concentration are attractive to investors who want to invest in a specific country, but prefer to rely on an experienced portfolio manager to select the stocks. The expenses associated with managing a portfolio are higher for international mutual funds than for other mutual funds because monitoring foreign firms from the United States is expensive. In addition, transaction costs from buying and selling stocks of foreign firms are higher. Nevertheless, many international stock funds have expense ratios that are less than 1.8 percent.

Some mutual funds invest in stocks of both foreign firms and U.S. firms. These are called "global mutual funds" to distinguish them from international mutual funds.

Socially Responsible Stock Funds. **Socially responsible stock funds** screen out firms viewed as offensive by some investors. For example, they may not invest in firms that produce cigarettes or guns or that pollute the environment.

18.1 Financial Planning Online: Index Mutual Funds

Go to
http://www.indexfunds.com/

This Web site provides news and other information about index mutual funds that can guide your investment decisions.

Even though the funds distributed the same amount to you, your taxes on the Index Fund distributions are $117 lower. Thus, your after-tax income from that fund is $117 higher than your income from the tech fund, as shown in Exhibit 18.2.

As the above example illustrates, individuals in higher tax brackets can reduce their tax liability by investing in mutual funds with low short-term capital gain distributions.

Capital Gain from Redeeming Shares.   You earn a capital gain if you redeem shares of a mutual fund when the share price exceeds the price at which you purchased the shares. For example, if you purchase 200 shares of a stock mutual fund at a price of $25 per share and sell the shares for $30, your capital gain will be:

$$
\begin{aligned}
\text{Capital Gain} &= (\text{Selling Price per Share} - \text{Purchase Price per Share}) \\
&\quad \times \text{Number of Shares} \\
&= (\$30 - \$25) \times 200 \\
&= \$1,000.
\end{aligned}
$$

If you held the shares for more than one year, you have a long-term capital gain. If you held them for one year or less, your gain is subject to your ordinary income tax rate.

Determining your capital gain is more difficult when you have reinvested distributions in the fund because each distribution results in the purchase of more shares at the prevailing price on that day. The capital gain on the shares purchased at the time of the distribution is dependent on the price you paid for them. Many investors rely on the mutual fund to report their capital gain after they redeem the shares. Now that many mutual fund companies allow you to review your account online, finding price information is simple.

Returns vary among stock mutual funds in any particular period. While they are normally affected by the general stock market conditions, stock mutual funds' returns could vary with the specific sector or industry in which the stocks are concentrated. For example, technology stocks performed better than other types of stocks in the late 1990s, so mutual funds focusing on technology stocks performed well at this time. In the 2001–2003 period, stocks as a group did not perform well. Because of the significant rise in price that technology stocks had experienced in the 1990s (resulting more from speculation than from actual increases in earnings) the price declines were even greater than for non-technology stocks. The same mutual funds whose performance was enhanced in the 1990s by focusing on technology stocks now suffered the greatest decline in performance.

Exhibit 18.2 Potential Tax Implications from Investing in Mutual Funds

	Index Mutual Fund	Technology Mutual Fund
Dividends	$800	$0
ST capital gain	0	900
LT capital gain	200	100
Total income	$1,000	$1,000
Tax on dividends (15%)	$120	$0
Tax on ST capital gains (28%)	0	252
Tax on LT capital gains (15%)	30	15
Total taxes	$150	$267
After-tax income	$850	$733

18.2 Financial Planning Online: Return from Investing in Mutual Funds

Go to
http://www.bloomberg.com/
markets/mutualfunds/index.
html

This Web site provides information on the top 25 mutual funds in the United States as well as several foreign countries.

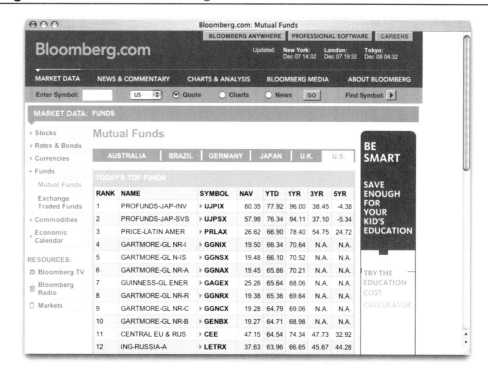

Since the returns are highly dependent on the performance of the sector in which the stock mutual fund is concentrated, be careful when comparing mutual funds. The difference between the performance of two stock mutual funds during a particular period may be attributed to the sector and not to the managers of the funds. Some investors tend to invest in whatever stock mutual fund performed well recently because they presume that the fund has the best portfolio managers. However, if the fund performed well just because its sector performed well, then it would be a mistake to judge the management based on past performance.

Risk from Investing in a Stock Mutual Fund

market risk
The susceptibility of a mutual fund's performance to general stock market conditions.

Although different types of stock mutual funds experience different performance levels in a given time period, they are all influenced by general stock market conditions. The performance of a stock mutual fund is dependent on the general movements in stock prices. When the stock market is weak, prices of stocks held by a stock fund decrease and the NAV of the fund declines as well. This susceptibility to the stock market is often referred to as **market risk**.

Focus on Ethics: Risk from Investing in Hedge Funds

hedge funds
Limited partnerships that manage portfolios of funds for wealthy individuals and financial institutions.

Hedge funds sell shares to wealthy individuals and financial institutions and use the proceeds to invest in various securities. In this way they serve a similar purpose to mutual funds, yet they are structured as limited partnerships in which investors have little or no control of the company's management. Hedge funds are not regulated by the SEC. While they strive to earn very high returns, they tend to make very risky investments that can lead to extremely poor returns. Hedge funds may invest not only in risky stocks, but also in a wide variety of investments including silver or other metals. They may take a short position in a stock by selling thousands of shares of a stock that they do not own. If this stock's price declines, the funds will earn a high return, but if the stock's price rises, it will experience a large loss. Hedge funds also commonly buy stocks on margin by sup-

porting their investment with borrowed funds. This strategy will increase the magnitude of the gain or the loss on the investment.

In the past, hedge funds required a minimum investment of $1 million, so most individuals were unable to invest in them. Recently, some mini-hedge funds have been created, which allow individuals to invest with a minimum of $50,000. Keep in mind that the fees for investing in hedge funds are very high and the hedge fund management can be suspect. Some former mutual fund managers barred from managing mutual funds by the Securities and Exchange Commission (SEC) as a result of fraudulent behavior have shifted to managing hedge funds, where SEC rules do not apply. While many hedge funds are managed by credible managers, most hedge funds are very risky. Do not consider investing in hedge funds unless you will not need the money for other purposes in the future and you fully recognize the risk involved.

Tradeoff between Expected Return and Risk of Stock Funds

Some investors are willing to tolerate risk from investing in a stock mutual fund when they expect that the mutual fund may offer a very high return. The tradeoff between the expected return and risk of a stock mutual fund is shown in Exhibit 18.3. On the conservative side, a stock index fund that represents a very broad index of stocks will perform similar to the market in general. Thus, its expected return is somewhat limited, but so is its risk. A growth stock fund offers potential for higher returns than a broad index fund, but it also has more risk (more potential for a large

Exhibit 18.3 Tradeoff between Expected Return and Risk

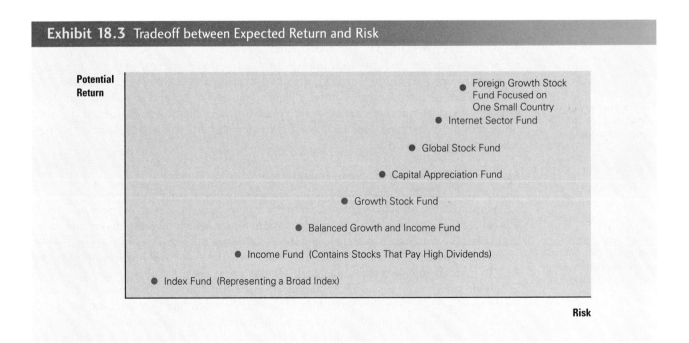

decline in value). A fund that invests only in growth stocks within one sector (such as a technology fund) has potential for a very high return, but it also exhibits high risk. A fund that invests in growth stocks of small firms in a small foreign country has even more potential return and risk.

Risk from Investing in a Bond Mutual Fund

Although different types of bond mutual funds will experience different performance levels in a given time period, they are all influenced by general bond market conditions. The performance of a bond mutual fund is dependent on the general movements in interest rates. When interest rates rise, prices of bonds held by a bond fund decrease, and the NAV of the fund declines. This susceptibility to interest rate movements is often referred to as **interest rate risk**.

interest rate risk
For a bond mutual fund, its susceptibility to interest rate movements.

The prices of all bonds change in response to interest rate movements, but the prices of longer-term bonds are the most sensitive, as discussed in Chapter 17. Thus, investors who want to reduce exposure to interest rate movements can select a bond fund that focuses on bonds with short terms to maturity. Conversely, investors who want to capitalize on an expected decline in interest rate movements can select a bond fund that focuses on long-term bonds.

The performance of many bond mutual funds is also dependent on the default risk of the individual bond holdings. Bond funds that invest most of their money in bonds with a high degree of default risk tend to offer a higher potential return to investors, but also exhibit a high degree of risk. Under favorable economic conditions, the issuers of those bonds may be able to cover their payments, and these bond funds will consequently perform very well. If economic conditions are weak, however, some of the bond issuers may default on their payments, and these bond funds will provide relatively low or even negative returns to their shareholders.

The exposure of a bond fund to default risk is independent of its exposure to interest rate risk, as illustrated in Exhibit 18.4. Some bond funds, such as long-term Treasury bond funds and long-term Ginnie Mae bond funds, have no (or low) default risk and a high level of interest rate risk. Other bond funds, such as short-term high-yield bond funds, have a low level of interest rate risk and a high level of default risk. Some bond funds, such as long-term high-yield bond funds, are highly exposed to both default risk and interest rate risk.

Exhibit 18.4 Classifying Bond Mutual Funds According to Interest Rate Risk and Default Risk

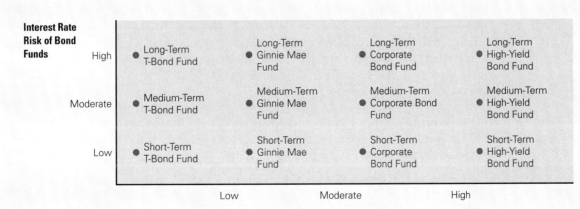

Exhibit 18.5 Tradeoff between Expected Return and Risk of Bond Mutual Funds

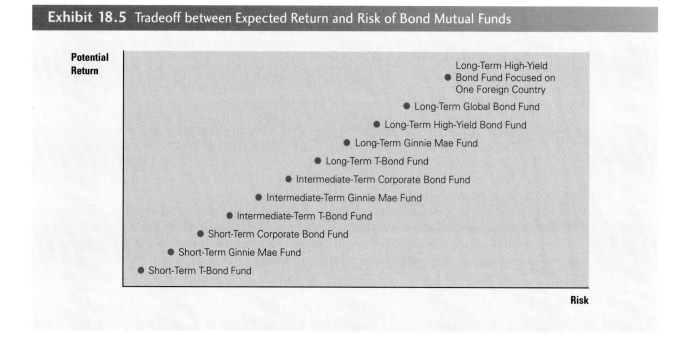

Tradeoff between Expected Return and Risk of Bond Funds

The tradeoff between the expected return and the risk of a bond mutual fund is shown in Exhibit 18.5. On the conservative side, a Treasury bond fund that holds Treasury bonds with a short term remaining until maturity has no exposure to default risk and limited exposure to interest rate risk. Thus, the prices of the bonds it holds are not very sensitive to external forces, so the NAV of the fund will not be very sensitive to these forces. The expected return on this fund is relatively low, however. An intermediate-term Ginnie Mae bond fund offers the potential for a higher return. Its bonds have a slight degree of default risk, however, and the intermediate term to maturity causes more exposure to interest rate risk than short terms to maturity. A high-yield bond fund that invests only in junk bonds with long terms to maturity has the potential for a very high return. Its value is subject to default risk, however, because the junk bonds could default. It is also subject to a high level of interest rate risk because of the long-term maturities. A bond fund that invests in bonds issued by risky firms in a small foreign country has even more potential return and risk.

DECIDING AMONG MUTUAL FUNDS

Your decision to purchase shares of a specific mutual fund should be made once you determine your investment objectives, evaluate your risk tolerance, and decide the fund characteristics that you want. The final step is to search for mutual funds that exhibit those desired characteristics.

Determining Your Preferred Mutual Fund Characteristics

When identifying the type of mutual fund you want, you will want to consider various fund characteristics.

Minimum Initial Investment. If you have a relatively small amount to invest (such as $1,000), you should limit your choices to mutual funds whose initial investment is equal to or below that level. Many funds allow an even smaller initial investment if the account is funded with a systematic investment plan, whereby you make a regular monthly investment in your account.

Investment Objective (Type of Fund). You must identify your investment goals. First, determine whether you are interested in a stock mutual fund or a bond mutual fund. If you want your investment to have high potential for increasing in value over time, you should consider capital appreciation funds. If you want periodic income, you should consider bond funds. Once you select a stock fund or a bond fund, you should select the particular type of fund that will match your investment objective. Funds vary according to their potential return and their risk, as mentioned earlier.

Investment Company. Whatever your investment objective, there are probably many investment companies that offer a suitable fund. One way to choose an investment company is by assessing the past performance of the type of mutual funds you are considering. Past performance is not necessarily a good indicator of future performance, however. A better approach may be to compare fees and expenses on the funds you are considering. You may want to screen your list of funds by removing the load funds from consideration. In addition, you should compare the funds' expense ratios, since some investment companies charge much lower expenses than others.

prospectus
A document that provides financial information about a mutual fund, including expenses and past performance.

investment objective
In a prospectus, a brief statement about the general goal of the mutual fund.

investment strategy
In a prospectus, a summary of the types of securities that are purchased by the mutual fund in order to achieve its objective.

Reviewing a Mutual Fund's Prospectus

For any mutual fund that you consider, you should obtain a **prospectus**, which is a document that provides financial information about the fund, including expenses and past performance. You can order the prospectus from the mutual fund company over the phone, by e-mail, or online in some cases. In fact, you may be able to download the prospectus from the Internet. The prospectus contains considerable information, as described in the next paragraphs.

Investment Objective. The **investment objective** is a brief statement about the general goal of the fund, such as capital appreciation (increase in value) of stocks or achieving returns that exceed that of the S&P 500 or some other index.

Investment Strategy. The **investment strategy** (also called investment policy) summarizes the types of securities that are purchased by the mutual fund in order to achieve its objective. For example, a fund's investment strategy may be to focus on large stocks, technology stocks, stocks that have a high level of growth, foreign stocks, Treasury bonds, corporate bonds, or other securities.

Past Performance. The prospectus will include the return on the fund over recent periods (such as the last year, the last three years, and the last five years). The performance is normally compared to a corresponding stock index (such as the S&P 500) or bond index, which is important since performance should be based on a comparison to general market movements. A stock mutual fund that earned a 15 percent annual return would normally be rated as a high performer, but during the late 1990s such a return would have been relatively low when compared to the stock market in general. Although the past performance offers some insight into the ability of the fund's managers to select stocks, it will not necessarily persist in the future.

Fees and Expenses. The prospectus will provide a breakdown of the following fees and expenses:

- The maximum load imposed on purchases of the fund's shares.

- The redemption fee or *back-end load* (if any) imposed when investors redeem their shares.

- Expenses incurred by the fund, including management fees resulting from monitoring the fund's portfolio, distribution fees resulting from the fund's advertising costs, and marketing costs that are paid to brokers who recommend the fund to investors. A fund can be classified as a no-load fund and yet still have substantial advertising and marketing fees.

The most important expense statistic mentioned in the prospectus is the expense ratio. Since it adjusts for the size of the fund, you can compare the efficiency of various mutual funds. The expense ratio may also be converted into the actual expenses that you would be charged if you had invested a specified amount in the fund (such as $1,000). The expense ratio may be as low as 0.1 percent for some funds and more than 4 percent for others. Expense ratios can change over time, so you should monitor them over time when investing in a mutual fund.

Risk. The prospectus of a stock fund typically states that the fund is subject to market risk, or the possibility of a general decline in the stock market, which can cause a decline in the value of the mutual fund. In addition, the prices of individual stocks within the fund may experience substantial declines in response to firm-specific problems. Bond funds normally mention their exposure to interest rate risk and default risk. These risks are stated so that investors understand that there is some uncertainty surrounding the future performance of the mutual fund and that the value of the mutual fund can decline over time.

Distribution of Dividends and Capital Gains. The prospectus explains how frequently the mutual fund makes distributions to investors. Most funds distribute their dividends to their shareholders quarterly and distribute their capital gains once a year (usually in December). The prospectus also describes the means by which dividends and capital gains are distributed.

Minimum Investment and Minimum Balance. The prospectus states the minimum investment that can be made in the fund. In addition, it may require that you maintain a minimum balance, as it is costly for a fund to maintain an account that has a very small balance.

How to Buy or Redeem Shares. The prospectus explains how you can invest in the fund by sending a check along with a completed application form (which is normally attached

18.3 Financial Planning Online: Mutual Fund Reports

Go to
http://moneycentral.
msn.com

Click on
"Fund Research" under
"Investing"

This Web site provides
a report for a mutual fund
that you specify. This
report allows you to review
key characteristics about
the fund, including its performance and expenses.

to the prospectus). If the mutual fund is part of a family of funds operated by a single investment company, the prospectus explains how you can call the investment company to transfer money from one fund to another within the family. The prospectus also explains how you can sell your shares back to the mutual fund. Normally you can send a letter asking the fund to redeem your shares. In some cases, you may be able to call the investment company to redeem your shares.

Making the Decision

Once you have narrowed your list to a small number of possible mutual funds, you can create a table to compare the important characteristics. This process will help you select the mutual fund that will best satisfy your preferences.

EXAMPLE

Stephanie Spratt has $2,000 to invest. She is interested in investing in both stocks and bonds. Since she has limited funds to invest at this time, a mutual fund is an attractive option. She wants to invest in stocks, but she also wants to keep her expenses low. She creates a list of possible mutual funds that focus on technology stocks and require a minimum investment of $1,000 that would satisfy her preferences. Using a prospectus for each fund that she downloaded online, she assesses the load fee, expense ratio, and past performance, as shown here:

Mutual Fund	Load Status	Expense Ratio	Recent Annual Performance
#1	No-load	1.5%	13%
#2	No-load	0.8%	12%
#3	No-load	2.0%	14%
#4	3% load	1.7%	11%

Stephanie immediately eliminates #4 because of its load and high expense ratio. She then removes #1 and #3 from consideration because of their high expense ratios. She selects #2 because it is a no-load fund and has a relatively low expense ratio. She does not place much weight on past performance in her assessment.

Stephanie also wants to invest $1,000 in a bond mutual fund. She is considering bond funds that contain AA-rated bonds. She is concerned about interest rate risk because she expects that interest rates may rise. She creates a list of possible bond funds that allow a very small minimum investment and evaluates information from the prospectuses:

Bond Fund	Load Status	Expense Ratio	Typical Terms to Maturity
#1	4% load	1.0%	6–8 years
#2	No-load	0.9%	15–20 years
#3	No-load	0.8%	5–7 years
#4	No-load	1.2%	5–7 years

Stephanie eliminates #1 because it has a load. She eliminates #2 because it focuses on bonds with long terms to maturity. She removes #4 from consideration because it has a relatively high expense ratio in comparison with #3. She decides to invest in #3 because it is a no-load fund, has a low expense ratio, and its bonds have a relatively short term to maturity, which reduces the amount of interest rate risk. She also prefers bond fund #3 because it is in the same family of mutual funds as the stock mutual fund that she just selected. Thus, she can easily transfer money between these two mutual funds. Stephanie sends her completed application and a $2,000 check to the mutual fund company.

QUOTATIONS OF MUTUAL FUNDS

Financial newspapers such as the *Wall Street Journal* publish price quotations of open-end mutual funds, as shown in Exhibit 18.6. When an investment company offers sev-

Exhibit 18.6 Open-End Mutual Fund Price Quotations

FUND	NAV	NET CHG	YTD %RET	3-YR %RET
StrAgg	8.07	0.06	2.5	15.5
StrConv	5.57	0.02	1.3	8.8
StrMod	6.87	0.05	1.9	12.9
✦Tg2010	88.46	0.09	0.4	3.6
✦Tg2015	76.74	0.08	0.3	6.9
✦Tg2025	52.20	0.09	0.1	12.3
✦TxFr Bond:Inv	10.78	0.01	0.1	3.2
✦Ultra	30.57	0.13	1.6	12.0
✦Util	13.73	0.05	2.5	20.3
Value	7.04	0.02	1.3	15.3
✦Vista	16.48	0.26	4.2	22.3
American Century Ist				
DivBnd	10.08	0.01	0.2	3.7
EqIndex	5.08	0.02	2.0	13.6
EqInc	7.92	0.01	1.3	12.7
Growth	21.17	0.13	2.1	12.4
IncGro	31.06	0.22	2.4	15.2
IntlDisc r	15.40	0.18	4.7	33.6
IntlGr	10.58	0.16	4.8	18.8
LgCoVal	6.61	0.01	1.7	15.1
RealEst	26.09	0.09	2.4	28.8
Select	38.95	0.11	1.4	10.3
SmallCo	10.02	0.08	2.2	28.6
SmCapVal	9.84	0.05	2.0	22.2
StrMod	6.87	0.05	1.9	13.1
Ultra	30.90	0.14	1.6	12.2
Value	7.04	0.01	1.3	15.5
American Funds Cl A				
BalA p	18.07	0.06	1.4	11.1
AmcpA p	19.42	0.07	1.6	14.6
AMutlA p	26.63	0.08	1.4	12.3
BondA p	13.27	0.02	0.4	6.8
CapIBA p	54.05	0.44	2.0	14.6
CapWA p	18.76	0.15	1.5	9.6
CapWGrA	37.78	0.44	3.3	24.5
EupacA p	42.74	0.59	4.0	25.3
FdInvA p	36.31	0.26	2.6	18.7
GovtA p	13.52	0.01	0.3	2.6
GwthA p	31.68	0.26	2.7	19.2
HI TrA p	12.16	0.03	0.5	13.6
HiInMuniA	15.57	...	0.1	5.6
ICAA p	31.92	0.13	1.8	13.7
IncoA p	18.40	0.10	1.6	13.5
IntBdA p	13.48	0.01	0.3	2.3
LtdTEBdA	15.26	...	0.1	3.0
N PerA p	29.66	0.35	3.6	20.6
NEcoA p	24.04	0.16	2.6	20.0
NwWrldA	40.22	0.60	3.9	29.3
SmCpA p	36.30	0.38	2.9	27.8
TECAA p	16.70	0.01	0.1	4.5
TEVAA p	16.53	0.01	0.1	3.3
TxExA p	12.46	0.01	0.1	4.5
WshA p	31.34	0.05	1.6	12.1

FUND	NAV	NET CHG	YTD %RET	3-YR %RET
Baird Funds				
IntBdInst	10.58	0.01	0.3	4.2
Barclays Global Inv				
BondIdx	9.67	0.01	0.3	3.7
LP2010	13.12	0.05	1.5	9.4
LP2020	16.16	0.08	2.0	11.9
LP2030	15.74	0.09	2.3	13.8
LP2040	18.63	0.10	2.5	15.3
S&P 500	153.15	0.60	2.1	13.7
Baron Funds				
Asset	56.85	0.25	1.0	21.4
AssetIns	28.34	0.13	1.4	19.0
Growth	46.07	0.22	1.5	20.8
Partners p	18.66	0.07	1.2	NS
SmCap	23.51	0.17	1.5	22.6
Bernstein Fds				
Ca Mu	14.19	0.02	0.2	2.7
DivMu	14.03	0.01	0.2	2.8
EmMkts	36.87	0.64	5.1	48.5
IntDur	13.21	0.03	0.3	4.2
IntVal2	25.12	0.38	4.5	24.6
NYMu	13.86	0.01	0.1	2.8
ShDivMu	12.48	0.01	0.1	1.5
ShtDur	12.35	0.01	0.2	1.9
TxMgdIntV	25.15	0.39	4.5	24.0
Berwynlnc	11.93	0.02	0.7	8.8
Bjurman,BarryMCGp	31.50	0.45	2.6	24.3
BlackRock Funds Blrk				
CoreBlk	9.55	0.01	0.3	4.1
CorePlTRBlk	10.18	0.01	0.3	4.2
IntBdBlk	9.26	...	0.3	3.4
LDurBlrk	9.88	0.01	0.3	1.9
BlackRock Funds Inst				
CoreBdTRIst	9.53	0.01	,0.3	3.9
IndexEql	24.49	0.10	2.1	13.8
IntGovtl	10.18	...	0.2	2.3
IntlBd	10.98	0.09	2.3	6.2
IntlOppl	38.51	0.71	4.5	35.9
IntTBdl	9.26	0.01	0.3	3.2
LowDurl	9.89	0.01	0.2	1.8
Managedl	10.09	...	0.3	4.0
PATxFInc	10.35	0.01	0.1	3.1
InvTr	13.35	0.06	2.0	14.5
SmCpGrl	17.91	0.17	2.2	22.5
TxFrInc	10.93	...	0.1	3.6
BlackRock Funds A				
AssetAllocA	15.28	0.10	1.9	14.0
Aurora	34.81	0.22	1.8	20.6
CoreBdTR A	9.54	0.01	0.3	3.6
ExcBlrk	548.87	3.39	2.3	10.5
GlRec p	70.11	1.13	5.9	56.6
GvtIncInvA	10.88	0.01	0.3	3.4
HiYInvA	7.87	0.01	0.2	13.8

FUND	NAV	NET CHG	YTD %RET	3-YR %RET
Gr&IncC t	31.68	0.20	2.1	13.9
GrowthA p	56.85	0.55	3.3	22.4
GrowthB t	58.51	0.57	3.2	21.5
GrowthC t	54.27	0.53	3.2	21.5
Calvert Group				
Inco p	16.79	0.01	0.2	7.7
IncomeB t	16.77	0.01	0.2	6.9
IncomeC t	16.78	0.02	0.2	6.9
IntlEqA p	21.73	0.21	3.8	19.8
LgCpGwth t	31.15	0.22	2.8	21.1
ShtDurIncA t	16.02	0.01	0.1	5.3
Social p	28.98	0.09	1.4	10.0
SocBd p	15.88	0.01	0.2	6.0
SocEq p	36.00	0.18	2.0	10.4
TxF Lt	10.58	...	0.1	1.6
CambiarOppInv	18.12	0.13	2.3	18.5
CausewayInst	17.28	0.21	4.2	26.7
CausewayInv	17.20	0.21	4.1	26.4
Century Funds				
SharesTrInst	34.13	0.13	1.3	13.7
SmCapInv	24.51	0.20	1.7	19.4
SmCapInst	24.76	0.20	1.7	19.8
ChaseGrwth	19.85	0.07	2.3	15.4
Chesapeake Funds				
CoreGr	17.26	0.09	2.0	16.3
Chestnt	344.64	0.95	2.2	9.8
CitiStreet Funds				
DivBond	11.72	0.02	0.3	4.4
IntlStk	15.95	0.16	4.1	20.4
LgCoStk	12.57	0.05	2.3	14.2
SmCoStk	14.64	0.15	2.2	20.8
Citizens Funds				
CitCGSt p	21.62	0.04	1.6	11.7
Clipper	88.95	0.22	0.9	7.3
Cohen & Steers				
✦InstlRlty	46.60	0.12	2.3	30.5
✦RltyIncA p	15.59	0.06	2.0	22.6
RltyIncB t	15.03	0.06	2.1	21.8
RltyIncC t	15.03	0.06	2.1	21.8
✦RltyShs	74.28	0.20	2.3	30.5
Colo Bonds	9.40	...	...	5.9
Columbia Class A				
21CentryA t	12.42	0.06	1.5	24.3
AcornA t	28.12	0.17	2.0	25.7
AcornSelA t	22.88	0.10	1.8	19.8
CATaxEA	7.66	...	0.2	4.7
ConSec A	17.35	0.11	1.6	12.9
CosvHiYldA p	8.51	0.01	0.3	6.9
FedSecA	10.54	0.01	0.2	3.0
FocEqA t	20.56	0.06	1.6	16.2
HYOppsA	4.52	...	0.1	12.4
IntlStkA p	17.49	0.21	4.4	20.4
IntValA	23.46	0.25	4.0	27.6

eral different mutual funds, its name is printed in bold, and the funds are listed below. For example, Fidelity is an investment company that offers growth funds, income funds, balance funds, international funds, and other types of funds. Each fund's NAV is shown in the second column, the net change in the NAV is shown in the third column, and the return over the year to date (YTD) is shown in the fourth column. For example, Baron Funds offers various mutual funds, including a growth fund, which has a net asset value of $45.85 per share. The net change in the net asset value during the previous day was $.45. The Fund has generated a return of 1 percent since the new calendar year, and a 20.7 return over the last three years.

Price quotations of closed-end funds are also provided in the *Wall Street Journal*, as shown in Exhibit 18.7. These closed-end funds are listed on the exchanges where they

Exhibit 18.7 Closed-End Fund Price Quotations

Tuesday, January 3, 2006

AMEX

STOCK (SYM)	DIV	LAST	NET CHG
Abrdn AP IncFd FAX	.42	5.94	0.14
AbrdnAusEq IAF	1.25e	12.73	-0.26
AbrdnGlobIncFd FCO	.72a	12.85	0.05
BancroftFd BCV	.75e	18	-0.05
BlkRkBIG Tr BCT	.90a	15	0.01
BlkRkCA Tr2 BCL	.79	13.78	0.06
BlkRkFL IQM Tr RFA	.85a	15.40	0.31
BlkRkMD Muni BZM	.86	16.90	-0.20
BlkRkMuniInco Tr2 BLE	1.01	16.60	-0.01
BlkRkNJ Tr RNJ	.84a	15.99	0.24
BlkRkNJ Muni BLJ	.94a	16.70	-0.08
BlkRkNY IQM Tr RNY	.88a	15.07	0.05
BlkRkNY MI Tr2 BFY	.71	13.29	0.04
BlkRkPA Tr BPS	.91	16.05	0.20
BlkRkS&P GlbEqu BQY	.90a	14.42	0.10
BlkRkVA Muni BHV	.87	17.20	-0.60
CIM HiYld CIM	.22m	4.05	-0.02
CastleFd CVF	.68a	23	...
CntlFdCan CEF	.01g	7.09	0.28
CntlSec CET	2.00e	23.99	0.19
CloughGlblFd GLV	1.44	28	0.90
CloughGlbEqFd GLQ n	1.32	23.77	0.02
ColCAInsMun CCA	.78m	13.87	0.14
ColinsMun CFX	.77m	13.28	0.22
CornstnStrat CLM	1.04	7.20	0.15
CornstnTtlRtn Fd CRF	2.11	15.03	0.24
DE AZ Mun Fd VAZ	.84a	15.38	-0.22
DE CO InsFd VCF	.96a	18.45	0.02
DE FL MunFd VFL	.96a	16.55	0.30
DE MN Fd II VMM	.87	15.06	0.04
DE MN Fd III VYM	.78	13.42	-0.04
DE MN Fd VMN	.78a	13.86	0.06
DreyfMunInc DMF	.56	8.92	0.02
EtnVncCA MIT CEV	.81	13.96	0.06
EtnVncFL MIT FEV	.73m	14.23	-0.07
EtnVncCA EVM	.77	13.40	0.21
EtnVncCA II EIA	.77m	14.41	...
EtnVncFL EIF	.71m	14.78	-0.14
EtnVncMA MAB	.77m	15.82	-0.38
EtnVncMI MIW	.75m	15.20	-0.29
EtnVncMuni EIM	.80m	14.87	-0.31
EtnVncMuni II EIV	.81m	16.36	-0.64
EtnVncNJ EMJ	.80m	17.05	-0.25
EtnVncNY ENX	.77	13.86	...
EtnVncNY II NYH	.70m	14.74	...
EtnVncOH EIO	.73	13.95	0.07
EtnVncPA EIP	.73m	16.15	-0.25

STOCK (SYM)	DIV	LAST	NET CHG
NuvMI NZW	.89	15.01	-0.11
NuvMO Prm NOM	.84a	17.59	0.09
NuvMuniIncoOpp NMZ	1.07a	16.11	0.01
NuvNJ NXJ	.86a	15.21	-0.04
NuvNJ Fd2 NUJ	.88a	16.52	0.02
NuvNY Fd2 NXK	.91a	16.22	0.16
NuvNC NRB	.88	17.14	0.10
NuvNC Fd2 NNO	.82a	15.39	-0.21
NuvNC Fd3 NII	.73	13.75	...
NuvOH NXI	.85a	17.05	0.20
NuvOH Fd2 NBJ	.80a	15.70	0.02
NuvOH Fd3 NVJ	.79m	15.05	-0.05
NuvPA NXM	.89a	15.65	-0.17
NuvPA Fd2 NVY	.80a	14.60	0.07
NuveenRlEst JRS	1.74	20.19	0.20
NuvVA NGB	.86	16.35	0.05
NuvVA Fd2 NNB	.86a	16.95	0.31
PachldrHi PHF	.90	8.65	0.15
PutnmCA Inv PCA	.66a	13.11	0.07
PutnmNYInv PMN	.53	11.86	-0.09
RMR FIRE Fd RFR	1.75	19.14	0.15
RMR HospFd RHR	1.50	18.55	0.34
RMR PfdDivFd RDR n	1.80	16.45	0.10
RMR RlEstFd RMR	1.20	13.32	0.17
ReavesUtilFd UTG	1.26	19.48	0.40
ScudderRE SRQ	1.58a	20.81	0.24
ScudderRE II SRO	1.26a	15.70	0.35
ThaiCapFd TF	.10e	9.34	0.35
VnKmMAInc VMV	.83a	15.73	-0.23
VnKmAdvII VKI	.83a	13.54	0.21
VnKmSelect VKL	.74a	12.36	0.04

NASDAQ

STOCK (SYM)	DIV	LAST	NET CHG
HnckJ Fnl JHFT	1.89e	16.80	0.12
RoyceFocus FUND	1.21e	9.65	0.12
S&P 500 Fd PEFX	.11e	9.19	-0.09

NYSE

STOCK (SYM)	DIV	LAST	NET CHG
ACM OppFd AOF	.44a	7.61	0.05
ACM IncFd ACG	.66	8.30	0.02
ACM MgdDlr ADF	.62	7.36	-0.07
ACM MgdInco AMF	.21	3.50	-0.01
ACM MuniSec AMU	.65	10.37	0.05
ASA ASA	1.40f	59.34	4.33
AdamsExp ADX	.86e	12.73	0.18
AdvntClymrFd AVK	2.06a	23.03	0.55

STOCK (SYM)	DIV	LAST	NET CHG
CalamosConvOp CHI	1.80a	20.04	0.23
CalamosGlblTot CGO n	.10p	14.16	-0.01
CalamosStratTot CSQ	1.17f	13.71	0.20
CapIncoStratFd CII	1.20	17.46	0.25
CntlEurRus Fd CEE	3.05e	43.65	1.19
ChrtwlDvdInco CWF	1.00	10.46	0.26
ChileFd CH s	6.21e	17.93	0.28
ChinaFund CHN	6.08e	24.77	1.59
CitigrpInvLnFd TLI	.84f	12.68	0.06
ChnStrAdvInco RLF	1.80a	20.94	0.55
ChnStrMjrs DVM n	1.20	17.41	0.38
ChnStrPrInco RPF	1.80a	20.36	0.37
ChnStrQuInco RQI	1.68a	19.64	0.40
ChnStrPfInco RNP	2.34a	26.11	0.26
ChnStrUtilFd RTU	1.38a	17.99	0.33
ChnStrSelUtil UTF	1.20	20.41	0.25
ChnStrTR RFI	1.32a	18.87	0.34
ChnStrWrldRlty RWF n	1.44	17.55	0.99
ColonlHilnco CXE	.44	6.57	...
ColonlIntmk CMK	.65a	8.22	0.07
ColonialIntr CIF	.31a	3.17	0.06
ColonlInvMun CXH	.62	10.53	0.03
ColonlMuni CMU	.37	5.41	0.03
CpHiYld VI HYT	1.20a	12.32	0.14
CpHiYld COY	.74	7.68	0.08
CpHiYld V HYV	1.27a	12.64	0.12
CpHiYld III CYE	.72	7.40	-0.06
CrSuisInco CIK x	.36	3.77	0.13
CrSuisHighYld DHY	.51	4.46	0.11
DebtStratFd DSU	.75	6.34	0.07
DfndStratFd DSF	.55e	15.85	0.29
DE InvDivInco DDF	.96a	11.65	0.07
DE InvGlbDiv DGF	.96a	13.20	-0.35
DiverIncStrat DVF n	1.65	16.18	0.33
DivCapRltyInco DCA n	1.26	12.82	0.32
DNP SelInc DNP	.84	10.35	-0.04
Dow30PremDiv DPD n	1.90f	18.28	0.13
DrmnClayDivInco DCS	1.30	18.40	0.32
DryfsHiYldFd DHF	.39	3.94	...
DreyfStMnBd DSM	.52	8.20	0.09
DreyfStrMuni LEO	.55	8.56	0.01
DTFTxFrInco DTF	.78	14.63	0.09
DufPhlpsBnd DUC	1.02	13.16	0.13
EtnVncTxMngOpp ETW n	.45p	17.70	0.50
EtnVncEqtyInco II EOS n	1.73	18.37	0.51
EtnVncEqtyInco EOI	1.64	19.10	0.62
EtnVncFltRte IncoTr EFT	1.40	17.07	0.20
EtnVnc MIT EVN	.90m	14.84	-0.22
EtnVncSrFltRte EFR	1.40	17.17	0.23

are traded. The special listing in the *Wall Street Journal* discloses the dividend of the fund in the second column, the last-reported price in the third column, and the change in the price per share in the fourth column. The premium or discount of the closed-end fund (relative to the price) is not reported. Consider the closed-end fund Central Securities Corp. (abbreviated as CntlSec; the symbol is CET), which invests in various stocks. It paid an annual dividend of $2.00 per share. Its last price (price at the time its shares were last traded) on the previous day was $23.99 per share. This reflects a gain of $.19 per share over the day.

In any particular period, some types of mutual funds perform better than others. For example, in some years large stocks perform well while small stocks perform poorly. In other years, smaller stocks perform better than large stocks. When investors want to

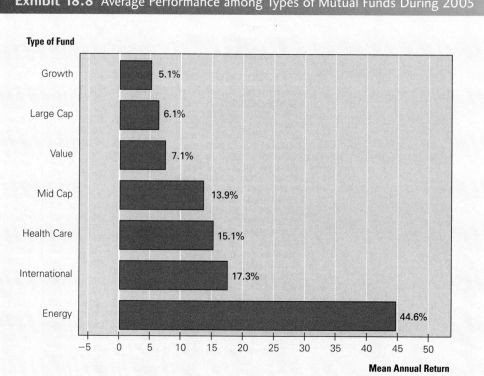

Exhibit 18.8 Average Performance among Types of Mutual Funds During 2005

Type of Fund

Growth   5.1%
Large Cap   6.1%
Value   7.1%
Mid Cap   13.9%
Health Care   15.1%
International 17.3%
Energy   44.6%

−5   0   5   10   15   20   25   30   35   40   45   50

Mean Annual Return

18.4 Financial Planning Online: Online Services by Mutual Funds

Go to
http://www.vanguard.com

This Web site provides
Vanguard history, philosophy and news information about investing, research on Funds and Stocks, Account types and Services, Opening an Account, Planning, and Education, Daily Fund Quotes, articles, brochures and online tools to help users with investment planning.

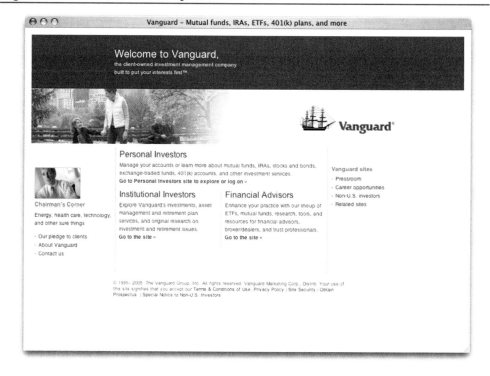

assess the performance of a mutual fund, they compare the return on that mutual fund to the average return for that same type of mutual fund. In this way, investors can determine whether their mutual fund was managed effectively. Exhibit 18.8 shows the average return of various types of mutual funds. Notice how the average return varies substantially among types of mutual funds. Growth funds earned relatively low returns (5.1 percent) on average, while mutual funds focused on energy companies earned very high returns (44.6 percent) on average. Thus, if you owned a growth fund that earned a return of 10 percent in this period, then the management of the fund was effective because their fund outperformed the average fund of that type. Conversely, if you owned an energy fund in this period that earned a return of 30 percent, then your fund performed worse than the average in the energy fund category.

There are various information sources that indicate the mean performance level among mutual funds. For example, Lipper indexes indicate the mean return for various types of mutual funds. These indexes are periodically reported in the *Wall Street Journal*. Investors also review the Lipper indexes to compare the performance of different types of mutual funds over time. You may want to compare small-cap growth funds and large-cap growth funds to determine which type of fund has been performing better lately.

DIVERSIFICATION AMONG MUTUAL FUNDS

If you plan to invest in more than one mutual fund, you may want to consider diversifying across several types of mutual funds to achieve a lower level of risk. When a stock mutual fund that contains large stocks is performing poorly, another stock mutual fund that contains small stocks may be performing well. Diversification benefits can be limited, though, since when the stock market declines, the values of most stock mutual funds decline as well. Therefore, diversifying among stock mutual funds that invest in U.S. stocks has only limited effectiveness in reducing risk.

18.5 Financial Planning Online: Diversifying among Mutual Funds

Go to
http://www.mfea.com

Click on
"Asset Allocation"

This Web site provides suggested asset allocation models that fit your financial situation and your degree of risk tolerance.

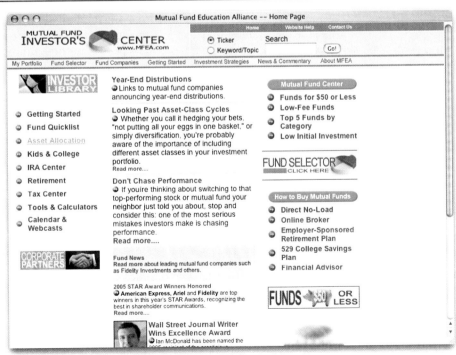

Diversification across bond mutual funds may result in less risk than investing in a bond fund that focuses only on long-term bonds. Virtually all bond funds are adversely affected by an increase in interest rates, however, so diversification among bond funds is not an effective means of reducing exposure to interest rate risk.

A more effective diversification strategy is to diversify across stock and bond mutual funds, as Stephanie Spratt chose to do earlier in the chapter. The returns of stock mutual funds and bond mutual funds are not highly correlated, so diversifying among stock and bond funds can be effective. When U.S. stock market conditions are poor, stock funds focused on U.S. stocks will perform poorly, but the bond funds may still perform well. If U.S. interest rates rise, the bond funds may perform poorly, but the stock funds may still perform well.

You may be able to reduce your overall risk further by diversifying among mutual funds that represent different countries. International stock funds tend to be susceptible to the market conditions of the countries (or regions) where the stocks are based and to the exchange rate movements of the currencies denominating those stocks against the dollar. Thus, the returns of international stock funds are less susceptible to U.S. stock market conditions. International bonds are primarily influenced by the interest rates of their respective countries, so they are also less susceptible to U.S. interest rate movements.

Consider a strategy of investing in the portfolio of mutual funds listed in the first column of Exhibit 18.9. The primary factor that affects each mutual fund's return is shown in the second column. Notice that each fund is primarily affected by a different factor, so one adverse condition (such as a weak U.S. market) will have only a limited adverse effect on your overall portfolio of mutual funds. Any adverse conditions in a single country should affect only a mutual fund focused on that country.

Diversification through Mutual Fund Supermarkets

mutual fund supermarket
An arrangement offered by some brokerage firms that enables investors to diversify among various mutual funds (from different mutual fund families) and to receive a summary statement for these funds on a consolidated basis.

A **mutual fund supermarket** enables investors to diversify among various mutual funds (from different mutual fund families) and receive summary statement information for these funds on a consolidated basis. Charles Schwab created the first mutual fund supermarket. Many other brokerage firms also offer them, including National Discount Brokers and DLJdirect. One disadvantage of some mutual fund supermarkets is that they charge high fees.

You can also achieve consolidated summary statements of all of your mutual funds by selecting all of your funds from a single family. To the extent that you select funds from a fund family that has low expenses and wide offerings (such as Vanguard), you can probably invest in all of the types of mutual funds you desire and reduce the expenses that you are indirectly charged.

Exhibit 18.9 Diversifying among Mutual Funds That Are Primarily Affected by Different Factors

Your Return from Investing in:	Is Primarily Affected by:
U.S. growth stock fund	U.S. stock market
U.S. corporate bond fund	U.S. interest rates
European stock fund	European stock markets and the value of the euro
Latin American stock fund	Latin American stock markets and the values of Latin American currencies
Australian bond fund	Australian interest rates and the value of the Australian dollar
Canadian bond fund	Canadian interest rates and the value of the Canadian dollar

HOW MUTUAL FUNDS FIT WITHIN YOUR FINANCIAL PLAN

The following are the key decisions about mutual funds that should be included within your financial plan:

- Should you consider investing in mutual funds?

- What types of mutual funds would you invest in?

Stephanie Spratt's first concern should be maintaining adequate liquidity and being able to make her existing loan payments. As she accumulates money, however, she plans to invest in mutual funds. Exhibit 18.10 provides an example of how mutual fund decisions apply to Stephanie's financial plan.

Exhibit 18.10 How Mutual Funds Fit within Stephanie Spratt's Financial Plan

GOALS FOR INVESTING IN MUTUAL FUNDS

1. Determine if and how I could benefit from investing in mutual funds.
2. If I decide to invest in mutual funds, determine what types of mutual funds to invest in.

ANALYSIS

Characteristics of Mutual Funds	Opinion
▪ I can invest small amounts over time.	Necessary for me
▪ Each fund focuses on a specific type of investment (growth stocks versus dividend-paying stocks, etc.).	Desirable
▪ Mutual fund managers decide how the money should be invested.	Desirable
▪ Investment is well diversified.	Desirable
▪ I can withdraw money if I need to.	Necessary for me

Type of Stock Mutual Fund	Opinion
Growth	Some potential for an increase in value.
Capital appreciation	Much potential for an increase in value, but may have high risk.
Equity income	Provides dividend income, but my objective is appreciation in value.
Balanced growth and income	Not as much potential for an increase in value as some other types of funds.
Sector	May consider in some periods if I believe one sector will perform well.
Technology	Much potential for an increase in value, but may have high risk.
Index	U.S. index funds should have less risk than many other types of funds.
International	Too risky for me at this time.

Type of Bond Mutual Fund	Opinion
Treasury	*Low risk, low return.*
Ginnie Mae	*Low risk, low return.*
Corporate bond (AA-rated bonds)	*Moderate risk, moderate return.*
High-yield bond	*Higher risk, higher potential return.*
Municipal bond	*Offers tax advantages, but my tax rate is still relatively low.*
Index bond	*Low risk, low return.*
International bond	*Higher risk, higher potential return.*

DECISIONS

Decision on Whether to Invest in Mutual Funds:

Mutual funds would allow me to invest small amounts of money at a time, and I could rely on the fund managers to make the investment decisions. I will likely invest most of my excess money in mutual funds.

Decision on Which Mutual Funds to Consider:

At this time, I would prefer stock mutual funds that offer much potential for capital appreciation. In particular, I believe that technology stocks should perform well because the prices of many technology stocks have declined lately and may be bargains. However, I am not confident about selecting any particular technology stocks myself and prefer to rely on a stock mutual fund manager who specializes in these stocks.

I prefer the AA-rated bond funds to the other bond mutual funds at this time because they offer adequate returns, and I think the risk is minimal right now. My financial situation and my preferences may change, so I may switch to other types of mutual funds. I will always select a specific mutual fund that not only achieves my investment objective, but also is a no-load fund and has a relatively low expense ratio.

DISCUSSION QUESTIONS

1. How would Stephanie's mutual fund investing decisions be different if she were a single mother of two children?

2. How would Stephanie's mutual fund investing decisions be affected if she were 35 years old? If she were 50 years old?

SUMMARY

The common types of stock mutual funds include growth funds, capital appreciation funds, income funds, sector funds, and index funds. The income funds typically have a lower expected return than the other funds and a lower level of risk. The capital appreciation funds tend to have a higher potential return than the other funds and a higher level of risk.

The common types of bond mutual funds are Treasury bond funds, Ginnie Mae funds, corporate bond funds, high-yield bond funds, and index bond funds. Treasury bond funds with short maturities have low potential return and low risk. High-yield bond funds have higher potential return and high risk (because some of their bonds may

default). Any bond funds that invest in long-term bonds are subject to a high level of interest rate risk.

When choosing among stock mutual funds, you should select a fund with a required initial investment that you can afford, an investment objective that satisfies your needs, and a relatively low expense ratio. The prospectus of each fund provides information on these characteristics. When choosing among bond mutual funds, you should select a fund with a required initial investment that you can afford, an investment objective that satisfies your needs, and a relatively low expense ratio.

Mutual fund quotations are provided in the *Wall Street Journal* and other business periodicals. These quotations can be used to review the prevailing prices, net asset values

(NAVs), expense ratios, and other characteristics. The quotations can also be used to assess recent performance.

When diversifying among mutual funds, recognize that most stock funds are affected by general stock market conditions, while most bond funds are affected by bond market (interest rate) conditions. You can achieve more effective diversification by investing across stock and bond mutual funds. You may also consider including international stock and bond funds to achieve a greater degree of diversification.

INTEGRATING THE KEY CONCEPTS

Your decision to invest in mutual funds not only relates to your other investment decisions, but also affects other parts of your financial plan. Before investing in mutual funds, you should consider your liquidity situation (Part 2), as you can sell a mutual fund when you need money. However, the value of a mutual fund may decline in some periods, and you may prefer to avoid selling the mutual fund during those periods.

The decision to invest in mutual funds should take into account your financing situation (Part 3). Pay off any personal loans before you invest in mutual funds, unless the return on the fund will exceed the interest rate incurred on the loans. If after considering your liquidity and your financing situation you still decide to invest in mutual funds, you need to decide whether the investment should be for your retirement account (Part 6). There are some tax advantages to that choice, but also some restrictions on when you have access to the money.

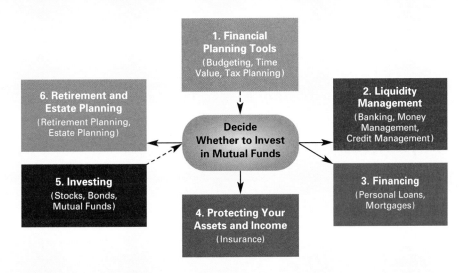

REVIEW QUESTIONS

1. What are mutual funds? What two broad categories of mutual funds exist, and how are they different? Do investors select the securities the mutual fund invests in?

2. List three reasons for investing in mutual funds.

3. What is a mutual fund's net asset value (NAV)? How is the NAV calculated and reported?

4. What is an open-end mutual fund? What types of companies usually manage open-end funds? Describe how these funds work on a day-to-day basis.

5. What is a closed-end fund? Describe how closed-end funds function.

6. What is the difference between no-load and load mutual funds? How do loads affect a fund's return?

Why do some investors purchase load funds? How does an investor purchase a no-load fund?

7. What kinds of expenses do mutual funds incur? How are expense ratios calculated? Why should investors pay attention to expense ratios?

8. Describe the three components of the expense ratio. How can a no-load fund compensate brokers?

9. List and briefly describe the different types of stock mutual funds.

10. Why do investors invest in index funds? Discuss the popularity of index fund investment as it relates to expenses. What tax advantage do index funds offer relative to other types of mutual funds?

11. List and briefly describe the types of bond mutual funds.

12. Why are some U.S. investors attracted to international and global bond funds? What risk is associated with these funds that investors are not subject to when investing strictly in U.S. bond funds? Discuss the expenses associated with international and global bond funds relative to domestic bond funds.

13. Describe the three ways a mutual fund can generate returns for investors.

14. Is a stock mutual fund's past performance necessarily an indicator of future performance? What type of risk affects all stock mutual funds? Describe the tradeoff between the expected return and risk of stock funds.

15. Discuss return and risk as they relate to bond mutual funds. What type of risk are all bond funds subject to? What other risk is associated with some bond funds? Describe the tradeoff between risk and the expected return of bond mutual funds.

16. What should investors consider when deciding whether to purchase shares of a mutual fund? What characteristics of a mutual fund should be considered? Briefly discuss each characteristic.

17. What is a prospectus? How does an investor obtain one? What information does a prospectus provide?

18. Where can an investor find price quotations for closed-end and open-end funds? What information will be provided in a quotation for open-end funds? What information will be provided in a quotation for closed-end funds?

19. Explain how Lipper indexes are used.

20. Discuss diversification among mutual funds. Describe some strategies that make diversification more effective. What is a mutual fund supermarket?

VIDEO QUESTIONS

1. What information does a mutual fund prospectus contain?

2. Where and how do you purchase mutual funds?

FINANCIAL PLANNING PROBLEMS

1. Hope invested $9,000 in a mutual fund at a time when the price per share was $30. The fund has a load fee of $300. How many shares did she purchase?

2. If Hope (from problem 1) had invested the same amount of money in a no-load fund with the same price per share, how many shares could she have purchased?

3. Hope later sells her shares in the mutual fund for $37 per share. What would her return be in each of the above cases (problems 1 and 2)?

4. Hunter invested $7,000 in shares of a load mutual fund. The load of the fund is 7 percent. When Hunter purchased the shares, the NAV per share was $70. A year later Hunter sold the shares at a NAV of $68 per share. What is Hunter's return from selling his shares in the mutual fund?

5. Mark owns a mutual fund that has an NAV of $45.00 per share and expenses of $1.45 per share. What is the expense ratio for Mark's mutual fund?

6. Rena purchased 200 shares of a no-load stock mutual fund. During the year she received $3 per share in dividend distributions, $200 in long-term capital gain distributions, and capital gains of $1,100 when she sold the stock after owning it eight months. What are the tax consequences of Rena's ownership of this stock fund? Rena is in a 35 percent marginal tax bracket.

7. Ronnie owns 600 shares of a stock mutual fund. This year he received dividend distributions of 60 stock mutual fund shares ($40 per share) and long-term capital gain distributions of 45 stock mutual fund shares (also $40 per share). What are the tax consequences of Ronnie's stock mutual fund ownership if he is in a 25 percent marginal tax bracket?

Ethical Dilemma

8. During the 1990s, mutual funds often engaged in a practice called "after-hours trading" that allowed some of their larger shareholders to reap profits or avoid losses in a manner not available to all investors. To understand how this practice works, one must remember that mutual fund prices (NAV) are based on the underlying prices of the securities in which they are invested. Mutual fund prices are established each day at 4 P.M., eastern time, when the market closes. For this reason, mutual fund orders to buy or sell must be placed by investors prior to 4 P.M. The after-hours trading practice allowed certain large

investors the opportunity to place and execute mutual fund trades after 4 P.M. Thus, if a news release occurred at 5 P.M. that would have a detrimental effect on the stock of a company held by a mutual fund, a large investor could sell the mutual fund shares based on a price prior to the announcement and, therefore, avoid a potential loss.

a. Ignoring the legal rulings recently established for after-hours trading, discuss the ethics of this practice.

b. If you had been a mutual fund investor in the 1990s and knew of the existence of this practice, would it have stopped you from investing in mutual funds? Discuss fully.

FINANCIAL PLANNING ONLINE EXERCISES

1. Go to http://www.indexfunds.com.

   a. Information on returns for various indexes for the previous trading session is displayed in a table called "Markets Today." The table shows the return for the index for a recent trading session. Click on "R 3000," which is the Russell 3000 index. Information is displayed on the composition of the index and its returns over various time periods. Assess the return performance of the Russell 3000 index.

   b. Now click on "S&P 500" to review information on the S&P 500 index. How do the returns for the S&P 500 compare with those for the Russell 3000 for corresponding periods? What could be the reason for any differences?

2. Go to http://biz.yahoo.com/p/tops/usstk.html.

   a. This Web site provides a list of the stock mutual funds that achieved the highest performance over various time periods. Examine the names under each time period and see if any names appear under more than one. Why do you think the same names do not appear on all of the lists? Which time period would give you more confidence in the managers of the fund? Why?

   b. Scroll down the list of top-performing funds to "Top Performers—5 Year." Obtain the profile for the first name on this list. You will obtain information on the returns for this fund for various time periods, the minimum initial investment, fees and expenses, Morningstar rating, NAV, and the lead fund manager. Then click on the second name on the 5-Year list. Compare the information on this fund with the earlier one.

3. Go to http://screen.yahoo.com/funds.html.

   a. Under "Category," select "Any"; for "Morningstar Rating," choose 4 Stars; for "Minimum Initial Investment," select less than $2,500; for "Total Expense Ratio," select less than 2%; for "Net Assets," choose "Any"; for "Turnover," choose "Any"; for "1 Yr Return," choose "up more than 25%"; and for "Rank in Category," select "top 10%." Click on "Find Funds." What funds meet your criteria?

   b. Obtain profiles for the top two funds on the list. Based on the information provided, which one would you choose? Why?

BUILDING YOUR OWN FINANCIAL PLAN

Mutual funds provide a relatively inexpensive investment medium for meeting many financial goals. With a relatively small investment, you can obtain diversification and receive professional management of your portfolio.

There are thousands of individual mutual funds that invest in a wide variety of portfolios ranging from very conservative bond portfolios to very aggressive funds. Fortunately, various Web sites provide information to help you select mutual funds that will best meet your individual financial goals.

In this case, you will explore one of these Web sites and begin the process of selecting some mutual funds that will help you reach the goals you established in Chapter 1.

Go to the worksheets at the end of this chapter, and to the CD-ROM accompanying this text, to continue building your financial plan.

THE SAMPSONS—A CONTINUING CASE

Over the last month, the Sampsons have been struggling with how to invest their savings to support their children's college education. They previously considered stocks and bonds and are now seriously considering investing their money in mutual funds. They find the prospect of relying on an investment professional's advice without having to pay for one-on-one service from a brokerage firm appealing. They are looking to you for advice on what type of funds would be appropriate and whether they should invest their savings in one mutual fund or in several.

Go to the worksheets at the end of this chapter, and to the CD-ROM accompanying this text, to continue this case.

Chapter 18: Building Your Own Financial Plan

GOALS

1. Determine if and how you could benefit from investing in mutual funds.
2. If you decide to invest in mutual funds, choose the best types of funds for your needs.

ANALYSIS

1. At http://www.smartmoney.com, click the tab marked "Funds." Under the heading "Top and Bottom Funds" review the performance of funds for various categories. Choose two or three that meet your goal needs. Enter your findings in the following chart:

Type of Stock Mutual Fund	Suitable Investment Option?	Reasoning
Growth		
Capital Appreciation		
Equity Income		
Balance Growth and Income		
Sector		
Technology		
Index		
International		

Type of Bond Mutual Fund	Suitable Investment Option?	Reasoning
Treasury		
Ginnie Mae		
Corporate Bond		
High-Yield Bond		
Municipal Bond		
Index Bond		
International Bond		

2. Return to http://www.smartmoney.com. Under "Funds" click on "Top 25 Funds." Click on the name of a fund you identified as meeting one or more of your goals. Answer the following questions and note other pertinent information about your fund.

a. On the "Snapshot" tab, what is the risk versus return relationship for your fund?

_____

_____

_____

b. On the "Return" tab, how does your fund's return compare to the return for its category over various time spans?

_____

_____

_____

c. On the "Expense" tab, what are the expenses for your fund?

_____

_____

_____

d. How do your fund's expenses compare to the expenses for this category?

_____

_____

_____

e. Under the "Purchase Info" tab, is this fund open to new investors?

_____

_____

_____

f. If so, what is the minimum purchase?

_____

_____

_____

g. What is the minimum subsequent purchase?

_____

_____

_____

h. Under the "Portfolio" tab, how long has the fund manager been in place?

DECISIONS

1. What is your decision regarding mutual funds? Explain why they are or are not a good investment for you?

2. If you decide to invest in mutual funds, what types of funds will you select? Why?

Chapter 18: The Sampsons—A Continuing Case

CASE QUESTIONS

1. Why might mutual funds be more appropriate investments for the Sampsons than individual stocks or bonds?

2. Should the Sampsons invest their savings in mutual funds? Why or why not?

3. What types of mutual funds should the Sampsons consider, given their investment objective?

Chapter 19

Asset Allocation

There is an old saying, "Do not put all of your eggs in one basket." Consider the case of Nicki and Jack Saizon. The Saizons worked for the same company in the telecommunications field. From that vantage point, they had seen the tremendous rise in telecom stocks in past years. They invested all of their savings, which up to that time had been invested conservatively in a certificate of deposit, into a telecommunications mutual fund. Hoping that this would be the way to quick wealth, they ignored the advice that they had read regarding diversification of an investment portfolio. The Saizons reasoned that diversification would limit their potential gain. Also, they expected some diversification benefits within the mutual fund they selected.

Within 2 years, their fund was worth half of their original investment. Nicki and Jack began to appreciate that the benefit of diversification—lower portfolio risk—far outweighed the potential gain they might have made by concentrating their investment in one sector.

Asset allocation is an important tool for investors. In prior chapters you learned about building your wealth by investing in stocks, bonds, and mutual funds. Now that you are familiar with each of these types of investments, you can determine how to distribute your money among the various types of financial assets. The primary goal of asset allocation is reducing your risk while still achieving an acceptable return on your investment.

The objectives of this chapter are to:

- Explain how diversification among assets can reduce risk
- Describe strategies that can be used to diversify among stocks
- Explain asset allocation strategies
- Identify factors that affect your asset allocation decisions

HOW DIVERSIFICATION REDUCES RISK

If you knew which investment would provide the highest return for a specific investment period, investment decisions would be easy. You would invest all of your money in that particular investment. In the real world, there is a tradeoff between risk and return when investing. Although the return on some investments (such as a Treasury security or a bank CD) is known for a specific investment period, these investments offer a relatively low rate of return. Many investments such as stocks, some types of bonds, and real estate offer the prospect of high rates of return, but their future return is uncertain.

asset allocation
The process of allocating money across financial assets (such as stocks, bonds, and mutual funds) with the objective of achieving a desired return while maintaining risk at a tolerable level.

Benefits of Portfolio Diversification

Because the returns from many types of investments are uncertain, it is wise to allocate your money across various types of investments so that you are not completely dependent on any one type. **Asset allocation** is the process of allocating money across financial assets (such as stocks, bonds, and mutual funds). The objective of asset allocation is to achieve your desired return on investments while maintaining your risk at a tolerable level.

Building a Portfolio. You can reduce your risk by investing in a **portfolio**, which is a set of multiple investments in different assets. For example, your portfolio may consist of various stocks, bonds, and real estate investments. By constructing a portfolio, you diversify across several investments rather than focus on a single investment. Investors who had all of their funds invested in Enron stock or bonds in 2001 or in WorldCom stock or bonds in 2002 lost all of their investment. Given the difficulty in anticipating when an investment might experience a major decline, you can at least reduce your exposure to any one stock by spreading your investment across several firms' stocks and bonds. A portfolio can reduce risk when its investments do not move in perfect tandem. Even if one investment experiences very poor performance, the other investments may perform well.

portfolio
A set of multiple investments in different assets.

insider information
Information known by insiders (such as managers) of a firm, but not known by investors.

Focus on Ethics: The Risk of Insider Trading

It can be tempting to seek **insider information** when deciding how to diversify your funds. For example, you might casually ask a friend for tips about the firm where they are employed, hoping that you can buy the stock before any significant news is released that will cause the stock price to rise.

Investors are legally bound to use only information that is publicly available. Nonetheless, some insiders, such as a firm's officers, directors, and employees, use non-public information when making personal investment decisions. There are many instances of a firm's executives purchasing or selling stock shortly before significant news was disclosed to the public. Certain Enron and WorldCom executives sold large amounts of shares before their respective firms went bankrupt. Samuel Waksal, the ex-CEO of ImClone Systems Inc., was accused of selling ImClone stock before publicly disclosing news in December 2001 that the Food and Drug Administration would not review the application for the firm's cancer drug.

The SEC investigates and prosecutes violations of the insider trading laws. Like the accounting scandals of 2002, insider trading undermines investor confidence. When there is insider trading, investors who play by the rules are at a disadvantage. You can

minimize your risk by using proper asset allocation. For example, if your assets are widely diversified among different types of mutual funds and other investments, you minimize your exposure to any one investment (such as a stock) that could experience a substantial decline in value once any negative news is released.

Determining Portfolio Benefits

To determine a portfolio's diversification benefits, you compare the return on the investments it consists of to the overall portfolio.

EXAMPLE   You are considering investing in a portfolio consisting of investments A and B. Exhibit 19.1 illustrates the portfolio diversification effect of using these two stocks. The exhibit shows the return per year for investments A and B, as well as for a portfolio with 50 percent of the investment allocated to A and 50 percent to B. The portfolio return in each year is simply the average return of A and B. Notice how the portfolio's range of returns is less than the range of returns of either stock. Also, notice that the portfolio's returns are less volatile over time than the returns of the individual stocks. Since the portfolio return is an average of A and B, it has a smoother trend than either individual investment. The smoother trend demonstrates that investing in the portfolio is less risky than investing in either individual investment. You decide to create a diversified portfolio of both investments to reduce your risk.

As the previous example illustrates, the main benefit of diversification is that it reduces the exposure of your investments to the adverse effects of any individual investment. In Exhibit 19.1, notice that when investment A experienced a return of −20 percent in year 2, the portfolio return was −5 percent. The adverse effects on the portfolio were limited because B's return was 10 percent during that year. Investment A's poor performance still affected the portfolio's performance, but less than if it had been the only investment. When B experienced a weak return (such as −15 percent in year 5), its poor performance was partially offset because A's performance was 5 percent in that year.

Factors That Influence Diversification Benefits

A portfolio's risk is often measured by its degree of volatility because the more volatile the returns, the more uncertain the future return on the portfolio. Some portfolios are more effective at reducing risk than others. By recognizing the factors that reduce a portfolio's risk, you can ensure that your portfolio exhibits these characteristics. The volatility of a portfolio's returns is influenced by the volatility of returns on each individual investment within the portfolio and by how similar the returns are among investments.

Volatility of Each Individual Investment. As Exhibit 19.2 illustrates, the more volatile the returns of individual investments in a portfolio are, the more volatile the portfolio's returns are over time (holding other factors constant). The left graph shows the returns of investment A (as in Exhibit 19.1), C, and an equal-weighted portfolio of A and C; the right graph shows the individual returns of investments A and D along with the return of

Exhibit 19.1 Example of Portfolio Diversification Effects

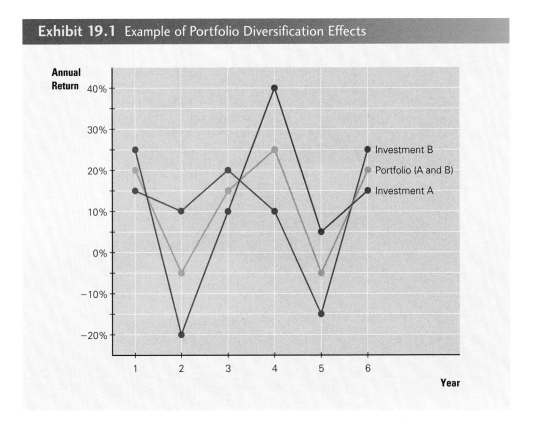

an equal-weighted portfolio of A and D. Comparing the returns of C on the left with the returns of D on the right, it is clear that C is much more volatile. For this reason, the portfolio of A and C (on the left) is more volatile than the portfolio of A and D (on the right).

Impact of Correlations among Investments. The more similar the returns of individual investments in a portfolio are, the more volatile the portfolio's returns are over time. This point is illustrated in Exhibit 19.3. The left graph shows the returns of A, E, and

Exhibit 19.2 Impact of an Investment's Volatility on Portfolio Diversification Effects

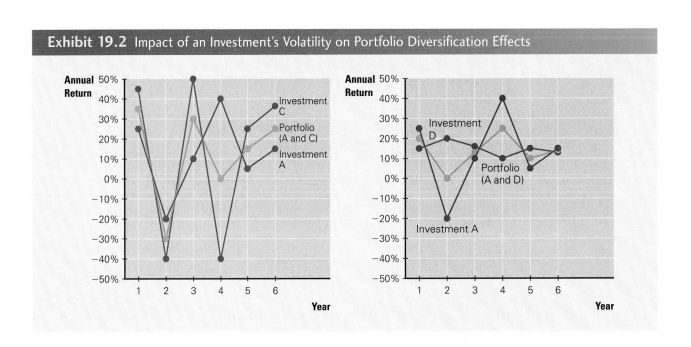

Exhibit 19.3 Impact of Correlations on Portfolio Diversification Effects

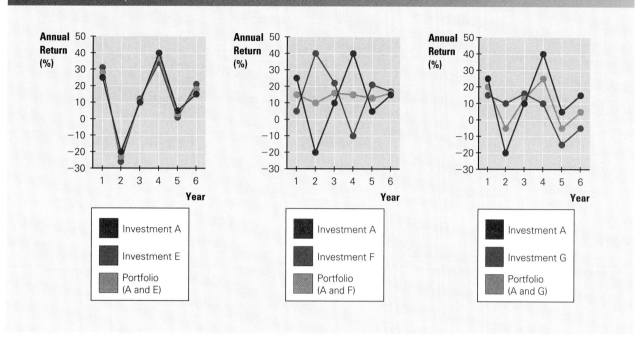

an equal-weighted portfolio of the two investments. Notice that the investments have very similar return patterns. When investment A performs well, so does E. When A performs poorly, so does E.

Consequently, the equal-weighted portfolio of A and E has a return pattern that is almost identical to that of either A or E. Thus, this portfolio exhibits limited diversification benefits.

The middle graph in Exhibit 19.3 shows the returns of A, F, and an equal-weighted portfolio of the two investments. Notice that the return patterns of the investments are opposite one another. When A performs well, F performs relatively poorly. When A performs poorly, F performs well. The returns of A and F are therefore negatively correlated. Consequently, the equal-weighted portfolio of A and F has a very stable return pattern because the returns of the stocks moved in opposite directions. Due to the negative correlation of returns, this portfolio offers substantial diversification benefits.

The right graph in Exhibit 19.3 shows the returns of A, G, and an equal-weighted portfolio of the two investments. Notice that the return patterns of the two stocks are independent of each other. That is, A's performance is not related to G's performance. The return pattern of the equal-weighted portfolio of A and G is more volatile than the returns of the portfolio of A and F (middle graph), but less volatile than the returns of the portfolio of A and E (left graph). Thus, the portfolio of investments A and G exhibits more diversification benefits than a portfolio of two investments that are positively related, but fewer diversification benefits than a portfolio of negatively correlated investments.

This discussion suggests that when you compile a portfolio you should avoid including investments that exhibit a high positive correlation. Although finding investments that are as negatively correlated as A and F may be difficult, you should at least consider investments whose values are not influenced by the same conditions. In reality, many investments are similarly influenced by economic conditions. If economic conditions deteriorate, most investments perform poorly. Nevertheless, some are influenced to a higher degree than others.

19.1 Financial Planning Online: Correlations among Stock Returns

Go to
http://finance.yahoo.com/
?u

Click on
"Charts" after inserting a stock symbol. Next, enter the symbol for another stock in the box labeled "Compare" and perform your own comparison.

This Web site provides a graph that shows the returns on two stocks so that you can compare their performance over time and determine their degree of correlation.

STRATEGIES FOR DIVERSIFYING

There are many different strategies for diversifying among investments. Some of the more popular strategies related to stocks are described here.

Diversification of Stocks across Industries

When you diversify your investments among stocks in different industries, you reduce your exposure to one particular industry. For example, you may invest in the stock of a firm in the publishing and music industry, the stock of a firm in the banking industry, the stock of a firm in the health care industry, and so on. When demand for books declines, conditions may still be favorable in the health care industry. Therefore, a portfolio of stocks diversified across industries is less risky than a portfolio of stocks that are all from the same industry.

The left graph in Exhibit 19.4 illustrates the diversification benefits of a portfolio consisting of two equally weighted stocks: Nike and IBM. Each of these firms is in a different industry and therefore is subjected to different industry conditions. Annual stock returns are shown for a recent period in which stock market conditions were mixed. Diversification is especially valuable during poor conditions. Notice that IBM experienced very poor performance in 2002, while Nike's stock return was not as poor. IBM's stock performed poorly in 2005, but Nike was neutral in that year. Overall, the poor performance of one stock in specific periods was partially offset by the other stock within the portfolio. Notice how the returns of the two-stock portfolio are less volatile than those of either individual stock.

When adding more stocks to the portfolio, the diversification benefits are even greater because the proportional investment in any stock is smaller. Thus, the portfolio is less exposed to poor performance of any single stock.

To illustrate how diversification benefits would be even stronger for a more diversified portfolio, the returns from investing in 500 large U.S. stocks (the S&P 500) are shown in the right graph of Exhibit 19.4. This trend is more stable than the trend of returns for the two-stock portfolio in the left graph. In general, a very diversified portfolio can reduce the potential for very large losses, but can also reduce the potential for very large gains.

Although diversification among stocks in different industries is more effective than diversification within an industry, the portfolio can still be highly susceptible to general economic conditions. Stocks exhibit market risk, or susceptibility to poor performance because of weak stock market conditions. A stock portfolio composed of stocks of U.S. firms based in different industries may perform poorly when economic conditions in the United States are weak. Thus, diversification will not necessarily prevent losses when economic conditions are poor, but it can limit the losses.

Diversification of Stocks across Countries

Because economic conditions (and therefore stock market conditions) vary among countries, you may achieve more favorable returns by diversifying your stock investments across countries. For example, you may wish to invest in a variety of U.S. stocks across different industries, European stocks, Asian stocks, and Latin American stocks. Many investment advisers recommend that you invest about 80 percent of your money in U.S. stocks and allocate 20 percent to foreign countries.

Diversifying among stocks based in different countries makes you less vulnerable to conditions in any one country. Economic conditions in countries can be interrelated, however. In some periods, all countries may simultaneously experience weak economic conditions, causing stocks in all countries to perform poorly at the same time. When investing in stocks outside the United States, recognize that they are typically even more volatile than U.S.-based stocks, as they are subject to more volatile economic conditions. Therefore, you should diversify among stocks within each foreign country rather than rely on a single stock in any foreign country.

Exhibit 19.4 Benefits of Portfolio Diversification

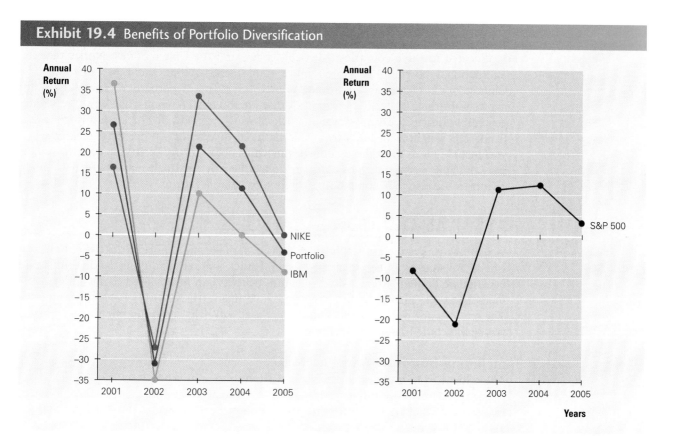

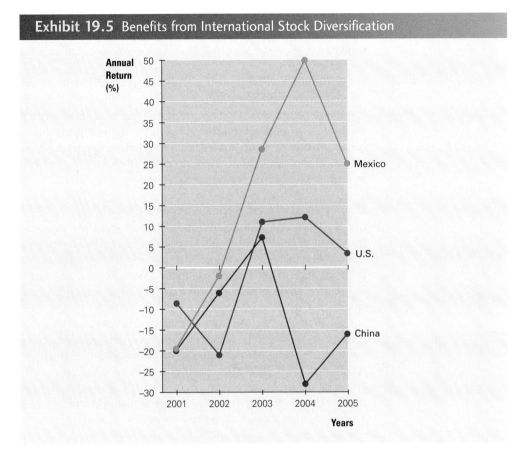

Exhibit 19.5 Benefits from International Stock Diversification

Exhibit 19.5 illustrates the benefits of a diversified international portfolio over the 2000–2002 period, when market conditions were generally mixed. An equal investment is allocated to three countries: Mexico, China, and the United States. Notice that the international portfolio generated more stable returns than the U.S. portfolio. The Chinese market generally performed poorly, but this was partially offset by the other markets. In the 2001–2002 period, all three markets were somewhat weak, reflecting general worldwide pessimism about stocks. In such periods, diversification is still beneficial. The potential benefits from international diversification are even greater when you include more than three countries in your stock portfolio. If you want to reduce risk, though, you should not concentrate too heavily on stock markets of developing countries because they commonly exhibit very volatile returns.

ASSET ALLOCATION STRATEGIES

When investors make asset allocation decisions, they should not restrict their choices to stocks. All stocks can be affected by general stock market conditions, so diversification benefits are limited. Greater diversification benefits can be achieved by including other financial assets, such as bonds, real estate investment trusts (REITs), and stock options. The size of your portfolio and knowledge level will help determine the financial assets you will include in your portfolio.

Including Bonds in Your Portfolio

The returns from investing in stocks and from investing in bonds are not highly correlated. Stock prices are influenced by each firm's expected future performance and general stock market conditions. Bond prices are inversely related to interest rates and are not directly influenced by stock market conditions. Therefore, by including bonds in your portfolio you can reduce your susceptibility to stock market conditions. The expected return on bonds is usually less than the return on stocks, however.

As you allocate more of your investment portfolio to bonds, you reduce your exposure to market risk, but increase your exposure to interest rate risk. Your portfolio is more susceptible to a decline in value when interest rates rise because the market values of your bonds will decline. Recall from Chapter 17 that you can limit your exposure to interest rate risk by investing in bonds with relatively short maturities because the prices of those bonds are less affected by interest rate movements than the prices of long-term bonds.

In general, the larger the proportion of your portfolio that is allocated to bonds, the lower your portfolio's overall risk (as measured by the volatility of returns). The portfolio's value will be more stable over time, and it is less likely to generate a loss in any given period. Investors who are close to retirement commonly allocate much of their portfolio to bonds because they are relying on it to provide them with periodic income. Conversely, investors who are 30 to 50 years old tend to focus their allocation on stocks because they can afford to take risks in order to strive for a high return on their portfolio.

Including Real Estate Investments in Your Portfolio

real estate investment trusts (REITs)
Trusts that pool investments from individuals and use the proceeds to invest in real estate.

Many individuals include real estate investments in their portfolio. One method of investing in real estate is to purchase a home and rent it out. Doing this requires a substantial investment of time and money, however. You must conduct credit checks on prospective renters and maintain the property in good condition. An alternative is to invest in **real estate investment trusts (REITs)**, which pool investments from individuals and use the proceeds to invest in real estate. REITs commonly invest in commercial real estate such as office buildings and shopping centers.

REITs are similar to closed-end mutual funds in that their shares are traded on stock exchanges; the value of the shares is based on the supply of shares for sale (by investors) and investor demand for the shares. REITs are popular among individual investors because the shares can be purchased with a small amount of money. For example, an investor could purchase 100 shares of a REIT priced at $30 per share for a total of $3,000 (computed as $30 × 100 shares). Another desirable characteristic of REITs is that they are managed by skilled real estate professionals who decide what properties to purchase and manage the maintenance of the properties.

equity REITs
REITs that invest money directly in properties.

mortgage REITs
REITs that invest in mortgage loans that help to finance the development of properties.

Types of REITs. REITs are classified according to how they invest their money. **Equity REITs** invest money directly in properties, while **mortgage REITs** invest in mortgage loans that help to finance the development of properties. The performance of an equity REIT is based on changes in the value of its property over time, so returns are influenced by general real estate conditions. The performance of a mortgage REIT is based on the interest payments it receives from the loans it provided.

Role of REITs in Asset Allocation. Individual investors may invest in REITs to further diversify their investment portfolios. When stock market and/or bond market conditions are poor, real estate conditions may still be favorable. Thus, REITs could perform well in a period when stocks or bonds are performing poorly. Consequently, a portfolio that contains stocks, bonds, and REITs may be less susceptible to major declines because it is unlikely that all three types of investments will simultaneously perform poorly.

Including Stock Options in Your Portfolio

stock option
An option to purchase or sell stocks under specified conditions.

When making your asset allocation decisions, you may want to consider **stock options**, which are options to purchase or sell stocks under specified conditions. Like stocks, stock options are traded on exchanges. Some employers include stock options in compensation packages, so you should be aware of them.

call option
Provides the right to purchase 100 shares of a specified stock at a specified price by a specified expiration date.

exercise (strike) price
The price at which a stock option is exercised.

Call Options. A **call option** on a stock provides the right to purchase 100 shares of a specified stock at a specified price (called the **exercise price** or **strike price**) by a specified expiration date. The advantage of a call option is that it locks in the price you have to pay to purchase the stock and also gives you the flexibility to let the option expire if you wish. The price that you pay when purchasing a call option is referred to as a **premium**. The premium of a call option is influenced by the number of investors who wish to buy call options on that particular stock. Investors can purchase call options through their brokerage firm, which charges a commission for executing the transaction.

EXAMPLE   On September 10, you pay a premium of $2 per share, or $200, to purchase a call option on Gamma stock. The stock price is currently $28. The call option gives you the right to buy 100 shares of Gamma stock at the exercise price of $30 at any time up until the end of November. Thus, no matter how much Gamma's stock price rises before the end of November, you can still buy the stock at $30 per share.

premium
The price that you pay when purchasing a stock option.

For every buyer of a call option, there must be a seller who is willing to sell the call option. The seller of a call option is obligated to sell the shares of the specified stock to the buyer for the exercise price if and when the buyer exercises the option.

EXAMPLE   Joan Montana sold you the call option on Gamma stock. Joan receives the $200 premium that you paid to buy the call option. She is obligated to sell 100 shares of stock to you for $30 per share if and when you exercise the call option.

Your net gain or loss from buying a call option can be determined by considering the amount received when you sell the stock, the amount you paid for the stock when exercising the option, and the amount you paid for the premium.

EXAMPLE   Recall that you paid a premium of $2 per share, or $200, to purchase the call option on Gamma stock. The price of Gamma stock increases from $28 to $35 per share by the end of November. You can exercise the option and then sell the stock in the market at its prevailing price of $35. Your gain is:

Amount Received from Selling the Stock ($35 × 100 shares)	$3,500
Amount Paid for Gamma Stock ($30 × 100 shares)	− $3,000
Amount Paid for the Premium ($2 × 100 shares)	− $200
Net Gain	= $300

Since you paid $200 for the call option and your net gain was $300, your return can be derived as your net gain divided by the amount of your investment:

Return	=	Net Gain/Amount of Investment
	=	$300/$200
	=	1.50, or 150%.

Joan does not own shares of Gamma stock, so she has to buy it in the market at $35 per share before selling it to you at $30 per share. Thus, her net gain (or loss) is:

Amount Received from Selling the Stock ($30 × 100 shares)	$3,000
Amount Paid for Gamma Stock ($35 × 100 shares)	− $3,500
Amount Received from the Premium ($2 × 100 shares)	+ $200
Net Gain	= − $300

Notice that the dollar amount of your gain is equal to the dollar amount of Joan's loss.

When investing in a call option on a stock rather than the stock itself, you can magnify your return. If you had purchased Gamma stock on September 10 at a price of $28 per share, your gain would have been $7 per share. The return from investing in the call option (150 percent) is much higher. However, the risk from investing in the call option is higher than the risk from investing in the stock itself.

put option
Provides the right to sell 100 shares of a specified stock at a specified price by a specified expiration date.

Put Options. A **put option** on a stock provides the right to sell 100 shares of a specified stock at a specified exercise price by a specified expiration date. You place an order for a put option in the same way that you place an order for a call option. The put option locks in the price at which you can sell the stock and also gives you the flexibility to let the option expire if you wish. You buy a put option when you expect the stock's price to decline.

EXAMPLE

On January 18, you pay a $300 premium to purchase a put option on Winger stock with an exercise price of $50 and that expires at the end of March. The stock price is currently $51 per share. The put option gives you the right to sell 100 shares of Winger stock at the exercise price of $50 at any time up until the end of March. Thus, no matter how much Winger's stock price decreases before the end of March, you can still sell the stock at $50 per share.

For every buyer of a put option, there must be a seller who is willing to sell the put option. The seller of a put option is obligated to buy the shares of the specified stock from the buyer of the put option for the exercise price if and when the buyer exercises the option.

The Role of Stock Options in Asset Allocation. Although stock options have become a popular investment for individual investors who want to achieve very high returns, options are still very risky and should therefore play only a minimal role (if any) in asset allocation. Since asset allocation is normally intended to limit exposure to any one type of investment, any allocation to stock options should be made with caution. Many stock options are never exercised, which means that the investment generates a return of −100 percent.

Nevertheless, there are some ways of using stock options to reduce the risk of your portfolio. Two of the more common methods are discussed next.

First, you can limit the risk of stocks you hold by purchasing put options on them.

EXAMPLE

You invested in 100 shares of Dragon.com stock a year ago. Although the stock has performed well, you think it may perform poorly in the near future. The present price of the stock is $40 per share. You decide to pay a premium of $3 per share, or $300, for a put option on Dragon.com stock with an exercise price of $38. If the stock price stays above $38 per share, you will not exercise the put option. Conversely, if the stock price falls below $38 per share, you can exercise the put option by selling the shares you are holding for $38 per share.

In this example, your purchase of a put option locked in a minimum price at which you could sell a stock you were holding, no matter how much that stock's price declined. Thus, you were able to reduce your portfolio's risk by limiting your potential loss on this stock.

covered call strategy
Selling call options on stock that you own.

You can also reduce your risk by selling call options on stocks you hold. Doing so is referred to as a **covered call strategy** because the call option you purchase is covered by stock that you already own.

EXAMPLE

Assume once again that you are concerned that the price of Dragon.com stock may decline in the near future. There is a call option available with an exercise price of $42 and a premium of $2. You decide to sell a call option on Dragon.com stock and receive a premium of $200 (computed as 2×100 shares). If the price of Dragon.com stock rises above $42 per share, the call option will be exercised, and you will have to sell the stock to fulfill your obligation. Yet you at least will sell the stock for a gain. Conversely, if the stock price remains below $42, the call option will not be exercised. In this case, the $200 that you earned from selling the call option can help offset the stock's poor performance, thereby reducing your potential losses from holding it.

How Asset Allocation Affects Risk

Some asset allocation strategies reduce risk to a greater degree than others. To maintain a very low level of risk, an asset allocation may emphasize money market funds, U.S. government bonds, and the stocks of large established U.S. stocks. These types of investments tend to have low risk, but also offer a relatively low rate of return. To strive for a higher return, the asset allocation should include more real estate and stocks of developing countries. Exhibit 19.6 compares different asset allocation strategies in terms of risk and potential return. Even the most conservative asset allocation strategy shown here could result in a loss over a given period because some of the investments included in the portfolio are subject to losses.

Benefits of Asset Allocation

To illustrate the potential benefits of asset allocation, Exhibit 19.7 shows the one-year returns on a wide variety of investments over the 2005 period. Investors who diversified only among U.S. stocks experienced decent performance during this period because of weak stock market conditions in the United States. However, real estate, non-U.S. stock markets, and precious metals generated relatively high returns. Therefore, investors who diversified internationally experienced better performance. In some other periods, some U.S. stocks performed better than real estate and better than international stock markets.

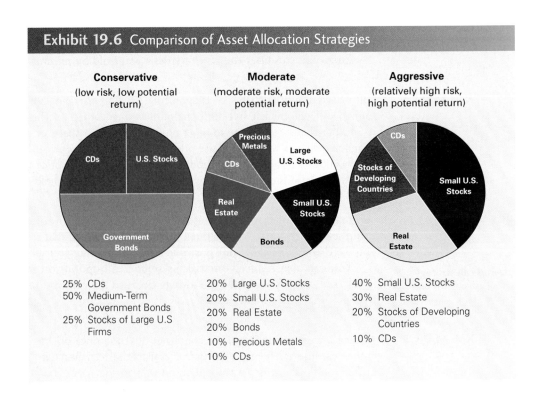

Exhibit 19.6 Comparison of Asset Allocation Strategies

Conservative
(low risk, low potential return)

Moderate
(moderate risk, moderate potential return)

Aggressive
(relatively high risk, high potential return)

25% CDs	20% Large U.S. Stocks	40% Small U.S. Stocks
50% Medium-Term Government Bonds	20% Small U.S. Stocks	30% Real Estate
25% Stocks of Large U.S Firms	20% Real Estate	20% Stocks of Developing Countries
	20% Bonds	10% CDs
	10% Precious Metals	
	10% CDs	

Exhibit 19.7 Returns of Investments in 2005

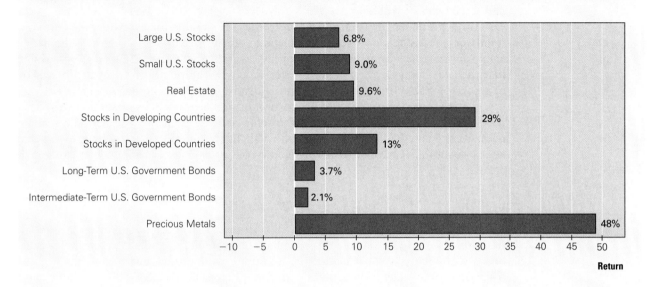

Investment	Return
Large U.S. Stocks	6.8%
Small U.S. Stocks	9.0%
Real Estate	9.6%
Stocks in Developing Countries	29%
Stocks in Developed Countries	13%
Long-Term U.S. Government Bonds	3.7%
Intermediate-Term U.S. Government Bonds	2.1%
Precious Metals	48%

Return

An Affordable Way to Conduct Asset Allocation

When allocating money across a set of financial assets, you are subject to transaction fees on each investment that you make. Thus, it can be costly to invest in a wide variety of investments. You can reduce your diversification costs by investing in mutual funds. Since a typical stock mutual fund contains more than 50 stocks, you can broadly diversify by investing in a few stock mutual funds.

For example, you could invest in a mutual fund focusing on stocks of large U.S. firms, another stock mutual fund that focuses on stocks of small U.S. firms, and a third stock mutual fund that focuses on a foreign country. You could also invest in a bond mutual fund that contains the types of bonds and maturities that you desire. You may also consider investing in a REIT to diversify your portfolio even further. With this type of portfolio, you can limit your exposure to adverse conditions such as a weak performance by a single firm, a single industry, or a single country, or an increase in interest rates.

FACTORS THAT AFFECT YOUR ASSET ALLOCATION DECISION

Your ideal asset allocation will likely not be appropriate for someone else because of differences in your personal characteristics and investment goals. The asset allocation decision hinges on several factors, including your stage in life and your risk tolerance.

Your Stage in Life

Investors who are early in their career path will need easy access to funds, so they should invest in relatively safe and liquid securities, such as money market investments. If you do not expect to need the invested funds in the near future, you may want to consider investing in a diversified portfolio of individual stocks, individual bonds, stock mutual funds, and bond mutual funds. Investors who expect to be working for many more years may invest in stocks of smaller firms and growth stock mutual funds, which have high growth potential. Conversely, investors nearing retirement age may allocate a larger proportion of money toward investments that will generate a fixed income, such as individual bonds, stock mutual funds containing high-dividend stocks, bond mutual funds, and some types of REITs.

Although no single asset allocation formula is suitable for everyone, the common trends in asset allocation over a lifetime are shown in Exhibit 19.8. Notice the heavy emphasis on stocks at an early stage of life, as individuals take some risk in the hope that they can increase their wealth. Over time, they gradually shift toward bonds or to stocks of stable firms that pay high dividends. The portfolio becomes less risky as it is changed to contain a higher proportion of bonds and stocks of stable firms. This portfolio is less likely to generate large returns, but it will provide periodic income upon retirement. In fact, your portfolio will likely be your main source of income after you retire. (Chapter 20 discusses the role of savings in retirement planning in detail.)

Your Degree of Risk Tolerance

Investors also vary in their degree of risk tolerance. If you are unwilling to take much risk, you should focus on safe investments. For example, you might invest in Treasury bonds with relatively short maturities. If you are willing to accept a moderate level of risk, you may consider a stock mutual fund that represents the S&P 500 stock index and large-cap stock mutual funds that invest in stocks of very large and stable firms. These investments offer more potential return than an investment in Treasury bonds, but they may also result in losses in some periods.

If you are willing to tolerate a higher degree of risk in order to strive for higher returns, you may consider individual stocks. Smaller stocks that are focused on technology tend to have potential for high returns, but they are also very risky. Even if you can tolerate a high level of risk, you should still diversify your investments. You might consider various mutual funds that have the potential of achieving a high return, but contain a diversified set of stocks, so you are not overly exposed to a single stock. Recall

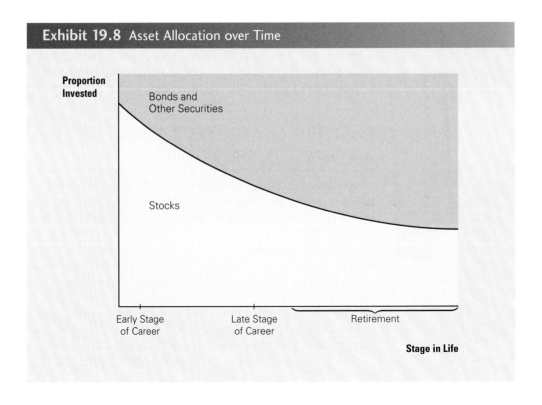

Exhibit 19.8 Asset Allocation over Time

from Chapter 18 that you can choose among various growth funds, capital appreciation funds, and even funds focused on various sectors such as health care or financial firms. You may also consider bond mutual funds that invest in corporate bonds. You can increase your potential return (and therefore your risk) by focusing on high-yield (junk) bond mutual funds with long terms to maturity.

Your Expectations about Economic Conditions

Your expectations about economic conditions also influence your asset allocation. If you expect strong stock market conditions, you may shift a larger proportion of your money into your stock mutual funds. Conversely, if you expect a temporary weakness in the stock market, you may shift a larger proportion of your money to your bond mutual funds. If you expect interest rates to decrease, you may consider shifting money from a bond mutual fund containing bonds with short maturities to one containing bonds with long maturities. You can easily shift money among mutual funds if the funds are part of the same family.

If you anticipate favorable real estate conditions, you may allocate some of your money to REITs. As time passes, your expectations may change, causing some types of financial assets to become more desirable than others. Over time, you should change the composition of your investment portfolio in response to changes in your market expectations, investment goals, and life circumstances.

Because it is nearly impossible to predict economic conditions, it is difficult to determine which types of investments will perform best in a given period. Consequently, you may be better off basing your asset allocation decisions completely on your stage in life and degree of risk tolerance. Then, once you establish a diversified portfolio of investments, you will need to revise the portfolio only when you enter a different stage in life or change your degree of risk tolerance.

19.2 Financial Planning Online: Advice on Your Asset Allocation

Go to
http://moneycentral.msn.com/investor/calcs/assetall/main.asp

This Web site provides a personal recommended asset allocation considering your income, your stage in life, and other characteristics once you input some basic information regarding your desired return and your degree of risk tolerance.

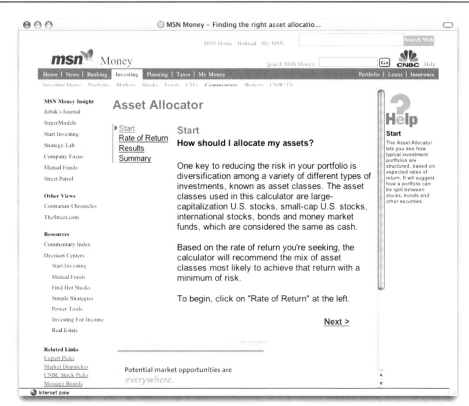

EXAMPLE

Stephanie Spratt wants to develop a long-term financial plan for allocating money to various financial assets. Specifically, she wants to set rough goals for the proportion of money that she will invest in stocks, bonds, and REITs over the next 10 years. Since she just recently started her career and may be working for another 30 years, she does not feel it is necessary to allocate a large proportion of her money to bonds at this time. She recognizes that bonds are typically safer than stocks, but plans to consider bond and stock mutual funds in the future. She recognizes that stocks are risky, but is comfortable taking some risk at this stage in her life. She plans to consider some equity income mutual funds, growth stock mutual funds, and international mutual funds.

As Stephanie accumulates more funds for investing over the next five years, she plans to invest in various stocks or stock mutual funds. She will invest in REITs only if her view of the real estate market throughout the United States becomes more favorable.

In 20 years, as she nears retirement, she will still consider market conditions, but will take a more conservative investment approach that reduces risk (and offers a lower potential return).

HOW ASSET ALLOCATION FITS WITHIN YOUR FINANCIAL PLAN

The following are the key asset allocation decisions that should be included within your financial plan:

1. Is your present asset allocation of investments appropriate?

2. How will you apply asset allocation in the future?

Exhibit 19.9 provides an example of how asset allocation decisions apply to Stephanie Spratt's financial plan. Stephanie's first concern is maintaining adequate liquidity and being able to make her existing loan payments. As she accumulates more money beyond what she needs for these purposes, she will allocate money to various investments.

Exhibit 19.9 How Asset Allocation Fits within Stephanie Spratt's Financial Plan

GOALS FOR ASSET ALLOCATION

1. Ensure that my present asset allocation is appropriate.
2. Determine a plan for asset allocation in the future as I accumulate more money.

ANALYSIS

Investment	Market Value of Investment	Proportion of Invested Funds Allocated to This Investment
Common stock	$3,000	$3,000/$5,000 = 60%
Stock mutual fund	1,000	$1,000/$5,000 = 20%
Bond mutual fund	1,000	$1,000/$5,000 = 20%
Total	$5,000	

DECISIONS

Decision on Whether My Present Asset Allocation Is Appropriate:

My present asset allocation is too heavily concentrated on one stock. With just $5,000 in investments, I should probably have all of my money invested in mutual funds so that my investments are more diversified.

I should consider selling the stock and investing the proceeds in a stock mutual fund. I already own shares of a mutual fund focused on technology firms. I will invest the proceeds from selling my stock in a different type of stock mutual fund so that I can achieve more diversification.

Decision on Asset Allocation in the Future:

Once I revise my asset allocation as described above, I will have $4,000 invested in stock mutual funds and $1,000 in bond mutual funds. This revision will result in a balance of 80 percent invested in stock funds and 20 percent invested in bond funds. The stock funds have a higher potential return than the bond funds. During the next few years, I will invest any extra money I have in stock or bond mutual funds, maintaining the same 80/20 ratio.

DISCUSSION QUESTIONS

1. How would Stephanie's asset allocation decisions be different if she were a single mother of two children?

2. How would Stephanie's asset allocation decisions be affected if she were 35 years old? If she were 50 years old?

SUMMARY

Asset allocation uses diversification to reduce your risk from investing. In general, a portfolio achieves more benefits when it is diversified among assets whose returns are less volatile and are not highly correlated with each other over time.

Common stock diversification strategies include diversifying among stocks across industries and among stocks across countries. You should consider using these two types of diversification so that you limit the exposure of your stock investments to any external forces that could affect their value.

Your asset allocation decision should not be restricted to stocks. Because bond returns are primarily influenced by interest rate movements rather than stock market conditions, they are not highly positively correlated with stock returns over time. Therefore, bonds can reduce the risk of an investment portfolio. Real estate investment trusts (REITs) are primarily influenced by real estate conditions and can also be useful for diversifying an investment portfolio.

Your asset allocation decision should take into account your stage in life, your degree of risk tolerance, and your expectations of economic conditions. If you are young, you may be more willing to invest in riskier securities to build wealth. If you are near retirement, you should consider investing more of your money in investments that can provide you with a stable income (dividends and interest payments) over time. If you are more willing to tolerate risk, you would invest in riskier stocks and bonds. Your asset allocation is also influenced by your expectations about future economic conditions. These expectations affect the expected performance of stocks, bonds, and REITs and therefore should shape your decision of how to allocate your money across these financial assets.

INTEGRATING THE KEY CONCEPTS

Your asset allocation decision is central to your other investment decisions and also affects other parts of your financial plan. Asset allocation affects your liquidity situation (Part 2) because some securities are more liquid than others. Even if you own some money market instruments to maintain liquidity, your asset allocation decision can achieve additional liquidity. For example, bonds and dividend-paying stocks provide periodic income. Some securities such as small stocks are subject to larger losses, and you may be less willing to sell those stocks when they perform poorly; consequently, small stocks are not liquid.

The asset allocation decision is related to financing (Part 3) because you should consider paying off any personal loans before you invest in some other assets. If, after considering your liquidity and financing situation, you decide to invest in securities or mutual funds, you need to decide whether the investment should be for your retirement account (Part 6). An asset allocation decision for retirement purposes is likely to be more conservative than short-term asset allocation decisions.

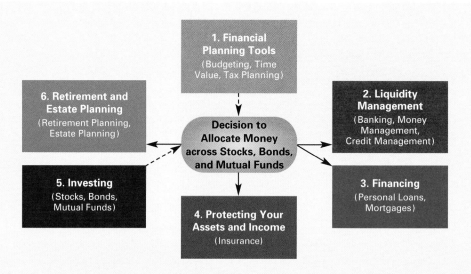

REVIEW QUESTIONS

1. Why is it important to diversify your financial holdings across financial assets? How does asset allocation enable you to accomplish diversification?

2. What is a portfolio? How does a diverse portfolio help reduce risk?

3. What factors influence a portfolio's risk? Explain.

4. Describe two strategies for diversifying a stock portfolio.

5. How can allocating some of your assets to bonds reduce the level of risk in your portfolio?

6. What are real estate investment trusts (REITs)? How are they classified? What are some attractive characteristics of REITs? How can REITs help diversify a portfolio?

7. What is a stock option? Why is it important for an investor to understand how stock options function?

8. Why can asset allocation be expensive? How can you reduce the costs?

9. Discuss the role that your stage in life plays in the asset allocation decision.

10. How does your risk tolerance affect the asset allocation decision?

11. How might your expectations of economic conditions influence your asset allocation? What is the problem with this strategy?

12. What is a stock option? Where are stock options traded? What is the exchange's role in the trade?

13. What is a call option? How does it work?

14. How is a gain or loss calculated from the trading of call options?

15. What is a put option? How does it work?

16. "There is a right way and a wrong way to use stock options in asset allocation." Evaluate this statement.

VIDEO QUESTIONS

1. Why should beginners diversify their investments among stocks, bonds, and mutual funds as explained in the segment?

2. How would investing in overseas markets give you an edge when diversifying?

3. As discussed in the segment, what is the role of a bond fund? How does it compare to stocks, and what is its role in a balanced portfolio?

FINANCIAL PLANNING PROBLEMS

1. Maryanne paid $300 for a call option on a stock. The option gives her the right to buy the stock for $27 per share until March 1. On February 15, the stock price rises to $32 per share, and Maryanne exercises her option. What is Maryanne's return from this transaction?

2. Chris purchased a call option on a stock for $200. The option gives him the right to purchase the stock at $30 per share until May 1. On May 1, the price of the stock is $28 per share. What is Chris's return on the stock option?

3. Teresa purchased a call option on a stock for $250. The option allows her to purchase the stock for $40 per share if she exercises the option by December 31. On December 15, the stock rises to $60 per share and Teresa exercises the option. What is Teresa's return?

Ethical Dilemma

4. Mike has decided that it is time he put his money to work for him. He has accumulated a substantial nest egg in a savings account at a local bank, but he realizes that with less than 3 percent interest he will never reach his goals. After doing some research he withdraws the money, opens an account at a local brokerage firm, and buys 500 shares of a large blue chip manufacturing company and 600 shares of a well-known retailing firm. From the beginning, his broker emphasizes that his portfolio is not sufficiently diversified with just two stocks. Over time, the broker convinces Mike to sell the shares of the two stocks to purchase stock in other companies. Two years later Mike owns stock in 14 different companies and views his portfolio as well diversified. His cousin, Ed, who has recently graduated from business school, looks at his portfolio and comments, "You are not very well diversified as 10 of the stocks you own are considered technology stocks." Mike tells Ed that he followed his broker's recommendations and sold his original stocks to purchase the new stocks in order to attain a diversified portfolio. Ed comments that the brokerage firm where Mike does business is noted as a specialist in technologies. Mike is disappointed because he thought he was getting good advice toward building a well-diversified portfolio. After all, Mike followed his broker's advice to the letter and why would his broker give a client bad advice?

a. Comment on Mike's broker's ethics in recommending the sale of the original stocks to purchase a portfolio weighted so heavily toward technologies. Include in your discussion reasons why the broker may have followed the course of action that he did.

b. To achieve diversification, what other course of action could Mike have taken that would not involve buying individual stocks in a variety of companies?

FINANCIAL PLANNING ONLINE EXERCISES

1. Go to http://finance.yahoo.com to determine how stocks are correlated with various indexes.

a. Enter "GE," the symbol for General Electric, and click "Go." Click "Basic Chart." Check the "S&P" box to compare S&P returns with the returns on GE for the past year. Click "Compare." What can you discern from this chart? You can choose various time periods from one day to five years. Repeat the exercise for some other time periods.

b. Add the Nasdaq and Dow indexes to the chart. Interpret the results and comment on GE's performance relative to the performances of the major indexes.

c. Click on "Technical Analysis." Add moving average information to the chart by clicking "200-day" and "50-day" under "Moving Avg." Interpret the current price of GE with respect to the 200-day and 50-day moving averages.

d. Click on "Basic Chart." Enter "IBM" in the "Compare" box. Click "Compare." The new chart will show a comparison of the returns on GE and IBM. Comment on the performance of GE and IBM and any interrelationship between the two.

2. Go to http://finance.yahoo.com.

a. Enter "NKE" and click "Go." Under "Quotes" click on "Options." Call and put options at various strike prices and expiration dates for Nike will be displayed. What is the pattern in premium costs for calls as the strike price increases? Why is this so?

b. Now review the premiums for put options as the strike price increases. Can you explain the relationship? How does this compare with what you observed with call premiums?

c. As the expiration period of put and call options increases, what is the effect on premiums? Why is this so?

3. Go to http://moneycentral.msn.com/investor/calcs/assetall/main.asp.

a. This Web site helps you determine an asset allocation strategy based on your specific situation. Click on "Rate of Return," then enter a desired rate of return of 8 percent. Click "Results." What is the recommended asset allocation that achieves a minimum amount of risk? What is the range of possible returns and risk of the recommended asset allocation? Are you comfortable with this allocation?

b. Now enter a desired rate of return of 11 percent. How does the recommended asset allocation change? Explain why the asset allocation changes the way it does. What is the range of possible returns and the risk now? How does this compare with the 8 percent desired rate of return scenario

BUILDING YOUR OWN FINANCIAL PLAN

Achieving the proper asset allocation balance in a portfolio is a significant part of any financial plan. Reviewing the selections you have made to meet your goals in investing, this case will help you determine the percentage of your funds that is allocated to each investment. Is your asset allocation conservative, moderate, or aggressive?

Asset allocation is an area of your personal financial plan that will change significantly as you get older and many of your goals have a shortened time horizon. Therefore, an annual review of your asset allocation is imperative.

Go to the worksheets at the end of this chapter, and to the CD-ROM accompanying this book, to continue building your financial plan.

THE SAMPSONS—A CONTINUING CASE

The Sampsons have been evaluating methods for investing money that will ultimately be used to support their children's college education. They have concluded that a mutual fund is better suited to their needs than investing in individual stocks or individual bonds. They are now seriously considering a biotechnology fund, which is composed of numerous biotechnology stocks. They have heard that biotechnology stocks can experience very high returns in some periods. They are not concerned about some biotechnology stocks performing poorly in any period because they have a mutual fund (rather than a single stock) and are therefore diversified.

Go to the worksheets at the end of this chapter, and to the CD-ROM that accompanies this text, to continue this case.

PART 5: BRAD BROOKS—A CONTINUING CASE

Between watching a financial news network on cable, reading articles in some business magazines, and listening to a co-worker recount his story of doubling his portfolio in six months, Brad is now convinced that his financial future lies in the stock market. His co-worker's windfall was in technology stocks, so Brad has focused his portfolio on three highly speculative technology stocks. He believes that the three stocks will give him adequate diversification with maximum growth potential.

Although he has heard that it might be a good idea to buy bonds for diversification purposes, he finds bonds boring and their returns too low. Brad read an article on how trading online with a margin account can increase his return, and he's interested in your opinion. Brad admits that he has virtually no knowledge of investing or time to do research, but a broker gives him lots of "hot tips." He believes that is all he really needs.

Brad has heard about misleading financial statements issued by some firms, but believes that even if companies misstate their financial condition, this will not affect their stock price.

Brad would like to hear what you think of his plan?

Go to the worksheets at the end of this chapter, and to the CD-ROM accompanying this text, to continue this case.

Chapter 19: Building Your Own Financial Plan

GOALS

1. Ensure that your current asset allocation is appropriate.
2. Determine a plan for future allocation.

ANALYSIS

1. Enter information about your current investments in the following chart. (If you input this information in the Excel template, the software will create a pie chart showing the market value of each investment.)

Type of Investment	Market Value of Investment	Goal(s) Met by Investment and Duration of Goal	Percentage of Funds Allocated to This Investment*
Checking Account			
Savings Account			
CDs			
Money Market			
Mutual Fund—Large Cap			
Mutual Fund—Small Cap			
Mutual Fund—International			
Mutual Fund—Corporate Bonds			
Mutual Fund—Government Bonds			
REITs			
Large Cap Stock			
Small Cap Stock			
International Stock (ADRs)			
Equity in Home			
Other Real Estate Holdings			
Investment in Collectibles (e.g., Antiques, Firearms, Art)			
Other Investment			
Other Investment			

(*continued*) Type of Investment	Market Value of Investment	Goal(s) Met by Investment and Duration of Goal	Percentage of Funds Allocated to This Investment*
Other Investment			
Other Investment			
Total Investments			

* To compute the percentage manually, take the dollar amount in the "Market Value Investment" column for each type of investment and divide it by the dollar amount for "Total Investments."

2. How would you rate your portfolio (i.e., conservative, moderate, or aggressive)?

_____

_____

_____

_____

3. Does the risk level of your portfolio correspond to your personal risk tolerance? If it does not correspond, what actions will you need to take to align the risk level of your portfolio and your own personal risk tolerance?

_____

_____

_____

_____

DECISIONS

1. Is your current asset allocation appropriate? If not, what changes will you make to better diversify your investments?

_____

_____

_____

_____

2. As you make additional investments in the future, how do you plan to allocate your assets?

_____

_____

_____

_____

Chapter 19: The Sampsons—A Continuing Case

CASE QUESTIONS

1. Advise the Sampsons regarding the soundness of their tentative decision to invest all of their children's college education money in a biotechnology mutual fund.

2. The Sampsons are aware that diversification is important. Therefore, they have decided that they will initially invest in one biotechnology mutual fund and then invest in three other biotechnology mutual funds as they accumulate more money. In this way, even if one mutual fund performs poorly, they expect that the other biotechnology mutual funds will perform well. How can the Sampsons diversify their investments more effectively?

3. A good friend of Dave's informed him that the company he works for will announce a new product that will revolutionize the industry the friend works in. Dave is very excited about the prospective jump in the stock price. He is ready to buy some stock in the friend's company. Advise Dave on this course of action.

Part 5: Brad Brooks—A Continuing Case

CASE QUESTIONS

1. Comment on each of the following elements of Brad's plan
   a. Level of diversification with three technology stocks

   _____

   _____

   _____

   b. View on bonds and not including them in his portfolio

   _____

   _____

   _____

   c. Trading online

   _____

   _____

   _____

   d. Margin trading

   _____

   _____

   _____

   e. Source of information ("hot tips")

   _____

   _____

   _____

2. Given Brad's lack of knowledge of investing and his limited time to learn or do research, what might be the best option for Brad to pursue and still get the benefit of the potential growth in the technology sector?

   _____

   _____

   _____

3. What factors will influence Brad's asset allocation? Based on these factors, what might be a suitable sample portfolio for Brad?

_____
_____
_____
_____

4. How would your answer to the sample portfolio part of question 3 be affected if Brad were
   a. 45 years old?

_____
_____
_____

   b. 60 years old?

_____
_____
_____

5. Explain to Brad why misleading financial statements may be more common than he believes and why misleading financial statements can negatively affect a stock's price.

_____
_____
_____
_____

6. Prepare a written or oral report on your findings and recommendations to Brad.

_____
_____
_____
_____
_____
_____
_____
_____
_____

Retirement and Estate Planning

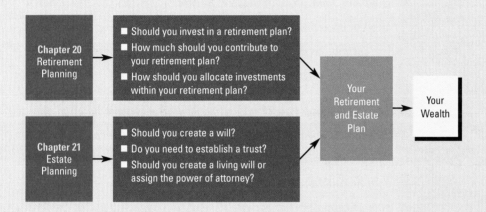

THE CHAPTERS IN THIS PART EXPLAIN HOW YOU CAN PROTECT THE wealth that you accumulate over time through effective financial planning. Chapter 20 explains how to plan effectively for your retirement so that you can maintain your wealth and live comfortably. Chapter 21 explains how you can pass on as much of your estate as possible to your heirs.

Retirement Planning

Patrick O'Toole, a divorcé, really wanted to retire at age 57. But, at 57, he was five years away from drawing Social Security, his mortgage still had 25 years of payments remaining, and after his divorce, he had only $225,000 accumulated in his retirement account. Even though he was unhappy in his present job, he needed to remain there as long as possible to build his retirement account.

Three years later Patrick had refinanced his mortgage and had only 15 years of payments remaining. In addition, his retirement assets had accumulated to $315,000. Patrick still had two years to go until he could draw early Social Security. At that time, he would be able to take a partial early retirement, although still not at the level of benefits he could have if he worked until age 65.

If you begin early in your working years to contribute to retirement plans, you can avoid the situation that Patrick was in. The quality and timing of your retirement will depend largely on your own decisions, even if your employer has a retirement plan available. It will take sound planning and diligent preparation to be financially prepared for retirement. This chapter describes the process and details some of the tools available to you.

The objectives of this chapter are to:

- Describe the role of Social Security

- Explain the difference between defined-benefit and defined-contribution retirement plans

- Present the key decisions you must make regarding retirement plans

- Introduce the retirement plans offered by employers

- Explain the retirement plans available for self-employed individuals

- Describe types of individual retirement accounts

- Illustrate how to estimate the savings you will have in your retirement account at the time you retire

- Show how to measure the tax benefits from contributing to a retirement account

SOCIAL SECURITY

Recall from Chapter 4 that Social Security is a federal program that taxes you during your working years and uses the funds to make payments to you upon retirement (subject to age and other requirements). It is intended to ensure that you receive some income once you retire and therefore is an important part of retirement planning. However, Social Security does not provide sufficient income to support the lifestyles of most individuals. Therefore, additional retirement planning is necessary to ensure that you can live comfortably when you retire. Before discussing other means of retirement planning, we will describe how Social Security functions.

Qualifying for Social Security

To qualify for Social Security benefits, you need to build up a total of 40 credits from contributing to Social Security over time through payroll taxes. You can earn four credits per year if your income is at least $920 per quarter. In addition to receiving income at retirement, you will also receive Social Security benefits if you become disabled, as discussed in Chapter 12, or if you are the survivor when the breadwinner of the household dies. If the person who qualified for Social Security dies (the household's main income earner), the following benefits are provided to the survivors:

- A one-time income payment to the spouse.

- Monthly income payments if the spouse is older than age 60 or has a child under the age of 16.

- Monthly income payments to children under the age of 18.

Social Security Taxes

As discussed in Chapter 4, your gross income is subject to a 7.65 percent FICA (Federal Insurance Contributions Act) tax. Your employer pays an additional tax of 7.65 percent of your gross income. Your FICA taxes are used to support Social Security and Medicare, the federal government's health insurance program. The Social Security tax is 6.2 percent of your gross income up to $90,000 in 2005 (this amount is adjusted periodically). The maximum that you pay per year for Social Security taxes is $5,580 (6.2 percent of $90,000). The Medicare tax of 1.45 percent of gross income is also included in FICA. There is no cap on the income level, however, so you and your employer must pay this tax on your gross income beyond $90,000. The FICA tax rates applied to various levels of gross income are shown in Exhibit 20.1.

			FICA Tax Rate	
Gross Income Level	FICA Tax Rate Imposed on You	FICA Tax Imposed on You	Imposed on Your Employer	FICA Tax Imposed on Your Employer
$20,000	7.65%	$1,530	7.65%	$1,530
30,000	7.65	2,295	7.65	2,295
40,000	7.65	3,060	7.65	3,060
50,000	7.65	3,825	7.65	3,825
60,000	7.65	4,590	7.65	4,590
70,000	7.65	5,355	7.65	5,355
80,000	7.65	6,120	7.65	6,120
90,000	7.65	6,885	7.65	6,885
100,000	7.65% of the first $90,000; 1.45% of the remainder	$7,030 [computed as $(.0765 \times \$90,000) + (0.145 \times 10,000)$]	7.65% of the first $90,000; 1.45% of the remainder	$7,030 [computed as $(0.765 \times \$90,000) + (0.145 \times \$10,000)$]

Exhibit 20.1 FICA Taxes on Various Income Levels

The taxes received by the Social Security program are distributed to current retirees. Thus, your payments to the Social Security program are not invested for your retirement. When you retire, you will receive Social Security payments contributed by individuals and their employers at that time.

Retirement Benefits

The amount of income that you receive from Social Security when you retire is dependent on the number of years you earned income and your average level of income. Social Security replaces about 42 percent of a worker's average annual income from his or her working years. Due to adjustments, however, this proportion is higher for individuals who had low-income levels and lower for those who had high-income levels.

At the age of 65, you can qualify for full retirement benefits. Starting in 2003, the eligibility age gradually increases until it reaches age 67. You can receive retirement benefits at age 62, but the benefits will be lower than if you wait until you reach full retirement age. As a general rule, though, early retirement will give you about the same total Social Security benefits over your lifetime as full retirement benefits.

You can earn other income while receiving Social Security benefits. If your income exceeds a specified limit (which is adjusted over time), however, a portion of your Social Security benefits will be taxed; the amount that is subject to taxes is dependent on how much other income you earn. The Social Security Administration estimates each individual's retirement benefits and sends this information annually to all individuals who will be receiving benefits.

Concern about Retirement Benefits in the Future

There is much debate about whether the Social Security program will be able to support retirees in the future. Today's retirees are now living longer, which means that the program must provide income over a longer period to individuals on average. In addition, there will be more retirees in the future and fewer workers to support them. When the generation of baby boomers begins retiring in the year 2011, much more funding will be needed to provide Social Security payments to all the retirees. Therefore, given the

20.1 Financial Planning Online: Request a Social Security Statement

Go to
http://www.ssa.gov/
top10.html

This Web site provides
a form that you can use to
request that a statement of
your lifetime earnings and
an estimate of your bene-
fits be mailed to you.

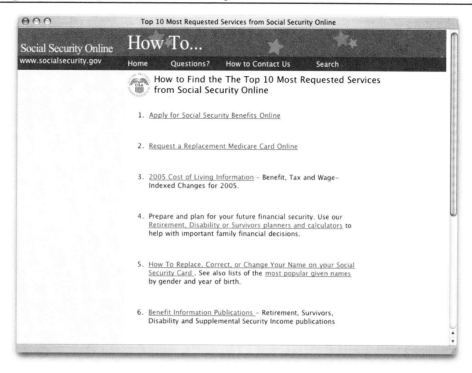

program's uncertain future, many individuals are relying less on Social Security income in their retirement planning.

Even if the Social Security program continues, many individuals will want more income after retirement than it provides. In 2005, the estimated average monthly Social Security payment was about $959. Thus, even if the Social Security program continues in its current form, its benefits are unlikely to be sufficient to provide a comfortable lifestyle for most people. For this reason, many individuals accumulate their own retirement assets either through an employer-sponsored retirement plan or by establishing an individual retirement account.

EMPLOYER-SPONSORED RETIREMENT PLANS

Employer-sponsored retirement plans are designed to help you save for retirement. Each pay period, you and/or your employer contribute money to a retirement account. The money in most of these accounts can be invested in a manner that you specify (within the range of possibilities offered by your specific plan). The money you contribute to the retirement plan is not taxed until you withdraw it from the account. If you withdraw money from the account before you reach a specific age, you will be subject to a penalty tax. Any money you withdraw from the retirement account after you retire is taxed as ordinary income.

Employer-sponsored retirement plans are classified as defined-benefit or defined-contribution plans.

Defined-Benefit Plans

defined-benefit plan
An employer-sponsored
retirement plan that
guarantees you a specific
amount of income when
you retire based on your
salary and years of
employment.

Defined-benefit plans guarantee you a specific amount of income when you retire, based on factors such as your salary and years of employment. Your employer makes all the

vested

Having a claim to a portion of the money in an employer-sponsored retirement account that has been reserved for you upon your retirement even if you leave the company.

contributions to the plan. The specific formula varies among employers. Guidelines also determine when employees are **vested**, which means that they have a claim to a portion of the retirement money that has been reserved for them upon retirement. For example, a firm may allow you to be 20 percent vested after two years, which means that 20 percent of the amount reserved for you through employer contributions will be maintained in your retirement account even if you leave the company. The percentage increases with the number of years with the employer, so you may be fully vested (able to retain 100 percent of your retirement account) after six years based on the guidelines of some retirement plans. Once you are fully vested, all money that is reserved for you each year will be maintained in your retirement account. These vesting rules encourage employees to stay at one firm for several years. One major advantage of a defined-benefit plan is that the benefits accumulate without the initiation of the employees. This helps employees who would not save money for retirement if they were given the money in the form of salary. Therefore, it ensures that the people save for their retirement.

Defined-Contribution Plans

defined-contribution plan

An employer-sponsored retirement plan that specifies guidelines under which you and/or your employer can contribute to your retirement account and that allows you to invest the funds as you wish.

Defined-contribution plans specify guidelines under which you and/or your employer can contribute to your retirement account. The benefits that you ultimately receive are determined by the performance of the money invested in your account. You can decide how you want the money to be invested. You can also change your investments over time.

As a result of their flexibility, defined-contribution plans have become very popular. In the last 10 years, many employers have shifted from defined-benefit to defined-contribution plans. This places more responsibility on the employees to contribute money and to decide how the contributions should be invested until their retirement. Therefore, you need to understand the potential benefits of a defined-contribution plan and how to estimate the potential retirement savings that can be accumulated under this plan.

The Decision to Contribute. Some people who have defined-contribution plans make the mistake of waiting too long before they save for retirement. They do not worry about saving for retirement at a young age because they believe that they can save later. With this rationale, they may spend all the money that they earn. Then, as they get older, they may be forced to catch up on investing for retirement, which could severely cut their funds available for spending. Yet, many people who do not have the discipline to start saving for retirement at a young age do not save for retirement as they get older. They may continually say that they will start saving next year, just because that is easier than saving for retirement now. The flexibility to postpone saving for retirement is one disadvantage of a defined-contribution plan for those people who lack the discipline to save on their own.

If you are willing to save, a logical approach is to start saving at an early age, contributing from every paycheck. The size of your contribution should increase as your salary increases. If you tend to spend whatever excess funds you have after covering all of your obligations, you should view retirement contributions as an obligation. If the contribution is taken directly out of your paycheck, you won't have it to spend. As you notice your retirement account accumulating funds, the saving process will become easier because you will see how your retirement account balance grows over time.

Benefits of a Defined-Contribution Plan. A defined-contribution plan provides you with many benefits. Any money contributed by your employer is like extra income paid to you beyond your salary. In addition, having a retirement account can encourage you to save money each pay period by directing a portion of your income to the account before you receive your paycheck.

Investing in a defined-contribution plan also offers tax benefits. The retirement account allows you to defer taxes on income paid by your employer because your contribution to your account is deducted from your pay before taxes are taken out. Also note that the income generated by your investments in a retirement account is not taxed until you withdraw the money after you retire. This tax benefit is very valuable because

20.2 Financial Planning Online: Retirement Expense Calculator

Go to

http://moneycentral.msn.
com/investor/calcs/
n_retireq/main.asp

This Web site provides
an estimate of your
expenses at retirement
based on your current
salary and expenses.

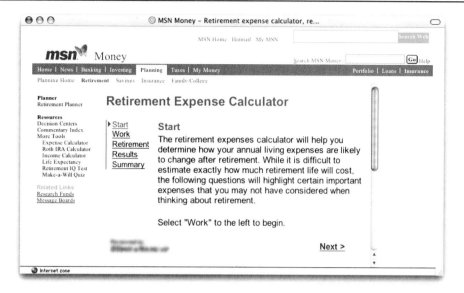

it provides you with more money that can be invested and accumulated. In addition, by
the time you are taxed on the investments (at retirement), you will likely be in a lower
tax bracket because you will have less income.

Investing Funds in Your Retirement Account. Most defined-contribution plans sponsored by employers allow some flexibility on how your retirement funds can be invested.
You can typically select from a variety of stock mutual funds, bond mutual funds, or
even money market funds. The amount of funds you accumulate will depend on how
your investment in the retirement account performs.

YOUR RETIREMENT PLANNING DECISIONS

Your key retirement planning decisions involve choosing a retirement plan, determining
how much to contribute, and allocating your contributions. There are several Web sites
that provide useful calculators that can help you make these decisions, such as
http://moneycentral.msn.com/retire/planner.asp and http://www.smartmoney.com/
retirement. Using the calculators can help you understand tradeoffs involved so that you
can make the retirement planning decisions that fit your specific needs. Each of your
retirement planning decisions is discussed next.

Which Retirement Plan Should You Pursue?

The retirement benefits from an employer-sponsored retirement plan vary among
employers. Some employer-sponsored plans allow you to invest more money than others. If your employer offers a retirement plan, that should be the first plan that you consider because your employer will likely contribute to it.

How Much to Contribute

Some retirement plans allow you to determine how much money (up to some specified
maximum level) to contribute to your retirement account. Although some individuals
like this freedom, others are not comfortable making this decision. A first step is to
determine your potential savings from contributing to your retirement plan. This
requires assumptions about how much you could contribute per year, the return you will
earn on your investments, and the number of years until your retirement, as illustrated
in the following example.

EXAMPLE

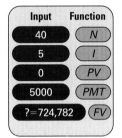

Input	Function
40	N
10	I
0	PV
5000	PMT
?=2,212,950	FV

Input	Function
40	N
5	I
0	PV
5000	PMT
?=724,782	FV

Stephanie Spratt is considering whether she should start saving toward her retirement. Although her retirement is 40 years away, she wants to ensure that she can live comfortably at that time. She decides to contribute $3,600 per year ($300 per month) to her retirement through her employer's defined-contribution plan. Her employer will provide a partial matching contribution of $1,400 per year. Therefore, the total contribution to her retirement account will be $5,000 per year. As a result of contributing to her retirement, Stephanie will have less spending money and will not have access to these savings until she retires in about 40 years. However, her annual contribution helps reduce her taxes now because the money she contributes is not subject to income taxes until she withdraws it at retirement.

Stephanie wants to determine how much money she will have in 40 years based on the total contribution of $5,000 per year. She expects to earn a return of 10 percent on her investment. She can use the future value of annuity tables (in Appendix B) to estimate the value of this annuity in 40 years. Her estimate of her savings at the time of her retirement is:

$$\text{Savings in Retirement Account} = \text{Annual Contribution} \times FVIFA \ (i = 10\%, n = 40)$$
$$= \$5,000 \times 442.59$$
$$= \$2,212,950.$$

Stephanie realizes that she may be overestimating her return, so she reestimates her savings based on a 5 percent return:

$$\text{Savings in Retirement Account} = \text{Annual Contribution} \times FVIFA \ (i = 5\%, n = 40)$$
$$= \$5,000 \times 120.797$$
$$= \$724,782.$$

Even with this more conservative estimate, Stephanie realizes that she will be able to accumulate more than $700,000 by the time she retires.

The amount that you try to save by the time you retire is partially dependent on the retirement income that you will need to live comfortably. There are various methods of determining the amount that you should save for your retirement. Among the important variables to consider are the levels of your existing assets and liabilities, whether you will be supporting anyone besides yourself at retirement, your personal needs, the expected price level of products at the time of your retirement, and the number of years you will live while retired. Various online calculators based on these factors are available.

Given the difficulty of estimating how much income you will need at retirement, a safe approach is to recognize that Social Security will not provide sufficient funds and to invest as much as you can on a consistent basis in your retirement plan. After maintaining enough funds for liquidity purposes, you should invest as much as possible in retirement accounts, especially when the contribution is matched by your employer.

How to Invest Your Contributions

When considering investment alternatives within a defined-contribution retirement plan, you do not have to worry about tax effects. All the money you withdraw from your retirement account at the time you retire will be taxed at your ordinary income tax rate, regardless of how it was earned. Most financial advisers suggest a diversified set of investments, such as investing most of the money in one or more stock mutual funds and investing the remainder in one or more bond mutual funds.

Your retirement plan investment decision should take into account the number of years until your retirement, as shown in Exhibit 20.2. If you are far from retirement, you might consider mutual funds that invest in stocks with high potential for growth (such as a capital appreciation fund, a technology fund, and maybe an international stock or

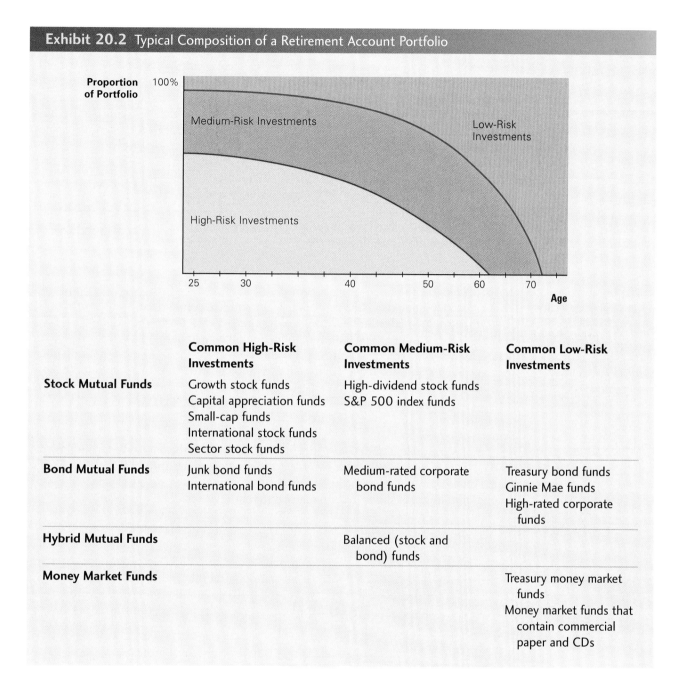

Exhibit 20.2 Typical Composition of a Retirement Account Portfolio

	Common High-Risk Investments	Common Medium-Risk Investments	Common Low-Risk Investments
Stock Mutual Funds	Growth stock funds Capital appreciation funds Small-cap funds International stock funds Sector stock funds	High-dividend stock funds S&P 500 index funds	
Bond Mutual Funds	Junk bond funds International bond funds	Medium-rated corporate bond funds	Treasury bond funds Ginnie Mae funds High-rated corporate funds
Hybrid Mutual Funds		Balanced (stock and bond) funds	
Money Market Funds			Treasury money market funds Money market funds that contain commercial paper and CDs

bond fund). If you are close to retirement, you might consider Ginnie Mae bond funds, Treasury bond funds, and a stock mutual fund that focuses on stocks of very large firms that pay high dividends. Remember, however, that any investment is subject to a possible decline in value. Some investments (such as a money market fund focused on Treasury bills or on bank certificates of deposit) are less risky, but also offer less potential return. Most retirement plans allow a wide variety of investment alternatives to suit various risk tolerances.

If you are young and far from retirement, you are in a position to take more risk with your investments. As you approach retirement, however, your investments should be more conservative. For example, you may shift some of your investment to Treasury bonds so that your retirement fund is less exposed to risk. Most people invest at least part of their retirement money in mutual funds. Regardless of the specific mutual funds in which you invest, one of the most important tips for accumulating more wealth by retirement is to avoid mutual funds with high expense ratios. If you start contributing to your retirement by age 30, you can accumulate an extra $200,000 or more by the time of retirement simply by choosing low-expense mutual funds. Put another way, the odds that you will run out of retirement savings is much higher if you choose high-expense mutual funds because your retirement savings will not likely accumulate to the same degree.

RETIREMENT PLANS OFFERED BY EMPLOYERS

Next we will take a close look at some of the more popular defined-contribution retirement plans offered by employers.

401(k) Plan

401(k) plan
A defined-contribution plan that allows employees to contribute a maximum of $14,000 ($18,000 if they are age 50 or older) per year on a pre-tax basis.

A **401(k) plan** is a defined-contribution plan established by firms for their employees. Under federal guidelines, the maximum amount that employees can contribute is $14,000 ($18,000 if they are age 50 or older) per year as of the year 2005. As a result of the Tax Relief Act of 2001, the maximum annual contribution allowed for the 401(k) plan is $15,000 in 2006 and will be adjusted beyond that time for inflation. Individuals over age 50 were able to make additional catch-up contributions of $4,000 in 2004 and that limit is $5,000 in 2006. You can usually start contributing after one year of employment. The money you contribute is deducted from your paycheck before taxes are assessed. Your 401(k) contributions are fully vested regardless of when you leave the firm.

Employers offer a set of investment alternatives for the money contributed to a 401(k). For example, you may be able to invest in one or more mutual funds. The mutual funds are not necessarily part of a single family, so you may be able to choose among mutual funds sponsored by many different investment companies.

Some firms allow a managed account in which an investment adviser provides you with investment advice and account allocation based on your risk tolerance. The program will prescribe a specific allocation of assets for you based on your risk tolerance. Each company relies on a different program, so the prescribed allocation could depend on the company where you have your 401(k) plan. There are advisory fees, which normally range from .2 percent to .8 percent per year.

Matching Contributions by Employers. Some 401(k) plans require the entire contribution to come from the employee with no matching contribution from the employer. Other employers match the employee's contribution. This means that if an employee contributes $400 per month, the employer will provide an additional $400 per month to the employee's retirement account. Or the firm may match a percentage of the employee's contribution. For example, if the employee contributes $400, the employer may contribute 50 percent of that amount, or an additional $200, to the employee's retirement account. The amount of matching (if any) provided by the employer has a large impact on the savings that the employee will have at retirement. More than 80 percent of all employers offering 401(k) plans match a portion or all of an employee's contributions.

Tax on Money Withdrawn from the Account. If you withdraw money from your 401(k) account before age 59½, you will be subject to a penalty equal to 10 percent of the amount withdrawn. Your withdrawal will also be taxed as regular income at your marginal income tax rate. However, if you are retired and over age 59½ when you withdraw the money, you may not have much other income and therefore will be in a very low marginal income tax bracket. Thus, the 401(k) plan allows you to defer paying taxes on the income you contributed for several years and may also allow you to pay a lower tax rate on the money once you withdraw it.

Focus on Ethics: 401(k) Investment Alternatives

In some cases, to participate in an employer's retirement plan, employees must invest their 401(k) contributions in their employer's stock. This type of retirement plan is not only unethical, but it leaves the employee's present and future wealth exposed if the firm's financial condition deteriorates.

The Enron case has made individuals well aware of this type of risk. Enron's stock declined abruptly, once investors became aware of fraudulent financial reporting. The retirement accounts of employees who had invested in Enron stock abruptly declined in value. Many of these employees not only lost their jobs when Enron went bankrupt, but also lost their retirement savings.

When setting up a retirement account through your employer, diversify your investments so that you are not highly exposed to conditions within a single firm or industry. Enron's demise adversely affected many energy stocks, while WorldCom's fraudulent accounting had a negative impact on many telecommunication stocks. Diversifying among mutual funds reduces your risk exposure.

Roth 401(k) Plan

Roth 401(k) plan
An alternative to a 401(k) account available to people employed by participating companies.

In 2006, the Roth 401(k) account was allowed as an alternative to the traditional 401(k) retirement account. The **Roth 401(k)** is available to people who are employed by firms that offer participation in the account. Income contributed to a Roth 401(k) is taxed at the contributor's marginal tax rate at the time of the contribution. The advantage to the Roth 401(k) is that funds are not taxed when withdrawn from the account, as they are when withdrawn from a traditional 401(k) account. In essence, the Roth 401(k) plan allows contributors to avoid paying taxes on the interest or capital gains generated by the account. There are no restrictions on income level in order to contribute to a Roth 401(k) account.

The decision to invest in a Roth 401(k) or traditional account may depend on your marginal tax rate today versus your expected tax rate when you withdraw funds after retirement. If you are currently in a very low marginal tax bracket, you may benefit from using the Roth 401(k) because the taxes on your contribution will be small and you will not be taxed on the funds at withdrawal. However, some people may prefer the traditional 401(k) because the tax benefit occurs now, which gives them more immediate disposable income. They may be less concerned about the tax benefit of the Roth 401(k) plan at their retirement, even if that benefit outweighs the immediate tax benefit from the traditional 401(k) plan.

403-b Plan

403-b plan
A defined-contribution plan allowing employees of nonprofit organizations to invest up to $15,000 of their income on a tax-deferred basis.

Nonprofit organizations such as educational institutions and charitable organizations offer **403-b plans**, which are very similar to 401(k) plans in that they allow you to invest a portion of your income on a tax-deferred basis. The maximum amount that you can contribute is dependent on your compensation and years of service, up to a limit of $15,000 in 2006 and beyond.

A 403-b plan allows you to choose investment alternatives. You will be penalized for withdrawals before age 59½, and when you withdraw the money at retirement, you will be taxed at your marginal tax rate.

Simplified Employee Plan (SEP)

Simplified Employee Plan (SEP)
A defined-contribution plan commonly offered by firms with 1 to 10 employees or used by self-employed people.

A **Simplified Employee Plan (SEP)** is commonly offered by firms with 1 to 10 employees. The employee is not allowed to make contributions. The employer can contribute up to 25 percent of the employee's annual income, up to a maximum annual contribution of $42,000 in 2005. SEPs give an employer much flexibility in determining how much money to contribute. The employer may establish your SEP account at an investment company, depository institution, or brokerage firm of your choice. If it is established at an investment company, you will be able to invest the money in a set of mutual funds that the company offers. If the account is established at a depository institution, you will be able to invest the money in CDs issued by the institution. If it is established at a brokerage firm, you may be able to invest in some individual stocks or mutual funds that you choose. Withdrawals should occur only after age 59½ to avoid a penalty, and the withdrawals are taxed at your marginal income tax rate at that time.

SIMPLE Plan

SIMPLE (Savings Incentive Match Plan for Employees) Plan
A defined-contribution plan intended for firms with 100 or fewer employees.

The **SIMPLE (Savings Incentive Match Plan for Employees) plan** is intended for firms with 100 or fewer employees. A SIMPLE account can be established at investment companies, depository institutions, or brokerage firms. The employee can contribute up to $10,000 in 2005 with the limit adjusted for inflation beyond 2005. As with the other retirement plans mentioned so far, this contribution is not taxed until the money is withdrawn from the account. Thus, a SIMPLE account is an effective means of deferring tax on income. In addition, the employer can match a portion of the employee's contribution. The SIMPLE plan allows catch-up contributions for employees who are age 50 or older. The catch-up amount is $2,000 in 2005, and is scheduled to rise to $2,500 in 2006.

Profit Sharing

profit sharing
A defined-contribution plan in which the employer makes contributions to employee retirement accounts based on a specified profit formula.

Some firms provide **profit sharing**, in which the employer makes contributions to employee retirement accounts based on a specified profit formula. The employer can contribute up to 25 percent of an employee's salary each year, up to a maximum annual amount of $42,000.

Employee Stock Ownership Plan (ESOP)

employee stock ownership plan (ESOP)
A retirement plan in which the employer contributes some of its own stock to the employee's retirement account.

With an **employee stock ownership plan (ESOP)**, the employer contributes some of its own stock to the employee's retirement account. A disadvantage of this plan is that it is focused on one stock; if this stock performs poorly, your retirement account will not be able to support your retirement. Recall from Chapter 19 that a diversified mutual fund is less susceptible to wide swings in value because it contains various stocks that are not likely to experience large downturns simultaneously. An ESOP is generally more risky than retirement plans invested in diversified mutual funds.

Managing Your Retirement Account after Leaving Your Employer

When you leave an employer, you may be able to retain your retirement account there if you have at least $5,000 in it. Another option is to transfer your assets tax-free into your new employer's retirement account, assuming that your new employer allows such transfers (most employers do). However, some employers charge high annual fees to manage transferred retirement plans.

rollover IRA
An individual retirement account (IRA) into which you can transfer your assets from your company retirement plan tax-free while avoiding early withdrawal penalties.

You can also create a **rollover IRA** by transferring your assets tax-free from your company retirement plan to an individual retirement account (IRA). You can initiate a rollover IRA by completing an application provided by various investment companies that sponsor mutual funds or by various brokerage firms. By transferring your retirement account into a rollover IRA, you can avoid cashing in your retirement account and therefore can continue to defer taxes and avoid the early withdrawal penalty.

RETIREMENT PLANS FOR SELF-EMPLOYED INDIVIDUALS

Two popular retirement plans for self-employed individuals are the Keogh Plan and the Simplified Employee Plan (SEP).

Keogh Plan

Keogh Plan
A retirement plan that enables self-employed individuals to contribute part of their pre-tax income to a retirement account.

The **Keogh plan** enables self-employed individuals to contribute part of their pre-tax income to a retirement account. An individual can contribute up to 25 percent of net income, up to a maximum annual contribution of $42,000. As with other retirement accounts, contributions are not taxed until they are withdrawn at the time of retirement. You can establish a Keogh plan by completing an application form provided by investment companies and some brokerage firms. Withdrawals can begin at age 59½, and you are responsible for determining how the plan's funds are invested.

Simplified Employee Plan (SEP)

Simplified Employee Plan (SEP)
A defined-contribution plan commonly offered by firms with 1 to 10 employees or used by self-employed people.

The **Simplified Employee Plan (SEP)** is also available for self-employed individuals. If you are self-employed, you can contribute up to 25 percent of your annual net income, up to a maximum annual contribution of $40,000. You can establish your SEP account at an investment company, depository institution, or brokerage firm of your choice. A SEP is easier to set up than a Keogh Plan.

INDIVIDUAL RETIREMENT ACCOUNTS

You should also consider opening an individual retirement account (IRA). There are two main types of IRAs: the traditional IRA and the Roth IRA.

Traditional IRA

traditional individual retirement account (IRA)
A retirement plan that enables individuals to invest $4,000 per year ($8,000 per year for married couples).

The **traditional individual retirement account (IRA)** enables you to save for your retirement, separate from any retirement plan provided by your employer. You can invest $4,000 per year ($8,000 per year for a married couple) in an IRA. As a result of the Tax Relief Act of 2001, the maximum annual contribution limit will be increased to $5,000 in 2008. The $5,000 level will be adjusted periodically for inflation. Individuals who are age 50 or older are allowed to make additional catch-up contributions of $1,000 per year. If you are covered by an employer-sponsored plan, and your gross income is above limits specified by the Internal Revenue Service, your IRA contribution is not tax-deductible. However, the income earned on your investments within the IRA is not taxed until you withdraw your money at retirement. You will not be taxed again on the initial investment when you withdraw that money at retirement. (If you are not covered by an employer-sponsored plan, your IRA contribution is tax-deductible unless your income is very high.)

When you contribute to an IRA, your investment choices will depend on the retirement plan sponsor. For example, if you set up your IRA at Vanguard, you can select among more than 60 mutual funds for your account.

You can withdraw funds from an IRA at age 59½ or later. You are taxed on the income earned by your investments at your ordinary income tax rate at the time you withdraw funds. If you withdraw the funds before age 59½, you are taxed not only at your ordinary income tax rate, but also are typically charged a penalty equal to 10 percent of the withdrawn funds.

Roth IRA

Roth IRA
A retirement plan that enables individuals who are under specific income limits to invest $4,000 per year ($8,000 per year for married couples).

The **Roth IRA** allows individuals who are under specific income limits to invest $4,000 per year ($8,000 per year for married couples). Due to the Tax Relief Act of 2001, the maximum annual contribution limit will be increased to $5,000 in 2008. Individuals who are age 50 or older can make additional catch-up contributions with the same limits as the traditional IRA. You can withdraw funds from the Roth IRA at age 59½ or later. You are taxed on money invested in the Roth IRA at the time of the contribution. However, you are not taxed when you withdraw the money, as long as you withdraw the money after age 59½ and the Roth IRA has been in existence for at least five years. These tax characteristics differ from the traditional IRA, in which you are not taxed when contributing (if you are under specific income limits), but are taxed when you withdraw the money after retirement. You can invest in both a Roth IRA and a traditional IRA, but you are limited to a total IRA contribution. For example, if you are single and invest the maximum amount in a Roth IRA this year, you cannot invest in a traditional IRA. If you invest $1,000 less than the maximum amount in a Roth IRA this year, you can also invest $1,000 in a traditional IRA. You need not maintain a specific allocation between the two types of IRAs each year, but you are subject to the maximum total contribution.

Individuals whose income exceeds specified limits are not eligible for the Roth IRA. For married taxpayers filing jointly, eligibility for the Roth IRA phases out from $150,000 to $160,000 of adjusted gross income. For single taxpayers, the Roth IRA phases out from $95,000 to $110,000 of adjusted gross income. Wealthy retirees may also find some additional benefits to a Roth IRA as a result of tax law changes taking effect in 2005. Because Roth IRAs have no required minimum distributions after age 70½, many retirees may wish to retain their Roth IRA or even add funds to it. The tax law changes make it easier to convert traditional IRAs to Roth IRAs, allowing additional funds to grow tax free.

Comparison of the Roth IRA and Traditional IRA

To illustrate the difference between the Roth IRA and the traditional IRA, we will consider the effects of investing $4,000 in each type of IRA.

Advantage of the Traditional IRA over the Roth IRA. The $4,000 that you contribute to a traditional IRA is sheltered from taxes until you withdraw money from your account. Conversely, you pay taxes on your income before you contribute $4,000 to a Roth IRA so that $4,000 is subject to taxes immediately. Assuming that you are in a 25 percent tax bracket, you would incur a tax of $1,000 now (computed as $4,000 × 25%) on the income contributed to a Roth IRA. Had you invested that income in a traditional IRA instead of a Roth IRA, you would not incur taxes on that income at this time.

Advantage of the Roth IRA over the Traditional IRA. IRA contributions should grow over time, assuming that you invest each year and that you earn a reasonable return. Assume that you are retired and withdraw $10,000 after several years of investing in your IRA. If you withdraw $10,000 from your Roth IRA, you will not pay any taxes on the amount withdrawn. Conversely, if you withdraw $10,000 from your traditional IRA, you will pay taxes on the amount withdrawn, based on your marginal income tax bracket. If your marginal tax bracket at that time is 25 percent, you will incur a tax of $2,500 (computed as $10,000 × 25%). Thus, you would incur a tax of $2,500 more than if you had withdrawn the money from a Roth IRA. Investment income accumulates on a tax-free basis in a Roth IRA, whereas money withdrawn from a traditional IRA is taxable.

Factors That Affect Your Choice. So which IRA is better? The answer depends on many factors, including what your marginal income tax rate is at the time you contribute money to your IRA and at the time that you withdraw money from your IRA. If you are in a high tax bracket now and expect to be in a very low tax bracket when you withdraw money from the IRA, you may be better off with the traditional IRA. Because you are not taxed on the initial contribution, you will receive your tax benefit when you are working and subject to a high tax rate. If you withdraw money from the IRA after you retire, and you do not have much other income, the money withdrawn from the IRA will be taxed at a low tax rate.

A counterargument is that if you save a substantial amount of money in your employer-sponsored account and your IRA, you will be withdrawing a large amount of money from your accounts every year after you retire, so you will likely be in a high tax bracket. In this case, you may be better off paying taxes on the income now with a Roth IRA (as you contribute to your retirement account) rather than later.

ANNUITIES

annuity
A financial contract that provides annual payments over a specified period.

When conducting your retirement planning, you should also consider investing in annuities. An **annuity** is a financial contract that provides annual payments until a specified year or for one's lifetime. The minimum investment in an annuity is usually $5,000. The investment in an annuity is not sheltered from income taxes. Thus, if you invest $5,000 in an annuity, you cannot reduce your taxable income by $5,000. The return on the investment in an annuity is tax-deferred, however, so any gains generated by the annuity are not taxed until the funds are paid to the investor. Although there are benefits from being able to defer the tax on your investment, they are smaller than the benefits from sheltering income by using a retirement account. Therefore, annuities are not suitable substitutes for retirement plans.

Fixed versus Variable Annuities

fixed annuity
An annuity that provides a specified return on your investment, so you know exactly how much money you will receive at a future point in time (such as retirement).

variable annuity
An annuity in which the return is based on the performance of the selected investment vehicles.

Annuities are classified as fixed or variable. **Fixed annuities** provide a specified return on your investment, so you know exactly how much money you will receive at a future point in time. **Variable annuities** allow you to allocate your investment among various sub-accounts (specific stock and bond portfolios), so the return is dependent on the performance of those investments. However, the variable annuities do not guarantee a specific return to you over time. The amount of money that you receive depends on the performance of the types of investment you selected. You may periodically change your allocation. You can withdraw your investment as a lump sum or as a series of payments over time.

Variable annuities commonly provide a death benefit, so that when you die, your heirs receive the account balance or the amount that you initially invested in the annuity, whichever is greater. In most cases, the value of your investments should increase over time, so the guarantee that your heirs will receive the amount that you initially invested is not extremely beneficial. Furthermore, the company who sells you the annuity charges you for this death benefit, and the amount that it charges is typically much more than the expected benefit.

Annuity Fees

surrender charge
A fee that may be imposed on any money withdrawn from an annuity.

The main disadvantage of annuities is the high fees charged by the financial institutions (primarily insurance companies) that sell and manage annuities. These fees include management fees that are charged every year (similar to those for a mutual fund) and a **surrender charge** that may be imposed on any money withdrawn in the first eight years or so. The surrender charge is intended to discourage withdrawals. Some annuities allow you to swap one type of annuity for another, but when you do, you are typically charged surrender fees. The surrender charges are especially high if you withdraw money shortly after you purchase the annuity, and decline over time. In addition, there may be "insurance fees" that are essentially commissions to salespeople for selling the annuities to you. These commissions commonly range from 5.75 to 8.25 percent of your investment. Some insurance companies have been criticized because their brokers aggressively sold annuities to customers without concern about the needs of their customers. Because brokers earn commissions on how much they sell, they may be tempted to make a sale without fully disclosing the disadvantages of annuities.

Some financial institutions now offer no-load annuities that do not charge commissions and also charge relatively low management fees. For example, Vanguard's variable annuity plan has total expenses between 0.58 and 0.86 percent of the investment per year, which are lower than what many mutual funds charge.

ESTIMATING YOUR FUTURE RETIREMENT SAVINGS

To determine how much you will have accumulated by retirement, you can calculate the future value of the amount of money you save.

Estimating the Future Value of One Investment

Recall from Chapter 3 that the future value of an investment today can be computed by using the future value interest factor (*FVIF*) table in Appendix B. You need the following information:

- The amount of the investment.

- The annual return that you expect on the investment.

- The time when the investment will end.

EXAMPLE

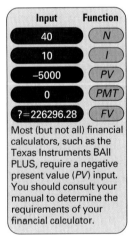

Most (but not all) financial calculators, such as the Texas Instruments BAII PLUS, require a negative present value (*PV*) input. You should consult your manual to determine the requirements of your financial calculator.

You consider investing $5,000 this year, and this investment will remain in your account until 40 years from now when you retire. You believe that you can earn a return of 10 percent per year on your investment. Based on this information, you expect the value of your investment in 40 years to be:

Value in 40 Years = Investment × *FVIF* (*i* = 10%, *n* = 40)

= $5,000 × 45.259

= $226,295.

It may surprise you that $5,000 can grow into more than a quarter of a million dollars if it is invested over a 40-year period. This should motivate you to consider saving for your retirement as soon as possible.

Relationship between Amount Saved Now and Retirement Savings. Consider how the amount you save now can affect your future savings. As Exhibit 20.3 shows, if you invested $10,000 instead of $5,000 today, your savings would grow to $452,590 in 40 years. The more you save today, the more money you will have at the time of your retirement.

Exhibit 20.3 Relationship between Savings Today and Amount of Money at Retirement (in 40 Years, Assuming a 10% Annual Return)

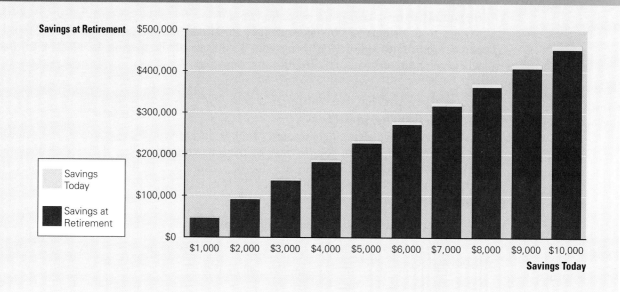

Relationship between Years of Saving and Your Retirement Savings. The amount of money you accumulate by the time you retire is also dependent on the number of years your savings are invested. As Exhibit 20.4 shows, the longer your savings are invested, the more they will be worth (assuming a positive rate of return) at retirement. If you invest $5,000 for 25 years instead of 40 years, it will be worth only $54,175.

Exhibit 20.4 Relationship between the Investment Period and Your Savings at Retirement (Assuming a $5,000 Investment and a 10% Annual Return)

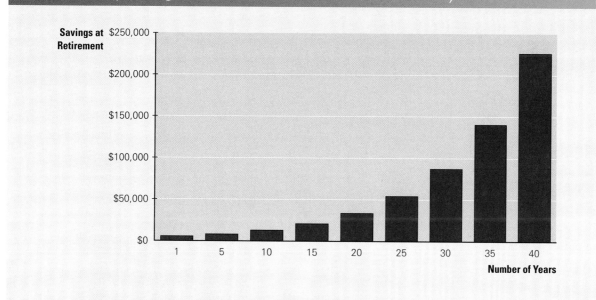

Relationship between Your Annual Return and Your Retirement Savings. The amount of money you will accumulate by the time you retire is also dependent on your annual return, as shown in Exhibit 20.5. Notice the sensitivity of your savings at retirement to the annual return. Two extra percentage points on the annual return can increase the savings from a single $5,000 investment by hundreds of thousands of dollars. With a 12 percent return instead of 10 percent, your $5,000 would be worth $465,200 in 40 years when you retire instead of $226,300.

Estimating the Future Value of a Set of Annual Investments

If you plan to save a specified amount of money every year for retirement, you can easily determine the value of your savings by the time you retire. Recall that a set of annual payments is an annuity. The future value of an annuity can be computed by using the future value interest factor of an annuity (*FVIFA*) table in Appendix B. You need the following information:

- The amount of the annual payment (investment)

- The annual return that you expect on the investments

- The time when the investments will end

EXAMPLE

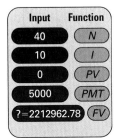

Input	Function
40	N
10	I
0	PV
5000	PMT
?=2212962.78	FV

You consider investing $5,000 at the end of each of the next 40 years to accumulate retirement savings. You anticipate that you can earn a return of 10 percent per year on your investments. Based on this information, you expect the value of your investments in 40 years to be:

Value in 40 Years = Annual Investment × *FVIFA* (*i* = 10%, *n* = 40)

= $5,000 × 442.59

= $2,212,950.

This is not a misprint. You will have more than $2 million in 40 years if you invest $5,000 each year for the next 40 years and earn a 10 percent annual return. The compounding of interest is very powerful and allows you to accumulate a large amount of funds over time with relatively small investments. Set aside income for your retirement as soon as possible so that you can benefit from the power of compounding.

Exhibit 20.5 Relationship between the Annual Return on Your Investment and Your Savings at Retirement (in 40 Years, Assuming a $5,000 Initial Investment)

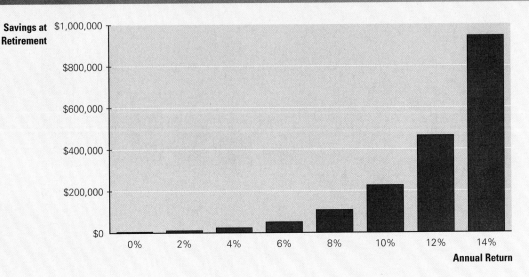

Relationship between Size of Annuity and Retirement Savings. Consider how the amount of your savings at retirement is affected by the amount that you save each year. As Exhibit 20.6 shows, for every extra $1,000 that you can save by the end of each year, you will accumulate an additional $442,590 at retirement.

Relationship between Years of Saving and Retirement Savings. The amount of money you will accumulate when saving money on an annual basis is also dependent on the number of years your investment remains in your retirement account. As Exhibit 20.7 shows, the longer your annual savings are invested, the more they will be worth at retire-

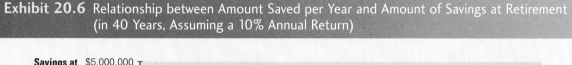

Exhibit 20.6 Relationship between Amount Saved per Year and Amount of Savings at Retirement (in 40 Years, Assuming a 10% Annual Return)

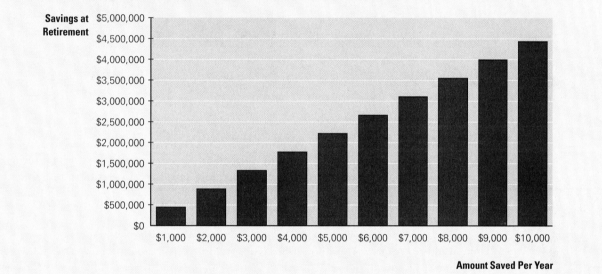

Exhibit 20.7 Relationship between the Number of Years You Invest Annual Savings and Your Savings at Retirement (Assuming a $5,000 Investment and a 10% Annual Return)

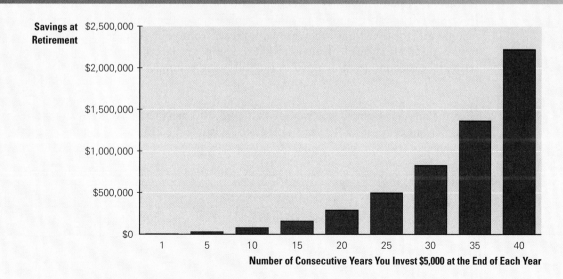

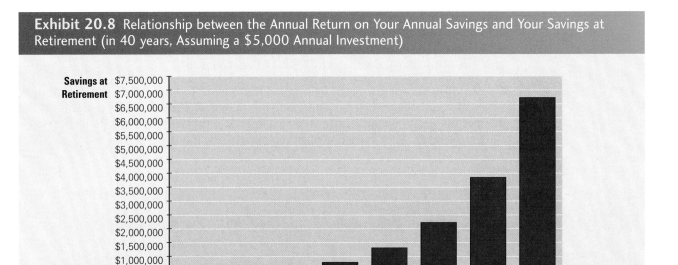

Exhibit 20.8 Relationship between the Annual Return on Your Annual Savings and Your Savings at Retirement (in 40 years, Assuming a $5,000 Annual Investment)

ment. If you plan to retire at age 65, notice that if you start saving $5,000 per year at age 25 (and therefore save for 40 years until retirement), you will save $857,850 more than if you wait until age 30 to start saving (and therefore save for 35 years until retirement).

Relationship between Your Annual Return and Your Savings at Retirement. The amount you will have at retirement is also dependent on the return you earn on your annual savings, as shown in Exhibit 20.8. Notice how sensitive your savings are to the annual return. Almost $1 million more is accumulated from an annual return of 10 percent than from an annual return of 8 percent. An annual return of 12 percent produces about $1.6 million more in accumulated savings than an annual return of 10 percent.

MEASURING THE TAX BENEFITS FROM A RETIREMENT ACCOUNT

If you can avoid or defer taxes when investing in your retirement, you will likely be able to save a much larger amount of money. Since some retirement contributions from your income are not taxed until they are withdrawn from your retirement account, you can reduce the present level of income taxes. The potential tax benefits of investing in a retirement account are illustrated in the following example.

EXAMPLE

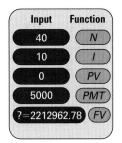

From the previous example, you can see that a $5,000 per year investment earning a return of 10 percent per year for 40 years would accumulate to $2,212,950. Using the future value of an annuity (*FVIFA*) table in Appendix B, your savings at retirement would be:

$$\text{Savings at Retirement} = \text{Annual Investment} \times FVIFA \ (i = 10\%, n = 40)$$
$$= \$5,000 \times 442.59$$
$$= \$2,212,950.$$

As you withdraw the money from your account after you retire, you will be taxed at your ordinary income tax rate, even though the investment appreciated over time due to capital gains. If you withdraw all of your money in one year, and are taxed at a 25 percent rate, your tax will be:

$$\text{Tax} = \text{Income} \times \text{Tax Rate}$$
$$= \$2,212,950 \times .25$$
$$= \$553,238.$$

You probably would not withdraw all your funds in one year, but this lump-sum withdrawal simplifies the example. Your income after taxes in this example would be:

$$\text{Income after Taxes} = \text{Taxable Income} - \text{Income Tax}$$
$$= \$2,212,950 - \$553,238$$
$$= \$1,659,712.$$

To compare the return from investing $5,000 in the retirement account to the return from investing $5,000 elsewhere, consider first that if you invest elsewhere, you will have an additional amount of taxable income of $5,000 each year. Assuming that your prevailing marginal income tax rate is 30 percent, you are subject to a tax of $1,500 each year. That leaves you with $3,500 that you can invest each year. Assume that you earn 10 percent on those annual savings invested over the next 40 years. Referring to the future value of annuity (*FVIFA*) table in Appendix B you will receive:

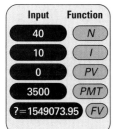

Input	Function
40	N
10	I
0	PV
3500	PMT
?=1549073.95	FV

$$\text{Savings at Retirement} = \text{Annual Investment} \times \textit{FVIFA} \ (i = 10\%, n = 40)$$
$$= \$3,500 \times 442.59$$
$$= \$1,549,065.$$

Next, consider that you will have to pay taxes when you cash in this investment. For many investments such as bonds or dividend-paying stocks, you would have been paying taxes every year over this 40-year period. Even if you had minimized taxes by choosing a stock that does not pay dividends, you would still pay a capital gains tax when you cash in the investment. Since you invested $3,500 per year, or a total of $140,000 over 40 years, your capital gain is:

$$\text{Capital Gain} = \text{Selling Price of Stock} - \text{Purchase Price of Stock}$$
$$= \$1,549,065 - \$140,000$$
$$= \$1,409,065.$$

Assuming a capital gains tax rate of 15 percent, your capital gains tax would be:

$$\text{Capital Gains Tax} = \text{Capital Gain} \times \text{Capital Gains Tax Rate}$$
$$= \$1,409,065 \times .15$$
$$= \$211,359.75$$

Therefore, after 40 years, you have:

$$\text{Value of Investment} = \text{Value of Investment before Taxes} - \text{Capital Gains Tax}$$
$$= \$1,549,065 - \$211,360$$
$$= \$1,337,705$$

Overall, investing $5,000 per year for the next 40 years in your retirement account will be worth over $322,000 more than if you invest $5,000 per year on your own. If you withdraw funds gradually from your retirement plan, the benefits of the retirement plan will be even greater because you will defer taxes longer. If you use a different annual return, you will get different results, but the advantage of the retirement account will remain. If you invest in something other than non-dividend-paying stocks on your own, the advantage of the retirement account will be even greater. Any investments on your own are subject to annual taxes on any ordinary income (dividend or interest payments), while income generated in the retirement account is not taxed until you withdraw the funds.

20.3 Financial Planning Online: How to Build Your Retirement Plan

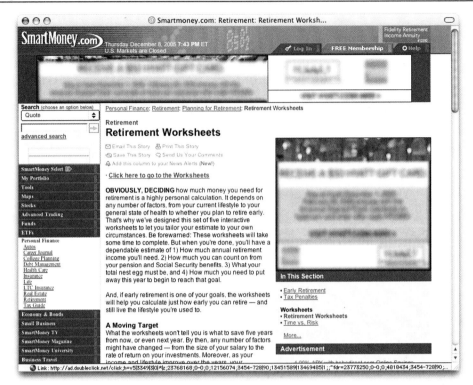

HOW RETIREMENT PLANNING FITS WITHIN YOUR FINANCIAL PLAN

The following are the key retirement planning decisions that should be included within your financial plan:

- Should you invest in a retirement plan?

- How much should you invest in a retirement plan?

- How should you allocate investments within your retirement plan?

Exhibit 20.9 provides an example of how the retirement planning decisions apply to Stephanie Spratt's financial plan.

Exhibit 20.9 How Retirement Planning Fits within Stephanie Spratt's Financial Plan

GOALS FOR RETIREMENT PLANNING

1. Ensure an adequate financial position at the time I retire.
2. Reduce the tax liability on my present income.

ANALYSIS

Type of Retirement Plan	Benefits
Employer's retirement plan	*I plan to contribute $3,600 of my income (tax-deferred) per year to my retirement plan. In addition, my employer provides a partial matching contribution of $1,400.*

Type of Retirement Plan	Benefits
Traditional IRA or Roth IRA	*I can contribute up to $4,000 of income per year (tax-deferred) to a traditional IRA. Alternatively, I could contribute up to $4,000 annually to a Roth IRA; in that case, the contribution occurs after taxes, but the withdrawal after retirement will not be taxed.*
Annuities	*I can contribute money to annuities to supplement any other retirement plan. The only tax advantage is that any income earned on the money invested is not taxed until I withdraw the money after retirement.*

DECISIONS

Decision on Whether I Should Engage in Retirement Planning:

Even if Social Security benefits are available when I retire, they will not be sufficient to provide the amount of financial support that I desire. Given the substantial tax benefits of a retirement plan, I should engage in retirement planning. I plan to take full advantage of my employer's retirement plan. I will contribute $3,600 per year and my employer will match with $1,400. The benefits of traditional and Roth IRAs are also substantial. Although I have not contributed to these retirement accounts in the past, I plan to do so as soon as possible. Annuities are not attractive to me at this point.

Decision on How Much to Contribute to Retirement:

I should attempt to contribute the maximum allowed to my employer's retirement plan and to a traditional or Roth IRA. These contributions will reduce the amount of money that I can dedicate toward savings and investments, but the tradeoff favors retirement contributions because of the tax advantages.

Decision on Asset Allocation within the Retirement Account:

I plan to invest the money slated for retirement in stock and bond mutual funds. I will invest about 70 or 80 percent of the money in a few diversified stock mutual funds and the remainder in a diversified corporate bond mutual fund.

DISCUSSION QUESTIONS

1. How would Stephanie's retirement planning decisions be different if she were a single mother of two children?

2. How would Stephanie's retirement planning decisions be affected if she were 35 years old? If she were 50 years old?

SUMMARY

Social Security provides income to qualified individuals to support them during their retirement. However, the income provided normally is not sufficient for most individuals to live comfortably. Therefore, individuals engage in retirement planning so that they will have additional sources of income when they retire.

Retirement plans sponsored by employers are normally classified as defined-benefit plans or defined-contribution plans. Defined-benefit plans guarantee a specific amount of income to employees upon retirement, based on factors such as their salary and number of years of service. Defined-contribution plans provide guidelines on the max-

imum amount that can be contributed to a retirement account. Individuals have the freedom to make decisions about how much to invest and how to invest for their retirement.

Two key retirement planning decisions are how much to contribute to your retirement plan and how to invest your contributions. When an employer is willing to match your retirement contribution, you should always contribute enough to take full advantage of the match. In addition, you should also try to contribute the maximum amount allowed, even if doing so means you will have less funds to invest in other ways. Most financial advisers suggest investing most of your contribution in one or more diversified stock mutual funds and putting the remainder in a diversified bond mutual fund. The specific allocation depends on your willingness to tolerate risk.

Retirement plans offered by employers include the 401(k) plan, 403-b plan, Simplified Employee Plan (SEP), SIMPLE, profit sharing, and ESOP. They offer similar types of benefits in that they encourage you to save for retirement and can defer your income from taxes. The specific eligibility requirements and other characteristics vary among retirement plans.

In addition to these retirement plans, some firms began to offer Roth 401(k) plans in 2006. The advantage of the Roth 401(k) is that the funds withdrawn at the time of retirement are not taxed. However, the income contributed to the plan is taxed. Individuals who have the choice of a traditional 401(k) versus the Roth 401(k) must compare the benefits of deferring taxes with the traditional 401(k) plan versus avoiding taxes upon withdrawal of retirement funds with the Roth 401(k) plan.

Self-employed individuals can use a Keogh plan, which allows them to contribute up to 25 percent of their net income, up to a maximum of $42,000. Alternatively, they can use a SEP, which also allows them to contribute up to $42,000.

In addition to retirement accounts offered by employers, individuals can also establish an individual retirement account (IRA), such as a traditional IRA or a Roth IRA.

Annuities are commonly used for retirement. Fixed annuities provide a specified return, while the return on variable annuities is dependent on the performance of the investment you select.

Your future savings from investing in a retirement account can easily be measured based on information regarding the amount you plan to invest each year, the annual return you expect, and the number of years until retirement. The future savings reflect the future value of an annuity.

The tax benefits from investing in a retirement account can be estimated by measuring the amount of retirement savings once they are converted to cash (and the income taxes are paid) versus the amount of savings if you had simply made investments without a retirement account. The tax benefits arise from deferring tax on income received from your employer until retirement and deferring tax on income earned from your contributions until retirement. Retirement accounts are the preferred investment in any comparison because of the tax advantages.

INTEGRATING THE KEY CONCEPTS

Your retirement planning affects other parts of your financial plan. If you build your retirement account when you are young, any funds that you invest in a retirement plan cannot be used for maintaining your liquidity (Part 2) or other investments (Part 5). Yet, by contributing to a retirement plan consistently over time, you are not forced to build wealth quickly shortly before you retire and are able to benefit from the power of compounding.

If you start saving for retirement at age 50 or later, you may take excessive risk in your efforts to quickly amass substantial wealth for your retirement. For example, you may decide to ignore the need for liquidity (Part 2) so that you can focus on investments that are expected to offer a high rate of return. This strategy could cause you to experience cash shortages in some periods. You may not be able to finance a car or a home (Part 3) because you would need to avoid interest payments and focus on accumulat-

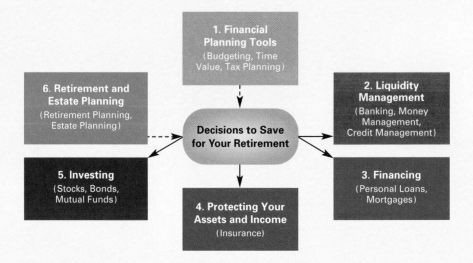

ing a lot of money quickly. You may also take excessive risk when making your investment decisions (Part 5), which could backfire. The advantage of retirement planning is that it allows you more time to build wealth for your retirement, so that you can make financing and investment decisions that are based on a long-term perspective.

REVIEW QUESTIONS

1. How does Social Security fit into retirement planning? How is Social Security funded? How does an individual qualify for Social Security benefits? When do you receive benefits?

2. How are the retirement benefits under Social Security calculated? Describe some factors that affect the amount of your benefits.

3. Discuss some of the concerns about the future of Social Security.

4. Describe how employer-sponsored retirement plans work in general.

5. What is a defined-benefit plan? What is vesting? What does it mean to be fully vested?

6. What is a defined-contribution plan? Why are some employers switching to this type of plan? List some of the benefits a defined-contribution plan offers to employees.

7. Briefly discuss the key retirement planning decisions an individual must make?

8. Discuss the general characteristics of a 401(k) plan. What is a 403-b plan?

9. Compare and contrast a Simplified Employee Plan (SEP) and a Savings Incentive Match Plan for Employees (SIMPLE).

10. Discuss profit-sharing and employee stock ownership (ESOP) plans.

11. Discuss the choices an employee has to manage a retirement account upon leaving an employer.

12. Briefly describe the two popular retirement plans for self-employed individuals.

13. Compare and contrast a traditional IRA with a Roth IRA. Discuss the advantages of each. What factors will affect your choice of IRAs?

14. What is an annuity? What is the difference between a fixed annuity and a variable annuity? What is the main disadvantage of annuities?

15. Why are retirement accounts more beneficial than other investments that could be used for retirement? Describe an effective strategy for retirement planning.

16. When estimating the future value of a retirement investment, what factors will affect the amount of funds available to you at retirement? Explain.

17. When estimating the future value of a set of annual investments, what factors will affect the amount of funds available to you at retirement?

18. Explain the tax benefits of investing within a retirement account versus investing outside a retirement account.

19. What is the main advantage of retirement planning?

VIDEO QUESTIONS

1. List the two main retirement rules and exceptions to these rules as explained in the video.

2. How can you increase your retirement income?

FINANCIAL PLANNING PROBLEMS

1. Barry has just become eligible for his employer-sponsored retirement plan. Barry is 35 and plans to retire at 65. Barry calculates that he can contribute $3,600 per year to his plan. Barry's employer will match this amount. If Barry can earn an 8 percent return on his investment, how much will he have at retirement?

Problem 2 requires a financial calculator.

2. How much would Barry (from problem 1) have at retirement if he had started this plan at age 25?

3. How much would Barry (from problem 1) have if he could earn a 10 percent return on his investment beginning at age 35?

4. Assuming an 8 percent return, how much would Barry (from problem 1) have if he could invest an additional $1,000 per year that his employer would match beginning at age 35?

5. Thomas is an attorney who earns $45,000 per year. What retirement plan should Thomas consider under the following circumstances?

   a. He works for a large private firm.

   b. He works at a university.

   c. He owns a small firm with employees.

6. How much will Marie have in her retirement account in 10 years if her contribution is $7,000 per year and the annual return on the account is 6 percent? How much of this amount represents interest?

7. Lloyd and his wife Jean have no retirement plan at work, but they contribute $4,000 each year to a tra-

ditional IRA. They are in a 25 percent marginal tax bracket. What tax savings will they realize for these contributions annually?

8. In need of extra cash, Troy and Lilly decide to withdraw $8,000 from their IRA. They are both 40 years old. They are in a 25 percent marginal tax bracket. What will be the tax consequences of this withdrawal?

9. Lisa and Mark married at age 22. Each year until their 30th birthdays, they put $4,000 into their IRAs. By age 30, they had bought a home and started a family. Although they continued to make contributions to their employer-sponsored retirement plans, they made no more contributions to their IRAs. If they receive an average annual return of 8 percent, how much will they have in their IRAs by age 60? What was their total investment?

10. Ricky and Sharon married at age 22, started a family, and bought a house. At age 30, they began making a contribution of $4,000 to an IRA. They continued making these contributions annually until age 60. If the average return on their investment was 8 percent, how much was in their IRA at age 60? What was their total investment?

11. Tilly would like to invest $2,500 in before-tax income each year in a retirement account or in alternative stock investments. Tilly likes the alternative investments because they provide her with more flexibility and a potentially higher return. Tilly would like to retire in 30 years. If she invests money in the retirement account, she can earn 7 percent annually. If she invests in alternative stock investments, she can earn 9 percent annually. Tilly is in the 25 percent marginal tax bracket.

   a. If Tilly invests all her money in the retirement account and withdraws all her income when she retires, what is her income after taxes?

   b. If Tilly invests all her money in alternative stock investments, what are her savings at retirement? (Hint: Remember that the income is taxed prior to investment.)

   c. Assuming a capital gains tax rate of 15 percent, what is the after-tax value of the alternative stock investment?

   d. Should Tilly invest her money in the retirement account or in the alternative stock investments?

Ethical Dilemma

12. Nancy and Al have been planning their retirement since they married in their early 20s. In their mid 40s and with two children in college, they are finding it harder to save and fear they will fall short of the savings needed to reach their retirement goals. Nancy's rich Uncle Charlie assures her she has nothing to worry about. "You are my favorite niece and because you are so good to me, I am leaving my entire estate to you." he said. Nancy and Al begin devoting considerable time and energy to making Uncle Charlie's golden years as enjoyable as possible. Factoring in their anticipated inheritance, Nancy and Al look forward to a comfortable retirement. Ten years later, Uncle Charlie passes away. At the reading of his will, Nancy is surprised to learn that Uncle Charlie made the same comment to her four cousins. As the will is read, all five of the cousins are horrified to find that Uncle Charlie left his entire estate, valued at over $2 million, to a home for stray cats.

   a. Fully discuss your views on the ethics of Uncle Charlie's actions.

   b. Looking at Nancy and Al's experience, what lessons about retirement planning can be learned?

FINANCIAL PLANNING ONLINE EXERCISES

1. Go to http://www.fool.com/money/allaboutiras/allaboutiras03.htm. After reading the comparison, use the regular IRA vs. Roth IRA calculator to determine which is better for you: a traditional (Regular) IRA or a Roth IRA. To perform the analysis, enter information based on your personal situation.

2. Go to http://www.ssa.gov/planners/calculators.htm. Click on "Quick Calculator." Enter your age in years and current total earnings for the year. Then select your benefit in today's dollars or inflated future dollars. What are your monthly Social Security benefits at age 62, 67, and 70?

BUILDING YOUR OWN FINANCIAL PLAN

Difficult as it may be to visualize, retirement really is "right around the corner." The reality is that the earlier you begin dealing with the issues of retirement, the more successful and enjoyable retirement will be.

You will very likely change jobs, if not careers, numerous times in your working life. Most of your employers will offer a defined-contribution plan, such as a 401(k), rather than a defined-benefit plan. It is therefore to your benefit to begin planning and executing a plan for your retirement as soon as possible. The tax benefits of retirement planning should serve as an additional motivator. The key decisions you need to make are how much to save each month, what type of plan(s) to contribute to, and how to allocate various retirement investments.

A retirement plan, like a portfolio, should be reviewed annually. You will probably not make major changes to your plan, but an annual review will help you to see whether you are on target to achieve your goals and retirement needs.

Go to the worksheets at the end of this chapter, and to the CD-ROM accompanying this text, to continue building your financial plan.

THE SAMPSONS—A CONTINUING CASE

Next on the Sampsons' financial planning checklist is saving for retirement. Dave's employer offers a 401(k) plan, but Dave has not participated in it up to this point. Now he wants to seriously consider contributing. His employer will allow him to invest about $7,000 of his salary per year and match his contribution up to $3,000, for a total contribution of $10,000 per year.

The retirement funds will be invested in one or more mutual funds. Dave's best guess is that the retirement fund investments will earn a return of 7 percent a year.

Go to the worksheets at the end of this chapter, and to the CD-ROM accompanying this text, to continue this case.

Chapter 20: Building Your Own Financial Plan

GOALS

1. Ensure an adequate financial position at the time you retire.
2. Reduce the tax liability on your present income.

ANALYSIS

1. Go to http://www.msn.com and click on the tab "Money," then click on "Site Map." Scroll down till you reach "Retirement" under "Planning Home." Click on "Retirement Planner." Use the calculator to determine the amount of savings you will need to retire.
2. Determine how much money you must save per year, the return you must earn, and the savings period to meet your goal for retirement savings. Experiment with different inputs in the following calculator in the Excel software.

Future Value of an Annuity

Payment per Period	
Number of Periods	
Interest Rate per Period	
Future Value	

Make any necessary adjustments to your personal cash flow statement.

Personal Cash Flow Statement

Cash Inflows	This Month
Disposable (after-tax) income	
Interest on deposits	
Dividend payments	
Other	
Total Cash Inflows	

Cash Outflows	
Rent/Mortgage	
Cable TV	
Electricity and water	
Telephone	

Cash Outflows (*continued*) | This Month

Cash Outflows (*continued*)	This Month
Groceries	
Health care insurance and expenses	
Clothing	
Car expenses (insurance, maintenance, and gas)	
Recreation	
Other	
Total Cash Outflows	
Net Cash Flows	

3. When examining retirement plans, keep in mind that tax benefits are important criteria. In the third column of the following table, indicate how suitable the plan options are for you.

Type of Retirement Plan	Benefits	Suitability
Employer's Retirement Plan	Employee contributions are tax-deferred; employer may match contributions.	
Traditional IRA or Roth IRA	Contribute up to $4,000 per year (tax-deferred) to a traditional IRA. Alternatively, contribute up to $4,000 annually to a Roth IRA after taxes; the withdrawal at retirement will not be taxed.	
Annuities	Contribute money to an annuity to supplement any other retirement plan. The only tax advantage is that any income earned on the investment is not taxed until withdrawal at retirement.	

4. Use the 401(K) planner worksheet to see how your savings can grow. The Excel software will present a complete analysis based on your input in the table below.

401(K) Planner

401(k) Contribution per Paycheck	
401(k) Employer match per Paycheck	
Paychecks per Year (12, 24, 26, and 52)	
Expected Annual Rate of Return	
Age as of the End of This Tax Year	

Anticipated Retirement Age	
Current Value of 401(k)	
Date (the "as of" Date for the Current Value)	
Enter the Date of the Year End	
Marginal Tax Rate (State plus Federal)	

Tax Deferred 401(k) Plan Growth

Age	Estimated 401(k) Value

Taxable Savings Plan Growth

Age	Estimated Savings Value

Pre-Tax Retirement Income*

From retirement age to 90 years old	
Monthly Income	

Pre-Tax Retirement Income*

From retirement age to 90 years old	
Monthly Income	

*The Excel software worksheets will calculate this information and create a chart showing your investment growth.

DECISIONS

1. How much savings do you need to support yourself during retirement?

2. How much will you contribute to your retirement? What type of plan(s) will you contribute to?

3. What are the present-day tax savings from your retirement planning?

Chapter 20: The Sampsons—A Continuing Case

CASE QUESTIONS

1. If Dave and his employer contribute a total of $10,000 annually, how much will that amount accumulate to over the next 30 years, at which time Dave and Sharon hope to retire?

Future Value of an Annuity

Contribution	$10,000
Years	30
Annual Rate of Return	
Future Value	

2. Assuming that Dave's marginal tax bracket is 25 percent, by how much should his federal taxes decline this year if he contributes $7,000 to his retirement account?

_____

_____

_____

3. The Sampsons' tax bracket has not changed. Assuming that Dave contributes $7,000 to his retirement account and that his taxes are lower as a result, by how much are Dave's cash flows reduced over the coming year? (Refer to your answer in question 2 when solving this problem.)

_____

_____

_____

4. If Dave contributes $7,000 to his retirement account, he will have less cash inflows as a result. How can the Sampsons afford to make this contribution? Suggest some ways that they may be able to offset the reduction in cash inflows by reexamining the cash flow statement you created for them in Chapter 2.

_____

_____

_____

5. Dave's employer has strongly urged him to invest his entire 401(k) contribution in the company's stock. Advise Dave on how to handle this situation.

_____

_____

_____

Chapter 21

Estate Planning

D amaris managed to accumulate an estate of over $3.5 million including a house worth $500,000 and investment assets of approximately $2 million. Her two children were aware of the value of their mother's estate, which they would inherit on a 50–50 basis. After her death they visited their attorney and learned that Damaris' estate would have to pay estate taxes on the $2.0 million in excess of the $1.5 million tax-exempt amount. The taxes on the excess $2.0 million would amount to $940,000. Failure to adequately take advantage of the estate-planning tools available to Damaris resulted in a high level of estate taxes, and a higher cost to her heirs.

Estate planning involves the planning and documentation of how your assets will be distributed either before or after you die. Estate planning is not just a tool for rich people. It is important for all individuals who want to ensure that their estate is distributed in the manner that they desire. This chapter explains several important estate-planning concepts as well as methods to reduce estate taxes.

The objectives of this chapter are to:

- Explain the use of a will
- Describe estate taxes
- Explain the use of trusts, gifts, and contributions
- Introduce other aspects of estate planning

PURPOSE OF A WILL

estate
The assets of a deceased person after all debts are paid.

estate planning
The act of planning for how your wealth will be allocated on or before your death.

will
A legal request for how your estate should be distributed upon your death. It can also identify a preferred guardian for any surviving children.

beneficiaries (heirs)
The persons specified in a will to receive a part of an estate.

intestate
The condition of dying without a will.

simple will
A will suitable for smaller estates that specifies that the entire estate be distributed to the person's spouse.

traditional marital share will
A will suitable for larger estates that distributes half of the estate to the spouse and the other half to any children or to a trust.

An **estate** represents a deceased person's assets after all debts are paid. At the time of a person's death, the estate is distributed according to that person's wishes. **Estate planning** is the act of planning how your wealth will be allocated on or before your death. One of the most important tasks in estate planning is the creation of a **will**, which is a legal request for how your estate should be distributed upon your death. It can also identify a preferred guardian for any surviving minor children.

Reasons for Having a Will

A will is critical to ensure that your estate is distributed in the manner that you desire. Once you have a positive net worth to be distributed upon your death, you should consider creating a will. In your will, you can specify the persons you want to receive your estate—referred to as your **beneficiaries** (or **heirs**). If you die **intestate** (without a will), the court will appoint a person (called an administrator) to distribute your estate according to the laws of your state. In that case, one family member may receive more than you intended, while others receive less. If there is no surviving spouse, the administrator would also decide who would assume responsibility for any children. Having an administrator also results in additional costs being imposed on the estate.

Creating a Valid Will

To create a valid will, you must be at least the minimum age, usually 18 or 21, depending on the state where you live. You must also be mentally competent and should not be subject to undue influence (threats) from others. A will is more likely to be challenged by potential heirs if there is some question about your competence or whether you were forced to designate one or more beneficiaries in the will. Some states require that the will be typed, although handwritten wills are accepted in other states. To be valid, a will must be dated and signed. Two or three witnesses who are not inheriting anything under the will must also witness the signing of the will. Although you are not required to hire a lawyer, you should still consider doing so to ensure that the will is created properly.

Common Types of Wills

A **simple will** specifies that the entire estate be distributed to a person's spouse. It may be sufficient for many married couples. If the estate is valued at more than $1 million, a simple will may not be appropriate because the estate in excess of $1 million could be subject to a high tax rate. A more appropriate will for large estates is the **traditional marital share will**, which distributes half of the estate to the spouse and the other half to any children or to a trust (to be discussed later in the chapter). This type of will is useful for minimizing taxes on the estate.

Key Components of a Will

A sample of a will is provided in Exhibit 21.1. The key components of a will are described next.

Distribution of the Estate. The will details how the estate should be distributed among the beneficiaries. Since you do not know what your estate will be worth, you may specify your desired distribution according to percentages of the estate. For example, you

Exhibit 21.1 A Sample Will

WILL of James T. Smith

I, James T. Smith of the City of Denver, Colorado, declare this to be my will.

ARTICLE 1
My wife, Karen A. Smith, and I have one child, Cheryl D. Smith.

ARTICLE 2 Payment of Debt and Taxes
I direct my Executor to pay my funeral expenses, my medical expenses, the costs of administration, and my debts.

ARTICLE 3 Distribution of the Estate
I direct that my estate be distributed to my wife, Karen A. Smith. If my wife predeceases me, my estate shall be distributed to my Trustee, to be managed as explained in Article 4.

ARTICLE 4 Trust for Children
4A. Purpose. This trust provides for the support of my daughter, Cheryl D. Smith, and any other children born to me.

4B. Use of Funds. The Trustee shall use as much of the trust income and principal as necessary to care for my child (or children). When the youngest of my children reaches the age of 25, the assets of this trust shall be split equally among the children.

4C. No Survivors. If no child of mine survives until age 25, assets of the trust shall be liquidated and 100 percent of the proceeds shall be donated to the San Diego Humane Society.

4D. Nomination of Trustee. I appoint my brother, Edward J. Smith, to serve as Trustee. If he is unable or unwilling to serve, I appoint my sister, Marie S. Smith, to serve as Trustee.

ARTICLE 5 Executor
I appoint my wife, Karen A. Smith, to serve as Executor. If she is unable or unwilling to serve, I appoint my brother, Edward J. Smith, to serve as Executor.

ARTICLE 6 Guardian
If my spouse does not survive me, I appoint my brother, Edward J. Smith, to serve as Guardian of my children. If he is unable to serve as Guardian, I appoint my sister, Marie S. Smith, to serve as Guardian.

ARTICLE 7 Power of Executor
My Executor has the right to receive payments, reinvest payments received, pay debts owed, pay taxes owed, and liquidate assets.

ARTICLE 8 Power of Trustee
My Trustee has the right to receive income generated by the trust, reinvest income received by the trust, sell assets in the trust, and use the proceeds to invest in other assets.

IN WITNESS WHEREOF, I hereby sign and declare this document to be my Will.

_____   _____
James T. Smith   Date

The above-named person signed in our presence, and in our opinion is mentally competent.

Signatures of Witnesses   Addresses of Witnesses

_____

Kenneth Tagan   44241 Lemon Street
                                          Denver, Colorado 80208

_____

Barbara Russell   101 Courtney Street
                                          Denver, Colorado 80208

21.1 Financial Planning Online: Quiz for Preparing Your Own Will

Go to

http://moneycentral.msn.
com/investor/calcs/
n_willq/main.asp

This Web site provides a quiz that indicates your ability to create your own will.

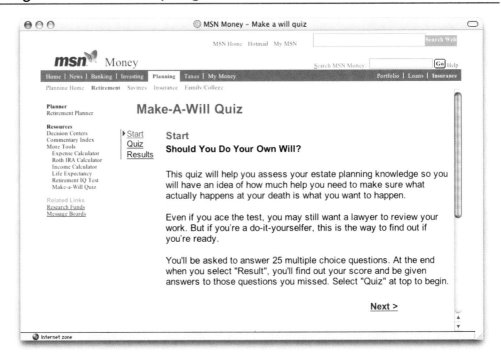

could specify that two people each receive 50 percent of the estate. Alternatively, you could specify that one person receive a specific dollar amount and that the other person receive the remainder of the estate.

executor (personal representative)
The person designated in a will to execute your instructions regarding the distribution of your assets.

Executor. In your will, you name an **executor** (also called a **personal representative**) to carry out your instructions regarding how your assets will be distributed. An executor may be required to collect any money owed to the estate, pay off any debts owed by the estate, sell specific assets (such as a home) that are part of the estate, and then distribute the proceeds as specified in the will. The executor must notify everyone who has an interest or potential interest in the estate. Most people select a family member, a friend, a business associate, a bank trust company employee, or an attorney as an executor. You should select an executor who would serve your interests in distributing the assets as specified in your will, who is capable of handling the process, and who is sufficiently organized to complete the process in a timely manner.

The executor must be a U.S. citizen, may not be a minor or convicted felon, and, under some states' laws, must reside in the same state as the person creating the will. The executor is entitled to be paid by the estate for services provided, but some executors elect not to charge the estate.

Guardian. If you are a parent, you should name a guardian, who will be assigned the responsibility of caring for the children and managing any estate left to the children. You should ensure that the person you select as guardian is willing to serve in

"Does it bother anyone else that we're burying half the Pharaoh's assets with him?"

http://www.cartoonresource.com

this capacity. Your will may specify an amount of money to be distributed to the guardian to care for the children.

Signature. Your signature is needed to validate the will and ensure that someone else does not create a fake will.

Letter of Last Instruction. You may also wish to prepare a **letter of last instruction**. This describes your preferences regarding funeral arrangements and indicates where you have stored any key financial documents such as mortgage and insurance contracts.

letter of last instruction
A supplement to a will that can describe your preferences regarding funeral arrangements and indicate where you have stored any key financial documents.

Focus on Ethics: Undue Influence on Wills
By now, you have learned to be aware of fraudulent or unethical behavior in all components of financial planning. Fraud and unethical behavior can even occur during the creation of a will. Consider the following examples:

- Christine, a 60-year-old mother of two, asks her oldest son for estate planning advice. He pressures her to leave much of the estate to him.

- Marguerite has already completed a will, which specifies that most of her estate will go to charity. She becomes terminally ill. Brooke, a frequent visitor at the hospital pressures Marguerite to include her in the will.

- Jarrod asks his son Jim (who is an attorney) for advice on creating a will. Jim misrepresents the rules about estates, which causes Jarrod to create a will that leaves a disproportionate amount of the estate to Jim.

- Tamara, a widow, has created a will that leaves her estate to her children and grandchildren. However, she recently met Jim, who has proposed marriage. Jim suggests that she leave her estate to him since he will be her husband.

These types of situations occur more frequently than you might think. If the court determines that there is fraud or some form of undue influence on the creator of the will, it may prevent the person who used fraudulent or unethical behavior from receiving any benefits. However, someone has to contest the will in order to have the court pursue an inquiry.

Consider creating a will without consulting potential beneficiaries. Meet with a financial planner who specializes in wills, and explain how you wish to allocate the estate among your heirs or others. The financial planner can design the will in a manner that achieves your goals. You can include all of your wishes in a will without discussing any of your wishes with anyone who is (or is not) named in the will.

Changing Your Will
You may need to change your will if you move to a different state because state laws regarding wills vary. If you get married or divorced after creating your will, you may also need to change it.

If you wish to make major changes to your will, you will probably need to create a new will. The new will must specify that you are revoking your previous will, so that you do not have multiple wills with conflicting instructions. When you wish to make only minor revisions to your will, you can add a **codicil**, which is a document that specifies changes in your existing will.

codicil
A document that specifies changes in an existing will.

Executing the Will during Probate
Probate is a legal process that ensures that when people die, their assets are distributed as they wish, and the guardianship of children is assigned as they wish. The purpose of the probate process is for the court to declare a will valid and ensure the orderly distribution of assets. To start the probate process, the executor files forms in a local probate court, provides a copy of the will, provides a list of the assets and debts of the deceased person, pays debts, and sells any assets that need to be liquidated. The executor typically

probate
A legal process that declares a will valid and ensures the orderly distribution of assets.

opens a bank account for the estate that is used to pay the debts of the deceased and to deposit proceeds from liquidating the assets. If the executor does not have time or is otherwise unable to perform these tasks, an attorney can be hired to complete them.

ESTATE TAXES

An estate may be subject to taxes before it is distributed to the beneficiaries. When a person dies and has a surviving spouse who jointly owned all the assets, the spouse becomes sole owner of the estate. In this case, the estate is not subject to taxes. If there is not a surviving spouse and the estate is to be distributed to the children or other beneficiaries, the estate is subject to taxes. The estate taxes are assessed after the value of the estate is determined during the probate process. You should estimate the estate taxes based on your net worth, so that you can take steps to minimize the tax liability upon your death.

Determining Estate Taxes

The estate's value is equal to the value of all the assets minus any existing liabilities (including a mortgage) and minus the funeral and administrative expenses. Life insurance proceeds from policies owned by the deceased are included in the estate and therefore may be subject to estate taxes.

A specified portion of an estate is exempt from estate taxes. During 2004 and 2005, the first $1 million of an estate could be distributed to children or others tax-free. The Tax Relief Act of 2001 increases the tax-exempt level to $2 million for 2006–2008, and $3.5 million in 2009.

Beyond the specific limit, federal estate taxes are imposed. The federal estate tax rates on the taxable part of the estate range from 45 to 48 percent. The Tax Relief Act of 2001 gradually reduces the maximum rate to 45 percent. In 2010, the estate tax will be repealed, but it could reappear in 2011 due to a sunset provision in the Tax Relief Act of 2001. There are several ways of reducing your exposure to high estate taxes, as explained later in the chapter.

Other Related Taxes

Several states impose inheritance taxes or state excise taxes on an estate, although these taxes are being phased out in some states. To avoid state taxes on an estate, residents of such states sometimes retire in other states that do not impose them.

Valuing Your Estate to Assess Potential Estate Taxes

Since the potential estate tax you could incur someday is dependent on the value of your estate, you should periodically calculate the value of your estate. Anyone who saves a relatively small amount of money every year can easily become a millionaire later in life due to the power of compounded interest. Therefore, many people will need estate planning to ensure that they can pass as much of their wealth as possible on to their beneficiaries. Once your net worth exceeds the tax-free limit, you should carefully plan your estate to minimize any potential tax liability.

TRUSTS, GIFTS, AND CONTRIBUTIONS

Estate planning commonly involves trusts, gifts, and contributions for the purpose of avoiding estate taxes. You may consider hiring an attorney to complete the proper documents.

Trusts

A **trust** is a legal document in which one person (called a **grantor**) transfers assets to another person (called a **trustee**), who manages the assets for designated beneficiaries.

trust
A legal document in which one person (the grantor) transfers assets to another (the trustee) who manages them for designated beneficiaries.

grantor
The person who creates a trust.

trustee
The person or institution named in a trust to manage the trust assets for the beneficiaries.

The grantor must select a trustee who is capable of managing the assets being transferred. Various types of investment firms can be hired to serve as trustees.

living trust
A trust in which you assign the management of your assets to a trustee while you are living.

Living Trusts. A **living trust** is a trust in which you assign the management of your assets to a trustee while you are living. You identify a trustee that you want to manage the assets (which includes making decisions on how to invest cash until it is needed or how to spend cash).

revocable living trust
A living trust that can be dissolved.

Revocable Living Trust. With a **revocable living trust**, you can dissolve or revoke the trust at any time because you are still the legal owner of the assets. For example, you may revoke a living trust if you decide that you want to manage the assets yourself. Alternatively, you may revoke a living trust so that you can replace the trustee. In this case, you would create a new living trust with a newly identified trustee.

By using a revocable living trust, you can avoid the probate process. You are still the legal owner of the assets, however, so you do not avoid estate taxes. The assets are still considered part of your estate.

irrevocable living trust
A living trust that cannot be changed, although it can provide income to the grantor.

Irrevocable Living Trust. An **irrevocable living trust** is a living trust that cannot be changed. This type of trust is a separate entity. It can provide income for you, but the assets in the trust are no longer legally yours. The assets are not considered part of your estate and therefore are not subject to estate taxes upon your death.

standard family trust (credit-shelter trust)
A trust established for children in a family.

testamentary trust
A trust created by a will.

Standard Family Trust. A **standard family trust** (also called a **credit-shelter trust**) is a trust established for children in a family. The standard family trust is just one of many types of **testamentary trusts**, or trusts created by wills. It is a popular type of trust because it can be used to avoid estate taxes in a manner somewhat similar to the irrevocable living trust, except that it is not structured as a living trust. Consider the following example.

EXAMPLE

Stephanie Spratt's parents earned a modest income before retiring. As a result of their diligent saving and the strong performance of their investments, they have about $2 million in assets and no will. If the estate is worth $2 million at the time it is passed on to Stephanie and her sister, a portion of the estate will be taxed. The Spratt family decides to meet with a financial planner.

With the financial planner's help, Mr. and Mrs. Spratt create a will declaring that they are each sole owners of specific assets. Mr. Spratt declares he is the owner of assets worth $1 million, and Mrs. Spratt declares she is the owner of the other assets, which are worth $1 million. Mr. Spratt specifies in the will that if he dies first, his assets are to be distributed to a standard family trust for the children.

The trust will be managed by a trustee and will provide Mrs. Spratt with income while she is alive, and ultimately it will provide income for her children. The assets in the trust will no longer be legally owned by Mrs. Spratt. These assets will ultimately be distributed to the children when they reach an age specified in the trust document. Therefore, Mrs. Spratt now legally owns $1 million in assets, rather than $2 million in assets. Upon her death, her estate will not exceed the maximum that can be passed on tax-free to her children.

The will could also state that if Mrs. Spratt dies first, her assets are to be distributed to a standard family trust. Since the Tax Relief Act of 2001 increases the estate tax exemption over time, the Spratts may not require the trust in the future.

gift
A tax-free distribution of up to $11,000 per year from one person to another.

Gifts

From an estate planning perspective, a **gift** is a tax-free distribution of funds from one person to another. The law currently allows up to $11,000 to pass by gift per year. The maximum amount of the gift allowed will increase in increments of $1,000 over time with inflation.

If your goal is to ultimately pass on your estate to your children, but you are concerned about estate taxes, you can reduce the size of your estate by giving $11,000 tax-free to each of your children each year. The recipient does not have to report the gift as income, and therefore it is not subject to taxes. If you are married, you and your spouse can each give $11,000 to each of your children and to others. Thus, a married couple with three children may give $66,000 in gifts to their children every year. Over a five-year period, the couple could give $330,000 to their three children without any tax consequences to the parents or the children. Such gifts are especially important for people whose estate value exceeds the tax-free limit. Frequent gifts may enable the parents to ensure that their estate is under the tax-free limit by the time of their death.

Contributions to Charitable Organizations

Many individuals wish to leave a portion of their estate to charitable organizations. Any money donated from an estate to charitable organizations is not subject to estate taxes. Consider an estate worth $200,000 more than the prevailing tax-free limit. If this entire estate is passed on to family members or other individuals, $200,000 of the estate will be subject to estate taxes. If $200,000 is donated to charitable organizations, however, none of the estate will be subject to estate taxes. Many individuals plan to leave donations for charitable organizations regardless of the tax implications, but it is nonetheless important to recognize the tax benefits.

OTHER ASPECTS OF ESTATE PLANNING

In addition to wills and trusts, estate planning also involves some other key decisions regarding a living will and power of attorney.

21.2 Financial Planning Online: How to Build Your Estate Plan

Go to
http://moneycentral.msn.
com/Content/
Retirementandwills/
Planyourestate/
Planyourestate.asp

This Web site provides
step-by-step instructions
for estate planning.

Living Will

living will
A legal document in which individuals specify their preferences if they become mentally or physically disabled.

A **living will** is a simple legal document in which individuals specify their preferences if they become mentally or physically disabled. For example, many individuals have a living will that expresses their desire not to be placed on life support if they become terminally ill. In this case, a living will also has financial implications because an estate could be charged with large medical bills resulting from life support. In this way, those who do not want to be kept alive by life support can ensure that their estate is used in the way that they prefer.

Power of Attorney

power of attorney
A legal document granting a person the power to make specific decisions for you in the event that you are incapable.

A **power of attorney** is a legal document granting a person the power to make specific decisions for you in the event that you are incapacitated. For example, you may name a family member or a close friend to make your investment and housing decisions if you become ill. You should name someone who you believe would act to serve your interests.

durable power of attorney for health care
A legal document granting a person the power to make specific health care decisions for you.

A **durable power of attorney for health care** is a legal document granting a person the power to make specific health care decisions for you. A durable power of attorney ensures that the person you identify has the power to make specific decisions regarding your health care in the event that you become incapacitated. While a living will states many of your preferences, a situation may arise that is not covered by your living will. A durable power of attorney for health care means that the necessary decisions will be made by someone who knows your preferences, rather than by a health care facility.

Maintaining Estate Plan Documents

Key documents such as your will, living will, and power of attorney should be kept in a safe, accessible place. You should tell the person (or people) you named as executor and granted power of attorney where you keep these documents so that they can be retrieved if and when they are needed.

21.3 Financial Planning Online: Legal Advice on Estate Planning

Go to
http://www.nolo.com

Click on
"Wills & Estate Planning"

This Web site provides a background on estate planning decisions and the terminology used in estate planning.

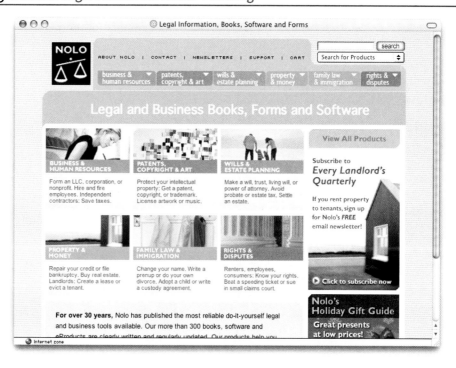

Here is a checklist of the important documents that you should keep together:

- Estate planning information, such as a will, living will, and power of attorney
- Life insurance policies and other insurance policies
- Retirement account information
- Home ownership and mortgage information
- Ownership of other real estate
- Personal property, such as cars or jewelry owned
- Mortgage information
- Personal loans
- Credit card debt information
- Ownership of businesses
- Personal legal documents
- The most recent personal tax filing
- Bank account information
- Investment information

HOW ESTATE PLANNING FITS WITHIN YOUR FINANCIAL PLAN

The following are the key decisions about estate planning that should be included within your financial plan:

- Should you create a will?
- How can you limit your estate taxes?
- Should you create a living will or designate an individual to have power of attorney?

Exhibit 21.2 provides an example of how estate planning decisions apply to Stephanie Spratt's financial plan.

Exhibit 21.2 How Estate Planning Fits within Stephanie Spratt's Financial Plan

GOALS FOR ESTATE PLANNING

1. *Create a will.*
2. *Establish a plan for trusts or gifts if my estate is subject to high taxes.*
3. *Decide whether I need to create a living will or assign power of attorney.*

ANALYSIS

Estate Planning and Related Issues

Issue	Status
Possible heirs to my estate?	*My sister and parents.*
Tax implications for my estate?	*Small estate at this point; exempt from taxes.*
Power of attorney necessary?	*Yes; I want someone to make decisions for me if I am unable.*
Living will necessary?	*Yes; I do not want to be placed on life support.*

DECISIONS

Decision Regarding a Will:

I will create a will that stipulates a contribution of $5,000 to a charity. I plan to make my parents my heirs if they are alive; otherwise, I will name my sister as the heir. I will designate my sister to be executor.

Decision Regarding Trusts and Gifts:

My estate is easily under the limit at which taxes are imposed, so it would not be subject to taxes at this point. Therefore, I do not need to consider establishing trusts or gifts at this time.

Decision on a Power of Attorney and Durable Power of Attorney:

I will assign my mother the power of attorney and the durable power of attorney. I will hire an attorney who can complete these documents along with my will in one or two hours.

DISCUSSION QUESTIONS

1. How would Stephanie's estate planning decisions be different if she were a single mother of two children?

2. How would Stephanie's estate planning decisions be affected if she were 35 years old? If she were 50 years old?

SUMMARY

A will is intended to make sure that your preferences are carried out after your death. It allows you to distribute your estate, select a guardian for your children, and select an executor to ensure that the will is executed properly.

Estate taxes are imposed on estates that exceed a tax-free limit. The limit will gradually increase over time, until it reaches $3.5 million in 2009.

Estate planning involves the use of trusts, gifts, and charitable contributions. Trusts can be structured so that a large estate can be passed on to the beneficiaries without being subjected to estate taxes. Gifts are tax-free payments that can be made on an annualized basis; they allow parents to pass on part of their wealth to their children every year. By making annual gifts, parents may reduce their wealth so that when they die, their estate will not be subject to estate taxes. An estate's contributions to charity are not subject to estate taxes.

In the event that you someday might be incapable of making decisions relating to your health and financial situation, you should consider creating a living will and power of attorney now. A living will is a legal document that allows

you to specify your health treatment preferences, such as that you do not want to be placed on life support. The power of attorney is a legal document that allows you to assign a person the power to make specific decisions for you if and when you are no longer capable of making these decisions.

INTEGRATING THE KEY CONCEPTS

Your estate planning decisions are related to other parts of your financial plan. For example, your estate planning decision to make $11,000 gifts to various family members each year reduces your liquidity. It also reduces the amount of funds available to pay off personal loans or a mortgage (Part 3) or to invest (Part 5). Yet making gifts may be more appropriate than paying off loans early or making more investments because it can help reduce the taxes on your estate. If you use the funds in some other way, the before-tax value of your estate may be larger, but your heirs will receive less due to the taxes imposed on the estate.

Your estate planning decisions may also be related to your life insurance decisions because you may not need as much life insurance if you have established a large estate.

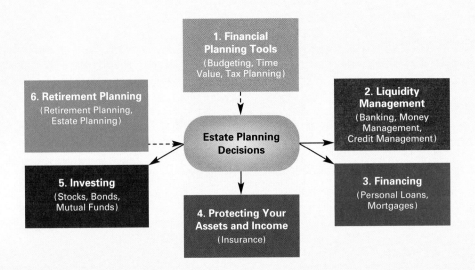

REVIEW QUESTIONS

1. What is an estate? What is estate planning? What is the main goal of estate planning?

2. What is a will? Why is a will important? What happens if a person dies without a will?

3. List the requirements for a valid will.

4. Describe two common types of wills.

5. List and briefly discuss the key components of a will.

6. When would you change your will? How can your will be changed?

7. What is probate? Describe the probate process.

8. Discuss estate taxes. When is an estate subject to and not subject to estate taxes? What is the range of federal estate tax rates? What other taxes may be levied against an estate?

9. Why is it important to calculate the value of your estate periodically?

10. Beyond the will, what does estate planning involve?

11. What is a trust? What is the difference between a living trust and a testamentary trust?

12. What is a revocable living trust? How can a revocable living trust be used to help your estate? How does a revocable living trust affect estate taxes?

13. What is an irrevocable living trust?

14. What is a standard family trust? Give an illustration.

15. How do gifts fit into estate planning?

16. How can contributions to charitable organizations help in estate planning?

17. What is a living will? What are its implications for estate planning?

18. What is a power of attorney?

19. What is a durable power of attorney for health care? Why is it needed even if you have a living will?

20. How should estate plan documents be maintained?

Ethical Dilemma

21. In the 19th century, people traveled the country selling tonics that were guaranteed to cure all the ailments of mankind. In the 21st century, the "snake oil salesmen" have been replaced with individuals making professional presentations on estate planning. At the conclusion of the presentation, they are prepared to sell you, for many hundreds of dollars, a kit that will show you how to do everything they have discussed without the expense of an attorney or tax professional.

One such group extols the virtues of a device called a charitable remainder trust (CRT). They tell you how you can establish it following their boilerplate template provided in their booklet. The CRT will allow you to make tax-deductible contributions to it during your lifetime, and upon your death, pass the CRT to a family foundation managed by your children. This will allow the assets to avoid estate taxes and probate. The presenter purports this to be a cost-effective way to pass on your assets to your children. All of what is said in the presentations concerning CRTs is true.

What the presenter does not say is that distributions from the family foundation can only be made to recognized charities. In other words, your own children will own the estate, but will not have access to it. These devices work well for a small percentage of the population, but for the majority of people they will not serve the purpose that the presenter alluded to.

a. Discuss how ethical you believe the presenter is being by not telling the full story. Keep in mind that what the presenter says is true, it is just not the whole truth.

b. If these seminars are the modern day version of the snake oil salesmen of the 19th century, who should you go to for estate planning advice?

FINANCIAL PLANNING ONLINE EXERCISE

1. Go to http://moneycentral.msn.com/retire/home.asp.

   a. Under "Retirement Tools" click "Make-a-Will Quiz." Taking this quiz will enable you to gauge your level of preparedness.

b. Go back. Under "Retirement Tools," click on "Retirement IQ Test." Take the test to determine your understanding of retirement issues.

c. Go back. Under "Retirement Tools," click on "Retirement Expense Calculator." Click on "Work" and enter data for various current and anticipated expenses you have. The calculator will provide you with the difference between expenses while working and in retirement.

d. Go back. Under "Retirement Tools," click on "Retirement Income Calculator." Choose a goal (e.g., preserving capital, spending capital, or growing capital). Click "Next." Enter the requested data in the screens provided. The "Results," "Details," and "Summary" links provide you with information on income flows and the estate that will remain for your heirs.

2. Go to http://www.nolo.com. Click on "Wills & Estate Planning" and then "Estate Taxes." Review the information provided on estate and gift taxes. What do you think the future of estate and gift taxes is? Why?

BUILDING YOUR OWN FINANCIAL PLAN

Wills, like life insurance, are something that many people mistakenly believe are necessary only if one is "wealthy." For today's college graduate, the accumulation of a $1 million estate is possible with disciplined savings. A will is necessary for anyone with positive net worth, and, as the chapter indicated, it is also necessary if you care about how and to whom your assets are distributed and to whom the guardianship of your children is assigned. Your key goals for estate planning are to create a will, establish a plan for trusts or gifts if your estate is subject to high taxes, and

decide whether you need to create a living will or assign power of attorney.

The key events that necessitate the review and/or change of your will are marriage, divorce, widowhood, parenthood, and grandparenthood. Significant changes in your assets (such as the receipt of a significant bequest from a friend or relative's will) may also necessitate a review and/or change of your will.

Go to the worksheets at the end of this chapter, and to the CD-ROM accompanying this text, to continue building your financial plan.

THE SAMPSONS—A CONTINUING CASE

Dave and Sharon want to make sure that their family is properly cared for in the event of their death. They recently purchased term life insurance and want to make sure that the funds are allocated to best serve their children in the long run. Specifically, they have set the following goals. First, they want to

make sure that a portion of the insurance proceeds is set aside for the children's education. Second, they want to make sure that the insurance proceeds are distributed evenly over several years, so that the children do not spend the money too quickly.

Go to the worksheets at the end of this chapter, and to the CD-ROM accompanying this text, to continue this case.

PART 6: BRAD BROOKS—A CONTINUING CASE

Brad tells you that he has revised his retirement plans. He would like to retire in 20 years instead of the original 30. His goal is to save $500,000 by that time. He is not taking advantage of his employer's retirement match; his employer will match retirement plan contributions up to $300 per month.

Factoring in the employer match, Brad could have a possible total annual retirement contribution of $7,200.

Brad also unveils his plans to provide for his two nephews' college education in the event of his death. He does not have a will and wonders if one is necessary.

Go to the worksheets at the end of this chapter, and to the CD-ROM accompanying this text, to complete this case.

Chapter 21: Building Your Own Financial Plan

GOALS

1. Create a will.
2. Establish a plan for trusts or gifts if your estate is subject to high taxes.
3. Decide whether to create a living will or assign power of attorney.

ANALYSIS

1. Go to http://www.msn.com and learn more about how equipped you are to create your own will by taking the "Make-a-Will Quiz." Click the "Money" tab then click "Site Map." Scroll down till you reach "Make-a-Will Quiz" under "Planning Home," "Retirement."
2. Determine the size of your estate by reviewing your personal balance sheet and filling out the table below. (If you enter this information in the Excel template, the software will create a pie chart based on your input.)

Gross Estate	Amounts
Cash	
Stocks and Bonds	
Notes and Mortgages	
Annuities	
Retirement Benefits	
Personal Residence	
Other Real Estate	
Insurance	
Automobiles	
Artwork	
Jewelry	
Other (Furniture, Collectibles, etc.)	
Gross Estate	

3. Next, consider the following estate planning issues. Indicate your action plan in the second column.

Issue	Status
Possible heirs and executor to my estate?	
Tax implications on my estate?	
Are trusts and gifts needed?	
Is power of attorney necessary?	
Is durable power of attorney necessary?	
Is a living will appropriate?	

DECISIONS

1. Will you create a will on your own or with an attorney's assistance? What special stipulations (for an heir, executor, or donations to charity) will you include?

_____

_____

_____

_____

_____

2. Do you need to establish trusts or gifts to reduce your estate's tax liability?

_____

_____

_____

_____

_____

3. Will you assign power of attorney and/or durable power of attorney?

_____

_____

_____

_____

_____

Chapter 21: The Sampsons—A Continuing Case

CASE QUESTIONS

1. Advise the Sampsons about how they can plan their estate to achieve their financial goals.

2. What important consideration are the Sampsons overlooking in their estate planning goals?

3. Dave recently met with an estate planner who offered to create an elaborate estate plan without asking Dave specific questions. What should Dave have done prior to meeting with the estate planner?

Part 6: Brad Brooks—A Continuing Case

CASE QUESTIONS

1. With regard to Brad's revised retirement plans:
   a. How much will he have in 30 years if he invests $300 per month at 8 percent? Do not consider the employer's matched contribution at this point.

Future Value of an Annuity

Payment per Year	
Number of Years	30
Annual Interest Rate	8%
Future Value	

   b. How much will he have to save per month at 8 percent to reach his $500,000 goal in 20 years? In 30 years?

Amount to be Accumulated	$500,000		Amount to be Accumulated	$500,000
Number of Years	20		Number of Years	30
Annual Interest Rate	8%		Annual Interest Rate	8%
Annual Deposit			Annual Deposit	
Monthly Deposit			Monthly Deposit	

   c. What impact could retiring 10 years earlier have on Brad's current standard of living?

   _____

   _____

   _____

   d. If Brad takes advantage of his employer's match, what will be the impact on his retirement savings (assume an 8 percent return)?

Future Value of an Annuity

Payment per Year	
Number of Years	20
Annual Interest Rate	8%
Future Value	

Future Value of an Annuity

Payment per Year	
Number of Years	20
Annual Interest Rate	8%
Future Value	

e. What other options are available to Brad to save for his retirement? Give the pros cons of each.

_____

_____

_____

_____

2. If Brad really wishes to provide for his nephews' college education, how can a will help him achieve that goal? What else might Brad consider to assure his nephews' college education?

_____

_____

_____

_____

3. How would your advice in questions 1 and 2 change if Brad were
    a. 45 years old?
    b. 60 years old?

_____

_____

_____

_____

4. Prepare a written or oral report on your findings and recommendations to Brad.

_____

_____

_____

_____

_____

_____

_____

_____

_____

_____

Synthesis of Financial Planning

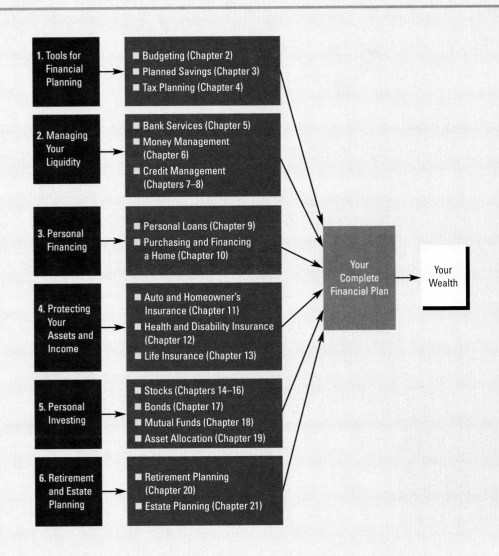

THIS PART SERVES AS A CAPSTONE BY SUMMARIZING THE KEY components of a financial plan. It also illustrates the interrelationships among the segments of a financial plan by highlighting how decisions regarding each component affect the other components.

Chapter 22

Integrating the Components of a Financial Plan

Now that you have completed your journey through the components of a financial plan, it is time for you to compile all this information and the many decisions you have made. Regarding your own personal financial situation, you have been asked to complete a number of assignments and online exercises throughout the previous chapters. Your first step is to determine the status of your personal finances. Establish your personal balance sheet, prepare the cash flow statement, establish your financial goals, and address your concerns. From there you can then analyze each part of the financial plan—your taxes, insurance, investments, retirement planning, estate planning—and establish a plan of action to help you accomplish each of your goals.

As explained throughout this text, each component of a financial plan impacts your ability to build wealth and achieve your financial goals. You have now learned many of the fundamentals relating to each component of a financial plan. This capstone chapter will help you integrate that knowledge into a cohesive financial plan.

The objectives of this chapter are to:

- Review the components of a financial plan
- Illustrate how a financial plan's components are integrated
- Provide an example of a financial plan

REVIEW OF COMPONENTS WITHIN A FINANCIAL PLAN

A key to financial planning is recognizing how the components of your financial plan are related. Each part of this text has focused on one of the six main components of your financial plan, which are illustrated once again in Exhibit 22.1. The decisions that you make regarding each component of your financial plan affect your cash flows and your wealth. The six components are summarized next, with information on how they are interrelated.

Budgeting

Recall that budgeting allows you to forecast how much money you will have at the end of each month so that you can determine how much you will be able to invest in assets. Most importantly, budgeting allows you to determine whether your cash outflows will exceed your cash inflows so that you can forecast any shortages in that month. Your spending decisions affect your budget, which affects every other component of your financial plan. Careful budgeting can prevent excessive spending and therefore help you achieve financial goals.

Budgeting Tradeoff. The more you spend, the less money you will have available for liquidity purposes, investments, or retirement saving. Thus, your budgeting decisions involve a tradeoff between spending today and allocating funds for the future. Your budget should attempt to ensure that you have net cash flows every month for savings or for retirement. The more funds you can allocate for the future, the more you will be able to benefit from compounded interest, and the more you will be able to spend in the future.

Managing Liquidity

You can prepare for anticipated cash shortages in any future month by ensuring that you have enough liquid assets to cover the deficiency. Some of the more liquid assets include a checking account, a savings account, a money market deposit account, and money market funds. The more funds you maintain in these types of assets, the more liquidity you will have to cover cash shortages. Even if you do not have sufficient liquid assets, you can cover a cash deficiency by obtaining short-term financing (such as using a credit card). If you maintain adequate liquidity, you will not need to borrow every time you need money. In this way, you can avoid major financial problems and therefore be more likely to achieve your financial goals.

Liquidity Tradeoff. Since liquid assets generate relatively low returns, you forgo earning a higher return. A checking account does not earn interest, and the other types of liquid assets have relatively low interest rates. If you choose to earn higher returns by investing all of your money in stocks or bonds, however, you may not have sufficient liquidity. Therefore, you should maintain just enough money in liquid assets to satisfy your liquidity needs; then you can earn a higher return on your other assets.

Personal Financing

Personal financing allows you to make purchases now without having the full amount of cash on hand. Thus, financing can increase the amount of your assets. Financing is especially useful for large purchases such as a car or a home.

Exhibit 22.1 Your Financial Transactions

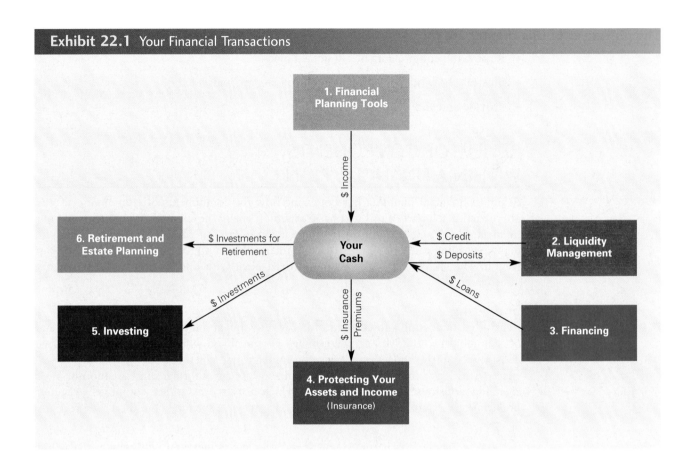

Personal Financing Tradeoff. One advantage of personal financing with a mortgage or home equity loan is that the interest payments are tax-deductible.

A disadvantage is that financing can cause budgeting problems. When you borrow to pay for a car, to purchase a home, or even to pay off a credit card balance, you affect your future budget, because the monthly loan payment means that you will have less cash available at the end of each month. Although a loan allows you to make purchases now, it restricts your spending or saving in future months while you are paying off the loan. Therefore, an excessive amount of financing can prevent you from achieving your financial goals. In addition, excessive financing may prevent you from paying off your loans on time, and therefore could damage your credit rating or cause you to file for bankruptcy.

It is easier to cover the monthly loan payment if you select financing with a relatively long maturity. But the longer the maturity, the longer the loan will be outstanding, and the more interest you will pay.

You may want to consider paying off a loan before its maturity so that you can avoid incurring any more interest expenses, especially when the interest rate charged is relatively high. You should not use all of your liquid funds to pay off a loan, however, because you will still need to maintain liquidity. Paying off loans rather than making additional investments is appropriate when the expected after-tax return on the investments you could make is lower than the interest rate you are paying on the loan.

Protecting Your Assets and Income

You can protect your assets or income by purchasing insurance. Recall from Chapters 11 and 12 that property and casualty insurance insures your assets (such as your car and home), health insurance covers health expenses, and disability insurance provides financial support if you become disabled. Life insurance (Chapter13) provides your family members or other named beneficiaries with financial support in the event of your death. Thus, insurance protects against events that could reduce your income or your wealth.

Insurance Tradeoff. Any money that is used to buy insurance cannot be used for other purposes such as investing in liquid assets, paying off loans, and making investments. Yet, your insurance needs should be given priority before investments. You need to have insurance to cover your car and your home. You may also need life insurance to provide financial support to a family member.

Managing Investments

When making investments, recall that your main choices are stocks, bonds, and mutual funds. If you want your investments to provide periodic income, you may consider investing in stocks that pay dividends. The stocks of large, well-known firms tend to pay relatively high dividends, as these firms are not growing as fast as smaller firms and can afford to pay out more of their earnings as dividends. Bonds also provide periodic income. If you do not need periodic income, you may consider investing in stocks of firms that do not pay dividends. These firms often are growing at a fast pace and therefore offer the potential for a large increase in the stock value over time.

Investment Tradeoff. By investing in the stocks of large, well-known firms, you may enhance your liquidity because you will receive dividend income and can easily sell the stocks if you need money. You can also enhance your liquidity by investing in Treasury bonds or highly rated corporate bonds because these bonds provide periodic income and can easily be sold if you need money. However, these investments typically do not generate as high a return as investments in stocks of smaller firms.

If you try to earn high returns by investing all of your money in stocks of smaller firms, you forgo some liquidity because the prices of these stocks are volatile, and you may want to avoid selling them when prices are relatively low. If you have sufficient liquid assets such as checking and savings accounts, however, you do not need additional liquidity from your investments in stocks.

Another concern about the stocks of smaller firms is that they can be very risky and are more likely to result in large losses than investments in stocks of large, well-known firms. You can invest in small stocks without being exposed to the specific risk of any individual stock by investing in a mutual fund that focuses on small stocks. When market conditions are weak, however, such funds can experience large losses, although not as much as a single stock of a small firm.

Whenever you use money for investments, you forgo the use of that money for some other purpose, such as investing in more liquid assets, paying off existing debt, investing in your retirement, or buying insurance. You should make investments only after you have sufficient liquidity and sufficient insurance to protect your existing assets. Investments are the key to building your wealth over time. By investing a portion of your income consistently over time, you are more likely to achieve your financial goals.

Retirement Planning

Retirement planning can ensure that you will have sufficient funds at the time you retire. As discussed in Chapter 20, there are a variety of plans available and many tax advantages to retirement savings.

Retirement Account Tradeoff. The more money you contribute to your retirement account now, the more money you will have when you reach retirement age. However, you should make sure you can afford whatever you decide to contribute. You need to have enough money to maintain sufficient liquidity so that you can afford any monthly loan payments before you contribute to your retirement.

When deciding whether to invest your money in current investments or in your retirement account, consider your goals. If you plan to use the investments for tuition or some other purpose in the near future, then you should not put this money in your retirement account. Funds invested in a retirement account are not liquid. Any money withdrawn early from a retirement account is subject to a penalty. One exception is the Roth IRA, which allows you to withdraw contributed dollars after five years without a penalty. If your goal is to save for retirement, you should allocate money to a retirement account. Although you will not have access to these funds, you are typically not taxed on contributions to your retirement account until the funds are withdrawn at the time of retirement. This deferral of taxes is very beneficial. In addition, some employers match part or all of your contribution to a retirement account.

Maintaining Your Financial Documents

To monitor your financial plan over time, you should store all finance-related documents in one place, such as a safe at home or a safety deposit box. The key documents are identified in Exhibit 22.2.

Exhibit 22.2 Documents Used for Financial Planning

Liquidity

- Certificates of deposit
- Bank account balances
- Any other money market securities owned

Financing

- Credit card account numbers
- Credit card balances
- Personal loan (such as car loan) agreements
- Mortgage loan agreement

Insurance

- Insurance policies
- Home inventory of items covered by homeowner's insurance

Investments

- Stock certificates
- Bonds
- Account balance showing the market value of stocks
- Account balance showing the market value of bonds
- Account balance showing the market value of mutual funds

Retirement and Estate Plans

- Retirement plan contracts
- Retirement account balances
- Will
- Trust agreements

22.1 Financial Planning Online: Insight about Financial Planning Concepts

Go to
http://www.kiplinger.com/
personalfinance

This Web site provides useful information about financial planning that can help you complete and refine your financial plan.

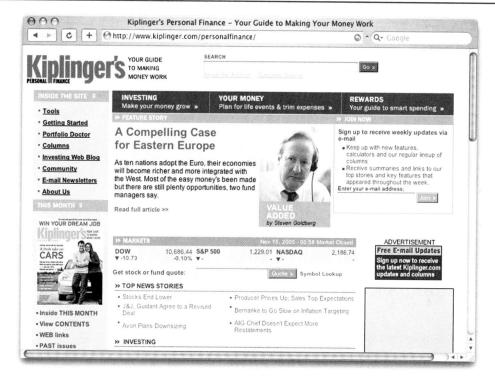

INTEGRATING THE COMPONENTS

At this point, you have sufficient background to complete all the components of your financial plan. As time passes, however, your financial position will change, and your financial goals will change as well. You will need to revise your financial plan periodically in order to meet your financial goals. The following example for Stephanie Spratt illustrates how an individual's financial position can change over time, how a financial plan may need to be revised as a result, and how the components of the financial plan are integrated.

EXAMPLE

Recall from Chapter 1 that Stephanie Spratt established the following goals:

- Purchase a new car within a year.
- Buy a home within a year.
- Make investments that will allow her wealth to grow over time.
- Build a large amount of savings by the time of her retirement in 20 to 40 years.

Stephanie purchased a new car and a new home this year. She also made some small investments. She has clearly made progress toward her goal of building a large amount of savings by the time she retires.

Recall from Chapter 2 that Stephanie originally had a relatively simple personal balance sheet. Her assets amounted to $9,000, and she had credit card debt of $2,000 as her only liability. Thus, her net worth was $7,000 at that time. Since she created the balance sheet shown in Chapter 2, her assets, liabilities, and net worth have changed substantially.

Stephanie's current personal balance sheet is compared to her personal balance sheet from Chapter 2 in Exhibit 22.3. Notice how her personal balance sheet has changed:

1. She purchased a home for $80,000 that still has a market value of $80,000.

2. She purchased a new car for $18,000 that currently has a market value of $15,000.

3. She recently used $2,000 of income to invest in two mutual funds, which are now valued at $2,100.

4. She recently started investing in her retirement account and has $800 in it.

The main changes in her liabilities are as follows:

1. Her purchase of a home required her to obtain a mortgage loan, which now has a balance of $71,000.

2. Her purchase of a car required her to obtain a car loan (she made a down payment of $1,000, has paid $2,000 of principal on the loan, and still owes $15,000).

3. She has a $1,000 credit card bill that she will pay off soon.

As Exhibit 22.3 shows, Stephanie's total assets are now $105,000. She increased her assets primarily by making financing decisions that also increased her liabilities. Exhibit 22.3 shows that her liabilities are now $87,000. Thus, her net worth is:

$$\text{Net Worth} = \text{Total Assets} - \text{Total Liabilities}$$
$$= \$105,000 - \$87,000$$
$$= \$18,000.$$

The increase in her net worth since the beginning of the year is mainly attributable to a bonus from her employer this year, which helped her cover the down payment on her house. Now that she has a car loan and a mortgage, she uses a large portion of her income to cover loan payments and will not be able to save much money.

As time passes, Stephanie hopes to invest in more stocks or other investments to increase her net worth. If the value of her home increases over time, her net worth will also grow. However, her car will likely decline in value over time, which will reduce the value of her assets and therefore reduce her net worth.

Budgeting

Stephanie's recent cash flow statement is shown in Exhibit 22.4. The major change in her cash inflows from Chapter 2 is that her disposable income is now higher as a result of a promotion and salary increase at work. The major changes in her cash outflows are as follows:

1. She no longer has a rent payment.

2. As a result of buying a new car, she now saves about $100 per month on car maintenance because the car dealer will do all maintenance at no charge for the next two years.

3. Primarily by discontinuing her health club membership and exercising at home, she has reduced her recreation expenses to about $500 per month (a reduction of $100 per month).

4. She now has a car loan payment of $412 each month.

5. She now has a mortgage loan payment of $688; with her property tax and her homeowner's insurance, her total payment for her home is $848 per month.

6. She just started paying for disability insurance ($10 per month) and life insurance ($10 per month).

7. She just started contributing $300 per month to her retirement account.

Exhibit 22.3 Update on Stephanie Spratt's Personal Balance Sheet

	Initial Personal Balance Sheet (from Chapter 2)	As of Today
Assets		
Liquid Assets		
Cash	$500	$200
Checking account	3,500	200
Money market deposit account	0	2,600
Total liquid assets	**$4,000**	**$3,000**
Household Assets		
Home	$0	$80,000
Car	1,000	15,000
Furniture	1,000	1,000
Total household assets	**$2,000**	**$96,000**
Investment Assets		
Stocks	$3,000	$3,100
Mutual funds	0	2,100
Investment in retirement account	0	800
Total investment assets	**$3,000**	**$6,000**
TOTAL ASSETS	**$9,000**	**$105,000**
Liabilities and Net Worth		
Current Liabilities		
Credit card balance	$2,000	$1,000
Total current liabilities	**$2,000**	**$1,000**
Long-Term Liabilities		
Car loan	$0	$15,000
Mortgage	0	71,000
Total long-term liabilities	**$0**	**$86,000**
TOTAL LIABILITIES	**$2,000**	**$87,000**
Net Worth	**$7,000**	**$18,000**

Budgeting Dilemma. While Stephanie's monthly cash inflows are now $500 higher than they were initially, her monthly cash outflows are $800 higher. Thus, her monthly net cash flows have declined from $400 to $100. This means that even though her salary (and therefore her cash inflows) increased, she has less money available after paying her bills and recreation expenses.

Budgeting Decision. Stephanie reviews her personal cash flow statement to determine how she is spending her money. Some of her cash flows are currently being invested in assets. Even if she does not invest any of her net cash flows now, her net worth will grow over time because she is paying down the debt on her home and on her car each month and is contributing to her retirement account.

Furthermore, she will now receive a tax refund from the IRS each year because she can itemize her mortgage expense. Overall, she decides that she is pleased with her cash flow situation. However, she decides to reassess the other components of her financial plan (as discussed below), which could affect her budget.

Long-Term Strategy for Budgeting. Some of Stephanie's budgeting is based on the bills that she incurs as a result of her car and home. Other parts of the budget are determined by the other components of her financial plan:

- The amount of cash (if any) allocated to liquid assets is dependent on her plan for managing liquidity.
- The amount of cash allocated to pay off existing loans is dependent on her plan for personal financing.
- The amount of cash allocated to insurance policies is dependent on her insurance planning.
- The amount of cash allocated to investments is dependent on her plan for investing.
- The amount of cash allocated to her retirement account is dependent on her retirement planning.

Managing Liquidity

Every two weeks, Stephanie's paycheck is direct deposited to her checking account. She writes checks to pay all her bills and to cover the other cash outflows specified in Exhibit 22.4; she also pays her credit card bill each month. She normally has about $100 at the end of the month after paying her bills and recreation expenses. Stephanie wants to ensure that she has sufficient liquidity. Her most convenient source of funds is her checking account; since her paycheck is deposited there, she knows she will have enough funds every month to pay her bills. If she had any other short-term debt, she would use her net cash flows to pay it off. She recently set up a money market deposit account (MMDA) and invested $2,600 in it. This account is her second most convenient source of funds; it allows her to write a limited number of checks in the event that unanticipated expenses occur.

Liquidity Dilemma. Stephanie must decide whether she should change her liquidity position. She considers these options.

Stephanie's Options If She Changes Her Liquidity	Advantage	Disadvantage
Reduce liquidity position by transferring money from her MMDA to a mutual fund	May earn a higher rate of return on her assets	Will have a smaller amount of liquid funds to cover unanticipated expenses
Increase liquidity position by transferring money from a mutual fund to her MMDA	May earn a lower rate of return on her assets	Will have a larger amount of liquid funds to cover unanticipated expenses

Liquidity Decision. Stephanie determines that she has access to sufficient funds to cover her liquidity needs. If she has any major unanticipated expenses beyond the funds in her MMDA, she could sell shares of the stock or the mutual funds that she owns. She decides to leave her liquidity position as is.

Exhibit 22.4 Update on Stephanie Spratt's Monthly Cash Flow Statement

	Initial Cash Flow Statement	Most Recent Cash Flow Statement	Change in the Cash Flow Statement
Cash Inflows			
Disposable (after-tax) income	$2,500	$3,000	+$500
Interest on deposits	0	0	No change
Dividend payments	0	0	No change
Total cash inflows	**$2,500**	**$3,000**	**+$500**
Cash Outflows			
Rent	$600	$0	– $600
Cable TV	50	50	No change
Electricity and water	60	80	+20
Telephone	60	60	No change
Groceries	300	300	No change
Health and disability insurance and expenses	130	140	+10
Clothing	100	100	No change
Car insurance and maintenance	200	100	–100
Recreation	600	500	–100
Car loan payment	0	412	+412
Mortgage payment (includes property taxes and insurance)	0	848	+848
Life insurance payment	0	10	+10
Contribution to retirement plan	0	300	+300
Total cash outflows			
	$2,100	$2,900	+$800
Net cash flows	**$400**	**$100**	**–$300**

Long-Term Strategy for Managing Liquidity. Stephanie's plan for managing liquidity is to continue using her checking account to cover bills and to use funds from the MMDA to cover any unanticipated expenses. She prefers not to invest any more funds in the MMDA because the interest rate is low. Thus, she will use any net cash flows she has at the end of the month for some other purpose. If she ever needs to withdraw funds from her MMDA, she will likely attempt to replenish that account once she has new net cash flows that can be invested in it.

Personal Financing

Stephanie has a car loan balance of $15,000 and a mortgage loan balance of $71,000. She has no need for any additional loans. The interest expenses on the mortgage are tax-deductible, but the interest expenses on the car loan are not. She considers paying off her car loan before it is due (about three years from now).

Financing Dilemma. Stephanie wants to pay off the car loan as soon as she has saved a sufficient amount of money. She realizes that to pay off this liability, she will need to reduce some of her assets. She outlines the following options for paying off her car loan early:

Stephanie's Options for Paying Off Her Car Loan Early	Advantage	Disadvantage
Withdraw funds from MMDA	Would be able to reduce or eliminate monthly car loan payment	Will no longer have adequate liquidity
Withdraw funds from retirement account	Would be able to reduce or eliminate monthly car loan payment	Will be charged a penalty and will no longer have funds set aside for retirement
Sell stock	Would be able to reduce or eliminate monthly car loan payment	Would forgo the potential to earn high returns on stock
Sell mutual funds	Would be able to reduce or eliminate monthly car loan payment	Would forgo the potential to earn high returns on a mutual fund

Financing Decision. Stephanie needs to maintain liquidity, so she eliminates the first option. She also eliminates the second option because she does not want to pay a penalty for early withdrawal and believes those funds should be reserved for retirement purposes.

The remaining options deserve more consideration. Stephanie's annual interest rate on the car loan is 7.60 percent. Once she has a large enough investment in stocks and mutual funds that she can pay off the car loan (perhaps a year from now), she will decide how to use that money as follows:

- If she thinks that the investments will earn an annual after-tax return of less than 7.60 percent, she will sell them and use the money to pay off the car loan. In this way, she will essentially earn a return of 7.60 percent with that money because she will be paying off debt for which she was being charged 7.60 percent.

- If she thinks that the investments will earn an annual after-tax return greater than 7.60 percent, she will keep them. She will not pay off the car loan because her investments are providing her with a higher return than the cost of the car loan.

Long-Term Strategy for Financing. Once Stephanie pays off her car loan, she will have an extra $412 per month (the amount of her car loan payment) that can be used to make more investments. She does not plan to buy another car until she can pay for it with cash. Her only other loan is her mortgage, which has a 15-year life. If she stays in the same home over the next 15 years, she will have paid off her mortgage by that time. In this case, she will have no debt after 15 years. She may consider buying a more expensive home in the near future and would likely obtain another 15-year mortgage. She does not mind having a mortgage because the interest payments are tax-deductible.

Insurance

Stephanie presently has auto, homeowner's, health, disability, and life insurance policies.

Insurance Dilemma. Stephanie recognizes that she needs insurance to cover her car, home, and health. In addition, she wants to protect her existing income in case she becomes disabled. She also wants to make sure that she can provide some financial support to her two nieces in the future.

Insurance Decision. Stephanie recently decided to purchase disability insurance to protect her income in case she becomes disabled. She also decided to purchase life insurance to fund her nieces' college education if she dies. She is pleased with her current employer-provided health insurance policy.

Long-Term Strategy for Insuance. Stephanie will maintain a high level of insurance to protect against liability resulting from owning her car or home. If she decides to have children in the future, she will purchase additional life insurance to ensure future financial support for her children. She will continue to review her policies to search for premium savings.

Managing Investments

Stephanie currently has an investment in one stock worth $3,100 and an investment in two mutual funds worth $2,100.

Investing Dilemma. If the one stock that Stephanie owns performs poorly in the future, the value of her investments (and therefore her net worth) could decline substantially. She expects the stock market to do well but is uncomfortable having an investment in a single stock.

She considers the following options:

Stephanie's Options If She Changes Her Investments	Advantage	Disadvantage
Sell stock; invest the proceeds in bonds	Lower risk	Lower expected return than from her stock
Sell stock; invest the proceeds in her MMDA	Lower risk and improved liquidity	Lower expected return than from her stock
Sell stock; invest the proceeds in a stock mutual fund	Lower risk	Lower expected return than from her stock

Investing Decision. All three possibilities offer lower risk than the stock, but given that Stephanie expects the stock market to perform well, she prefers a stock mutual fund. She is not relying on the investment to provide periodic income at this time and wants an investment that could increase in value over time. She decides to sell her 100 shares of stock at the prevailing market value of $3,100 and to invest the proceeds in her stock mutual fund to achieve greater diversification. This transaction reflects a shift of $3,100 on her personal balance sheet from stocks to mutual funds. She incurs a transaction fee of $20 for selling the shares.

Long-Term Strategy for Investing. Stephanie considers using most of her $100 in net cash flows each month to purchase additional shares of the stock mutual fund in which she recently invested. She does not specify the amount she will invest because she recognizes that in some months she may face unanticipated expenses that will need to be covered. Once her car loan is paid off, she will have an additional $412 in net cash flows per month that she can invest in the stock mutual fund or in other investments.

Protecting and Maintaining Wealth

Stephanie recently started to contribute to a retirement account. This account is beneficial because her contributions will not be taxed until the funds are withdrawn during retirement. In addition, this account should grow in value if she consistently contributes to it each month and selects investments that appreciate in value over time.

Retirement Contribution Dilemma. Recently, Stephanie started contributing $300 per month to her retirement account, which is partially matched by a contribution from her employer. She could also establish an individual retirement account (IRA), up to a limit of $4,000 per year. However, she cannot use any of the contributed funds until she retires.

She considers the following options:

Stephanie's Options Regarding Her Retirement Account	Advantage	Disadvantage
Do not contribute any funds to her retirement account	Can use all net cash flows for other purposes	Forgo tax benefits and matching contribution from employer; will have no money set aside for retirement
Continue to contribute $300 per month	Benefit from partial matching contribution, and achieve some tax benefits	Could use the $300 for other purposes
Contribute $300 per month and establish an IRA	Increased tax benefits	Could use the funds for other purposes

Retirement Contribution Decision. Stephanie wants to know how much more she will have in 40 years (when she hopes to retire) if she saves an additional $100 per month ($1,200 per year). She expects to earn an annual return of 10 percent per year if she invests in an IRA. She can use the future value annuity table in Appendix B to determine the future value of her extra contribution. The *FVIFA* for a 10 percent interest rate and a period of 40 years is 442.59. In 40 years, her extra contribution of $1,200 per year would accumulate to be worth:

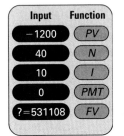

Input	Function
−1200	PV
40	N
10	I
0	PMT
?=531108	FV

$$\text{Extra Savings at Retirement} = \text{Extra Amount Invested} \times FVIFA_{i,n}$$
$$= \$1,200 \times 442.59$$
$$= \$531,108.$$

She decides to save the additional $100 per month since it will result in $531,108 more at retirement. She also realizes that contributing the extra amount will provide present-day tax benefits. Contributing the extra $100 will reduce her net cash flows, however, so she may have more difficulty meeting her liquidity needs, will be less likely to pay off her existing car loan quickly, and will have less money to spend on recreation. Yet, by accepting these disadvantages in the short run, she can receive major tax benefits and ensure a high level of wealth when she retires. Stephanie's view is that any dollar invested in a retirement account is more valuable than a dollar invested in a nonretirement account because of the tax advantages.

Long-Term Strategy for Retirement Contributions. Stephanie plans to invest the maximum allowed in her retirement account so that she can take full advantage of the tax benefits. The maximum annual limit on her retirement contribution is dependent on her income. As her income increases over time, she will be able to increase her monthly contribution up to the maximum limit. She would also like to contribute the maximum amount ($3,000 per year) to her IRA, but cannot afford to contribute that amount.

FINANCIAL PLAN

Stephanie Spratt's financial plan is illustrated in Exhibit 22.5. It incorporates her most recent decisions (discussed earlier in this chapter). Her budget plan determines how she will use her cash inflows. Notice how she adjusts her budget plan in response to decisions regarding other components of her financial plan.

A review of Stephanie's financial plan shows that she is building her wealth over time in four ways:

1. She is increasing her equity investment in her car as she makes monthly payments on her car loan.

2. She is increasing her equity investment in her home as she makes monthly payments on her mortgage loan.

3. She is increasing her investment in a mutual fund as she uses the net cash flows each month to buy more shares.

4. She is increasing her retirement account assets as she makes monthly contributions.

If Stephanie follows the financial plan she has created, she will pay off her car loan within a year or two. She will also pay off her mortgage loan in 15 years and then will not have any remaining debt. In addition, she will continue to use her net cash flows to make investments in either stock or bond mutual funds. Her retirement account contributions ensure that she will have substantial wealth by the time she retires.

Stephanie's wealth may also increase for other reasons. The value of her home, mutual fund, and any investments she makes for her retirement account may increase over time. Overall, Stephanie's financial plan should provide her with sufficient wealth so that she can afford a very comfortable lifestyle in the future.

22.2 Financial Planning Online: A Synthesized Financial Plan

Go to
http://quicken.com/
banking_and_credit/
savings _calc/

This Web site provides a synthesized financial planning assessment for you, including tax planning, money management, insuring your assets, and investing.

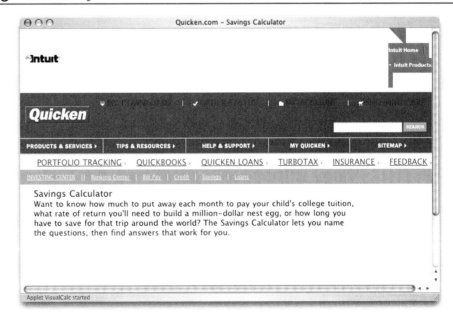

Exhibit 22.5 Stephanie Spratt's Financial Plan

BUDGET PLAN

My monthly salary of $3,000 after taxes is direct deposited to my checking account. I will use this account to cover all bills and other expenses. My total expenses (including recreation) should be about $2,900 per month. This leaves me with net cash flows of $100. I will also receive an annual tax refund of about $3,000. The taxes I pay during the year will exceed my tax liability, as the interest payments on my mortgage will reduce my taxable income.

I will use the net cash flows each month to cover any unanticipated expenses that occurred during the month. My second priority is to use the net cash flows to keep about $2,600 in my money market deposit account (MMDA) to ensure liquidity. If this account is already at that level, I will use the net cash flows to invest in an individual retirement account (IRA).

PLAN FOR MANAGING LIQUIDITY

Since my salary is direct deposited to my checking account, I have a convenient means of covering my expenses. My backup source of liquidity is my MMDA, which currently contains $2,600; I will maintain the account balance at about that level to ensure liquidity. If I ever need more money than is in this account, I could rely on my net cash flows. In addition, I could sell some shares of my mutual fund, or I could cover some expenses with a credit card; since I would have an extra month before the credit card bill arrives.

PLAN FOR FINANCING

I have two finance payments: a monthly car loan payment of $412, and a monthly mortgage payment of $848 (including property taxes and homeowner's insurance). I would like to pay off the car loan early if possible. The interest rate on that loan is 7.60 percent, and the interest is not tax-deductible. The principal remaining on the car loan will decrease over time as I pay down the debt with my monthly payments.

I may consider selling my shares of the mutual fund and using the proceeds to pay off part of the car loan. My decision will depend on whether I believe the mutual fund can provide a higher return to me than the cost of the car loan.

When I pay off the car loan, my cash outflows will be reduced by $412 per month. Thus, I should have more net cash flows that I can use to make investments or spend in other ways.

INSURANCE PLAN

I have car insurance that covers the car and limits my liability. I have homeowner's insurance that covers the full market value of my home. I have health insurance through my employer. I have disability insurance that will provide financial support if I become disabled. I have life insurance, with my two nieces named as the beneficiaries. If I decide to have children in the future, I will purchase additional life insurance in which they would be named as the beneficiaries.

INVESTMENT PLAN

I currently have $6,000 in investments. This amount should increase over time as I use my net cash flows of about $100 each month to invest in an IRA or buy more shares of the mutual fund. I may sell my shares of the mutual fund someday to pay off part of my car loan. Once I pay off the car loan, I will have an additional $412 per month that I can use to make investments. My net cash flows should also increase over time as my salary increases, and most of the net cash flows will be directed toward investments over time.

When I make additional investments, I will consider those that have tax advantages. Since I am not relying on investments to provide me with income at this point, I will only consider investing in mutual funds that do not pay out high dividend and capital gain distributions. A stock index mutual fund that focuses on small stocks may be ideal for me because these types of stocks typically do not pay dividends. In addition, an index fund does not trade stocks frequently and therefore does not generate large capital gain distributions. This type of mutual fund provides most of its potential return in the form of an increase in the fund's value over time. I would not pay taxes on this type of capital gain until I sell the mutual fund.

I will focus on mutual funds rather than stocks to achieve diversification. If I invest in any individual stocks in the future, I will only consider stocks that pay no dividends and have more potential to increase in value.

If I consider investing in bonds in the future, I may invest in a Treasury bond fund or a municipal bond fund. Before selecting a bond fund, I will determine whether municipal bonds would offer me a higher after-tax yield (because of their tax advantage) than other types of bonds.

RETIREMENT PLAN

I just recently began to contribute $300 per month to my retirement account; my employer will provide a partial match of $1,400 per year so that the total contribution will be $5,000 per year. If I work over the next 40 years and earn 5 percent a year on this investment, the future value of my contributions will be:

$$\text{Savings at Retirement} = \text{Amount Invested} \times \text{FVIFA}_{i, n}$$
$$= \$5,000 \times 120.797$$
$$= \$724,782.$$

If I have children, I may not work full-time for the entire 40 years, so I may not be able to invest $5,000 per year for 40 years. In addition, the return on the retirement fund may be less than 5 percent a year. Therefore, I may be overestimating my future savings. Consequently, I should maximize my contributions now while I am working full-time.

SUMMARY

A financial plan consists of a budget (Part 1), a plan for managing liquidity (Part 2), a financing plan (Part 3), an insurance plan (Part 4), an investment plan (Part 5), and a plan for retirement and estate planning (Part 6). The budget determines how you will spend or invest your money. Your plan for managing liquidity will ensure that you can cover any unanticipated expenses. Your financing plan is used to finance large purchases. Financing also involves decisions that affect the interest rate you are charged and the duration of any loans. Your plan for protecting your assets and income involves decisions as to what types of insurance to purchase, how much insurance to buy, how much to periodically invest in your retirement account, and how to distribute your estate to your heirs. Your investment plan determines how much you allocate toward investments and how you allocate money across different types of investments.

The components of a financial plan are integrated in that they depend on each other. The budget plan is dependent on the other components of the financial plan. The amount of money available for any part of the plan is dependent on how much money is used for liquidity purposes, to make loan (financing) payments, to make investments, to buy insurance, or to contribute to retirement accounts. The more money you allocate toward any part of the financial plan, the less money you have for the other parts. Thus, a key aspect of financial planning is to decide which components of the financial plan deserve the highest priority, because the decisions made about those components will influence the decisions for the others.

The example featuring Stephanie Spratt's financial plan shows how the plan can be segmented into the six components. The example also illustrates how the components are integrated so that a decision about any one component can only be made after considering the others. As time passes and financial conditions change, you should continuously reevaluate your financial plan.

INTEGRATING THE KEY CONCEPTS

As this chapter showed, all parts of the financial plan are related. The financial planning tools (Part 1) allow you to budget, apply time value calculations (measure how money grows over time), and assess the tax effects of various planning decisions. Your money and credit management (Part 2) allows you to establish liquidity as a cushion in case your cash outflows exceed your cash inflows in a particular month. This cushion should always be maintained before you consider any other financial planning decisions. Your financing decisions (Part 3) determine how much you will borrow and dictate what you can afford to purchase.

Your insurance decisions (Part 4) determine how much money is needed to protect your assets or income. Therefore, they affect the amount of funds you have to pay off loans (Part 3) or to make investments (Part 5). Your investment decisions (Part 5) are related to the financing decisions in Part 3, as you should first consider whether the money to be invested could be put to better use by paying off any personal loans. Your investment decisions in Part 5 should take into account whether the money you have to invest should be used for your retirement account (Part 6).

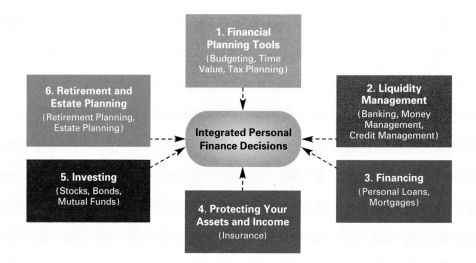

REVIEW QUESTIONS

1. Why is it important to integrate the components of your financial plan?

2. How does budgeting fit into your financial plan? How is your financial plan affected by your spending? What is the budgeting tradeoff?

3. Discuss how managing liquidity fits into your financial plan. What is the liquidity tradeoff?

4. Describe some advantages and disadvantages of using personal financing to achieve your financial goals. What is the personal financing tradeoff?

5. How does managing your investments fit into your financial plan? What is the investment tradeoff?

6. Discuss some methods for maintaining and protecting your wealth. What is the insurance tradeoff? What is the retirement account tradeoff?

7. How does time affect your financial plan?

8. What do you think happens to your budget when your financial position changes?

9. You have a $7,000 balance on your car loan at 11 percent interest. Your favorite aunt has just left you $10,000 in her will. You can put the money in a money market account at your bank and pay off your car loan, or you can invest the money in mutual

funds. What factors must you consider in making your decision?

10. In the previous question, you decide to pay off the car loan and invest the difference. Now you no longer have a $350 per month car payment. Suggest some ways you might use these additional funds.

11. You have some extra cash in your budget that you wish to invest. You have narrowed your choices to a single stock, Treasury bonds, or stock mutual funds. What characteristics of each investment alternative should you consider in making your decision?

12. How does purchasing car insurance and homeowner's insurance help protect and maintain your wealth?

13. How does purchasing sufficient health insurance and disability insurance help protect and maintain your wealth?

14. How does life insurance protect your wealth? Who needs life insurance?

FINANCIAL PLANNING PROBLEMS

1. Judy has just received $12,500 as an inheritance from her uncle and is considering ways to use the money. Judy's car is one year old, and her monthly

payment is $304. She owes 48 more payments. The amount to pay off the loan is $12,460. How much will Judy save in interest if she pays off her car loan now?

2. Judy (from problem 1) is also considering investing the $12,500 in a certificate of deposit (CD). She is guaranteed a return of 4 percent on a four-year CD. How much would Judy earn from the CD? Which of the two alternatives offers the better return?

3. Judy (from problem 1) pays off her car loan and now must decide how she wants to invest the extra $3,648 per year that she budgeted for car payments. She decides to invest this additional amount in her employer-sponsored retirement plan. Currently, the plan is averaging a 12 percent annual return. Judy has 15 years until retirement. How much more money will she have at retirement if she invests this additional amount?

4. Judy (from problem 1) believes that another benefit of investing the extra $3,648 in her employer-sponsored retirement plan is the tax savings. Judy is in a 25 percent marginal tax bracket. How much will investing in this manner save her in taxes annually? Assuming she remains in a 25 percent marginal tax bracket until she retires, how much will it save her in total over the next 15 years, ignoring the time value of the tax savings?

FINANCIAL PLANNING ONLINE EXERCISE

1. Go to http://missourifamilies.org/mofamquiz/ checkup.htm and take the Family Financial Health Check Up. Based on your results, establish two goals to improve your financial health.

BUILDING YOUR OWN FINANCIAL PLAN

Congratulations. By completing the preceding 21 *Building Your Own Financial Plan* exercises, you have created a comprehensive financial plan. At this point, using the Excel-based software that accompanies your book, you should print out your completed plan and store it in a safe place.

As with any plan, periodic review and modification of your financial plan are essential. Many of the exercises have included prompts for when decisions should be reviewed or modified. The worksheets provided with this chapter and on the CD-ROM will assist you in establishing your own timing for this review, tracking your progress toward meeting your goals, and keeping track of the location of important documents. Setting a specific time to do this review is

helpful in preventing procrastination. For example, while watching bowl games on New Year's Day, review your portfolio using your laptop. Establish a time that is practical and comfortable for you. The important thing is that you do the review on schedule and then follow up by making any necessary changes indicated by your review. Use the Excel spreadsheets that accompany this text to change your financial plan as needed.

Remember that good financial planning is the result of informed decisions rather than luck.

Go to the worksheets at the end of this chapter, and to the CD-ROM accompanying this text, to complete building your financial plan.

THE SAMPSONS—A CONTINUING CASE

With your help, Dave and Sharon Sampson have now established a financial plan. Among their key financial planning decisions are the following:

- **Budgeting.** They decided to revise their budget to make it possible to start saving. By reducing their spending on recreation, they freed up funds to be saved for a down payment on Sharon's new car and the children's college education.

- **Liquidity.** They paid off the credit card balance to avoid the high interest charges they were accumulating by carrying their balance from month to month.

- **Financing.** They obtained a four-year car loan to finance Sharon's new car. In addition, they considered refinancing their mortgage, but it was not feasible to do so. They may refinance the mortgage if they decide to live in their home for a long time or if interest rates decline further.

- **Protecting Their Wealth.** They decided to in crease their car insurance, reduce the deductible on their homeowner's insurance, and buy disability insurance. They also purchased a life insurance policy for Dave. They decided that Dave should invest at least $3,000 per year in his retirement account since his employer matches the contribution up to that amount. They made a will that designates a trustee who can allocate the estate to ensure that the children's college education is covered and that the children receive the benefits in small amounts (so they do not spend their inheritance too quickly).

- **Investments.** They decided not to buy individual stocks for now, because of the risk involved. They decided that they will invest their savings for their children's education in mutual funds. They will not invest all the money in one mutual fund or one type of fund, but will diversify among several types of mutual funds.

Now that Dave and Sharon have completed their financial plan, they are relieved that they have a plan to deal with their budget, liquidity, financing, investing, insurance, and retirement.

Go to the worksheets at the end of this chapter, and to the CD-ROM accompanying this text, to complete this case.

Chapter 22: Building Your Own Financial Plan

GOALS

1. Review your completed financial plan.
2. Record the location of your important documents.

ANALYSIS

1. Congratulations! You have completed your financial plan. Remember that financial planning is an ongoing task. Use the following table as a reminder to review key parts of your financial plan.

Item	When Reviewed	Date of Review
Short-Term Goals	As needed	
Intermediate-Term Goals	Annually	
Long-Term Goals	Annually	
Personal Cash Flow Statement	Annually	
Personal Balance Sheet	Annually	
Tax Situation	Annually, before year end	
Selection of Financial Institution	Biannually	
Credit Report	Annually	
Loans	As needed	
Risk Tolerance	Every 2–3 years	
Portfolio and Asset Allocation (Including Stocks, Bonds, and Money Market Instruments)	Annually	
Property and Casualty Insurance Needs	Annually	
Insurance Needs (Life, Health, Auto)	As dictated by critical events	
Retirement Plan	Annually	
Will and Estate Planning	As dictated by critical events	

2. Now that your plan is complete, store it for safekeeping. Along with your financial plan, keep a record of the location of your key assets and financial documents. Use the following worksheet as a guide.

Location of Important Documents

Estate Related	Location
Wills/Trusts	
Letter of Last Instruction	
Other	
Other	

Insurance	
Life	
Health	
Disability	
Auto	
Other	
Other	

Certificates and Deeds	
Automobile Titles	
Real Estate Deeds	
Birth Certificates	
Marriage Certificate	
Passports	
Other	
Other	

Investments and Savings	
Certificates of Deposit	
Stock Certificates	
Passbooks	
Mutual Fund Records	
Other	
Other	

Tax Records	**Location**
Last Year's Tax Return	
Last Seven Years of Tax Records	
Other	
Other	

Loans and Credit Cards	
Loan Notes (Still Outstanding)	
List of Credit Card Numbers	
Other	
Other	

3. Students who have completed the software worksheets throughout the semester can print out the final versions of the critical financial planning documents for safekeeping.

- Click on the tab "Your Documents" for the goals you've established in Chapter 1 and your final version of this document, as well as your personal cash flow statement and personal balance sheet from Chapter 2 and the final version of these documents. Access your asset allocation chart. Evaluate these documents to see how your financial plans have evolved throughout the course.

- Click on the tab "Your Decisions" for a summary of the decisions you have made in each chapter.

  Store printouts of the above documents, along with your home inventory, schedule for reviewing your financial plan, and location of important documents in a safe place.

Chapter 22: The Sampsons—A Continuing Case

CASE QUESTIONS

1. Explain how the Sampsons' budgeting affects all of their other financial planning decisions.

2. How are the Sampsons' liquidity and investment decisions related?

3. In what ways are the Sampsons' financing and investing decisions related? What should they do in the future before asking advice from investment advisers?

4. Explain how the Sampsons' retirement planning decisions are related to their investing decisions.

5. How likely is it that the Sampsons will achieve their financial goals now that they have captured them in a financial plan? What activity must they periodically undertake?

Your Career

DETERMINING YOUR CAREER PATH

What career path is optimal for you? Review the factors described here that you should consider when deciding your career path. Then, access the sources of information that are identified below to help make your selection.

Factors That May Affect Your Career Path

Perhaps the obvious first step in determining your career path is to consider your interests, and then identify the careers that fit your interests. Most people identify several possible career interests, which makes the decision difficult. However, you may be able to screen your list based on the following factors.

Educational and Skill Requirements. Some jobs may seem interesting, but require more education and training than you are prepared to acquire. For example, the training required to be a doctor may be too extensive and time-consuming. In addition, the entrance requirements are very high. Review the education and skills that are needed for each career that appeals to you. From your list of possible career paths, focus on those in which you already have or would be willing to achieve the necessary background, education, and skills.

Job Availability. There are some career paths that people think they would like to follow and could do so successfully, but the paths have a limited supply of open positions relative to applicants. For example, many people want to be actors or actresses, or waiters at very expensive restaurants. Consider the number of job positions available compared to the number of applicants pursuing those jobs.

Compensation. Most people consider compensation to be an important criterion when considering job positions. There are some career tracks that may be enjoyable but do not provide sufficient compensation. Information on compensation for various types of jobs is available on many Web sites. For example, at http://www.careerjournal.com you can insert the type of job position that you are curious about and obtain salary ranges for that position in a particular location in the United States.

Sources of Information That Can Help
You Select Your Career Path

Consider the following sources of information as you attempt to establish your list of career options from which to select your optimal career path.

Books on Careers. There are many books that identify careers and describe the necessary skills for each one. Some books provide a broad overview, while others are more detailed. A broad overview is usually ideal when you are first identifying the various types of careers that exist. Then once you narrow down the list, you can find a book that focuses on your chosen field, such as medicine, engineering, social work, and so on.

Courses. Your college courses are a vital source of information about related careers. Courses in accounting can help you understand the nature of the work accountants do, nursing classes provide insight into the job descriptions of nurses, and courses in sociology may help you understand the job of social workers. Even courses that are broader in scope, for example, courses in management, may be applicable to many different types of jobs, including those of accountants, nurses, and social workers. If you enjoyed your basic management course, you may like a job in which you are involved in managing people, production processes, or services.

Job Experience. Internships allow some exposure to a particular type of job and allow you to learn what tasks people in a field do as part of their daily work. Such experience is especially useful because many jobs are likely to differ from your perception.

Contacts. For any specific job description in which you are interested, identify people who you know in that field. Set up an informational interview so that you can ask detailed questions about the job.

The Internet. Much information on careers is available on the Internet. To explore the types of careers that are available, and the skills needed for each, go to http://www.careers.org to learn about jobs in numerous fields, including finance, law, management, construction, health, agriculture, and broadcasting. Some Web sites such as http://www.careerbuilder.com list the most popular job categories so that you can determine the types of job positions that are frequently available. Be careful, however, to note the size of the pool of applicants for any type of job you are interested in. It is much easier to land the job you want (assuming you have the requisite skills) when the number of openings is large compared to the number of qualified people interested in that position.

At some point, you have to narrow your choices, so that you can spend more time focused on the careers that intrigue you the most. The Internet is very valuable in offering insight even after you narrow your choices. For example, http://www.monster.com offers targeted advice for many different fields.

Personality Tests. You can get feedback on the type of career that fits you based on a personality test. Some of these tests are expensive, and there are mixed views about whether they can more accurately pinpoint a job that fits your personality than if you simply use the criteria described above. Some tests are offered for free online, such as the personality test at http://www.findtherightcareer.com. Be aware that the free tests normally do not offer as detailed an analysis as the tests that you pay for.

GETTING THE SKILLS YOU NEED

Once you decide on the type of position you want, your next step is to determine the training and education you will need to qualify for it.

Training

To gather general information, go to Web sites such as America's Career InfoNet (http://www.acinet.org/acinet) and the Bureau of Labor Statistic's site (http://www.bls.gov/k12). There you will discover what training is needed for a specific job description and how to obtain it.

Be careful when reviewing the information about various training courses that are available. Much information found on Web sites specifically devoted to training is provided by companies that want to sell you training. For this reason, carefully evaluate whether the training offered will get you the job that you want. As an extreme example, some companies provide training for modeling or acting. People are well aware of celebrities who became very rich by modeling or acting. However, taking a few courses is unlikely to lead to major success in those fields. Try to determine whether the market truly rewards people who pay for training by a particular company before you pay for it.

The training by some companies may be certified, which could distinguish it from others. However, a certificate does not always mean that the training is valuable or will lead to employment. In some cases, there may simply be fewer jobs than the number of people who are properly trained. In other cases, the training will not qualify you for a specific job position.

Education

Colleges and universities provide training in the form of education. Web sites such as http://www.CollegeBoard.com profile careers by college major, to help you consider your career path and the education it requires. A degree in a career-oriented major, such as accounting or business, will prepare you for a job in that specific field. A liberal arts degree, on the other hand, will allow you to choose from a broad range of careers in areas such as marketing, journalism, teaching, and publishing.

The reputations of universities vary substantially, and some universities may be much more credible than others in preparing you for a specific job position. Some jobs require that your degree be acquired from an accredited university. Therefore, it may be important to learn about whether the university you plan to attend is accredited. Because there are different accreditation agencies, it is important to determine the type of accreditation that would be important for the specific type of job that you plan to pursue.

Learn as much as you can about the college or department of the university in which you are considering taking courses. What percentage of the recent graduates pass a standardized exam that must be taken after graduation (for fields like accounting and law)? Are recent graduates being hired in the field that you wish to enter when you graduate? You may be able to get answers to these questions from the department where you would be taking courses.

Expanding Your Education

A master's degree or a Ph.D. provides you with additional knowledge and skills that may allow you to qualify for better jobs. However, there are costs associated with pursuing such degrees, and you must weigh them against the potential benefits.

Costs.   The cost of a graduate degree is substantial, and should be estimated carefully before you make your decision to pursue. Because the cost varies substantially among programs, you may find a program that is less expensive than others and yet satisfies your needs. Consider tuition and fees, room and board, and the opportunity cost of pursuing the degree. If you enroll in a full-time program, your opportunity cost is the salary that you could have earned if you worked during that time. You may also find it necessary to give up some social activities as well.

Benefits.   Individuals often pursue a master's degree or doctorate to increase their marketability. There are many job positions that require a degree beyond a bachelor of arts or a bachelor of science. If your goal is to increase your marketability, determine whether an additional degree truly results in better job opportunities. In addition, determine what type of degree would make the biggest difference. For example, engineers commonly obtain a master's in business administration (MBA) rather than a master's in engineering because the MBA is intended to give them stronger management skills. In this way, the degree certifies skills in managing other people.

If you decide to pursue a master's or doctorate, determine if the university you select would make a big difference in your marketability. Some programs have a national or international reputation, while others are known only within a local area.

CHANGING YOUR CAREER

Many people do not realize the career that would make them happy until they have pursued the wrong career. In some cases, they can use their existing experience in a new career, while in other cases, they must be retrained. The obvious barrier to switching careers is the amount of time that is already invested in a particular career. In addition, if training is necessary, the costs of changing careers may be high. Nevertheless, people should seriously consider switching if they truly believe a different career would be more satisfying, but first they should obtain detailed information about the new job description.

Be realistic in assessing any career switch; look closely at your expectations. Would you really be more satisfied? How much training is involved? Would you have to stop working while you are retrained? How long will it take you to get a job once you are retrained? Is the compensation higher or lower in the new career versus your existing career? Are there more chances for advancement? Is there more job security?

Self-Employment

At some point in your life, you might decide that you want to leave your current job in order to be self-employed. There are millions of people who started their own businesses and are much more satisfied than when they were employed by a firm or government agency. Self-employment, however, is not for everyone; some people are excellent workers but are not effective at creating business ideas or running a business.

First, to start your own business, you need a business plan that will be successful. Normally, this requires the creation of a product or service that is more desirable to customers than other products or services that are already offered in the market. Your advantage may be creating a product that you can offer at a lower price than similar products in the market. Alternatively, your advantage may be higher quality. Keep in mind that competitors may be quick to adjust once you start your business and it may be more difficult than you anticipated to gain market share. A business is accountable to its customers, and if it does not satisfy customers, it will not survive.

CRITERIA USED TO ASSESS APPLICANTS

When you pursue a job, you will likely be competing against many other applicants. By recognizing what the employer is seeking, you may be able to distinguish yourself from the other applicants. Understanding the criteria that employers use to assess applicants will help you determine whether you possess the right qualifications for the job.

Your Application

An application may request general information about your education background, such as the schools you attended, and your major and/or minor in college. It may also request information about your previous work experience. Applications are used to determine whether applicants have the knowledge and the experience to perform well in the job position.

Your Resume

Your resume should provide your educational background and work experience. Companies receive numerous resumes for job positions, so it helps to describe succinctly the skills that may help you stand out from other applicants. If you obtain the skills and training that you need to pursue the job that you desire, creating a resume is relatively easy. Most career Web sites offer tips on how you can improve your resume (for example, http://resume.monster.com). You can also post your resume on many Web sites such as http://www.monster.com and http://www.careers.com.

Your Interview

The interview process helps an employer obtain additional information such as how you interact with people and respond to specific situations. Various personality traits can be assessed, such as:

- your punctuality

- your ability to work with others

- your ability to communicate

- your ability to grasp concepts

- your listening skills

- your ability to recognize your limitations

- your ability to take orders

- your ability to give orders

- your potential as a leader

There are numerous books and Web sites that offer advice about various aspects of the interview, such as grooming, body language, etiquette, and even answering tough questions about deficiencies in your resume. Another source of up-to-date information on interviewing is the career center at your college or university, which often offer seminars on effective interview techniques.

CONCLUSION

You have control over your career path. If you follow guidelines such as those described above, you can increase your chances of achieving the job and career path that you want. However, keep in mind that your career aspirations and opportunities change over time. Therefore, your career planning does not end with your first job, but continues throughout your career path, and even plays a role in your decision to retire someday.

Appendix B

Financial Tables

Table B-1   Future Value Interest Factors for $1 Compounded at i Percent for n Periods:
$$FV = PV \times FVIF_{i,n}$$

Table B-2   Present Value Interest Factors for $1 Discounted at i Percent for n Periods:
$$PV = FV \times PVIF_{i,n}$$

Table B-3   Future Value Interest Factors for a $1 Annuity Compounded at i Percent for n Periods:
$$FVA = PMT \times FVIFA_{i,n}$$

Table B-4   Present Value Interest Factors for a $1 Annuity Discounted at i Percent for n Periods:
$$PVA = PMT \times PVIFA_{i,n}$$

Table B-1 Future Value Interest Factors for $1 Compounded at i Percent for n Periods: $FV = PV \times FVIF_{i,n}$

Period	1%	2%	3%	4%	5%	6%	7%	8%	9%	10%	11%	12%	13%	14%	15%	16%	17%	18%	19%	20%
1	1.010	1.020	1.030	1.040	1.050	1.060	1.070	1.080	1.090	1.100	1.110	1.120	1.130	1.140	1.150	1.160	1.170	1.180	1.190	1.200
2	1.020	1.040	1.061	1.082	1.102	1.124	1.145	1.166	1.188	1.210	1.232	1.254	1.277	1.300	1.322	1.346	1.369	1.392	1.416	1.440
3	1.030	1.061	1.093	1.125	1.158	1.191	1.225	1.260	1.295	1.331	1.368	1.405	1.443	1.482	1.521	1.561	1.602	1.643	1.685	1.728
4	1.041	1.082	1.126	1.170	1.216	1.262	1.311	1.360	1.412	1.464	1.518	1.574	1.630	1.689	1.749	1.811	1.874	1.939	2.005	2.074
5	1.051	1.104	1.159	1.217	1.276	1.338	1.403	1.469	1.539	1.611	1.685	1.762	1.842	1.925	2.011	2.100	2.192	2.288	2.386	2.488
6	1.062	1.126	1.194	1.265	1.340	1.419	1.501	1.587	1.677	1.772	1.870	1.974	2.082	2.195	2.313	2.436	2.565	2.700	2.840	2.986
7	1.072	1.149	1.230	1.316	1.407	1.504	1.606	1.714	1.828	1.949	2.076	2.211	2.353	2.502	2.660	2.826	3.001	3.185	3.379	3.583
8	1.083	1.172	1.267	1.369	1.477	1.594	1.718	1.851	1.993	2.144	2.305	2.476	2.658	2.853	3.059	3.278	3.511	3.759	4.021	4.300
9	1.094	1.195	1.305	1.423	1.551	1.689	1.838	1.999	2.172	2.358	2.558	2.773	3.004	3.252	3.518	3.803	4.108	4.435	4.785	5.160
10	1.105	1.219	1.344	1.480	1.629	1.791	1.967	2.159	2.367	2.594	2.839	3.106	3.395	3.707	4.046	4.411	4.807	5.234	5.695	6.192
11	1.116	1.243	1.384	1.539	1.710	1.898	2.105	2.332	2.580	2.853	3.152	3.479	3.836	4.226	4.652	5.117	5.624	6.176	6.777	7.430
12	1.127	1.268	1.426	1.601	1.796	2.012	2.252	2.518	2.813	3.138	3.498	3.896	4.334	4.818	5.350	5.936	6.580	7.288	8.064	8.916
13	1.138	1.294	1.469	1.665	1.886	2.133	2.410	2.720	3.066	3.452	3.883	4.363	4.898	5.492	6.153	6.886	7.699	8.599	9.596	10.699
14	1.149	1.319	1.513	1.732	1.980	2.261	2.579	2.937	3.342	3.797	4.310	4.887	5.535	6.261	7.076	7.987	9.007	10.147	11.420	12.839
15	1.161	1.346	1.558	1.801	2.079	2.397	2.759	3.172	3.642	4.177	4.785	5.474	6.254	7.138	8.137	9.265	10.539	11.974	13.589	15.407
16	1.173	1.373	1.605	1.873	2.183	2.540	2.952	3.426	3.970	4.595	5.311	6.130	7.067	8.137	9.358	10.748	12.330	14.129	16.171	18.488
17	1.184	1.400	1.653	1.948	2.292	2.693	3.159	3.700	4.328	5.054	5.895	6.866	7.986	9.276	10.761	12.468	14.426	16.672	19.244	22.186
18	1.196	1.428	1.702	2.026	2.407	2.854	3.380	3.996	4.717	5.560	6.543	7.690	9.024	10.575	12.375	14.462	16.879	19.673	22.900	26.623
19	1.208	1.457	1.754	2.107	2.527	3.026	3.616	4.316	5.142	6.116	7.263	8.613	10.197	12.055	14.232	16.776	19.748	23.214	27.251	31.948
20	1.220	1.486	1.806	2.191	2.653	3.207	3.870	4.661	5.604	6.727	8.062	9.646	11.523	13.743	16.366	19.461	23.105	27.393	32.429	38.337
21	1.232	1.516	1.860	2.279	2.786	3.399	4.140	5.034	6.109	7.400	8.949	10.804	13.021	15.667	18.821	22.574	27.033	32.323	38.591	46.005
22	1.245	1.546	1.916	2.370	2.925	3.603	4.430	5.436	6.658	8.140	9.933	12.100	14.713	17.861	21.644	26.186	31.629	38.141	45.923	55.205
23	1.257	1.577	1.974	2.465	3.071	3.820	4.740	5.871	7.258	8.954	11.026	13.552	16.626	20.361	24.891	30.376	37.005	45.007	54.648	66.247
24	1.270	1.608	2.033	2.563	3.225	4.049	5.072	6.341	7.911	9.850	12.239	15.178	18.788	23.212	28.625	35.236	43.296	53.108	65.031	79.496
25	1.282	1.641	2.094	2.666	3.386	4.292	5.427	6.848	8.623	10.834	13.585	17.000	21.230	26.461	32.918	40.874	50.656	62.667	77.387	95.395
30	1.348	1.811	2.427	3.243	4.322	5.743	7.612	10.062	13.267	17.449	22.892	29.960	39.115	50.949	66.210	85.849	111.061	143.367	184.672	237.373
35	1.417	2.000	2.814	3.946	5.516	7.686	10.676	14.785	20.413	28.102	38.574	52.799	72.066	98.097	133.172	180.311	243.495	327.988	440.691	590.657
40	1.489	2.208	3.262	4.801	7.040	10.285	14.974	21.724	31.408	45.258	64.999	93.049	132.776	188.876	267.856	378.715	533.846	750.353	1051.642	1469.740
45	1.565	2.438	3.781	5.841	8.985	13.764	21.002	31.920	48.325	72.888	109.527	163.985	244.629	363.662	538.752	795.429	1170.425	1716.619	2509.583	3657.176
50	1.645	2.691	4.384	7.106	11.467	18.419	29.456	46.900	74.354	117.386	184.559	288.996	450.711	700.197	1083.619	1670.669	2566.080	3927.189	5988.730	9100.191

Table B-1 (Continued)

Period	21%	22%	23%	24%	25%	26%	27%	28%	29%	30%	31%	32%	33%	34%	35%	40%	45%	50%
1	1.210	1.220	1.230	1.240	1.250	1.260	1.270	1.280	1.290	1.300	1.310	1.320	1.330	1.340	1.350	1.400	1.450	1.500
2	1.464	1.488	1.513	1.538	1.562	1.588	1.613	1.638	1.664	1.690	1.716	1.742	1.769	1.796	1.822	1.960	2.102	2.250
3	1.772	1.816	1.861	1.907	1.953	2.000	2.048	2.097	2.147	2.197	2.248	2.300	2.353	2.406	2.460	2.744	3.049	3.375
4	2.144	2.215	2.289	2.364	2.441	2.520	2.601	2.684	2.769	2.856	2.945	3.036	3.129	3.224	3.321	3.842	4.421	5.063
5	2.594	2.703	2.815	2.932	3.052	3.176	3.304	3.436	3.572	3.713	3.858	4.007	4.162	4.320	4.484	5.378	6.410	7.594
6	3.138	3.297	3.463	3.635	3.815	4.001	4.196	4.398	4.608	4.827	5.054	5.290	5.535	5.789	6.053	7.530	9.294	11.391
7	3.797	4.023	4.259	4.508	4.768	5.042	5.329	5.629	5.945	6.275	6.621	6.983	7.361	7.758	8.172	10.541	13.476	17.086
8	4.595	4.908	5.239	5.589	5.960	6.353	6.767	7.206	7.669	8.157	8.673	9.217	9.791	10.395	11.032	14.758	19.541	25.629
9	5.560	5.987	6.444	6.931	7.451	8.004	8.595	9.223	9.893	10.604	11.362	12.166	13.022	13.930	14.894	20.661	28.334	38.443
10	6.727	7.305	7.926	8.594	9.313	10.086	10.915	11.806	12.761	13.786	14.884	16.060	17.319	18.666	20.106	28.925	41.085	57.665
11	8.140	8.912	9.749	10.657	11.642	12.708	13.862	15.112	16.462	17.921	19.498	21.199	23.034	25.012	27.144	40.495	59.573	86.498
12	9.850	10.872	11.991	13.215	14.552	16.012	17.605	19.343	21.236	23.298	25.542	27.982	30.635	33.516	36.644	56.694	86.380	129.746
13	11.918	13.264	14.749	16.386	18.190	20.175	22.359	24.759	27.395	30.287	33.460	36.937	40.745	44.912	49.469	79.371	125.251	194.620
14	14.421	16.182	18.141	20.319	22.737	25.420	28.395	31.691	35.339	39.373	43.832	48.756	54.190	60.181	66.784	111.119	181.614	291.929
15	17.449	19.742	22.314	25.195	28.422	32.030	36.062	40.565	45.587	51.185	57.420	64.358	72.073	80.643	90.158	155.567	263.341	437.894
16	21.113	24.085	27.446	31.242	35.527	40.357	45.799	51.923	58.808	66.541	75.220	84.953	95.857	108.061	121.713	217.793	381.844	656.841
17	25.547	29.384	33.758	38.740	44.409	50.850	58.165	66.461	75.862	86.503	98.539	112.138	127.490	144.802	164.312	304.911	553.674	985.261
18	30.912	35.848	41.523	48.038	55.511	64.071	73.869	85.070	97.862	112.454	129.086	148.022	169.561	194.035	221.822	426.875	802.826	1477.892
19	37.404	43.735	51.073	59.567	69.389	80.730	93.813	108.890	126.242	146.190	169.102	195.389	225.517	260.006	299.459	597.625	1164.098	2216.838
20	45.258	53.357	62.820	73.863	86.736	101.720	119.143	139.379	162.852	190.047	221.523	257.913	299.937	348.408	404.270	836.674	1687.942	3325.257
21	54.762	65.095	77.268	91.591	108.420	128.167	151.312	178.405	210.079	247.061	290.196	340.446	398.916	466.867	545.764	1171.343	2447.515	4987.883
22	66.262	79.416	95.040	113.572	135.525	161.490	192.165	228.358	271.002	321.178	380.156	449.388	530.558	625.601	736.781	1639.878	3548.896	7481.824
23	80.178	96.887	116.899	140.829	169.407	203.477	244.050	292.298	349.592	417.531	498.004	593.192	705.642	838.305	994.653	2295.829	5145.898	11222.738
24	97.015	118.203	143.786	174.628	211.758	256.381	309.943	374.141	450.974	542.791	652.385	783.013	938.504	1123.328	1342.781	3214.158	7461.547	16834.109
25	117.388	144.207	176.857	216.539	264.698	323.040	393.628	478.901	581.756	705.627	854.623	1033.577	1248.210	1505.258	1812.754	4499.816	10819.242	25251.164
30	304.471	389.748	497.904	634.810	807.793	1025.904	1300.477	1645.488	2078.208	2619.936	3297.081	4142.008	5194.516	6503.285	8128.426	24201.043	69348.375	191751.000
35	789.716	1053.370	1401.749	1861.020	2465.189	3258.053	4296.547	5653.840	7423.988	9727.598	12719.918	16598.906	21617.363	28096.695	36448.051	130158.687	*	*
40	2048.309	2846.941	3946.340	5455.797	7523.156	10346.879	14195.051	19426.418	26520.723	36117.754	49072.621	66519.313	89962.188	121388.437	163433.875	700022.688	*	*
45	5312.758	7694.418	11110.121	15994.316	22958.844	32859.457	46897.973	66748.500	94739.937	134102.187	*	*	*	*	*	*	*	*
50	13779.844	20795.680	31278.301	46889.207	70064.812	104354.562	154942.687	229345.875	338440.000	497910.125	*	*	*	*	*	*	*	*

*Not shown because of space limitations.

Table B-2 Present Value Interest Factors for $1 Compounded at i Percent for n Periods: $PV = FV \times FVIF_{i,n}$

Period	1%	2%	3%	4%	5%	6%	7%	8%	9%	10%	11%	12%	13%	14%	15%	16%	17%	18%	19%	20%
1	.990	.980	.971	.962	.952	.943	.935	.926	.917	.909	.901	.893	.885	.877	.870	.862	.855	.847	.840	.833
2	.980	.961	.943	.925	.907	.890	.873	.857	.842	.826	.812	.797	.783	.769	.756	.743	.731	.718	.706	.694
3	.971	.942	.915	.889	.864	.840	.816	.794	.772	.751	.731	.712	.693	.675	.658	.641	.624	.609	.593	.579
4	.961	.924	.888	.855	.823	.792	.763	.735	.708	.683	.659	.636	.613	.592	.572	.552	.534	.516	.499	.482
5	.951	.906	.863	.822	.784	.747	.713	.681	.650	.621	.593	.567	.543	.519	.497	.476	.456	.437	.419	.402
6	.942	.888	.837	.790	.746	.705	.666	.630	.596	.564	.535	.507	.480	.456	.432	.410	.390	.370	.352	.335
7	.933	.871	.813	.760	.711	.665	.623	.583	.547	.513	.482	.452	.425	.400	.376	.354	.333	.314	.296	.279
8	.923	.853	.789	.731	.677	.627	.582	.540	.502	.467	.434	.404	.376	.351	.327	.305	.285	.266	.249	.233
9	.914	.837	.766	.703	.645	.592	.544	.500	.460	.424	.391	.361	.333	.308	.284	.263	.243	.225	.209	.194
10	.905	.820	.744	.676	.614	.558	.508	.463	.422	.386	.352	.322	.295	.270	.247	.227	.208	.191	.176	.162
11	.896	.804	.722	.650	.585	.527	.475	.429	.388	.350	.317	.287	.261	.237	.215	.195	.178	.162	.148	.135
12	.887	.789	.701	.625	.557	.497	.444	.397	.356	.319	.286	.257	.231	.208	.187	.168	.152	.137	.124	.112
13	.879	.773	.681	.601	.530	.469	.415	.368	.326	.290	.258	.229	.204	.182	.163	.145	.130	.116	.104	.093
14	.870	.758	.661	.577	.505	.442	.388	.340	.299	.263	.232	.205	.181	.160	.141	.125	.111	.099	.088	.078
15	.861	.743	.642	.555	.481	.417	.362	.315	.275	.239	.209	.183	.160	.140	.123	.108	.095	.084	.074	.065
16	.853	.728	.623	.534	.458	.394	.339	.292	.252	.218	.188	.163	.141	.123	.107	.093	.081	.071	.062	.054
17	.844	.714	.605	.513	.436	.371	.317	.270	.231	.198	.170	.146	.125	.108	.093	.080	.069	.060	.052	.045
18	.836	.700	.587	.494	.416	.350	.296	.250	.212	.180	.153	.130	.111	.095	.081	.069	.059	.051	.044	.038
19	.828	.686	.570	.475	.396	.331	.277	.232	.194	.164	.138	.116	.098	.083	.070	.060	.051	.043	.037	.031
20	.820	.673	.554	.456	.377	.312	.258	.215	.178	.149	.124	.104	.087	.073	.061	.051	.043	.037	.031	.026
21	.811	.660	.538	.439	.359	.294	.242	.199	.164	.135	.112	.093	.077	.064	.053	.044	.037	.031	.026	.022
22	.803	.647	.522	.422	.342	.278	.226	.184	.150	.123	.101	.083	.068	.056	.046	.038	.032	.026	.022	.018
23	.795	.634	.507	.406	.326	.262	.211	.170	.138	.112	.091	.074	.060	.049	.040	.033	.027	.022	.018	.015
24	.788	.622	.492	.390	.310	.247	.197	.158	.126	.102	.082	.066	.053	.043	.035	.028	.023	.019	.015	.013
25	.780	.610	.478	.375	.295	.233	.184	.146	.116	.092	.074	.059	.047	.038	.030	.024	.020	.016	.013	.010
30	.742	.552	.412	.308	.231	.174	.131	.099	.075	.057	.044	.033	.026	.020	.015	.012	.009	.007	.005	.004
35	.706	.500	.355	.253	.181	.130	.094	.068	.049	.036	.026	.019	.014	.010	.008	.006	.004	.003	.002	.002
40	.672	.453	.307	.208	.142	.097	.067	.046	.032	.022	.015	.011	.008	.005	.004	.003	.002	.001	.001	.001
45	.639	.410	.264	.171	.111	.073	.048	.031	.021	.014	.009	.006	.004	.003	.002	.001	.001	.001	*	*
50	.608	.372	.228	.141	.087	.054	.034	.021	.013	.009	.005	.003	.002	.001	.001	.001	*	*	*	*

*$PVIF$ is zero to three decimal places.

Table B-2 (Continued)

Period	21%	22%	23%	24%	25%	26%	27%	28%	29%	30%	31%	32%	33%	34%	35%	40%	45%	50%
1	.826	.820	.813	.806	.800	.794	.787	.781	.775	.769	.763	.758	.752	.746	.741	.714	.690	.667
2	.683	.672	.661	.650	.640	.630	.620	.610	.601	.592	.583	.574	.565	.557	.549	.510	.476	.444
3	.564	.551	.537	.524	.512	.500	.488	.477	.466	.455	.445	.435	.425	.416	.406	.364	.328	.296
4	.467	.451	.437	.423	.410	.397	.384	.373	.361	.350	.340	.329	.320	.310	.301	.260	.226	.198
5	.386	.370	.355	.341	.328	.315	.303	.291	.280	.269	.259	.250	.240	.231	.223	.186	.156	.132
6	.319	.303	.289	.275	.262	.250	.238	.227	.217	.207	.198	.189	.181	.173	.165	.133	.108	.088
7	.263	.249	.235	.222	.210	.198	.188	.178	.168	.159	.151	.143	.136	.129	.122	.095	.074	.059
8	.218	.204	.191	.179	.168	.157	.148	.139	.130	.123	.115	.108	.102	.096	.091	.068	.051	.039
9	.180	.167	.155	.144	.134	.125	.116	.108	.101	.094	.088	.082	.077	.072	.067	.048	.035	.026
10	.149	.137	.126	.116	.107	.099	.092	.085	.078	.073	.067	.062	.058	.054	.050	.035	.024	.017
11	.123	.112	.103	.094	.086	.079	.072	.066	.061	.056	.051	.047	.043	.040	.037	.025	.017	.012
12	.102	.092	.083	.076	.069	.062	.057	.052	.047	.043	.039	.036	.033	.030	.027	.018	.012	.008
13	.084	.075	.068	.061	.055	.050	.045	.040	.037	.033	.030	.027	.025	.022	.020	.013	.008	.005
14	.069	.062	.055	.049	.044	.039	.035	.032	.028	.025	.023	.021	.018	.017	.015	.009	.006	.003
15	.057	.051	.045	.040	.035	.031	.028	.025	.022	.020	.017	.016	.014	.012	.011	.006	.004	.002
16	.047	.042	.036	.032	.028	.025	.022	.019	.017	.015	.013	.012	.010	.009	.008	.005	.003	.002
17	.039	.034	.030	.026	.023	.020	.017	.015	.013	.012	.010	.009	.008	.007	.006	.003	.002	.001
18	.032	.028	.024	.021	.018	.016	.014	.012	.010	.009	.008	.007	.006	.005	.005	.002	.001	.001
19	.027	.023	.020	.017	.014	.012	.011	.009	.008	.007	.006	.005	.004	.004	.003	.002	.001	*
20	.022	.019	.016	.014	.012	.010	.008	.007	.006	.005	.005	.004	.003	.003	.002	.001	.001	*
21	.018	.015	.013	.011	.009	.008	.007	.006	.005	.004	.003	.003	.003	.002	.002	.001	.001	*
22	.015	.013	.011	.009	.007	.006	.005	.004	.004	.003	.003	.002	.002	.002	.001	.001	*	*
23	.012	.010	.009	.007	.006	.005	.004	.003	.003	.002	.002	.002	.001	.001	.001	*	*	*
24	.010	.008	.007	.006	.005	.004	.003	.003	.002	.002	.002	.001	.001	.001	.001	*	*	*
25	.009	.007	.006	.005	.004	.003	.003	.002	.002	.001	.001	.001	.001	.001	.001	*	*	*
30	.003	.003	.002	.002	.001	.001	.001	.001	*	*	*	*	*	*	*	*	*	*
35	.001	.001	.001	.001	*	*	*	*	*	*	*	*	*	*	*	*	*	*
40	*	*	*	*	*	*	*	*	*	*	*	*	*	*	*	*	*	*
45	*	*	*	*	*	*	*	*	*	*	*	*	*	*	*	*	*	*
50	*	*	*	*	*	*	*	*	*	*	*	*	*	*	*	*	*	*

*PV/F is zero to three decimal places.

639

Table B-3 Future Value Interest Factors for $1 Annuity Compounded at *i* Percent for *n* Periods: $FVA = PMT \times FVIFA_{i,n}$

Period	1%	2%	3%	4%	5%	6%	7%	8%	9%	10%	11%	12%	13%	14%	15%	16%	17%	18%	19%	20%
1	1.000	1.000	1.000	1.000	1.000	1.000	1.000	1.000	1.000	1.000	1.000	1.000	1.000	1.000	1.000	1.000	1.000	1.000	1.000	1.000
2	2.010	2.020	2.030	2.040	2.050	2.060	2.070	2.080	2.090	2.100	2.110	2.120	2.130	2.140	2.150	2.160	2.170	2.180	2.190	2.200
3	3.030	3.060	3.091	3.122	3.152	3.184	3.215	3.246	3.278	3.310	3.342	3.374	3.407	3.440	3.472	3.506	3.539	3.572	3.606	3.640
4	4.060	4.122	4.184	4.246	4.310	4.375	4.440	4.506	4.573	4.641	4.710	4.779	4.850	4.921	4.993	5.066	5.141	5.215	5.291	5.368
5	5.101	5.204	5.309	5.416	5.526	5.637	5.751	5.867	5.985	6.105	6.228	6.353	6.480	6.610	6.742	6.877	7.014	7.154	7.297	7.442
6	6.152	6.308	6.468	6.633	6.802	6.975	7.153	7.336	7.523	7.716	7.913	8.115	8.323	8.535	8.754	8.977	9.207	9.442	9.683	9.930
7	7.214	7.434	7.662	7.898	8.142	8.394	8.654	8.923	9.200	9.487	9.783	10.089	10.405	10.730	11.067	11.414	11.772	12.141	12.523	12.916
8	8.286	8.583	8.892	9.214	9.549	9.897	10.260	10.637	11.028	11.436	11.859	12.300	12.757	13.233	13.727	14.240	14.773	15.327	15.902	16.499
9	9.368	9.755	10.159	10.583	11.027	11.491	11.978	12.488	13.021	13.579	14.164	14.776	15.416	16.085	16.786	17.518	18.285	19.086	19.923	20.799
10	10.462	10.950	11.464	12.006	12.578	13.181	13.816	14.487	15.193	15.937	16.722	17.549	18.420	19.337	20.304	21.321	22.393	23.521	24.709	25.959
11	11.567	12.169	12.808	13.486	14.207	14.972	15.784	16.645	17.560	18.531	19.561	20.655	21.814	23.044	24.349	25.733	27.200	28.755	30.403	32.150
12	12.682	13.412	14.192	15.026	15.917	16.870	17.888	18.977	20.141	21.384	22.713	24.133	25.650	27.271	29.001	30.850	32.824	34.931	37.180	39.580
13	13.809	14.680	15.613	16.627	17.713	18.882	20.141	21.495	22.953	24.523	26.211	28.029	29.984	32.088	34.352	36.786	39.404	42.218	45.244	48.496
14	14.947	15.974	17.086	18.292	19.598	21.015	22.550	24.215	26.019	27.975	30.095	32.392	34.882	37.581	40.504	43.672	47.102	50.818	54.841	59.196
15	16.097	17.293	18.599	20.023	21.578	23.276	25.129	27.152	29.361	31.772	34.405	37.280	40.417	43.842	47.580	51.659	56.109	60.965	66.260	72.035
16	17.258	18.639	20.157	21.824	23.657	25.672	27.888	30.324	33.003	35.949	39.190	42.753	46.671	50.980	55.717	60.925	66.648	72.938	79.850	87.442
17	18.430	20.012	21.761	23.697	25.840	28.213	30.840	33.750	36.973	40.544	44.500	48.883	53.738	59.117	65.075	71.673	78.978	87.067	96.021	105.930
18	19.614	21.412	23.414	25.645	28.132	30.905	33.999	37.450	41.301	45.599	50.396	55.749	61.724	68.393	75.836	84.140	93.404	103.739	115.265	128.116
19	20.811	22.840	25.117	27.671	30.539	33.760	37.379	41.446	46.018	51.158	56.939	63.439	70.748	78.968	88.211	98.603	110.283	123.412	138.165	154.739
20	22.019	24.297	26.870	29.778	33.066	36.785	40.995	45.762	51.159	57.274	64.202	72.052	80.946	91.024	102.443	115.379	130.031	146.626	165.417	186.687
21	23.239	25.783	28.676	31.969	35.719	39.992	44.865	50.422	56.764	64.002	72.264	81.698	92.468	104.767	118.809	134.840	153.136	174.019	197.846	225.024
22	24.471	27.299	30.536	34.248	38.505	43.392	49.005	55.456	62.872	71.402	81.213	92.502	105.489	120.434	137.630	157.414	180.169	206.342	236.436	271.028
23	25.716	28.845	32.452	36.618	41.430	46.995	53.435	60.893	69.531	79.542	91.147	104.602	120.203	138.295	159.274	183.600	211.798	244.483	282.359	326.234
24	26.973	30.421	34.426	39.082	44.501	50.815	58.176	66.764	76.789	88.496	102.173	118.154	136.829	158.656	184.166	213.976	248.803	289.490	337.007	392.480
25	28.243	32.030	36.459	41.645	47.726	54.864	63.248	73.105	84.699	98.346	114.412	133.333	155.616	181.867	212.790	249.212	292.099	342.598	402.038	471.976
30	34.784	40.567	47.575	56.084	66.438	79.057	94.459	113.282	136.305	164.491	199.018	241.330	293.192	356.778	434.738	530.306	647.423	790.932	966.698	1181.865
35	41.659	49.994	60.461	73.651	90.318	111.432	138.234	172.314	215.705	271.018	341.583	431.658	546.663	693.552	881.152	1120.699	1426.448	1816.607	2314.173	2948.294
40	48.885	60.401	75.400	95.024	120.797	154.758	199.630	259.052	337.872	442.580	581.812	767.080	1013.667	1341.979	1779.048	2360.724	3134.412	4163.094	5529.711	7343.715
45	56.479	71.891	92.718	121.027	159.695	212.737	285.741	386.497	525.840	718.881	986.613	1358.208	1874.086	2590.464	3585.031	4965.191	6879.008	9531.258	13203.105	18280.914
50	64.461	84.577	112.794	152.664	209.341	290.325	406.516	573.756	815.051	1163.865	1668.723	2399.975	3459.344	4994.301	7217.488	10435.449	15088.805	21812.273	31514.492	45496.094

Table B-3 (Continued)

Period	21%	22%	23%	24%	25%	26%	27%	28%	29%	30%	31%	32%	33%	34%	35%	40%	45%	50%
1	1.000	1.000	1.000	1.000	1.000	1.000	1.000	1.000	1.000	1.000	1.000	1.000	1.000	1.000	1.000	1.000	1.000	1.000
2	2.210	2.220	2.230	2.240	2.250	2.260	2.270	2.280	2.290	2.300	2.310	2.320	2.330	2.340	2.350	2.400	2.450	2.500
3	3.674	3.708	3.743	3.778	3.813	3.848	3.883	3.918	3.954	3.990	4.026	4.062	4.099	4.136	4.172	4.360	4.552	4.750
4	5.446	5.524	5.604	5.684	5.766	5.848	5.931	6.016	6.101	6.187	6.274	6.362	6.452	6.542	6.633	7.104	7.601	8.125
5	7.589	7.740	7.893	8.048	8.207	8.368	8.533	8.700	8.870	9.043	9.219	9.398	9.581	9.766	9.954	10.946	12.022	13.188
6	10.183	10.442	10.708	10.980	11.259	11.544	11.837	12.136	12.442	12.756	13.077	13.406	13.742	14.086	14.438	16.324	18.431	20.781
7	13.321	13.740	14.171	14.615	15.073	15.546	16.032	16.534	17.051	17.583	18.131	18.696	19.277	19.876	20.492	23.853	27.725	32.172
8	17.119	17.762	18.430	19.123	19.842	20.588	21.361	22.163	22.995	23.858	24.752	25.678	26.638	27.633	28.664	34.395	41.202	49.258
9	21.714	22.670	23.669	24.712	25.802	26.940	28.129	29.369	30.664	32.015	33.425	34.895	36.429	38.028	39.696	49.152	60.743	74.887
10	27.274	28.657	30.113	31.643	33.253	34.945	36.723	38.592	40.556	42.619	44.786	47.062	49.451	51.958	54.590	69.813	89.077	113.330
11	34.001	35.962	38.039	40.238	42.566	45.030	47.639	50.398	53.318	56.405	59.670	63.121	66.769	70.624	74.696	98.739	130.161	170.995
12	42.141	44.873	47.787	50.895	54.208	57.738	61.501	65.510	69.780	74.326	79.167	84.320	89.803	95.636	101.840	139.234	189.734	257.493
13	51.991	55.745	59.778	64.109	68.760	73.750	79.106	84.853	91.016	97.624	104.709	112.302	120.438	129.152	138.484	195.928	276.114	387.239
14	63.909	69.009	74.528	80.496	86.949	93.925	101.465	109.611	118.411	127.912	138.169	149.239	161.183	174.063	187.953	275.299	401.365	581.858
15	78.330	85.191	92.669	100.815	109.687	119.346	129.860	141.302	153.750	167.285	182.001	197.996	215.373	234.245	254.737	386.418	582.980	873.788
16	95.779	104.933	114.983	126.010	138.109	151.375	165.922	181.867	199.337	218.470	239.421	262.354	287.446	314.888	344.895	541.985	846.321	1311.681
17	116.892	129.019	142.428	157.252	173.636	191.733	211.721	233.790	258.145	285.011	314.642	347.307	383.303	422.949	466.608	759.778	1228.165	1968.522
18	142.439	158.403	176.187	195.993	218.045	242.583	269.885	300.250	334.006	371.514	413.180	459.445	510.792	567.751	630.920	1064.689	1781.838	2953.783
19	173.351	194.251	217.710	244.031	273.556	306.654	343.754	385.321	431.888	483.968	542.266	607.467	680.354	761.786	852.741	1491.563	2584.665	4431.672
20	210.755	237.986	268.783	303.598	342.945	387.384	437.568	494.210	558.110	630.157	711.368	802.856	905.870	1021.792	1152.200	2089.188	3748.763	6648.508
21	256.013	291.343	331.603	377.461	429.681	489.104	556.710	633.589	720.962	820.204	932.891	1060.769	1205.807	1370.201	1556.470	2925.862	5436.703	9973.762
22	310.775	356.438	408.871	469.052	538.101	617.270	708.022	811.993	931.040	1067.265	1223.087	1401.215	1604.724	1837.068	2102.234	4097.203	7884.215	14961.645
23	377.038	435.854	503.911	582.624	673.626	778.760	900.187	1040.351	1202.042	1388.443	1603.243	1850.603	2135.282	2462.669	2839.014	5737.078	11433.109	22443.469
24	457.215	532.741	620.810	723.453	843.032	982.237	1144.237	1332.649	1551.634	1805.975	2101.247	2443.795	2840.924	3300.974	3833.667	8032.906	16579.008	33666.207
25	554.230	660.944	764.596	898.082	1054.791	1238.617	1454.180	1706.790	2002.608	2348.765	2753.631	3226.808	3779.428	4424.301	5176.445	11247.062	24040.555	50500.316
30	1445.111	1767.044	2160.459	2640.881	3227.172	3941.953	4812.891	5873.172	7162.785	8729.805	10632.543	12940.672	15737.945	19124.434	23221.258	60500.207	154105.313	383500.000
35	3755.814	4783.520	6090.227	7750.094	9856.746	12527.160	15909.480	20188.742	25596.512	32422.090	41028.887	51868.563	65504.199	82634.625	104134.500	325394.688	*	*
40	9749.141	12936.141	17153.691	22728.367	30088.621	39791.957	52570.707	69376.562	91447.375	120389.375	*	*	*	*	*	*	*	*
45	25294.223	34970.230	48300.660	66638.937	91831.312	126378.937	173692.875	238894.312	326686.375	447005.062	*	*	*	*	*	*	*	*

*Not shown because of space limitations.

641

Table B-4 Present Value Interest Factors for $1 Annuity Discounted at *i* Percent for *n* Periods: $PVA = PMT \times PVIFA_{i,n}$

Period	1%	2%	3%	4%	5%	6%	7%	8%	9%	10%	11%	12%	13%	14%	15%	16%	17%	18%	19%	20%
1	.990	.980	.971	.962	.952	.943	.935	.926	.917	.909	.901	.893	.885	.877	.870	.862	.855	.847	.840	.833
2	1.970	1.942	1.913	1.886	1.859	1.833	1.808	1.783	1.759	1.736	1.713	1.690	1.668	1.647	1.626	1.605	1.585	1.566	1.547	1.528
3	2.941	2.884	2.829	2.775	2.723	2.673	2.624	2.577	2.531	2.487	2.444	2.402	2.361	2.322	2.283	2.246	2.210	2.174	2.140	2.106
4	3.902	3.808	3.717	3.630	3.546	3.465	3.387	3.312	3.240	3.170	3.102	3.037	2.974	2.914	2.855	2.798	2.743	2.690	2.639	2.589
5	4.853	4.713	4.580	4.452	4.329	4.212	4.100	3.993	3.890	3.791	3.696	3.605	3.517	3.433	3.352	3.274	3.199	3.127	3.058	2.991
6	5.795	5.601	5.417	5.242	5.076	4.917	4.767	4.623	4.486	4.355	4.231	4.111	3.998	3.889	3.784	3.685	3.589	3.498	3.410	3.326
7	6.728	6.472	6.230	6.002	5.786	5.582	5.389	5.206	5.033	4.868	4.712	4.564	4.423	4.288	4.160	4.039	3.922	3.812	3.706	3.605
8	7.652	7.326	7.020	6.733	6.463	6.210	5.971	5.747	5.535	5.335	5.146	4.968	4.799	4.639	4.487	4.344	4.207	4.078	3.954	3.837
9	8.566	8.162	7.786	7.435	7.108	6.802	6.515	6.247	5.995	5.759	5.537	5.328	5.132	4.946	4.772	4.607	4.451	4.303	4.163	4.031
10	9.471	8.983	8.530	8.111	7.722	7.360	7.024	6.710	6.418	6.145	5.889	5.650	5.426	5.216	5.019	4.833	4.659	4.494	4.339	4.192
11	10.368	9.787	9.253	8.760	8.306	7.887	7.499	7.139	6.805	6.495	6.207	5.938	5.687	5.453	5.234	5.029	4.836	4.656	4.486	4.327
12	11.255	10.575	9.954	9.385	8.863	8.384	7.943	7.536	7.161	6.814	6.492	6.194	5.918	5.660	5.421	5.197	4.988	4.793	4.611	4.439
13	12.134	11.348	10.635	9.986	9.394	8.853	8.358	7.904	7.487	7.013	6.750	6.424	6.122	5.842	5.583	5.342	5.118	4.910	4.715	4.533
14	13.004	12.106	11.296	10.563	9.899	9.295	8.745	8.244	7.786	7.367	6.982	6.628	6.302	6.002	5.724	5.468	5.229	5.008	4.802	4.611
15	13.865	12.849	11.938	11.118	10.380	9.712	9.108	8.560	8.061	7.606	7.191	6.811	6.462	6.142	5.847	5.575	5.324	5.092	4.876	4.675
16	14.718	13.578	12.561	11.652	10.838	10.106	9.447	8.851	8.313	7.824	7.379	6.974	6.604	6.265	5.954	5.668	5.405	5.162	4.938	4.730
17	15.562	14.292	13.166	12.166	11.274	10.477	9.763	9.122	8.544	8.022	7.549	7.120	6.729	6.373	6.047	5.749	5.475	5.222	4.990	4.775
18	16.398	14.992	13.754	12.659	11.690	10.828	10.059	9.372	8.756	8.201	7.702	7.250	6.840	6.467	6.128	5.818	5.534	5.273	5.033	4.812
19	17.226	15.679	14.324	13.134	12.085	11.158	10.336	9.604	8.950	8.365	7.839	7.366	6.938	6.550	6.198	5.877	5.584	5.316	5.070	4.843
20	18.046	16.352	14.878	13.590	12.462	11.470	10.594	9.818	9.129	8.514	7.963	7.469	7.025	6.623	6.259	5.929	5.628	5.353	5.101	4.870
21	18.857	17.011	15.415	14.029	12.821	11.764	10.836	10.017	9.292	8.649	8.075	7.562	7.102	6.687	6.312	5.973	5.665	5.384	5.127	4.891
22	19.661	17.658	15.937	14.451	13.163	12.042	11.061	10.201	9.442	8.772	8.176	7.645	7.170	6.743	6.359	6.011	5.696	5.410	5.149	4.909
23	20.456	18.292	16.444	14.857	13.489	12.303	11.272	10.371	9.580	8.883	8.266	7.718	7.230	6.792	6.399	6.044	5.723	5.432	5.167	4.925
24	21.244	18.914	16.936	15.247	13.799	12.550	11.469	10.529	9.707	8.985	8.348	7.784	7.283	6.835	6.434	6.073	5.746	5.451	5.182	4.937
25	22.023	19.524	17.413	15.622	14.094	12.783	11.654	10.675	9.823	9.077	8.422	7.843	7.330	6.873	6.464	6.097	5.766	5.467	5.195	4.948
30	25.808	22.396	19.601	17.292	15.373	13.765	12.409	11.258	10.274	9.427	8.694	8.055	7.496	7.003	6.566	6.177	5.829	5.517	5.235	4.979
35	29.409	24.999	21.487	18.665	16.374	14.498	12.948	11.655	10.567	9.644	8.855	8.176	7.586	7.070	6.617	6.215	5.858	5.539	5.251	4.992
40	32.835	27.356	23.115	19.793	17.159	15.046	13.332	11.925	10.757	9.779	8.951	8.244	7.634	7.105	6.642	6.233	5.871	5.548	5.258	4.997
45	36.095	29.490	24.519	20.720	17.774	15.456	13.606	12.108	10.881	9.863	9.008	8.283	7.661	7.123	6.654	6.242	5.877	5.552	5.261	4.999
50	39.196	31.424	25.730	21.482	18.256	15.762	13.801	12.233	10.962	9.915	9.042	8.304	7.675	7.133	6.661	6.246	5.880	5.554	5.262	4.999

Table B-4 (Continued)

Period	21%	22%	23%	24%	25%	26%	27%	28%	29%	30%	31%	32%	33%	34%	35%	40%	45%	50%
1	.826	.820	.813	.806	.800	.794	.787	.781	.775	.769	.763	.758	.752	.746	.741	.714	.690	.667
2	1.509	1.492	1.474	1.457	1.440	1.424	1.407	1.392	1.376	1.361	1.346	1.331	1.317	1.303	1.289	1.224	1.165	1.111
3	2.074	2.042	2.011	1.981	1.952	1.923	1.896	1.868	1.842	1.816	1.791	1.766	1.742	1.719	1.696	1.589	1.493	1.407
4	2.540	2.494	2.448	2.404	2.362	2.320	2.280	2.241	2.203	2.166	2.130	2.096	2.062	2.029	1.997	1.849	1.720	1.605
5	2.926	2.864	2.803	2.745	2.689	2.635	2.583	2.532	2.483	2.436	2.390	2.345	2.302	2.260	2.220	2.035	1.876	1.737
6	3.245	3.167	3.092	3.020	2.951	2.885	2.821	2.759	2.700	2.643	2.588	2.534	2.483	2.433	2.385	2.168	1.983	1.824
7	3.508	3.416	3.327	3.242	3.161	3.083	3.009	2.937	2.868	2.802	2.739	2.677	2.619	2.562	2.508	2.263	2.057	1.883
8	3.726	3.619	3.518	3.421	3.329	3.241	3.156	3.076	2.999	2.925	2.854	2.786	2.721	2.658	2.598	2.331	2.109	1.922
9	3.905	3.786	3.673	3.566	3.463	3.366	3.273	3.184	3.100	3.019	2.942	2.868	2.798	2.730	2.665	2.379	2.144	1.948
10	4.054	3.923	3.799	3.682	3.570	3.465	3.364	3.269	3.178	3.092	3.009	2.930	2.855	2.784	2.715	2.414	2.168	1.965
11	4.177	4.035	3.902	3.776	3.656	3.544	3.437	3.335	3.239	3.147	3.060	2.978	2.899	2.824	2.752	2.438	2.185	1.977
12	4.278	4.127	3.985	3.851	3.725	3.606	3.493	3.387	3.286	3.190	3.100	3.013	2.931	2.853	2.779	2.456	2.196	1.985
13	4.362	4.203	4.053	3.912	3.780	3.656	3.538	3.427	3.322	3.223	3.129	3.040	2.956	2.876	2.799	2.469	2.204	1.990
14	4.432	4.265	4.108	3.962	3.824	3.695	3.573	3.459	3.351	3.249	3.152	3.061	2.974	2.892	2.814	2.478	2.210	1.993
15	4.489	4.315	4.153	4.001	3.859	3.726	3.601	3.483	3.373	3.268	3.170	3.076	2.988	2.905	2.825	2.484	2.214	1.995
16	4.536	4.357	4.189	4.033	3.887	3.751	3.623	3.503	3.390	3.283	3.183	3.088	2.999	2.914	2.834	2.489	2.216	1.997
17	4.576	4.391	4.219	4.059	3.910	3.771	3.640	3.518	3.403	3.295	3.193	3.097	3.007	2.921	2.840	2.492	2.218	1.998
18	4.608	4.419	4.243	4.080	3.928	3.786	3.654	3.529	3.413	3.304	3.201	3.104	3.012	2.926	2.844	2.494	2.219	1.999
19	4.635	4.442	4.263	4.097	3.942	3.799	3.664	3.539	3.421	3.311	3.207	3.109	3.017	2.930	2.848	2.496	2.220	1.999
20	4.657	4.460	4.279	4.110	3.954	3.808	3.673	3.546	3.427	3.316	3.211	3.113	3.020	2.933	2.850	2.497	2.221	1.999
21	4.675	4.476	4.292	4.121	3.963	3.816	3.679	3.551	3.432	3.320	3.215	3.116	3.023	2.935	2.852	2.498	2.221	2.000
22	4.690	4.488	4.302	4.130	3.970	3.822	3.684	3.556	3.436	3.323	3.217	3.118	3.025	2.936	2.853	2.498	2.222	2.000
23	4.703	4.499	4.311	4.137	3.976	3.827	3.689	3.559	3.438	3.325	3.219	3.120	3.026	2.938	2.854	2.499	2.222	2.000
24	4.713	4.507	4.318	4.143	3.981	3.831	3.692	3.562	3.441	3.327	3.221	3.121	3.027	2.939	2.855	2.499	2.222	2.000
25	4.721	4.514	4.323	4.147	3.985	3.834	3.694	3.564	3.442	3.329	3.222	3.122	3.028	2.939	2.856	2.499	2.222	2.000
30	4.746	4.534	4.339	4.160	3.995	3.842	3.701	3.569	3.447	3.332	3.225	3.124	3.030	2.941	2.857	2.500	2.222	2.000
35	4.756	4.541	4.345	4.164	3.998	3.845	3.703	3.571	3.448	3.333	3.226	3.125	3.030	2.941	2.857	2.500	2.222	2.000
40	4.760	4.544	4.347	4.166	3.999	3.846	3.703	3.571	3.448	3.333	3.226	3.125	3.030	2.941	2.857	2.500	2.222	2.000
45	4.761	4.545	4.347	4.166	4.000	3.846	3.704	3.571	3.448	3.333	3.226	3.125	3.030	2.941	2.857	2.500	2.222	2.000
50	4.762	4.545	4.348	4.167	4.000	3.846	3.704	3.571	3.448	3.333	3.226	3.125	3.030	2.941	2.857	2.500	2.222	2.000

Index

Credits

Chapter 1:

Page 1:   © 2006 PhotoDisc Red. All Rights Reserved.

Page 12 (bottom): Reproduced with permission of Yahoo! Inc. © 2006 by Yahoo! Inc.
              YAHOO! and the YAHOO! logo are trademarks of Yahoo! Inc.

Page 12 (top): Courtesy www.cartoonstock.com.

Chapter 2:

Page 24:   © 2006 PhotoDisc. All Rights Reserved.

Page 33:   Courtesy The Federal Reserve Bank of Dallas.

Page 34, 35: Screen shot reprinted by permission from FinanCenter, Inc.

Chapter 3:

Page 57:   © 2006 Brand X Pictures. All Rights Reserved.

Page 62:   Reproduced with permission of Yahoo! Inc. © 2006 by Yahoo! Inc.
              YAHOO! and the YAHOO! logo are trademarks of Yahoo! Inc.

Page 67:   Screen shot reprinted by permission from Microsoft Corporation.

Chapter 4:

Page 85:   © 2006 PhotoDisc. All Rights Reserved.

Page 87, 89, 90, 92, 94, 95, 99: Courtesy of irs.gov.

Page 97:   Reproduced with permission of Yahoo! Inc. © 2006 by Yahoo! Inc.
              YAHOO! and the YAHOO! logo are trademarks of Yahoo! Inc.

Page 105:   Reproduced with permission of Intuit.com

Page 112:   Courtesy www.comics.com.

Chapter 5:

Page 122:   © 2006 PhotoDisc Red. All Rights Reserved.

Page 128:   Courtesy www.cartoonstock.com.

Page 130:   Courtesy The Federal Reserve Bank of Chicago.

Page 131:   Reproduced with permission of Yahoo! Inc. © 2006 by Yahoo! Inc.
              YAHOO! and the YAHOO! logo are trademarks of Yahoo! Inc.

Page 132, 137, 138: © 2006 Bloomberg L.P. All Rights Reserved. Reprinted with
              permission. Visit www.Bloomberg.com.

Chapter 6:

Page 149:   © 2006 LWA-Dann Tardif/Zefa/Corbis. All Rights Reserved.

Page 152:   © The New Yorker Collection 1998 Michael Maslin from
              cartoonbank.com. All Rights Reserved.

Page 155:   Courtesy Bankrate.com.

Page 157:   © 2006 Dow Jones & Company, Inc. All Rights Reserved.

Page 159:   Screen shot reprinted by permission from RMS Reprint Management
              Services.

Page 160:   Courtesy The Federal Reserve Bank of Chicago.

Chapter 7:

Page 173:   © 2006 Don Mason/Corbis. All Rights Reserved.
Page 176:   Courtesy The Federal Reserve Bank of Philadelphia.
Page 179, 187: Reproduced with permission of Federal Trade Commission.
Page 187:   © 2006 United Features Syndicate, Inc. All Rights Reserved. Reproduced with permission.

Chapter 8:

Page 197:   © 2006 Spencer Grant/Photo Edit. All Rights Reserved.
Page 199:   Reproduced with permission of Yahoo! Inc. © 2006 by Yahoo! Inc. YAHOO! and the YAHOO! logo are trademarks of Yahoo! Inc.
Page 200:   © 2006 United Media. All Rights Reserved. Reproduced with permission
Page 201:   Screen shot reprinted by permission from RMS Reprint Management Services.
Page 206, 209: Courtesy The Federal Reserve Bank of Chicago.
Page 207:   Courtesy Bankrate.com.
Page 211:   Reproduced with permission of Free Financial Advice.

Chapter 9:

Page 223:   © 2006 Pearson Education/PH College. All Rights Reserved.
Page 226:   Reproduced with permission of Digital Federal Credit Union.
Page 227:   Courtesy www.cartoonstock.com.
Page 228:   Courtesy of LendingTree, Inc.
Page 233   Reproduced with permission of GMAC Mortgage.
Page 235, 239: Reproduced with permission of Yahoo! Inc. © 2006 by Yahoo! Inc. YAHOO! and the YAHOO! logo are trademarks of Yahoo! Inc.
Page 236:   Courtesy Kelley Blue Book, kbb.com.
Page 237, 241: Reproduced with permission of Bankrate.com.
Page 244:   © 2006 Bloomberg L.P. All Rights Reserved. Reprinted with permission. Visit www.Bloomberg.com

Chapter 10:

Page 255:   © 2006 Beth Anderson. All Rights Reserved.
Page 257 top: © The New Yorker Collection 1997 Michael Maslin from cartoonbank.com. All Rights Reserved.
Page 258:   Screen shot reprinted by permission from FinanCenter, Inc.
Page 259, 265, 277: Reproduced with permission of Yahoo! Inc. © 2006 by Yahoo! Inc. YAHOO! and the YAHOO! logo are trademarks of Yahoo! Inc.
Page 260:   Courtesy National Association of Realtors, www.realtor.com.
Page 263, 268: © 2003 Bloomberg L.P. All Rights Reserved. Reprinted with permission. Visit www.Bloomberg .com.
Page 271:   Reproduced with permission of The Federal Reserve.

Chapter 11:

Page 298:   © 2006 David Young-Wolff/Photo Edit. All Rights Reserved.
Page 302:   Reproduced with permission of A.M. Best Company.
Page 307:   Reproduced with permission of Yahoo! Inc. © 2006 by Yahoo! Inc. YAHOO! and the YAHOO! logo are trademarks of Yahoo! Inc.
Page 315:   © 2006 United Media. All Rights Reserved. Reproduced with permission.
Page 318, 319: © 2006 Insurance.com. All Rights Reserved.

Chapter 12:

Page 335:   © 2006 Jose Luis Pelaez, Inc./Corbis. All Rights Reserved.
Page 339:   Courtesy Cartoon Resource.
Page 341:   © 2005 Individual Health Plans.
Page 345:   Courtesy medicare.gov.

Chapter 13:

Page 363:   © 2006 Getty RF. All Rights Reserved.
Page 369, 377: Screen shot reprinted by permission from Microsoft Corporation.
Page 370:   Screen shot reprinted by permission from FinanCenter, Inc.

Chapter 14:

Page 394:   © 2006 Digital Vision. All Rights Reserved.
Page 396:   Courtesy IPO.com.
Page 397:   Reproduced with permission of Yahoo! Inc. © 2006 by Yahoo! Inc.
             YAHOO! and the YAHOO! logo are trademarks of Yahoo! Inc.
Page 405:   Courtesy www.cartoonstock.com.

Chapter 15:

Page 419:   © 2006 Bill Aron/Photo Edit. All Rights Reserved.
Page 420:   © 2006 Dow Jones & Company, Inc. All Rights Reserved.
Page 421:   © 2006 Bloomberg L.P. All Rights Reserved. Reprinted with permission.
             Visit www.Bloomberg.com.
Page 425:   Courtesy www.cartoonstock.com.
Page 426:   © 2006 Value Line Publishing, Inc.
Page 427, 433, 436: Reproduced with permission of Yahoo! Inc. © 2006 by Yahoo!
             Inc. YAHOO! and the YAHOO! logo are trademarks of Yahoo! Inc.
Page 429:   Courtesy OECD, www.oecd.org.

Chapter 16:

Page 449:   © 2006 Stone/Getty Images. All Rights Reserved.
Page 453:   Courtesy Pritchett Cartoons.
Page 454, 459: Reproduced with permission of Yahoo! Inc. © 2006 by Yahoo! Inc.
             YAHOO! and the YAHOO! logo are trademarks of Yahoo! Inc.
Page 455:   © 2006 E*TRADE Group, Inc. All Rights Reserved.
Page 458:   © 2006 Dow Jones & Company, Inc. All Rights Reserved.
Page 459:   © 2003 Bloomberg L.P. All Rights Reserved. Reprinted with permission.
             Visit www.Bloomberg.com.

Chapter 17:

Page 469:   © 2006 Digital Vision. All Rights Reserved.
Page 471:   Screen shot reprinted by permission from FinanCenter, Inc.
Page 473:   © 2006 Bloomberg L.P. All Rights Reserved. Reprinted with permission.
             Visit www.Bloomberg.com.
Page 475:   © 2006 Dow Jones & Company, Inc. All Rights Reserved.
Page 477:   Courtesy BusinessWeek, Copyright © 2006, by The McGraw-Hill
             Companies Inc. All Rights Reserved.
Page 481:   © 2003 Robert Mankoff from cartoonbank.com. All Rights Reserved.

Chapter 18:

Page 495: © 2006 Getty Images, Inc. All Rights Reserved.

Page 501: © 2006 Index Funds, Inc. All Rights Reserved.

Page 505: © 2006 Bloomberg L.P. All Rights Reserved. Reprinted with permission. Visit www.Bloomberg.com.

Page 506: Courtesy www.cartoonstock.com.

Page 510: Screen shot reprinted by permission from Microsoft Corporation.

Page 512, 513: © 2006 Dow Jones & Company, Inc. All Rights Reserved.

Page 514: © 2006 The Vanguard Group, Inc. All Rights Reserved. Vanguard Marketing Corporation, Distributor. Reprinted with permission from The Vanguard Group.

Page 515: © Copyright 2006 The Mutual Fund Education Alliance. All Rights Reserved.

Chapter 19:

Page 527: © 2006 Tony Freeman/Photo Edit. All Rights Reserved

Page 529: © The New Yorker Collection 1997 Mike Twohy from cartoonbank.com. All Rights Reserved.

Page 532: Reproduced with permission of Yahoo! Inc. © 2006 by Yahoo! Inc. YAHOO! and the YAHOO! logo are trademarks of Yahoo! Inc.

Page 541: Screen shot reprinted by permission from Microsoft Corporation.

Chapter 20:

Page 554: © 2006 PhotoDisc. All Rights Reserved.

Page 557: Courtesy www.ssa.gov.

Page 559: Screen shot reprinted by permission from Microsoft Corporation.

Page 562: © 2006 United Features Syndicate, Inc. All Rights Reserved. Reproduced with permission.

Page 574: Reproduced with permission of Smartmoney.com.

Chapter 21:

Page 585: © 2006 Getty Images, Inc. All Rights Reserved.

Page 588, 592: Screen shot reprinted by permission from Microsoft Corporation.

Page 588: Courtesy Cartoon Resource.

Page 593: Copyright © 2006 Nolo. Reproduced with permission.

Chapter 22:

Page 606: © 2006 Digital Vision. All Rights Reserved.

Page 611: Reprinted with permission from Kiplinger.com © 2003 The Kiplinger Washington Editors, Inc.

Page 619: © 2006 Intuit Inc. Reproduced with permission.

(continued from inside the front cover)